The Caravan

Abdallah Azzam, the Palestinian cleric who led the mobilization of Arab fighters to Afghanistan in the 1980s, played a crucial role in the internationalization of the jihadi movement. Killed in mysterious circumstances in 1989 in Peshawar in Pakistan, he remains one of the most influential jihadi ideologues of all time.

Here, in the first in-depth biography of Azzam, Thomas Hegghammer explains how Azzam came to play this role and why jihadism went global at this particular time. It traces Azzam's extraordinary life journey from a West Bank village to the battlefields of Afghanistan, telling the story of a man who knew all the leading Islamists of his time and frequented princes, CIA agents, and Cat Stevens the pop star. It is, however, also a story of displacement, exclusion, and repression which suggests that jihadism went global for fundamentally local reasons.

THOMAS HEGGHAMMER is a Senior Research Fellow at the Norwegian Defence Research Establishment (FFI) and Adjunct Professor in the Department of Political Science at the University of Oslo. Trained in Middle Eastern Studies at the University of Oxford and the Sciences Po, Paris, he is the author of the prize-winning book *Jihad in Saudi Arabia* (Cambridge University Press, 2010) and is the editor of *Jihadi Culture* (Cambridge University Press, 2017). He has conducted extensive fieldwork in the Middle East, including interviews with former militants, and he has testified on jihadism in front of the US Congress and the British Parliament.

Azzam on horseback (*al-Bunyan al-Marsus* magazine, no. 31 p. 38).

The Caravan

Abdallah Azzam and the Rise of Global Jihad

THOMAS HEGGHAMMER
Norwegian Defence Research Establishment (FFI)

CAMBRIDGE
UNIVERSITY PRESS

University Printing House, Cambridge CB2 8BS, United Kingdom

One Liberty Plaza, 20th Floor, New York, NY 10006, USA

477 Williamstown Road, Port Melbourne, VIC 3207, Australia

314–321, 3rd Floor, Plot 3, Splendor Forum, Jasola District Centre, New Delhi – 110025, India

79 Anson Road, #06–04/06, Singapore 079906

Cambridge University Press is part of the University of Cambridge.

It furthers the University's mission by disseminating knowledge in the pursuit of education, learning, and research at the highest international levels of excellence.

www.cambridge.org
Information on this title: www.cambridge.org/9780521765954
DOI: 10.1017/9781139049375

© Thomas Hegghammer 2020

This publication is in copyright. Subject to statutory exception and to the provisions of relevant collective licensing agreements, no reproduction of any part may take place without the written permission of Cambridge University Press.

First published 2020
Reprinted 2020

Printed in the United Kingdom by TJ International Ltd. Padstow Cornwall

A catalogue record for this publication is available from the British Library.

ISBN 978-0-521-76595-4 Hardback

Cambridge University Press has no responsibility for the persistence or accuracy of URLs for external or third-party internet websites referred to in this publication and does not guarantee that any content on such websites is, or will remain, accurate or appropriate.

Every effort has been made to contact the relevant copyright holders for the images reproduced in this book. In the event of any error, the publisher will be pleased to make corrections in any reprints or future editions.

To Arne and Haldis

Contents

Timelines	*page* ix
List of Maps	xiii
List of Illustrations	xiv
List of Table and Figure	xvi
Acknowledgments	xvii
Introduction	1
Prologue	9
1 Palestinian	11
2 Brother	28
3 Fighter	47
4 Scholar	66
5 Vagabond	88
6 Writer	125
7 Pioneer	143
8 Diplomat	172
9 Manager	205
10 Recruiter	244
11 Ideologue	288
12 *Mujahid*	328
13 Resident	369
14 Enemy	409

15	Martyr	436
16	Icon	463
	Conclusion	493
	Note on Sources	509
	Overview of Abdallah Azzam's Works	511

Notes 515
Bibliography 647
Index 682

Timelines

Azzam's life

Life events		Political events
Born in al-Sila al-Harithiyya (West Bank)	1941	
	1942	
	1943	
	1944	
	1945	
	1946	
	1947	
	1948	Palestine War
	1949	
	1950	
	1951	
	1952	
Joins Muslim Brotherhood	1953	
	1954	Muslim Brotherhood banned in Egypt
	1955	
	1956	
Enrolls in Kadoorie Agricultural School in Tulkarm (West Bank)	1957	
	1958	
	1959	
Graduates from Kadoorie, teaches in Adir (Jordan)	1960	
Starts teaching in Burqin (West Bank)	1961	
Enrolls at Damascus University (distance learning)	1962	Muslim World League founded in Mecca

(*cont.*)

Life events		Political events
	1963	Ba'thist coup in Syria
	1964	
Marries Samira Awatila	1965	
Graduates from Damascus University	1966	Sayyid Qutb executed in Egypt
Emigrates to Amman, moves to Baha (Saudi Arabia)	1967	Six Day War
Returns to Amman, teaches in high school	1968	
Joins the Fedayin in northern Jordan	1969	
Demobilizes, works in Jordanian Awqaf Ministry	1970	Black September in Jordan
Moves to Cairo for Ph.D.	1971	
	1972	
Gets Ph.D., starts teaching at Jordan University	1973	Yom Kippur War, oil crisis, Afghan monarchy toppled
	1974	
	1975	
	1976	
Publishes first book	1977	
Makes first trip to the United States, meets Bin Ladin	1978	Afghan Communist coup
	1979	Russian invasion of Afghanistan, Iranian revolution
Emigrates to Mecca	1980	
Visits Yemen, Emigrates to Islamabad	1981	
	1982	
	1983	
Founds Services Bureau, *al-Jihad* magazine	1984	
	1985	
Moves to Peshawar	1986	
	1987	Outbreak of Palestinian Intifada
	1988	
Is assassinated in Peshawar	1989	Russian withdrawal from Afghanistan

Afghanistan war

Political–military events		Azzam activities
	1980	
	1981	Meets al-Sananiri in Jeddah (around March)
		Meets al-Sananiri in Mecca (around August)
		Meets Sayyaf (October), moves to Islamabad (November)
	1982	
	1983	Publishes *Signs of the Merciful*
Badr project (February)	1984	
Founding of Services Bureau (September)		
Launch of *al-Jihad* magazine (December)		
	1985	Publishes *Defense of Muslim Lands*
	1986	
Battle of Zhawar (April)		Moves to Peshawar (May–June)
Sada camp for Arabs founded (July)		
al-Ma'sada camp founded (October)		
	1987	
Battle of Jaji (May–June)		
al-Qaida starts forming (winter)	1988	

(*cont.*)

Political–military events	Azzam activities
First record of al-Qaida organization (September)	Visits Massoud in Panjshir (September)
	Dispute with Ahmad Sa'id Khadr (December)
1989	
Battle of Jalalabad (March–May)	
	Assassination (24 November)

Maps

1: Middle East and South West Asia *page* xxi
2: West Bank and Jordan xxii
3: Afghanistan–Pakistan border areas xxiii
4: Afghanistan xxiii

Illustrations

1 Abdallah Azzam's native village, al-Sila al-Harithiyya, in 2008. View from the southeast, with the road from Jenin in the foreground (Thomas Hegghammer). *page* 271
2 Abdallah Azzam as a young schoolteacher, around 1961 (*al-Jihad* magazine, no. 74 p. 31). 271
3 Abdallah Azzam as a teacher in Amman, around 1968 (Azzam family collection). 272
4 Abdallah Azzam and his children in Cairo, around 1972 (Azzam family collection). 272
5 Cover of Abdallah Azzam's book *The Red Cancer*, published 1980 (Internet Archive image). 273
6 Azzam lecturing at the University of Da'wa and Jihad, around 1985 (*al-Jihad* magazine, no. 64 p. 22). 274
7 Azzam relaxing during a visit to an Afghan Mujahidin camp, early 1980s (*al-Bunyan al-Marsus* magazine, no. 30 p. 28). 274
8 Azzam writing, location unknown, mid-1980s (*al-Jihad* magazine, no. 65 p. 7). 275
9 Cover of the first edition of Abdallah Azzam's book *The Defense of Muslim Lands*, published in Peshawar in March 1985 (*al-Jihad* magazine, no. 7 p. 3). 276
10 Cover of *al-Jihad* magazine in March 1986. Cat Stevens in the picture below on the left (*al-Jihad* magazine, no. 17 p. 1). 277
11 Advertisement for propaganda materials in *al-Jihad* magazine, September 1987. Among the products on offer is a cassette tape containing "*Anashid* of jihad by the British Muslim preacher Yusuf Islam [Cat Stevens]." (*al-Jihad* magazine, no. 34 p. 29). 278
12 Facsimile of *al-Jihad* magazine report on the al-Sada camp in August 1986 (*al-Jihad* magazine, no. 21 p. 33). 279

List of Illustrations

13 Abdallah Azzam, Tamim al-Adnani, Gulbuddin
    Hekmatyar, and Abd Rabb al-Rasul Sayyaf at Jaji in
    May 1987 (*al-Jihad* magazine, no. 31 p. 18). 279
14 Abdallah Azzam in Afghanistan in the mid-1980s
    (*al-Bunyan al-Marsus* magazine, no. 30 p. 26). 280
15 Abdallah Azzam (middle) with Ahmed Shah Massoud
    (second from left), Azzam's son Ibrahim (far left), and
    Azzam's aide and driver Abu Harith (far right). Fifth man
    unidentified (*al-Bunyan al-Marsus* magazine, no. 30 p. 17). 281
16 Ahmed Shah Massoud, Burhanuddin Rabbani, and
    Abdallah Azzam inspecting Massoud's troops in the
    Panjshir valley, September 1988 (*al-Bunyan al-Marsus*
    magazine, no. 30 p. 24). 281
17 Abdallah Azzam speaking about Palestine in the Muslim
    Student Union Centre in Islamabad during the "Solidarity
    week with global movements of liberation," November 1985
    (*al-Bunyan al-Marsus* magazine, no. 5 p. 14). 282
18 Abdallah Azzam and Rachid Ghannouchi in Peshawar in
    1989 (*al-Bunyan al-Marsus* magazine, no. 30 p. 22). 283
19 Abdallah Azzam and his father Yusuf Azzam in Peshawar,
    around 1988 (Azzam family collection). 284
20 The wreck of Abdallah Azzam's car after the assassination
    on 24 November 1989 (*al-Bunyan al-Marsus* magazine,
    no. 30 p. 6). 284
21 Drawing from *al-Bunyan al-Marsus* magazine of the area
    around the site of Abdallah Azzam's assassination in
    Peshawar on 24 November 1989. Azzam's house on the
    left; the Sab' al-Layl mosque on the right (*al-Bunyan al-
    Marsus* magazine, no. 30 pp. 6–7). 285
22 Abd Rabb al-Rasul Sayyaf grieving before the dead body of
    Abdallah Azzam in Pabbi on the evening of the day of his
    assassination (*al-Jihad* magazine, no. 74 p. 29). 285
23 Pro-al-Qaida photo montage from around 2011 showing
    Abdallah Azzam (far right) alongside (from left) Usama Bin
    Ladin, Abu Yahya al-Libi, Abu Mus'ab al-Zarqawi, and
    Ayman al-Zawahiri (jihadi website). 286
24 The author and Hudhayfa Azzam in Amman, July 2018
    (Thomas Hegghammer). 287

Table and Figure

Table

10.1 Author's Best Estimate of the Number of Foreign Fighters
in 1980s Afghanistan   *page* 267

Figure

10.1 Approximate number of Arabs present in Peshawar and
Afghanistan, 1979–1989   268

Acknowledgments

"Smell it!" he said, as he passed me the bloodstained jacket. "Can you smell it? The musk? The blood of martyrs smells of musk." I could not for the life of me sense anything other than a whiff of old garment. Not that I knew what musk smelled like, for that matter. I was holding the jacket that Abdallah Azzam had worn on the day of his assassination in 1989, and I was in the Azzam family house in Amman with Hudhayfa, his oldest surviving son. It was September 2006, and I had come to interview Hudhayfa for my doctoral dissertation on jihadism in Saudi Arabia, a story in which his father was an important support actor. I had just had dinner prepared by Azzam's widow, so the smell of roasted chicken made the olfactory challenge even harder. "I know you probably don't believe this stuff," Hudhayfa said, breaking the silence. "You would, though, if you had been to Afghanistan."

At that moment I realized my next book would have to be about the jacket's owner. I already knew that Abdallah Azzam was a towering figure in the history of Islamism. I had encountered his name numerous times in my research on al-Qaida, starting in July 2001, when, as a young intern at the Norwegian Defence Research Establishment (FFI), my boss Brynjar Lia put me to work on something called "the Bin Laden network." By August 2001 I had learned about Azzam, the Services Bureau, and the Afghan Arabs, and I had discovered Azzam.com, the main English-language jihadi website at the time. Over the following years, as I immersed myself in the world of jihadi literature, collecting texts and films, I saw the Azzam folder on my hard drive grow conspicuously large. When I started going to Saudi Arabia in 2004 for my Ph.D. research (which became the book *Jihad in Saudi Arabia*), many of my interviewees highlighted Azzam's inspirational role.

In late 2007 I was able to devote myself fully to writing Azzam's biography thanks to a postdoctoral fellowship and a travel grant from Princeton University, where I enjoyed the generous support of Bernard

Haykel. I was then allowed to continue my research at Harvard Kennedy School's Belfer Center thanks to the hospitality of Monica Duffy Toft and Steven Miller. The next year (2009–2010) a William D. Loughlin fellowship at the Institute for Advanced Study in Princeton allowed me to keep working on Azzam and to bounce ideas off Patricia Crone, Avishai Margalit, and other great minds at the Institute. Then, having written half the book, I put the project on hold because the Arab Spring and the Syria war gave me too many other things to do. In late 2015 I was able to get back to it, thanks to my FFI bosses Espen Berg-Knutsen and Espen Skjelland, who allowed me to withdraw to the attic of the Norwegian Nobel Institute, where Olav Njølstad kindly hosted me.

I have many other people to thank for helping to make this book a reality; most of all my family. My wife Målfrid has not only put up with a great deal of absent-mindedness and agonizing; she has also pushed me when I needed it and provided feedback on the manuscript. My parents Tone and Odd have supported and encouraged me over a lifetime, including on this project. My greatest source of joy and energy along the way have been Arne and Haldis. As every writing parent knows, few things relieve writer's angst like the rolling laughter of a five-year old – except perhaps a "Dad, the book's gonna be great" from a boy aged seven.

The other family that deserves my gratitude is Abdallah Azzam's own. I owe special thanks to Hudhayfa Azzam and Abdallah Anas, who were extremely generous with their time and knowledge. Abdallah Anas even accompanied me to Afghanistan in December 2017 to help arrange a meeting with Abd Rabb al-Rasul Sayyaf. I am also very grateful to Umm Muhammad, Abu Mujahid, and Abu Suhayb for their hospitality. They knew that I was not going to write a hagiography, but they still opened up their homes to me. I have tried to repay their trust by staying as objective and accurate as possible, though I realize they may not agree with all of my assessments.

I have also benefited tremendously from the help of colleagues in the field. Stéphane Lacroix and Brynjar Lia have long been my closest intellectual sparring partners, and their influence is all over this manuscript. Brynjar also provided detailed comments, down to the diacritics in the footnotes, on the entire final draft. My former supervisor Gilles Kepel also provided important support and inspiration, especially in the project's early stages. I am also very

Acknowledgments   xix

grateful to those who participated in the day-long "murder board" on the first draft of this book in September 2017 in Oslo: Abdallah Anas, Leah Farrall, Stéphane Lacroix, Nelly Lahoud, Brynjar Lia, Will McCants (in absentia), Petter Nesser, Don Rassler, Anne Stenersen, and Alex Strick van Linschoten. Each took days off their schedule to discuss and comment on my manuscript, a large favor I hope to repay in due course.

Many colleagues shared sources and ideas with me over the years. Christopher Anzalone sent me a steady stream of Azzam-related material he came across in his research. I also received crucial documents from Peter Bergen, J. M. Berger, Alexander De la Paz, Brian Fishman, Seamus Hughes, Evan Kohlmann, Felix Kuehn, Alex Strick van Linschoten, Truls Tønnessen, and Joas Wagemakers. The following people all shared ideas and insights: the late Mariam Abou Zahab, As'ad AbuKhalil, Eran Benedek, James Brandon, Jean-Charles Brisard, Steven Brooke, Vahid Brown, Romain Caillet, David Cook, Michael Cook, Michael Crawford, Yusuf al-Dayni, Renaud Detalle, Gilles Dorronsoro, Jean-Pierre Filiu, Tore Hamming, Hassan Hassan, Steffen Hertog, Bruce Hoffman, Timothy Holman, Seamus Hughes, Saba Imtiaz, Gregory Johnsen, Shashank Joshi, Shiraz Maher, Andrew March, Mathias Müller, the late Reuven Paz, Thomas Pierret, Bernard Rougier, Olivier Roy, Ronald Sandee, Saud al-Sarhan, Rachel Simon, Charles D. Smith, Aymenn al-Tamimi, Asgeir Ueland, Bertrand Valeyre, Lorenzo Vidino, Lawrence Wright, and Aaron Zelin.

Several others helped me in various ways. Erik Skare shared sources and did a formidable job with the preliminary copyediting of the manuscript. Zachary Johnson, Sumayya Doqa, Michael Boyce, Samna Zia, and Mohammad Arshad Zia all provided valuable research assistance at different stages in the project. Azmi Saleh at the Kadoorie College in Tulkarm scanned and sent me Azzam's school records. Synnøve Eifring and the other librarians at FFI were always there to expedite my strange literature requests. Norwegian embassy personnel assisted me on my field trips, especially Hanne Ulrichsen in Amman in 2008 and Ambassador Mari Skåre in Kabul in 2017.

I also thank the many people who agreed to be interviewed for this book. The list of names in the Note on Sources (see the end of the book) does not give justice to the scale of the goodwill from which I benefited. Behind each name is the memory of one or more warm encounters in which someone took time off a busy schedule for no other benefit than to help improve our collective understanding of history.

Finally, I thank the team at Cambridge University Press: Marigold Acland, who accepted the project; Maria Marsh, who took over after Marigold's retirement; and Daniel Brown, who saw it through at the end. My brilliant and eagle-eyed copyeditors Mary Starkey and Shirley Rhodes greatly improved the manuscript and saved me from many embarrassments. Many thanks also to Abigail Walkington and Natasha Whelan for their assistance in the production process. I also thank Obaydah Amer, the translator of the Arabic edition of this book, for very helpful comments and corrections.

This project has been so long in the making and involved so many generous people that there are almost certainly some I have forgotten to mention. I hope they will forgive me, as I hope you readers will forgive me for other errors and inaccuracies that have slipped into the book. It has been a long journey, and I have learned a lot. I have even found out what musk smells like.

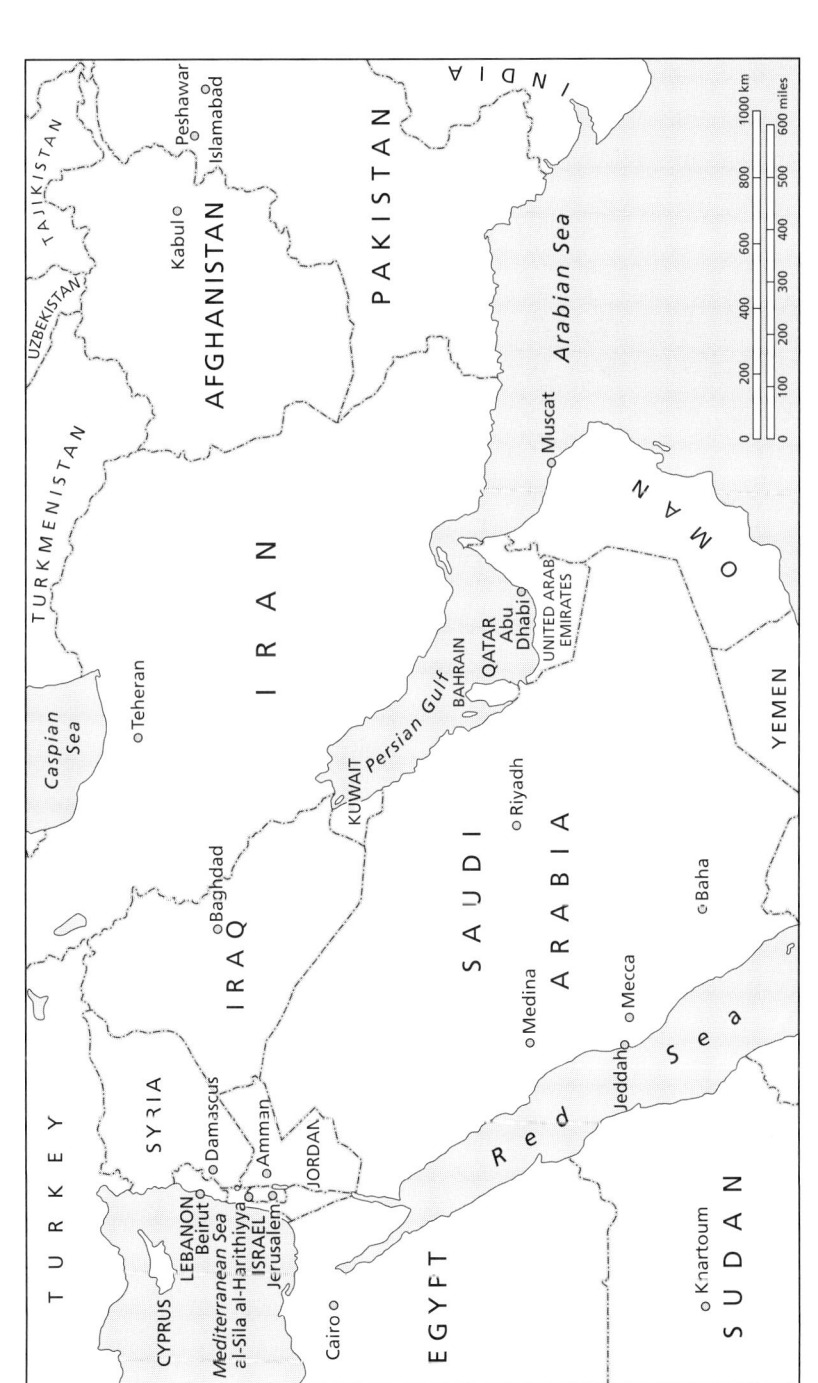

Map 1: Middle East and South West Asia

Map 2: West Bank and Jordan

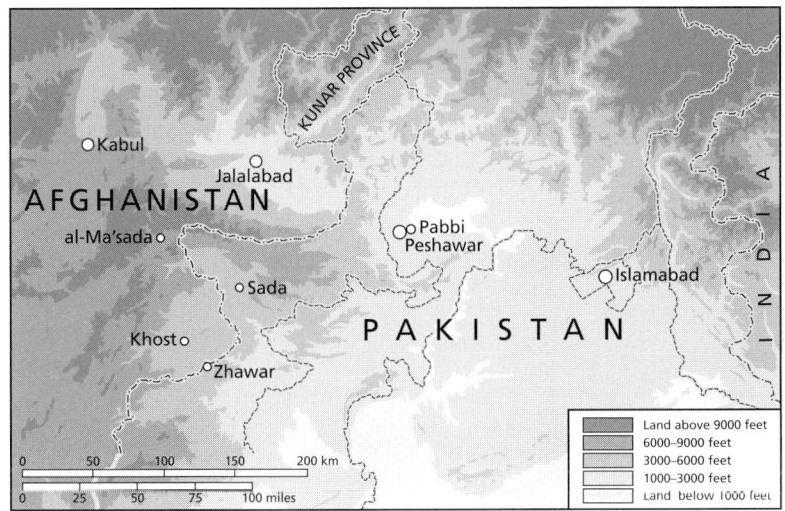

Map 3: Afghanistan–Pakistan border areas

Map 4: Afghanistan

Introduction

This book is about why jihadism went global. It is a biography of Abdallah Azzam, the Palestinian ideologue who led the recruitment of Arab fighters to Afghanistan in the 1980s. It is also a history of the Afghan Arabs, the world's first truly global foreign-fighter mobilization. The Afghan jihad is widely recognized as the Big Bang in the globalization of jihadism, but we have not really understood why the Arabs joined it. The deep answer, as we shall see, lies neither in Islamic theology nor in international politics, but in the domestic politics of the postwar Arab world.[1]

This is also the story of a life stranger than fiction. It is the tale of a Palestinian who devoted his life to a war in Central Asia, a farmer who became a globetrotting war recruiter, and a professor who came to love military life. It is the account of a radical ideologue who not only befriended virtually all the leading Islamists of his time, but also met royals, CIA agents, and Cat Stevens the pop star. His story will take us to unexpected places such as California, southern Italy, and Venezuela, and bring us into underground apartments, lavish palaces, and dark mountain caves. It will end literally with a bang: a bomb assassination that remains the greatest murder mystery in the history of jihadism.

What happened in the 1980s is still relevant because the Soviet–Afghan war is the cradle of today's jihadi movement. That was where al-Qaida was born, and that was where famous leaders such as Usama Bin Ladin started their militant careers. The networks forged in Afghanistan became the backbone of the jihadi movement in the 1990s and 2000s, with former Afghan Arabs filling key roles in most jihadi groups. Intellectually, too, the Afghan jihad played a vital role, both as an incubator for key ideas and as the source environment for the jihadi subculture we know today. As the jihadi strategist Abu Mus'ab al-Suri later said, "This was a turning in Muslim history. People met, thoughts and perspectives met. Groups fought out their rivalries, and different thoughts and ideas competed. It was a kind of birthplace. Much of what you see today is a result of this period."[2]

At the same time, the mobilization to Afghanistan is something of a mystery, because nothing like it had happened before. Earlier decades saw multiple conflicts in the Muslim world – from Algeria in the west to the Philippines in the east – but none attracted foreign fighters on anywhere near the scale of Afghanistan. There had been Islamist foreign fighters in the 1948 Palestine war, but they enjoyed state support and came mainly from neighbouring countries. Indeed, since its emergence in the early twentieth century, the Islamist movement had been preoccupied with domestic politics. The 1960s saw the emergence of radical Islamists who were more open to the use of violence, but they too were focused on domestic political change. In short, as late as the 1970s virtually all radical Islamist politics was local. Then – all of a sudden, as it were – thousands of foreign fighters from all over the world decided to join the anti-Soviet war in Afghanistan. They came from Venezuela, Sweden, Australia, and South Africa, and from over forty other countries in between. Most, of course, came from the Arab world, and made the term "Afghan Arabs" shorthand for all the foreign volunteers.[3]

The Afghan jihad is also fascinating from a comparative perspective, because it produced what may be the most transnational rebel movement in modern history. No other ideological family has fostered a set of militant groups as large, as mobile, and as resilient as the jihadi movement. The leftist revolutionaries of the twentieth century had more impact because they captured large states, but Marxist rebel groups did not operate militarily across borders nearly as much as the jihadis have done in recent decades. Far-left terrorist groups in 1970s and 1980s Europe were highly mobile, but they were much smaller and less lethal than groups such as al-Qaida and Islamic State. As such, the jihadis are an anomaly in a world of largely parochial rebel movements, and should pique the curiosity of anyone interested in international politics.

Recent decades have seen extensive research on jihadism, but the formative event – the Arab involvement in Afghanistan – has not been fully explained. When it is not described as something that simply happened, the Arab mobilization to Afghanistan is explained by some combination of government encouragement and the search for a safe haven. Some scholars, such as Gilles Kepel and Peter Mandaville, emphasize the role of geopolitics and government encouragement, especially from Saudi Arabia.[4] Others, such as Fawaz Gerges and Bernard Rougier, highlight Afghanistan's role as a safe haven for Islamist revolutionaries under pressure at home.[5] What most accounts have in common is the view that the foreign fighters were really domestic revolutionaries in exile. Put differently, the Arab mobilization to Afghanistan has been viewed as a natural continuation of the ideas of the Egyptian ideologue Sayyid Qutb (d. 1966) that dominated radical Islamist thinking in the 1960s and 1970s.

However, the Arab involvement in Afghanistan represented a rupture from Qutb's ideas, because Qutb talked about regime change, not about other Muslims' wars of national liberation. The Afghan Arabs went to fight non-Muslim invaders in Afghanistan – a qualitatively different endeavour from that of toppling Muslim regimes. Thus the call to fight in Afghanistan represented a change of priorities in Islamist thought, away from fighting corrupt Muslim rulers at home and toward fighting infidel invaders abroad. This shift from revolutionary to pan-Islamist mobilization cries out for an explanation.

In describing this shift, many writers have highlighted the role of Abdallah Azzam, the Palestinian preacher who spent the 1980s recruiting Arabs to the Afghan jihad from his base in Peshawar in Pakistan.[6] Azzam is widely credited with having played a major role in bringing the Arabs to Afghanistan; he has been called "the spiritual father of the Afghan Arabs," "the sheikh of the Arab Mujahidin," and "the hero of the Arab Jihad in Afghanistan."[7] However, the claim has not been subjected to careful scrutiny. How do we know that there were not other actors or forces that brought the Arabs to Afghanistan? And if Azzam really was important, then how did he get involved, and how was he able to exert such influence? A close examination of Azzam's life thus promises to yield important insights into how the Arab mobilization happened, and, by extension, why the Islamist foreign-fighter phenomenon emerged when it did.

There are other reasons to study Abdallah Azzam closely. For one thing, he remains one of the most revered figures in the world of radical Islamism. On almost every metric, Azzam is one of the most influential jihadi ideologues of all time, as we shall see in Chapter 16. For another, his life closely tags the history of Islamism in the late twentieth century, so he is a useful prism for viewing that history. As we shall see, Azzam found himself, often by coincidence, in many of the places where history was being made in this period.

Yet the literature on Azzam is remarkably small. There is only one English-language book about him – Muhammad Haniff Hassan's *Father of Jihad* – and it concentrates on his ideology, not his biography.[8] Other than that, the Western academic literature on Azzam is currently limited to about six articles, a three-part report, and a book chapter.[9] To this list must be added a certain number of magazine articles, op-eds, blog posts, and the like.[10] For comparison, there are at least five biographies in English of Usama Bin Ladin, while Sayyid Qutb is so widely studied that there are two books *about* the books about him.[11] The Arabic-language literature on Azzam is larger than the English-language one, but it is mostly hagiographic, so I will come back to it below in my review of primary sources. This has not only left Azzam shrouded in a fog of unanswered factual questions – such as: Who killed him? Did he found al-Qaida? Did he write the Hamas charter? – it has also left us with a limited understanding of his wider historical role and contribution.

The book will try to fill these gaps by exploring three main lines of inquiry. The first is about the basic facts of Azzam's biography. Where did he come from, and what shaped him as a thinker? What motivated the big decisions in his life, such as his move to Pakistan in 1981? And what were his opinions? The second concerns the sources of Azzam's influence. Why did he become so influential? What did he do to recruit so many people to Afghanistan? Why did his ideas catch on the way they did? The third question set concerns the mechanisms of the Arab mobilization to Afghanistan. Who were the first movers and what got them involved? By which networks, methods, and resources were subsequent recruits drawn in? And last but not least, what exactly was Azzam's contribution?

Answering these questions required working roughly two-thirds as a historian and one-third as a social scientist. Much of the work was an inductive, historiographical process of locating, assessing, and reconciling sources to identify key actors and events. This is especially true of my approach to the factual questions about Azzam's trajectory. Addressing the second and third sets of questions – about ideological influence and the Arab–Afghan mobilization – involved a more analytical approach. For example, to assess Azzam's relative importance as a recruiter and organizer, I had to identify the other actors who contributed, think of metrics of contribution, and then compare Azzam to the others.

Finding relevant sources involved a lot of detective work. For the questions about the Arab Afghan mobilization, there was a rich secondary literature to work with, thanks to the recent books by Peter Tomsen, Alex Strick van Linschoten and Felix Kuehn, Vahid Brown and Don Rassler, Leah Farrall and Mustafa Hamid, and Anne Stenersen.[12] However, for the first two sets of questions I had to rely mainly on primary sources, collected over a long period from many different places.

A crucial source was Azzam's own writings and lectures. This is a corpus of many thousand pages of text and several hundred hours of recorded lectures. I collected most of it from the internet and from university libraries in the USA and Middle East. I believe I have a full collection, but I cannot be certain, because the Azzam corpus is large and unwieldy. Only a small part of it was published in book form in his lifetime. The rest is posthumous editions of unpublished manuscripts, transcriptions of lectures, compilations of articles, and recorded lectures that his supporters took it on themselves to make available after he died. However, this editorial work was decentralized, resulting in transcribed lectures presented as books, medleys and extracts presented as independent works, and multiple title discrepancies. Disentangling all this has been laborious, and establishing a full chronology was impossible, because many of the documents are undated. At the end of the book I provide a list of his major works, and on the book website (www.azzambook.net) I provide a more detailed list of sources as well as the documents themselves.

Another vital source was Islamist biographies of Azzam. Particularly useful were six book-length works in Arabic, which I treat here as primary sources, because they are hagiographic and were authored by people who were Afghan Arabs and/or Muslim Brothers themselves. They include Husni Jarrar's *The Martyr Abdallah Azzam* (1990), Bashir Abu Rumman and Abdallah Sa'id's *The Scholar, Mujahid, Martyr and Sheikh Abdallah Azzam* (1990), Muhammad Amir's *The Mujahid Sheikh Abdallah Azzam* (1990), Fayiz Azzam's *The Martyr Abdallah Azzam between Birth and Martyrdom* (1991), Adnan al-Nahawi's *Abdallah Azzam: Events and Positions* (1994), and, last but not least, Mahmud Azzam's *The Doctor and Martyr Abdallah Yusuf Azzam* (2012).[13] Several of these books contain testimonies and primary sources collected in the first few years after Azzam's death, and two of them were written by family members of Azzam who were with him in Pakistan (Fayiz and Mahmud Azzam are his nephews). Another key source was *Through Contemporary Eyes*, a 650-page collection of articles, statements, and letters published in the aftermath of Azzam's death.[14] I also drew on the many article-length biographies in English and Arabic that have circulated on Islamist websites.[15] In addition, I collected theses written about him by sympathizers at schools such as the Islamic University in Gaza.[16]

A third key source was my own interviews with people who knew Azzam or observed the Afghanistan war up close. I spoke to around seventy people, including some living legends of modern Islamism such as Abd Rabb al-Rasul Sayyaf in Afghanistan and Abu Muhammad al-Maqdisi in Amman. I went to Azzam's native village, al-Sila al-Harithiyya, where his brother, cousin, and other family members showed me the places he frequented growing up. I went to Amman several times to interview Azzam's son Hudhayfa and other family members. I did not get to meet his widow, Umm Muhammad, but she answered questions by intermediary. In London I spoke at length with Azzam's son-in-law Boudjema Bounoua (better known as Abdallah Anas). In Peshawar I met Jamal Isma'il and Ahmad Zaidan, who had worked with Azzam on *al-Jihad* magazine. I talked to former Central Intelligence Agency (CIA) operatives, a former Saudi intelligence official, and a former official of the Pakistani ISI. I also interviewed former students of Azzam's, veteran Muslim Brotherhood members, and Western NGO workers who were in Peshawar in the 1980s.

I also examined the broader corpus of books, magazines, and videos produced by the Afghan Arab community in the 1980s and 1990s. It includes several dozen memoirs, travel accounts, and other types of books. A key source was Basil Muhammad's *Pages from the Record of the Arab Supporters in Afghanistan* (1991), a detailed history of the Arabs in Afghanistan from 1980 to 1987.[17] Arabs in Peshawar also produced magazines; Azzam's own *al-Jihad* magazine is the best known, but there were many others. I also perused jihadi propaganda films from the 1980s, including the productions of the Egyptian filmmaker Isam Diraz, who was embedded with Arab fighters in Afghanistan in the late 1980s.

Some of this material has been available in the nooks and crannies of the internet, but for other things I had to go off the beaten track. In Kabul I trawled bookshops for old editions of Azzam's books. I went to

Peshawar to browse local newspapers from the 1980s, and to Riyadh to find jihadi magazines in libraries and private collections. I contacted the schools Azzam had attended asking for his enrollment dates, in response to which the Kadoorie College in Tulkarm kindly sent me copies of his entire file, complete with his application letter from 1957 and his grade transcripts. I also made an effort to obtain government documents, submitting Freedom of Information Act requests about Azzam to the CIA, the Federal Bureau of Investigation (FBI), and the US Customs and Border Protection.

Still, some sources were left unexploited. The language barrier prevented me from accessing the substantial literature on Azzam in Turkish. I also failed to obtain interviews with a few key individuals who knew Azzam well, notably Isma'il al-Shatti' and Rachid Ghannouchi. I also did not fully exploit Jordan as a fieldwork site; there are many former students of Azzam's and veteran Jordanian Muslim Brothers I did not interview. Similarly, there is more work to be done on the Afghan and Pakistani side of the Afghan Arab story. Still, this book presents quite a bit of new evidence that should help us address some important historical questions.

The book's main finding is that jihadism went global in the 1980s because Islamists had been excluded from domestic politics in preceding decades. Constrained at home, some Islamists turned to an arena in which they faced less government interference – namely, transnational activism for pan-Islamic causes. By the late 1970s a whole new movement of pan-Islamist activists had emerged, one that promoted a victim narrative about worldwide Muslim suffering and provided assistance to faraway Muslim countries through Islamic charities. Then, in the 1980s, hardliners such as Abdallah Azzam interpreted the notion of Muslim solidarity militarily, saying that Muslims should also *fight* for each other. This message resonated with many because Muslim solidarity activism was already in vogue.

Abdallah Azzam did not cause the transnationalization of jihad, but few individuals played a more important part. His clerical training and Muslim Brotherhood background gave him a religious authority and contact network that no other Arab in 1980s Peshawar possessed. The Afghan Arab phenomenon would have emerged without him, but he made it substantially larger than it would have been. Azzam is also partly responsible for the subsequent rise of transnational jihadi terrorism, not because he advocated such tactics, but because he helped undermine traditional authorities on matters of jihad. Azzam's key message in the 1980s was that Muslims should go and fight in Afghanistan even if their governments or parents objected. This helped produce a movement that could not be controlled, and would descend further and further into radicalism. As such, the story of the globalization of jihad is a lesson in unintended consequences for both governments and Islamists.

The book consists of sixteen chapters which are ordered chronologically and form two natural parts. Chapters 1 through 6 cover Azzam's pre-Afghanistan period, while Chapters 7 through 15 deal with his time in Afghanistan. In the first part, each chapter covers an aspect of his background that helps understand his subsequent influence. These are: his background as a Palestinian, Muslim Brother, Fedayin fighter, Islamic scholar, itinerant dissident, and author. In the second part, each chapter deals with a role that he played in the Afghan jihad and that helps us assess his contribution to the mobilization. He was – partly in this order – an early mover, diplomat, manager, recruiter, ideologue, military man, resident, object of controversy, and assassination target. Chapter 16 is an epilogue about his contested legacy.

In 1987, two years before his death, Azzam wrote a short book titled *Join the Caravan*, which called on all able-bodied Muslims to fight in Afghanistan.[18] The book became an instant classic of jihadi literature, and is still widely read today. The expression "joining the caravan" has since entered the jihadi lexicon as a synonym for joining the jihadi movement. Azzam's caravan grew larger than anyone could have imagined. This is the story of how it got moving.

Prologue

Like every Friday morning, Sheikh Abdallah had been up since before sunrise to pray and read the Qur'an, and he had already clocked up several hours in his study. He took a last look at his notes and went to put on clean new clothes. As the imam of Peshawar's "Arab mosque," he was due to give the Friday sermon to hundreds of people in a little over an hour. The calendar read 24 November 1989, the clock half past eleven.

He was in a good mood. The night before he had finally secured a truce agreement between Hekmatyar and Rabbani, the Afghan Mujahidin leaders who had been practically at war for the past six months. He was looking forward to announcing the peace from the pulpit and then going to Islamabad to celebrate with all the Mujahidin leaders. He was also pleased to have his eldest son Muhammad back in the house; the latter had just come back from Amman after accompanying his grandfather to their native Palestine. Azzam was so upbeat he had not even minded that Hudhayfa and Ibrahim, his two other teenage sons, had asked to leave the Qur'an-reading session early this morning to play sports.

At noon he was ready to go. He put on his jacket, then looked at his watch. "Hudhayfa, where are you? Can you still take us?" he shouted. His son peeked into the hallway with an embarrassed smile. "What, you haven't washed yet? Never mind, Muhammad can take us. You join us there later." He went out to the courtyard and jumped into the passenger seat of his dark red Chevrolet Vega. The mosque was just around the corner, but the roads were pedestrian-unfriendly, so they always took the car. Muhammad got in the front, Ibrahim in the back.

It was now ten past twelve. As their car pulled out from the yard, five-year-old Mus'ab came running, keen to ride with the big boys. "Father, can I please also come?" "No, my son, please go back into the house." With Muhammad behind the wheel, the car headed slowly down the residential street, then right up Arbab Road, and then right again onto Grand Trunk Road. Fifty meters up, they exited on the right, in the direction of the mosque. Then, all of a sudden, there was a flash of light and a deafening explosion. A large bomb ripped the car apart from underneath. Abdallah Azzam's jihad in Afghanistan was over.

1 | *Palestinian*

Abdallah Azzam's involvement in the Afghan jihad would have been less intriguing if he had been from a quiet corner of the Arab world such as Morocco or Oman. But Azzam was from Palestine, the site of one of the most bitter national liberation struggles of the late twentieth century. He had even been personally affected by Israel's territorial expansion through his family's loss of land in 1948 and his emigration to Jordan during the Six Day War of 1967. Why, then, did he fight for the liberation of Afghanistan and not Palestine? Why would any man join a faraway war while his own country is under occupation?

This chapter deals with Azzam's Palestinian years – that is, from the early 1940s to the late 1960s. We will look at his upbringing on the West Bank, his experiences with the wars of 1948 and 1967, and his thinking on the Palestinian struggle. We will see that Azzam's Palestinian background was a central part of his identity, and that he remained deeply committed to the Palestinian cause throughout his life. However, after Jordan's crackdown on the Fedayin guerrillas in 1970, he lost faith in the idea that Israel could be defeated by paramilitary efforts from outside the Territories. He later rationalized his involvement in Afghanistan as a first stage in a long-term strategy to liberate Jerusalem, one that involved building a strong Muslim army in Afghanistan and conquering Palestine by conventional war. In the 1980s Azzam grappled with the dilemma of trying to leverage his Palestinian background for recruitment to Afghanistan while fending off accusations that he had abandoned the Palestinian cause.

Fighting Farmers

Abdallah Azzam was born on 14 November 1941 in the village of al-Sila al-Harithiyya in the northern West Bank, some 10 kilometers northwest of Jenin.[1] Al-Sila, as locals call it for short, sits on a cluster of hills on the southern flank of the Jezreel Valley plain, a vast green expanse of prime agricultural land. Back in the 1940s al-Sila was a community of some 1,800 inhabitants, mostly farmers, who used the southern strip of the plain for grazing livestock and growing apricots, olives, and almonds.[2]

The Azzam family had deep roots in the area, but few claims to fame.[3] Azzam means "very resolved," and was the name of a man who had come from the Ramallah area and settled in al-Sila when the village was founded generations ago.[4] The Azzams belonged to the al-Shawahina tribe of the al-Rifa'i tribal confederation that hailed back to the early Islamic historical figure Husayn bin Ali bin Abi Talib.[5] The Azzams were one of five branches of the al-Shawahina tribe represented in al-Sila, most of whom lived in a part of the village called the al-Shawahina district.[6] The Azzams were respected in the village; Abdallah's great-uncle Salih Mahmud Azzam long served as its mayor.

Abdallah grew up in an entirely ordinary household. His father, Yusuf Mustafa Yusuf Azzam (ca. 1901–1990), was a farmer who supplemented his income by running a small butcher's store on the side.[7] His mother, Zakiya Salih Husayn al-Ahmad (ca. 1901–1988) was from another farming family from al-Sila. Azzam's family was not poor; in 1957 it had a land holding of 150 decars, a decent plot at the time.[8] However, they were far from affluent; when Abdallah went to boarding school in the late 1950s, his father had trouble paying the yearly fee of 30 Jordanian dinars. He would have had to quit after the first year had it not been for his strong academic performance, which made the headmaster agree to waive his fees.[9] Moreover, when Azzam was in his early twenties he kept only the bare minimum of his teacher's salary and gave the rest to his father.

By all accounts Azzam had a happy and harmonious childhood. He was the last addition to the family, born when his parents were both around forty years old.[10] As such he enjoyed the care and attention of not only his parents, but also of his two older sisters, Bahja and Jamila.[11] As the youngest, he was also less involved in the farmwork than his two older brothers Abd al-Qadir and Abd al-Malik, which probably gave him more time to pursue his intellectual interests. He is widely described as a bookish and well-behaved child, who was particularly close to his sister Jamila and to his mother Zakiya, whose hand he kissed every morning.

Azzam's home region was bucolic, but also politically charged. The Jezreel Valley plain is one of the most fertile agricultural areas of the entire Levant, making it a prized possession for those who control it.[12] When Azzam was born the area had been under foreign domination for centuries; first by the Ottomans, then, from 1922, by the British Mandate. The region therefore had a history of resistance activism. In the mid-eighteenth century northern Palestine enjoyed near autonomy from the Ottomans under the rebellious sheikhdom of Zahir al-Umar.[13] In 1799 locals had fought Napoleon's invading forces on the Jezreel Valley plain.[14] In the nineteenth century Ottoman administrators reported difficulties collecting tax from the area.[15] During the Arab revolt against the British in the late 1930s, the Nablus–Tulkarm–Jenin region was a centre of resistance referred to by the British as the "Triangle of Death."[16]

The Arab revolt was fresh in al-Sila's collective memory when Azzam was growing up. Residents had been involved in the insurgency; according to one of his Islamist biographers, al-Sila was a "striving village" (*qariya mujahida*) with "a noble role in jihad."[17] Azzam himself later noted that when the 1948 war broke out there were still some hundred rifles left in the village from the 1930s.[18] In 1935 the legendary fighter and Palestinian national hero Sheikh Izz al-Din al-Qassam had been killed by British forces near Ya'bad, just 10 kilometers southwest of al-Sila. Al-Sila was also the hometown of Yusuf Abu Durra, one of the heroes of the revolt.[19] Abu Durra had been a student and companion of Izz al-Din al-Qassam and rose to the top ranks of the resistance in 1936.

Azzam's family had direct experience with both the vicissitudes of the British occupation and the resistance to it. His father later recounted that "the English tried to burn our house in the past after they beat my uncle before my eyes and broke his ribs. They accused him of supporting the *mujahidin*, and they demanded that the village pay a fine of 60 pounds."[20] This led Abdallah's father, who had previously spent time in the Ottoman army, to take up arms: "The English were occupying the land, and when the revolution against them began, I sold my cattle and went on foot to Jordan and from there to Syria to Aleppo and the Peninsula to buy a rifle. I paid 100 Palestinian dinars, a vast amount in those days."[21] We do not know exactly what he did with the rifle; he does not appear to have joined the core of the resistance, but Azzam's hagiographers were keen to stress that his father had "waged jihad in Palestine."[22]

Losing Land

Shortly after Abdallah turned six, war returned to Palestine. On 29 November 1947 the United Nations General Assembly approved the Partition Plan for Palestine, prompting armed rebellion by Arab Palestinians. Violence erupted in December 1947, and escalated in the spring until, on 14 May 1948, Israel declared independence. The following day, forces from Egypt, Iraq, Jordan, Lebanon, and Syria invaded in an attempt to prevent the establishment of a Jewish state. The attempt failed, and the armistice agreements of early 1949 drew new borders, known as the Green Line, which gave Israel more territory than the UN plan had envisaged. What remained of the West Bank fell under Jordanian rule. More importantly, the war displaced some 700,000 Palestinians, creating a refugee problem that remains unsolved today.[23] Known as the *nakba* (catastrophe) among Palestinians and the "War of Liberation" among Israelis, the 1948 war is one of the most important events in the modern history of the Middle East.

Abdallah Azzam was not physically affected by the 1948 war; his family was neither harmed nor displaced. There was little if any fighting in al-Sila, although the area immediately to the north, from the Jezreel Valley plain in the west to the town of Beit She'an (Baysan) in the east, saw heavy fighting in April and May 1948. By mid-May the Haganah (the precursor to the Israel Defence Force) had seized the Jezreel Valley plain – Palestinian territory under the UN Partition Plan – and cleared it of Arab inhabitants, some 7,000 in all.[24] In late May 1948 the Israeli so-called Golani Brigade moved south to capture Jenin. In the ensuing battle of Jenin (1–3 June) Iraqi forces and local fighters pushed back the Israeli offensive in a rare case of Arab high performance in the war.[25] Benny Morris described it as a "nasty defeat; superior IDF forces had been routed by a small number of Iraqis and irregulars."[26] There were no major hostilities in the area during the rest of the conflict.

Although the physical destruction was limited, locals were affected by the war in at least two important ways. One was through loss of land. According to Azzam's own account, formal ownership of the southern part of the Jezreel Valley plain had fallen into the hands of two Christian families, the Sarsaq and Matran, through bureaucratic maneuvering under the Ottomans.[27] Unaware of the legal technicalities, residents of al-Sila continued to till the land as their own, as they had done for centuries. In 1948 Zionists then bought the land from the

Christian families, and took control of it. Many villagers were affected, and Azzam later wrote: "[The Jezreel Valley plain] included the land of my father and my grandfather and the people in my village."[28]

In his memoirs Azzam also writes that Jewish militias committed atrocities against Palestinian farmers who defied the change in land ownership in 1948–1949. "On one occasion," he claims, "a group of young men went down to reap the wheat that they had sown [earlier that spring]. Then Jewish fighters seized them, cut their stomachs open, filled them with wheat and put the bodies on iron poles as an example to others."[29] It is difficult to find independent confirmation of this story. The historiography of the 1948 war does contain reports of gun massacres, torture, and rape, but not butchery of the kind described by Azzam.[30] In any case, the Jewish acquisition of the valley had a psychological effect on Palestinians in the area, if only because the latter had such a clear view of the plain from their hillside homes. As Azzam biographer Husni Jarrar, himself from Jenin, notes: "Wherever the martyr moved as a child, before his eyes was the Jezreel Valley plain, seized by the Jews through international conspiracies ... He grew up seeing the land of his village occupied and cultivated by the Jews right before his very eyes, as they reaped its fruits and enjoyed its goods."[31]

A second effect of the war was the influx of refugees from neighboring areas captured by Israel. According to Walid Khalidi, Jenin governorate absorbed some 100,000 of the 700,000 Palestinian refugees of 1948.[32] Many of the refugees were temporarily sheltered by local families while they looked for new places to live. The Azzams opened their house to a man named Abdallah Awatila and his family, who had been evicted from the village of Umm al-Shuf near Haifa.[33] The two families went back a long time, because Abdallah Awatila's grandfather had lived in al-Sila several decades earlier.[34] One of the daughters in the refugee family later wrote, "When Palestine was occupied in 1948, my family fled to Jenin ... and when [Azzam's] father and other elders in his family heard this, they went to Jenin looking for them. They brought them to their village and put them up in their houses."[35] The refugee family stayed at the Azzams' house in al-Sila for three years before moving to the village of Dayr al-Ghusun near Tulkarm. The Azzams thus felt the human consequences of the displacement of 1948 up close.

After the 1948 war, Sila residents found themselves right on the border with Israel, as a result of which they would experience conflicts with Israeli farmers and occasional incursions by the Israeli military. One source of conflict was cattle – now the main resource of many of Sila's farmers – going astray and being confiscated by Israelis.[36] Another frustration was Israeli military patrols, which Azzam said he saw come to his house on many a night.[37] Azzam writes that he saw a certain Qasim Dawasa being killed by an Israeli patrol right outside the family's house. He also notes that Jordanian authorities did little to protect al-Sila residents' interests, often dismissing reports of cattle theft and Israeli incursions.

Something else happened during the war that would influence Azzam's worldview. One day in the spring of 1948 he noticed some people in the mosque whom he had not seen before and who spoke differently.[38] They were Muslim Brothers from Syria and Iraq who had come to fight alongside the Palestinians. The prospect of a Jewish state in Palestine, including in Islam's second-holiest city, Jerusalem, angered Muslims across the region. Muslim religious leaders declared a jihad to repel the intruders, and Arab regimes cast the issue as a concern for all Arabs. As a result, some 3,000–5,000 volunteer fighters from Egypt, Jordan, Syria, Lebanon, and Iraq joined the Palestine war.[39] The Jewish side also had some 5,000 foreign war volunteers; these were known as the *machal*, a Hebrew acronym for "volunteers from outside the land."[40] The 1948 war was a highly internationalized conflict for its time, and the volunteers on the Muslim side represent an early precedent for the Islamist foreign fighting of the late twentieth century.

At the same time, the Muslim foreign fighters of 1948 differed from the Afghan Arabs of the 1980s in three main ways. For one thing, most came from territories immediately bordering the war zone, not from faraway places. (There was a substantial contingent of Bosnians, but they were former members of German SS units who were stranded in prisoner camps in Italy after World War II and were recruited to the Palestine war by the Syrian army.)[41] Second, the mobilization was largely state organized. Most volunteers fought in the Army of Salvation (Jaysh al-Inqadh), an irregular force created by the Arab League in late 1947. All of its weaponry and supplies were paid for by Arab League governments, volunteers were enlisted in official recruitment centres, and many were trained at military bases by Syrian and Iraqi officers.[42] Third, most foreign fighters in 1948 were not especially religious. When the Army of Salvation disbanded in July 1948, its men were allegedly "deserting en masse, getting drunk, firing off their weapons and harassing visiting officials."[43] The Army's leader, the Syrian officer-adventurer Fawzi Qawuqji, was not an Islamist, nor were the many Druze, Ismailis, and Circassians in the force.[44] Fighters were also well paid (18 Palestinian pounds per month) and may thus have been partly motivated by profit.[45] As Azzam himself later noted, "True Islam did not enter the battles of 1948."[46]

This is not to say that there were no Islamist volunteers. Between 500 and 1,000 Muslim Brothers from Egypt, Syria, Iraq, and Jordan fought in the war.[47] The Brotherhood movement had been an active supporter of the Arab struggle in Palestine since the 1930s revolt, and when the 1948 war approached all the branches launched a volunteer recruitment effort.[48] The recruits entered in different capacities. The Syrians, Iraqis, and Jordanian Brothers were part of the Army of Salvation.[49] The Egyptian Brothers, on the other hand, fought largely independently in the southern part of Palestine. The Brotherhood contingent was small compared both with the organization's overall membership and with its fiery rhetoric on Palestine. As Levenberg noted, the Egyptian brotherhood "was able to dispatch no more than a few hundred volunteers for the jihad in Palestine, from a follower mass of hundreds of thousands of people. The explanation must be found in the Society's unwillingness, rather than its inability, to dispatch many Holy Warriors to Palestine."[50]

Still, the Muslim Brotherhood's participation in the 1948 war came to be seen inside the movement as a heroic effort. To subsequent hardliners such as Azzam, the jihad of 1948 was evidence that the Brotherhood's true calling included warfare and not only peaceful political activism. For Azzam, the 1948 war was a brief golden age when the Islamist movement actually fought for Palestine, before leaving the resistance effort to nationalists and leftists. He also saw the war and its aftermath as evidence of the Arab regimes' hostility to Islamists. In 1989 he said:

Hassan al-Banna sent four brigades from Egypt. A brigade came from the Muslim Brotherhood from Iraq, led by Sawwaf, Muhammad Mahmud al-Sawwaf, and a brigade from Syria led by Muhammad al-Siba'i, and a brigade from Jordan led by Abd al-Latif Abu Qura. But what were the results? They made great sacrifices and demonstrated heroic exploits. The results were that

Banna was killed! In Egypt. And the youth who had been waging jihad in Palestine in Egyptian tanks were taken and put in prison.[51]

To Azzam, in other words, the war of 1948 had offered a glimpse of what the Islamist movement could achieve militarily if it was not obstructed by governments and if it collaborated across borders.

School and Family

In the spring of 1957, at age fifteen, Abdallah Azzam graduated from al-Sila al-Harithiyya middle school. He then enrolled briefly in Jenin high school, before changing to the Kadoorie Agricultural School in Tulkarm.[52] This decision appears to have been a trade-off between Azzam's academic aspirations and economic realities. At the time there were no universities in Jordan and Palestine, and his family likely had neither plans nor means to send him abroad. The choice, then, was between a regular high school followed by nothing and a vocational one that would give him skills for use right upon graduation.

Besides, Kadoorie was no ordinary vocational school. It was quite prestigious, and probably more competitive than the high school in Jenin. It was one of two schools established in the early 1930s by the Jewish philanthropist Ellis Kadoorie.[53] One, in Tulkarm, catered for Arab students, while the other, in Kfar Tavor east of Nazareth, was for Jews. The latter is well known in Israel due to its prominent alumni, such as former prime minister Yitzhak Rabin and former foreign minister Yigal Allon. Kadoorie taught a combination of technical subjects and regular academic ones, including Arabic, maths, and English. It was a boarding school, but Azzam probably went home most weekends. He spent many an evening in Kadoorie reading the Qur'an, for he was working hard to learn the holy book by heart, a milestone he would only reach in the mid-1960s.[54]

After graduation in the spring of 1960, he was sent by the school to work as a teacher in the remote Jordanian village of Adir. Kadoorie students were required to spend the first year after graduation teaching in a local school somewhere in Jordan. Azzam had reportedly wanted a placement closer to home, but a dispute with the headmaster reportedly led to him being appointed to a remote school.[55] Located near the central Jordanian city of Karak 90 kilometers south of Amman, Adir represented a veritable exile for the young Azzam, although probably also an opportunity for more reading of religious books.

In 1961 he moved back to al-Sila, and that autumn he began teaching in a secondary school in the village of Burqin just west of Jenin.[56] He taught Islamic education, agriculture, and sciences, although one of his pupils later said that he found ways to talk about Islam in all the classes.[57] He also worked as an agricultural supervisor in Burqin, putting his Kadoorie education to use.[58] The commute between al-Sila and Burqin soon proved too time-consuming, so he moved to Jenin, where he rented a room with two friends from the Muslim Brotherhood.[59] In this period he also started giving Friday sermons in the local mosque. He would practice his speeches at home, standing on a chair or box and reading them out to himself.[60]

Now that he had an income of his own, he could start contemplating a university education in Islamic Law.[61] At this time no institution in Jordan offered university degrees in Islamic Studies, so the options were Cairo or Damascus.[62] Azzam chose the latter, because it had a more active Muslim Brotherhood scene than Cairo at the time. In the autumn of 1962 he enrolled as a student in the faculty of Shari'a at Damascus University. He would spend the next four years studying toward a *license* (Bachelor's degree) in Islamic Law. However, he could not afford to live there as a full-time student, so he stayed in the West Bank and kept his teaching job in Burqin, while going to Damascus every once in a while for exams and other formalities.[63]

He soon had an even better reason to stay: On 27 July 1965 he married Samira Abdallah Awatila, a daughter of the family who had stayed with the Azzams in May 1948.[64] They had become engaged in late 1963, when she was thirteen years old, which was quite early by the standards of 1960s Palestine.[65] Samira later described the engagement as follows: "I was born in the house of Sheikh Abdallah's sister ... We later left for Tulkarem and he happened to have been there studying. He visited us once, and three days later, his father asked for my hand in marriage."[66] Azzam himself later said that he had been attracted to her relative conservatism:

I searched for a religiously observant girl to marry, and I found a girl who wore a headscarf covering two-thirds of her hair and a robe covering her knees. So I said, "Hold on, this girl is a saint!" [compared with other girls]. I tried to dress her in a long robe to cover the part below her knees, but then a battle erupted between me and her mother; fortunately I came out victorious.[67]

Around 1965, in preparation for life as a family man, Azzam had a small house constructed in al-Sila after designing it himself.[68] In late May 1966 the young couple had a daughter, Fatima, their only child born in Palestine. The second child, Wafa, was born in Amman in early August 1967. In early 1969 they had their first son, Muhammad, after which Abdallah and Samira would be known as Abu Muhammad and Umm Muhammad – father and mother of Muhammad – in accordance with the Arab tradition of taking a nickname (*kunya*) after one's first-born son. Over the next fifteen years the couple would have five more children: Hudhayfa (b. 1972 in Cairo), Ibrahim (b. 1974 in Amman), Sumayya (b. 1975 in Amman), Hamza (b. 1977 in Amman), and Mus'ab (b. 1984 in Islamabad).[69]

In 1966 Azzam graduated from Damascus University and settled in for what promised to be a fairly quiet life as a teacher on the West Bank.[70] He hoped one day to continue his religious studies at the graduate level, but in the meantime he was bound up with family life, teaching, and *da'wa* work (proselytizing) with the Muslim Brotherhood branch in Jenin (see next chapter). Indeed most of Azzam's life choices up until 1967 suggest that he was rather attached to his hometown. He might well have settled for good in the Jenin area, had history not wanted it otherwise.

Fleeing to Jordan

In late May 1967, following escalating tensions with Israel, Egypt closed the Straits of Tiran, expelled UN peacekeepers in Sinai, and amassed forces on the Israeli border. On Monday 5 June, Israel, fearing an Egyptian attack, launched what it called a preemptive strike on the Egyptian Air Force, prompting Egypt, Jordan, and Syria to engage Israel militarily. However, within six days the Israel Defense Forces (IDF) had destroyed the combined Arab air force, repelled the Arab armies, and seized Sinai, the West Bank, and the Golan Heights. The Six Day War was a watershed event that changed the map of the Middle East and brought Palestinian territories under direct Israeli occupation.

This time al-Sila would be directly affected. In the afternoon of 5 June a motorized infantry battalion entered the village on its way southeast toward Jenin, where Jordanian forces had retreated and would be defeated the next morning.[71] Azzam was around at the time. He had been "among the people who observed the events most closely," and he briefly took up arms together with a group of friends.[72] They fired a few shots at the Israeli vehicles with old Lee Enfield rifles before giving up:

I was in our village, and the Jewish, or Israeli, tanks entered, near us. Not a single bullet was fired against the tanks. At all. We knew nothing about war, RPGs, or that kind of thing. We had an English rifle, I held it, there were a bunch of boys in secondary school, I took them and went down to stand before the tanks. So a Jordanian sergeant came and said, "Guys, come back, come back. The tanks are rolling forward, they will crush you and keep going. What are you going to do with the tanks?"[73]

Azzam's hagiographers would later embellish the story, saying that he and his men "stood before the Israeli tanks," that "some of the sheikh's followers fell as martyrs in the confrontations with the Jews," and that their position "was incinerated by an Israeli tank shell" just after they left it.[74] There is no evidence, however, that Azzam or any of his friends were physically hurt in the Six Day War.[75]

Instead of taking up arms, Azzam decided to leave the West Bank for Jordan. In later hagiographies his decision was presented as a purely political one, motivated by an aversion to living under Jewish occupation. However, an important part of the circumstances was that his family was already in Amman on vacation when the war broke out. His wife later said:

We were visiting the sheikh's sister in Amman on 25 May 1967, and I was with him and his father, and after five days I and his father were left in his sister's house. His visa had expired so he went back to the West Bank to go back to work in the school, and after five days the West Bank was occupied, and we stayed in Amman and he on the West Bank . . . The sheikh only stayed a few days before he fled al-Sila to Jordan on foot together with an old man who knew the roads.[76]

In any case, Azzam was probably not forced to leave Palestine. Most of his relatives stayed in the village, and no coercive evictions were reported in al-Sila in 1967.[77] Generally, forced evictions were less common in 1967 than they had been in 1948. In a survey conducted among refugees in Jordan in 1970, four in five refugee families said that they were not evicted by force, while 85 percent reported no casualties in the family.[78] This is not to say that Azzam's departure was a choice of convenience; in the heat of the moment there would have been much uncertainty about what the future would bring, especially since the previous war in 1948 really had brought mass evictions.

The 1967 war was a turning point in Azzam's life. He was now a refugee – in fact, he would never again set foot in Palestine. Moreover, the occupation angered him and planted the idea of armed resistance. We have no evidence of Azzam taking part in, or even seeking, weapons training prior to June 1967. From this point, however, "the idea of training and using of weapons to confront the Jews began preoccupying his mind."[79] It would take just eighteen months before Azzam was carrying a Kalashnikov on the Jordanian–Israeli border, as we shall see in Chapter 3.

The Six Day War was also a pivotal event in the history of the modern Middle East. It had several repercussions, three of which were particularly significant for the rise of transnational Islamism. First, the military defeat delegitimized the Arab republics and their secular ideologies, thereby making Islamism a relatively more attractive ideological product. As Fouad Ajami and others have argued, the war became a catalyst for the emergence of the Islamist Zeitgeist in the late twentieth century.[80] Second, the occupation of significantly more Arab territory and all of Jerusalem increased the potency of Palestine as a symbol of Muslim suffering. Finally, the war displaced yet more Palestinians, increasing the size and geographical extent of the Palestinian diaspora. The Six Day War led some 320,000 people to leave the West Bank and Gaza Strip, mostly for Jordan.[81] Although this second exodus was smaller than that of 1948, it almost doubled the number of Palestinians living abroad, since two-thirds of the 700,000 displaced in 1948 had resettled in other parts of Mandate Palestine.[82] Over the following decades the diaspora would expand geographically as Palestinians sought work and education in new places.

The Palestinian refugee phenomenon facilitated transnational political activism through at least two mechanisms. First, Palestinian networks served as conduits for transnational flows of people and ideas. The fact that many diaspora Palestinians were highly educated and that many worked as teachers gave these networks even more salience.[83] A pertinent illustration of this diaspora effect is that when Azzam arrived in Pakistan in the early 1980s there were already many

Palestinian students there, several of whom became his first recruits in the Services Bureau.[84] Second, the diaspora produced political entrepreneurs and activists with a more transnational outlook and skillset than non-exiled activists. Palestinian activists in exile had to develop communication and recruitment tactics adapted to cross-border activism. The effects of this transnationalism were first observed on the Palestinian left, whose activities in the 1960s and 1970s were highly transnational; it was notably they who pioneered the use of international terrorist tactics in this period.[85] Palestinian Islamist groups would never conduct international operations in the same way, but individuals such as Azzam would become capable transnational activists.

Views on Palestine

Although Abdullah Azzam left Palestine in 1967 and became famous for his role in Afghanistan, the Palestinian cause occupied a central place in his mind and strategic worldview. Unlike subsequent Palestinian ideologues of transnational jihad, such as Abu Qatada al-Filastini or Abu Muhammad al-Maqdisi, Azzam gave no theological reasons for not fighting in Palestine, only pragmatic ones.[86] He deeply resented the occupation of his homeland and wished to take part in its liberation. If he did not personally fight Israel more often, it is because he did not have the opportunity. As late as 1989 he declared, "I am Palestinian, and if I found a way to Palestine and to al-Aqsa, I would fight there."[87]

Palestine appears to have been on Azzam's mind throughout his life. Both his earliest and last books – notably the *Red Cancer* (1980) and *Hamas: Historical Roots and Charter* (1990) – were about Palestine. The rest of his intellectual production is full of references to the Palestinian struggle, and there are numerous quotes by Azzam on the conflict's importance.[88] Even in the mid-1980s, when Azzam did not publish much on Palestine, he spoke about it in private. As one Afghan Arab recalled: "The sheikh would sit with us in the training camp, and he would always talk about the jihad in Palestine when he was in Sada on the border; about the conspiracies that had befallen the brothers in Palestine since the beginning of the jihad, about how the jihad in Palestine had collapsed after 68–69."[89]

For Azzam, the liberation of Jerusalem was an inescapable religious duty. "Palestine is a matter of creed [*aqida*]," he often said, suggesting that one could not be a Muslim and not want to fight for the liberation of Palestine.[90] He often lamented the fact that he had had to leave the jihad in Palestine after Black September in 1970, and declared that "we will not have peace of mind until we return to the jihad in Palestine."[91] For Azzam, Palestine was not just important; it had priority over other struggles in the Islamic world. Even in the midst of the Afghan jihad he stated outright that "Palestine is more important than Afghanistan" (*filastin awla min afghanistan*), and that "all Arabs who are able to fight in Palestine must do it. Those who are not able to do so must go to Afghanistan."[92] Azzam was thus quite open about the fact that jihad in Afghanistan was not his first choice. As one biographer described it, "the sheikh's body was in Afghanistan, but his spirit was suspended over Nablus and Jerusalem."[93]

Azzam was often accused by other activists of having abandoned his homeland in favor of Afghanistan. One biographer asked rhetorically: "[Azzam's] talk on the importance of jihad in Palestine lead us to the question that many people ask: How could the martyr Abdallah Azzam leave the land of *ribat* and jihad around al-Aqsa in Palestine and move his efforts and his jihad to Afghanistan?"[94] Another wrote: "Many of those who do not know the martyred imam well and who have not studied his writings think – wrongly – that the sheikh's heart swerved to Afghanistan and that he forgot Palestine. I heard several of our brothers in Palestine say this in all seriousness."[95]

Azzam was conscious of this criticism, and was somewhat defensive about it. For example, he opened one of his many articles on Palestine in *al-Jihad* magazine by saying: "Our presence in Afghanistan does not mean that we have forgotten Palestine."[96] His defense was to argue that circumstance had prevented him from fighting in the Palestinian Territories, and that the war for Kabul was a means to the long-term end of liberating Jerusalem. He cited two main reasons for why he had not been able to fight more in Palestine. The first was that the armed Palestinian resistance, in his view, had been hijacked by leftists. Bitterness against the PLO is a major theme in Azzam's ideological production, as we shall see in later chapters; on no other topic is he as vitriolic and sarcastic (and entertaining) as when he discusses Palestinians leftists. These people, he argues, are responsible for the failure of the Palestinian struggle, because they have turned the Palestinian people away from Islam with their imported ideologies. In Azzam's view, only a truly Islamic army can defeat Israel. In the late

1960s, when Palestinians had a window of opportunity to confront Israel, he argued, the Palestinian resistance was dominated by secularists, and the Islamists were too weak to make a difference.

His second reason was that the battlefield had been physically inaccessible since the early 1970s. Not only did Israel guard its borders extremely well; her immediate neighbours Egypt, Jordan, Syria, and Lebanon prevented prospective fighters from even getting within striking distance of Israel.[97] For him personally, it had been even more difficult because he had also been thrown out of Jordan in 1981.[98] Azzam was bitter about the role of Arab governments in the Palestinian struggle. In his view, Arab rulers had done nothing but exploit Palestine for their own benefit: "I have not seen an issue with which traders have done more trading, with which the speculators have made more profit, and whose true friends have been oppressed more than in Palestine."[99]

Azzam was thus basically saying that he had not had a choice of where to fight. He summed up his trajectory as follows:

God aroused in my heart the great hope to taste the sweetness of jihad in Palestine in 1969–1970. Afterwards, the activity of sacrifice was eradicated in Jordan, the borders were closed, jihad waned, and jihadist thinking was forbidden. I thought, "Where is the jihad?" I found a parcel of land called Afghanistan, and I tried getting there. God showed me the way there.[100]

Thus Azzam came close to describing his own involvement in Afghanistan as mere opportunism. "For me," he wrote, "Afghanistan is not greater than Palestine, and Kabul is not holier than Hebron, but it was an opportunity I grasped after the oppressors expelled me ... so I went out to the land in which I found a path for *da'wa* and a space to move."[101] The bottom line for Azzam was that it was better to wage jihad in Afghanistan than not to wage jihad at all:

We are like a people whose mosque has been destroyed, and who has become exposed to rain and whirlwinds and storms. When the time for Friday prayer has come, are we allowed to drop the Friday prayer with the excuse that our mosque has been destroyed? Or do we go to the mosque in the neighboring village and perform our duty?[102]

Azzam subsequently articulated a strategic argument according to which the jihad in Afghanistan was a necessary stage in a process that would eventually lead to the liberation of Palestine. "He considered that the jihad in Afghanistan ... was just a means to the end of jihad in

Palestine," as one biographer put it.¹⁰³ According to Azzam's pragmatic argument, victory in Afghanistan would strengthen the *umma* militarily through two mechanisms. The first was morale-boosting. Afghanistan, he argued, was the *umma*'s best opportunity since 1948 to build a purely Islamic resistance movement. The Afghan jihad could thus serve as inspiration for the Muslim nation and mobilize it for the eventual liberation of Palestine. The second mechanism was acquisition of territory. The only way to build a Muslim army strong enough to reconquer Jerusalem, he argued, was to have a contiguous piece of territory – a solid base (*qaʿida sulba*) – on which to train and equip fighters. The best candidate for such a base was in Afghanistan. He said: "Those who think that the jihad in Afghanistan is a distraction of the Islamic cause in Palestine are confused and misled and do not understand how one prepares leaders, how one builds a movement, how one founds a core around which a big Muslim army can be gathered to cleanse the earth of the big corruption."¹⁰⁴

At a lecture in Germany in the late 1980s, Azzam was confronted by a Palestinian member of the audience, who disapproved of his insistence that people should go and fight in Afghanistan. "I think the priority for us youth should be Palestine, declaring jihad in our homeland. So why has jihad not been declared there yet? I think it is wrong to invite us to Afghanistan; Afghanistan has its own youth and its own people. So let jihad be declared in Palestine."¹⁰⁵ In an unusual loss of composure, Azzam fired back:

My brother. Does jihad not require preparation? Sons of Palestine who want jihad – do you not want to train yourselves? Where will you train? In Jordan? So that they may slaughter you? Are you allowed to carry a bullet in Jordan? Or in Syria with Hafiz al-Assad? Or with Husni Mubarak? ... Do you not live in the real world? Are you going to *fly* from the East Bank to the West Bank?¹⁰⁶

Azzam later said the Palestine had been a "cold issue" (*qadiya barida*) between 1970 and the outbreak of the Intifada in late 1987, but his own interest in the cause did not peter out.¹⁰⁷ As a preacher in Jordan in the 1970s, he spoke regularly about the need to fight Israel, "preparing [the students] for the day they would meet the enemy and end the occupation of the Muslim *umma* in Palestine."¹⁰⁸ In Afghanistan in the 1980s he also talked regularly about Palestine both in public and in private. However, it was only after the outbreak of the Intifada – or the "jihad of the Intifada" as he called it – that he got back to more hands-on activism for the cause. In the last two years of his life he wrote extensively on Palestine, fundraised for Hamas, and trained Palestinians in Afghanistan with a view to sending them back to the Territories for operations, as we shall see in Chapter 14.

Of the political actors in the Palestinian theater, Azzam appears to have dealt only with the Muslim Brotherhood and, later, Hamas. He despised the PLO and other Palestinian leftists, whom he saw as godless traitors (although he was happy to subscribe to PLO newsletters for information from the Territories). He also appears to have had few links with Palestinian Islamic Jihad (PIJ), Hamas's smaller sibling on the Palestinian Islamist scene. As far as we know, he was not in contact with Islamic Jihad leaders such as Fathi Shqaqi, few if any Islamic Jihad members went to Afghanistan in the 1980s, and Azzam does not feature much if at all in PIJ publications.[109]

As we have seen, Azzam's Palestinian background was less at odds with his involvement in Afghanistan than it might seem. Instead, it may have predisposed or nudged him toward transnationalism in several ways. For one thing, it shaped his thinking. The Israeli occupation constituted a personal grievance which Arab nation-states proved unable to address; he concluded from this that a pan-Islamic effort was the only way forward. For another, his refugee status made him more mobile, because he had already been uprooted, and his residency rights in new host countries were fragile. Had Azzam been an East Bank Jordanian, he probably could not have been expelled from Jordan so easily in 1980, and he might thus not have ended up in Pakistan. Finally, his Palestinian origin afforded him certain advantages in the transnational arena. Palestine's status as a symbol of Muslim suffering probably gave him a certain emotional leverage vis-à-vis wealthy Muslim donors. Moreover, Palestinian diaspora networks provided him with logistical support for his travels and with information from faraway places. Of course, Azzam's Palestinian background does not explain his transnationalism; most other Palestinians in exile did not end up doing what he did. To understand his peculiar path, we must consider other aspects of his background – not least his relationship with the Muslim Brotherhood.

2 | Brother

Abdallah Azzam did not support the Afghan struggle for humanitarian reasons; he did it because he believed that God would punish him if he did not. He was a deeply religious man and a committed Islamist who believed that most problems in the Muslim world would be solved if people took religion more seriously. More specifically, he was a lifelong member of the Muslim Brotherhood, the Middle East's leading Islamist organization in the second half of the twentieth century. "My creed has been that of the Muslim Brotherhood for thirty-six years," Azzam wrote in 1988.[1]

This chapter looks at Azzam's involvement with the Muslim Brotherhood in the 1950s and 1960s, the ideologically formative phase of his career. It covers his recruitment as a young teenager, his political activities on the West Bank, his encounters with the Syrian Brotherhood during his student years in Damascus, and his intellectual admiration for Sayyid Qutb. Azzam's Brotherhood background is crucial for understanding his subsequent activities; it shaped not only his ideological outlook, but also his career opportunities and personal trajectory. As we shall see throughout this book, his Brotherhood network would come into play at almost every key juncture of his life, and it would help him fundraise and recruit for the Afghan cause.

Religious Inclinations

"The sheikh was not like the people of his time or his peers," one of Azzam's hagiographers noted.[2] Even if we adjust for the tendency to retroactively ascribe piety to clerics, Azzam does seem to have been unusually religious as a child. He himself said he became religious at age seven or eight.[3] His mother recalled how, at nine years old, he meticulously kept all his prayers, which was unusual even in their relatively pious household. "One night," she later said, "I woke up and went to check on him, and there he was, praying. I said, 'My boy, get back in bed and get some rest!' whereupon he replied, 'There's no better rest for the spirit than this.'"[4] One of his sisters said he could not enjoy almonds from the field like other children, because he did not have the farmer's permission.

[He was] constantly making sure that nothing forbidden entered his mouth. He would sometimes go out on the hills with some of his peers when the weather was nice, when the scent of flowers filled the noses, and the earth was spring green – a breathtaking natural scenery – and you would find him sitting next to a water source performing ablution, then praying excessively on the green grass ... meanwhile you would find his peers having fun stealing green almonds from nearby fields. Then they would come to the sheikh and put it in his hands and say to him: "Why are you not eating with us, Abdallah?" And he would respond: "I don't eat sinful things!"[5]

Azzam was more religious than both his parents and his siblings, which suggests that his religious inclination was at least partly a personality trait and not a result of peer pressure. His parents were pious, believing Muslims, but they were not nearly as obsessive in religious matters as he was. According to Azzam's nephew and biographer:

Azzam's mother had not memorized anything from the Qur'an other than [Surat] al-Fatiha, while his father had only memorized a few short Suras ... But the thing that really shows their simplicity is that when his father prayed with his mother at home, she would ask at the beginning that they not spend so much time reciting the Qur'an. Then in the first *rak'a* he would read Surat al-Ikhlas, and in the second Surat al-Falaq; and then it would hardly be over before the old lady got up in front of him and said, "Old man, why did you spend so much time on the Qur'an verses?"[6]

Azzam himself later expressed frustration with his parents' popular Islam:

I was watching some of the movements that my mother did during prayer; I considered them *bid'a* (religious innovation) so I say to her, "These movements are not those of the Prophet." She replied, "Sheikh Ma'ani told us to do it this way." She meant Sheikh Ma'ani, that Azharite man from the Jordanian city of Ma'an who once worked as a teacher and imam in the mosque of our village. What can I do with my mother when she listens to Sheikh Ma'ani and not to me even though my diploma is higher than Sheikh Ma'ani's?[7]

However, Azzam later said he had learned one thing from his father in the religious domain, namely to get up in the middle of every night for the optional night prayer: "I learned how to get up in the night [to pray] as a child from my father. I would see him get up at night regularly, so I got used to it, and I did not stop as an adult."[8]

Indeed, he only became more observant with time, especially after he joined the Muslim Brotherhood. The sources are full of anecdotes about his pious behavior as a young man, such as his frequent mosque attendance or his reading of the Qur'an by himself during lunch breaks instead of chatting with colleagues. Humam Sa'id, who studied with Azzam in Damascus, said, "He had features and characteristics I had not seen in others before; he did *dhikr* [short invocations] all the time, in fact I don't remember if ever I saw him not doing *dhikr*. He even did it during the exams and while he was studying."[9] Azzam's religiosity was unusual for his time. The 1950s and 1960s were the golden era of Arab nationalism, a period in which religion was considered distinctly old-fashioned. "I cannot remember a single schoolgirl in my village who wore the veil," Azzam later wrote. "And in Cairo University, with its 50,000 female students, there was a single girl who wore proper [*shar'i*] dress, and that was Sayyid Qutb's niece."[10]

Azzam was also one of very few Palestinians to study Islamic Law in the 1960s. At the faculty of Shari'a in Damascus in 1968 there was only one Palestinian out of over 1,200 students (about a quarter of whom were foreigners).[11] At al-Azhar's Shari'a faculty in 1968 there were somewhat more Palestinians (20 out of 278 foreigners), but this was just a fraction of the number of Palestinians in the regular Egyptian universities.[12] We also know that religious vocations were not very sought after in Transjordan in this period. In Richard Antoun's classic anthropological study of the East Bank village preacher Luqman, we learn that mosque preachers were so poorly paid in the 1950s and 1960s that they had inspired a saying: "There are three things unseen to the eye – the legs of the snake, the eyes of the scorpion, and the bread of the preacher."[13] In 1959, only four of the twenty-five villages in the area Antoun worked in even had a preacher.[14]

The leftist Zeitgeist of the 1950s and 1960s also kept the membership of the Muslim Brotherhood in Jordan rather small. Declassified documents from the Jordanian Security Services indicate that between

1948 and 1967 the Brotherhood recruited a total of no more than a thousand members in the entire West Bank, and no more than 150 in the Jenin, Tulkarm, Qalqilya, and Anabta branches combined.[15] Thus at any given time in this period there were probably not more than 500 Muslim Brothers in the entire West Bank, and 75 members in the Jenin area.[16] By contrast, the Communist Party had twice or three times as many registered members in the West Bank.[17] As one Islamist writer lamented, "in those days most people were infected by nationalism and Nasserism and imported socialist ideas ... all their culture came from the Voice of the Arabs radio station which they listened to at all times."[18] Another observed, "Palestine and the Arab world worshiped [Gamal] Abdel Nasser and considered him a saviour for this *umma*. It was as if people thought [the angel] Gabriel would descend when he gave speeches."[19]

The relative weakness of the Brotherhood was entirely due to low recruit supply, because the Jordanian Brotherhood was subject to relatively less repression than both its foreign sister organizations and its domestic competitors. In Egypt the Brotherhood was banned and severely repressed from 1954 onward, but in Jordan all parties *except* the Brotherhood were outlawed in 1957. From its foundation with the king's blessing in 1945, the Brotherhood enjoyed a relatively good relationship with the regime, which saw it as a useful counterweight to the political left. The Brotherhood participated in all parliamentary elections in this period, and did not have an underground paramilitary structure comparable to the Secret Apparatus of the Egyptian Brotherhood.[20] Still, Islamists were far outnumbered by the left. It would take a long time for the Brothers' predicament to improve. Over the next couple of decades Islamists in Jordan and Palestine would remain politically marginal, especially among students and other youth. As we shall see in Chapter 5, it was not until the mid-1970s that the student body at the University of Jordan acquired a substantial Islamist component. Azzam's sustained commitment to the weaker side in this political struggle is indicative of a deep and genuine ideological conviction.

With the Jenin Brothers

Azzam joined the Muslim Brotherhood in 1954, at which time the Jordanian branch of the movement had been around for roughly a decade. First founded in Egypt in 1928 by Hasan al-Banna, the Muslim Brotherhood spread in the 1940s to several other countries in the region. The first offices in the Levant were founded in Jerusalem and Amman in 1945 by the Egyptian activist Sa'id Ramadan and the Syrian Abd al-Latif Abu Qura respectively.[21] After 1948 the West Bank and East Bank branches became part of the Jordanian Brotherhood under Abu Qura's leadership, and in the late 1940s and early 1950s local branches emerged across Transjordan, including in Jenin. Jordanian Brothers were strongly influenced by their Egyptian colleagues, and shared the latter's political strategy of Islamizing society "from below" – that is, through education and grassroots activism.

The Jenin branch had reportedly been founded in the early 1950s by a group of five individuals consisting of Tawfiq Jarrar (mufti of Jenin and leader of the branch), his brother Faris Jarrar, Shafiq As'ad Abd al-Hadi, Sa'id Bilal, and Muhammad Fu'ad Abu Zayd (who had studied in Cairo and Damascus in the early 1950s).[22] The branch had its own little center known as the Da'wa House (*dar al-da'wa*) in downtown Jenin, where the senior members held gatherings and lectures for young recruits. They also helped set up small study circles in the surrounding villages such as Qabatiyya, Sanur, Ya'bad, and Kfar Ra'i.

The largest of the village circles was in al-Sila, due to the presence of a local schoolteacher named Shafiq As'ad Abd al-Hadi. A well-known member of the Brotherhood's Jenin branch, Abd al-Hadi had worked as a teacher in al-Sila his entire career, with the exception of a year spent teaching in Saudi Arabia in 1952.[24] Around 1954 the twelve-year-old Azzam came to his attention.[25] Abd al-Hadi must have seen the young, bright, and devout Abdallah as a precious recruit. He took on the role of the latter's mentor and introduced him to the ideological literature of the Brotherhood. Azzam came to hold Abd al-Hadi in very high esteem. When Abd al-Hadi died some time in the mid-1950s, Azzam gave a speech at his funeral. As one source described it, "he stood – still in his early teens – on the grave of his teacher and mentor and praised him in an impromptu speech, impressing listeners with an eloquence which far exceeded that of others of his generation and age."[26] More than ten years later, when Azzam completed his senior thesis in Islamic Law at the University of Damascus, he dedicated it to Abd al-Hadi.[27]

In line with the Brotherhood's strategy of Islamization from below, Abd al-Hadi encouraged Azzam to set up a local study group for other teenagers in al-Sila. Azzam took up the challenge with enthusiasm, and rapidly became the most active young Brother in his village.[28] From very early on he started giving lectures about Islam to other young people in the local mosque. Husni Jarrar, a young Muslim Brother from Jenin, recalls:

> We would visit al-Sila al-Harithiyya regularly and meet the brothers in their houses and sometimes in the olive groves around the village. We would spend moments with them in the obedience of God, the best moments of my life. In those days Sheikh Abdallah Azzam was the smallest of the group in age and size, but the most active.[29]

During this time Azzam got his first experience with *da'wa* – that is, reaching out to people and persuading them to become more religious (or to convert if they are non-Muslim). *Da'wa*, which means "inviting" or "calling," is considered a fundamental part of Islamic practice; many Islamic universities teach it as a discipline, and there is a massive body of books and manuals on the topic.[23] For Islamists, *da'wa* is a central preoccupation, because it is the principal mechanism by which they can increase their political and cultural influence. For many organizations, such as the Muslim Brotherhood, *da'wa* can also effectively be a form of recruitment. In practical terms, *da'wa* can be performed in a wide variety of ways, from writing books giving lectures, via organizing events and convening meetings, to traveling around and knocking on doors. Azzam and his companions would travel around the northern West Bank seeking out young people in mosques and other places. Azzam enjoyed *da'wa* very much, and it would become his passion from the early 1970s onward.

Shafiq Abd al-Hadi also introduced Azzam to the Muslim Brothers in Jenin. There Azzam found a second mentor in Sheikh Fayiz Jarrar, the most senior member of the branch. He began coming frequently to the center to attend Jarrar's lectures and gatherings.[30] Azzam also started accompanying Jarrar on his *da'wa* trips in the countryside.[31] Azzam was impressed by Jarrar's energy and devotion, especially after the latter spent seventy days in prison for his activities yet continued to devote all his spare time to the youth in the center.[32] One of their contemporaries recalls that "[Azzam's] attachment to [Jarrar] was such that he would kiss his hand every time they met. The sheikh forbade it, but Azzam would tell the people around him:

'This is the man who guided us and educated us in *da'wa*, so how can I not kiss his hand?'"[33]

Azzam's enthusiasm for the cause was even noticed by Muhammad Abd al-Rahman Khalifa, the general supervisor (*al-muraqib al-'amm*) of the Muslim Brotherhood in Transjordan. Khalifa would become a legend in the Jordanian Brotherhood by serving in this role for over forty years, from 1953 to 1994. In the 1950s Khalifa and other senior Brotherhood officials traveled regularly to Palestinian towns and cities to meet with local branches.[34] As Khalifa himself recalled:

> On one of my visits to the Brotherhood branch [*shu'ba*] in Jenin in the 1950s, I was sitting with the deputy of the branch when a young boy came over and said: "I am Abdallah Azzam from al-Sila al-Harithiyya and from the Muslim Brotherhood. I am in seventh grade, and I have formed a study circle [*usra*] with my relatives and friends who meet in the local mosque. I invite you to visit us." So I promised to do so on my next trip to Jenin. When I went there the next time, I visited al-Sila during afternoon prayer, and I found Abdallah Azzam and his group sitting in a corner of the mosque. They were so happy with my visit. I still remember the meeting and the good impression it left on me.[35]

As time went by, Azzam became more involved with the Brotherhood in Jenin. While in high school in Tulkarm, he would often stop by the Da'wa House in Jenin on his way home on family visits.[36] In 1961, after he had started his teaching job in the village of Burqin, he was allowed to rent a room in the Brotherhood center in Jenin together with two friends, Ali Humayd and Ahmad al-Hajj Ali.[37] This allowed him to devote more time to the cause. In addition to the regular meetings and *da'wa* tours, Azzam and his comrades began touring Jenin and the villages collecting charitable donations and distributing them to the poor.[38] The activity was called *qirsh al-khayr*, or "penny of charity."

Bookish by nature, Azzam also delved deep into the world of Islamist literature. One of his contemporaries remembers him devouring Muslim Brotherhood publications, especially the works of Hasan al-Banna, Abd al-Qadir Awda, Sayyid Qutb, and Muhammad Qutb.[39] His wife later noted that "in those days he loved knowledge and never tired of reading, day and night, especially the books by Hasan al-Banna and other famous scholars."[40]

Perhaps because of his youth, Azzam did not hold positions of responsibility within the Jordanian Brotherhood in this period. His name does not appear in Jordanian intelligence reports on the leadership of the Jenin branch before 1967.[41] He also does not figure prominently in the main historical accounts of the Islamist movement in Jordan and Palestine in this period. For example, al-Ubaydi's *History of the Brotherhood in Palestine and Jordan between 1945 and 1970* only mentions Azzam in connection with the Fedayin operations in 1969–1970.[42] He also did not make a mark as a writer in this period; we know of no publications by him predating 1976 except for his BA thesis (1966) and Ph.D. dissertation (1973). Nevertheless, by the early 1960s Azzam was a full-fledged Muslim Brother and thoroughly socialized into the Islamist community in Jenin.

By this time, the armed Palestinian struggle against Israel had been effectively taken over by the Palestinian left, to the great chagrin of the Islamists. Although the Palestine Liberation Organization (PLO) was never secular in the European sense – several PLO leaders had Islamist sympathies – they were viewed by the Brotherhood as a secularizing, and thus corrupting, influence on society and on the Palestinian struggle.[43] Azzam himself would come to deeply resent what he viewed as the Communist hijacking of the Palestinian cause, and the "culture war" between leftists and Islamists became an ideologically formative influence on him.

Commuting to Damascus

As mentioned in the previous chapter, the lack of options for higher religious studies in Jordan forced Azzam to choose between Damascus and Cairo. When he chose Damascus, it was not so much that it was geographically closer, but because it was the "world capital" of the Muslim Brotherhood movement at the time. In Egypt the organization had faced severe government repression since the crackdown of 1954, and Nasser had brought al-Azhar University under tight state control through the education reform of 1961.[44] In Syria, by contrast, the Brotherhood enjoyed relative freedom, at least until the Baathist coup of 1963.[45] Thus Egyptian Brothers such as Sa'id Ramadan sought refuge in Syria and published from Damascus, while the Syrian Brotherhood issued statements on behalf of all Muslim Brotherhood organizations.[46]

Moreover, the faculty of Shari'a at Damascus University was a well-known Brotherhood bastion. The faculty had been founded in 1954 by Mustafa Siba'i, a member of parliament and the leader of the Syrian Brotherhood since its foundation in 1945.[47] Up until the mid-1960s virtually all the faculty's professors were affiliated with the Brotherhood. Most had been trained at al-Azhar or the Sorbonne rather than extracted from local *ulama* families.[48] The first two deans of the faculty were grand old men of the Syrian Brotherhood, namely, Siba'i (until 1958) and Muhammad al-Mubarak (until 1964). In the late 1950s and early 1960s Friday sermons in the university mosque were delivered by Isam al-Attar, the de facto leader (since 1958) of the Syrian Brotherhood.[49] The Brotherhood's grasp of the institution would gradually loosen from the mid-1960s onward until eliminated in the late 1970s.[50]

The Brotherhood influence was reflected in the relatively modern curriculum. The faculty's stated purpose was not simply to transmit traditional religious heritage, but to train modern experts on Islamic law who could deal with real-world challenges.[51] One of the faculty's intellectual trademarks thus became comparative legal studies, especially the comparison of Shari'a and Common Law.[52] As we shall see in Chapter 6, Azzam himself would write a BA thesis exactly on this template. Moreover, as much as a third of the curriculum was devoted to non-religious topics such as Syrian law, history, economics, and foreign languages.[53] However, until the late 1980s the faculty offered only undergraduate degrees, which is why Azzam later went to al-Azhar for graduate study.[54]

The Brotherhood presence at the Shari'a faculty reflected the enormous importance that Islamists attached (and continue to attach) to the issue of legislation. The main political objective of all Brotherhood branches in the region was the Islamization of the legal system. It was, to put it simply, the beginning and the end of all Islamist conversations about politics. Most of the ideological literature produced around this time was essentially about why Islamic law is a good thing and how the Islamist movement should go about introducing it. Most other issues – whether they related to foreign policy, economics, or culture – were of secondary importance, for in an Islamic political system, it was assumed, solutions to these other problems would emerge naturally.

Azzam too was consumed with this question at this time, as he later explained in a lecture:

We studied at university in Syria, in the college of Shari'a, we were reading Law as well as Shari'a; the Syrian civil law is taken from the Egyptian law, which has French roots. And when they wanted in Jordan to implement this law, they went and they brought it letter by letter, God blinded their hearts, and they wrote "issued in Damascus" on this or that date, they didn't write "issued in Amman," they wrote "issued in Damascus"! The issue of law is very, very important, and legislating by something other than what God has revealed is *kufr* that departs from Islam, strays from Islam, and is this not the least we can expect from a Muslim, that he condemns with his heart, that he does not approve it with his heart?[55]

The problem, of course, was that none of the governments in power at the time wanted to Islamize the legal system to an extent that would satisfy the Islamists, and this put the various Brotherhood branches periodically into confrontation with their respective regimes.

Azzam arrived in Damascus just as the relationship between the Brotherhood and the Syrian government began to deteriorate significantly.[56] The coup of 1963 brought a Ba'thist regime, which was more explicitly secular than previous governments. It also introduced several controversial economic policies which affected merchants, an important Brotherhood support base in Syria. Protests soon erupted, especially in Hama, where a radical Brotherhood faction had been forming around a figure named Muhammad al-Hamid, the imam of the Sultan mosque. The faction included several young men who would later become very prominent figures on the national and regional Islamist scene, not least Marwan Hadid and Sa'id Hawa.[57]

In mid-1963, following unrest in Hama and Aleppo, the Syrian Brotherhood was outlawed. In October its leader Isam al-Attar was briefly arrested for accusing the president of atheism.[58] March and April 1964 saw a month-long general strike and violent clashes in Hama and Aleppo, culminating with the famous police shelling of the Sultan mosque where a group of hard core demonstrators, led by Marwan Hadid, were holed up.[59] In the autumn of 1964 Isam al-Attar was forced into exile when Syrian authorities denied him reentry to the country following a trip to Mecca. In early 1965 unrest spread to Damascus, although demonstrations there did not get quite as violent as in the northwest.[60] In 1966 the situation calmed down, but in May 1967 there were further strikes and demonstrations following the publication of an anti-Islamist article in an army magazine.[61]

The events of the mid-1960s caused the Syrian Brotherhood to fragment into three regionally defined parts: a moderate Damascus-based wing led by the exiled Isam al-Attar, a radical wing based in Hama led by Marwan Hadid, and a semi-radical wing in Aleppo under the unofficial leadership first of Abd al-Fattah Abu Ghuda and later of Adnan Sa'd al-Din.[62] The dispute between the Damascus and Hama branches mirrored that between the "Bannaists" and "Qutbists" in Egypt and centered on the issue of whether to use violence against the government. In the 1960s and 1970s the Hama and Aleppo branches collaborated, and both took part in the insurgency of the late 1970s and early 1980s.[63]

As far as we know, Azzam neither witnessed nor participated in any of the unrest in the mid-1960s, because he spent his time between al-Sila and Damascus, while most of the action was in Hama and Aleppo. That said, he was well aware of what was going on, because he was in close touch with the Syrian Brotherhood during his time in the country. He attended lectures by the top Brotherhood leaders Isam al-Attar and Mustafa Siba'i (d. 1964) and got to know up-and-coming Syrian brothers such as Ali al-Bayanuni and Sa'id Hawa.[64] He got on particularly well with Hawa, and stayed in touch with him in later years.[65] In 1984 Hawa wrote an endorsement for Azzam's landmark fatwa on jihad in Afghanistan. When Hawa died in 1989, Azzam wrote an obituary in which he recalled first meeting Hawa in Damascus in his student days and, later, visiting him in his house in 1971.[66] Azzam also made friends with other foreign students who later became prominent Muslim Brothers, such as the Jordanian Humam Sa'id.[67]

Azzam also knew the prominent Syrian revolutionary Marwan Hadid, although the two had actually first met in Palestine, not in Syria.[68] At some point in the early or mid-1960s Hadid had visited the Muslim Brothers in Jenin, and the two were briefly introduced. It appears that their paths did not cross in Syria during Azzam's university days, but in 1971, during a trip to Syria, Azzam visited Hadid in his secret hideout in Damascus shortly before the latter was captured by Syrian security forces.[69] Azzam subsequently harbored great respect for Marwan Hadid; Azzam's book *'ibar wa basa'ir li'l-jihad fi'l-'asr al-hadir* (Lessons and Insights on Jihad in the Current Age, 1986) was dedicated to him. Azzam later said Hadid was the bravest person he ever met.[70]

Upon graduation from Damascus in 1966, Azzam returned to his teaching job in Burqin, and he continued to play an active role among the Brothers in Jenin.[71] This was a time of mounting tension between leftists and Islamists in Palestine and elsewhere. A particular incident in March 1967 left a big impression on Azzam. During a pro-Nasser demonstration in Jenin, a man entered the Muslim Brotherhood center, tore apart the religious books, and threw them in the street.[72] Azzam was there to see the torn pages float in the streets of Jenin. It was the first of many bad experiences that he would have with leftists over the years.

Azzam's politicization in 1965 and 1966 was further accelerated by the political events in Egypt, where the Brotherhood's mother branch faced a major and brutal crackdown under President Nasser.[73] After allegedly uncovering an Islamist coup attempt in 1965, the Egyptian government proceeded to arrest, and brutally interrogate, thousands of suspected Brotherhood members. The crackdown culminated in late August 1966 with the trial and execution of three leading Brotherhood figures, including the prominent ideologue Sayyid Qutb.

The news of Qutb's execution shocked Azzam, and may have prompted his first act of political dissidence: a protest telegram to the Egyptian government. "I remember the day I heard about [Qutb's] death sentence," Azzam later wrote. "I was so upset I sent a telegram to Nasser saying 'the *da'wa* will not stop, the martyrs are immortal, and history is merciless.'"[74] He later described the process in more detail:

I wrote an express telegram and directed it to Gamal Abdel Nasser, and I sent it through the post office in the village. It basically threatened and menaced Abdel Nasser and said history will not be merciful. But the village postmaster returned it, telling me off. So I wrote it again under a false name, and I sent it, but I have no idea if it ever arrived.[75]

According to Azzam, the incident did not go unnoticed by Jordanian authorities:

The security services wrote to the postmaster, he was a friend of mine, and they said to him, "Who is this?" He said, "This is the man who sent it." They said, "We went back to the village registry and there is no such name in al-Sila (which I am from), the name isn't there." Here I should mention the name; it was Muhammad Salim Adnan ... so my name was not put on the [no-fly] list at the airport.[76]

The telegram anecdote is not corroborated by other sources, but there is little reason to doubt that Azzam was angered by the news of Qutb's execution.

It did not help that many leftists reportedly celebrated the execution of Sayyid Qutb, whom they saw as a dangerous reactionary. According to a Palestinian Islamist author, some people in Nablus reportedly distributed the local delicacy *kunafa* (a sweet and salty cheesecake) to mark the occasion.[77] In Burqin, at the secondary school where Azzam was teaching, one of the teachers reportedly handed out sweets to the children to celebrate the execution. This was said to have made Azzam furious, and other colleagues had to intervene to prevent a fight.[78]

Qutbist

Azzam was upset because Sayyid Qutb was his main inspiration. Some time in the 1980s, Azzam said:

No author of books on Islamic thought has influenced me more than Sayyid Qutb. I am grateful to God almighty for elucidating my mind and opening my heart to the study of Sayyid Qutb. [God] sent me Sayyid Qutb for ideas [*fikriyyan*], Ibn Taymiyya for creed ['*aqdiyyan*], Ibn Qayyim for spirituality [*ruhiyyan*], and al-Nawawi for jurisprudence [*fiqhiyyan*]. These are the four who have influenced me most deeply in my life.[79]

To be sure, Azzam spoke highly of other Muslim Brotherhood writers too. Like any good Muslim Brother he read Hasan al-Banna with enthusiasm and celebrated him in later writings.[80] His wife said that in the mid-1960s "one of his greatest inspirations was the books of the martyr Hasan al-Banna."[81] He was also influenced in the 1960s by Muhammad Qutb, Sayyid's brother, as well as the Syrian Mustafa al-Siba'i and the Egyptian Yusuf al-Qaradawi, but Sayyid Qutb held a special place in Azzam's intellectual universe.

Azzam had started reading Qutb relatively late, in 1965, as a result of the media coverage of the latter's trial that year.[82] However, Azzam became a lifelong admirer, and Qutb's ideological influence is visible in a great number of his writings. Azzam later said that when he first read Sayyid Qutb's book *The Future Belongs to This Religion* in 1965, he thought Qutb was "living in the dreams."[83] Some fifteen years later, after the Islamist movement had started sweeping the region, Azzam changed his mind and wrote a book of his own entitled *Islam and the Future of Mankind* (1980), a clear reference to Qutb.

Azzam, of course, was hardly alone in his admiration for Sayyid Qutb. This frail teacher from the Egyptian countryside wrote a series of books in the 1950 and 1960s that would make him one of the most influential Islamist thinkers of the modern era. His ideas about Muslim societies being in a state of ungodly ignorance (*jahiliyya*) and about the need to establish an Islamic state based on divine sovereignty (*hakimiyya*) influenced generations of Islamists inside and outside Egypt. His decade-long incarceration, torture, and eventual execution by Nasser's regime made him a martyr and a powerful symbol of resilience the face of oppression.

Qutb had a rather interesting, if tragic, life.[84] He was born in 1906 in a village in Asyut province to a family of landowners who were both religious and politically aware. His father was active in Mustafa Kamil's National Party and hosted meetings in the family home. (Perhaps as a result, three of Sayyid's four siblings – Muhammad, Amina, and Hamida – also became prominent Brotherhood activists.) Sayyid was encouraged to memorize the Qur'an at an early age, but he came to view traditional religious education as backward. At age thirteen he moved with his family to Cairo, where he developed a passion for literature and poetry, and later trained at a teachers' college. He worked first as a teacher (from 1933 to 1940) and then as a civil servant in the Ministry of Education. In this period he wrote many works of fiction, poetry, and literary criticism. After 1945 his writings became more political, but he was still more of a nationalist than an Islamist.

In 1948 the Ministry sent him to the United States to study education, and he spent two years at the Colorado State College of Education in Greeley.[85] He also traveled around the USA and visited Europe on his way home. His encounter with what he saw as a decadent Western culture deepened Qutb's conviction that Islam offered a superior societal model. In his book *The America I Have Seen* (1951) he offered a long list of complaints about American society, from its materialism, sexual promiscuity, and racism to its shallow cinema, disrespectful funeral practices, and bad haircuts. On his return to Cairo in 1950 he took up his old job in the Education Ministry, but started frequenting Muslim Brotherhood circles and began to write extensively about Islam and politics. He notably started working on his *magnum opus*, a six-volume Qur'an commentary titled *In the Shade of the Qur'an*, which took him a decade to complete. Around 1953 Qutb left the Ministry and formally joined the Muslim Brotherhood, which made him the editor-in-chief of the group's weekly magazine, *al-Ikhwan al-Muslimun*. By the mid-1950s Qutb had published several books on Islam and politics, including *Social Justice in Islam* (1949), *The Battle between Islam and Capitalism* (1951), *World Peace and Islam* (1951), *Islamic Studies* (1953), and the first instalment of *In the Shade of the Qur'an* (1954). Starting in 1951 Qutb had also been writing for Islamist magazines such as *al-Risala*, al-Da'wa, and *al-Liwa' al-Jadid*.

In the early 1950s the Brotherhood was a widely popular movement in active opposition to the British presence in Egypt. The Islamists enjoyed common cause with the so-called Free Officers who would topple the Egyptian king in 1952, and Qutb was in personal contact with Gamal Abd al-Nasser and other Free Officers both before and after the revolution. However, relations soon soured because the two movements had very different views on the role of Islam in politics. Over the next few decades the Brotherhood would suffer heavy repression under Nasser's regime. This was primarily because Nasser led an authoritarian regime which suppressed all forms of political opposition. However, it was also because he faced a real security threat from radical elements inside the Brotherhood, especially former members of its "Special Section" (*al-nidham al-khass*), better known as the Secret Apparatus (*al-jihaz al-sirri*).

The Secret Apparatus had been the Muslim Brotherhood's paramilitary wing. Established in the late 1930s (the date is disputed), it was particularly active in the late 1940s, when it carried out dozens of bombings and assassinations against police and British targets.[86] It was also responsible for the recruitment and dispatch of Brotherhood volunteers to Palestine in 1948. After Hasan al-Hudaybi took over as supreme guide in 1950 he sought to dissolve the unit, which he viewed as a liability for the organization. He succeeded only partially, and a clandestine version of it survived until its eventual dissolution in the late 1960s.[87] Sayyid Qutb himself was not a member of the Secret Apparatus, but he was an important ideological inspiration. Abdallah Azzam would later become friends with several former members of the Secret Apparatus, notably Kamal al-Sananiri, Abd al-Aziz Ali, and Salah Hasan. This was no coincidence, because Azzam shared these men's hardline views and military mindset.

As many autocrats do, Nasser dealt with the threat from the radical fringe by suppressing the entire movement. The repression of the Brotherhood began in earnest in early 1954, when the government banned the organization and briefly arrested many of its cadres, including Qutb. In the autumn of that year, following an assassination attempt on Nasser that was blamed on the Brotherhood, the government cracked down fiercely on the organization and sent Qutb and many others to prison. Qutb would spend the next ten years in jail, undergoing brutal torture and long periods of solitary confinement. He also witnessed the mistreatment of other inmates, and was especially marked by an episode in 1957 in which prison guards, claiming to be repressing a prison riot, killed over twenty Brotherhood prisoners in their cells. Qutb was released in late 1964, but rearrested only eight months later in connection with the above-mentioned coup plot against Nasser. After a show trial he was sentenced to death, and hanged in August 1966.

The prison experience radicalized Qutb – as it did many other Islamists – and made him conclude that the Egyptian regime was corrupt beyond repair. It was in this period that he wrote his most explicitly revolutionary texts. In 1964 he notably published *Milestones*, a short book that would become one of the great classics of radical Islamist literature. *Milestones* was essentially a call to action which said that Muslims must remove governments that abuse power and do not "rule according to what God has revealed." Only this way can Muslim society be brought out of the age of ignorance and into a prosperous and just social order. The book is not very explicit about which methods should be used to remove such governments, but it does say that "there should be a vanguard which sets out with determination" and that "when the abovementioned obstacles and practical difficulties are put in its way, it has no recourse but to remove them by force."[88] Qutb also argues that "those who say that Islamic jihad was merely for the defence of the homeland of Islam" are wrong, and that jihad can also be waged to liberate Muslims from domestic oppression. It is not difficult to see how it could be interpreted as a call for revolutionary violence.

The revolutionary call was just one of many themes in Qutb's vast ideological output. He also wrote extensively about theology, about his vision of an Islamic society, and about Islamic civilization and its place in the world. To supporters such as Abdallah Azzam, the appeal of Qutb's writings lay probably not so much in the call to arms but in the holistic vision he presented and in the persuasive way he combined scriptural evidence and perceptive political analysis to support his argument. At the same time, it was the revolutionary spirit of *Milestones* that set Qutb apart from other Muslim Brotherhood writers. Qutb's radicalism and death for the cause gave him a reputational "edge" that other, more pragmatic Islamist figures lacked. There are many prolific writers and many risk-taking activists, but few are both at the same time. This combination of attributes was something that Abdallah Azzam would come to share with Sayyid Qutb.

Sayyid Qutb was one of the few leading Brotherhood figures of the postwar period that Azzam never had a chance to meet. Had Qutb not been imprisoned, their paths would probably have crossed, because Qutb did have contact with the Jordanian Brotherhood. In 1954 he attended a Muslim Brotherhood conference in Jerusalem where he met Muhammad Khalifa, the leader of the Brotherhood in Jordan – the same Khalifa who came to visit the young Azzam in al-Sila a while later.[89] Azzam no doubt regretted not having had the chance to meet Qutb. When he moved to Cairo in 1971, one of the first things he did was to reach out to the Qutb family, represented by Sayyid's sister Amina Qutb (see Chapter 4). When Sayyid's brother Muhammad Qutb came out of prison in October 1971, Azzam met with him at the earliest opportunity.[90]

In the meantime, Azzam found a number of other ways to celebrate Qutb. In 1969, for example, when he was fighting with the Fedayin in northern Jordan, he and his companions wrote Qutb's name on missiles they fired against Israeli targets. In August 1970 they marked the four-year anniversary of Qutb's execution by launching what they called "the Sayyid Qutb operation" against an Israeli tank patrol.[91] Azzam also wrote articles praising Qutb and his ideas long after the latter's death. In 1981, for example, Azzam wrote an article in *al-Mujtama'* vigorously defending Qutb against the accusation – leveled by Nasir al-Din al-Albani in a previous article – that Qutb was inspired by Sufism (more on this in Chapter 5).[92] In the autumn of 1986 he wrote a glowing eulogy of Qutb in *al-Jihad* magazine to mark the twentieth anniversary of his execution.[93] Later he also wrote a short biography of Qutb. Azzam's followers subsequently compiled these three texts into a single manuscript and published it posthumously as a book titled *The Giant of Islamic Thought (The Martyr Sayyid Qutb)*.[94]

The Qutbist influence is visible in a great number of Azzam's writings and lectures. He features particularly prominently in Azzam's pre-Afghanistan writings such as the *Islam: the Future of Mankind* and

The Red Cancer. In the 1980s Azzam recorded a forty-hour lecture series titled *In the Shade of Surat al-Tawba*, which was a commentary on Surat al-Tawba in the Qur'an. Not only did the title and approach echo Qutb's *In the Shade of the Qur'an*, Azzam also relies heavily on Qutb's analysis of the same Sura. At least as important as the citations and allusions is the substantive Qutbist influence we can see in Azzam's thinking. Azzam's own view of Islam as a perfect social model and superior civilization, his preoccupation with Islamic legislation, and his critical attitude to Arab regimes all echo Qutb. He also used Qutbist terminology such as *jahiliyya* and *hakimiyya* extensively; in fact, after Azzam's death an Islamist author wrote an entire book titled *The Concept of* Hakimiyya *in the Thought of Abdallah Azzam*.[95] Azzam also mentioned Qutb repeatedly in his lectures, and he encouraged students to read Qutb. In the training camps of Afghanistan he recommended to trainees that they take half an hour after Fajr prayer to read *In the Shade of the Qur'an*.[96]

This lifelong admiration notwithstanding, Qutb featured somewhat less prominently in Azzam's later writings, because Qutb had little to say about national liberation struggles such as the Afghan jihad, and about military strategy more generally. Azzam brought him up when he spoke about broader issues, but he is rarely cited in Azzam's texts about Afghanistan.

When Azzam graduated from Damascus University in 1967 he had been an active member of the Muslim Brotherhood for over ten years, and he had met many of its senior figures in Jordan and Syria. Still, his career in the organization had only just begun. Over the next decade and a half he would rise to the highest ranks of the Jordanian branch, build a vast regional network of Brotherhood contacts, and make a name for himself as a hard-hitting Islamist writer. In the 1980s he would drift away from the Brotherhood because the latter did not want to get directly involved in the recruitment of foreign fighters to Afghanistan, but he never formally broke with them. After his assassination there was a small deluge of obituaries written by prominent Brotherhood leaders, as we shall see in Chapter 14.

Azzam's affiliation with the Brotherhood is crucial for understanding his trajectory. Aside from shaping his beliefs and worldview, the Brotherhood offered international connections that helped Azzam out and steered him in certain directions at key points of his life. As we shall see in subsequent chapters, Azzam likely got his Ph.D. scholarship and his teaching job in part because of his brotherhood credentials. When he was thrown out of Jordan in 1981, it was through Brotherhood connections that he secured new jobs, first in Saudi Arabia and then in Pakistan. And in Pakistan, of course, Azzam would use his Brotherhood connections for all they were worth in his effort to mobilize Arab support for the Afghan jihad. In the short term, however, the Brotherhood would get him involved in a more action-filled endeavor.

3 Fighter

When Azzam was in Afghanistan in the 1980s, he often stressed that he was no newcomer to warfare. "I tasted the sweetness of jihad in 1969 and 1970. [From then on,] my heart remained passionately attached to jihad wherever it may be in the worlds."[1] But what exactly did this military experience consist of, and how did he get involved? This chapter examines Azzam's time as a guerrilla fighter on the Jordanian–Israeli border in the late 1960s. It looks at how the military effort started, how Azzam was recruited, what he did on the frontlines, and how he fared in the events of Black September in 1970. We will see that Azzam fought not with leftist Palestinians, but with a little-known Islamist wing of the Fedayin movement. This group included Muslim Brotherhood members from several other countries, making it a little-known early case of Islamist foreign fighting. The experience, while short-lived, affected Azzam's political outlook and added to his credibility as a recruiter in the 1980s.

Islamist Fedayin

The term Fedayin means "those who sacrifice themselves," and in the context of the Arab–Israeli conflict it refers to the militants who conducted border raids against Israel between 1948 and 1970.[2] These raids came in two main waves: the first on the Egyptian–Israeli border in the 1950s, and the second on the Jordanian–Israeli border – and to a lesser extent from Syria and Lebanon – in the late 1960s.[3] It was in the latter that we would find Abdallah Azzam.

The second Fedayin wave began in early 1968 after Fatah had failed to mount an insurgency in the West Bank and decided to "heat up the Jordanian and Syrian fronts" instead.[4] The movement gained momentum after the famous battle of Karama on 21 March 1968, in which Palestinian guerrillas and Jordanian troops inflicted significant casualties on the Israel Defense Forces (twenty-eight deaths and the destruction of four tanks and an aircraft).[5] Although the Arabs lost five times as many men, they viewed the battle as a psychological victory, and it sparked unprecedented volunteering for the Fedayin: By June 1968 some 3,000 fighters were mobilized along the Jordanian–Israeli border, from Umm Qays in the north to Wadi Araba in the south.[6] The guerrillas received weapons and military training from Egypt, Iraq, and Syria, and Fatah leaders traveled to Vietnam to learn guerrilla tactics.[7] Similar activity occurred in southern Syria and Lebanon in the autumn of 1968, but the Jordanian front was by far the most active, with an average of over 200 cross-border attacks per month throughout 1969.[8] The effort initially had the Jordanian regime's blessing – after the battle of Karama, King Hussein famously declared, "We are all Fedayin" – but the relationship would come to a bitter end in Black September in 1970, when the Jordanian government cracked down on the Fedayin, killing several thousand Palestinians.

Although the Fedayin in the late 1960s were predominantly leftist, they included a small Muslim Brotherhood component with volunteers from across the Middle East.[9] The Islamist Fedayin are barely mentioned in the existing literature, because they were militarily insignificant.[10] They numbered just a few hundred from a Fedayin movement of over 10,000.[11] Still, they merit attention, because they represent a little-known chapter in the Muslim Brotherhood's history and an important early instance of Islamist foreign fighting.

The Brotherhood's involvement with the Fedayin was basically an attempt to meet the demand among its younger members for action on the Palestinian front, and to avoid being outshone by the leftists. The Arab defeat in 1967 had sparked a desire among younger Islamists to take military action against Israel. Ahmad Nawfal later said, "In 1968, immediately after al-Karama, we put pressure on the leadership, saying we have to train, at least we have to be prepared."[12] Ibrahim Ghusheh, a Jordanian Muslim Brother at the time, later described the mood:

The world had changed; and we began to meet with the MB Movement's youth in Irbid and Amman, and to ask ourselves, what the outcome and solutions [to the Israeli occupation] were ... At the time, we were young men in our thirties. We were angry because these resolutions were mere explanations of the events of 1967 together with slogans calling for Arab and Islamic unity. [They] failed to give us an outlet for our anger, failing to call for the building of an Islamic resistance structure as a prelude to action. During this period, the Fatah movement grasped exactly what was going on ...

The Fatah Movement decided to start the battle and fill this void. This was a wise and farsighted decision.[13]

The pressure led the Brotherhood's Executive Office in Cairo to convene a series of meetings in late 1968 or early 1969 between the region's Brotherhood branches to discuss the issue of joining the Fedayin.[14] According to Abdallah Abu Izza, who participated in the process as a representative of the Palestinian Brotherhood, a first meeting was held in Cairo, followed by a second one in Amman. Discussions were tough, because the different national branches did not agree on whether and how to participate. The pressure for action was reportedly strongest among the Muslim Brothers in Jordan, Sudan, Kuwait, and among Egyptian Brothers outside Egypt. Lebanese and Iraqi brothers were initially hesitant, but eventually came on board. The Syrian Brotherhood, represented by Isam al-Attar, tried the longest to stay out, citing financial difficulties and a recent travel ban, but agreed to contribute a small contingent. Meanwhile the Palestinian Brotherhood was firmly opposed on several grounds, the main one being that such a military project was doomed to face opposition from Arab states and lead to the weakening of the Islamic resistance effort.[15] The Palestinian Brothers agreed to provide a small financial contribution, but refused to send members to participate in the fighting.[16] According to Abu Izza the Sudanese Brothers, represented by Uthman Khalid Madawi and Muhammad Salih Umar, were particularly keen on the Fedayin project, at one point pressing the Iraqi delegation to specify its contribution. When the Iraqis said that they had already donated 300 Iraqi dinars to the training-camp project, the Sudanese complained that it was far too little. The Lebanese Brotherhood, represented by Fathi Yakan, agreed at the meeting to send fighters, but he later had to retract his support due to opposition from other Lebanese Brothers. In the end, the Brotherhood Fedayin project proceeded with participation from the Jordanian, Sudanese, Syrian, Kuwaiti, and Iraqi Brotherhood, with a few independent Egyptian Brothers.[17]

In early 1969 the Brotherhood struck an agreement with Fatah that allowed the former to set up separate training camps and military bases so long as they operated officially under the name and command of Fatah's al-Asifa forces.[18] They began with two training camps, the first in the Dibbin woods near Jerash, and the second in Zarqa, closer to

Amman. Both were adjacent to or inside existing Fatah training facilities. Dibbin was a good location for training camps because it was halfway between Amman and the northern fronts and because the hills and the umbrella pine trees offered protection and camouflage. There was also a Palestinian refugee camp in Jerash right next door which provided recruits and supplies to the Fedayin. Ahmad Nawfal later said, "The group elected ten people, I was one of them, and we trained in the toughest of Fatah's training camps: in Zarqa and in the woods of Jerash. It was a training camp with trainers the likes of which I have never seen ... the leader was a lieutenant named Salah."[19] This was Salah Hasan (aka Abu Amr), a veteran Egyptian Brother with a background from the Secret Apparatus who had studied under Hasan al-Banna and fought in Palestine in 1948 and around Suez in the early 1950s.[20] He had high ambitions for the new project. "In one of our meetings," one trainee later said, "[Hassan] told us that we in the MB Movement should establish a fighting 'Jihadi' force, no less important than that of the Viet Cong; the communist armed resistance in Vietnam."[21]

Sometime in early or mid-1969 the Brotherhood also set up bases further north near the Israeli border.[22] Officially called the Western Unit, these camps became known as the Bases of the Sheikhs (*qawa'id al-shuyukh*) because they included senior Brotherhood figures such as Ishaq al-Farhan (Jordan), Muhammad Salih Umar (Sudan), Uthman Khalid Madawi (Sudan), and Isam Sharabini (Egypt).[23] There appear to have been four main camps, at least two of which were named after places in Palestine: one (the largest) was called Jerusalem while another was called Gaza.[24]

The precise extent and location of these installations is difficult to reconstruct from the sources. Most testimonies speak of four main camps, but there also seem to have been a number of forward operating bases and training camps. The sources also cite a number of different place names, many of which are for small locations which are not marked on regular maps.[25] His comrade Ahmad Nawfal said:

In Marw was the Bayt al-Maqdis base, whose *amir* and leader was Sheikh Dr. Abdallah Azzam; here we had a base in these areas and hills, in Mughayyir as well, in Bayt Yafa we had a base, in the Rafid area we had a base, as well as three training camps: a winter one in Azraq, a summer one in Dibbin, and a third training camp in the Aluk area. And in Aghwar we had a group of forward bases.[26]

The camps were formally under the supervision of a Fatah official named Mundhir al-Dajani, but they were staffed and led by Muslim Brothers and enjoyed full operational autonomy.[27] The Bases of the Sheikhs were quite small; each housed a few dozen people, which means that the total number of Islamist Fedayin was probably in the order of around a hundred people.

The Islamist Fedayin were a multinational group. Many of the fighters were Jordanians, but there were also volunteers from Egypt, Sudan, Syria, Yemen, Lebanon, Kuwait, Iraq, and Palestine.[28] This was not so much the result of a spontaneous popular mobilization as the product of the abovementioned agreement between different Brotherhood country branches to each contribute fighters. The Jordanians included several subsequently prominent figures such as Abdallah Azzam, Ahmad Nawfal, Dhib Anis, and Abd al-Mun'im Abu Zant.[29] Among the Syrians were people such as Abd al-Sattar Za'im, who later became a prominent member of the Combatant Vanguard (al-Tali'a al-Muqatila) group in Syria.

The general leader of the Islamist Fedayin was the veteran Egyptian brother Abd al-Aziz Ali (aka Abu Usama al-Misri), who already in 1969 was something of a legend in Muslim Brotherhood circles.[30] A former member of the Egyptian Secret Apparatus, he had fought in Palestine in 1948 as well as against the British in the Suez Canal zone in the early 1950s.[31] A military man through and through, he brought some of the best paramilitary expertise that the Brotherhood had to offer and was thus a natural leader for the Bases of the Sheikhs. It is worth noting that Abd al-Aziz Ali would continue to be involved in various Islamist military efforts. In the 1970s he supported Islamist rebels in Yemen and Eritrea. In the early 1980s he was involved in supporting the Islamist uprisings in Syria, and helped train Syrian Muslim Brothers (including Abu Mus'ab al-Suri) in Baghdad. As we shall see in Chapter 12, he also turned up in Afghanistan in the mid-1980s to serve as training-camp instructor and military advisor for Abdallah Azzam and the other Arabs. Abd al-Aziz Ali's remarkable military career thus stretched from the 1940s to the 1980s, and links together a long series of Islamist military adventures in the postwar period. He represented to some extent the Muslim Brotherhood's institutional memory in military affairs and helped transmit know-how across conflicts and generations.[32] Ali's precise role within the Brotherhood in the later years is unclear, but his career suggests that the Muslim Brotherhood had at least an unofficial military cadre operating throughout the 1960s, 1970s, and 1980s.

The Islamist Fedayin also attracted short visits by prominent Brotherhood figures from across the region who were anxious to see the first Islamist military effort against Israel since 1948. The Egyptian Brother Tawfiq al-Wa'i describes one such inspection trip:

> The [Egyptian] Brotherhood formed a delegation to visit the camps and to get a sense of the action taking place there and learn about its shortfalls and needs. I was one of the three people charged with visiting the camp, and that was the first time I met Brother Abdallah Azzam. I had heard of him before from the Palestinian brothers, and we would meet again in Kuwait, Saudi Arabia, Pakistan, Afghanistan, Jordan, Europe, and Egypt.[33]

Top brotherhood leaders such as Muhammad Khalifa and Isam al-Attar also came to inspect the young recruits. Al-Attar later said, "All the Muslim Brotherhood cadres in Jordan and Syria visited the camps or participated in the fighting."[34] The legendary Marwan Hadid also trained there for a short while.[35] Many visitors seem to have only inspected the Dibbin and Zarqa camps, and thus Azzam, who was in the north, appears not to have met neither al-Attar nor Hadid at this time.[36] However, a number of other prominent brothers did meet Azzam, including Abd al-Rahman Abd al-Khaliq, Isma'il al-Shatti, and Jasim al-Yasin.[37] All these visitors later wrote enthusiastically about their time in the camps and about meeting Azzam there.[38]

The Jordanian camps thus appear to have served as an important socialization arena for young Brotherhood cadres from across the region. The networks forged here would last for decades, and Azzam himself would stay in touch with several of his Fedayin comrades his whole life. Ahmad Nawfal notably became a close colleague at Jordan University, while Isma'il al-Shatti became editor of *al-Mujtama'* magazine and published Azzam's articles in the 1970s and 1980s.

Becoming a *Mujahid*

As we saw in Chapter 1, Azzam had fled Palestine during the Six Day War and arrived in Jordan on foot. He must have had difficulties finding a job in Amman, because in the early autumn of 1967 he moved to Saudi Arabia to teach for a year (see next chapter). The following summer he moved back to Amman and found a job as a teacher in the al-Taj secondary school in the Jabal al-Taj area of Amman.[39] The influx of West Bank refugees had dramatically increased the demand for teachers in Jordan. Azzam taught the morning shift, for in this period schools offered two sessions per day to accommodate all the new students from the West Bank.[40]

In mid-1968 the Fedayin movement was gaining momentum, and the following winter Azzam began to seriously contemplate joining the action. In his subsequent memoirs he says he decided to join the Fedayin after experiencing something of a political epiphany in the middle of the night. One night in early 1969, according to him,[41]

I was woken up in the middle of the night by a group of leftists chanting a nationalist *nashid* that stirred my emotions: "My country, my country, my country." The echo of the song reverberated through the night. This had a deep effect on my heart, and I said [to myself], "Should you not be ashamed, Abdallah? Do those people hold their country more dear than we do?" So I decided that instant to begin the jihad, at whatever cost.[42]

Then, in March or April 1969, Azzam joined the Fedayin. In the words of Azzam's wife, "the Muslim Brotherhood announced the opening of the Bases of the Sheikhs in northern Jordan, and he left teaching two months before the year was over and joined the jihad."[43]

The decision drew the family into economic uncertainty. Here is Samira's account of her less-than-glorious life as a *mujahid*'s wife:

He told me, "Prepare yourself, in two days we will go. Keep the plan secret. I don't want you to reveal it, because I want to take you to a place near your cousin's house in Jerash so you will be out of sight from my family and so I can come visit you in my breaks without anyone seeing me. I want to announce to my parents that I have gone to Egypt to continue my studies there, so that the news does not spread" ... so he left me as I was eight months pregnant with Muhammad, and I had only a week's worth of supplies. He said, "I'm going, and I will come to you every month with what you need" ... After four months he asked that I move to Zarqa to live with one of the sisters whose husband, who was a *mujahid* like [Azzam], wanted me to be with her. It was tough because she was angry with her husband for leaving his job and joining the jihad. I tried my best to support her and mend relations between her and her husband. I did not have anything against it, but she looked at me and said, "But you will stay in a single room without a kitchen" ... so he took me and the few earthly possessions I had, and we left, and I stayed in this mudbrick room which was four meters by two-and-a-half meters for me and my three children ... in this room I washed clothes and dishes, I cooked, I slept, I received guests. But by God I felt happiness engulf my heart and soul ... The sheikh always looked at me affectionately, feeling that he had made things difficult for me by making me live in his room. He gave 14 dinars per month for me and the three children ... he came home during his breaks, but it was only four days per month.[44]

The decision was also met with disapproval from many in the family. His cousin Fayiz Azzam later wrote:

I still remember the day when a group of relatives, including his father, came to persuade him to leave his path. In those days, jihad was seen as a little odd, especially for an employed, educated man of good family. The view of most people was that jihad is for the unemployed! This was in the village of Rasifa where his sister lived. His father told him: "Son, I was hoping that you would become a great judge in Amman, and here you are with small kids and youth in the mountains." Then [the father] and the mother began to weep. Azzam got angry and stood up and said: "I am inviting you to heaven and you are inviting me to hell!?" From that day, his view was that one does not need parental permission [to wage jihad].[45]

Azzam's father later said that he had been pressured by Israeli authorities to dissuade his son from fighting:

When [the Jews] learned that Abdallah had a link with [the Fedayin], they came to us and tried to bribe us with money to stop Abdallah's jihadi activities, and when they failed, they started threatening us with punishments and penalties, and they asked me to bring him back to Palestine. I said, you say you are a powerful state, so go and get him yourselves.[46]

This claim is hard to verify, but in any case, Azzam's father had other reasons to talk his son out of war, notably a concern for the latter's well-being and economic future.

While Azzam argued with his parents, Samira reportedly suffered the condescending looks of her female relatives and friends. Fayiz Azzam noted that "the views and respect of the women toward his wife and his children changed because she had been the wife of a civil servant, and was now the wife of a *mujahid* moving around in the mountains with small children."[47] She herself later said that her husband "always asked

Fighter

whether any friends or relatives were visiting me, and I said 'Some are, others are not, because they frown on me as the wife of a small *mujahid* who has no possessions in this world.'"[48] Later on, of course, the tables would turn. In the 1980s Azzam became the family hero, and many of his male relatives joined him as volunteer fighters in Afghanistan. Even his aging parents moved to Peshawar in the late 1980s.

Life in the Camps

After he had parked his pregnant wife and their children in Jerash, Azzam headed to boot camp in the Dibbin woods. He appears to have been part of the very first group of around ten Brotherhood members who trained in the new camp.[49] We lack detailed accounts of this particular facility, but we know that the Fatah camps in Dibbin typically processed a few dozen recruits at the time and offered spartan conditions. Recruits slept in tents under the umbrella pines and followed a strictly regimented program lasting from sunrise to sunset.[50] They started the day with a pre-breakfast run at 5 a.m. and spent the day receiving training in light weapons, maneuvers, and close combat before winding down in the evening with ideological discussions. The Muslim Brotherhood camp would have been similar, except with Qur'an reading and other religious activities instead of Marxist instruction. Military life was quite a change for the young academic, but he enjoyed it:

> The training lasted four months ... and I remember being full only once. For the whole four months and a half we had bread for breakfast, lunch and dinner ... yes we were hungry a lot, but it was one of the best times of my life. We felt like kings ... because we had been liberated of everything and nobody had power over us.[51]

Others also found the training demanding. Here is Ibrahim Ghusheh:

> We went training for a few days in a brothers' camp in Zarqa. I remember once when I was with Brother Fayz al-Hazina and others, Salah Hassan (Abu Amr) asked us to carry out a maneuver, walking on foot and carrying arms, for a distance of 60 km. We were young men unaccustomed to walking. So after this walk, we stayed two days suffering from swollen feet.[52]

After initial training, Azzam moved to the Bases of the Sheikhs in the north. The bases needed to be relatively close to the Israeli border, but they could not be too close or too exposed, or else they would be bombed by Israeli planes. The Islamist Fedayin operated in the far northwest of Jordan, where the relatively narrow Yarmuk river cuts through the hilly landscape to form a natural border between Jordan and Israel. Some of the camps and forward bases were literally caves. Around 2008, for a documentary on Azzam's life, Ahmad Nawfal took the al-Jazeera journalist Yasir Abu Hilala on a tour of some of the areas in which the Islamist Fedayin operated. In the documentary we see Nawfal interviewed on a hillside overlooking what appears to be the Yarmuk river valley, and we can see Abu Hilala walk down a long tunnel and come out from a cave opening at the other end.[53]

We can get a sense of life in such camps from the testimony of the Belgian journalist Gérard Chaliand, who spent time with leftist Fedayin in Jordan around 1969. One of the places he visited was a camp belonging to the Popular Democratic Front for the Liberation of Palestine (PDFLP) in roughly the same area as the Bases of the Sheikhs:

North-west of Irbid, in a PDF[LP] base set up in a vast cave. Four in the morning and still dark. The deep blackness of the sky is pierced with myriads of glittering stars – a night almost as beautiful as the magnificent nights of the Sahara. Opposite the camp, on the invisible far bank of the river, the lights of the Israeli kibbutzim. A three-mile run in the night, followed by quarter of an hour's physical training. Breakfast consists of hard biscuits, green olives and scalding tea. Dawn breaks, revealing a narrow bare defile dominated by the camp. In the distance to the north, the Golan heights are dimly visible. The desiccated hills are sparsely dotted with poplars. The cave shelters about fifteen *fedayeen*, with their equipment and stocks of food. Under a solitary tree squats an anti-aircraft gun – a Dikitiriov . . . The base, the fifth of its type, has been in existence for about three weeks at the time of writing. The base consists of twenty-five *fedayeen* including those who are away for operations or in village working-parties. The group has carried out forty operations, in ten of which it had no fighting to do. Camp rations consist basically of starch foods (haricot beans, lentils, potatoes, pasta), eggs, tomatoes and tinned foods (sardines, corned beef). Meat is only eaten once a week.[54]

Chaliand also writes that PDFLP's military bases were typically manned by about forty-five guerrillas.[55] The Bases of the Sheikhs were probably not much larger, which means that the four Islamist camps probably held a total of between 100 and 200 fighters at any one time.

As a twenty-eight-year old Shari'a graduate and longtime Brotherhood member, Azzam was a relatively senior figure among the fighters, which is probably why he was appointed commander (*amir*) of the Jerusalem base in Marw.[56] A visitor later mentioned Azzam as one of the three "prominent" people in the camps, alongside Ahmad Nawfal and Dhib Anis.[57] However, Azzam was still a relative novice in military matters. As one of his comrades, Muhammad Nur, later recounted:

> Once, when he was with the *mujahidin* in Jordan, the sheikh made a slight mistake in a military matter in the Bayt al-Maqdis base where he was the leader and responsible for the group. When martyr Abu Amr – the trainer of the group – was angry with him, the sheikh stood up, gave a military salute and declared that he was willing to take any reprimand he deserved.[58]

Soon, however, Azzam got the hang of things and began instructing others. The Kuwaiti Muslim Brother Isma'il al-Shatti later wrote:

> I still remember you on the plateaus and mountains of Irbid, between its caves and rocks, and in the Jordan Valley, and on the banks of Yarmuk. You were wearing khaki and carrying the Kalashnikov, and you always had the Qur'an in your breast pocket. I can still feel your strong grip around my hand as you taught me how to take aim, how to fire a shell, and how to shoot. I still remember your tears dripping on your beard as you wept for your brothers who fell as martyrs in the operations.[59]

Azzam also took part in fighting in this period. He participated in several raids on Israeli targets along the border just like the other Fedayin. His memoirs and other sources speak of "many operations" and present the Islamist camps as a serious military effort. They had decent military equipment, including aerial maps of the border region.[60] According to one of Azzam's hagiographers, Yasir Arafat himself supposedly asked Fatah for "operations like those of the sheikhs."[61] According to Ahmad Nawfal:

> The sheikh took part in many operations, but one of them was in the Baqura area, it was one of the most prominent operations he undertook. They bombed him with planes all day, and the sheikh's clothes were ripped from shrapnel and bullets, but no injury or martyrdom was written for him … I remember it was during Ramadan, one of the seasons of jihad, and we would go down every day seeking martyrdom, seeking jihad, but God had not prescribed it for us. Every day we undertook sniper operations. The

sheikh took part in most of the large operations, in addition to the ones I said happened daily.⁶²

However, the military contribution of the Islamist Fedayin should not be exaggerated. The Muslim Brothers were but a small fraction of the Fedayin movement, and there is no evidence – except in a handful of pro-Brotherhood writings – that they made any mark whatsoever on the overall military effort. It is telling that all the written accounts of the Islamist Fedayin cite the same three incidents as evidence of their bravery. First was the "battle of al-Mashru'," a gun battle with the IDF in 1969 from which the *mujahidin* only barely escaped alive.⁶³ A small group of fighters, including Azzam, had attacked an IDF target but found themselves cut off and holed up under a bridge, with one fighter gravely wounded. They were saved by the Jordanian army, which opened a massive round of artillery fire as cover. A Jordanian commander was injured in the process, earning the gratitude of Azzam and his comrades.⁶⁴ Second was the "battle of 5 June 1970," in which a group of six fighters led by Azzam himself confronted two tanks and a minesweeper, killing at least twelve IDF soldiers.⁶⁵ Azzam recounts:

> Dayan had sent a Canadian and an American correspondent to accompany them on the border and show them that the Fedayeen operations had finished. Then [the *mujahidin*] came out on them like *jinn* from underground and shelled them and wounded the two journalists; the Jews admitted to losing twelve soldiers but the enemy losses were much higher than this.⁶⁶

Third was the "Sayyid Qutb operation," which took place on 29 August 1970 to mark the four-year anniversary of Qutb's execution. It must also have been one of their last operations. Azzam recounts:

> Abu Amr (Salah Hasan) was preparing a missile operation which he called "the Sayyid Qutb operation" against a patrol of several tanks. He made the plan and checked the location and rigged the missiles which he was going to trigger with an electric fuse, but he was ambushed by the Jews, and a battle erupted in which Abu Amr fell a martyr together with Mahmud al-Barqawi and Zuhayr Qayshu (from Hama). The date of their martyrdom coincided with that of Sayyid Qutb, namely 29 August.⁶⁷

Of the three operations highlighted by Azzam, only the second can be described as a success. The fact that he chose to list two blatant defeats among his most memorable battles suggests that their record as a fighting force was meager.

The sources say thirteen fighters were killed in combat during the camps' existence. We know the names of nine of these: Salah Hasan (Egypt), Mahdi al-Idlibi (Hama, Syria), Nasr Isa (Hama, Syria), Zuhayr Qayshu (Hama, Syria), Ridwan Krishan (Ma'an, Jordan), Ridwan Bal'a (Damascus, Syria), Muhammad Sa'id Ba'abbad (Yemen), Mahmud al-Barqawi (Palestine), and Abu al-Hasan Ibrahim al-Ghazzi (Palestine).[68] Having fighters from so many different countries posed a practical problem – that of repatriating the dead. The body of Salah Hasan, for example, had to be taken to Kuwait, where his Egyptian family lived.[69] Abd al-Mun'im Abu Zant later described how he and Azzam took Hasan's body to the Ashrafiyya hospital in Amman for transportation to Kuwait.[70] On another occasion, Azzam brought the body of Zuhayr Qayshu to Syria:

As for the funeral of Zuhayr, I brought [the body] to Hama in Syria and stayed there several days as a guest of Marwan Hadid. While I was there, another burial party was brought to Hama, that of Nasr Isa, the brother of Dr. Rashid Isa, who spent time with us in Palestine accompanying a group of brothers from Hama. Together with us at the time was Abd al-Sattar Za'im.[71]

Of course, this type of transnational undertaking was costly and impractical, and the practice was abandoned in future conflicts involving Islamist foreign fighters. In 1980s Afghanistan, fallen foreign fighters were buried on site or in cemeteries in the region.

Abdallah Azzam appears to have taken on the role of a religious authority in the camps. Dawud Jarrar recalled that "Abdallah Azzam was in [the Dibbin] base, leading us in prayer and speaking to us about *da'wa* and jihad."[72] Muhammad Nur said, "I lived with the martyr for about a month in Jordan in the *mujahidin* bases ... he practiced what he believed in, by words and deeds; verbally with morning and evening classes, lectures, and private and general meetings."[73] Azzam also gave religious pep talks before military operations. For example, right before entering the battle of Mashru', Azzam "asked us to perform ablution and pray two *ruk'a*s and remember God and purify our intentions. Then he gave a sermon explaining why we were fighting the Jews and urged us to seek martyrdom."[74] When Azzam was off duty, he combined family visits with lectures in mosques in Irbid and in Zarqa about his activities in the camps. The mayor of Zarqa later talked about Azzam's visits:

The people of Zarqa were delighted with his wonderful speeches in the Umar Ibn Khattab mosque ... he would come to the Umar mosque from the Fedayin bases, not to brandish his weapons in the streets, because it was about religion for him. We saw him in the Umar mosque talking about the martyrs who had fallen near the Land of the Night Journey ... He spoke at times about a martyr from Yemen, at other times about a martyr from Syria. One day he took out from his pocket a handkerchief stained with the blood of a martyr from Hama, and he swore, "By God I can smell musk from the blood of this martyr more than ten days after his martyrdom" ... he said that prior to his operation against the Jews, this martyr had darkened his eyelids with lemon leaves. His *mujahidin* friends asked, "Why are you doing this?" He said ... "Because I am about to meet the virgins of Paradise."[75]

We see here that in 1969 Azzam was already taking on the role he would be famous for during the Afghan jihad, namely, as a preacher who brings news and martyrdom stories from the battlefront to the people. The account also shows that the narrative theme of martyrdom miracles – such as the martyr's blood smelling of musk – was not something he invented in the 1980s. He would develop the theme much more in later books such as *Signs of the Merciful in the Afghan Jihad* (1983), but it was clearly already on his mind in the 1960s. We also see here Azzam using the presentational device he would use again in the 1980s, that of bringing a bloodstained personal item from a dead fighter.

Friction with Leftists

The Islamist Fedayin were in constant conflict with their leftist counterparts, especially the more hardline leftists in the Popular Front for the Liberation of Palestine (PFLP). Relations had soured from the beginning after the PFLP confiscated two brand-new Land Rovers that the Kuwaiti Brothers had donated to the Islamist Fedayin effort. According to Abu Izza, the Land Rovers "were parked at the entrance of the Islamic Center Charity Association in the middle of Amman when the men from the Popular Front came and took them in broad daylight, and that was the end of the story."[76]

More friction ensued, because the Bases of the Sheikhs were surrounded by PFLP Fedayin bases. The Irbid area was the PFLP's heartland in Jordan, and during Black September the organization would declare a "People's Socialist Republic" in the area.[77] As one might expect, relations were bad, with leftists and Islamists arguing and trading insults whenever they met, although never turning violent. In Azzam's words: "Sometimes we would encounter a group of them and we would stop and make the call to prayer, and they would chant leftist slogans back."[78] He also said: "We were surrounded on four sides: on three of them were PLO factions, on the fourth were the Jews. By God, we had to guard against the leftists more than against the Jews."[79] He added:

In their bases, we saw them from up close, with their nicknames such as Abu Jahl, Abu Lahab, Mao, Guevara, and Ho Chi Minh!! And their watchwords were curses of religion and the Lord. As for their food, they would shoot dogs with their guns and eat them, because for them there was no difference between dogs and sheep; the distinction was a superstition brought by a man from the desert named Muhammad, peace and blessings be upon him. We saw them when Muslim weapons-carrying *mujahid* youth called to prayer in the Fedayin gatherings, the sons of Lenin and Mao Tse Tung would babble on and raise their voices saying, "I don't care, I am an internationalist Marxist-Leninist" ... The socialist revolutionaries have no values or manners. They had so many mistresses!! They beguiled them in the name of Palestine. You would enter their bases, especially in the offices in the cities such as Amman you would see [the women] wearing tight trousers sleeping to music and waking to Oud strings mixed with Beatles and Hippies music!![80]

In the spring of 1970 Azzam got into trouble after giving a flaming anti-Communist sermon in a mosque in Irbid. Around the time of Lenin's hundredth birthday (22 April) leftist Fedayin groups had put up posters all around town featuring the Russian revolutionary's picture. Azzam found it all distasteful, and delivered a Friday sermon criticizing Communism in general and Lenin in particular.[81] Azzam said that the incident had him summoned to a PLO military tribunal to explain himself. He saw it as an opportunity to speak his mind and deliver some insults. He later boasted of asking his inquisitors, "Who is Che Guevara?" and "What is the religion of Fatah?" When they replied, "Guevara is a noble freedom fighter and Fatah does not have a religion," Azzam reportedly said, "My religion is Islam, and Guevara is under my foot."[82]

It was therefore probably just as well that Azzam did not run into any of the European leftists who were training with the Fedayin around this time. In 1969 and 1970 a substantial number – probably over a hundred – young Communists from Europe traveled to Jordan to train with the PFLP and other groups. These foreign fighters came partly out of solidarity with the Palestinian cause and partly in a quest for military training. Most famous is probably the ten-strong delegation from the Rote Armee Fraktion, including Andreas Baader and Ulrike Meinhof, who trained in a Fatah camp west of Amman in the summer of 1970.[83] Another well-documented case was that of Gunnar Ekberg, a Swedish intelligence officer who, as part of his infiltration of the Swedish far left, ended up with training with the PFLP in Jordan.[84] However, there is no evidence of contact between the Europeans and the Brotherhood Fedayin.

While relations with other Fedayin were tense, Azzam and his comrades "had good relations with the Jordanian army, which respected us and ... cooperated very well with us."[85] He noted that a certain Major-General Khalaf Rafi', the man responsible for border security in the Ghor region, "would stop his car if he saw one of us."[86] The Islamist Fedayin cooperated with the Jordanian army at the tactical level, as illustrated in the account of the battle of Mashru'. The Islamists also appear to have got on well with the locals in the Marw area. Azzam and his comrades were very respectful of the locals and their property; they later stressed that they had never helped themselves to fruit from the orchards around the camps, even though they had little food.[87] Azzam later wrote:

There was also a strong link and deep love between us and the locals, especially those near our camps. I especially remember the Ubaydat family in Rafid and Hartha, who treated us like their sons ... They took an admirable stance when the Jordanian army went in to strike our camps, and they said: "Over our dead bodies. We know them as teachers to our children, as imams and preachers in our mosques and as protectors of our villages and fields" ... One of their sons had heard of us from his family and his village and tribe, and come to like us; later he rose to high office in the state, even to the office of prime minister, and he was a good supporter of us if bad rumors spread or the campaigns against us intensified.[88]

Avoiding Black September

By early 1970 the PLO had become a state within a state in Jordan, to the great frustration of the regime. Ever since 1968 there had been friction and occasional clashes between Fedayin and Jordanian security forces. From February 1970 onward, PLO–regime relations deteriorated significantly, and violent clashes increased in frequency. It all culminated in September 1970, when a series of assassination attempts on King Hussein and the spectacular hijacking of four airliners at the Dawson's Field airstrip near Zarqa by the PFLP prompted the regime to crack down on the Fedayin for good. For ten days in late September, Jordanian forces assaulted and defeated most of the Fedayin in fighting that killed thousands of people. These events, known as Black September, marked the end of Fedayin activity in Jordan. Still, some factions held out until July 1971 when the Jordanian army and air force defeated them in a final showdown in the Dibbin woods and Ajlun mountains.[89]

The Islamist Fedayin managed to stay out of the conflict by laying down their arms early during the confrontation.[90] The Muslim Brotherhood saw the fighting as *fitna* (sedition) and had an interest in preserving good relations with the government. Later, Bassam al-Umush, a prominent Brotherhood figure, wrote that the Brotherhood had turned down an invitation from PLO to join forces against the regime:

I recall that Yasser Arafat sent for three Brotherhood leaders in Jordan, including Dhib Anis. He met with them in Jabal al-Hussein in Amman and told them about his intention to carry out a military operation against King Hussein under the pretext that the regime was against the resistance. The Brotherhood and specially Dhib Anis refused that notion. They told him, "you have no right to do so. Our guns are directed for action in Palestine." Abu-Ammar [Arafat] became very angry. There was not any regional background behind the Brotherhood's stance in the September war. It is not true to say that it was a stance dictated by the East Jordanian trend inside the movement. It was a collective stance taken by the Brotherhood.[91]

The fighters in the camps agreed with the Brotherhood leadership's policy of neutrality and demobilized voluntarily. Azzam recounts:

We gathered together, the brothers responsible for the young men, and decided that if the army clashed with the Fedayin, we would not enter into this conflict ... in which we feared forbidden blood would be spilled ... the battle was not clear, and the banner was not Islamic ... fighting the army was not acceptable, neither legally, logically, nor pragmatically. So we chose to remain neutral. Then the conversation turned to the dangers that lurked in the next stage, and the uncertainty surrounding the next few nights. But God's eye watched over this group ... and by God's great fortune ... none of us was hurt despite the fact that many civilians were killed, tortured, and imprisoned.[92]

The Islamist Fedayin camps remained operative right up until the final crackdown of mid-September 1970, and Azzam was there all along. When the situation exploded on 15 September, Azzam was home on leave:

I remember at the time I was in Irbid, because our base was near Irbid and my family was living in Irbid, and I was on leave and sitting at home when the crackdown begun. So we brought the women to the refuge under the house, meaning the women of the neighborhood inside trenches and refuges, while the men sat in the rooms, and the missiles struck and destroyed one house after the other. And there was a drunkard neighbor who threw himself in with the women.[93]

Black September made a big impression on Azzam. It left him deeply disappointed with the regional political order and pessimistic about the short-term prospects of the Palestinian struggle. It also made him more critical of governments in the region, including that of Jordan. In his writings on Black September, Azzam fiercely criticized the Jordanian, Egyptian, and Syrian governments for chasing the "Palestinian youth" – by which he meant the PLO militias – out of their countries and into Lebanon.[94] Although he would not express his views in public until much later, he thought that King Hussein had been much too heavy-handed in the suppression of the Fedayin, and he resented the regime's ban on anti-Israeli military activity from Jordan. After Black September he remarked, "[Possessing] a bullet became a crime, anyone who had one could be brought to military court; the same with mines and bombs."[95]

Because the Brotherhood pulled out of the confrontation in time, Black September did not harm Azzam's career prospects. On the contrary, his time in the camps helped him, because it raised his status inside the Brotherhood, which was represented in several key institutions such as the Ministry of Education and in the University of Jordan. Moreover, in the autumn of 1970, Ishaq al-Farhan, a prominent Muslim Brother and personal friend of Azzam's who had spent time in the Fedayin camps, became minister of education. Al-Farhan wanted to Islamize the education system, and openly admitted that he gave

Muslim Brothers preference in hiring decisions in the Ministry.[96] When Azzam got a teaching position in the Shariʿa faculty at the University of Jordan just months after Black September, al-Farhan almost certainly had a hand in it.[97] Al-Farhan may also have personally intervened to get Azzam the scholarship for his Ph.D. in Cairo, as one source says that "al-Farhan sent him to al-Azhar."[98]

The Fedayin experience also inspired Azzam. It gave him a taste of military life with all its emotional rewards: the sense of purpose, the thrill of adventure, the pride of making it through hardship, and the pleasure of camaraderie. It also persuaded him that the Islamist movement still had fighting spirit, especially among its younger members; it was only a matter of finding the right context to ignite it. It would take another decade before that opportunity arose. In the meantime, Azzam would start a new, academic chapter in his life.

4 | Scholar

"I asked some brothers in Pakistan how many Shari'a professors from the Arab world have visited Peshawar even once to show interest in the situation of Muslims, and the answer was of the kind that makes the soul shrink."[1] As in this quotation from 1983, Azzam often complained about being virtually the only Islamic scholar among the Afghan Arabs. While this made him lonely, it also gave him a special position and influence within the Afghan Arab community. Moreover, his scholarly credentials gave weight to his political writings, and help explain why his ideas gained such traction. But what exactly did these credentials consist of, and what type of scholar was he? This chapter examines Azzam's academic career. It starts with a brief look at his personality, and continues with an account of his year in Saudi Arabia in the late 1960s, his doctoral student days at al-Azhar in Cairo, and his tenure at the University of Jordan in the 1970s. We will see that Azzam was an intellectual who studied at some of the most prestigious religious schools of his time. He was too involved in Muslim Brotherhood activism to become an academic superstar, but his credentials became essential to the authority and influence he commanded in the Afghan jihad in the 1980s.

Academic Temperament

After high school, there never seems to have been any doubt in Azzam's mind that he wanted to become a religious scholar. He pursued his ambition with relentless determination in challenging circumstances. He completed his entire undergraduate and early graduate education in his spare time; he first studied Islamic Law at the University of Damascus while working as a teacher in Palestine, and he later read for a Master's degree from the trenches of the Jordan Valley. None of this was necessary or expected by his peers. Nobody else in his family had done it before him, and a degree in religion was no requirement for high office in the Muslim Brotherhood.

By all accounts, Azzam had been bookish from an early age. Anecdotes from both his early and later life describe an individual who was studious, self-disciplined, and austere. Azzam the child is described in hagiographies as unusually interested in religious study. His older sister later said, "He was always carrying a book, night and day, and I would sometimes come into him at night and he would lie on his mattress, having fallen asleep reading, with his small gas lamp on."[2]

Some sources portray Azzam as something of a child prodigy who excelled at all levels in the school system.[3] Such claims should be taken with a pinch of salt, because nearly all biographies of Islamic scholars describe their subjects as pious little geniuses when young. However, Azzam did stand out in academic ability from his peers. His original school records from Kadoorie show that he did have very good grades, although not the best in his class. Moreover, reaching the highest echelons of the Islamic education system in his time – without having a single scholar in his family – speaks to a high cognitive ability. As we shall see, he also wrote very fast and in an advanced language register. People who worked with him in the 1980s also said he had a remarkable memory for numbers and dates.[4]

His self-discipline, on the other hand, is undisputable. His friends and family said he always carried books around, and used every spare moment to read. When he worked as a schoolteacher, he reportedly spent his lunch breaks reading instead of chatting with the other teachers. In the Fedayin camps, his wife later said, "He made a program for his studies during the breaks and at night. When he came home during his breaks, and it was only four days per month, his book never left his hand, even when he was eating. This became a habit till the last days of his life."[5] He was also a meticulous reader who took careful and systematic notes. According to his wife, again, "He never did anything without writing it down in the form of keywords so he could retrieve it if need be. And he would write down quotes that he liked, and take out some Hadiths for later use in his lectures."[6]

Azzam's devotion to religious study came at his family's expense. Although he no doubt cared about and provided materially for his family, his work usually had priority. His wife later joked: "I often threatened to pour the food on his book if he did not put it down while we ate; sometimes he would apologize, while other times he would say: 'I have a lecture in a little bit that I have to prepare for, so excuse me and let me read while I eat.' So we would leave him."[7] Although his wife later described him as a "wonderfully kind husband and a caring father," he was not a particularly involved parent by modern standards.[8] His daughter Wafa described her relationship with her father as somewhat distant: "He treated us as would a caring and advising teacher, he was respectful and affective. I felt a lot of things inside me but I could not speak to him because we were in such awe of him. There was not a lot of beating, but instead advice and guidance."[9] A friend of the family added to the picture of a relatively stern father:

He urged them to memorize the Qur'an and would go over it with them. He did not like them to laugh and joke, and he did not like chitchat. He liked exercise and swimming and encouraged his children to do the same ... he encouraged his wife and children to read and to listen to classes and lectures, and to read magazines, especially *al-Mujtama'*. He took them to a lot of lectures ... he taught his children good manners and to keep their tongue. For example, he would sometimes say to them: "He who can keep quiet for an hour will get 100 rupees."[10]

At the same time, he was not an authoritarian head of family. His wife later said that he was patient both with her and their children if they did not behave quite as conservatively as he wanted. "He persuaded us gradually," she later said, recalling a period early in their marriage when she used to listen to music on the radio, and he tolerated it for a long time even though he did not like it. Eventually, through gentle prodding, he persuaded her to stop listening.[11]

In Islamist hagiographies, Azzam is also widely described as an ascete, a humble man who cared little for earthly possessions. "Believe me when I tell you that I hate buying new things, new clothes, and the like," he once said.[12] Like many jihadist leaders after him, Azzam would gain respect and legitimacy by forsaking material comfort for the cause. "Luxury is the first enemy of jihad," he reportedly used to say.[13] He also developed ascetic habits, deliberately exposing himself to cold and depriving himself of food. Azzam's wife later said:

Since getting married and even prior to traveling to Pakistan, he was preparing himself for jihad and a hard life. During the cold winter days he used to go out and pray the morning prayers and insisted on using cold water to perform his ablution. He would only eat one type of food, and sometimes only have one meal. Sometimes, he would only eat bread. He was getting himself used to life in the mountains and to becoming a *mujahid*. Most times he owned two pairs of trousers: he would wear one and wash the other. Nevertheless, he was always clean and well groomed.[14]

Later he wrote:

The soul is never satisfied. Satisfying your desires is like satisfying the thirsty person who went to drink water from the sea – the more he drinks, the thirstier he gets, since the water is salty … Therefore, it should be everyone's goal to be abstinent from worldly pleasures and to fight their desires, since it is impossible for the soul to rise and ascend except if it dominates over its desires and whims. The soul that becomes a prisoner to its desires will never be able to face the enemy on the battlefield. So, if you wish to remain travelling upon the path to Allah, hold yourself back.[15]

As we saw in Chapter 2, Azzam had obtained an undergraduate degree in Islamic Law from Damascus University in 1966. He then put his studies on hold, probably because he was too busy with family and work. However, the war of 1967 set him on a new path with more time for religious study.

Wahhabi Exposure

In the early autumn of 1967, a couple of months after fleeing to Amman, Azzam moved to the town of Baha in southwestern Saudi Arabia. He had been offered a job in the local institute for religious science (*al-ma'had al-'ilmi*), where he would teach for a full academic year.[16] The institutes for religious sciences were a specifically Saudi institution set up in the 1950s to bring Wahhabi religious education to the provinces.[17] They were basically religious high schools that prepared students for careers as Wahhabi preachers or teachers, or for further religious study. It was not uncommon for Muslim Brothers from the Levant to teach in Saudi institutes for religious science in the 1960s and 1970s. For example, the Syrian Sa'id Hawa spent five years in the late 1960s teaching in the same type of school in Hofuf and Medina.[18] Precisely how Azzam's job was arranged is unclear. We only have the testimony of his wife, who said, "He was authorized by the Emir of the Baha and Zafir region to do *da'wa* in the region," and that he helped train local preachers and set up a Qur'an memorization program for children.[19] The year in Baha must have exposed Azzam to Wahhabi ideas, because the institutes for religious sciences were, as Nabil Mouline put it, "designed to groom students in accordance with the most orthodox precepts of Hanbali-Wahhabism."[20]

Azzam's time in Saudi Arabia may help explain the traces of Salafism in his later discourse, as we shall see in subsequent chapters. Wahhabism is usually considered a substrand of Salafism, a theological movement widely viewed as distinct from the Muslim Brotherhood. Salafis – thus called because they claim to emulate the *salaf* ("predecessors"), meaning the earliest Muslims – represent a heterogeneous phenomenon, but they have usually been more literalist, less pragmatic, and less politically confrontational than the Muslim Brothers.[21] In many countries Salafis and Muslim Brothers have also formed distinct social networks and organizations. These differences have led both analysts and activists to speak of the divide between Salafis and Ikhwanis (Brotherhood activists) as one of the most salient dividing lines in the modern Islamist landscape.[22] However, this distinction has not always been clear-cut, as amalgams of Ikhwanism and Salafism have periodically emerged.[23] As we shall see in Chapters 5 and 11, Azzam would come to represent the case of a Salafi-influenced Muslim Brother.

Just prior to moving to Baha, Azzam enrolled in a Master's programme in Islamic Law at the University of al-Azhar in Cairo.[24] His plan was to complete the degree by distance learning, as he had done with this first degree in Damascus. In Baha he had enough time to complete the first year of the Master's degree. When he moved back to Amman in mid-1968 he continued with the second-year curriculum, but stopped studying when he joined the Fedayin in the spring of 1969. The following winter he decided to try to complete the degree while fighting in northern Jordan:

During our stay in the camps, some of the Brothers advised me to continue my studies to obtain a Master's degree at al-Azhar. I said to them, "Did we come here to wage jihad or did we come to study and learn?" But in the end I agreed with my brothers at their insistence, despite the fact that we did not have the required books in the camps. And so I went and took the exams, with God's help, for in those days you did not need to prepare a Master's thesis, it was enough to take exams. And then I went back to the base again.[25]

Abd al-Rahman Abd al-Khaliq later recalled, "I knew him in the bases of the *mujahidin* in Jordan; his books were with him, for he was following higher studies at al-Azhar, and the Kalashnikov was always by his side."[26]

The exams brought Azzam to Cairo in the spring of 1970. Even though he probably spent at most a few weeks there, it was enough to get a taste of big-city life and the atmosphere at al-Azhar. He also got a glimpse of the secularism of Nasser's Egypt, which appalled him; years later, he said in a lecture:

This took place in a time when nobody in Egypt was able to utter anything concerning Islam. Trust me, I saw it with my own eyes. During the last days of Gamal Abdel Nasser's rule, I was completing my Master's degree in Egypt. At this time, our brothers in Egypt were not allowed to enforce the wearing of Islamic dress upon their wives. It reached a stage where any house in which a woman wore long clothes would be under Secret Services surveillance. At this time, there were approximately 40,000 girls studying in Cairo University, but nobody except one wore Islamic dress.[27]

Doctorate at al-Azhar

When Azzam demobilized from the Fedayin and reverted to "civilian life" in late 1970, his academic future was still uncertain. He did not have much money, he had a family to support, and there was no Ph.D. program in Islamic Law in Jordan. Fortunately for him, Jordan at this point was in the process of building up its academic sector, and the Ministry of Education offered Ph.D. scholarships for Jordanians to study at institutions abroad. There was a need for people with doctorates in Islamic Law because the College of Shari'a had only recently been incorporated into Jordan University and sought to become a fully accredited Ph.D.-granting institution. At some point in the winter of 1970–1971 Azzam was awarded a scholarship to do a doctorate at al-Azhar.[28] He jumped at the opportunity, and moved to Cairo with his family in the late summer of 1971.

Azzam arrived in a changing Egypt. In October 1970 President Gamal Abdel Nasser had died, and Anwar Sadat had taken over. The new leader was to break with a number of his predecessor's key policies. In May 1971 he announced his so-called Corrective Movement, which involved, among other things, the purging of senior Nasserist officials, a certain reining in of the security services, and a move away from the

Soviet Union (culminating with the July 1972 expulsion of 25,000 Soviet advisors).[29] Later he would embark on a policy of economic liberalization, and eventually even sign a peace treaty with Israel.

Crucially for our story, Sadat also took a softer stance on Islamists. The early 1970s would see a gradual transformation of the relationship between the regime and the Muslim Brotherhood from one of extreme hostility to one of apprehensive coexistence. The secular Nasser regime had ruthlessly suppressed the Muslim Brotherhood since the early 1950s, imprisoning hundreds in hard-labor camps, subjecting many to horrific torture, and executing suspected coup-plotters. The second half of the 1960s saw a particularly brutal crackdown which included the execution of Sayyid Qutb in 1966 and the imprisonment of virtually all the remaining cadres of the organization. By 1971, however, Sadat had come to see the Brotherhood as less of a threat, and he recognized that many Egyptians were becoming more religious. He also hoped to enlist the support of Islamists to marginalize the leftist opposition. Thus in the summer of 1971, right before Azzam arrived, Sadat started releasing many imprisoned Islamists, including almost all of the Muslim Brothers in labor camps.[30] Over the coming years more would be released, in trickles, until the most senior figures came out in 1974. In 1971 the regime also authorized the organization of religious summer camps, and in 1972 it became legal to form Islamic associations, including Islamic student societies.[31] The Muslim Brotherhood itself was not formally legalized under Sadat – nor under Mubarak for that matter – but it started to operate openly from 1974 onwards.[32]

The rapprochement between the regime and the Brotherhood was made easier by the latter's ideological moderation. By around 1970 the Egyptian Muslim Brotherhood had abandoned revolutionary violence, in both theory and practice. That year the Brotherhood's supreme guide, Hasan al-Hudaybi, wrote a famous book titled *Preachers, not Judges*, in which he argued that Islamists should be in the business of proselytization, education, and social work, not coup-making.[33] The Secret Apparatus was effectively dismantled, and the leadership worked to purge the organization of its most militant elements.[34] These developments helped persuade Sadat that the Brotherhood no longer posed an existential threat to the regime.

The ideological shift reflected the rise to prominence of the "Bannaists" over the "Qutbists" in the leadership of the Brotherhood. There had long been a debate inside the Brotherhood over whether to pursue political change slowly though grassroots activism, as advocated by Hasan al-Banna, or rapidly through confrontation with the regime, as suggested by Sayyid Qutb. Although these two positions are better understood as opposing ends of a spectrum rather than two distinct camps, the terms Bannaist and Qutbist have been used by academics and Islamists alike as synonyms for pragmatists and hardliners.[35] An important part of this debate was the question of the conditions for *takfir* (excommunication), because it had implications for the use of violence. If a given person or group of people could be considered outside the fold of Islam, then their blood could legitimately be spilled. The *takfir* debate mostly revolved around the status of leaders and regimes, although a radical fringe was ready to declare *takfir* on entire segments of the population if the latter did not share their hardline views.

Despite the ascendancy of Bannaism, there would still remain, within the Egyptian Muslim Brotherhood, a Qutbist wing with more hawkish views than al-Hudaybi. It included figures such as Muhammad Qutb, former members of the Secret Apparatus, and many others. We will meet several of them later in this book because they tended to get involved in international projects such as support for the Afghan jihad. These figures were more hostile to secular regimes than al-Hudaybi was – many privately considered the Egyptian government un-Islamic – but they did not advocate revolutionary action, and kept their heads down so as not to get the Brotherhood into trouble again. Some of them had Salafi leanings and interacted more with Islamists in Saudi Arabia. It is no coincidence that Sayyid Qutb's brother Muhammad, who became the main representative of the Qutbist wing of the Egyptian Muslim Brotherhood, moved to Mecca within months of his release from prison in 1971.[36]

Moreover, there were Islamists with views so radical that they were outside of the Muslim Brotherhood altogether. These were people such as Salih Sirriya, who led a failed coup attempt in 1974, and Shukri Mustafa, whose cult-like group Jama'at al-Muslimin (aka al-Takfir wa'l-Hijra) kidnapped and killed the Egyptian minister Muhammad al-Dhahabi in 1977.[37] They were by no means a homogeneous crowd. Salih Sirriya was a Palestinian student and former member of Hizb al-Tahrir who sought to undertake a classic Lenin-style coup to Islamize Egypt from above.[38] Shukri Mustafa was a former low-level Brotherhood activist from Asyut who came to hold a maximalist *takfiri* position according to which anyone who did not declare *takfir* on an infidel was an infidel himself, which basically meant everybody except Mustafa's own group.[39] There were other activists too who considered the regime infidel and the Brotherhood too moderate; the young Ayman al-Zawahiri appears to have been part of one such group from the late 1960s onward.[40] Later in the 1970s these grouplets would coalesce into a more substantial militant movement from which Sadat's assassins would spring.

When Azzam was in Cairo there was little violent unrest, but fierce ideological debates raged under the surface. Azzam later described the atmosphere among the Islamists as one of *fitna* (discord), a very strong term that connotes political–religious chaos:

After looking at this issue a lot, the issue of legislating by something other than what God has revealed, and truly, this preoccupied me a lot, because I was doing a doctorate when the factions came out of prison during the Sadat days. One group came out declaring *takfir* on all people, one group separated themselves from people altogether, and one group saying to everyone "anyone who says there is no God but Allah and Muhammad is his Prophet is a Muslim." So the issue preoccupied me, and one group was not praying in the mosques, and frankly there was great discord, and this young man Shukri Mustafa, may God have mercy on his soul, whom Sadat executed in the Takfir wa'l-Hijra case about the killing of al-Dhahabi, adopted the *takfiri* view, he considered that anyone who did not enter his group was an infidel outside the community. They relied on the rule "he who does not excommunicate the infidel is himself an infidel, and whoever doubts the infidelity of the infidel is himself an infidel."[41]

Azzam was talking from experience, because he met some of the extremists personally and was himself declared an infidel:

By God, one of the youth came to see me, he liked me, he was Jordanian, he had adopted Shukri Mustafa [as a leader], and he liked him and his views. I have never seen a human being with as strong a conviction as this young man. He was studying pharmacology, and he would sometimes come and have breakfast with me in Cairo. One day after he had met Shukri Mustafa he came to see me, and he started talking, and I was discussing with him, and then came the time for prayer. I saw him like this, clearly uncomfortable praying behind me. So I said to him, "Please, come here and pray in my place." On the days where I was supposed to lead the prayer, he said, "I have already prayed." I said to him, "What is your opinion of me?" He said, "You mean honestly?" I said, "Yes, honestly." He said, "I consider you an infidel." "Why, my son? What's the issue?" He said, "You're from the Muslim Brotherhood." So we said, "OK", and he said, "Everyone in the Muslim Brotherhood is an infidel." "Why?" He said, "Because you don't declare al-Hudaybi an infidel" ... And indeed, he was caught up with the Shukri Mustafa case and was sentenced to fifteen years, and he is still in prison today.[42]

Such encounters were the exception, though, because Azzam did not frequent the radical fringes of the Egyptian Islamist scene. He almost certainly did not meet Shukri Mustafa himself, who was in Asyut in the early 1970s. There is also no evidence that he met Muhammad Faraj, Khalid al-Islambuli, Ayman al-Zawahiri, Salih Sirriyya, or any of the other subsequently famous revolutionaries at this time. They were all younger than Azzam and attended other universities.

Azzam studied at al-Azhar University, a thousand-year-old institution located in the eastern part of central Cairo. Around 1970 al-Azhar was the most prestigious place of religious learning in the world of Sunni Islam. In 1961 Nasser had brought it under government control, made it part of the regular university system, and established the office of Grand Imam of al-Azhar to serve as the primary religious authority in Egypt.[43] Al-Azhar as an institution was thus effectively coopted by the state, and its scholars instrumentalized to discourage radical Islamist activism. Under Nasser, for example, sheikhs from al-Azhar were brought to the prisons to persuade detained activists to recognize the government.[44] Similarly, after Sadat's assassination in 1981, the sheikh of al-Azhar, Jadd al-Haqq, issued a fatwa denouncing revolutionary violence.[45] For this reason, and perhaps because students with formal religious training are generally not drawn to militancy, al-Azhar was never a hotbed of Islamist radicalism in Egypt. Militants were more often recruited from the regular universities, especially from the science and engineering faculties.[46]

Al-Azhar was not unaffected by the tense political atmosphere. Around this time it took a somewhat more assertive stance in favor of giving Islam a larger role in society. In 1971, after Sadat announced that work would begin on a new permanent constitution, al-Azhar became a vocal proponent of Shari'a as the sole source of legislation.[47] According to Malika Zeghal, some Azharite scholars also adopted a more openly Islamist discourse in this period.[48]

The university gradually also became a player in the political struggle between leftists and Islamists.[49] The sheikh of al-Azhar, Muhammad Muhammad al-Fahham, came out publicly denouncing the leftists.[50] In 1972 and 1973, when there were tensions and skirmishes between leftists and Islamists on Egyptian campuses, some students at al-Azhar participated on the Islamist side.[51] It is not clear whether Azzam was one of them, but the events must have reminded him of his own run-ins with leftist Fedayin just a few years earlier. Jordanian politics also caught up with him in Cairo. On 28 November 1971, not long after Azzam's arrival in Cairo, operatives from a PFLP faction named Black September assassinated the Jordanian prime minister, Wasfi al-Tal, outside the Sheraton hotel in Cairo.[52] The attack was revenge for the crackdown a year earlier, and was the first in a series of international terrorist attacks by the group.

However, Azzam did not focus much on politics, because he spent most of his time studying. In the foreword of his doctoral thesis he described his time in Cairo:

The hours [spent on this thesis] have been a blessing in which I have tasted the sweetness of scientific research while I have immersed myself in the pages a not inconsiderable amount of time ... And these have truly been among the most beautiful days of my life. God allowed me to learn things that I have never learned in my life. The gracious Lord allowed me to isolate myself this period to prepare my thesis, my investigation, and my research. And I have benefited greatly from the Egyptian National Library and the Library of al-Azhar.[53]

He took advantage of Cairo's great bookstores to build a personal library that would later serve him in Jordan and in Pakistan. Like many budding academics, he liked to browse bookshops, and often bought books he could not really afford:

During this period I was looking out for the first editions of books on principles of jurisprudence in the old bookshops, and if I came across one I would buy it even if it was expensive ... I tried not to miss any old work of reference I came across or saw displayed in the shops. I added to my library a valuable collection of these old works of reference that did not leave anything to those who came after.[54]

He also had a family to look after. He had four children (his son Hudhayfa was born in Cairo in 1972) to feed, clothe, and educate. The family lived a frugal existence in cheap Cairo apartments, although they could afford to have a maid to come and help his wife.[55] He also paid for private religious tuition for his children. His wife later said, "He was interested in educating the children and teaching them Arabic, and he brought them teachers of Arabic and Qur'an memorization. [Our son] Muhammad memorized a section and a half when he was three years old."[56] In addition, Azzam himself read the Qur'an with the children every morning after the morning prayer. According to Isma'il al-Shatti, the four-year-old Muhammad would quote expressions from Sayyid Qutb without knowing what they meant.[57] Muhammad also reportedly memorized the Qur'an at age eleven.[58]

For his doctoral dissertation, Azzam chose to work on Islamic Law, specifically the subfield of Islamic sciences known as principles of jurisprudence (*usul al-fiqh*). According to *The Oxford Dictionary of Islam*, *usul al-fiqh* is "the body of principles and investigative methodologies through which practical legal rules are developed from the foundational sources."[59] This was a natural continuation of his Bachelor's degree in Islamic Law at the University of Damascus which he had completed some four years earlier.

At al-Azhar, Azzam worked under the supervision of Abd al-Ghani Abd al-Khaliq, the head of the department of *usul al-fiqh*. A prominent legal scholar in his mid-sixties, Abd al-Khaliq was best known for a work titled *Proofs of the Sunna* (*hujjiyat al-sunna*). He also had a reputation for being friendly toward foreign students. He would let students use his large library, and would often give books away.[60] Azzam himself would later acquire a similar reputation, and it is possible that he learned good teaching ethics from his doctoral advisor. Azzam's positive interactions with scholars may have contributed to his deep respect for the profession; one biographer noted that "Azzam had great respect for the scholars; [disrespecting them] was a red line for him."[61] Moreover, "he was careful to avoid any enmity between him and other scholars."[62]

At the very end of 1972 Azzam completed his thesis.[63] While most students at al-Azhar needed three to five years to finish their doctorates, Azzam did it in sixteen months, and his thesis was over 600 pages long.[64] It is not clear why he was in such a hurry to finish; perhaps he simply enjoyed working hard and making the most of his time. He defended it on 29 March 1973 in a three-hour viva voce examination in one of the halls of al-Azhar. His thesis committee consisted of Muhammad al-Sayis, Ibrahim al-Shahawi, and his supervisor Abd al-

Ghani Abd al-Khaliq.[65] They had a number of critical remarks and suggestions, as is customary, but overall the assessment was positive. It emerged that he probably worked a little too fast, because one of the criticisms at this thesis defense was that he had included in the background chapter "many things that were outside the topic of the thesis and made it unnecessarily long."[66] Still, he passed with the highest possible grade, "first rank of honor."[67] Azzam was proud to declare that "I had the fortune of being the first to specialize in this science – *usul al-fiqh* – among the people of my home country Jordan."[68] We will look at the content of the thesis in Chapter 6.

Networking in Cairo

Al-Azhar was an international place, and Azzam, who, despite his studiousness was a sociable person, made many new connections. One of his contemporaries said that "his network among the foreign students – from Syria, Saudi Arabia, Jordan, and Palestine – was a wide one; the sheikh forged many friendships."[69] He also strengthened existing friendships, because he found himself in Cairo with several people he knew from before. One was Fadl Abbas, a Jordanian Muslim Brother from Amman.[70] Another was Ahmad Nawfal, a Jordanian Muslim Brother who had been in the Fedayin camps with Azzam, and who became a close lifelong friend.[71] Another good friend was Isma'il al-Shatti, a Kuwaiti Muslim Brother who had also been with Azzam in the Fedayin camps. Al-Shatti later wrote:

> We met again in the Cairo of [Caliph] al-Mu'izz when the tyrants were in power and the truthful people in prison. And we spent time as brothers on the same path. We were one heart, idea, and movement: we did not take notice of all the evil surrounding us ... We spent five years on the same road. We learned a lot ... I remember your small children, Fatima, Wafa and Muhammad, that I teasingly called "my lambs." I still remember your son Muhammad whom we called Abu Dharr.[72]

Azzam also overlapped at al-Azhar with other individuals who later became prominent Islamist figures, although he did not meet them at the time. One was Umar Abd al-Rahman (aka "the blind sheikh"), the spiritual leader of the militant Egyptian group al-Jama'a al-Islamiyya.[73] Abd al-Rahman would visit Peshawar in the late 1980s and meet Azzam there, but they did not know each other in Cairo. Another was Abd Rabb al-Rasul Sayyaf, the future Afghan Mujahidin leader who would become a close collaborator of Azzam's in the 1980s.[74] A third figure who was at al-Azhar around this time was Ahmad Yasin, the Palestinian founder of Hamas. One source says Azzam and Yasin met in Cairo, but this is uncertain.[75]

Azzam did, however, spend considerable time with prominent members of the Egyptian Muslim Brotherhood. According to a fellow student, Azzam "got to know the leading figures of the *daʿwa* in Egypt, the figures who were around at the time, he was in touch with them all. The most prominent of them was Muhammad Qutb, but there were of course many others."[76] Another friend of Azzam's later said: "We spent years with the Qutb family and the Hudaybi family, and sometimes with Zaynab al-Ghazzali."[77] Some leaders, such as Hasan al-Hudaybi and Kamal al-Sananiri, were in prison the whole time Azzam was in Cairo, but he was close to their families. Azzam and other young Muslim Brothers took pride in "helping the families of imprisoned Muslim Brothers."[78] His wife later said that he "used to collect money for the family of Sayyid Qutb and [his sister] Amina Qutb and others after they came out of prison."[79]

Azzam was close enough to the Qutb family to be let in on their personal life dramas, such as Muhammad Qutb's preparations to leave for Saudi Arabia and Amina Qutb's agonizing over her imprisoned fiancé, Kamal al-Sananiri:

I still remember those nervous days in the house of Dr. Muhammad Qutb in 1973 when he wanted to leave Egypt. His sister Hamida had just got married or was about to, and there was no other legally responsible male relative in the house except Dr. Muhammad. Amina [Qutb] was living a nerve-wrecking and heart-breaking existence. She traveled with her brother Muhammad to Saudi Arabia, and on Mount Arafat she made supplication from her confused and burning heart, and Kamal al-Sananiri came out [from prison] on the same day, the Day of Arafah [2 January 1974].[80]

Azzam would stay in touch with all these people throughout the 1970s and 1980s; Muhammad Qutb would travel to America with Azzam in 1978, and become his department colleague in Mecca in 1981. Kamal al-Sananiri would persuade Azzam to join the Afghan jihad in 1981. Al-Ghazzali visited him in Peshawar in 1985 and gave an interview to *al-Jihad* magazine. When Azzam died, Amina Qutb called Azzam's wife, and wrote a condolence letter that was published in Brotherhood magazines.[81]

It is clear from these connections that Azzam identified with the Qutbist wing of the Muslim Brotherhood. His writings from the 1970s also show him as a tough-talking conservative. In 1973 – at his Ph.D. defense, no less – he lambasted "the people of this generation of successors that have abandoned prayer, seeking the vanities of this world saying we will be forgiven, and that is because they are busy with the nonsense written in the stupid magazines and depraved newspapers."[82] His subsequent writings are replete with declarations of *takfir* on secular Arab leaders and leftists, such as: "He who embraces nationalist principles leaves Islam"[83] and "let it be clear from the start that those who legislate by something other than God's revelation are infidels [*kuffar*]."[84] These positions are far removed from the message of *Preachers, not Judges*, so Azzam must have quietly disagreed with Hasan al-Hudaybi and other Bannaists during his time in Cairo.

According to one of his hagiographers, Azzam was followed closely by Egyptian intelligence while in Cairo. The police harassment was reportedly such that Azzam and his family had to move from apartment to apartment, keeping their clothes in their bags in case they had to leave quickly.[85] The same source suggests that this had to do with the telegram Azzam allegedly sent to President Nasser criticizing him for the execution of Sayyid Qutb.[86] However, if Azzam had the attention of Egyptian security services – which is possible – it probably had more to do with his frequenting senior Muslim Brotherhood activists than with the telegram, which he had sent anonymously anyway.

Azzam, in other words, came away from Cairo as a classically trained scholar of Islamic Law with impeccable credentials. He later said, "God opened the road for me to complete the Master's degree and the Doctorate in the days of Abdul Nasser ... we waged war on Abdel Nasser through the diploma we obtained from his country."[87]

Teaching in Amman

In the summer of 1973 Azzam returned to Amman. He initially worked in the media department of the Ministry of Religious Endowments, because his Ph.D. scholarship contract stipulated a year of government service upon completion. However, after just a few months the minister allowed Azzam to take up the job he really wanted, which was as lecturer in the Shari'a department at the University of Jordan.[88]

It was not a lucrative position. As his wife later described it, "We were living a frugal life after our return from Egypt. In our house there was nothing but a naked space, and a tiny bit of furniture and personal belongings." She also told an anecdote about how Azzam's mother had come to visit and helped herself to one of the few possessions she had left: "[His] mother came to visit, she looked around, and there were some of my personal belongings (a gift from a friend). She took it and gave it to her daughter, and I [was so upset I] had to get up and leave the room." Azzam, however, handled the situation with humor and affection: "Abdallah followed me, and he looked at me and said: 'it's difficult, isn't it? I know, but it is my mother.' After they left and he saw how sad I was, he told me jokingly: Would you accept me instead of what my mother took from you?"[89]

At some point in the mid-1970s he had saved enough money to buy a larger house in the Suwailih area not far from the University of Jordan. Azzam became a well-known figure in the neighborhood, and was well liked. His nephew later told the story of how, one day, one of Azzam's children was hit by a car right outside their house. The driver took the boy to the nearest hospital and then went back to inform Azzam. Knowing that Azzam was a prominent sheikh, he was nervous about the latter's reaction, but Azzam just said, "Don't worry, it's not your fault. By God, if he had died, I would not have asked anything from you. I know that you would not want to harm a chicken."[90] Azzam also involved himself in local neighborhood activities. One of his main projects was raising funds for the construction of a local mosque, because there was none in his part of Suwailih when he moved there. This became the Abd al-Rahman bin Awf mosque, which soon became, and still remains, a major Muslim Brotherhood hub in Amman.[91] He reportedly founded several other mosques in Amman, notably the Ammar bin Yasir mosque in the Kamaliyya district.[92]

According to his wife, getting the Ph.D. had made Azzam snap into a different, more determined mode. He had probably never been a progressive family man, but from now his work had priority over everything:

In the beginning of my life with him, he was interested in the children, in educating them and teaching them about Islam. He was very careful to always give them some of his time, however little. This was before the doctorate ... after he obtained the doctorate, all his time went to *da'wa* and *irshad*. He was keen to exploit every minute of the day, although he tried to give his children at least a minute, despite being very busy with the jihad. He was away from the house for many days. When I raised the issue with him, he would say: "Umm Muhammad, I have prepared you for this type of day so that you can preside over the household and educate the children; if God had not blessed me with such a good wife, I could not have performed my duties of *da'wa* and jihad." He would encourage me with these words so that I fill my role. I then understood why he had taken such an interest in us in the beginning of our life together. So I relied on God alone to sort out the many issues that arose when he was away.[93]

Azzam found great satisfaction in his new role as an Islamic educator, and he would teach at the University of Jordan for the next seven years. Located on a pleasant, tree-filled campus in northwestern Amman, the University of Jordan was the country's only university. It had roughly 12,000 students, many of whom were Palestinians who had come from the Territories to study or whose families had fled to Jordan in 1967.[94] Politically, the campus was still relatively quiet compared with its sister institutions in Cairo. The Shari'a department was one of the largest departments, with a total of some 1,500–2,000 undergraduate students and several dozen professors.[95] As many as a third of the teaching staff in the department were Muslim Brothers, some of whom were known as relative hardliners, such as Ahmad Nawfal, Muhammad Abu Faris, and Humam Sa'id.[96]

Azzam lectured primarily on subjects related to Islamic Law, but also on more political and contemporary topics, such as "The Muslim World Today." He soon acquired a reputation as a great speaker and an attentive teacher. Some of his lecture notes from that time have survived, and suggest that he was a structured and meticulous lecturer.[97] His classes were often oversubscribed, and attracted many students from other departments. Sometimes people came from outside the university to listen to him.[98] According to several former students, he was, together with his close friend and colleague Ahmad Nawfal, the most popular lecturer in the department.[99]

No recordings of Azzam's lectures in the 1970s have survived, but the many videotaped lectures from the 1980s show a highly capable orator: confident, engaging, knowledgeable, and charismatic. His lectures were also famously popular, as his former student Jihan Bakeer later recalled:

One of the most famous [professors] and most loved by the students was Dr. Azzam. He was kind and so down to earth. The course title was "The Muslim World Today"; it was the summer semester of my sophomore year 1978. The classroom was one of the biggest in the faculty, there were over fifty or sixty students ... I never saw a class of his less than overloaded, and when he gave lectures out of curricula on certain occasions like the birthday of the prophet Mohammad (p.b.h) you would need to be an hour early to find a seat in the largest lecture room in the University.[100]

Azzam appears to have had a gift for connecting with young people. He could be stern and serious on the podium, but in personal interactions he was friendly and down-to-earth. Many former students describe him as more likeable and interesting than the other professors; one student said, "This doctor is different from other doctors with diplomas ... he is a man of the people – in the university he would sit with his students and followers [... and they] would not feel that there was any difference between him and them."[101] It does not show in the videos that we have of him, but several sources insist that Azzam had a good sense of humor and joked a lot.[102] "The sheikh was not stiff in his life at all," one former student insisted.[103] Moreover, in personal encounters with young people, Azzam was tolerant of dissenting opinions, and even religious doubt. A young member of his extended family recalls discussing politics and religion with him in the early 1980s and finding him surprisingly open to dialogue. When the teenager expressed skepticism of both the Muslim Brotherhood and the Arab involvement in Afghanistan, his embarrassed father (a cousin of Azzam) told him to tone it down, but Azzam said calmly, "Let him speak. He is entitled to his own opinions. Not everyone agrees on these issues."[104]

For Azzam, teaching was a 24/7 commitment, and he spent a lot of time with his students outside of class. He deliberately chose to live in the Suwailih district near the university so that his home would be accessible to the students.[105] "There was no strict separation," one source said, "between his private and his public life. His house was his students' house as well."[106] According to Kazim Ayish, one of his former students, "The doctor's house was almost like a public place, given the number of people who passed through. He was continuously hosting people, whether they were neighbors and locals, people from the Arab and Islamic world, or students from the university."[107] Azzam was so hospitable that, at times, his wife thought it could be a bit much. She later said Azzam put his students first and his own family second:

It was to the point where he preferred his children in the department at Jordan University, who were getting their education from him, he preferred them over his own children. A number of times, by God, I was putting out food, and none [of us in the family] had touched it, we hadn't eaten; but he would just take the food [and bring it to the students].[108]

Because Azzam spent so much time with students, including female ones, his wife's friends speculated that he might end up taking a second wife. Samira was not opposed to the idea on principle, but considered the chances of this happening to be slim because her husband worked so much:

When the sheikh was teaching in the university in Jordan, the women warned me that he might marry again, because the university was mixed gender ... They told me to watch out, but how could I watch out? Should I stalk him on campus? How would I watch out when I only see him one hour per day? How would he even have the time to marry another? I remember he once asked me, "What will you do if I marry again?" I said, "I won't do anything, but I have one condition, and that is to have a house to myself ... I will not lie and say she is my sister and that I love her, because jealousy is not conducive to friendship and I will not be better than the women of the Prophet, between whom there were problems even though they were married to the Prophet."[109]

Azzam contributed to the Islamization of the student population at the University of Jordan in the 1970s. Aside from conveying Islamist ideas in his lectures, he encouraged conservative behavior on campus. He segregated his classrooms by gender, and he encouraged women to wear the face veil (*niqab*), neither of which was common practice in the early 1970s.[110] A former student said, "I remember him standing alone in the university advocating the covering of the face. He told them, 'I will not argue with you over the Islamic ruling, but university regulations give female students personal freedom in what to wear, and just as you allow liberal dress, you must allow others to wear what they want.'"[111] Another said that "when he began teaching at Jordan University, signs of an Islamic awakening started appearing, first in the Shari'a department, and then in the other departments."[112]

A milestone was reached in 1976 when Islamists wrested control of the Student Union from leftists. To be sure, this was not all Azzam's work; Islamism was on the rise across the Middle East at this time, and there were other Muslim Brotherhood professors who also wielded influence. For a while, from 1976 to 1978, even the president of the university was a Muslim Brother: Ishaq al-Farhan.[113] Perhaps the most tangible effect of his efforts was the Islamization of Palestinian students in Jordan. Many of those who studied with him at this period went on to join Hamas and take part in the Palestinian Intifada in the late 1980s. Speaking in 2009, the Jordanian Muslim Brother Kazim Ayish said Hamas cadres today "include at least a hundred people who studied with Abdallah Azzam."[114] Muhammad Kazim Sawalha, a UK-based Hamas-linked activist who studied at Jordan University in 1980, said: "There's a whole generation of preachers active today, who undertook the Palestininan Intifada in the West Bank and Gaza, a whole generation who was influenced by Sheikh Abdallah Azzam."[115] One biography summed up Azzam's influence by noting that he educated a "vast number of students who came to have a prominent role in leading the process of education, reform, and change in the region."[116]

However, Azzam's educational efforts did not stop at the campus gate. He spent much time on *da'wa* work across the country. He lectured widely in Amman and other parts of Jordan to a variety of audiences. He spoke frequently at Yarmuk University in Irbid, as well as in mosques and youth centers across the country. He also took part in typical Brotherhood organizational work, visiting Brotherhood study circles (*usar*) and helping organize religious summer camps for students.[117] Mansur Hayyari later recalled:

In Jordan in the mid-1970s we used to accompany each other to Qur'an memorization centers to encourage the youth in lectures and meetings ... And [Azzam] really had their ear because he spoke with his heart before his tongue ... and was very tactful in speaking to people, with a sweet and charming smile ... and he was friendly to the brothers who preceded him in the *da'wa*, especially if they were older than him, and he would always ask his brothers for advice and make note of it.[118]

Azzam loved *da'wa* work, and by all accounts he was very good at it. Like any skilled proselytizer, he would address his audience in plain language with references familiar to them. In his writings and recorded lectures we find many rhetorical vignettes that we can assume he also used in his informal talks. He notably used a lot of allegories, a staple of *da'wa* rhetoric. For example, he might compare God to an intelligence service or a university dean:

> Had it been the case that we dealt with Allah, feared Allah in our gatherings just as we would fear an intelligence agent, we would pay close attention to every word that came out of our mouths. So, we fear some soldier – this intelligence agent – more than we fear Allah, as the Angels record every single word that we speak. We do not consider this, and we are not afraid when we speak. However, if it were said to us that in this gathering, there is an intelligence agent present, we would pay close attention to every single word that comes out of our mouths. So, fear of a single intelligence agent has become more than it is of Allah. If we were to deal with Allah as having the same power that the dean of the college has – with his ability to pass, fail, accept, reject as he pleased – our behavior with Him would be quite different, indeed. If we were to deal with Allah as if He were like the ruler of a country who gives visas, money, jobs, provision, etc. – if we were to deal with Allah in such a manner, human beings would look so insignificant in our eyes.[119]

Or he might compare the heart to glass that can be soiled by too much dirt:

> The heart is like glass – do you not see the lamp? The glass lamp, or the windshield of the car ... the windshield of the car has wipers and wiper fluid installed for it. So, whenever it becomes dirty, you press the button, and the fluid comes out, and the wipers clean it: "Follow a bad deed with a good deed, and it will wipe it out." However, if you splash into a pit of mud, how can you clean your windshield?"[120]

At other times he would guilt-trip his listeners with anecdotes of very pious people:

> At times, I would pray a normal prayer with the people behind me, so I would elongate the prayer. The youth would then come to me and say (the hadith): "Whoever leads the people in prayer should go easy on them" – the youth! And there was an old man behind me who was between 90 and 100 years of age – his face filled with light – and he would say to me: "Keep making the prayer long and do not answer them." A man of 90 years getting pleasure out of a long prayer, and a youth of 20, who probably practices karate and judo, cannot handle the same prayer ... Because, what stands up to pray is the heart, and what stands up for sports are simply the body and muscles.[121]

Azzam was thus an Islamic scholar of some stature even before making his name with the Afghan jihad. Although not a giant in the broader field of Islamic scholarship, he was respected in clerical circles and well known among Muslim Brothers in the region. His scholarly credentials and ability to connect with the young later became major assets in his recruitment efforts for Afghanistan. In the meantime, his ability to influence people would cause him problems.

5 Vagabond

By the end of the 1970s Azzam had done really quite well considering his humble background. At barely forty years old he had a big house, a university job, and a leading position in the Jordanian Muslim Brotherhood. Soon after, in 1981, he would leave all of this behind for an uncertain future in Pakistan. Why? This chapter will look at Azzam's career in the late 1970s and the events that took him to Islamabad. It examines his political activities in Jordan, his international travel, his departure from Jordan, his time in Saudi Arabia, and his move to Pakistan. We will see how the Jordanian government's attempts to silence Azzam helped turn him into a rootless citizen of the Muslim world. Once pressured out of Jordan, his trajectory was shaped by his Muslim Brotherhood connections and by the pan-Islamist ideas that flourished in western Saudi Arabia at this time.

The Sayyid Qutb of Jordan

Azzam did not just wake up one morning and say, "I'll skip work and join the Afghan jihad." The transition to Pakistan was a two-stage process in which he was first forced into exile, and only then – with less to lose – decided to try his luck in South Asia. His departure from Jordan was a consequence of his increasingly bold political activism. Azzam was never just a university lecturer in Amman; he was also a prominent member of the Muslim Brotherhood with hardline views. He was a strict conservative, a fierce anti-secularist, and an ardent supporter of jihad against Israel. This earned him the nickname the "Sayyid Qutb of Jordan," something he must have been quietly pleased about, given his admiration for the Egyptian ideologue.[1]

Azzam had risen quickly in the ranks of the Jordanian Brotherhood after his return from Egypt. Even though he was only in his thirties, he had impeccable credentials: an active member since age twelve, a former Fedayin fighter, and a respected scholar with a Ph.D. from al-Azhar.

At some point in the mid-1970s he was elected into the group's Consultative Council (*majlis al-shura*), a governing body of forty members.[2] He was eventually also made part of the seven-member Executive Committee, the organization's steering organ. This committee was subject only to the authority of Muhammad Khalifa, but the latter was more of a figurehead who left most of the managing decisions to the Executive Committee. Here is how Ibrahim Gharaybeh, a former Muslim Brotherhood member, describes Azzam's election:

> At that time, a new leadership was elected, represented by Jordanian university professors Abdallah Azzam, Ahmad Nawfal, Mohammad Abu-Faris, and Humam Saeed, in addition to Ibrahim Khreisat who was a schoolteacher subsequently elected to parliament in 1989. It was a youthful leadership inspired by the ideas of Sayed Qutb and influenced by the participation of many of its members in combat on the side of the guerilla organizations (1967–1970) ... This leadership maintained its control of the Brotherhood until the mid-80s, although Abdallah Azzam and Ahmad Nawfal left. It faced competition from another, less influential group represented by Is'hak Farhan, Youssef al-Adhm, and Ahmad al-Azaydeh.[3]

At the end of this quotation, Gharaybeh is hinting at a very important aspect of the internal politics of the Jordanian Brotherhood in the 1970s and beyond, namely, the tension between the so-called hawks and doves. The schism was analogous to that between Bannaists and Qutbists in Egypt, and was primarily about accommodation versus confrontation with the government, but also about hard and soft approaches to other issues. The tensions had surfaced in the late 1960s with the growing popularity of Sayyid Qutb's writings, the humiliation of the 1967 war, and the dilemmas raised by the Brotherhood's repression in Egypt and Syria. As we saw in Chapter 3, there had already been disagreement over the extent of the Jordanian Brotherhood's involvement with the Fedayin.

In the autumn of 1970 the atmosphere became acrimonious when Ishaq al-Farhan accepted the position as education minister in Wasfi al-Tal's new cabinet. A fierce debate erupted about whether a Brotherhood member should participate in government, especially so soon after Black September. A group of dissenters, led by Muhammad Abu Faris and Humam Sa'id, criticized al-Farhan vehemently for taking part in a manifestly non-Islamic system of government, one whose hand was also stained with Palestinian blood from the recent crackdown. To make his point, Abu Faris wrote a book titled *Participation in the Government of the Jahiliyya Regimes*, drawing heavily on Qutb and to a lesser extent on Hizb al-Tahrir founder Taqi al-Din Nabhani.[4] Al-Farhan's supporters countered with arguments from a book by Umar al-Ashqar titled *The Ruling on Participation in the Ministry and Representative Assemblies*.[5] It was a classic debate over opposition versus participation as strategies of political influence.

Ishaq al-Farhan did not yield; the US-trained academic served as minister of education in two governments and then as minister of religious endowments.[6] Ironically, having al-Farhan in these positions probably helped the hardliners wield influence. For example, Azzam may have got some of his jobs in the 1970s (such as his 1970 appointment at Jordan University and his job at the Ministry of Religious Endowments in mid-1973) because of al-Farhan. Moreover, al-Farhan would probably not have become president of the University of Jordan – where he was in a position to allow Brotherhood activities on campus – if he had not previously served as minister. Still, a long-lasting internal antagonism emerged, separating pragmatists such as al-Farhan, Yusuf al-Azm, Ahmad al-Azayda, and Bassam al-Amush from hardliners such as Muhammad Abu Faris, Humam Sa'id, Ahmad Nawfal, Ibrahim Khraysat, Dhib Anis, and Muhammad Ibrahim Shaqra'.

The Qutbists appear to have been the stronger camp in 1970s Jordan. This was unlike the situation in Egypt, where Bannaists such as Hasan al-Hudaybi and Omar al-Tilmisani presided. At the same time, however, Jordan did not have Egypt's violent revolutionary fringe. There had been less animosity between the Brotherhood and the regime in Jordan because the latter was not leftist and secular, as in Egypt. Moreover, on two important occasions (in 1957 during the Nasserist coup attempt against King Hussein and in 1970 during Black September) the Brotherhood had actively and tacitly supported the regime against the leftists, something for which King Hussein was grateful. The Jordanian regime probably tolerated the existence of a strong Qutbist current because it was confident that the latter would not produce a violent revolutionary offshoot.

This said, there had been a brief attempt to form an Islamist revolutionary group in Jordan in the early 1970s.[7] In 1973 Mohammad Ra'fat Sa'id Salih, a former Brotherhood member who had radicalized during his studies in Saudi Arabia, set up a group called the Vanguard of Islamic Revival (Tali'at al-Ba'th al-Islami). He was able to attract a small number of recruits, but the group disbanded before it got going because its founder had second thoughts, allegedly after being dissuaded by Sheikh Nasir al-Din al-Albani.[8]

Abdallah Azzam himself sat squarely in the hawkish camp, if not at the radical end of it. He had always been a hardliner in Brotherhood strategy debates, although never to the point of advocating immediate revolutionary action. Like other Qutbist Brothers, his attitude toward Arab governments was one of defiant coexistence, meaning that he accepted living under a non-Islamic regime for the purpose of *da'wa* work, but he would not collaborate with it and would never hesitate to verbally condemn what he saw as un-Islamic policies. It was this attitude that eventually got him into trouble with the Jordanian government.

Azzam had several things in common with the other hawks, in particular his relative youth and his background from the Fedayin camps. Abu Rumman and Abu Hanieh argue that the Fedayin experience had a formative effect on the Qutbist current in the Jordanian brotherhood, because it represented the first attempt to depart from the organization's moderate line, and it had helped forge strong bonds between participants.[9] Over time, though, the hardliners would include many others who did not have this particular background.

An interesting feature of the Qutbist Brotherhood current in the 1970s was its openness to Salafism; in fact, Abu Rumman and Abu Hanieh described the ideology of the Jordanian Brotherhood hawks as a "Qutbist salafism."[10] Azzam, for example, is on record as saying, "I am salafi in my belief and thought."[11] This is noteworthy because Ikhwanism (from *ikhwan*, "Brotherhood") and Salafism are usually considered distinct and partly competing ideological traditions, as noted in Chapter 4. In the political domain, the Brotherhood has historically been more pragmatic and willing to trade principles for participation than the Salafis. However, on cultural, social, and ritual matters there is scope for overlap, and socially conservative Muslim Brothers have often had much in common with Salafists. As Stéphane Lacroix showed in the book *Awakening Islam*, Saudi Arabia witnessed, in the 1970s and 1980s, the rise of an Islamist movement (the so-called Sahwa) which represented an amalgam of Ikhwanism and Salafism.[12] A similar cross-pollination appears to have happened in Jordan and other countries in the same period, most likely as a result of increased contact with Saudi scholars. A key figure behind the growth of Salafi ideas in Jordan was Muhammad Ibrahim Shaqra', a Brotherhood member who taught at the University of Medina in the 1960s and came back influenced by Salafism.[13]

Abu Rumman and Abu Hanieh report an illustrative – and historically very interesting – example of the Jordanian Qutbists' openness to Salafi thought. They say it was the Zarqa branch of the Muslim Brotherhood – where Abdallah Azzam was active – that first invited Nasir al-Din al-Albani to Jordan in 1973. Al-Albani (1919–1999) was a Syrian Salafi scholar of Albanian origin who came to play a very important role in the growth of apolitical, so-called quietist Salafism in the 1980s and 1990s.[14] He had taught at the University of Medina in the early 1960s, but returned to Syria in 1963 because of theological disagreements with Wahhabi clerics. In 1979 he moved to Jordan to escape repression in Syria. Before that, however, he had extensive contacts with the Jordanian Brotherhood. According to Abu Rumman and Abu Hanieh:

While living in Syria, al-Albani was close to the Damascene Salafists inside the Syrian Brotherhood; the majority of his lessons were conducted through the facilitation of the Muslim Brotherhood there. Indeed, he would enter the Jordanian Islamist scene through a "gateway" opened and facilitated by the Muslim Brotherhood. Sheikh al-Albani began to make monthly visits to Jordan on invitation from the "Qutubian Salafists" inside the Jordanian Muslim Brotherhood, and particularly the Zarqa Branch headed by Dib Anis, in order for Sheikh al-Albani to give lessons and lectures to its members. Several of the leaders in the Muslim Brotherhood also attended these lessons including Azzam Abdullah [sic], Ahmad Nawfal, Abdullah al-Qaryiouti, Faisal al-Jawabirah, Yousef al-Barqawi, Abdul Raouf al-'Aboushi, amongst others.[15]

However, relations between the Jordanian Brothers and al-Albani soured in the mid-1970s over ideological differences. Around this time, al-Albani articulated a number of unconventional religious opinions based on his own strict literalist interpretation of Hadith. The Brotherhood responded by calling for boycotts of al-Albani's lessons and publishing diatribes against him in *al-Mujtama'* magazine.[16] The most controversial of al-Albani's statements was his famous Palestine fatwa from 1974, in which he ruled that Palestinians must leave Palestine and abandon the land to the Jews for the time being.[17]

Needless to say, this was extremely unpopular among the Muslim Brothers in Jordan, most of whom were Palestinians and sworn supporters of jihad against Israel. Another issue that caused bad blood between the two parties was al-Albani's pointing out that some of Sayyid Qutb's writings showed Sufi influences. Al-Albani was essentially correct, and the same point has since been made by academics such as Olivier Carré.[18] However, to the Muslim Brotherhood, who venerated Qutb and disliked Sufis, this was sacrilege. According to Abu Rumman and Abu Hanieh:

> By the middle of the 1970s, the Brotherhood's leadership commenced with publishing internal flyers and memos that cautioned members from attending Sheikh al-Albani's meetings, lectures and lessons. They, and particularly Dr. Mohammad Abu Fares and Abdullah Azzam, began to attack al-Albani during their lessons and sermons in an attempt to fend off al-Albani's increasingly growing appeal with members of the Brotherhood.[19]

Azzam had an ambiguous relationship with al-Albani. On the one hand he really respected the latter's knowledge of Hadith, and he was one of the most positively inclined to al-Albani among the Muslim Brothers. He said, "Shaykh Nasir ad-Din al-Albani had a great effect on my thinking, in my beliefs, in clarifying my beliefs, in my extracting the authentic texts, in researching. I cannot write a weak [*da'if*] hadith in a single one of my books."[20] On the other hand, he could not stomach al-Albani's views on Palestine and criticism of Sayyid Qutb. Hence he wrote:

> I am of those who studied at the hands of the Shaykh, and I benefited greatly from him in the areas of 'Aqidah and researching texts – the authentic texts. Because of this, I shudder whenever I come across a weak hadith, as there is no way that I can place a weak hadith in any of my books. I cannot stand to do this! Subhan Allah, I took from him – may Allah reward him – even I differ from him in many of the Fiqh opinions that he held. I do not agree with most of his Fiqh opinions, as he held many strange positions.[21]

Al-Albani himself confirmed the special relationship with Azzam:

> Abdullah Azzam was here [in Amman] with the Muslim Brothers. A short while ago, seven or eight years ago, the Muslim Brotherhood decided to boycott me. They boycotted my lectures and my call, and Abdullah Azzam was the only one from the Muslim Brotherhood who always came to my lectures with a small notebook and a very small pen. Once the decision of boycotting my lectures came, he never appeared again. I once happened to

meet him in the Suhayb mosque outside the prayer. I greeted him and he shamefully greeted back because he didn't want to break the agreement. I then said to him: "Is it this what Islam commands you?" He said: "The summer clouds will soon brighten up."[22]

However, the Sayyid Qutb issue soured their relationship. Al-Albani later said:

"What is the intention with this boycott?" He then said: "You have made *takfir* upon Sayyid Qutb!" – and this is the point. I asked him: "How?" He answered: "You say that he speaks in accordance with *wahdat al-Wujud* in the chapter 'al-Hadid' and 'al-Ikhlas.'" I then said: "Yes, he has said some things that the Sufis say. The only thing one could understand from it is that he speaks in accordance with *wahdat al-wujud*. However, according to our principles we do not do *takfir* upon a person who falls into *kufr* before he has received the truth ... you could have sent someone in order to find out if it is true that I am making *takfir* upon Sayyid Qutb or not. Sayyid Qutb says this and that here and there." He had an outbreak and said: "The man believes in Allah, his messenger and Tawhid!" We then said to him: "O dear brother, we do not refute the truth he said, rather the incorrect." Despite this session, he spread two–three articles in the Kuwaiti journal *al-Mujtama'* with big headlines: "Shaykh al-Albani makes *Takfir* upon Sayyid Qutb."[23]

In the late 1970s Azzam was a Muslim Brother through and through, and he had ambitions in the organization. He was intellectually open to figures such as al-Albani, but when push came to shove, he sided with the Brotherhood. He was a rising star in the organization, and his subsequent fall from grace would be all the more hard to bear.

International Travel

Azzam's activities were not confined to Jordan. In the late 1970s he visited several other countries in the Middle East and the West, including the USA and Italy. Although it was nothing compared to what he would be doing in the 1980s, he was already becoming a seasoned traveler with a growing international network.

Azzam's travels reflected the increasing connectivity between Islamists around the world. The 1970s saw a growing number of interactions across borders, in the form of more young Islamists studying abroad, more preachers lecturing in other countries, more Islamic organizations hosting international seminars, and more Hajj pilgrims.

Of course, transnational connections were by no means new. Mecca had always been a meeting place for pilgrims and a venue for Islamic congresses, and al-Azhar had attracted international students for centuries. The Egyptian Muslim Brotherhood had spread to other countries in the 1930s and 1940s by sending preachers such as Saʿid Ramadan abroad and influencing foreign students in Cairo such as Mustafa al-Sibaʿi. In 1948 Brotherhood members from several countries had met on the battlefield in Palestine. After Nasser's 1954 crackdown several leading Brothers had moved to Damascus. And throughout the 1950s and 1960s many Muslim Brothers from the Middle East had gone to Saudi Arabia for study or work. Muslim World League (MWL) conferences in the 1960s had brought together scholars and Islamist leaders, including senior Muslim Brothers, from across the Muslim world.[24] And as we have seen, in 1969–1970 Muslim Brothers came to Jordan from all over the region to join or observe the Fedayin effort.

What was new was the frequency and range of the interactions. In the past, preachers had visited other countries irregularly and infrequently. In the 1940s and 1950s only the most senior preachers and activists seem to have gone abroad on a regular basis. In the 1970s we start seeing more international conferences, seminars, and lecture series where mid-level Islamic scholars and activists would also attend. Moreover, in previous decades most cross-border interactions occurred within regions, typically within the Cairo–Mecca–Damascus triangle or within South Asia. In the 1970s there was more interaction across regions; between the Middle East and South Asia, and between the Middle East and the West.

Several factors account for this Islamist globalization process. One was technology. Between 1940 and 1980 the cost of ocean freight, air transport, and telephone calls fell steadily.[25] We know that this trend affected the Muslim world, because, between 1965 and 1975, the annual number of pilgrims to Mecca rose from 250,000 to 900,000 and the percentage of pilgrims traveling by air increased from 20 to 60 percent.[26] Moreover, the cost of printing decreased, making it easier for Islamist organizations to produce and distribute books and magazines.

Another factor was the general increase in Islamist activity in the Middle East. In many countries, including Jordan and its neighbors, the size of the Islamist community grew steadily in the 1970s, so that by the late 1970s there were simply more activists than there had been a decade or two earlier. Moreover, in key countries such as Egypt, state repression of Islamists eased somewhat, leaving groups such as the Muslim Brotherhood able to organize more activities than they had in the 1950s and 1960s. This resulted in more seminars and meetings, hence a larger market for speakers such as Abdallah Azzam.

A third reason was the growth in the number of Islamic organizations in the West. Muslim immigration to Europe and the United States increased considerably in the postwar period, as did the number of Muslim students in the West. The number of mosques and Islamic community organizations increased steadily from the 1960s onward. From the mid-1970s onward, the MWL sought to connect with, finance, and influence several of these organizations, such as the US-based Muslim Students' Association.[27] As a result of this, the number of seminars and events in the West featuring speakers from the Middle East and South Asia went up from the mid-1970s onward.

Meanwhile, Azzam's reputation had started to spread outside Jordan's borders. Isam al-Attar, the exiled leader of the Syrian Muslim Brotherhood, says he heard of Azzam from his base in Aachen in Germany, in the mid-1970s: "I heard there was this young man in Jordan who was very energetic and courageous."[28] In the late 1970s Azzam also became more active on the publishing front, which put his name on the map and generated speaking invitations.

Azzam gladly seized these new opportunities. A regular destination was Saudi Arabia, where he went for the pilgrimage practically every year, sometimes taking students.[29] Hajj was not only a ritual, it was also an occasion to meet scholars and preachers from other countries. There would always be seminars and other events on the margins of the Hajj celebrations. We know, for example, that during the Hajj in 1975 Azzam spoke in the tent of the Council of Great Scholars about the need to combat polytheism in the form of man-made legislation.[30] Just as Muhammad bin Abd al-Wahhab had fought grave worshiping, he argued, so today one should fight man-made laws. In 1978 he was also invited to speak at Imam University in Riyadh.[31] Another destination was Cairo, though it is not clear how often he went there. One source said, "In Egypt, the Islamic movement in universities, they were sometimes during their summer camps or cultural week and they were inviting him to speak."[32] On at least one point between 1975 and 1978 he was there for the annual gathering of the Egyptian Brotherhood's student branch.[33]

Azzam also traveled to the West at least twice in the late 1970s. At the end of 1977 he notably went to the United States for meetings with Islamic student societies there. He is documented as having been in Indianapolis on 1 January 1978 for a meeting at the University of Indiana's Islamic Teaching Center (ITC).[34] The subsequent report in the Center's newsletter is worth quoting in full:

In line with the nature of its activities, the ITC opened the year 1978 with an exchange of views with eminent Muslim Scholars from the overseas. Received by the Director General and the staff of the Islamic Teaching Center on January 1, the following guests attended a meeting in the prayer room of the Center.
 Mohd Qutb, Professor of Education, King Abdul Aziz University, Mecca.
 Dr. Abdullah Al-Azzam, Professor of Shariah, University of Jordan, Amman.
 Shaikh Tais al-Jumaili, Imam and teacher, Central Mosque Kuwait.
 Shaikh Saud al-Finaisan, Assistant Dean of Students, Muhammad bin Saud University, Riyadh.
 Also present at the meeting were the leading officials of the MSA, the NAIT and the ICS. Director General Dr. El-Tigani Abugideiri, briefed the guests on the objectives, activities and achievements of the Center and emphasized its crucial role in the work of Da'wah in this part of the world. The guests showed a lively interest in the progress of the Center and in the course of the briefing put searching questions in regard to the nature of interaction between Muslim Da'wah workers and the American people and its long-range effects on the work of Da'wa in this country. The meeting ended at the time of Zuhr prayer.[35]

Aside from being the first known mention of Azzam in an English-language publication, this report is interesting because of the names of Azzam's three travel companions. Muhammad Qutb was Sayyid Qutb's brother and one of the most respected scholars in the entire Muslim Brotherhood movement. The two others, Tais al-Jumayli and Saud al-Funaysan, were also well-known Muslim Brotherhood-linked scholars.[36] Azzam's presence in the delegation suggests that by 1977 he was already considered a senior figure in the Brotherhood community.

The four men had likely come for the annual conference of the Muslim Arab Youth Association (MAYA), which took place during the Christmas break of 1977 in Bloomington, Indiana, just 100 kilometers southwest of Indianapolis.[37] Another article in the same newsletter says that Tais al-Jumayli – one of the three who were in Indianapolis with Azzam – "attended the [MAYA] conference and stayed for about three weeks visiting local chapters of the MSA."[38] We do not know whether Azzam, Qutb, and al-Funaysan accompanied al-Jumayli for the whole three weeks, but it is possible.

Intriguingly, the Indianapolis meeting was probably also attended by the young Usama Bin Ladin. The millionaire's son was a Muslim Brotherhood sympathizer in this period; he had been introduced to Brotherhood ideas in his early teens by a Syrian gym teacher at the al-Thagr School in Jeddah.[39] In her 2009 memoir *Growing up Bin Laden*, Bin Ladin's wife Najwa says she accompanied her husband on a trip to Indianapolis in 1979, where the latter met with Azzam:

> Pregnant, and busy with two babies, I remember few details of our travel, other than we passed through London before flying to a place I had never heard of, a state in America called Indiana. Osama told me that he was meeting with a man by the name of Abdullah Azzam ... We were there for only two weeks, and for one of those weeks, Osama was away in Los Angeles to meet with some men in that city.[40]

Later in the book she adds, "I suddenly remembered that Abdallah Azzam was the man my husband had met in America when we had paid a visit to that state of Indiana."[41] Steve Coll has since shown that Bin Ladin's US trip is corroborated by several other sources.[42] This allows us to suggest with some confidence that the very first meeting between Abdallah Azzam and Usama Bin Ladin happened in Indianapolis, Indiana, of all places, in early 1978.

We cannot be certain, however, because there are some contradictory sources. In December 1989 Bin Ladin himself said, "I saw Azzam the first time during Hajj over nine years ago when he was giving a lecture in Mina."[43] However, it is more likely that Bin Ladin failed to mention their US meeting than it is that his wife completely made up something as specific as the Indianapolis encounter. Another source says that Bin Ladin visited Azzam at his house in Amman in the "late 1970s," which conceivably could have been before 1978. However, if Bin Ladin had already met Azzam and knew he could visit him any time in Amman, it seems unlikely he would make a detour to Indianapolis to see him. On balance, Azzam and Bin Ladin most likely did meet – or at least crossed paths – for the first time in Indianapolis.

We also know that Azzam attended a conference in Perugia in Italy, on 30 and 31 December 1979, organized by the Italian Muslim Students' Association. There he met Rachid Ghannouchi, the Tunisian Muslim Brotherhood leader and future president of Tunisia, and the two struck up a close friendship. They had met once before in Amman in 1968, "but the special relationship really began ... in Perugia," Ghannouchi later wrote.[44] They would stay in touch for the next decade, meeting again at conferences in Oklahoma City in 1988 and in Kuwait and Lahore in 1989.[45] In August 1989 Ghannouchi visited Azzam in Peshawar and gave an interview to *al-Jihad* magazine.[46] A picture taken on that trip shows Azzam and Ghannouchi together, smiling (see Illustration 18).[47] When Azzam died, Ghannouchi wrote no less than three obituaries for him, one in *al-Sharq al-Awsat*, one in *al-Mujtama'*, and one in *al-Bunyan al-Marsus*.[48] Ghannouchi's 1993 book *Public Freedoms in the Islamic State* was dedicated to, among others, "the martyrs everywhere, first and foremost the dear brother Abdallah Azzam, martyr of Islam in the jihad against Communist imperialism."[49]

At the Perugia conference, Ghannouchi later recalled, the topic of the day was the Iranian revolution, and Azzam was very enthusiastic about it.[50] He considered the revolution an inspiring example of Islamic law implemented. This was a view shared by many Muslim Brothers, but Azzam was among the most supportive.[51] Ibrahim Ghusheh recounts:

At the outset of the Iranian revolution, the Muslim Brothers were delighted, for it stirred the emotions of the Arab and Islamic public ... the MB movement called for a celebration and a huge demonstration in Amman ... During this celebration, a number of the Brotherhood leaders delivered speeches in the Grand Husseini mosque. I attended this demonstration and joined the march. I recall that among the Brothers' icons, the one most enthusiastic about Iran's Islamic revolution was the *Mujahid* 'Abdallah 'Azzam. Afterwards, I heard that when 'Abdallah 'Azzam left for Afghanistan to support the Mujahideen there, he changed his mind regarding the Islamic revolution, because he saw that it was dominated by the Shi'ite dimension through establishing the authority of the Ja'fari jurisprudence.[52]

Azzam would indeed change his mind about the Iranian revolution and come to see Khomeini as misguided.[53] His daughter Fatima later wrote,

"The day that the Islamic revolution in Iran exploded, you were following the news of the jihad there, and God knows you were elated. You did not know how Shia-centric they would be, and when you realized that, you were sad and disappointed."[54] By the late 1980s he saw Iran as just another authoritarian Middle Eastern state.[55]

Expulsion from Jordan

By the end of the 1970s Azzam had become a visible figure on the Jordanian Islamist scene. He was popular among students, his off-campus lectures attracted large audiences, and he had started to publish books and articles. He had strong opinions about many things, and was not at all afraid to voice them. He was very interested in international politics, and former students have described him as having an almost encyclopedic knowledge of the political situation in Muslim countries around the world. According to his wife, Azzam had always been "reading a wide range of newspapers and magazines of all orientations."[56] In 1978 or earlier he began teaching a course at the university titled "The Muslim World Today."[57] It offered a highly politicized analysis of the history of the Middle East in the twentieth century, one that attributed most of the region's ills to Western and Jewish conspiracies against Muslims. It also consisted of long diatribes against Communism and secularism, which he saw as the main ideological enemies of the Islamist project.[58]

In the late 1970s Azzam also began criticizing the Jordanian government more explicitly, placing himself on the radar of the security services. The two main recurring issues were, not surprisingly, Islamic law and the Palestinian struggle. Azzam considered the Jordanian political system to be un-Islamic, and said as much in public. At one point, during a visit by King Hussein to the university campus, Azzam attracted attention by refusing to stand up while the national anthem was being played.[59] He also accused the Jordanian regime of being against the Palestinian resistance, and of having a secret relationship with Israel.[60] Azzam also had local bones to pick with the government, such as its refusal to establish a Shari'a department at Yarmuk University in Irbid after that university was founded in 1976.[61] In 1980 he criticized the Jordanian government's support for Iraq in the Iran–Iraq war, which he saw as a US plot to weaken the new Iranian regime.[62] However, what reportedly raised the government's concern the most was his role in mobilizing protests against the plan to introduce compulsory military service for women. According to his son Hudhayfa, Azzam helped spark widespread protests in Amman. Hudhayfa remembers observing the demonstrations and seeing people turn cars upside down.[63]

Azzam was also worked up about the political situation in neighboring Syria, where the confrontation between the radical wing of the Muslim Brotherhood and Hafiz al-Assad's regime had escalated severely in 1979.[64] The government's heavy-handed repression, which would culminate with the Hama massacre in February 1982, incensed Muslim Brothers across the region. Azzam criticized the Syrian government in his lectures, and, according to his nephew Fayiz, went so far as to declare the Alawites infidels.[65] This attracted the attention of Syrian intelligence officials in Amman. Several sources mention an alleged episode in which a Syrian hit team reportedly fired shots at his house to scare him.[66] His son Hudhayfa later said that the Syrians had actually tried twice to assassinate him in this period: once by firing shots, and once by placing "a bomb under his house large enough to destroy the house, but the bomb was discovered at the last minute."[67] It is difficult to verify these claims, and it is not clear why Syrian security services would prioritize Azzam, but in any case, by 1980 he was seen by the Jordanian regime as a troublemaker. As one biographer noted:

His activities caught the attention of the [Jordanian] security services. They began to follow him, and they questioned him every now and then. Some religious scholars advised him to be careful so that they wouldn't expel him from the university, but the sheikh would reply, "I am prepared to sell falafels to my students at the gates of the university."[68]

Azzam later said the government attempted twice in 1980 to have him fired from his post, but he managed to stay.[69]

Then, in the autumn of 1980, an incident happened that would seal his professional fate. One of the Jordanian newspapers printed a cartoon mocking Iranian clerics by depicting them as American agents.[70] It pushed all of Azzam's buttons – his sympathy for the Iranian revolution, his respect for religious clerics, and his anti-Americanism. Furious, he picked up the phone, called up the editor, and demanded that he print an apology the next day. The editor interpreted it as a threat and notified the government, which proceeded to fire Azzam from the university. Here is how one of Azzam's hagiographers describes the chain of events:

Things stayed this way till September of 1980, when a caricature in one of the Jordanian newspapers caught the sheikh's attention. It depicted religious scholars with long beards carrying American M-16s, and under the caricature it said "agents for the Americans." So the sheikh called the owner of the newspaper and said "My name is Abdallah Azzam, I'm a teacher in the College of Shari'a, and today you published a caricature in your newspaper that defames Islam and scholars of Islam. Tomorrow you have to publish an apology; if not, beware of the consequences,"[71] before hanging up. The owner of the newspaper was not an ordinary man, but had connections to the Jordanian prime minister and Jordanian military chief of staff, Madar Badran, and he called the latter immediately to say that Abdallah Azzam had threatened him. Madar Badran had been waiting for an incident like this, and he decided to have Azzam fired from the university immediately ... And he did it, just like that, without consulting with any disciplinary body, the higher education ministry or the administration of the university ... Then a government delegation came to the sheikh and said, "The government does not want to fire you from the university, it wants you to continue, but to stay away from politics. Go to your class, explain your topic without going into this or that or the other." He replied, "I am not a teacher of chemistry or physics or mathematics – I teach Islamic Shari'a. Do you want me to teach the religion that was revealed to Muhammad bin Abdallah? Then I am ready." But they said no ... And from the Brotherhood came Abd al-Rahman Khalifa (Abu Majid), the general supervisor of the Muslim Brotherhood. He told the sheikh, "We are ready to bring all the Muslim brothers into the streets to protest your dismissal." But the sheikh refused, because he did not want our brothers to get into trouble because of him.[72]

According to a slightly different account, Azzam was himself asked to apologize to the newspaper editor, but he flatly refused, saying, "By God, if *he* came and kissed my hand, I would not accept his apology."[73] This time the game was over. "In October 1980," Azzam later said, "a letter arrived sealed with the words 'top secret' written on the envelope. I opened it and there was a decision by the military ruler and prime minister at that time, Madar Badran, to expel me from Jordan University."[74] Later he also wrote:

I was at the University of Jordan, and I was fired, thank God, by a decree from the general military ruler the prime minister with reference to article 24 or 27, I forget, for my personal convictions!! This prime minister ordered the firing of Dr. Abdallah Azzam from the University of Jordan, for his personal convictions ... he said "Go to Mecca, Hajj is coming up" ... so they threw us out of the University of Jordan and I came to Afghanistan, thanks to God.[75]

The precise circumstances of Azzam's departure are unclear, for we only have his side of the story, but there is little reason to doubt that he was forced to leave. The Jordanian regime at this time was no stranger to censoring opinions and suppressing political opposition through non-democratic means. It was less repressive toward Islamists than the Syrian or Egyptian regimes – many observers even say that the government promoted the Brotherhood as a bulwark against the left – but there was a limit to what the regime would tolerate from the Muslim Brothers.[76] It had previously banned preachers such as Ibrahim Zayd from giving sermons, and later it would force other hardline brothers such as Ruhayyil al-Gharaybeh to leave their jobs at Jordan University.[77] Nevertheless, Azzam appears to have been the first high-profile Brotherhood casualty. His Palestinian background likely affected the way in which he was treated, because Palestinian immigrants were considered second-class citizens by the Transjordanian-dominated regime.

The accounts by Azzam and his hagiographers all blame the government for his expulsion, but the truth is that he was also betrayed by his own – that is to say, the Muslim Brotherhood in Jordan. The Brotherhood had long had a tacit understanding with the Jordanian government by which they were allowed to operate freely if they did not rock the boat. Azzam's increasingly vocal criticism of the regime threatened to upset that delicate balance, and some Brothers feared that he could drag the whole organization into a confrontation with the regime. Thus the Brotherhood actually encouraged him to leave Jordan. Jamal Isma'il later said:

The leadership of Islamic movement, Ikhwan al-Muslimin in Jordan, because of its policy not to have confrontation with regime or with the government, they advised him many times, that no, we need you here, but we don't need your activities which can bring confrontation with the government for any reason. They suggested him to go out of Jordan. Either Mecca, Jeddah, Abha – they had no objection or observations – but they did not want him to stay in Jordan, because they were thinking that due to your presence in Jordan, maybe due to your activities or lectures here, the authorities they will come and arrest you. And we don't want to confront with the regime in the current situation. Therefore you go, and defuse the tension here.[78]

The Jordanian researcher Hasan Abu Hanieh has corroborated Isma'il's claim, saying that the Brotherhood was secretly pleased that Azzam left Jordan.[79]

After Azzam's death, a fascinating document emerged from his personal archive that sheds light on the internal conflict.[80] The seven-page letter, undated but likely from 1980, is addressed to the Shura Council and complains that parts of the Brotherhood are working against him.[81] In the opening part of the letter, Azzam summarized his complaint as follows:

> I see in the *da'wa* a strange policy by which every means is used to silence and marginalize dissenting views, so that the group is led by a handful of people who agree on everything ... I have noticed through tens of examples that I have personally experienced with pain and sadness that some of the Brothers seek nothing else but to stop me from taking votes in the Shura Council or in the Office ... I have long felt that when I sit down with some of them, it is like I am sitting down with a university dean who lies in wait to turn small infractions into crimes ... If I was able to live outside this *da'wa*, I would [but I can't].

He then offered an eighteen-point list of complaints. One of them was that he felt excluded from key activities:

> For three years I have been completely cut off from the activities section [*qism al-'amilin*], and I have not been part of a working group [*katiba*] nor made any trips, nor attended any organizational meetings. The excuse offered by this Brother is that Abdallah is busy with the university section ... even though you know what I do in the university section and what my role is there ... I say cut off from the activities department even though all the Brothers who work with the university section ... are invited to working groups and trips and other things ... I felt they were treating me like a small child, insulting my intellect.

He also said he felt ignored in meetings:

> My words are distorted and ignored. If I suggest an opinion, the head of the session opposes it, so I stay quiet. Sometimes I consider proposing the opposite of what I really mean just to see him take the opposite view [i.e. my real view] ... After the weekly session I am sometimes upset all day, and sometimes I am tired mentally and physically.

He then complained about being monitored and marginalized for his views:

> in the Chechen mosque Abu [redacted] only let me preach once, and after the sermon one of his students submitted a report to the monitoring section saying that people had told [me] off. [Then] they came to my house to divide the morning lessons, like spoils, and they divided them so that I lost mine,

with the argument that I was bad for the *da'wa* with my lessons and my opinions.

The intrigues even affected his family affairs:

For my daughter's engagement party, when I was distributing invitation cards, the unit deputy went ... to my friends and said, "What's with the extravagance, where is the austerity?" – even though nobody knew what I wanted to do at that point – he was just turning them against me so that some of them would not attend the engagement party. And at our house, when the Qur'ans were distributed, one of the guests said, "This is fine Sunna," the unit deputy said, "Chocolate would have been better; if I married off my daughter, I would just do that" ... Then his wife, who is responsible for the women's section, stood in the Islamic Center and angrily told off Umm Muhammad for this wedding and the supposed wrongdoings that happened there – and God knows no infractions on the Shari'a occurred ... Then a female student ... came to our house to ask whether it was true that my daughter had been photographed. Umm Muhammad said, "Yes, but did you know how the photo was taken? Nobody was there except the groom, my daughter, me, his mother and the photographer Anas bin Abi Anas" [who was less than ten years old].

He concluded, however, by underlining his loyalty to the organization:

Brothers: I am very sorry to take of your precious time ... I wanted to keep this inside me ... but finally I decided to tell you, because I have seen this tendency inside the group. I follow your orders even though I am accused of disobedience, and I stand where you command.

The letter shows that Azzam had been mired in a bitter internal conflict with parts of the Jordanian Brotherhood for several years before leaving the country. He was seen by influential leaders as something of a troublemaker, and they had been working systematically to marginalize and silence him. The tone of the letter and the intimate nature of some of the examples suggest that Azzam took the conflict very personally, and that he was profoundly disappointed by his comrades. The document also suggests that Azzam was in a position of weakness, and that he was not a real contender for the leadership of the Brotherhood in Jordan, as has sometimes been suggested.[82]

The document also sheds rare light on the strict hierarchy and discipline inside the Brotherhood. This was not a free-flowing popular movement, but a very tightly run ship – one that was not prepared to tolerate rabble-rousers. This part of Azzam's story has been glossed over by all the involved parties; neither the Brotherhood leadership, nor Azzam, nor any of his hagiographers ever mentioned it in public after his departure from Jordan. Instead, they all kept up appearances and pretended to be on good terms. When Azzam was assassinated in 1989, the Jordanian Brotherhood organized a large memorial service in Amman and issued statements celebrating him, as we shall see in Chapter 15.

Azzam later said he was grateful for what happened because it set him on a new course: "There was a decision to expel me from Jordan University ... and, praise God, this opened a door of mercy for me."[83] This gratitude was almost certainly a case of cognitive dissonance reduction, the tendency we all have to tweak our description of the past to make our life stories more consistent. Despite his conflict with the Brotherhood, there is little question that Azzam left Jordan against his will. As his friend Jamal Isma'il later said: "Abdallah Azzam was not in favor of leaving Jordan – he was in favor of staying there, working anything in Jordan, or writing books or articles, but not to leave Jordan, because he want to be with his students, or with Islamic movement in Jordan, recruiting them, or promoting them."[84] Nobody can say for sure, but it seems unlikely that Azzam would have invested himself in the Afghan jihad the way he did if he had been allowed to stay in Jordan. He might have become peripherally involved and perhaps gone to Peshawar on short visits, but he had too much going on in Amman to leave everything behind voluntarily.

Either way, in the autumn of 1980 Azzam had to start looking for a new place to go, because he needed a job. Without an income, he had to borrow money to support his family. In fact, when he left Jordan he had accumulated a debt of 15,000 Jordanian dinars with an Islamist businessman.[85] The most promising job market was Saudi Arabia, but Azzam was initially not very keen on the idea.[86] He was persuaded after meeting a Saudi professor named Muhammad al-Muslih in Amman. Al-Muslih was a Muslim Brotherhood-linked professor at the University of Abha who happened to be in Jordan in the autumn of 1980 to recruit lecturers and Ph.D. students.[87] He first suggested that Azzam come to Abha, an offer Azzam politely declined. Then, al-Muslih said, "Okay, if you don't want to come to our university in Abha, I can arrange another contract for you in Mecca ... or in Jeddah, King Abd al-Aziz University. I know the dean of that university, he is my friend."[88] Thus it was that in late 1980, probably in October or November, the Azzam family packed their bags and moved to Mecca.

With Pan-Islamists in Saudi Arabia

By the time Azzam left Jordan, a new Islamist current had begun to gain strength in the Middle East, one whose center of gravity was in western Saudi Arabia, where Azzam was about to settle. This was pan-Islamism; a strand of Islamism aimed at promoting Muslim solidarity.

Pan-Islamism in the broad sense was nothing new.[89] The idea that all Muslims are one people is as old as Islam (see Qu'ran 3:110), and since the nineteenth century political actors have harnessed the notion of the *umma* for a variety of purposes. The pan-Islamist movement described here must therefore be distinguished from earlier manifestations of pan-Islamism, such as the early twentieth-century attempts to restore the Caliphate and the 1960s foreign policy doctrine of Saudi King Faisal. Caliphists sought a formal political union of Muslim countries; King Faisal sought foreign-policy coordination among Muslim governments. The pan-Islamist movement of the 1970s sought neither; its aim was to foster popular awareness about Muslims' standing in the world and cooperation between Muslims worldwide.

The pan-Islamist movement that emerged in the 1970s was motivated by three basic ideas: that all Muslims are one people; that this people is under assault by non-Muslim forces; and that Muslims in different countries should help one another. These ideas were already present in the worldview of the Muslim Brotherhood and other Islamists, but until the 1970s they had been subordinate to the objective of Islamizing their respective nation-states. The various national Brotherhood branches had operated to a large extent as vertically separated silos, with most political activities taking place within countries. In the late 1970s, however, there emerged a new class of Islamists preoccupied with building horizontal connections between countries.

Sociologically speaking, these Muslim internationalists resembled the Westerners working in the United Nations and the international NGO community, in the sense that they constituted a multinational network of professionals devoted to transnational activism. Like their Western counterparts, the pan-Islamic activists were a mixed and loosely connected community; some worked in international Islamic organizations such as the Muslim World League, some worked in

Islamic charities, some were academics, and some were cadres in the Muslim Brotherhood. Many were either residents of, or frequent visitors to, the Hijazi city triangle of Mecca, Medina, and Jeddah. As we shall see, Azzam's transition to Afghanistan was facilitated at every step by pan-Islamist activists and organizations in the Hijaz. Moreover, Azzam's own thinking would be greatly influenced by the pan-Islamist notion of Islamic solidarity (*al-tadamun al-islami*).

The pan-Islamist movement owed its emergence to a combination of regional and domestic Saudi political developments. The movement emerged in the late 1960s in a cluster of religious institutions in western Saudi Arabia, a key component of which were the international Islamic organizations (IIOs), such as the Muslim World League (MWL), the Organization of the Islamic Conference (OIC), and their various subsidiary organizations such as the World Association of Muslim Youth (WAMY). The MWL was established in Mecca in 1962 as a marriage of convenience between scholars concerned with the post-Ottoman fragmentation of the Muslim world and a Saudi government keen to promote its conservative Wahhabi brand of Islam. It was a non-governmental organization aimed at coordinating international *da'wa* activities and promoting cooperation between Muslim countries in the religious and cultural domain.[90] It would later become an umbrella organization for a plethora of cultural, educational, and humanitarian organizations. The MWL had no parallel in other parts of the world, but it might be described, at least in terms of its ambitions, as a mixture of the Vatican and UNESCO for the Islamic world. (In fact, MWL is an observer with consultative status in UNESCO and the UN Economic and Social Council.) The OIC, by contrast, was an intergovernmental organization – a Muslim United Nations General Assembly of sorts. It was established in Jeddah in 1969 on the initiative of King Faisal, who saw it as a diplomatic instrument in the ideological power struggle against the leftist President Nasser of Egypt.[91]

Another important part of the Hijazi pan-Islamist cluster was the universities, in particular the International Islamic University in Medina (founded 1961), King Abd al-Aziz University in Jeddah (founded 1967), and the College of Shari'a in Mecca, renamed Umm al-Qura University in 1981. They were founded to meet the kingdom's growing educational needs during a phase of rapid economic growth. These institutions had a relatively multinational student body from the start, because their location near the Muslim holy places coupled with scholarship opportunities made them attractive to international students. The University of Medina also had an explicit international mandate, namely to train new generations of religious scholars from all corners of the Muslim world. Thus by the early 1970s the Mecca–Medina–Jeddah triangle was home to the world's largest concentration of Islamic religious institutions.

Because Saudi Arabia lacked educated manpower at this time, a substantial proportion of the staff in these institutions were foreign nationals, notably Muslim Brotherhood activists from Syria and Egypt who had sought political refuge in the kingdom. A first wave of immigration had occurred in the late 1950s and early 1960s following crackdowns on the Brotherhood in Egypt (1954 onward), Iraq (1958 onward), and Syria (1958 onward). A trickle of immigrants continued throughout the 1960s, until a second major wave of Egyptians arrived in the early 1970s following Sadat's release of Egyptian Muslim Brothers from prison. These well-educated men found employment in Saudi schools and universities, and formed the backbone of the kingdom's education system in the 1960s and 1970s. Exiled Muslim Brothers notably filled many teaching positions at King Abd al-Aziz University in Jeddah and its Mecca annex, and they were strongly represented in the International Islamic University of Medina.[92] They would also make up a significant portion of the staff in the international Islamic organizations. The Hijaz, already quite cosmopolitan as a result of the pilgrimage and maritime trade, became one large melting pot of Islamists from across the region. A similar process occurred also in the smaller Gulf states Kuwait, Qatar, and the United Arab Emirates, though on a smaller scale.[93] Here also, Muslim Brothers from the Arab republics would find refuge and populate the education sector. In Kuwait in particular, the Muslim Brotherhood notably came to play a prominent role in Islamic charities such as the Kuwaiti Red Crescent, which, as we shall see, became deeply involved in the Afghan jihad in the 1980s.

The incentive for these people to devote their energy to international activism was strengthened by their limited prospect of influence in any domestic political arena. The exiled Muslim Brothers were unwelcome in their home countries. The Saudi Islamists in the Hijaz, for their part, were politically peripheral to a system where real decisions were taken by royals in Riyadh, and where the highest religious prestige was reserved for the Wahhabi *ulama* in the central Najd region. The Hijaz-based Islamists thus constituted a marginalized elite. They did, however, have the opportunity to work internationally. The Muslim World League was mandated with the global promotion of Muslim solidarity and enjoyed a generous budget for this purpose, especially after the 1973 oil crisis. The yearly revenues of the MWL increased steadily from around 7 million Saudi riyals ($1.9 million) in 1972/73 to around 45 million Saudi riyals ($12 million) in 1979–1980.[94]

The IIOs offered an institutional platform for the exportation of ideas and personnel, and Saudi leniency toward Islamists allowed them to receive visitors from abroad. With limited prospects for domestic political influence and an opportunity to work internationally, these activists devoted themselves to transnational activism and the promotion of pan-Islamist ideas. The Hijazi activists had a strong interest in increasing public awareness of global Muslim affairs. Put simply, the higher the importance attached to pan-Islamic issues by the public and by incumbent elites, the larger the budgets and political role of the IIOs.

To get a sense of the activities of the IIOs, we can take a closer look at the Muslim World League. A 1981 book marking the twenty-year anniversary of the MWL listed the fifteen main activities in which it is engaged (I am paraphrasing):

1. Working for the implementation of Shari'a.
2. Organizing conferences for scholars from around the world so as to bring about exchange of views and coordination of efforts.
3. Making the most of the Hajj season to increase religious awareness, through lectures and seminars.
4. Organizing the "Global Islamic Session" every Hajj season.
5. Organizing introductions and mingling opportunities between the different Hajj delegations.
6. Encouraging preachers around the world to spread Islam, and supporting them materially and equipping them with what they need.
7. Distributing copies of the Qur'an.
8. Distributing Islamic books in different languages.
9. Supporting Islamic media foundations.
10. Sending delegations to all regions of the Muslim world and to the regions with Muslim minorities to study their problems, with the aim of knowing their requirements and extending a helping hand to them.

11. Supporting all Islamic organizations and foundations that have a link to the League and coordinating their efforts.
12. Supporting Islamic writing and purchasing Islamic books.
13. Spreading Islamic education by establishing Islamic schools and institutes in all parts of the "Muslim homeland" (*al-watan al-islami*).
14. Working to spreading the language of the Qur'an so that it can become a language of mutual understanding between Muslims.
15. Working to cleanse Muslim media generally of elements alien to the spirit of Islam."[95]

Another important thing the MWL did was to organize, at its headquarters in Mecca, something called the "religious and cultural season," a two-week series of lectures and meetings around Hajj when many foreign visitors were in town anyway. From 1965 to 1980 the MWL organized some 250 lectures and seminars with scholars and Islamist figures from around the world.[96] From 1972 onward each religious and cultural season included a special "global Islamic session" (*nadwa islamiyya 'alamiyya*) in which "scholars and men of Islamic thought" from different countries would discuss selected religious and political topics and produce resolutions and recommendations at the end.[97]

Starting in the mid-1970s, the Muslim World League played a particularly active role in setting up Islamic organizations outside the Middle East. In 1974 it organized a large conference in Mecca on the theme of "Islamic Organizations in the World," which led directly to the setting up of several new regional organizations in the following few years, such as the Union of Islamic Societies in Australia (1975), the African Islamic Coordination Council (1976), and the North American Islamic Coordination Council (1977), "in addition to a large number of high councils for Islamic organizations at the regional level."[98] This effort was accompanied by a series of large MWL-organized conferences in places as diverse as Nouakchott in Mauritania (1976), Newark, New Jersey (1977), and Port of Spain in Trinidad (1977).[99] Moreover, the 1970s also saw the establishment of MWL offices in fourteen countries around the world: Jakarta in Indonesia (1973), Amman in Jordan (1974), Nouakchott in Mauritania (1974), Libreville in Gabon (1974), Port Louis in Mauritius (1974), Copenhagen in Denmark (1974), New York in the USA (1974), Brazzaville in West Congo (1975), San

Fernando in Trinidad and Tobago (1976), Islamabad and Karachi in Pakistan (1977), Dakar in Senegal (1977), Paris in France (1977), Mogadishu in Somalia (1980), and Kuala Lumpur in Malaysia (no date).[100] In the 1980s and 1990s the MWL would also establish offices in Bangladesh, the Maldives, Burundi, the Comoros, Kenya, Mozambique, Nigeria, Senegal, South Africa, Tanzania, Uganda, Togo, Sudan, the United Kingdom, Russia, Austria, Italy, Canada, and Australia. This was in addition to cultural centers in Spain, Argentina, Belgium, the Netherlands, Switzerland, Sweden, Brazil, Guinea-Bissau, Benin, Niger, South Korea, and Bosnia-Herzegovina.[101]

In addition to building an international organizational infrastructure, the pan-Islamists constructed an identity discourse emphasizing the unity of the Muslim nation and highlighting outside threats.[102] Like many other identity discourses it was alarmist, self-victimizing, conspiratorial, and chauvinistic. It was a victim narrative that highlighted cases of Muslim suffering around the world, paying particular attention to interreligious conflicts.[103] No one ideologue can be credited with articulating the discourse; rather, it developed gradually through incremental rhetorical escalation. Many of its themes echoed those of earlier pan-Islamists and anti-colonial activists, but the Hijazi pan-Islamist discourse was more alarmist and more global in outlook than any of its predecessors. The following extract from a speech by Muslim World League secretary-general Muhammad Ali Harakan from April 1980 is representative:

Jihad is the key to Muslims' success and felicity, especially when their sacred shrines are under the Zionist occupation in Palestine, when millions of Muslims are suffering suppression, oppression, injustices, torture and even facing death and extermination campaigns in Burma, Philippines, Patani, USSR, Cambodia, Vietnam, Cyprus, Afghanistan, etc. This responsibility becomes even more binding and pressing when we consider the malicious campaigns being waged against Islam and Muslims by Zionism, Communism, Free Masonry, Qadianism, Bahaism and Christian Missionaries.[104]

Here is Harakan again in 1981:

In these blessed historical moments ... begins an important and dangerous phase in the course of the blessed Islamic jihad in the face of all the dangers and conspiracies which threaten Islam's *umma* politically, militarily, ideologically, and socially. It is a stage that requires candor, realism, and solidarity to face all these dangers, as well as the realization that the danger that threatens any one Islamic location militarily, politically, or ideologically is one that threatens the Islamic sphere [*al-wujud al-islami*] in its large extent from one ocean to another. The security and the responsibility to confront and repel this danger thus cannot under any circumstances be the responsibility of a limited section or part of the Islamic entity; rather it is the responsibility of the entire Islamic *umma*.[105]

In 1981 the MWL published a book celebrating twenty years of accomplishments:

The League's media has lived through the issues and events that the Islamic *umma* has gone through over the past two decades. In all these cases, it has been a significant voice in these issues and events, and a pulpit that has conveyed to the world the positions of Muslims everywhere on the issues that preoccupy them, and that has communicated their realities and their fate. The League's media has supported and still recognizes the issues concerning the oppressed Muslim minorities around the world, especially the following: the Muslims in the Philippines, the Muslims in Cyprus, the Muslims in Russia, the Muslims in Communist China, the Muslims in Eritrea, and the Muslims in Burma.[106]

The same book stated:

The enemies of Islam are doing their utmost to wage conspiracies to separate Muslims from their religion and break their unity and brotherhood and weaken their strength. The League considers itself the organization that represents Muslim peoples, with all the issues and problems that they suffer from as a result of these conspiracies. And in this domain the League explained, through its founding council and various conferences and seminars which it organized or helped put together, the Muslim point of view in various political, military, economic, social, and other issues, and it drew up a plan to resolve them by supporting the parties that have a direct link to these issues, notably: (1) the Jerusalem and Palestine issue; (2) the Afghanistan issue; (3) the issue of Muslims in the southern Philippines; (4) the issue of the Muslims in Burma; (5) the issue of the Muslims of Fatani, the issue of Muslims in Lebanon, and the issue of Muslims in Cambodia and Vietnam.[107]

Harakan's successor Umar Nasif was a little less flamboyant, but here is the opening paragraph of a 1992 book commemorating the MWL's activities: "Since its emergence, the Islamic *umma* has faced different challenges, internal and external, and it has confronted many political, ideological, and social conspiracies aiming to tarnish Islam and Muslims, and seeking to eliminate the Islamic personality everywhere on earth."[108]

Variations on this message were spread through a large propaganda effort, at the heart of which were Islamic magazines with a wide distribution. Most important was the Muslim World League weekly *News of the Muslim World* and the monthly *Journal of the Muslim World League*, published in both Arabic and English. Many other IIOs had their own magazines. Both the quality and distribution of these magazines increased markedly in the late 1970s as a result of increased budgets and new technologies. By the early 1980s they were printed on glossy paper and were full of close-up color photographs of wounded Muslim women and children. Every magazine contained calls for charitable donations to the causes covered.

Several Arab governments tolerated the diffusion of pan-Islamist propaganda because it vilified primarily non-Muslim powers, not Muslim governments. For Muslim politicians there was little to gain and much to lose by trying to stem pan-Islamist populism. Instead, allowing or encouraging it had the benefit of diverting attention from domestic political problems. As a result, some governments, especially Saudi Arabia, were periodically caught in bidding games with the pan-Islamist community over declared concern for the well-being of the Muslim nation.[109]

The Hijazi pan-Islamists also sought to practice pan-Islamic solidarity by providing aid to Muslims in need around the world. The 1970s and early 1980s thus saw the growth of a vast network of Islamic charities, most of which were administered by IIOs.[110] Much like secular Western charities, these organizations monitored the humanitarian situation around the Muslim world and were prepared to rapidly deploy resources to any area in the event of a crisis.

The pan-Islamists did not have a military agenda. Many of their adherents no doubt approved of armed resistance to non-Muslim aggression, but their own activism was of the soft kind. Their idea of helping the Muslim nation was limited to raising awareness of Muslim suffering and providing various forms of educational, developmental, and humanitarian support to Muslims abroad. As we shall see, however, the ideas they promoted – that the Muslim nation is under siege and that Muslims should help each other – lent themselves very easily to a military interpretation. Soon, scholars such as Abdallah Azzam would start asking why the assistance should not include military support.

While the driving force behind the rise of pan-Islamist ideas in the late 1970s was the Hijaz-based internationalists, the Muslim Brotherhood also developed a somewhat more international discourse and activity portfolio in this period. Pan-Islamist ideas had always been part of Muslim Brotherhood ideology and discourse, but in the late 1970s they became more pronounced. This internationalization was highly visible in their publications. Just like the MWL magazines, Brotherhood magazines were full of articles conveying a sense of an *umma* under siege.[111] For example, the two flagship Muslim Brotherhood magazines, *al-Mujtama'* (published in Kuwait from 1969) and *al-Da'wa* (produced in Egypt from 1976), both include extensive coverage of wars involving Muslims in the late 1970s and early 1980s. *Al-Da'wa* notably had a regular section titled "Our Islamic Nation" containing news reports about suffering Muslims in places such as the Philippines, Eritrea, and the Soviet Union.[112] This new international rhetoric was accompanied by frequent expressions of hostility to the West. Brotherhood writers in this period described the West often in religious – as opposed to political – terms, and they spoke much about "new Crusades," a perceived Christian cultural and geopolitical onslaught against Islam.[113] For example, as early as November 1979, *al-Mujtama'* ran a front-cover story titled "The Crusader Threat to the Arabian Gulf."

Moreover, in this period the Egyptian Muslim Brotherhood also launched an international network-building effort. Starting in the late 1970s, the secretariat of the general guide, known as the Guidance Office (*maktab al-irshad*), began to liaise more systematically with Brotherhood branches abroad. The key figure behind this enterprise was Mustafa Mashhur, a Brotherhood veteran and former member of the Secret Aapparatus who would himself become general guide in the 1990s.[114] Helped by other Secret Apparatus alumni, such as Kamal al-Sananiri and Ahmad al-Malt, al-Mashhur embarked on a network-building effort in the late 1970s that would culminate with the foundation of the Muslim Brotherhood's International Organization (*al-tanzim al-duwali*) in 1981–1982.[115] Their objective was to reestablish some of the cross-country cooperation that had existed among Brotherhood branches in the 1930s, 1940s, and 1960s and to expand the Brotherhood's international influence. The group around Mustafa Mashhur became the core in a wider international network of Muslim Brothers preoccupied by international as opposed to domestic politics.

There were several reasons for the Egyptian Muslim Brotherhood's international turn in the late 1970s. One was the sheer growth of the movement. As Pargeter notes, al-Mashhur and his comrades were "driven by the fact that once they left prison [in the early 1970s] they discovered that other Ikhwani branches had flourished whilst their own had withered."[116] Another reason was all the money that had become available in the Gulf after the oil boom; going international was a way for cash-strapped Islamists to tap into that resource. International politics also offered opportunities to win popular support; the Egyptian–Israeli peace agreement was notably highly unpopular in Egypt. Last but not least was the Sadat regime's constraining of the Brotherhood's domestic political activities. In the late 1970s the Egyptian Brothers were out of prison and free to operate, but there were clear red lines as far as domestic politics was concerned. Expanding "outward," on the other hand, was relatively risk-free, as it posed no immediate threat to the Egyptian government.

Abdallah Azzam thus arrived in the Hijaz at a time when the pan-Islamist movement was in high gear and when the Egyptian Brotherhood was building its international organization. In the social circles he was about to enter there would have been much talk about the external threats to the Muslim nation and the ways to address them. For the next year, from late 1980 to late 1981, Azzam would live and work in the holy city of Mecca in western Saudi Arabia. His new job was with King Abd al-Aziz University's Shari'a department, which was located on the campus of what used to be the College of Shari'a in the Abidiyya district in the city's southeast. In 1971 the College of Shari'a had been incorporated into King Abd al-Aziz University (whose main campus was in Jeddah) to house the university's religious departments. In 1981 these departments again became a separate institution under its current name, Umm al-Qura University. Azzam found an apartment in the Aziziyya district a little further north, just 3 kilometers east of the Great Mosque. For a deeply religious person such as Azzam, it was not a bad setup.

It was probably also intellectually inspiring. At his new department, Azzam found himself with several of the most prominent Brotherhood-affiliated scholars in the region. There were the three Syrian scholars Muhammad al-Mubarak, Ali al-Tantawi, and Abd al-Rahman Habannaka, as well as prominent Egyptian figures such as Muhammad al-Ghazzali and Sayyid Sabiq.[117] Last but not least there was Muhammad

Qutb, Sayyid Qutb's brother, whom Azzam knew well from the 1970s. This was in addition to all the other famous scholars who lived in or visited Mecca, such as the Saudi clerics Abd al-Aziz Bin Baz and Muhammad bin al-Uthaymin.

Azzam's life in Saudi Arabia revolved around teaching, preaching, and writing. In 1980 and 1981 he published several articles in *al-Mujtama'*, a Muslim Brotherhood magazine that was published in Kuwait and had a wide distribution across the Arab world. Azzam had published there in part because he knew the editor, Isma'il al-Shatti, well; they had studied together in Cairo in the early 1970s. Azzam also appears to have been following international political developments closely, especially the events in Syria, Yemen, Afghanistan, and Egypt. We do not know very much about his social life in this period, other than that he got on particularly well with a certain Abdallah Nasir al-Alwan, who taught in the same department. They would stay in touch after Azzam went to Afghanistan; al-Alwan would contribute articles to *al-Jihad* magazine, and Azzam wrote an obituary for al-Alwan when the latter died in 1987.[118] Azzam was also in touch with people who worked in the international Islamic organizations, such as the Egyptian Kamal al-Helbawy, who worked for the World Association of Muslim Youth in Jeddah at this period.[119] They too would meet again in Peshawar in the late 1980s.

Azzam also met the twenty-three-year old Usama Bin Ladin at this time, but they were not very close. Bin Ladin lived in Jeddah and studied business administration at King Abd al-Aziz University's main campus in the same city, while Azzam taught religious subjects in Mecca. Bin Ladin was thus not Azzam's student, but he probably attended one or more of his lectures.[120] One source says that Bin Ladin met Azzam in a lecture series on Islamic culture, which is plausible because we know this was a topic that Azzam liked to teach.[121] It is also a topic that may have been taught on the Jeddah campus, because Islamic Culture was often compulsory in Saudi universities regardless of degree program. Still, judging from the personal notebook retrieved from Bin Ladin's hideout in Abbottabad in the late 2000s, Azzam was not a major intellectual influence on him in the 1970s or early 1980s.[122]

At the same time, Bin Ladin was not just a random Saudi student to Azzam. The two men had already met in 1978, and during Azzam's time in the kingdom they occasionally interacted on a private basis.

Azzam later wrote about having been at Usama Bin Ladin's house in Jeddah at one point in 1981.[123] And Azzam's wife later said, "I knew Bin Laden's wives before settling in Pakistan because we were living in Saudi Arabia where we used to meet them."[124] However, it was not until after Azzam moved to Pakistan that the two families became really close, as we shall see in Chapter 9.

Interestingly, I have found no mention of Juhayman al-Utaybi or the 1979 Mecca rebellion in any of Azzam's writings or speeches. In November 1979, just a year before Azzam moved to Mecca, the Great Mosque was seized by armed apocalyptic zealots who believed the end of times had come and who sought to consecrate one of their members as the Mahdi.[125] They took hundreds of worshipers hostage and barricaded themselves inside while they waited for the prophecy to materialize. It took Saudi security forces a full two weeks to dislodge them, and by the end several hundred people were dead. The Mecca incident was so shocking and spectacular that Azzam could not possibly have been unaware of it. If he did not devote it any attention, it was probably because he considered the rebels ideologically beyond the pale and therefore irrelevant. At this point in his intellectual trajectory, Azzam was primarily interested in foreign theaters of jihad.

Leaving for Pakistan

Azzam would only teach one full semester at King Abd al-Aziz University – the spring semester of 1981 – because later that autumn he would be on the move again.[126] It was clear to him almost from the start that Saudi Arabia would only be a temporary station on the way to something else. For one thing, his family did not like living in Mecca. His son Hudhayfa later said that he and his siblings felt out of place and that they found Saudis to be unwelcoming of foreigners.[127] For another, Azzam himself was understimulated. Kamal al-Helbawy says that Azzam confided to him at the time that he was bored and was looking for something more interesting to do.[128] Later, in Afghanistan, Azzam declared: "I was a university professor and I lived next to the Great Mosque in Mecca, but God knows that these kinds of places [in Afghanistan] are dearer to me than my life in Mecca."[129] Also, he did not see a great professional future for himself in the kingdom. He only had five-year work contract with King Abd al-Aziz University, and his wife later said the university "had been making plans to get rid of him" as early as 1981.[130] Finally, there was a lot going on in the Muslim world, and Azzam may have felt that his new job did not contribute to the causes he cared about. In Amman he had at least been able to influence a new generation of Palestinian students; in Jeddah he was mainly teaching Saudis, and he was a minor figure in a country chock full of clerics.

Azzam himself later said he had wanted to get involved in a military struggle, but he was not sure which one. He eventually narrowed the choice down to two options: Yemen or Afghanistan: "I looked for a battlefield [*saha*], and there was a jihad in Yemen and a jihad in Afghanistan, and I said, 'let's go to one of the two battlefronts and start practicing our vocation, which is jihad.'"[131] On another occasion he said, "[My expulsion from Jordan] opened a door of mercy for me ... and I looked around me when longing for jihad was always pulling me, so I looked for it, there was Jihad in Yemen where [the] Islamic movement were fighting the Communists, and there was Jihad in Afghanistan, so I decided I should go to one of these countries."[132]

Yemen was a candidate because of the civil war between the Yemen Arab Republic in the north and the Communist People's Democratic Republic of Yemen in the south. In 1979 fighting had erupted over the south's support for leftist rebels in the north. The worst fighting soon ended after the Arab League intervened to negotiate, but the conflict simmered as the Communist south kept supplying the rebels in the north with weapons. Azzam read about the Yemen conflict in the news and in magazines such as *al-Mujtama'*, and he likely knew the Yemeni Muslim Brotherhood leader Abd al-Majid Zindani, at least by reputation. The conflict appealed to Azzam in part because it offered an opportunity to fight Communists, whom he hated. At some point in 1981 Azzam actually traveled to Yemen to see the situation for himself. In 1989 he wrote a martyr biography of a dead Yemeni fighter in Afghanistan in which he said:

Eight years ago I met him in his house in Ma'rib with a group of his brothers; roaring lions gathered under a single roof, good Islamic learning, great manners, courage, and modesty ... they slaughtered a lamb or two in my honor. Then, close to sunset, we headed outside Ma'rib and they showed me the area where the Communists advancing from the south had attacked ... Then I left this house to which my heart had become attached, and I went home.[133]

Unfortunately Azzam never wrote much about this trip or about his thinking regarding Yemen as a destination. It is also not clear to what extent the Yemen conflict received foreign fighters or other visitors such as Azzam.

The other candidate was Afghanistan. We know from student testimonies that Azzam was following the Afghanistan conflict closely from early 1980 if not before. In the summer of 1980 Jamal Isma'il heard Azzam lecture in Amman about "Palestine, Afghanistan, and the situation in Islamic countries":

In that lecture which he delivered in the culture week at Jordan University, he talked about the Soviet invasion of Afghanistan which happened in December 1979; nearly six to seven months after that, he was speaking about the brave Afghan *mujahidin*, their achievements, their needs, how to support them, what to do for them, and how to collect donations for them.[134]

In fact, Azzam himself wrote in 1980 that some people in Jordan were accusing him of "inciting the students and sending them to Afghanistan."[135] Azzam also had Afghans among his students in Mecca. The Afghan Mujahidin leader Abd Rabb al-Rasul Sayyaf says he first heard of Abdallah Azzam in the spring of 1981 from fellow Afghans in Mecca: "I heard about him when he was teaching in Mecca. Not before that. Because some of our Afghan students were studying there in Mecca, in Umm al-Qura, and they were speaking about Abdallah Azzam, about his lectures, about his thinking, and about his thought about Afghan jihad."[136]

Still, both Yemen and Afghanistan were unusual destinations for an Arab Islamist in 1981, if only because there was so much else going on in the region at the time. The period from 1979 to 1982 was an extremely eventful one; it saw the Iranian revolution, the Camp David accords, the siege of Mecca, the Iran–Iraq war, the Lebanese civil war, the Syrian uprising, the Israeli incursions into Lebanon, and the assassination of Anwar Sadat, to mention just the main ones. Further afield there were other conflicts such as that in the Philippines. If Azzam singled out Yemen and Afghanistan, it was probably due to a combination of accessibility and the presence of a Communist enemy.

What tipped the balance in favor of Afghanistan was the influence of Kamal al-Sananiri, an Egyptian Muslim Brother whom Azzam knew well from his Cairo days. The sixty-three-year-old al-Sananiri was a legend in the organization.[137] He had studied under Hasan al-Banna, served in the Secret Apparatus in the late 1940s, fought in Palestine in 1948, and conducted operations in the Suez Canal area in the early 1950s. In early 1954 he helped organize large demonstrations in Cairo and was consequently arrested in Nasser's crackdown on the Brotherhood that year. Because he was a prominent alumnus of the Secret Apparatus, he would spend the next twenty years in prison under harsh conditions. While in prison he became engaged to Amina Qutb, and it was at the tail end of this imprisonment that Abdallah Azzam helped Amina in Cairo, as we saw in the previous chapter.

After his release from prison in January 1974 he reconnected with the Brotherhood, and took a particular interest in transnational work. In 1979 he quit his day job in an engineering company and devoted himself fully to the Islamic call.[138] He worked closely with Mustafa Mashhur and Ahmad al-Malt to build the Brotherhood's International Organization. He became something of a Brotherhood diplomat, traveling extensively to Kuwait, Saudi Arabia, Lebanon, and elsewhere to bring the various regional branches closer together. His assistant in this period, Abdallah al-Aqil, later wrote: "After his release, I had many meetings with him in Egypt and outside ... He was concerned with uniting the ranks of the Ikhwan all over the world. I worked with him under his command in many areas ... His tours in Arab and Islamic countries and elsewhere are renowned, and he left an unforgettable impact on the people he met."[139] When he died, *al-Mujtama‘* magazine carried a statement saying, "The International Organization of the Muslim Brotherhood announces to the Islamic world the death of the *mujahid*, martyr, and brother Muhammad Kamal al-Din al-Sananiri, one of the pioneers of the Islamic movement in the world."[140]

In the spring of 1981 al-Sananiri was the Muslim Brotherhood's envoy to the Afghan jihad (more on this in Chapter 7). On his way to his second study trip in Peshawar he stopped in Saudi Arabia for meetings with other Muslim Brothers. One of the people he contacted was Abdallah Azzam, and the two met in Jeddah. Al-Sananiri was keen to get Azzam involved in his Afghanistan work. "We had a strong connection from the Cairo days," Azzam later wrote. "He told me: this is not your homeland. Pack your bags and come to Afghanistan. And thus I began preparing myself to join him there."[141] Meanwhile, al-Sananiri was confident that he had persuaded Azzam; according to one of his travel companions, he told the Mujahidin leaders in Peshawar, "We will send you one of the leaders of the Islamic movement . . . Abdallah Azzam."[142]

Later in the summer, on the return leg from the same Peshawar trip, al-Sananiri met Azzam in the Great Mosque in Mecca, reportedly by coincidence. His wife later said, "The sheikh and I were in the Great Mosque before the morning prayer, at about 2.30 or 3 a.m., performing *umra*. As we were doing this, whom did I see other than this man who was hugging him and greeting him warmly."[143] Al-Sananiri was glowing with enthusiasm for the Afghan jihad. He told Azzam again, "Abdallah, your place is there, not here. Pack your bags and trust in God." Al-Sananiri said he would follow soon: "I will sort out my things, get my wife, and join you."[144] They talked some more, and in the end Azzam was persuaded. He agreed to accompany al-Sananiri on his flight to Pakistan for an initial exploration trip.[145] Al-Sananiri headed back to Egypt, promising to return to Saudi a few weeks later. But al-Sananiri did not return as planned, because he was arrested by Egyptian police on 4 September.[146]

In mid-September 1981 Azzam went to Pakistan as planned, hoping that al-Sananiri would be released and eventually join him. While waiting for al-Sananiri, Azzam looked around Peshawar for himself and gave a lecture at Peshawar University.[147] He also made a trip to the border, which made a big impression: "When I stood on the peaks of Afghanistan I could not believe it! I was a Palestinian, having suffered repeated losses in the Arab world. And I saw victories and I saw myself on top. I could not believe it."[148] The Afghan jihad, he was now convinced, was "the beginning of a renaissance (*nahda*)" and a potential "historical turning point for the world as a whole".[149] All he needed was for al-Sananiri to arrive so the two could start working together. But al-Sananiri never came; he would die in prison on 6 November 1981, reportedly from torture.[150] As someone later put it, "Sheikh Abdallah Azzam lost his leader."[151]

In the meantime Azzam returned home, determined to move to Pakistan, but there were practical hurdles. He needed a way to support himself in the long term, and he was bound by a five-year contract with King Abd al-Aziz University.[152] The perfect opportunity soon arose, as his wife later explained:

On the first day after the summer vacation he went to the university, and he found an announcement hanging on the wall saying there was a new cooperation between King Abd al-Aziz University and Pakistani universities and that King Abd al-Aziz University and Medina University would send professors there to teach the Qur'an and Arabic in Pakistan. "Interested professors can register with the Human Resources department." So he said, "God arranged this for me," and he went and signed up, as the first person.[153]

Not long after, around 11 October 1981, he met another person in Mecca who would become a close collaborator in the years to come: the Afghan Mujahidin leader Abd Rabb al-Rasul Sayyaf.[154] Sayyaf later said:

In the period of Hajj I met him [in Mecca]. I had a speech there and . . . after the meeting he met me and he introduced himself [saying] "I am Abdallah Azzam." I had a picture from him before and I knew him before that, so he told me that I want to come and participate in jihad. I told him, "You are welcome," and [he said] "I will come to Islamabad, the International University" . . . So after some time he came to Islamabad and . . . I received him for the first time in our office.[155]

The story of Azzam's transition to Pakistan illustrates the crucial role of the Hijaz region as an international Islamist hub in the early 1980s. This was a place where many connections were made, and it was a platform from which international Islamic organizations were spreading their global network. In the years to come, Azzam himself would use this platform to recruit and fundraise for the Afghan jihad.

There was also a reason why Azzam in particular moved to Pakistan, as the only Islamic scholar from the Arab world to do so at this time. He simply had less to lose than the others. Azzam faced what economists would call a lower opportunity cost than his peers: Most scholars with his level of qualifications and experience had secure, well-paid jobs and families embedded in their respective communities. Leaving everything behind for a life on the frontlines was very costly. Azzam, by contrast, did not have this; by the time he decided to move to Pakistan, he was a two-time refugee with a temporary job and a family unhappy in their new country. He was the only Islamist vagabond with a Ph.D. from al-Azhar.

Azzam's involvement in the Afghan jihad was thus the result of both push and pull factors: autocrats pushed him out and pan-Islamists pulled him in. If he had not lost his job and been pressured to leave Jordan, he would most likely have grown old in Amman. Similarly, if the Egyptian Brotherhood had not sent Kamal al-Sananiri to Peshawar first, Azzam might not have been inspired to go there. And if the Muslim World League had not offered job opportunities for Arab scholars in Islamabad, he might not have been able to go. Of course, none of this is to say that Azzam was a passive victim of the circumstances. He had already made it quite clear through his writings where he stood politically.

6 Writer

Abdallah Azzam would become so famous for his books on the Afghan jihad that it is easy to forget that he had an earlier publishing career. This chapter looks at the things Azzam wrote in his pre-Afghanistan years, and what they tell us about his worldview. His subsequent work, which deals mainly with Afghanistan and matters relating to jihad, will be dealt with in Chapter 11. In the following, we will look at the main themes in his pre-Afghanistan production: Islamic law, education, anti-quietism, anti-Communism, and Islamic supremacy. We will see that Azzam's output became sharply more political in the late 1970s, and that he was especially concerned with the threat to Islam from foreign ideologies such as leftism and Western liberalism. In Azzam's worldview, politics was primarily a struggle between religions, not between states or other interest groups. He was also a chauvinist on Islam's behalf as well as a believer in a broad range of anti-Semitic conspiracy theories. At the time these were entirely mainstream views within the Muslim Brotherhood, and to some extent in Arab politics more broadly, so he was not yet a particularly original thinker.

Azzam's literary production prior to 1982 is quite small compared to that of his Afghanistan years. He began publishing late; he was around thirty-five years old when his first articles appeared in *al-Mujtama'* magazine. As far as we know, there are not even any unpublished writings by him from before this time other than his BA and Ph.D. theses. If he wrote letters, booklets, op-eds, or anything else prior to 1975, those have yet to surface, which is unlikely given the considerable efforts by his supporters to collect and publish his works. His pre-Afghanistan writing career has two distinct phases. From 1967 through 1977 he addressed relatively apolitical topics such as Islamic law and Islamic education. From 1978 through 1981 he wrote a series of very polemical works, attacking leftists, liberals, and other Islamists.

Islamic Law

The earliest known works by Azzam are his academic works on Islamic law. The first is his BA thesis from Damascus University titled "Marriage Dissolution in Islamic Jurisprudence and Civil Law," which he submitted in the spring of 1967. The text sheds valuable light on his early political views and intellectual influences. At 47,000 words it also shows a very prolific author in the making. It is not clear why he chose to write on divorce, but the topic may simply have been suggested to him by his supervisor, Abd al-Rahman al-Sabuni, who was a specialist on Islamic family law in addition to being an active member of the Syrian Muslim Brotherhood.[1] The approach of the thesis fell squarely in the comparative legal tradition that was the trademark of the Shari'a faculty in Damascus (see Chapter 2).

Most of the text is rather technical, but there is politics between the lines. The thesis notably begins with a section highlighting the decline of family values in the West. Azzam lists Western data on divorce and children born out of wedlock, cites French sociologist Paul Bureau's book *Toward Moral Bankruptcy*, and shakes his head at Scandinavians: "Statistics show that one in seven marriages in Sweden end with divorce, and in Norway one in every six marriages end. It is not uncommon in Denmark to find women in their thirties who have been married two or three times."[2] Western moral laxitude is then contrasted with the Islamic position on family and divorce. Azzam's argument is that Islamic law is the best antidote to family dissolution, and that too much secular legislation might bring Western moral ills to the Muslim world. This theme of Islam's superiority over other beliefs and cultures is a staple of Islamist thinking and one that Azzam would return to in his 1980 book *Islam and the Future of Mankind*.

We can see already in this student work that Azzam read quite widely on modern history and politics. He was reasonably familiar with the Western intellectual tradition, some misconceptions about Western society notwithstanding. He also read and spoke fluent English. Already in this thesis, Azzam cited relevant Western academic literature, and his book *Islam and the Future of Mankind* (1980) is packed with references to Western works of literature, philosophy, and politics. This is partly testimony to his educational background; the Kadoorie College in Tulkarm, where he studied agriculture, was a secular school and one of the best in Palestine, and the faculty of Shari'a in Damascus was well known for its relatively progressive curriculum, which included social science, foreign languages, and civil law.

The thesis leaves little doubt about the twenty-five-year-old Azzam's Muslim Brotherhood sympathies. In addition to revealing his social conservatism, it also shows his familiarity with the writings of Brotherhood ideologues such as Mustafa Siba'i, Muhammad Qutb, and Yusuf al-Qaradawi. No author, however, is treated with more deference than Sayyid Qutb. Azzam introduces him as "the great Islamic writer, the giant, and martyr Sayyid Qutb" and subsequently refers to him variously as "the great writer," "the giant thinker," "the great professor and martyr," "the great writer and martyr," and "the giant of Islamic thought in the twentieth century."[3]

Azzam's next known written product is his Ph.D. thesis from 1973 at al-Azhar University. Titled "The Implications of the Book and the Sunna for Legal Rulings," it was a highly technical study comparing legal reasoning across the four schools of Islamic jurisprudence. It showed that the Hanafi school differed from the Maliki, Shafi'i, and Hanbali schools in how it reconciled general principles and the different branches inside the school. While the latter three represented a deductive approach in which the general principles were established first and the branches developed from the principles, in Hanafism it was the other way around. As Azzam himself put it:

In my research I clarify the distinction between the method of the Hanafis and the method of the rest, which they called the procedure of the theologians [al-mutakallimin]. As for the method of the Hanafis, in their principles, the starting point was to follow the branches of their imams, and to extract the rules from these [branches] with the idea that these were the rules that were originally in their imams' minds when they spread out into different branches. Thus when a branch of jurisprudence departs from the fundamental rule they had posited, they tried to modify the rule and specify it so that the rule was consistent and balanced with the branches. As for the rest, they operated differently with regard to establishing their rules and extracting their principles. They posited the basic rules and then from these they deduced the branches.[4]

The general insight was not new, so Azzam's academic contribution was to demonstrate it in detail and to systematize the evidence. The thesis was well received by the examiners, but it has not gone down in history as a pioneering work of Islamic legal literature. It was never published as a book in Azzam's lifetime.[5] Doctoral theses in Islamic Law at the time were probably not expected to be particularly innovative, because in practice it was a vocational training that prepared candidates for careers as judges and educators.

The thesis shows that Azzam had received a strong and broad Islamic legal education and possessed a good overview of the four legal traditions. The speed at which he researched and wrote the thesis – he took sixteen months to produce over 600 pages of finished text – also suggests that he had memorized not just the Qur'an but also substantial parts of the Hadith literature. All of this would serve him well in his subsequent work as a preacher and a writer. The thesis also gave Azzam a particularly deep insight into Hanafi jurisprudence, which would help him in Afghanistan.

The text also reveals important aspects of Azzam's legal and political thinking that recur in his later works. Most important was his anti-modernism. In his introduction, he stressed that he had spent much time digging up pre-twentieth-century books and manuscripts, and that "these old references were the founding pillar on which the argument in my thesis rests. As for the modern references, I only consulted them to see in which way they agreed or differed with the old ones."[6] We see here Azzam's skepticism of twentieth-century Islamic legal analysis and his tendency to prefer the classical sources. Here and in several other works, he strongly insinuates that modern Islamic scholars have distorted the original teachings of Islam. This idea would become crucial in Azzam's 1984 fatwa on foreign fighting, because there too he would bypass modern interpretations and rely only on the classical sources.

A second feature of his worldview that shines through his Ph.D. is his nostalgia for the Ottoman Empire. In his view, the Ottoman state – which he called the "High State" (*al-dawla al-ulya*, the Ottomans' own term) or simply "the state" (*al-dawla*) – had been a true Islamic caliphate, and its dissolution was a great tragedy. For example, he wrote:

> I began preparing the research in the Egyptian National Library, where I obtained a list of the books in stock on *usul al-fiqh* ... But I was saddened when I saw that most of these references were printed in the time of the Great State which governed by God's Shari'a, protected the sanctuary of his religion, and guarded the principles of his legislation, namely the Ottoman state, toward

which we used to harbor so much resentment and malice, because it has been imprinted in our minds through our studies of the fabricated history which the orientalists penned, through which they conveyed their hate and poisonous fury, to the point where the name of this Great State became "the Sick Man" and branded its era, which represented Islam, an era of decline – thus belittling us. And the Masonic Dönmeh Jews who were behind the fall of the last rule of God on earth, portrayed themselves as the free and the great of the followers of the Committee of Union and Progress and the Young Turks and the like. Then I stopped exploring the printed books and entered the manuscript department in the same library and looked at pretty much every manuscript on *usul* [*al-fiqh*] – except one that I saw just the other day when I went to skim the registry of the manuscript department. And my pain increased when I discovered the forgotten truth that most of these manuscripts were written in the time of this state which has been maliciously and falsely named an age of decline.[7]

Ottoman Caliphate nostalgia is a recurring theme in Azzam's ideological production. In 1987, in the midst of the Afghan jihad, he would publish a book titled *The Lost Beacon*, which was a eulogy of the Ottoman state and a scathing attack on its secular Kemalist successor.[8]

Islamic Education

Azzam's first writing project after finishing his Ph.D. and moving to Amman was about the importance of Islamic education. In 1975 he published a series of articles on the topic in *al-Mujtama'* magazine, and the same year he published a book titled *The Creed and its Effect on Building the Generation*.[9] The book must have been well received in Brotherhood circles, because in 1977 it was also published by Dar al-I'tisam press in Cairo. The Egyptian edition included a foreword by the famous sheikh Muhammad Mutawalli al-Sha'rawi, the most popular scholar of the official religious establishment under Sadat.

The Creed was a short but passionate defense of Islamic education in the modern world. The central message is that it is crucial to instill strong faith and a proper understanding of the creed in the young from an early age. Most of the nine-chapter text is relatively abstract and focuses on describing the various elements of the creed and laying out its scriptural basis. Perhaps the most interesting part is chapter 8, which explains what happens to a society that does not take Islamic education seriously. Potential ills include (1) extreme wealth inequality; (2)

government oppression; (3) moral depravity; (4) psychological problems; (5) fear of world annihilation by nuclear weapons; and (6) community fragmentation. This is not to mention number (7):

Certain manifestations of rebellion that reflect the confusion, angst, and tiredness of mankind, such as the Beatles and the hippies, who have come to represent a great danger to the security of America and Europe, holding gatherings of millions of people from all social classes in public (where they eat and drink and defecate and have intercourse in one place, in the middle of the street).[10]

The book places Azzam squarely in the Muslim Brotherhood intellectual tradition. The topic itself, religious education, was central to the Brotherhood's ideology.[11] Moreover, it copiously cites Sayyid Qutb and other Muslim Brotherhood thinkers. *The Creed* also hints in several places at Azzam's personal interactions with prominent Muslim Brothers. For example, at one point he highlights Amina Qutb and obliquely references Kamal al-Sananiri as examples of proper Islamic conduct: "This woman, who was proposed to first by a prince and then by an ambassador, but who refused both, only to get engaged to one of those convicted to life with hard labor in 1963, and she waited ten years – the longest engagement in history – until her fiancé came out of prison so they could marry."[12] At another point in the text Azzam mentions the Sudanese Muslim brother Muhammad Salih Umar, who had fought with him among the Fedayin in the late 1960s.[13]

It is no coincidence that his first book was about Islamic education, because this was perhaps his greatest passion. He was a teacher for most of his professional life, and by all accounts he thrived in the presence of young people. He would also return to the theme of Islamic education in many of his subsequent writings and sermons till the end of his life.

Anti-Quietism

In the meantime, however, Azzam was ready to go more polemical. Around 1978 a highly controversial book titled *The Islamic Call* was published in Amman under the pseudonym "Sadiq Amin."[14] The book was a call to support the Muslim Brotherhood as well an attack on the Brotherhood's ideological competitors in the Islamist field, notably the Tabligh movement, Hizb al-Tahrir, and the followers of Nasir al-Din al-Albani. These movements represent what we may call "quietist" strands of Islamism insofar as they were preoccupied with theological matters and were less confrontational than the Brotherhood toward political authorities. The book criticized these other movements for spending too much time on small, irrelevant things at a time when the Islamic world faced major political threats. In Sadiq Amin's view these other efforts were misguided, and the Muslim Brotherhood was the only real Islamist game in town.

It has long been suspected that Azzam wrote or co-authored *The Islamic Call* but used a pseudonym to avoid trouble for himself and the Brotherhood.[15] "It was an open secret that this was Azzam's book," the Saudi former Muslim Brother Jamal Khashoggi later said.[16] The big online repository of jihadi literature, Minbar al-Tawhid wa'l-Jihad, includes *The Islamic Call* in the Azzam folder. Abu Rumman and Abu Hanieh, who take Azzam's authorship for granted, summarized the book's message as follows:

Perhaps the largest attack against Hizb ut-Tahrir, from within the Muslim Brotherhood, came from Sheikh 'Abdullah 'Azzam, who attacked Hizb ut-Tahrir's approach and its insistence on focusing on intellectual issues, while it neglected all matters related to realistic and the practical spheres. Sheikh 'Azzam accused the party of taking a path that "turned the party's work and activities into a frigid, never-ending dialectic; and, it has cornered itself within the confines of a debate that has no beginning and no end, and which has no effect or impact on peoples' reality or lives, particularly in light of the dearth of its members' rhetoric, and their prioritization of debate and talk over all matters practical." 'Abdullah 'Azzam also harshly criticized Hizb ut-Tahrir's "call for support" approach, as well as the manner in which they dealt with other issues, such as permitting women as members in the party's ranks, allowing non-Muslims in their shura councils, and permitting the kissing of and shaking of hands with foreign women. He also attacked the party over matters related to certain aspects of religious Islamic jurisprudence, such as denying the authoritative authenticity of al-khabar al-wahid (Hadith of the Prophet viewed as lacking in chain of transmittance), and that which is associated between this notion and the disbelief in "'adhab al-qabr" (torment of the grave), as well as the party's stance on the rise and re-emergence of the Antichrist.[17]

The circumstantial evidence for his authorship is compelling. For one thing, several of his closest family members – including his wife, his daughter Fatima, and his son-in-law Abdallah Anas – have said that he wrote all of it.[18] For another, Azzam appears to have used the pseudonym Sadiq Amin elsewhere. Several articles in *al-Jihad* magazine in the late 1980s were signed "Sadiq Amin," and we know that Azzam would write pseudonymously in *al-Jihad* to make it look as if the magazine had more contributors.[19] According to Abu Rumman and Abu Hanieh, "Sadeq Amin is the pseudonym that Dr. 'Abdullah Azzam is known by within the circles of the Muslim Brotherhood."[20] One of the copies of the book in the Jordan University library has "Abdallah Azzam" scribbled right under "Sadiq Amin" on one of the introductory pages.[21] Third, Azzam fits the profile: the book was published on a Muslim Brotherhood-affiliated press in Amman, and Azzam was an Amman-based Brotherhood preacher and writer. He had also already quarreled with the quietist Salafi Nasir al-Din al-Albani, as we saw in the previous chapter. Finally, the content of the book is consistent with Azzam's other known opinions, as well as with the overarching theme of his other books around this time, namely, that of ideological threats to the Islamist project.

At the same time, we cannot be fully certain, because Azzam himself insisted that he only wrote one chapter of the book. Jamal Isma'il said he asked Azzam directly in the autumn of 1983:

> In Peshawar once, I asked him directly, in a gathering for Arab students ... I said to him, "Dr. Abdallah ... you have been accused of writing this book, and you did not write your name, you have written Dr. Sadiq Amin, just to be safe from the criticism which can come out of this book." He smiled and he said, "I am not the real author of this book, but I really participated in one chapter; the one chapter which I have wrote, it was the fifth chapter, which did not say any single word about any Islamic movement. It was generally about Islam and what is needed and the current situation in the Islamic countries. I did not say anything. The one who wrote about other, different groups, he was not me, he was someone; originally he was member of Hizb al-Tahrir, but he quit them and he joined Muslim Brotherhood. Due to his knowledge about Hizb al-Tahrir, he wrote this, and due to my lectures in Amman at Jordanian University, I was quoting this book, and due to my lectures and my quotations from that book, many people came to know about that book from my lectures. Brothers in Hizb al-Tahrir they were thinking that I was the author of that book. I didn't; if I [had] authored it, I'll say it in front of everybody, and in front of almighty Allah, that yes I'm the one who authored it, but I am telling you the truth that I did not at least write that chapter which is criticizing the other groups."[22]

Another piece of evidence suggests that Azzam was indeed only a co-author of the book. In the letter he sent to the Brotherhood leadership in 1980 (see Chapter 5) he complained that "the book I co-authored, *The Islamic Call*" was not taught enough.[23] This letter was never intended for public consumption, and the reference to the book was unsolicited, so the claim is credible. This said, it is possible that he wrote more than one chapter, and that he later tried to downplay his contribution. It has not yet emerged who his co-author may have been.

Anti-Communism

The issue that probably preoccupied Azzam the most in the pre-Afghanistan period was the ideological threat from the Arab left. Decades of political competition with leftist factions in Palestine had made him extremely hostile to leftism in all its forms. In 1980 he published a book titled *The Red Cancer*, in which he elaborated on the evils of Communism and its manifestations in the Arab world.[24] *The Red Cancer* became Azzam's most famous pre-Afghanistan book; it was published in several editions and reportedly in tens of thousands of copies. It had a particularly warm reception among Palestinian Islamists; according to Jamal Isma'il, "it was so much distributed in Palestine at that time, because [of] the struggle between the leftist PLO supporters and the Islamists."[25] Isma'il also says he had read the book before coming to Jordan in the summer of 1980.

The Red Cancer is a highly interesting read because it contains more politics and less theology than Azzam's previous works. It is the first book to give us real insight into his geopolitical views in this period. The book starts broadly, with three chapters on the origins and history of Marxism before narrowing in on the history of Communism in the Muslim world in general and in Palestine in particular. Its main argument is that Communism is a Jewish ploy to weaken Islam. Much of the book is in fact spent explaining how the Jews founded Communism and spread it around the world. "The Bolshevik revolution was Jewish in ideology, planning, funding and execution," Azzam asserts. "Its philosopher and thinker was Marx, the grandson of the Jewish rabbi Mordechai Marx, and likewise with Lenin, who changed Marx's words into reality and revolution."[26] He goes on to add, "As for the funding [of the revolution], it was Jewish; the Brooklyn area of eastern New York was the plotting base for the revolution; Trotsky was from there, and this area is still the center for the Jewish plotting to destroy mankind."[27] He also argues that Jews have largely controlled Soviet policy throughout the history of the Soviet Union, and that wherever Communism spread, Jews were involved; in short, "all Communist revolutions in the world are Jewish."[28] It is no surprise, therefore, that "the Jews orchestrated the organization and formation of Communist parties in the Arab world; they are its leaders and planners."[29] Naturally, then, Communists in Palestine became a fifth column during the establishment of Israel:

In 1939, the Communists established the National Liberation League; its secretary was the Jewish Ben Faski, and his aide was Tawfiq Tawbi. Its aim was the eviction of Britain and the establishment of a joint Arab–Jewish government. In the 1948 war the members of the National Liberation League became leaders of armed bands that slaughtered the Palestinian people ... the zealous Communists defended the Jews and stood beside them; among them was the lawyer Ibrahim Bakr in Nasiriyya and Fu'ad Nisar in Jaffa and other Arab Communist leaders in Palestine.[30]

Azzam also argues that Communism harbors a particular hostility toward Muslims and has worked to undermine Islam. The fifth chapter includes a long section on "Communist massacres of Muslims" in which he asserts that "History has never seen anything like the butcheries which Communists committed against Muslims," citing examples from the Caucasus, Xinjiang, and Yugoslavia. Worst of all, in Azzam's view, is that Communists and Jews brought down the Ottoman Empire.[31] Here he points to the presence of several so-called Dönmeh Jews in the Young Turk movement which led to the establishment of modern Turkey. (The Dönmeh were a group of Jews based in Thessaloniki who converted to Islam in the seventeenth century but were suspected of having retained their Jewish beliefs.) As we saw in the earlier section on his Ph.D. thesis, Azzam was a big admirer of the Ottoman state.

To be sure, Azzam does not only blame the Jews. In the ninth chapter he offers nine additional reasons which facilitated the spread of Communism in the Muslim world. The first, he argues, was Western imperialism, which made the Muslim world more receptive to Communism by oppressing Muslims so much that they looked to Communism for liberation. It is clear from *The Red Cancer* that Azzam was both very anti-Western and very anti-American in 1980:

Muslims have suffered the ills of Western imperialism especially by Britain and France ... then America took their place in imperialism hidden and visible, and the West sucked up the blood of Muslims, plundered its homelands, trampled on its sanctities and violated its [women's] honor. This produced rancor and enmity to the West in the heart of all who believe in this religion.[32]

The second reason for Communism's spread was

the [Westernized] systems of education ... on which the West relied in the Muslim world. The media focus on disgraceful sexuality and on spreading nudity and mixing of the sexes has led to gender chaos [al-fawda al-jinsiya] ... and Communism can only thrive in such an environment. Likewise, the media's emphasis on destroying and distorting the image of Islamic scholars has become a major obstacle between the [new] generation and those who present them this religion.[33]

Reasons three, four, and five for the spread of Communism were "the taking of Jews and their supporters as allies," "social ills and the great decline in living standards," and "the spread of corrupt doctrine and [false] superstitious myths in the name of Islam" respectively.[34] The sixth reason was "the treason of Islamic scholars, i.e. the scholars' passivity in the face of the tyrants' oppression." Azzam argued that modern scholars "justify and embellish the actions of the rulers." He highlighted the Camp David accords of September 1978, saying: "When the Camp David treaty was signed, opinions were issued by al-Azhar scholars who bought the verses of God at a small price, opinions which supported peace and stood beside the President. The Communists gathered these fatwas and commented, 'Did we not say "religion is the opium of the people"?'"[35] The seventh reason for Communism's spread was "Muslims' abandonment of jihad." In Azzam's view, "the Palestinian revolution is the clearest example of this. When the Muslims retreated, the secular leaders were pushed to the forefront."[36] The eighth reason was "the nationalist movements' adoption of secularism." Azzam argued that "all the nationalist parties in the Muslim-Arab world are Communist in reality and content, although they are nationalist in name and appearance."[37] The ninth and final contributing cause was "the Muslim countries' indifference to the missions to the Eastern bloc," which had allowed Arab Communists to go to the Soviet Union for training and indoctrination.[38]

To illustrate the corrosive influence that Arab leftists are having on Muslim societies, Azzam supplements his analysis with personal anecdotes from his time with the Fedayin:

And they began to cultivate revolutionary culture in the youth!! The culture of Mao and Guevara. The revolutionary doctrine of Lenin and Stalin, the views of Marx, and the life of Castro. They taught the youth twenty key terms ... imperialism, bourgeoisie, demagogy, proletariat ... the youth thought they possessed something new and they substituted it for God's religion ... so the battle changed from a jihad against the Jews and a struggle in God's path to a claim for territory and holy sites ... to a war against reactionism (the religion of God), to an internal conflict brought to every house between brothers, between father and son, daughter and mother ... Officials from the Communist organization the "Partisans" ... began lecturing in the Professional Association Complex in 1969–1970 saying, "Our enemies are imperialism and Zionism, not the noble Jews!!" On 10 April 1970 revolutionary factions in Amman celebrated for a whole week the hundred-year anniversary of Lenin's birth. There was no intersection, no door, no shop, no magazine, where they did not stick posters of the great Lenin!! The state of disbelief was taking root in the land ... The socialist revolutionaries have no values or manners. They had so many mistresses!! They beguiled them in the name of Palestine. You would enter their bases, especially in the offices in the cities such as Amman you would see them wearing tight trousers, sleeping to tunes of music and waking to Oud strings mixed with Beatles and Hippies music!! And in a demonstration [at] the University of Jordan in 1979 they were saying with loud voices, "Our demands are bread, security, freedom, and gender equality." I saw a young man approach them and some of the local agitators began appearing, and this good man said, "Brothers and sisters, I speak to you in the name of Islam," whereupon one of the misled socialist revolutionaries got up and shouted, "Our demands are clear, reactionism we don't want to hear," i.e. we don't want to see Islam.[39]

Still, Azzam ends on a positive note for his Islamist readers, insisting that Communism is bound to fall, and that the sooner Muslims take religion more seriously the sooner this will happen. He outlines a four-pronged "Program for returning to God":

1. Working with an ideologically balanced Islamic group that is based on *tawhid* [God's oneness] and that knows the global plots against it.
2. The Islamic group begins with jihad, and is the spark that ignites the energy of the *umma*.
3. The battle led by the Islamic movement continues.
4. The battle will end with victory for the Muslim people whom the [Islamic] movement leads and [for whom] it will establish an Islamic state.[40]

Azzam was thus in 1979 already envisaging military jihad as a way to rid the Muslim world of Communism and reclaim Muslim lands. He seems to have believed that the jihad would not happen by itself, but would have to be initiated and led by an Islamic vanguard organization which would inspire the masses and establish an Islamic state.

Some time after the publication of *The Red Cancer*, perhaps a year or two later, Azzam wrote a similar but shorter text entitled *Arab Nationalism*.[41] It is not clear exactly when or in which form it was published, but it featured in posthumous collections of Azzam's works, and the content suggests that it was written in the early 1980s. It is structured similarly to *The Red Cancer*, taking us from the movement's origin to the present day. The argument is slightly more nuanced, and he quotes academics such as George Antonius and Albert Hourani extensively, but he still gives the Jews a significant historical role.

Azzam sees Arab nationalism essentially as a Western import, but he also gives local actors a good part of the blame. He traces the origin of the rise of nationalism in the Muslim world to Napoleon's campaign in Egypt, and attributes the rise of Arab nationalism to four causes:

> The main one was the West's attempt to marginalize Islam ... and put another unit in its place. After the failure of the Crusades, the West wanted to employ ideas instead of weapons to facilitate the Western encroachment on our lands, notably after Napoleon's campaign in Egypt. Second was the ambition of Muhammad Ali Pasha and Ibrahim Pasha to create an Arab nationalist empire. Third was the elimination of Muslim Turkey so that the West could seize its possessions. Fourth was the attempt by Christians to bring down Turkey because it imposed the *jizya* [tax on non-Muslims] on them as well as some exceptional duties corresponding to the paying of *zakat* and military service to protect the Islamic state.[42]

Interestingly, Azzam is quite critical of the "Pioneers of Islamic Revival" Jamal al-Din al-Afghani, Muhammad Abduh, and Abd al-Rahman al-Kawakibi, whom he blames for helping bring down the Ottoman Empire. In this book too, Azzam expresses bitter resentment at the dissolution of the Caliphate:

> Here we have to point to three preachers who wore the garb of *ulama* and were known in the whole world as advocates of Muslim unity, although at the same time they attacked Turkey and sought to bring down the edifice of the Caliphate ... the ideas of these three represented a preliminary step to

secularization. As Albert Hourani says, their views was an aqueduct by which secularism reached the Islamic world. They broke the psychological barriers between infidels and Muslims and Muslim souls became able to receive imported ideas, foremost of which was nationalism ... Then came Muhammad Abduh's students who deepened this current and led society with their secularism.[43]

Azzam soon reverts to blaming external forces, however. He links both Arab nationalism and pan-Turkism to foreign influences, saying, "Both nationalisms were raised in foreign nurseries; Arab nationalism grew up in American nurseries, and in the American university, whereas Turanism grew up in Masonic and Jewish circles supervised by Spanish, Polish and Italian Jews."[44] He adds that "all the Arab nationalist leaders were non-Muslims ... of Christian origin."[45]

He goes on to declare nationalism of all kinds un-Islamic, and produces a whole list of reasons: "Nationalism values unity based on nationality and location rather than creed"; "Nationalism prefers the Christian Arab over the Pakistani or Turkish Muslim"; "Arab nationalism allies with infidels and follows infidel leaders; they prefer the message of Michel Aflaq and George Habash and their professors Nietzsche and Rousseau over any other, even that of God's Prophet"; "Arab nationalism does not accept Islamic laws"; "Arab nationalists see Arab nationalism as a new religion"; "Arab nationalism prefers *jahiliyya* over Islam"; and "Arab nationalism is a new Taghut (a new idol)."[46] He then spells out the implication, which is that all nationalists are infidels:

Based on the abovementioned evidence, Arab nationalism, or any other nationalism ... is *kufr*. He who embraces nationalist principles leaves Islam; and his slaughtered meat cannot be eaten, a nationalist girl cannot be wed [to a Muslim], and a nationalist man cannot marry the girls of Muslims, [his dead body] cannot be washed and shrouded and prayed over, it cannot be buried in a Muslim cemetery; one should not answer his greeting saying "peace," and one should not say "God to bless his soul" when he dies ... If a man embraces nationalism when he is married to a Muslim, they must divorce; if they continue to have sexual relations, that is considered fornication and the children that result are bastards.[47]

As far as declarations of *takfir* go, it hardly gets more explicit than this. It is noteworthy because a nationalist is not necessarily an atheist, so Azzam is effectively declaring as infidels people who could be claiming to be Muslims. Incidentally, the passage is not unique: Elsewhere in the same text, he says of the Egyptian writer Taha Hussain that he "was expelled from university due to his blatant unbelief [*kufruhu al-sarih*]" which he displayed by writing the book *On Pre-Islamic Poetry*.[48] Moreover, as we shall see in Chapter 11, he said similar things of other people. In other words, Azzam had *takfiri* tendencies insofar as he publicly declared certain categories of Muslims as infidels.

Toward the end of *Arab Nationalism* he elaborates on the negative effects of this phenomenon on Muslim societies. In Azzam's view, Arab nationalism separates Arabs from other Muslims, leads to the fragmentation of the Arab world, strengthens Israel, causes "decline in most social, political, economic and military domains," and leads to the "emergence of a generation with no identity and no principles."[49]

Islamic Supremacy

The last book Azzam published in his pre-Afghanistan period was *Islam and the Future of Mankind*, which made the case for Islam's superiority over other belief systems. The introduction is dated 10 October 1980, which means he completed it right around the time when he was expelled from Jordan to Saudi Arabia.[50] He also published two articles in *al-Mujtama'* magazine based on the manuscript.[51]

Islam and the Future of Mankind was probably intended as a work of *da'wa* literature – in other words, a book designed to persuade young people to become practicing Muslims. The book starts from the premise that humanity is in a state of crisis – "a misery from which it can no longer find an escape" – with problems accumulating in multiple domains, and many people experiencing existential angst.[52] Azzam's basic message is that Islam is the only answer to these problems and therefore represents the future of mankind. He offers four main arguments in support of this claim, each of which becomes a section in the book:

1 – this religion is the one that best fits Man and suits his nature;
2 – the breakdown of Western civilization;
3 – the textual tidings in the Book and the prophetic tradition;
4 – the material tidings on the ground and man's return to religion.

These are but the tip of the iceberg of reasons that make us assert that this creed is the oasis in which humanity will find rest.[53]

The most interesting part of the book is arguably the second one, in which he contends that Western civilization is spiritually bankrupt. In this section he quotes a remarkable number of Western thinkers, including Henri Bergson, Georg Hegel, Friedrich Nietzsche, August Comte, Bernard Shaw, Alexis Carrel, Bertrand Russell, Jacob Moreno, Ernest Hemingway, Arthur Schopenhauer, Albert Camus, Arthur Miller, Jean-Paul Sartre, Eugene Ionesco, Martin Heidegger, Søren Kierkegaard, Niccolò Machiavelli, Lloyd Osborne, Colin Wilson, and several others. He quotes so many that one could be forgiven for suspecting that he is namedropping to persuade the reader. While Azzam did read widely, including in the Western intellectual tradition, he likely did not read all these writers. A look at the footnotes suggests that he is relying heavily on secondary sources in Arabic, especially a book titled *Chaos of the World in Contemporary Western Theatre* by Imad al-Din Khalil as well as the books *We and the West* and *Our Road to Victory* by Rachid Ghannouchi.[54]

Azzam offers a very negative assessment of Western thought. Although he never really defines "Western thought" – it is unclear whether he is referring mainly to Christianity, secularism, liberalism, capitalism, or something else – he blames it for a whole range of ills. In his view Western thought has brought little but spiritual emptiness and disasters such as the world wars. The spiritual vacuum in turn has many negative consequences, including but not limited to "alcohol abuse, drug addiction, mental illnesses, rebellion and uncivil behaviour, crime, sexual promiscuity, venereal disease, and suicide."[55] He goes on to cite statistics from the USA and Sweden on several of these phenomena, and he repeats the example of the Beatles and the hippies that he mentioned in his first book, *The Creed*.[56] He goes as far as to say that "in the West, people do not know why they live, as suggested by a poll in America in which people were asked, 'What is your goal in life?', and 80 percent said 'I don't know' and 20 percent said 'To accumulate money.'"[57] Azzam says that intellectuals in the West have begun to understand the vacuousness of their own thinking and have started calling for a return to religion. As evidence he cites statistics showing that 70 percent of members of the Italian Communist Party go to church, and that Pope John Paul was warmly received in Communist Poland in 1979.[58]

Azzam's optimism on Islam's behalf only increases as the book progresses, and toward the end he says, "The Western Crusaders, the Eastern Atheists, and Global Zionism fear the rise of the Islamic movement."[59] As evidence he cites, among other things, Hamilton Gibb's classic 1932 book *Whither Islam*, which, Azzam says, was written "by a group of orientalists who held a conference at Princeton" about the rise of Islamist movements. Azzam also quotes former Israeli prime minister David Ben-Gurion as allegedly saying, "We do not fear socialism or nationalism or kingdoms in the region, but we fear Islam, this giant which has slept for a long time and is starting to wake up in the region. I fear that there will appear another Muhammad in the region." It is not clear whether Ben-Gurion ever actually said this, and it is hard to verify because Azzam is sloppy with the references. In any case, the section is interesting because it puts into sharp relief Azzam's geopolitical worldview, namely that there is a global competition for influence going on between four groups: the Western Crusaders, the Eastern Atheists, the Global Zionists, and the Muslims. Of these, the Zionists (whom Azzam often simply calls "the Jews") are the most dangerous, not least because they conspire with the others against the Muslims. In general it is noteworthy how rarely Azzam speaks of states as independent actors or mentions material resources as an object of competition. It would seem that in his view almost everything that happens in world politics is the result of ideological macro-groups vying for influence. Azzam would probably have warmly embraced Samuel Huntington's notion of a clash of civilizations.

It is important to note that few if any of these views were unique to Azzam. In this period many Muslim Brothers wrote about similar themes and expressed a similar worldview.[60] Azzam's writings in the 1970s are particularly reminiscent of the work of Muhammad Qutb. As Masami Nishino noted, Muhammad Qutb's writings also expressed "a negative view of the history of Western Christianity, Jewish conspiracy theories ... condemnation of modern Western ideologies ... denunciation of the existing regimes in the Middle East, and a worldview in which the US confronts Islam."[61] Azzam, in other words, was intellectually firmly positioned within a Muslim Brotherhood tradition, and he had not yet shown the intellectual independence that he would display in his Afghanistan years.

The Abdallah Azzam who moved to Pakistan in the autumn of 1981 was a man who firmly believed in God, in the truth of the Islamic message, and in the superiority of Islam as a system for organizing society. He was also a man who saw Islam as ideologically and militarily besieged by hostile forces, foremost of which were the Jews and their Communist agents. He also saw the early 1980s as a momentous time when big things were going to be decided, although he was no apocalypticist.

Azzam also arrived in Pakistan as an established writer with at least three books under his belt – five if we include *The Islamic Call* and *Arab Nationalism* – and seven articles in *al-Mujtama'*, the flagship journal of the Muslim Brotherhood. It would be a stretch to say he was famous, but he was probably known to many committed Muslim Brothers in the Middle East, especially in Jordan and Palestine. This publishing record was an asset in several ways: he knew how to write books, he had connections in the publishing world, and he had a certain following. This meant he could get books out quickly once he got to Pakistan, and that his books would be taken more seriously than if he was a first-time author writing from Islamabad. As we shall see, he would indeed hit the ground running.

7 | Pioneer

It was late November 1981 and a mild afternoon when Abdallah Azzam stepped off the plane at Islamabad International Airport.[1] With him were his wife Samira, their seven children, and God knows how much luggage. A representative of the Islamic University of Islamabad greeted them in the arrivals hall and took them to a guest house close to campus. The next day Azzam called Sayyaf's Islamabad office and arranged for a trip to Peshawar the upcoming weekend.[2] Peshawar was where the action was; it was the base of the Afghan Mujahidin parties and the launching pad for most humanitarian and military support operations. The city was not yet the bustling international playground it later became, but the signs of cosmopolitanism were already showing. But what exactly was going on in the Afghan jihad when Azzam arrived? Were there Arabs already, and if so, how had they become involved?

This chapter examines the Arab involvement in the first few years of the Afghanistan war. After a brief look at Azzam's life in Islamabad, it will describe the outreach efforts of the Afghan Mujahidin, the initial Arab response, and the arrival of the first foreign fighters. We will see that Azzam was among the first Arabs to get involved – though not the very first – and that the number of Arab fighters remained low till 1984, in part because nobody was making a concerted effort to recruit them.

Settling in

The Azzam family settled in quickly in Islamabad, where they would live for the next four-and-a-half years. It was a big change. They did not speak the local languages, and Islamabad was as different from Mecca as one could possibly imagine. The Saudi city was hilly, ancient, and spiritual, while Islamabad was flat, artificial, and full of bureaucrats. Built in the 1960s to serve as the young nation's administrative capital, the city was famous for its soullessness.

After some time in university accommodation, the Azzams moved into a house in the F8 sector in northwestern Islamabad, just a couple of kilometers south of the Faisal mosque.[3] It was a residential area with several embassies and a number of Arab families, which probably eased the culture shock for his wife and children. One of Azzam's neighbours was Muhammad Salim al-Hamud (Abu Mazin), a senior official in the Saudi embassy who would later collaborate with Azzam on jihad-related projects in and around Peshawar.[4] There were also other Palestinians, because the PLO mission to Islamabad was in the area. Azzam later boasted that he once had a Palestinian neighbor who hated Islamists, but who changed his view and joined the jihad after being invited to Azzam's house.[5]

For Azzam, Islamabad was just a base, and he sought to spend as much time as possible in Peshawar. A three-hour drive to the northeast, it was too far for a daily commute, so he would go there at weekends, staying at Abd Rabb al-Rasul Sayyaf's house. "He was coming and staying in the nighttime with me in Peshawar, every Thursday he was coming and Friday he was going back to Islamabad," Sayyaf later said.[6] Jamal Isma'il, a Palestinian student in Peshawar at the time, said:

> From '81 to '84 I was seeing him whenever he came to give *jum'a* prayer in Peshawar. Minimum once a month, sometimes four Fridays in a month. There was no specified mosque. In the Student Union we had *jum'a* prayer, sometimes he would come there. To the Center for Arab Students. He would come to Peshawar on Thursdays. He would call in the day before and say, "Tomorrow I'm giving a speech."[7]

He would later compress his teaching commitments into the first few days of the week (Saturday, Sunday, and Monday) so that he could leave for Peshawar on Monday afternoon and stay until Friday.[8] In 1984 he compressed it further: "I took a sabbatical to join the jihad. I only went to the university in Islamabad on Saturdays and Sundays, while spending the rest of the week either in Peshawar or on the nearby fronts."[9] Azzam occasionally also brought his family to Peshawar in the early years. He wanted them to see the refugee camps and get a sense of what was going on. As we shall see in Chapter 13 the entire household would get involved with the jihad in one way or another.[10]

Azzam would have spent more time in Peshawar were it not for his new job as lecturer in the faculty of Shari'a in the Islamic University of

Islamabad (IUI). It was difficult to sneak away, because at this time the IUI was a small operation. It had been set up only a year previously, in November 1980, with an enrollment of just nine students in the first semester.[11] When Azzam arrived there were only about 200 students.[12] It did not yet have its own campus, but was based within Qaid-e Azam University in northeastern Islamabad. Only when the King Faisal mosque complex neared completion in the mid-1980s did the Islamic University get its own premises under the mosque courtyard. The complex, known today as the old campus, is located at a beautiful site at the foot of the Margalla hills in northwest Islamabad.

The university expanded quickly in the first half of the 1980s, because it was a prestige project of Pakistani president Zia ul Haq's and a key part of his Islamization policy. The IUI had been set up to offer a modern place of higher Islamic learning in the country's capital, as a supplement to the traditional religious schools in other parts of Pakistan. It brought together several smaller institutes, such as the Institute of Shari'a in Qaid-e Azam University, the Islamic Research Institute, and the Institute of Languages.[13] Part of the mission was to bridge the secular and religious higher education systems so that future Pakistani civil servants could study subjects such as engineering and management while still getting a good Islamic education. Another part of the mission was to streamline the training of preachers who could proselytize across Pakistan and beyond.

The IUI also had an international mission; it was intended as an Asian version of the International Islamic University of Medina, which for years had attracted students from around the world. In 1985 the IUI would therefore be renamed the International Islamic University of Islamabad (IIUI). According to a former student, about a third of the approximately 200 faculty were from the Arab world, primarily Egypt, and most worked in the religious departments.[14] Of the 800–900 students in the mid-1980s, some 60 percent were foreigners. Most were from Asia, but there were also around fifty Arabs.[15]

The funding was also international. For starters, Saudi Arabia had paid for the construction of the entire King Faisal mosque complex, at an estimated cost of over 130 million Saudi riyals.[16] Another source of external funding was the salaries of foreign staff, because visiting Arab faculty were "sponsored teachers" paid by their home institutions.[17] Azzam, who was technically on loan, thus received his salary from King Abd al-Aziz University in Jeddah until he left the IIUI in 1986.

Aside from providing a stable income, the Islamic University was a good fit for Azzam in several ways. The philosophy behind it – offering Islamic education adapted to the modern world – was in line with his own Muslim Brotherhood-inspired thinking about religious education. Perhaps for the same reason, several of the Pakistani professors had links to the Jamaat-e Islami, the Muslim Brotherhood's Pakistani sister organization. Moreover, the IUI placed great emphasis on training preachers for *da'wa* work, one of Azzam's pet interests. Finally, the university's international profile suited Azzam's pan-Islamist worldview.

Azzam taught mainly Islamic jurisprudence plus some Arabic language classes.[18] He taught all his classes in Arabic, which was common in the Shari'a faculty (elsewhere in the university the main language of instruction was English). He did not teach any courses explicitly about politics, such as the one he had taught at Jordan University, but he would often find a way to talk about politics in his lectures on Islamic Law; he struck one Pakistani student as having a vast knowledge about the situation in various Muslim countries around the world.[19] The same student said that the university sometimes organized trips to the Afghan refugee camps around Peshawar, and that Azzam was the only teacher who went with the students.[20]

Azzam's signature down-to-earth teaching style made him popular with students.[21] "His house in Islamabad was open to everybody," one former student said. "I saw brothers from Africa and the Philippines in there; he was helping the brothers getting ready to start university."[22] According to Abdallah Anas, who arrived in Islamabad in 1983:

Studying with Abdallah Azzam did not involve academic hours. Studying with him was a process. Studying with him was a lifestyle. The class or topic he was teaching at the university, if there wasn't enough time and the bell rang etc., you wouldn't see him two days later for him to finish explaining; no, the students would follow him back to his house. And he never got bored or exhausted. He had Turkish students, Malaysian students, Arab students, Egyptians, Syrians, Iraqis – the university in Islamabad was full of nationalities. People like Secretary Necmettin Erbakan, Umar al-Faruq can testify to this ... so at his house you'd find five to ten people, drinking, eating, discussing.[23]

A former student remembered him as extremely punctual, and as someone who never canceled classes, in spite of his frequent travels.[24] He even took the time to personally reply to letters from prospective students asking about how to enroll.[25] As far as we know, Azzam also got along well with his colleagues and the university administration during his tenure at IUI. He could probably have had a long career there if he had not been preoccupied with the war in Afghanistan.[26]

Vicious Conflict

When Azzam arrived, the Soviet–Afghan war had been going on for almost two years. In fact, there had been conflict in Afghanistan for much longer. The situation had started deteriorating in 1973, when Muhammad Dawud Khan, a left-leaning Pashtun nationalist, overturned the Afghan monarchy and introduced controversial economic and social reforms. He succeeded in little other than accumulating enemies at home and abroad, and by the mid-1970s he faced opposition from both Islamists and Communists, the former backed by Pakistan and the latter supported by the Soviet Union. The Islamist opposition became known as the Mujahidin, and enjoyed a safe haven in Peshawar from the mid-1970s onward.

The Mujahidin remained weak until April 1978 when the Afghan Communist Party deposed Dawud in the so-called Saur Revolution. Under the leadership of Nur Muhammad Taraki, the Afghan Communists – whom Olivier Roy compared to the Pol Pot regime in Cambodia – introduced radical agrarian reforms and other laws that were deeply unpopular in the countryside.[27] The regime handled dissent with ruthless repression. Real and imagined opposition activists were detained, tortured, and executed on a massive scale. In 1978 and 1979 alone, between 50,000 and 100,000 Afghan citizens disappeared in the crackdowns. As a result, armed opposition began to grow in the summer of 1978, gained momentum the following spring, and became a full-blown insurgency by the autumn of 1979.

It was to quell this insurgency and save the Communist regime that the Red Army intervened on Christmas Eve 1979 and installed their protégé Babrak Karmal. However, the Soviet intervention turned the conflict into a whole different ballgame. It was no longer an obscure civil war, but an international conflict of major geopolitical consequence. The invasion also poured fuel on the fire of the insurgency, because the conflict was now perceived by Afghans as a fight against foreign occupation and not just a domestic power dispute.

With more fighting came more civilian suffering, especially since the Soviet approach to counterinsurgency was so heavy-handed that one scholar called it a strategy of "rubbleization."[28] Carpet bombings, razed villages, mass executions, torture, starvation, disease, and landmines caused horrific casualties and created masses of refugees. Astonishingly for a country with high birth rates, Afghanistan's population actually declined during the war from 13.3 million 1979 to 11.5 million in 1987.[29] Within a year of the invasion some 1.4 million Afghans had fled to the refugee camps of Peshawar. By the end of the decade between 1 and 2 million Afghans were dead and around 7.5 million – over half the population – was displaced.[30] Thus by the time Azzam arrived, the Afghanistan war had been world news for quite some time.

Afghan Outreach

International awareness of the war had been further increased by the outreach efforts of the Afghan Mujahidin. From the mid-1970s the Afghan Islamist opposition had been reaching out to the outside world for money, weapons, and diplomatic support. It was not a coordinated operation, because the various Mujahidin parties ran parallel initiatives, partly in competition with one another, but the combined international footprint was considerable. They targeted two main regions: the Arab world and the West, playing the Muslim solidarity card in the former and the anti-Communist card in the latter.

Although the Afghan jihad was widely perceived in the West as a national liberation struggle, the Afghan Mujahidin neither presented nor saw themselves simply as a nationalist movement in need of external support. Instead, their external messaging emphasized the global ramifications of the war and the Afghan people's membership in wider transnational communities, especially that of the *umma* – the Muslim nation. To Muslim audiences, the Mujahidin played up Afghanistan's centuries-old connections to the rest of the Muslim world, the global threat from Communism, and the historical, almost cosmic, significance of the conflict. As Simon Wolfgang Fuchs put it, "they considered it a pioneering effort with implications for all other Muslim contexts that would expand on the achievements of the Iranian Revolution."[31] Another theme in their messaging was the Afghan people's bravery under material destitution; here was a poor but pious nation facing up to a technologically advanced superpower. Aside from showing their moral fiber, this image suggested that the Afghan people had no ulterior material motive; all they wanted was for Islam to be victorious. They just needed a little help from their more fortunate Muslim friends.

Their outreach strategy had several elements, the most basic of which was to travel and speak about the situation in Afghanistan. The Gulf was a particularly important destination. Here is a list of some of the visits made by Mujahidin representatives in the 1979–1981 period:

- In February and March 1979, an Afghan named Muhammed Alim visited Kuwait, where he gave interviews with *al-Siyasa* and other newspapers and "conferred with a number of prominent Kuwaiti personalities including the Kuwaiti minister for Islamic affairs sheikh Jassem al-Hajji."[32]
- In April 1979 Jalaluddin Haqqani sent a delegation of Afghans to Abu Dhabi in the United Arab Emirates.[33]
- In mid-June 1979 Burhanuddin Rabbani went to Jeddah and gave talks and interviews to the *al-Medina*, *al-Riyadh*, and *Saudi Gazette* newspapers.[34]
- In the spring of 1980 a large delegation led by Abd Rabb al-Rasul Sayyaf visited the UAE and other Gulf countries. During the trip, "the delegation made direct contact with Arabs in the Gulf who came to support the Afghan jihad."[35]
- In October 1980 Sayyaf went to Mecca for the Hajj season and delivered a prominent speech at one of the conferences organized by the Muslim World League.[36]
- In December 1980 several Mujahidin representatives were present at the founding meeting of the short-lived Islamic People's League in Cairo.[37]
- In late January 1981 Sayyaf spoke at the third Islamic Summit Conference in Ta'if, which gathered the foreign ministers of all Muslim-majority countries.[38]
- In October 1981 Sayyaf again went to Mecca to speak at MWL events. It was on this trip that he met Azzam (see Chapter 5).

It was not only senior Mujahidin commanders who traveled abroad like this. Sometimes ordinary Afghan expatriates in the Gulf were tasked with fundraising. Alex Strick van Linschoten interviewed an Afghan who had worked in Kuwait in the late 1970s and who, on a visit to Quetta in 1979, was given a letter from the Mujahidin parties with which to raise funds in Kuwait. After one month in Kuwait he had collected around $25,000, 200 pairs of shoes, and 300 blankets, and been given a six-month visa for Kuwait to continue his work.[39]

A second element of the strategy was to set up information offices abroad that could lobby, fundraise, and disseminate publications. Starting in the late 1970s the main Mujahidin parties set up offices in many countries around the world, including in the Gulf.[40] In mid-1978, for example, Jalaluddin Haqqani sent several representatives to Saudi Arabia and United Arab Emirates to establish information offices.[41] By 1980 those representatives had set up, among other things, a donor program to support the families of Afghan fighters killed on Haqqani's fronts.[42] Similar offices existed in other Gulf countries; in one source we read of a certain Muhammad Sadiq Qurashi who served as the "representative of the Afghan Mujahidin in Kuwait."[43] In the West, the network of Mujahidin information offices was even larger. As early as 1977 Afghans in Karlsruhe and Bochum in Germany had started publishing anti-Communist newsletters in Dari and Pashto. In 1980 pro-Hekmatyar activists set up the Information Bureau of Afghan Mujahidin in Bonn in Germany. This organization was very active throughout the war, and it made Bonn the center of gravity of the Mujahidin's information apparatus in the West. By the mid-1980s numerous other offices had emerged across Europe and the USA.[44] The Mujahidin also established information offices in Pakistan that specialized in conveying news from Afghanistan to an international audience. Early examples include the Afghan Information Center (established in 1980), Afghan Islamic Press (1982), and the Cultural Council of Afghanistan Jihad (1983).

A third key element of the outreach strategy was publications. The Afghan Mujahidin were extremely prolific; they published somewhere between 200 and 300 different magazine titles during the 1980s.[45] Most were in Dari and Pashto and for Afghan consumption, but at least forty-five magazines were in foreign languages: twenty-two in Arabic, fifteen in English, three in Turkish, and one each in Russian, French, German, Dutch, and Danish.[46] Most of the pro-Mujahidin magazines were published in the late 1980s, but by 1984 there were already ten different foreign-language magazines: five in Arabic, four in English, and one in Turkish. Thanks to generous external funding, several of the magazines were lavishly produced, with plenty of color photographs.[47]

By late 1981 no less than three Arabic-language Mujahidin magazines were available in the Gulf. The first was *al-Mawqif* (the Stance), a monthly magazine produced from as early as 1979 by a Hekmatyar-affiliated Afghan student in Mecca named Muhammad Zaman Muzamil.[48] The second was the monthly *al-Nafir al-Amm* (the General March), which was published from February 1981 by the administration of the new Ittihad government.[49] It was produced in Peshawar, printed in Lahore, and distributed for free in the Gulf countries. Muzamil, who was involved in this magazine as well, said they used the same address list they had compiled for the distribution of *al-Mawqif*. The third early magazine was *Sawt al-Jihad* (the Voice of Jihad), published from July 1981 by Rabbani's Jamiat-e Islami.[50] It was also produced in Peshawar, printed in Lahore, and distributed in the Gulf. According to Ahmad Zaidan, the "administration of fatwa in Saudi Arabia"[51] subscribed to 1,000 copies of every issue.

The Mujahidin also produced audiovisual propaganda from the start. For example, on his trip to Jeddah in 1979 Rabbani brought pictures of destroyed Afghan villages which he gave to *al-Medina* newspaper for publication.[52] Starting in 1981 if not before, the Mujahidin would also produce videos that could be screened abroad in connection with fundraising rallies and the like.[53] Dozens of such videos would be produced in the course of the 1980s. For example, in 1986 Sayyaf's magazine *al-Bunyan al-Marsus* included an advertisement for the fifth Arabic-language film in a series called "al-Shahada," complete with screenshots and the teaser phrase "Martyr stories ... virgins of paradise ... and the smell of musk."[54]

A fourth element of the strategy was accessibility to visitors. Especially in the early days of the war, the Afghan Mujahidin parties went to great lengths to accommodate visitors who turned up at their offices in Peshawar. Both Arabs and Westerners could turn up in the city unannounced and obtain meetings with most Mujahidin parties in a matter of days. Realizing that good "customer service" could help sway donors and other supporters, the big parties had a dedicated infrastructure for visitor reception, complete with reception rooms, interpreters and guides to show people around refugee camps, and the like. Jere Van Dyk, for example, went to a refugee camp in Peshawar in October 1981 to find that it already had a person whose job was to show visitors around.[55]

The early outreach efforts were helped by the many preexisting links between the Mujahidin and the Arab world.[56] The oldest links were with the Muslim Brotherhood in Egypt, but in the 1970s the connections with the Gulf had grown stronger. One reason was the expanding education sector in Saudi Arabia, which brought a good number of Afghan students to the kingdom in the 1970s, several of whom later joined the Mujahidin.[57] Another mechanism was the international Islamic organizations such as the Muslim World League, which had brought several Afghans to their meetings in Saudi Arabia in the 1970s and also counted some Afghans among their employees.[58] In addition, pilgrimage brought hundreds of Afghans to Mecca every year, and the 1970s oil boom had spurred labour migration from Afghanistan to the Gulf.

Links went in the other direction, too, in the form of Arabs who had spent time in Afghanistan or Pakistan before the war. A steady trickle of Arab preachers had come for *da'wa* work inside Afghanistan, and hundreds of Arab students had attended Pakistani universities in the 1970s. In 1981 there were notably between 150 and 200 Arab students at the University of Peshawar, mostly from low-income countries such as Sudan, Egypt, Yemen, Iraq, Syria, Jordan, and Palestine.[59] The Palestinians in Pakistan were from above average politically active families, because the PLO paid for the education of siblings of fallen fighters.[60] As we shall see in Chapter 9, some of them became involved in the early running of Abdallah Azzam's Services Bureau.

The Afghan Mujahidin's outreach machinery had thus been up and running for some time when Azzam arrived. Substantial numbers of people in the Arab world would have heard of the suffering of the Afghan people, the heroic resistance of the Mujahidin, and their pleas for material and financial support.

Pan-Islamist Response

The audience that responded first and most enthusiastically to these pleas were the pan-Islamists – the Islamic internationalists described in Chapter 5. The Soviet invasion pushed all their buttons; here was a veritable takeover of a Muslim country by an infidel superpower, horrific war crimes against defenseless civilians, and a humanitarian crisis of massive proportions. In addition, the local resistance force was dominated by Islamists, making Afghanistan an almost perfect arena for pan-Islamic solidarity displays.

Private donors were among the first to go. Soon after the invasion, wealthy Gulf Arabs started traveling to Pakistan to give money for relief work or to the Mujahidin. Some went to Lahore or Islamabad to give money to the Pakistani Islamist group Jamaat-e-Islami. One of these early donors was Usama Bin Ladin, as we shall see in Chapter 9. Another was a Kuwaiti named Abdallah al-Mutawwa' (aka Abu Badr) who "would pay Jamaat-e Islami in Pakistan and tell them to spend it as they see fit, because they were at the forefront of events, and because Hekmatyar had the biggest number of fighters, and he was one of the members of Islamic Movement."[61] Other donors went straight to Peshawar to hand over cash to refugee-camp administrators or to Mujahidin parties. When Jere Van Dyk visited a refugee camp in 1981, his guide boasted that "the Saudi Arabians and our other brothers give us so much money."[62] The French journalist Edward Girardet, who was in Peshawar from 1979 onward, later wrote:

Within days [of the invasion] money and humanitarian aid was flowing in. Businessmen from Saudi Arabia and the Gulf dressed in their white thaubs with red-and-white keffieh headdresses often flew into Peshawar to disperse relief or cash in person among the refugees ... I often encountered Arabs in the offices of the mujahideen with their luxury four-by-four, tinted glass vehicles parked outside. Such generosity quickly became more organized with the establishment of new Islamic aid agencies.[63]

Another category of early movers was the charity workers. The first Arab-run Islamic charities in Peshawar were the Saudi Red Crescent (SRC) and the Kuwaiti Red Crescent (KRC), which began operating in November 1980 and in mid-1981 respectively.[64] They were followed by the International Islamic Relief Organization (IIRO) in 1983, and then by several other organizations from 1984 onward. Although these organizations handled large sums of money, their permanent Arab staff was small; in the early years they probably counted dozens of people.

We know little about the early charity workers except Nasir al-Rashid, who was the first director of the Saudi Red Crescent in Peshawar.[65] He had been treasurer at the SRC's central office, and moved to Peshawar very early, probably in 1980, and he became something of a legend in the Afghan Arab community.[66] Azzam's book *Signs of the Merciful* (1983) praises al-Rashid for supporting Mujahidin combat units directly. Azzam writes that al-Rashid had used his personal funds to purchase 1,000 tents with blankets for the Mujahidin after seeing 4,000 fighters in the Warsak camp during the winter with no tents or blankets.[67] He did the same again for the fighters in the Abu Bakr al-Siddiq camp, where 2,500 Mujahidin were stuck in the winter with no shelter or blankets.

A few Arab doctors also came in the early years to work in clinics and hospitals in the Peshawar area. One of the first was Ayman al-Zawahiri, the Egyptian doctor and subsequent al-Qaida leader, who spent two months in Peshawar in mid-1980:

My connection with Afghanistan began in the summer of 1980 by a twist of fate, when I was temporarily filling in for one of my colleagues at Al Sayyidah Zaynab Clinic [in Cairo]. One night the clinic director asked me if I would like to travel to Pakistan to contribute, through my work as a surgeon, to the medical relief effort among the Afghan refugees. I immediately agreed because I saw this as an opportunity to get to know one of the arenas of jihad that might be a base for jihad in Egypt and the Arab region ... I left for Peshawar, Pakistan, in the company of a colleague who was an anesthetist. We were soon followed by another colleague who specialized in plastic surgery. We were the first three Arabs to arrive there to participate in relief work among the Afghan refugees.[68]

Later, al-Zawahiri would move to Peshawar and work for several years in the Kuwaiti Red Crescent hospital, as we shall see in Chapter 14.

A third major player to take an early interest in the Afghan jihad was the Muslim World League (MWL). As the pan-Islamist organization par excellence, the MWL had followed the situation in Afghanistan closely, and when the Russians invaded it moved fast to whip up support for the Mujahidin. Its conferences in Kuala Lumpur in January 1980 and in Mecca in June both passed resolutions describing the fight against the Soviet occupation as a jihad and calling for the international Muslim community to support it with "all types of material and financial assistance."[69]

Interestingly and importantly, the MWL's rhetoric on Afghanistan in 1980 had strong military overtones. At the MWL conference in Kuala Lumpur on 11–14 January 1980, the participants agreed on eight points; they

1) condemned the Soviet invasion;
2) called for an immediate withdrawal;

3) called on Muslims in the Soviet Union to put pressure on their government;
4) called on all Muslims to condemn [this] "humiliation of the Muslim Umma";
5) expressed support for the Afghan people in their jihad;
6) called on the international community to not recognize any new "collaborator regime" in Afghanistan;
7) called on the MWL, the OIC, and other Islamic organizations to "mobilize all the resources of the Muslim *umma* and supply the Afghan people with all types of material and financial assistance in their heroic jihad";
8) called on the MWL in Mecca "to take all necessary measures, and, as quickly as possible, organize a conference for all the world's Islamic organizations to discuss what practical measures need to be taken."[70]

The next MWL conference was in Mecca in June 1980, and here the war rhetoric was even more explicit.[71] There were four agenda points: (1) Islamic solidarity; (2) Islam in confrontation with contemporary ideological currents; (3) jihad; and (4) Islamic *da'wa*. This was the first time in the history of MWL conferences that a major agenda point was explicitly titled "jihad."[72] Moreover, one of the resolutions under the topic "Islamic Solidarity" called on Muslim states "to incite a spirit of jihad in the Islamic armies, to set up coordination mechanisms between them, and to establish joint war materiel production, so that the Muslim *umma* is able to defend itself, protect its rights, and repel the aggression against its lands."[73]

These statements show that the MWL's rhetoric about Islamic solidarity became more militaristic around 1980. Islamic solidarity was no longer just about providing aid, but also military support. In the past the MWL had used fiery rhetoric, especially on the Palestinian issue, but it had never gone as far as to explicitly propose joint military operations and coordination of weapons industries. It is also worth noting that, in 1981, when the MWL published a book to mark its twentieth anniversary, the title was *The Muslim World League: Twenty Years on the Road of Da'wa and Jihad*.[74] The militarization of the MWL's rhetoric is significant because it helps explain why Abdallah Azzam's foreign-fighter doctrine would come to resonate so strongly in the 1980s.

In the summer of 1981 the MWL dispatched a high-level delegation to Pakistan to find out more about the situation. One of the delegates, a certain Muhammad al-Majdhub, later wrote a book about his experiences, titled *Unforgettable Memories with the Mujahidin and the Emigrants in Afghanistan*.[75] It offers a detailed description of Peshawar some four months before Azzam arrived, and is thus worth rendering here in some detail.

Al-Majdhub was a seventy-four-year-old Syrian who combined his job as a professor at the University of Medina with international *da'wa* work for the MWL. In the summer of 1981 he had been scheduled to go to Indonesia to train local preachers. The trip was canceled at the last minute, and al-Majdhub was asked instead to accompany the deputy director of MWL and two others on a trip to Peshawar. The delegation consisted of Muhammad al-Majdhub, Sheikh Ali Mushrif al-Amri, and Sheikh Abdallah al-Sanyur. On 2 July 1981 they flew from Medina to Jeddah and on to Karachi, and by car from there to Peshawar.

On arrival they checked in at Green's hotel, where they noticed several Westerners among the other guests.[76] The first afternoon, while strolling outside, they were approached by a Palestinian-Jordanian medical student at the University of Peshawar who had overheard them speaking Arabic. He had been there for several years, and told them about the situation. The next morning a group of seven Afghan sheikhs showed up unsolicited to their hotel. They spoke Arabic and wanted to talk about the process of unifying the Afghan organizations. The Afghans also said that a delegation from Saudi Arabia had arrived a few days earlier to help mediate between them.[77]

Over the next week or so, Majdhub and his colleagues met with almost all the Afghan Mujahidin leaders at their respective headquarters: Yunus Khalis, Abd Rabb al-Rasul Sayyaf, Nasrallah Mansur, Muhammad Nabi, Ahmad Gailani, Sibghatullah Mujaddidi, Burhanuddin Rabbani, and Gulbuddin Hekmatyar – in that order. They knew Sayyaf already, because they had attended the Islamic Summit Conference in Ta'if in January 1981, where Sayyaf had spoken.[78] The MWL representatives were disappointed at the level of discord and backstabbing between the leaders. Khalis told them there had been fighting between the Afghan factions in Afghanistan, which shocked them. Sayyaf criticized two of the parties in the union vehemently – Majdhub does not say which ones – accusing one of them of corruption.[79] Mansur spoke extensively about his disagreement with

Nabi and his reasons for leaving the Harakat. Nabi, for his part, went on about how bad Hekmatyar was. Hekmatyar, who, unlike most of the others spoke to them through a translator, struck them as less sympathetic than the others.

During their two- or three-week stay in Peshawar, Majdhub and his colleagues also visited a refugee camp, attended Friday prayers at different mosques, and toured Peshawar University. They also visited a military camp in the Peshawar area belonging to one of the two Hizb-e Islami parties (Majdhub does not specify which). In the camp they met several Arabic-speaking Afghans who had studied or worked in Saudi Arabia. Done with Peshawar, Majdhub and his colleagues headed to Lahore, where they visited some of the Saudi-funded religious schools, before heading to Karachi and then back to Saudi Arabia. It is worth noting that the Peshawar visit takes up only about half the book, and that Majdhub is also very interested in the educational and *da'wa* activities in Lahore. He was not, in other words, exclusively interested in the Afghan jihad the way Azzam and others would become. If anything, Majdhub left Pakistan disappointed with the infighting and lack of coordination between the Mujahidin parties. Still, the MWL would later expand its operations in Peshawar, first in 1983 by deploying the International Islamic Relief Organization, and later, in 1985, by setting up a regular MWL office. The MWL also kept monitoring and publishing about the Afghan jihad throughout the decade.

Another actor to get involved early was the Egyptian Muslim Brotherhood, which had longstanding connections to Afghan Islamists and an increasingly pan-Islamist worldview. As we shall see in later chapters, the Brotherhood would provide extensive political and humanitarian support to the Afghan jihad, but was careful not to get directly implicated in foreign-fighter recruitment and other military activities. The involvement began in mid-1980, when, as we saw in Chapter 5, the Office of the Supreme Guide dispatched Kamal al-Sananiri to Pakistan to help negotiate between the Afghan Mujahidin leaders and assess the prospects for further Brotherhood involvement.[80] (One source suggests that al-Sananiri may have gone to Afghanistan as early as 1978 or 1979, but this is unconfirmed.[81]) Al-Sananiri's contact point in Pakistan was the Brotherhood's sister organization in Pakistan, the Jamaat-e Islami. He stayed in their guest house in Peshawar, and was accompanied much of the time by Khalil al-Hamidi, a Jamaat-e Islami official who spoke fluent Arabic.[82] Al-Hamidi was something of an ambassador to the Arab world within Jamaat-e Islami; he had previously translated Abu A'la al-Mawdudi's works into Arabic, and he used to go to Mecca for Hajj each year as a representative of Jamaat-e Islami.[83] Another key initial contact was Abd Rabb al-Rasul Sayyaf, whom al-Sananiri had met in Mecca before going to Pakistan. The two men met four or five times in Peshawar as part of al-Sananiri's tour of the various Mujahidin party offices.[84] According to Azzam, al-Sananiri "stayed for forty days trying to unite the four factions: Hekmatyar, Rabbani, Khalis, Sayyaf, and almost reached a solution."[85]

In the spring of 1981 al-Sananiri went back to Peshawar again, and it was on the way to and from this trip that he met Azzam, first in Jeddah and then in Mecca, as we saw in Chapter 5. On this second trip he appears to have led a delegation of Muslim Brothers that included, among others, the Jordanian Dhib Anis.[86] This time he stayed three or four months in Pakistan, focusing on mediating between the Afghan Mujahidin party leaders.[87] Al-Sananiri was well liked by the Mujahidin leaders. Later in 1981, when al-Sananiri died in an Egyptian prison, the Afghan Mujahidin organized a memorial service in the Mahabbat Khan mosque attended by hundreds of people.[88] Sayyaf's magazine *al-Bunyan al-Marsus* later published an article about him as well as a book review of the poetry collection by his widow, Amina Qutb.[89] There are many similarities between al-Sananiri and Azzam in terms of the role they played on the political scene in Peshawar. As we shall see in the next chapter, Azzam would take over where al-Sananiri had left off in terms of serving as the main Arab negotiator between the Afghan Mujahidin.

It was not only al-Sananiri and Azzam who would serve as negotiators. Several other Muslim Brothers took part in the various unification processes between the Afghan Mujahidin in the first half of the 1980s. As one Brotherhood historian noted, "[Azzam] worked to bring together the leaders of the Mujahidin and to unite their ranks, in cooperation with preachers from the Brotherhood such as Muhammad Kamal al-Din al-Sananiri, Ahmad al-Malt, Mustafa Mashhur, Muhammad Abd al-Rahman Khalifa, Sa'id Hawa, and others."[90] The main negotiation event was in 1984, when the unification process had come to a complete standstill. A group of senior Arabs in Peshawar proposed appointing an international committee of senior clerics to choose a leader for the union. The Mujahidin grudgingly agreed, and a committee of seventeen scholars from the

Middle East was invited to Peshawar. The committee consisted almost entirely of Muslim Brotherhood-linked figures, including Abu Badr al-Mutawwa' (Kuwait), Ahmad Bazigh al-Yasin (Kuwait), Yusuf al-Fulayj (Kuwait), Saqr al-Murri (UAE), Abd al-Rahman al-Jawdar (Bahrain), Abd al-Majid al-Zindani (Yemen), Abdallah al-Zayid (Saudi), Abd al-Ilah al-Mu'ayyad (Saudi), Yusuf al-Azm (Jordan), Mustafa Mashhur (Egypt), Abdallah al-Ansari (Qatar), Isa bin Abdallah Al Khalifa (Bahrain), Muhammad Salih al-Rayyis (UAE), and Muhammad Mahmud al-Sawwaf (Syria).[91] These men came to Peshawar and deliberated for an entire month before choosing Abd Rabb al-Rasul Sayyaf. They had the Mujahidin leaders sign a paper in advance promising to respect whatever decision was made, but this did not prevent the union from breaking up again shortly afterward. Azzam was later critical of the involvement of the seventeen Arab scholars in 1984:

When the committee of seventeen came to examine the affair of the union, I told them, "Brothers, do you want the union or do you want jihad? The jihad is now dissolving and weakened, because this man" – and I pointed to Hekmatyar who was present, as was Sayyaf – "this man cannot find food for his fronts. So support the union, and support the jihad." However, the brothers were insisting on the union ... They paid millions of dollars to the union, and then they left.[92]

A last Arab attempt at keeping to the alliance together was made in November 1984, again with Brotherhood figures involved.[93] This time the committee was smaller and the members more senior. It included the Great Imam of Mecca, a few old-guard Muslim Brothers, and officials from the Saudi embassy in Islamabad. This time they succeeded, albeit with a different, less ambitious unification agenda. Instead of having one leader, the new organization, to be called the World Alliance for the Liberation of Afghanistan, would have a joint leadership consisting of Sayyaf, Rabbani, Hekmatyar, and Yunus Khalis. This model would stay in place for several years. Even though these negotiation processes were no resounding success, the Brotherhood maintained close links with the four Islamist Mujahidin parties, especially that of Sayyaf. A good indication of their ties was when the Brotherhood's supreme guide Omar al-Tilmisani died in 1986 and *al-Bunyan al-Marsus* published a full-page condolence notice where the text was superimposed on a large image of al-Tilmisani's face.[94]

Later in the 1980s the Brotherhood's main role in Peshawar was as a provider of humanitarian support. Around 1984 the Egyptian

Brotherhood gained control of the Egyptian Doctors' Syndicate, which enabled it to deploy medical resources to Pakistan in a more systematic way.[95] Over the following years the Brotherhood developed a strong presence in the Islamic NGO sector in Peshawar. According to the Libyan former Afghan Arab Noman Benothman, "all the NGOs and sources of money were controlled by the Muslim Brotherhood"; this is likely an exaggeration, but the Brotherhood was indeed prominently represented.[96] Writing about MWL activities in early 1980s Peshawar, Gilles Dorronsoro noted that "local employees were generally identified with the Muslim Brotherhood. Additionally, the Saudi Red Crescent was funded directly by the Saudi government, but here too the personnel often belonged to the Muslim Brotherhood tendency."[97] In the late 1980s the Brotherhood's main representative in Peshawar was the Egyptian Kamal al-Helbawy, who by his own account was in charge of all the Brotherhood's activities in Peshawar from 1988 to the early 1990s.[98] Another important Brotherhood representative in Pakistan was the Egyptian Ahmad al-Assal, who worked at the International Islamic University of Islamabad, later becoming its director.[99]

The Brotherhood also raised awareness about the Afghan cause through publications. Brotherhood-linked magazines such as *al-Mujtama'* reported from Afghanistan even before the Soviet intervention. In May 1979 it published a story titled "With our Brother Mujahidin of Afghanistan, in Pictures," and in June 1979 it devoted the front page to Afghanistan with the headline "The Islamic Revolution in Afghanistan: Between Starting Point and Objective."[100] *Al-Mujtama'* kept covering Afghanistan in detail throughout the war, as did other Islamist magazines such as *Liwa' al-Islam, al-Balagh, al-Nur, al-Akhbar*, and *al-Muslimun*.[101] In addition, several prominent Brotherhood figures would also write books and articles about the Afghan jihad. In the early years the Palestinian-Kuwaiti sheikh Ahmad al-Qattan wrote influential books about Afghanistan, and later Muhammad Qutb followed suit.[102]

This is why many of the Arabs who did become involved in military activities had a Muslim Brotherhood background. In many cases these were young people who had frequented Muslim Brotherhood circles, but were not strictly speaking members or Brotherhood representatives. In other cases it was members who simply disobeyed the official guidelines and left for Afghanistan on their own.[103] In a few cases they were Brotherhood members who had come to Peshawar for humanitarian work, but who "sneaked to battlegrounds, fought, and returned before being busted."[104] Thus the Muslim Brotherhood played a very important role in facilitating the Afghan Arab mobilization. As Mustafa Hamid put it, "Yes, Azzam was Ikhwan, Sayyaf was the leader of Ikhwan in Afghanistan and Maktab al-Khadamat was essentially an Ikhwan project. Abu Abdullah [Usama Bin Ladin] too was initially Ikhwan."[105] However, as we shall see in the next chapter, the Brotherhood as an organization was careful not to get directly involved in the recruitment of fighters.

The First Fighters

Some Arabs also came to fight in the first few years of the war, but they were few in number and we know little about them. There are two main ways to reconstruct the early flow of war volunteers. One is to collect snapshot assessments by informed observers of the size of the Arab contingent before 1985. I collected twenty-two such assessments, most of which suggest that we are dealing with dozens rather than hundreds of individuals. The other estimation strategy consists of collecting data on individuals who are documented as having been present in the early years. I compiled a dataset with the names and arrival dates of as many early Afghan Arabs in combat roles as I could find in the sources. I found references to ninety individuals who arrived at some point between mid-1978 and the end of 1984. If we break down this group of ninety confirmed individuals by year of reported arrival, we get seven in 1979, one in 1980, nineteen in 1981, one in 1982, seven in 1983, and fifty-six in 1984. In combination, these data suggest that Arab fighters were on the ground from as early as 1979, but that their numbers did not exceed 100 until 1984. When Azzam arrived in late 1981, roughly twenty-five Arabs had already gone to Afghanistan to fight, but most of them had stayed only a short while.

It is unclear who the very first Arab fighters in Afghanistan were. One candidate is an unidentified "small group of young men," who, according to Mustafa Hamid, "took part in battles in Afghanistan" as early as mid-1978.[106] Another is Mustafa Hamid himself (see below), who by his own account spent a month and a half in Paktika and Paktia with two other Egyptian friends in the summer of 1979. It is not clear, however, whether they participated in combat on this trip. A third candidate is a certain "Hamdi," an

Egyptian former combat pilot who is described in one source as "maybe the first Arab to ever set foot on the land of the Afghan jihad."[107] He reportedly joined the Mujahidin "at the beginning of the Soviet invasion," that is, in early 1980, and stayed in the field for about four years until he was severely wounded. A fourth candidate is Isam Abd al-Hakim, a Tunisian student in France who went to Afghanistan in 1980 and fought in Khost and Paghman before being captured in 1983 by Afghan Communist forces and spending five years in prison in Kabul.[108] He is described in one source as "the first Arab *mujahid* in all of Afghanistan," but Abd al-Hakim himself later said in an interview that there had been two other Arabs before him.[109] A fifth candidate is Rachid Rochman (or Rashid al-Rahman), an Egyptian ex-officer who met the American journalist Jere Van Dyk in October 1981 among Haqqani's forces in Paktika.[110] Rochman had been there for a while, but it is not clear for how long. Which of these five candidate one considers the very first Afghan Arab depends on how one interprets the sources.

We do not know very much about the earliest Arab fighters, but a few cases are sufficiently well documented to merit a closer look. One is that of Mustafa Hamid, also known as Abu Walid al-Masri. He was an Egyptian from Minya who had moved to the Gulf in the early 1970s to seek work as a car mechanic, because he could not find work as an engineer in Egypt.[111] After a short time in Kuwait he settled in Abu Dhabi, where he started an auto repair shop. In the mid-1970s he became more religious – or rather, he returned to religion, because he had been active in the Muslim Brotherhood as a young teenager. In 1975 he started going to Mecca for pilgrimage and frequenting Islamist circles in Abu Dhabi.

In 1978 he and an Egyptian friend named Isma'il decided to go to Lebanon, hoping to find Islamist members of Fatah with whom they could wage jihad against Israel.[112] They had been encouraged by an Abu Dhabi-based sheikh named Abd al-Badi' Saqr, who had told them jihad was an individual duty.[113] However, they did not find the atmosphere sufficiently religious, and returned to Abu Dhabi after a few months.[114] At this point Azzam started working as a journalist for *al-Fajr* magazine. He continued to explore options for jihad; at one point he contacted Muslim Brotherhood representatives in the UAE to inquire, unsuccessfully, about Islamist groups to join in Lebanon.

In late 1978 or early 1979 he had started frequenting a mosque in Abu Dhabi whose imam, Muhammad Tahir, happened to be from Herat in Afghanistan.[115] Through the imam and his son he learned about the Communist coup in Afghanistan, a country he was somewhat familiar with already, having attended a speech by then King Zahir Shah in Cairo back in 1960. In April 1979 a delegation of Afghan religious leaders from Paktia came to the UAE and visited Sheikh Tahir's mosque. This was the same delegation that Haqqani had sent to raise funds in the Gulf (see earlier in this chapter). Hamid met with them, and became very interested in traveling to Afghanistan. When Sheikh Tahir's son Sayyid Ahmad returned from his own Afghanistan trip in May 1979 with a personal invitation letter from Jalaluddin Haqqani to Mustafa Hamid, there was no longer any question.

In June 1979 Hamid went to Afghanistan via Karachi and Peshawar together with his friend Isma'il and at least one more Egyptian friend.[116] Muhammad Tahir, the Afghan imam, also traveled with them.[117] They would spend a month and a half in Afghanistan, first in Urgun in Paktika province and then to Paktia province, to Jalaluddin Haqqani's fronts.[118] Back in the UAE, Hamid would continue his work as a journalist while supporting the efforts of Haqqani and his representatives to raise funds for Afghanistan in the Gulf. Hamid helped facilitate visits by Mujahidin leaders and wrote about the Afghanistan war in his columns. In the autumn of 1981 Hamid returned to Afghanistan, this time for good.

After this, Hamid spent much time with Haqqani's forces in Paktia province, combining his military activities with a part-time job as a journalist reporting for the UAE daily *al-Ittihad*. A trained engineer-turned-journalist, Hamid was a resourceful and entrepreneurial individual who from day one in Afghanistan would work to improve things around him. He had a lot of ideas about how the Afghan Mujahidin and the Arabs could do things better, and produced a steady flow of concept papers for circulation among military and political leaders in the Peshawar community. He was also an opinionated person who did not hesitate to speak what he saw as truth to power.

All these things made Hamid something of an outsider with few close allies in the Afghan Arab community. He appears to have been seen as a mixture of warrior-intellectual and self-appointed whistleblower who always had interesting things to say, but who also annoyed many people. According to Basil Muhammad,

[Hamid's contributions] angered many, and made him several enemies!... It seems that Abu Walid's independence from any of the Islamic groups or organizations helped him greatly in [his] intellectual liberation, and to excel in terms of quickly understanding the secrets of the arena and its backgrounds. He thus acquired early and unique experience that made him a school in his own right, which existed for consecutive years, independent of any Arab front.[119]

Hamid was not particularly close to Azzam, although they knew of and respected one another. According to Hamid, they first met in Peshawar in 1984, which is surprisingly late given that the Afghan Arab community was small and they had both been around since 1981.[120] Hamid later wrote that he disagreed with Azzam on many issues, and that he particularly disliked what he saw as Azzam's excessive deference to the Mujahidin leaders. Hamid reportedly wrote several columns in *al-Ittihad* criticizing Abdallah Azzam during the war. Azzam for his part made few if any references in his own writings to Mustafa Hamid.

Another early traveler was Nur al-Din al-Jaza'iri, a young Algerian student of religion at the University of Medina in Saudi Arabia. Some time in late 1981 or early 1982, Abd Rabb al-Rasul Sayyaf came to Medina to give a lecture about Afghanistan. Al-Jaza'iri met with him and was inspired to go to Afghanistan; his biography says he and Sayyaf "agreed on jihad."[121] Before leaving he also consulted with his supervisor at the university, Sheikh Abu Bakr al-Jaza'iri, who supported the idea. Abdallah Azzam later said that Abu Bakr al-Jaza'iri used to "send" Nur al-Din to fight in Afghanistan.[122]

Thus in the summer of 1982 he went to Peshawar and into Afghanistan, but he returned to Medina in time for Hajj and to continue his studies. The next summer vacation he returned to Afghanistan, again intending to return to Saudi Arabia for the Hajj season in September. However, he was killed in battle in mid-1983 in Paghman near Kabul, and is described in some sources as the very first Arab martyr in Afghanistan.[123]

A third well-documented trajectory is that of Boudjema Bounoua, better known as Abdallah Anas. He had grown up in the western Algerian countryside, attending religious schools, and joined the Muslim Brotherhood in the late 1970s while doing his military service.[124] In 1981, at age twenty-three, he went to Mecca for Hajj and theological instruction, and liked it so much he came back the next two Hajj seasons. In 1982 and 1983 he worked in Mecca for an organization called the Foundation for Assisting Turkish Pilgrims and Muslims from Europe, America and Australia, which helped pilgrims with practical matters during their visit. He had obtained the job through a man named Fu'ad Abu Nasif; they had met in theology lectures in Mecca, and ended up working together in Mecca guiding pilgrims. Anas was also interested in religious studies, and was following classes with various sheikhs in Mecca and Medina such as Abd al-Aziz Bin Baz, Abu Bakr bin Jabir al-Jaza'iri, and Atiyya Salim.[125]

While studying in Medina in 1982, Abdallah Anas met the above-mentioned Nur al-Din al-Jaza'iri, who talked to him about Afghanistan. When Anas returned the next Hajj season, he learned that Nur al-Din had died in Afghanistan. At this point Anas was merely curious about Afghanistan, but he became more interested after another friend, named Nur al-Din al-Gharbi, said he had seen Nur al-Din al-Jaza'iri in a dream, walking toward a great, beautiful door. In the dream, al-Jaza'iri knocked on the door, whereupon a doorman opened the door and let him into a wonderful garden. Then, still in the same dream, Nur al-Din al-Gharbi tried to do the same, but this time the doorman asked, "Do you have a visa?" "Yes," he replied, "I have a passport and a visa." But the doorman said, "No, I don't mean this kind of visa." Nur al-Din al-Gharbi and Abdallah Anas later concluded that the "visa" signified martyrdom.

Shortly afterward, during Hajj, in September 1983, Anas met Abdallah Azzam by chance at the Zamzam well in the Mecca mosque.[126] Anas had recently read one of Azzam's articles about Afghanistan in *al-Mujtama'* magazine, so he took the opportunity to ask how he could get to Afghanistan.[127] "It's very easy," Azzam said. "You go to Pakistan – for you can't go straight to Afghanistan – and I will help you from there."[128] Azzam also offered to provide funding, because there were people, he said, who were not able to go and fight themselves, but wanted to support the jihad financially. Anas declined, saying he had the means.[129] Two or three weeks later, once he got his paycheck, he began making preparations. He initially had problems getting a visa for Pakistan, because the consulate in Jeddah told him he had to go back to Algeria and apply for a visa there. But then he met a Pakistani Ph.D. student who helped him get a seven-day visa through family members at the consulate. Then he flew from Jeddah to Kuwait, from there to Karachi, and on to Islamabad.

Absent Structures

The heterogeneous and haphazard trajectories of Mustafa Hamid, Nur al-Din, and Abdallah Anas speak to the absence of systematic recruitment of Arab fighters in the early 1980s. In fact, there does not appear to have been any organized foreign-fighter recruitment to speak of prior to 1984.

For one thing, what little we know about the early travelers suggests a bottom-up mobilization. Jalaluddin Haqqani, who hosted several of the early fighters, said they had come "by personal motive only."[130] Moreover, their points of departure are scattered, not clustered, suggesting an absence of systematic recruitment. Most seem to have been the only individual or group from their respective locations: the Tunisian man from Tunisia, Mustafa Hamid and his two friends from Abu Dhabi, a group of Salafis from London, a few people from Syria and Iraq, a few students from Peshawar University, Abdallah Azzam from Mecca, Nur al-Din al-Jaza'iri from Medina, Abu Hafs and Rajab from Yemen, Abdallah Anas from Algeria (via Mecca), and Abd al-Wahhab al-Ghamidi from Jeddah.[131]

For another, if we look closely at the actors most likely to have engaged in organized recruitment, we see that they called for support, but not for fighters. This is notably the case with the Afghan Mujahidin, who were not very interested in attracting foreign fighters, because they already had enough men. As they noted in a statement in January 1980, "there are now 150,000 men fighting in Afghanistan, and there are 300,000 others ready to fight if they got weapons."[132] At a press conference in Abu Dhabi in 1980, Mujahidin leaders explicitly said, "We do not need Arab volunteers, we need money."[133] With one notable exception – discussed below – the Afghan Mujahidin never issued public calls for foreign fighters during the war. Their outreach activities almost certainly inspired some Arabs to travel, and they never discouraged people who expressed an interest in going, but they generally did not ask foreigners to come and fight.

The Mujahidin parties differed in their attitudes toward foreign fighters who turned up at the door. Most parties – including those of Hekmatyar, Rabbani, Gailani, Mujaddidi, and Muhammadi – would rather not have foreign fighters. They might give visitors a tour of the frontlines for the purpose of fundraising, but they were generally reluctant to let them train, let alone integrate them in their forces. Sayyaf, by contrast, appears to have been quite willing to let people train. When Azzam began helping Arabs in Peshawar join the fight in 1984, Sayyaf became his primary Afghan contact. However, Sayyaf's party had a limited military presence inside Afghanistan in the early 1980s, so he did not really have serious forces to integrate the foreign fighters into. The only Afghan party that wholeheartedly welcomed foreign fighters in the early years was Yunus Khalis's Hizb-e Islami – or, more precisely, his commander Jalaluddin Haqqani. According to Mustafa Hamid, "While a number of parties accepted Arabs, it was really only Haqqani and Khalis who said 'Yes, you can join us as fighters.' The other groups tended to keep the Arabs away from the fighting."[134] Haqqani received Arab volunteers before any other Afghan party, and it was he who hosted Mustafa Hamid in June 1979, as well as most of the Arabs who came in the 1979–1982 period.

Haqqani is also the only Afghan Mujahidin commander who is on the record as having called for foreign fighters in the early years. He took several initiatives to recruit Arab fighters as early as 1979 and 1980. In May 1979 he sent Mustafa Hamid a personal letter of invitation after he heard that Hamid had met with some of his representatives in Abu Dhabi the previous month. Moreover, in 1980, when a delegation representing the newly formed union of Mujahidin parties visited Abu Dhabi, Haqqani allegedly pushed for Sayyaf to call for Arab war volunteers. Here is how Mustafa Hamid describes the episode:

Jalaluddin Haqqani ... was among those in the delegation that travelled to Abu Dhabi and who wanted Arabs to come and join the jihad. He asked Sayyaf to call for Arab volunteers to come to Afghanistan, arguing, "the Arabs will not know what we need unless they come here." Sayyaf agreed to Haqqani's request and said he would call for volunteers at a press conference he was to hold in Abu Dhabi. But other Afghan leaders said, "We do not need Arab volunteers, we need money." I attended this press conference and Sayyaf did not call for Arab volunteers.[135]

Moreover, as Vahid Brown and Don Rassler uncovered, Haqqani gave an interview in 1980 in which he suggested that jihad in

Afghanistan was an individual duty for non-Afghans: "There is a tendency in most of the Islamic countries which wish to help us to present aid and food as a kind of jihad. Some even think that this is the best kind of jihad. This, however, does not absolve the Muslim of the duty to offer himself for the jihad."[136] This is a significant statement, because it makes a theological claim similar to that for which Azzam would be famous, namely that jihad in Afghanistan is an individual obligation for all Muslims. It is a radical position, because it implies that every able-bodied Muslim in the world should go and fight in Afghanistan, and that those who do not are committing a grave sin. Haqqani's statement raises an interesting debate about the ideological origins of Azzam's foreign-fighter doctrine, which we shall return to in Chapter 10.

Together with Sayyaf, Haqqani would become the most important host for Arabs during the crucial first six or seven years of the war. The two catered for slightly different types of clients: while Sayyaf had most of the rookie training camps, Haqqani offered more opportunities for serious fighting. It was not uncommon for Arabs to start in Sayyaf's camps and end up on Haqqani's fronts. Haqqani is also uniformly described in the Arabic sources as very friendly and welcoming. Basil Muhammad quotes a certain Abu Hafs al-Masri, who first trained in the Badr camp with Sayyaf and later joined Haqqani:

I then met Abd al-Rahman al-Masri, may God have mercy on him, who had been there months before me. He told me about the fronts of Sheikh Jalal al-Din and how he treated the Arabs, and I found a real difference in the treatment. The group of Mr. Sayyaf makes you feel like a guest only … You stick to your tasks, and then you return to your country. When I heard about Sheikh Jalal al-Din from Abd al-Rahman, his treatment of the brothers, and their participation in training and operations, I told him: "I will go with you, God willing."[137]

The significance of Haqqani's availability as a host should not be underestimated. Called "the Ho Chi Minh of Islam" by a French reporter, Haqqani was a powerful military commander.[138] According to Mohammad Yousaf, he disposed of "some forty to fifty subordinates under his direction, with probably 10,000 Mujahideen spread over the border district between Ali Khel and Zhawar."[139] Without Haqqani, the Afghan Arabs would have had fewer opportunities to gain real combat experience. This, in turn, might have dampened recruitment, because we know that the stories of actual Arab war exploits, such as the battle of Jaji in the spring of 1987, increased the flow of foreign fighters to Afghanistan. Some of the major battles in Afghan Arab history, such as the battle of Zhawar in April 1986, occurred on Haqqani's territory. Haqqani also became an important early ally of Azzam's. They probably met relatively soon after the latter's arrival in Pakistan, because Haqqani is a key source for Azzam's first book, *Signs of the Merciful*, which was researched in 1982. In April 1986 Azzam even wrote his will in Haqqani's presence prior to the battle of Zhawar (see Chapter 13). In a counterfactual Afghan jihad with a less hospitable Haqqani, the history of the Afghan Arabs might have looked quite different.

Haqqani's openness to Arab fighters is puzzling for a number of reasons. For one, he had very few preexisting links with the Arab world. He had not lived in the Middle East like Rabbani, Sayyaf, and Mujaddidi, and apart from a trip to Mecca in the early 1970s there is no record of him traveling anywhere outside Afghanistan or Pakistan prior to 1979. For another, Haqqani was less ideologically radical than many of the Arabs he was hosting. Unlike Hekmatyar and most of the Arabs, Haqqani had nothing against Westerners; he hosted several of them in his ranks and he treated them with courtesy. He was also socially more liberal than many of his fellow Afghan mullahs; at one point he persuaded a group of them to have their photograph taken, saying, "Islam is not a closed religion; when it is necessary, one can take photographs."[140] Amin Wardak, the Sufi-oriented Gailani commander who despised Hekmatyar for his radicalism, spoke very highly of Haqqani, describing him above all as a pragmatist. According to Wardak, "He speaks Arabic and hosted Arabs who came to support him, but without rejecting the Westerners. He would receive anyone who could bring him their support. Even if he had good relations with the Arabs, he does not have the same ideology."[141]

There seem to be two main reasons why Haqqani was more open to foreign volunteers than other commanders. One is quite simply that his territories were closer to the border, so they were relatively accessible from Peshawar. Basil Muhammad noted, "Sheikh Jalal al-Din Haqqani was the most convenient at this time. He was known for his initiative in jihad, his hard work, and his positive dealings with those who wanted to join the jihad. Moreover, Pakistan was near his fronts."[142] A second hypothesis is that Haqqani may have been short of qualified local manpower. According to Amin Wardak, in the three mountainous provinces Khost, Paktia, and Paktika, men had for decades been exempt from military service. This was allegedly a reward for the population having helped King Nadir Shah into power in the early twentieth century. Over time, however, this exemption turned the local population into inferior fighters, because they did not get exposure to modern weaponry and experience of military life. For this reason, Wardak says, Haqqani was always keen to recruit officers and fighters from other provinces, or from the Peshawar refugee population. He was also very welcoming to deserters from the Afghan army.[143]

In assessing Haqqani's significance, it is important not to conflate his role as a host with his work as an international recruiter. Even though he welcomed foreign fighters, and even though he encouraged some individuals such as Mustafa Hamid to go to Afghanistan, it would be a stretch to say that he ran a foreign-fighter recruitment operation in the early 1980s. He rarely left Pakistan, he did not produce Arabic-language recruitment propaganda, and he had a limited reception infrastructure in Peshawar. Moreover, there is no evidence that any early foreign fighters other than Mustafa Hamid and his two friends were inspired to go to Afghanistan by Haqqani. Haqqani, in other words, does not seem to have made a systematic effort to recruit foreign fighters from abroad.

One might also have expected some of the early Afghan Arabs to mount a recruitment effort, but we know of only one such attempt in the early years, and it was unsuccessful. In 1983 or early 1984 Mustafa Hamid appears to have tried to set up an office in Peshawar called the "global Islamic office" (*al-maktab al-'alami al-islami*) to better organize the reception of Arab war volunteers.[144] However, nothing ever came of it. Hamid says his proposal was dismissed by Sayyaf because the latter had already taken a strong dislike to him. The real reason, however, probably lies with his lack of resources and political connections. Such an organization would have required substantial start-up capital as well as the goodwill of the Afghan Mujahidin leaders, and Hamid had neither. In 1984, at age thirty-nine, Hamid was a junior figure with no political or religious credentials. He did not have the ear of any wealthy donor in the Middle East, nor did he have the religious or political authority to get other people on board. It probably did not help that he was an undiplomatic person. Thus, even though he was one of the first fighters and an important voice in the Afghan Arab community, Mustafa Hamid was no international recruiter.

As we have seen, Muslims did not rush to defend Afghanistan when the Soviets invaded. It took over four years for the number of Arab war volunteers to reach 100, and several of the early arrivals only stayed for a short while. This indicates that foreign fighting was not a widespread activity in those days, and that it was not the mere existence of the war, but the hard recruitment work of entrepreneurs inside the conflict that would eventually bring large numbers of volunteers. In the early years, however, nobody was making a concerted, organized effort to recruit Arab fighters.

As someone who first visited in September 1981 and settled in late November, Azzam was definitely an early mover, but he was not the first. He was roughly the fiftieth Arab to visit Peshawar to inspect the jihad, and he may have been approximately the tenth Arab to join it on a long-term basis. However, Azzam did not come as a foreign fighter; he came as a university professor who hoped to use his spare time to help the Afghan Mujahidin in other ways. He would eventually come to realize that there was an untapped potential for foreign-fighter recruitment, but in the meantime he was busy navigating the complex politics of the Afghan jihad.

8 | Diplomat

"His beard was black in the beginning of the jihad, but after only two years, his entire beard was grey and white," one of Azzam's nephews later wrote.[1] Azzam was only forty years old, so what took such a toll on his beard? This chapter will look at what he did in his first few years in Pakistan. We will see that he spent most of his time serving as a kind of Islamist diplomat, mediating between bickering Mujahidin leaders and lobbying governments and donors to support the Afghan jihad. The chapter looks in turn at the four main actors with whom Azzam had dealings in this period: the Afghan Mujahidin, foreign governments, Westerners, and Islamic NGOs.

The results of Azzam's diplomatic efforts would be mixed. On the one hand, he succeeded in drawing Arab attention to the Afghan jihad and in becoming a central figure in the Islamic charity sector in Peshawar. On the other, he failed to unite the Afghan Mujahidin, and proved unable to convince the Muslim Brotherhood to support the war militarily. Still, all this networking provided him with contacts and political capital that would later help him build the Services Bureau and bring Arab volunteers. Meanwhile, Azzam kept government actors at arm's length, and neither he nor other Afghan Arabs received direct support from Western intelligence services. He shunned the many Westerners in Peshawar and worked against their humanitarian projects, which he saw as having a Christian missionary agenda.

Uniting Afghans

Azzam's top priority upon arrival was to connect with the Afghan Mujahidin to learn about the military and political situation. Sayyaf later recalled:

I remember when he came for the first time to Islamabad; he came to me in my office while the martyr Hajj Abd al-Ghani was there. I told him, "Sheikh

Abdallah, this man was the first to shell the Russian embassy in Kabul by RPG." He stood up and kissed the hands of Sheikh Abd al-Ghani. He was burning with desire for the frontlines.[2]

He spent early 1982 going from reception room to reception room in Peshawar, meeting with as many Afghan Mujahidin leaders as his time allowed. He also made a point of speaking to foot soldiers and field commanders to learn about the situation inside Afghanistan. Muhammad Yasir, a senior aide to Sayyaf, later said:

I was with him most of the time, especially in the beginning ... He was meticulous about recording the history of the jihad; whenever we sat down, he wanted to make the most of it, taking out notebook and pen and making us tell him the history of the jihad ... and making us talk about the miracles of the martyrs.[3]

Azzam's main Afghan contacts in the early days were Sayyaf and Jalaluddin Haqqani, but he was in touch with most, and perhaps all, of the parties. We get a sense of his contact surface with the Mujahidin from his first Afghanistan-related book, *Signs of the Merciful in the Afghan Jihad*, published in late 1983 (and described in more detail in Chapter 11). The book relays stories of divine miracles observed in Afghanistan, and attributes each anecdote to a named person, allowing us to identify some of the people he met in 1982 and 1983. The book cites over forty different Afghans from several different parties, from foot soldiers to senior commanders. Haqqani and his men are strongly represented.

Azzam displayed affection and respect for Afghans from the start, always speaking highly of their courage and commitment to jihad. This was not a given, because there would be no shortage of Arab volunteers who looked down on Afghans and wanted little to do with them. Moreover, Azzam always insisted that Arabs were only guests, and that they should be respectful of their Afghan hosts. To his mind this implied that everything the Arabs did in Afghanistan needed to be in service of the Afghans, and with their explicit permission. Azzam's respect for the Afghan Mujahidin was largely mutual. He enjoyed the respect of most Afghan Mujahidin leaders because he was a senior cleric, an eloquent Arabic speaker, and a relatively humble interlocutor. For these reasons – and because there was no other Arab of comparable stature in Peshawar – he was quickly drawn into intra-Afghan politics as a mediator. He would spend much of 1982 and 1983 on the frustrating task of uniting the Afghan Mujahidin.

This was difficult, because the Mujahidin were fragmented. Infighting plagued the Afghan resistance throughout the war. The fragmentation reflected Afghanistan's complex social fabric, with its many interest groups separated along regional, ethnic, tribal, religious, and social lines. The Mujahidin were also pulled apart by differences over ideology and strategy, as well as by their leaders' ambitions and personalities. The head of the Pakistani ISI at the time said that in his work on the Afghan jihad, 75 percent of his time went on negotiating between Afghan leaders.[4]

The landscape of Mujahidin parties evolved continuously from the mid-1970s to the late 1980s through a bewildering series of splits and unifications. The total number of entities that emerged in this period is somewhere between 50 and 100, with most lasting only a few months. The evolution of Afghan Mujahidin parties is a story so complex that it is not worth rendering in detail here.[5] Suffice to say that in the early 1980s the number of Sunni factions hovered between five and ten, and that it was only around 1985 that it stabilized at seven main parties, known as the "Peshawar seven." The leaders of these parties – known in Western intelligence circles as the "Seven Dwarfs" – were Burhanuddin Rabbani, Gulbuddin Hekmatyar, Yunus Khalis, Ahmad Gailani, Sibghatullah Mujaddidi, Muhammad Nabi Muhammadi, and Abd Rabb al-Rasul Sayyaf. To these must be added the Shiite parties, which had a similarly complex history but stabilized at eight, the so-called "Teheran eight."

The list of Sunni Mujahidin parties could be sliced analytically in different ways. An ideological distinction has often been drawn between the four Islamist or "radical" parties of Rabbani, Hekmatyar, Khalis, and Sayyaf and the three traditionalist or "moderate" parties of Gailani, Mujaddidi, and Muhammadi. Emphasizing organizational structure, Olivier Roy distinguished between the loosely structured parties (Gailani, Mujaddidi, and Muhammadi), the dominant party (Rabbani), and the very homogeneous party of the Leninist type (Hekmatyar).[6] Kevin Bell distinguished between the "clerical parties" (Khalis and Muhammadi) which included many madrasa-educated members, the "Sufi parties" (Gailani and Mujaddidi), and the "Kabul Islamists" (Rabbani and Hekmatyar).[7] To some extent the parties could also be distinguished according to their respective geographical strongholds inside Afghanistan.[8] Rabbani's Jamiat had a strong presence in the entire north, especially in the northeast. The south was dominated by the

Harakat of Muhammadi, while the center west of Kabul was the base of the Shiite groups. In the east the map was a lot messier, with Khalis, Hekmatyar, Gailani, Mujaddidi, and (to a much lesser extent) Sayyaf holding scattered pockets of territory.[9] The strength of groups also ebbed and flowed with the tide of money.

In the early years Azzam loyally supported and promoted Abd Rabb al-Rasul Sayyaf, both in Peshawar and abroad. The charismatic, Arabic-speaking Sayyaf had been chosen as the figurehead of the Afghan Mujahidin in 1980 and remained the default leader in most subsequent unification attempts.[10] As such, he was, in Azzam's eyes, the ultimate authority in the Afghan jihad. When Azzam went abroad, he sometimes went as Sayyaf's representative; "In that time," Sayyaf later said, "I gave him also a letter [saying] that Mr. Abdallah Azzam is authorized to speak on behalf of Mujahidin."[11] Azzam and Sayyaf developed a good relationship; "He was my very, very close friend and close brother; I pray for [him] continuously," Sayyaf later said.[12] However, if Azzam worked primarily with Sayyaf in these early years, it was mainly because he represented Afghan unity, not because of a unique personal or ideological bond. Azzam got along well with all four "hardline" leaders: Sayyaf, Hekmatyar, Rabbani, and Khalis. In fact, later in the 1980s Hekmatyar became Azzam's closest associate among the Mujahidin, as we shall see in Chapter 15.[13]

The early 1980s saw a lot of negotiations between Mujahidin parties, because at this time the external funding was increasing, and many donors pressured the Mujahidin to unite. This led to a tremendous amount of politicking as the Mujahidin scrambled to provide some semblance of unity. Every three to six months a new union was announced, each with a different set of participants, and each with a different name (usually some variant of *ittihad*, "union"). In 1982 the Afghans agreed on a somewhat more stable union, but it was a dysfunctional one. The parties did not trust each other enough to let any one of them accrue power, so the union had a rotating presidency, with a new president every month. This made for an organization with very limited executive power and ability to plan ahead. It also produced a steady stream of intra-Mujahidin crises and disputes that required defusing. Relations between the party leaders were generally tense, with constant insults, backstabbings, and character assassinations.[14] There was often fighting inside Afghanistan between units from different parties.[15]

Abdallah Azzam was keen to bring the Mujahidin together, because he assumed that unity would be better for the war effort. As the most senior Afghan Arab based in Pakistan, he was brought in to help with the negotiations. He did the work of any good diplomat: chairing meetings, acting as go-between, and staying in touch with all sides in the dispute. Bringing the Mujahidin together became his prime objective: "I had a passion to unite Sayyaf and Hekmatyar because I saw them as the most honest and able to lead the jihad, so I tried endlessly to unite them, and for a while we almost did."[16]

The fundamental problem with the unification line was that, in practice, it involved a reallocation of resources away from the big, old parties of Hekmatyar and Rabbani and onto a new central government led by Sayyaf. Hekmatyar and Rabbani already had established resource streams from the Arab world, but under a union many of the same donors would divert their funds to Sayyaf instead. Sayyaf did distribute the resources to the other parties, but Hekmatyar and Rabbani felt that they always got a raw deal, because they had more fighters inside Afghanistan to take care of. In addition, negotiations were marred by information problems, notably the lack of transparency about the budget of the "central government" and the poor insight into what each party was doing inside Afghanistan. As a result, parties often felt that they did not get what they deserved. No mediator was ever able to find a distribution key that all could agree on. Later, Azzam openly admitted he had been wrong to insist on supporting the union:

> The leaders of the parties saw with their own eyes how the union was gradually absorbing their leaders and growing, and they were torn to pieces in their midst while seeing their parties shrinking after they had worked so hard to make them grow. Anger rose, and the gap widened between Sheikh Sayyaf on the one side, and Hekmatyar and Rabbani on the other. It was because the Hizb-e Islami and the Jamaat-e Islami were the backbone of the Afghan jihad. I was writing in *al-Mujtama'* magazine: Support the Union, donate to the Union. And every article that I wrote was like a dagger in the heart of Hekmatyar and Rabbani, and I did not realize that I was weakening their parties through my work.[17]

It had taken Azzam a while to realize just how large Hekmatyar and Rabbani's military presence inside Afghanistan was compared to that of Sayyaf. He had a eureka moment in the autumn of 1984 when Abdallah Anas returned from a fact-finding mission to eastern and northern Afghanistan (see next chapter) and told him that Sayyaf had neither a military presence nor any political support to speak of inside the country. Thus from early 1985 onward, Azzam relaxed his support for Sayyaf and adopted a more neutral approach to the various Mujahidin parties. From here onward, he would pursue a strategy providing Arab support directly to the Afghan fronts instead of distributing it via the intermediary of the Mujahidin parties in Peshawar.

Azzam's shift to a more neutral stance disappointed Sayyaf. The latter's deputy Muhammad Yasir was furious at both Abdallah Anas and Abdallah Azzam for suggesting that his party was weak inside Afghanistan.[18] He reportedly "led a fierce attack against Abdallah Azzam in Peshawar, saying Abdallah Anas has harmed us more than the Russians."[19] Yasir himself later said, "Azzam and I debated on some issues to do with Mujahidin relations, and the debate escalated to the point of anger."[20] At the same time, Azzam scored few points with Hekmatyar, who still suspected him of supporting Sayyaf. Abdallah Anas says he met with several of the top leaders in the Hizb-e Islami in 1985 and found them very hostile. Hekmatyar's deputy, Engineer Salam, was particularly angry, suggesting that Azzam was serving the agenda of the Americans.[21]

All these intrigues left Azzam tired and disillusioned with Afghan politics: For the next few years he shied away from intra-Mujahidin politics and advised other Arabs to do the same:

[An] issue that the sheikh would raise and insist on continuously ... was that the Arab should not believe what an Afghan says of another Afghan, because they are mired in factionalism, and one of them might lie to support his party, and some might defend the mistakes committed by his group. So the Arab *mujahid* must remain respectful with all of them and stay out of the factionalism.[22]

Azzam did not disengage from the Afghan Mujahidin in the mid-1980s; he only scaled down his peacemaking efforts. He remained in close touch with all the Islamist Mujahidin leaders, and at the end of the 1980s he would return briefly to mediation by attempting to unite Hekmatyar and Massoud (see Chapter 14). In the meantime he had other challenges to deal with.

Navigating Geopolitics

The Soviet invasion turned an Afghan civil conflict into a major geopolitical issue that would prompt massive external interference. As a result, Azzam found himself navigating a complex landscape of government actors from multiple countries. Because he did it quite well, and because international support for the Afghan Mujahidin was so strong, the Afghan Arabs would come to enjoy an almost friction-free operating environment.

The Afghan Mujahidin had broad and strong international backing, because their struggle fitted several preexisting ideological agendas. For the USA and other Western countries the Mujahidin were a bulwark against Communism and an opportunity to inflict damage on the Soviet Union. For conservative Muslim governments the Mujahidin were defenders of Islam against foreign aggression and atheist ideology. For much of the political left in the West the Mujahidin led an anti-imperialist fight for self-determination. Meanwhile, Afghanistan's neighbor Pakistan had its own set of reasons to support the Mujahidin, notably the fear of a Soviet march on the Indian Ocean, the need for strategic depth and US goodwill in its ongoing competition with India, and a desire to appear as a defender of Islam.[23] As a result, many countries supported the Afghan Mujahidin in various ways, and the total amount of material assistance reached staggering proportions, somewhere in the order of $10 billion.[24] Far from everything reached the Mujahidin, because the pipeline leaked through corruption, notably in Pakistan, but the willingness to fund the Afghan resistance was high, especially from the mid-1980s onward.

The support for the Mujahidin was a poorly kept secret. In the Muslim world, several countries boasted of their support for the Afghan resistance and met openly with Mujahidin leaders. The same happened in the West: In early 1980, for example, Jimmy Carter's national security advisor, Zbigniew Brzezinski, went to a Pakistani military outpost in the Khyber Pass and posed for a now-famous photograph in which he pointed a Kalashnikov toward Afghanistan. On a similar visit in October 1981, UK prime minister Margaret Thatcher "shook hands across the border with an Afghan Government militiaman" and "gingerly touched a Soviet machine gun," according to the *New York Times*.[25] In March 1982 US president Ronald Reagan dedicated the launch of the space shuttle *Columbia* to "the people of Afghanistan."[26] In 1983 Reagan received a delegation of six Afghan Mujahidin leaders in the Oval Office, where he referred to them as freedom fighters.[27] Even the Hollywood film *Rambo III* (1988), featuring Sylvester Stallone in the role of a rogue US fighter in

Afghanistan, would include a title card at the end stating that "this film is dedicated to the brave Mujahideen fighters of Afghanistan." Gestures such as these sent a clear signal to allied governments and to non-state actors that it was perfectly legitimate, indeed desirable, to support the Mujahidin.

The three main players in the game to support the Mujahidin were the United States, Saudi Arabia, and Pakistan. Other countries also contributed – Egypt and China, for example, supplied weapons; Britain and France shared intelligence; and Iran helped the Shiites – but America, Saudi Arabia, and Pakistan did the heavy lifting.[28] (John Cooley has also suggested that Israel was "involved in both training and supply of the Mujahidin," but he provides no corroborating evidence.[29]) Put simply, the USA and Saudi Arabia provided the money, while Pakistan took care of the distribution. The bulk of the money and equipment was basically handed over to the Pakistani Inter-Services Intelligence (ISI), which passed it on to select elements of the Afghan Mujahidin. ISI, under the leadership of General Akhar Abdul Rehman (from 1979) and Hamid Gul (from 1987), had by far the deepest involvement with the Afghan Mujahidin and the best situational awareness. As the leading historian of the ISI put it, "the ISI was in no way acting as junior partners of the CIA; on the contrary, the ISI was leading the struggle for Afghanistan in the 1980s."[30] Its Afghanistan bureau, based at the Ojhri camp outside Rawalpindi, had a staff of around 500 people and three main departments: operations, logistics, and psychological operations.[31] The bureau was led from 1983 to 1987 by Brigadier Mohammad Yousaf, who later detailed his experiences in the book *Afghanistan: The Bear Trap*.

Most countries backing the Afghan jihad paid little attention to the Arab foreign fighters in the 1980s, because the latter were never numerous enough to make a military difference. Moreover, the phenomenon of "foreign-fighter blowback" – the tendency for radicalized foreign fighters to cause security problems on their return – was completely unknown at this time. Most countries were thus willing to let the Afghan Arabs go about their business so long as they did not hamper the larger support operation. This was notably the case with the Gulf countries, Algeria, and Western countries.[32]

That said, policies toward foreign fighters varied from hostile to supportive. Arab republics such as Egypt and Syria, which had experience with domestic militancy, actively prevented people from going. A common myth holds that they tried to get rid of their militants by letting them go to Afghanistan, but it is unsupported by evidence. On the contrary, we know that they outlawed publications from Peshawar, imposed travel bans, and detained returnees.[33] By contrast, Saudi Arabia provided a degree of active encouragement and facilitation, though not as much as has often been claimed. For a while, the state-owned airline Saudia offered subsidized plane tickets between Saudi Arabia and Pakistan.[34] The measure was likely intended to ease the financial burden on charities operating in Pakistan, but it also helped war volunteers. In the late 1980s there was reportedly also an Office for Afghan Mujahidin in Riyadh (on 60th Street in Malazz) which advised on various ways to support the Afghan jihad, including on how to travel there.[35] The head of Saudi foreign intelligence at the time, Prince Turki al-Faisal, later said that "some [of the Saudis] registered with the embassy. We gave them a telephone number to call if they were in trouble."[36] However, he also insisted that "there was a humanitarian rationale for allowing Saudis to go ... there was no intention on the part of the Saudi government, ever, to mobilize fighters."[37]

Pakistan also offered a relatively friction-free operating environment. Islamabad did try to keep a hand on the steering wheel by requiring charities to register, by requiring visas from all visitors, and by not officially allowing foreigners to cross the border into Afghanistan. For example, when Abdallah Anas applied for a visa for Pakistan in 1983, a friend told him to avoid mentioning the Afghan jihad in his visa interview, because this would lead to the application being rejected; instead, he said he was going to the yearly Tabligh conference in Rawalpindi.[38] However, all these barriers were easy to circumvent: there were few background checks into the charity and visa applications, and the policing of the Afghan border was weak.

For much of the war, Azzam was able to maintain decent relations with the key government actors in the Peshawar theater. He had a functional, if distant, relationship with the Pakistanis. The Arabic sources mention few meetings between Azzam and Pakistani officials. In his own writings, he generally describes the Pakistani government as something to be worked around, not with. Pakistani officials, for their part, have not indicated contact with Azzam in their writings and interviews.[39] Former ISI director Hamid Gul later insisted that his agency never trained Arabs and had no direct contact with Abdallah Azzam or Usama Bin Ladin.[40] While it seems implausible that there was no contact at all, there probably was not close coordination.[41] On the contrary, Azzam's relationship with Pakistani authorities became conflictual at times, as we shall see in Chapter 14.

Azzam's relationship with the Saudis was closer, but not quite as intimate as some authors have suggested.[42] Azzam was personal friends with the Saudi ambassador to Pakistan, Tawfiq Khalid Alamdar, and his assistant, Muhammad Salim al-Hamud (Abu Mazin).[43] The latter was also Azzam's neighbor in Islamabad in the early 1980s. As we shall see later in this chapter, Azzam worked with these officials on a few joint projects between the Services Bureau and Saudi charities. However, these were ad hoc efforts, and there is little to suggest that he cooperated systematically with Saudi officials, much less served as an intelligence asset. There is also no evidence of direct Saudi government funding of the Services Bureau.[44] Prince Turki al-Faisal, the director of Saudi foreign intelligence in the 1980s, insisted years later that "Abdullah Azzam was never supported by me or the [General Intelligence Directorate]."[45] Besides, as we shall see in Chapter 14, the Saudi government distanced itself from Azzam in the late 1980s.

Usama Bin Ladin, on the other hand, worked more closely with Saudi intelligence. Prince Turki's deputy Ahmed Badeeb said, "We were happy with him. He was our man. He was doing all that we ask him."[46] Badeeb, a childhood friend of Bin Ladin's, said the latter's "role in Afghanistan ... was to build roads in the country [to] make easy the delivery of weapons to the mujahidin."[47] Steve Coll assessed that Bin Ladin "had a substantial relationship with Saudi intelligence" and that he "operated as a semiofficial liaison between the GID, the international Islamist religious networks [... and] Saudi-backed Afghan commanders, such as Sayyaf."[48] This does not mean that all of Bin Ladin's activities in Afghanistan were directed by Saudi intelligence; the al-Ma'sada project and the al-Qaida organization (see Chapter 12) were almost certainly not.

Azzam for his part was probably too skeptical of Muslim governments to work very closely with them. He had long seen Arab states as Western constructions that had all abandoned the Palestinian cause and mostly failed to implement Islamic law. By the 1980s he was also effectively stateless. He felt no loyalty to any nation-state, and was not afraid to say so:

No tyrant has power over me, and no interest ties me to any Arab state, even with Jordan, whose nationality I hold. I haven't been to Jordan in four years; I haven't seen my house in Amman nor my family in this period. No power on earth can exert psychological, moral, or material pressure on me, even Pakistan, whose land I live on, for if they come after me I will just go into Afghanistan.[49]

Azzam did not work with Western security services, although he unknowingly met with at least two Western intelligence officials. One was a CIA case officer who, around June 1988, found himself at a large reception for Mujahidin leaders in Peshawar where Azzam was also in attendance.[50] The other was Alastair Crooke, a British official in Pakistan from 1985 to 1988, who said he also met with Azzam a couple of times in Peshawar as part of his information-gathering duties.[51] It would have been unthinkable for Azzam to knowingly collaborate with Western services. He was very hostile to the West (see Chapter 11), and he once wrote that "he who is an agent for American ... or English intelligence ... is an infidel outside the creed."[52] As Ayman al-Zawahiri later wrote in one of his books, "Is it possible that the martyr Abdallah Azzam was a US collaborator when in fact he never stopped inciting young men against the United States and used to back Hamas with all the resources at his disposal?"[53]

In theory, of course, Western governments may have supported the Afghan Arabs in other ways. This topic merits in-depth examination, because one of the most popular narratives about the Afghanistan war is that America trained the Afghan Arabs – perhaps even created al-Qaida – only to see the radicals turn against them. The book that did the most to propagate this view was John Cooley's *Unholy Wars*, which went a long way toward suggesting that the CIA orchestrated both the recruitment and the training of the Arab volunteers in Afghanistan.[54] Many other writers have made similar allegations.[55]

In reality, it is very unlikely that the CIA collaborated directly with Arab fighters in 1980s Afghanistan, for several reasons. First, there was no reason for Langley to support the Arabs, because they were militarily insignificant. As we will see in Chapter 12, it was Afghans who won the war, and Arabs never made up more than 1 percent of the anti-Soviet fighting force. Jack Devine, who led the Afghan Task Force in the CIA in the late 1980s, later said, "Bin Ladin was a minor blip on our screen."[56] Similarly, Thomas Twetten, head of the Near East Division of the CIA's Directorate of Operations, said, "We considered that the Arab volunteers were a problem for the Afghans and the Pakistanis, and that it was not in our interest to monitor their very small contribution. Our assessment was that they were not training to perpetrate terrorist acts once they were back on Arab or North African territory. We were not collecting intelligence on them."[57]

Second, the CIA station in Islamabad had limited capacity. Its operation in Pakistan was large in financial terms, but small in personnel. It never counted more than ten people, and of these most dealt with the Pakistani regime and nuclear program.[58] In the late 1980s the station had only three people covering the Afghanistan war, and most of their time was spent dealing with the Pakistani ISI and senior Afghan commanders to ensure that weapons shipments were transmitted properly.[59]

Third, no proof exists of collaboration between the CIA and the Afghan Arabs.[60] No record or interview to this effect has surfaced in the three decades since the Afghanistan war. Two of the three CIA field officers working on Afghanistan in the late 1980s have said that they did not deal with Arabs (the third officer has not given interviews).[61] In his memoirs, Milt Bearden, who was one of the three, hardly mentions Arabs, and when he does, he describes them in ways that hardly suggest collaboration.[62] To the extent that they paid attention to the Arabs, it was as a source of problems in the Afghan theater.[63]

Fourth, testimonies by Arab and Pakistani intelligence officials who *did* have contact with Afghan Arabs suggest that the American services were kept apart. Saudi GID official Ahmed Badeeb told Steve Coll that "the humanitarian aid – that was completely separate from the Americans; And we insist[ed] that the Americans will not get to that, get involved – especially in the beginning – because some of the Islamist mujahidin objected to direct contact with Western infidels."[64] The head of the Pakistani ISI's Afghan Bureau said the Americans were not even involved with the Afghan Mujahidin. "It was ... a cardinal rule of Pakistan's policy that no Americans ever become involved with the distribution of funds or arms once they arrived in the country."[65] He also wrote:

Let me demolish a myth that has been built up by Soviet propaganda and many journalists ... No American or Chinese instructor was ever involved in giving training on any kind of weapon or equipment to the Mujahideen ... it was always our Pakistani teams who trained the Mujahideen ... The US did, however, have a role in training our Army instructors.[66]

Fifth, the Afghan Arabs were by all accounts self-sufficient as far as military expertise was concerned. Multiple sources describe the training and the life in the camps in minute detail, and there is virtually no trace of Western instructors or equipment in these sources. The instructors described in these accounts are all Arabs – bar a few Afghans and Pakistanis. As we shall see in Chapter 12, most of the trainers had received their training in the Arab world, often as former army or police officers.

Last but not least, Afghan Arabs themselves have firmly dismissed the idea that Western services supported anyone among them. Mustafa Hamid, for example, insisted that ISI kept the CIA out and managed all relations with Afghan Mujahidin.[67] Usama Bin Ladin said in 1999, "The Americans are lying when they say that they cooperated with us in the past, and we challenge them to show any evidence of this."[68] Abu Mus'ab al-Suri said, "It is a big lie that the Afghan Arabs were formed with the backing of the CIA, whose minions were Bin Laden and Azzam ... the accusation that bin Laden was an employee of the CIA [is false]."[69] Abdallah Anas wrote, "I never learned, until my departure from Afghanistan, about the rumors concerning the CIA's involvement in the Afghan jihad through secret circles. I don't know, but what is known and clear is that the main supply depots for the jihad were in the bases of the Pakistani army in Peshawar."[70] And Ayman al-Zawahiri wrote, "The truth that everyone should learn is that the United States did not give one penny to the [Arab] mujahideen. Is it possible that Osama bin Laden who, in his lectures in the year 1987, called for the boycott of U.S. goods ... is U.S. agent in Afghanistan?"[71]

In fact, to many Arabs the idea of colluding with America was so alien that they even doubted that the USA was supporting the *Afghan* Mujahidin. Azzam, for example, praised Hekmatyar for saying that "we have not received any help from America, and there is no link between us."[72] Similarly, in 1988, Azzam's deputy Tamim al-Adnani insisted that he had never seen any American weapons in Afghanistan, except for the Stinger missiles, which, he said, the Afghan Mujahidin had to pay for, at $70,000 apiece. Besides, he claimed, the Americans had deliberately given the Afghans a low-quality type of Stinger which was easy to avoid.[73] Likewise, in a speech in Saudi Arabia in 1989, Usama Bin Ladin said, "Although weapons have reached [the Mujahidin], they have not been made in America but have rather come from the East. What is the American contribution? What share of support in the region comes from them? That I don't know ... it is all rumour."[74] Attitudes like these show how anti-American the Afghan Arabs were and how unlikely it is that they knowingly cooperated with the US government.

What about other Western services? Both the British and the French had a substantial intelligence presence on the ground in Afghanistan and Pakistan. They supplied smaller resources than the Americans, but traveled more than the Americans inside Afghanistan proper.[75] According to a former CIA official, the British were more active than the French and "wanted to be in on the US operation."[76] Larry Crandall, the head of the USAID's Cross-Border Humanitarian Assistance Program, says, "The Brits were involved too, but mainly with weapons."[77] Mark Curtis describes a substantial British contribution, saying, among other things, that Britain worked closely with the CIA on a number of projects, trained Afghan Mujahidin in northern England, and supplied Blowpipe missiles left over from the Falklands war.[78] Other authors, such as Shashank Joshi, suggest a more limited contribution centered on support to Ahmed Shah Massoud in Panjshir.[79] Alastair Crooke, a British official in Pakistan in the mid-1980s, says, "The British had a special relationship with the Tajiks [i.e. Massoud], but kept in touch with everyone."[80] In any case, there is little to suggest that the British trained or provided resources directly to Arabs.[81]

Of the Western services, the French appear to have had the best networks of informants. They also seem to have paid the most attention to the foreign fighters, though without dealing directly with them. Jean-Christophe Notin, who wrote a 935-page history of the French involvement in Afghanistan from 1979 to 2011, notes that that DGSE (Direction Général de la Sécurité Extérieure) station chief Thibault started keeping an eye on the Services Bureau "as soon as he realized the scale of the Arab influx to Pakistan, presumably around 1985–1986."[82] His assessment was that the Arabs were not much to worry about because most came from a background of unemployment, because they "are not taking part in combat."[83] Notin also describes the moment, in October 1988, when the French services – possibly as the first of all the Western agencies – became aware of Bin Ladin:

In Peshawar, a source indicates in October to Matthias [the DGSE representative in Peshawar] that "a certain Bin Ladin who lives not far from you, is training Arabs." The Frenchman ends up passing him in the street a few times: "He was impossible to miss; very tall, long beard, and scraggy like a wolf." The commander reports the Saudi's activities to the central office and is surprised by the lack of follow-up information. He mentions it to the station chief, who has no knowledge of neither Bin Ladin nor of French jihadis. "Nobody knew about Bin Ladin in Peshawar," Matthias says.[84]

Overall, it seems clear that Western services had only cursory knowledge of the Arab presence in Afghanistan and did not consider it significant enough to support.

None of this is to say that US policy in Afghanistan was unproblematic. For one thing, around three-quarters of the US support for the Afghan Mujahidin went to the four Islamist parties of Hekmatyar, Sayyaf, Khalis, and Rabbani.[85] As Coll noted, the policy "effectively eliminated all the secular, leftist and royalist political parties that had first formed when Afghan refugees fled communist rule."[86] The CIA was heavily criticized for this policy during the 1980s by people inside and outside the US government, but the agency insisted that these were the militarily strongest parties and the ones with the most support in the population.[87] The strategy was effective in the short term, but strengthened the more uncompromising part of the Afghan resistance for the longer term.

Another, less well-known, aspect of US policy toward Afghanistan was the support for information operations with Islamist content. For one thing, as J. M. Berger noted, "the State Department's United States Information Agency produced hours of propaganda films promoting the mujahideen and their struggle."[88] For another, the USAID funded and commissioned Afghan schoolbooks with pro-jihad content.[89] Similarly, in 1984 the CIA collaborated with the ISI on a scheme to distribute 10,000 Russian-language copies of the Qur'an into Uzbekistan from across the border in Afghanistan. The project was initiated by the ISI, and the CIA agreed only reluctantly, but the agency reportedly provided both the copies and the rubber boats with which to ship them across the Amu River into Uzbekistan.[90]

Third, the United States did little if anything to limit the recruitment of foreign fighters. As we shall see in Chapter 10, Azzam and other recruiters and fundraisers enjoyed near-complete operational freedom in the United States; they traveled back and forth between the USA and Pakistan without any problems, they held recruitment rallies across the USA, and they set up US bank accounts and transferred money as they pleased. There is also no indication that any US citizens who fought in Afghanistan were obstructed in their travels. The same was true all over the West. Abdurraheem Green later described his reception on returning to London from jihad in Afghanistan at the end of the 1980s:

> On my return from Afghanistan I recall walking through British airport customs dressed in my Kandahari outfit with compulsory Pakol, the legendary cap of the mujahideen. "Where have you been?" asked a customs officer. "Fighting jihad in Afghanistan," I replied with a smile. "I see! Well I just need to check that if you don't mind. They seem to be used quite often for smuggling drugs." He unrolled the pakol and found nothing. "Welcome back sir!"[91]

In lower levels of the US government there appears to have been awareness of a problem in the making. Former CIA analyst Cynthia Storer later said, "The important developments were noted and appropriate concern was raised ... there was even a *National Intelligence Daily* article in the early-to-mid 1980s that highlighted the potential threat posed by the presence of Islamic extremist organizations in Afghanistan."[92] However, little was done at the strategic level, because, as Milt Bearden noted, "there was little concern at the time over the role of the Afghan Arabs in Pakistan or Afghanistan."[93]

A fourth problematic aspect of US policy in Afghanistan in the 1980s was the misuse of charities for military and intelligence purposes. To be sure, the Western charities were not misused as egregiously as the Islamic ones, but some Western NGOs were certainly used as cover. According to Kurt Lohbeck: "The distribution of humanitarian aid and the covert operations of the CIA frequently became so intertwined that it was difficult to separate them."[94] The United States Agency for International Development (USAID) notably appears to have been a storefront for the covert military assistance. Larry Crandall, the former director of the USAID's Cross-Border Humanitarian Assistance Program, later said that USAID, the CIA, and the ISI were "just one happy family ... We weren't interested in all the handholding, this was serious business ... defeat the Soviets ... That's really what was going on, all this missionary crap ... we didn't have time or inclination for it."[95]

Avoiding Westerners

Azzam stayed clear of Western spies, but there were other Westerners he could not ignore, namely the many NGO workers, journalists, and adventurers who also descended on Peshawar. As we shall see, Azzam met several of them, but he resented their presence and avoided them if he could.

The Western volunteers came to support the Afghan jihad before the Arabs. Westerners had started trickling in as early as 1979, and by the time Azzam first visited in late 1981 there were over a hundred Europeans and Americans working in Peshawar or inside Afghanistan. Edwards noted that during his stay in 1983–1984 "there had been many foreigners [in Peshawar], the vast majority of them Europeans and Americans."[96] Later the proportions shifted and the Arabs became more numerous. Swedish journalist Börje Almqvist recalls that in 1983 Western NGOs in University Town – the main expatriate area of Peshawar – were struggling to meet the increase in rental prices caused by the influx of Arabs.[97] Estimates of the peak size of the Western NGO community in Peshawar differ widely, from a few dozen organizations and 200 people to 265 organizations and almost 2,000 people.[98] To these must be added a few dozen journalists and adventurers. In any case, the Westerners outnumbered the Arabs in the early 1980s, but the tables turned in the second half of the decade.

The Westerners came for largely the same reasons as the Arabs: to assist Afghans and help the Mujahidin beat the Russians. The humanitarian aid was not neutral, because almost all of it went to civilians in rebel-controlled areas, thus constituting a form of non-lethal aid to the Mujahidin. Moreover, most of the media and NGO reporting was done from inside Mujahidin territory by people who were usually sympathetic to the resistance. In addition, many Western volunteers did more than distribute aid and write newspaper reports; several organizations, especially the right-wing American advocacy NGOs, provided military equipment directly to combatants.[99]

There was even a small number of non-Muslim Western war volunteers among the Afghan Mujahidin. One was the Frenchman Patrice Franceschi, who fought for several years with the Yunus Khalis-affiliated commander Amin Wardak.[100] Lohbeck also writes that "every few months would see a down-and-out soldier of fortune arrive who wanted to go to war."[101] He mentions a Polish man named Lech Zondek, who "showed up in Peshawar determined to train the mujahidin in hand-to-hand combat," and an East German "who had escaped from prison and brought his hatred of the Soviets and his military training with him, [and who] actually led Afghans into battle in the Kandahar area."[102] Paul Overby, a left-wing American adventurer who went to Afghanistan in 1988, later wrote, "My secret wish was to fight."[103] Thus it was not as if foreign fighters and militarized aid was something only the Arabs provided; many others were doing it.

Even though they were on the same side in the war, Arab Islamists did not consider the Westerners as allies. According to a former USAID official, "Islamic funded health and education NGOs declined to join in coordination efforts with USAID and other donors."[104] Azzam often lamented the presence of Western NGOs and contrasted their large efforts with that of Islamic NGOs, presumably to guilt-trip donors. For example, in 1983 he wrote, "On the field of jihad there is not a single Muslim doctor, except for a group of about ten Afghans. There are about a thousand battlefronts. Meanwhile, the field is swarmed by missionary delegations and some field hospitals from America, France, Germany, and Britain."[105] He kept an eye on the evolution of the Western presence, taking note of relevant statistics. In 1986 he wrote:

Most of the medical services depend on the Western Crusader organizations ... above all the International Red Cross and Caritas. There is the missionary "Interaid Hospital" as well as first-aid centers. There are care centers in Peshawar (Hayatabad) with some hundred beds. In Peshawar alone there are about 500 workers. The Red Cross Center in Peshawar did 3,500 operations in 1982, most of them leg amputations.[106] ...

The Crusader organizations are covering Afghanistan from east to west; they have no competition. For example, in Balkh province (Mazar e Sharif) there has been a French delegation for four years; they have even built a hospital ... and in Panjshir, the French have built eight health units and bring medicine from Chitral. The French have 116 doctors working with them, and the Swedes have 90 nurses and 110 doctors working there. Last summer it was expected that 60 French doctors and 120–200 American doctors would join them.[107]

To Azzam and many other Afghan Arabs the Western NGOs were not just competitors in aid provision, but a threat to Afghanistan in several ways. For one thing, they had a morally corrupting influence on Afghan society. Azzam said that Western doctors encouraged sexual promiscuity among Afghan women by giving them contraceptive pills, and that female Western NGO workers were tempting Afghan *mujahidin* by doing things like bathing in the river right in front of them.[108]

Other articles in *al-Jihad* magazine said that the "Crusaders" were distributing drugs and pornography and contributing to the spread of sexual diseases in Afghanistan.[109] For another, the Western NGOs were all part of a systematic effort to Christianize Afghanistan. Azzam wrote in 1986 that "some thirty international Crusader organizations have arrived in Peshawar, and the World Church [*al-kanisa al-'alamiyya*] is behind almost all of them."[110] The alleged missionary activities of Western NGOs in Afghanistan was a major theme in *al-Jihad* magazine in the late 1980s.[111] Third, the Western NGOs were engaged in spying and other hostile activities. *Al-Jihad* magazine notably claimed in at least two articles that Western NGOs regularly amputated healthy limbs to weaken the Afghan Mujahidin. In January 1986 it said 3,500 *mujahidin* had their legs amputated by the Red Cross as part of this scheme.[112]

For these reasons, Azzam and other Afghan Arabs were keen to expel Western NGOs from Afghanistan and Peshawar. In at least one case they succeeded. In late 1984 Azzam was disappointed when a fact-finding mission from the Services Bureau found a well-established mission of the French NGO Médecins sans Frontières in northern Afghanistan. The delegation leader Abdallah Anas later said:

This was 1984, we were the first Arabs to arrive in the Balkh region. I was struck by the fact that the French organization MSF was already there, they had preceded us by four years. There were both men and women. I got angry, started reproaching the local leader for allowing these people in. The leader listened quietly, and when I was done he took me quietly by the hand to a nearby cave complex and showed me wounded *mujahidin*. "You want me to send the medical help back? We didn't see any Arabs or Muslims all this time."[113]

In 1985 Azzam recruited an Arab doctor – a Libyan named Salih al-Farisi who had come to Peshawar from London – to go to Mazar-e Sharif so that the locals would have no excuse for using the services of the French Crusaders:

Brother Abdullah [Anas] came to us from Mazar-i-Sharif and said, "We need only one Arab doctor to expel the French team from there." We chose Dr. Salih as this doctor ... as soon as Dr. Salih arrived in Mazar-i-Sharif, the frontline Commander there, Abdullah, who was in charge of over 1,000 Mujahideen, issued a fatwa saying that it was no longer permissible for a Muslim to sit with the French, speak to them or be treated by them, for now the Arabs had arrived. Thus, all of a sudden, the land shunned the French and it became a different land. Before, the French had been welcomed with the hearts of the Afghans, but now they were discarded and distanced like the distanced camels ... Therefore, the French decided to leave and take their hospital equipment with them.[114]

Later, Azzam would refer to this episode by saying that "we stood before the Crusaders and made them retreat from inside Afghanistan."[115] For Azzam, in other words, it was more important to keep Afghanistan free of Western cultural influences than to provide the best possible healthcare to Afghans.

Azzam generally opposed collaboration with non-Muslim organizations, and he appears to have avoided personal interactions with Westerners. Still, we know of at least eight Westerners who met with him in Pakistan or Afghanistan in the 1980s. Two were intelligence operatives: the abovementioned CIA officer and Alastair Crooke. Five were journalists and aid workers that Azzam met by coincidence in the field: a French journalist named Christian Robin, an unnamed Japanese journalist, an unnamed Italian journalist, a French doctor named "Malson," and a French doctor named "Eveline Ghuti."[116] The last three were converts to Islam, and "Eveline Ghuti" reportedly converted in Azzam's presence. The only person reported to have had more than fleeting interactions with Azzam was a (hitherto unidentified) Swede who worked for the Swedish Afghanistan Committee in Peshawar.[117] This list is probably not exhaustive, but in any case his contact surface with Westerners was very small compared with his overall network.

Although Azzam mistrusted Westerners, he rarely turned them away, and he was sometimes impressed by them. In an early article in *al-Jihad* magazine, Azzam described his meeting with the Frenchman Christian Robin by the Lija camp near Khost on 17 July 1985:

> The young man was blond, tall, blue eyed, and with a clear complexion. He said to us in English: "Do any of you know English?" I replied: "What do you need?" He said: "Did I get my suitcase from Lija?" I asked him: "Who are you?" He said: "I am Christian Robin, I am from France, sent as a reporter from the French News agency Si'ma, and I've stayed in Afghanistan four and a half months; in Wardak, and Ghazni, and Khawsat. I asked, "Do you believe in God?" He said, "Yes, and my faith increased in Afghanistan, especially when I saw the Kalashnikovs bringing down airplanes" ... And this Catholic reporter told me that the jihad in Afghanistan will succeed

because God is with the *mujahidin*. I asked him: "How did you survive in Afghanistan in spite of the difficult terrain and heat?" He told me: "It is easy. I eat bread and tea for breakfast, and tea and bread for lunch, and bread and tea for dinner ... So I asked him: "Did you enjoy your trip?" He said: "It is the best trip I have ever had in my life." I asked him why, and he said: "I really like the Afghan people because they are generous, courageous, and religious. The Afghanis stare death in the face, and I was amazed to see missiles falling from airplanes like rain and they would go about their business normally" ... I asked him about "There is no God but Allah, and Muhammed is his prophet", if he believed in those words. He said, "I believe in the first part of it, but about Muhammad, I need to read more about it" ... We kept talking, when he told me that he was returning to Peshawar to see a telegram that came from France which stated that his mother was dying. And he insisted that he wanted to come back to Afghanistan. And I was surprised to see this Catholic reporter, who was very patient with the harsh life here in Afghanistan ... I saw the cuts on his body, made during a bombardment on the Lija camp. The Mujahidin told me of this incident previously. They told me that this French journalist was hit, which is a miracle of jihad, because he was non-Muslim and the only one in the camp to be hit. So I was comparing this journalist to the Arab Muslim journalists ... who do not bother to come here to see the situation for themselves.[118]

Other Arabs were more hostile to Westerners. Anthony Davis talked about the "visceral anti-Westernism" of the Arabs, who "were seldom backward in threatening Western aid workers and journalists with death."[119] According to historian Jean-Christophe Notin, "Many French humanitarian workers crossed paths with Arabs in Peshawar, often taking insults from Algerians who saw them as colonial intruders."[120] There are numerous anecdotes of unpleasant encounters. The French academic Olivier Roy says he was once told "go home, dirty infidel!" by a North African in Peshawar.[121] Roy also met a group of French-speaking Arabs in Nuristan in 1985 who asked him "what the hell" he was doing there.[122] The same year, Christian Destremeau and Jean-Pierre Perrin were called infidels and told to leave by three "black Muslims" in Jawar.[123] The journalist Edward Girardet mentions the case of a French photographer who was beaten up in Kunar in 1989 by three African-American Muslims from New York.[124] Also in Kunar, a UN team was reportedly chased by Arabs at gunpoint in 1989.[125] Steve McCurry, a US photographer, describes an unpleasant encounter with Arabs near Jalalabad in 1989.[126] Girardet also describes an encounter with Arabs in Jalalabad in 1989, one of whom was a "strikingly tall man" whom Girardet later suspected was Usama Bin Ladin himself.[127] The man took the time to talk to them, but he was unfriendly and said upon departure, "If I see you again, I'll kill you." These hostilities notwithstanding, it seems that no Westerners were killed or kidnapped by Afghan Arabs in the 1980s.

Girardet has provided one of the most detailed descriptions of relations between Westerners and Arabs in Peshawar:

> During the first several years of the occupation, the only Arabs I saw were those managing on-the-ground operations of the Islamic aid agencies. They had their offices in University Town, and also in Islamabad ... By the mid-1980s, I began to notice more Arabi [sic] and black African Muslims dressed in *jalabiyas* or *thaubs* and sandals wandering around University Town. Some of them, barely out of their teens, could not even grow beards. These were no humanitarians ... they spoke mainly Arabic and almost always walked in groups ... Occasionally I managed to get into conversations with some of the English speakers, but they harboured a deep loathing for the *kafirs* ... They almost never gave their names – or if they did, these were clearly noms de guerre. Nor did they ever shake hands ... Once I succeeded in chatting with a Briton of Pakistani background. He had a Yorkshire accent from the north of England and seemed grateful to be able to speak in his native tongue. He had come to fight because of what he had seen on television and read in the papers. Afghanistan was discussed in the mosques back in the UK, and some had talked about joining the jihad ... others with whom I talked were less friendly. One man in his late twenties with thin spectacles and a scornful look could have been Algerian. Passing him in the street as he and two other jihadists were returning from the mosque, I heard them speaking French ... Quite a few, I was aware, had come out from the Paris suburbs or cities such as Marseille ... I asked one if he was French but he pretended not to understand. When I persisted, he suddenly blurted out: "Qu'est-ce que tu veux?" ... "We don't like you people ... You have nothing to do here".[128]

As Girardet's account shows, it was not only Arabs from the Middle East who were hostile to Westerners. Foreign fighters who had come to Peshawar from Europe and the USA were also hostile, suggesting that the phenomenon of anti-Westernism among young Muslims in the West already existed in the 1980s.

There was not always outright hostility, however. Jere Van Dyk got on well with "Rachid Rochman," the Egyptian he met in Afghanistan in 1981.[129] Peregrine Hodson, who met an Algerian in late 1984, described relatively amicable encounters.[130] Similarly, Paul Overby got along very well with an African-American Muslim foreign fighter from Illinois named Shamsideen whom he met in Qandahar province in 1988.[131] Nancy Dupree, who worked in refugee camps in Peshawar in the late 1980s, recalls being approached by Usama Bin Ladin, who wanted her help in obtaining heavy engineering equipment. "He was very polite and very shy," she later recalled.[132] On the whole, though, there simply was not very much interaction between Westerners and Arabs. Peter Tomsen, the former US Special Envoy to Afghanistan from 1989 to 1992, said, "The Arabs always kept away from foreigners in Peshawar. I never saw any of them."[133] It is telling that most of the Western accounts published at the time contain very few references to Arabs; most of the testimonies we have were published years later, when the Afghan Arabs had become a hot topic. The lack of interaction suited Azzam well, for he preferred to work with "his own" – that is, the other Islamists in Peshawar.

Lobbying Islamists

Azzam spent much of his time in Peshawar dealing with Islamist actors and organizations that were not directly involved in the military effort, but could provide other kinds of support. He lobbied four sets of actors in particular: the Islamic charities, senior Saudi clerics, the Muslim Brotherhood, and, to a lesser extent, Pakistani Islamists. He constantly sought to draw these actors into the war effort and into collaboration with his own organization, the Services Bureau.

Azzam had the most success with the charities; he used his connections, credentials, and networking skills to become a central player on the constantly expanding Islamist NGO scene in Peshawar. The first charities had set up shop in 1980, and by the late 1980s there were between ten and thirty different Islamic charities, depending on one's inclusion criteria. The precise composition of the Islamist NGO scene in Peshawar is difficult to reconstruct, because it involved a variety of subsidiary organizations, ad hoc projects, and name changes.[134] Generally speaking, there were ten key organizations (ordered here by their start date): (1) the Saudi Red Crescent, (2) the Kuwaiti Red Crescent, (3) the Saudi Relief Committee, (4) the Kuwaiti Relief Committee, (5) the Islamic Da'wa Committee, (6) the Islamic Relief Agency, (7) Human Concern International, (8) the International Islamic Relief Organization, (9) Muslim Aid, and (10) the Islamic

Benevolence Committee.[135] With the exception of Muslim Aid (UK), Human Concern International (Canada), and the Islamic Relief Agency (Sudan), all these charities were headquartered in Saudi Arabia or Kuwait. We lack good data, but it seems that the International Islamic Relief Organization (the Muslim World League's flagship charity) and the Saudi Relief Committee had the deepest pockets, with yearly budgets in the order of tens of millions of dollars.[136]

The Islamic NGO community in Peshawar was a collaborative one. Most of the leaders and senior operators knew each other, people regularly traded favors informally, and it was common to switch roles and affiliations. Azzam himself was well connected because he was a professor of Islamic Law and because he had preexisting links to the Hijazi pan-Islamist community from which most charities emerged. As director of his own NGO, the Services Bureau, Azzam would work with other Islamic NGOs on many specific projects in the domains of aid and education. He was an active participant in – and convener of – conferences in Peshawar, where representatives from Islamic NGOs gathered to discuss things like education, aid, and reconstruction.[137] Azzam also used *al-Jihad* magazine to promote other charities, especially Human Concern International, the Kuwaiti Red Crescent, and Muslim Aid.[138]

Azzam also succeeded in placing several of his friends and associates in positions of responsibility in other charities. For example, Abu al-Hasan al-Madani, who had represented the Services Bureau in the meeting at the Saudi embassy, went on to become director of the Saudi Red Crescent in Peshawar some six months later.[139] Al-Madani, whose real name was Wa'il Julaydan, was a US-educated Saudi from Medina and a close friend of Usama Bin Ladin. Azzam notably used the "placement" strategy to control the Muslim World League's activities in Peshawar. He had longstanding connections to the MWL, and he was friends with Umar Nasif, the organization's director-general from 1985.[140] In 1986 Azzam persuaded the MWL to open an office in Peshawar, to be financed by Usama Bin Ladin and directed by Jamal Khalifa – another Saudi from Medina and a friend of Azzam and Bin Ladin.[141] The next year another key Services Bureau member, Abu al-Rida al-Suri, joined the MWL office.[142] Getting control of the MWL was particularly useful because it had diplomatic status in Pakistan, which meant that foreign envoys did not need visas, and resources could be moved more easily in and out of the country.[143] Basil Muhammad notes that the MWL office "would function as an umbrella to facilitate the work and free movement of the brothers in Pakistan."[144] Similarly, Abu al-Rida al-Suri said outright that the MWL office was opened "as a cover so that the brothers could work under its name and move freely around Pakistan."[145]

Among the Islamic NGOs in Peshawar, the line between humanitarian and military support was notoriously blurred. Throughout the war, individual Arabs switched between fighting and aid provision, and charities knowingly used aid money on military equipment or assisted with military logistics. Azzam played an entrepreneurial role in this domain, using his connections to get charities to support projects of a more military character. According to a former Afghan Arab, "the Islamic foundations provided support in the jihadi field by supporting the fronts financially through the Arab lions in the Services Bureau."[146]

One of the Services Bureau's main partners in these endeavors was the Saudi Relief Committee, which, according to Ahmad Zaidan, "worked among Afghan Mujahideen by providing them with ammunition, guns, and whatever else they needed."[147] For example, in the spring of 1985 Azzam learned that weapons shipments were lingering on the Pakistani side of the border, and decided to do something about it. He approached the head of the Saudi Relief Committee, asking him to use *zakat* money (charitable donations) to transport the weapons:

I went to the head of the Relief Committee, the brother Salih al-Dhayf, and I told him: the weapons are piling up on the border ... I asked [him], "You have funds of *zakat* and jihad at your disposal – can you pay to have these weapons moved?" He said, "Who can guarantee that the money will be spent for this purpose?" I answered, "I can. We have the Arab youth who came in order to die in the cause of God, and who are prepared to oversee the transportation of munitions and weapons." So Sheikh Salih al-Dhayf said, "Let us think about it for three days." I returned [after three days] for a meeting attended by the Saudi ambassador Tawfiq Khalid Alamdar, Abu Mazin [Muhammad al-Hamud], who was responsible for the Afghan office at the embassy, Salih al-Dhayf, and Abu al-Hassan al-Madani. I presented my case again, and everyone agreed that the Relief Committee had to support the project. I told them, "This is Wa'il Julaydan, whom you know, and whose family you know. He is a trusted young man who is the link between the Services Bureau and the Saudi Relief Committee, which is responsible for the transportation." They listened in approval, and Wa'il began the process of overseeing the transportation.[148]

In a speech in Saudi Arabia in 1988, Usama Bin Ladin highlighted the contribution of the Saudi Relief Committee:

> They conducted 3,000 portages – 3,000 portages! – each about seven kilometres as they carried weapons into Afghanistan. Aid organizations used their personnel – apparently calculating these portages exactly – this much was shipped to this mountain, that much elsewhere. When the Afghans had confirmed that the weapons arrived, the Saudi Relief Committee would compensate [the porters] for the expenses.[149]

Other charities did similar things. The Saudi Red Crescent, for example, brought in the construction equipment that Usama Bin Ladin used to build his al-Ma'sada camp in late 1986: "We entered [the bulldozers] in the name of the Mujahidin through the Saudi Red Crescent. The ambassador, God bless him, Abu Muhammad (Tawfiq Khalid Alamdar) helped us a lot in bringing them in."[150] Similarly, in 1989 a certain Sheikh Akil, who directed the Saudi Red Crescent in Quetta, gave an Arab fighter named Ibrahim al-Ata "large quantities of heavy blankets, thick coats, military boots, dried dates, medicine, religious books and luxurious Qur'ans which the wise among the Afghans were eager to get."[151] The Muslim World League and its charity, the International Islamic Relief Organization (IIRO), offered similar support. Yet others were implicated; a former Afghan Arab said several charities "provided support in the jihadi field . . . especially the Benevolence Committee . . . and the Kuwaiti Red Crescent."[152]

This involvement is illustrated by the internal records from al-Ma'sada, the camp Bin Ladin established in 1986 and which became the precursor of al-Qaida. In the spring of 1987 Bin Ladin and his comrades kept written records of the purchase of supplies, the inventory of weapons, and the like. This internal archive, which has been preserved in the so-called Tareekh Musadat collection (see Chapter 12), contains at least eleven documents on formal letterheads from organizations such as the Saudi Red Crescent, the Kuwaiti Red Crescent, Muslim Aid for Afghan Refugees, and the International Islamic Relief Organization.[153] They include things like a note of passage for a generator issued by Wa'il Julaydan on an official Saudi Red Crescent letter and a salary sheet from the Saudi Red Crescent, with Abu Rida, Abu Ubayda, and three others listed as recipients.

In addition to helping provide supplies, charities allowed marked ambulances to be used to smuggle fighters and military equipment past

Pakistani checkpoints. Abdallah Azzam was personally involved in this practice. At one point he wanted to bring two Arab visitors across the border to see the Mujahidin, but the Pakistani border guards had not let them through. But "the sheikh was bent on getting them into Afghanistan with the Mujahidin, so he headed to one of the medical points by the border, dressed the two of them up as doctors, and they rode together in one of the ambulances. They entered the border crossing with the siren on."[154] On another occasion, according to a fighter named Abu Mahmud, "we were in a position overlooking the enemy directly. After two days – it was towards the end of November [1986] – Sheikh Abdullah sent for us. We were seven and took the ambulance to go to him."[155] Several of the Islamic charities willingly collaborated. For example, a Services Bureau member named Ali Ghuzlan later recounted how Usama Bin Ladin borrowed a car from the Saudi Red Crescent to get to the Ma'sada camp inside Afghanistan: "We arrived from Saudi Arabia on the same plane, the five of us ... We took an ambulance from Hassan Al-Madani in Peshawar (actually one of the Saudi Red Crescent cars). We drove the car to al-Ma'sada."[156]

The widespread acceptance of such practices came from the pan-Islamist conviction that aid and jihad are two sides of the same coin, because both are about helping fellow Muslims in need. We must also bear in mind that the Afghan jihad was a dirty war with extensive human rights abuses and neglect of the Geneva conventions on both sides of the conflict. In any case, the Afghan jihad became the cradle of the "charity–terrorism financing nexus" that led to so many controversies and lawsuits in the post-9/11 era. It was in this period that Islamic charities developed the militant ties and problematic practices that led some of them to lend support, wittingly and unwittingly, to more radical organizations such as al-Qaida in the 1990s.

Azzam also spent some time soliciting the support of senior Saudi clerics, notably Abd al-Aziz Bin Baz. The two may have met already in the 1970s on Azzam's trips to Mecca, and they certainly met several times in the 1980s. They also exchanged letters. Azzam had a lot of respect for Bin Baz:

I love him like I love my father and mother; you might be surprised by the high esteem in which I hold this man, for this scholar has a white hand [sic] toward Muslims in many places around the world. The biggest piece of evidence for that is his fatwa in support of the Muslim Brotherhood on the day the battle erupted between them and the Syrian regime in the early 1980s, his famous fatwa in support of jihad in in all places [*fi biqa' al-ard*], and his urging Muslims to support the Mujahidin financially.[157]

Realizing that Bin Baz had a lot of influence, Azzam wanted him to put his theological weight behind the Afghan Arab mobilization. During Hajj in 1984 he asked Bin Baz to endorse his fatwa declaring the Afghan jihad an individual obligation, and even though he did not obtain it, he namedropped Bin Baz in the introduction to *The Defense of Muslim Lands* (the book version of the fatwa). Bin Baz never visited Peshawar (he was blind and rarely left the kingdom), but he did publish three statements in *al-Jihad* magazine calling on Muslims to support the Afghan jihad financially, and fight if they wish.[158]

However, Bin Baz never openly supported the position that fighting is an individual obligation for non-Afghans, but rather issued vague calls on people to support the war (see Chapter 11). Still, Bin Baz probably talked more about the Afghan jihad than most senior figures in the Saudi establishment, so even his half-hearted support was valuable. Azzam himself considered that Bin Baz had made a very important contribution:

Shaykh Ibn Baz, God has truly given him insight, if He Wills, and God Knows best. God has benefited Islam and the Muslims through him more than most people, and God Knows best. I do not think that anyone on Earth has benefited – other than the rulers, those who possess millions – has benefited the Afghan Jihad like Shaykh Ibn Baz has.[159]

In one domain Azzam's diplomatic efforts did fall short, and that was in his attempts to persuade the Muslim Brotherhood to support the Afghan jihad militarily. The official Muslim Brotherhood organizations were very careful not to get directly involved with military side of the Afghan jihad. This was not because they did not support it, but because they feared reactions from their governments.[160] In countries such as Egypt and Jordan the Brotherhood enjoyed hard-won but precarious political freedoms, and their leaders knew that any involvement with violence might give their respective autocrats an excuse to limit their operating space. The senior Egyptian Brother Abd al-Mun'im Abu al-Futuh later insisted, "None of the Egyptian Brotherhood members fought there since their instructions forbade it," and Kamal al-Helbawy said, "We were only there as medical personnel."[161]

In the early 1980s Azzam tried hard to get the Muslim Brotherhood in Jordan to recruit fighters for Afghanistan and to get fellow clerics to join him in Afghanistan, but he failed in both efforts. On his last trip to Jordan, in 1984, he reportedly made a last attempt to persuade the Jordanian Brotherhood to recruit war volunteers, only to be rebuffed by the general supervisor, Muhammad Khalifa.[162] He then lowered his bid by asking for preachers instead of fighters: In late 1984 he reportedly sent a letter to the Jordanian Brotherhood asking them to send sixty preachers to Afghanistan to help teach Afghans more about Islam.[163] This request was not met either, but Azzam did not give up. According to his nephew Mahmud Azzam,

> [Abdallah Azzam] repeated the request in 1986 in a meeting that brought the sheikh together with some brothers from the Guidance Office, including Professor Mustafa Mashhur and Dr. Ahmad al-Malt. I was present at the meeting, where he said, "Send me sixty preachers who know the jurisprudence of jihad and *da'wa* and I promise you I will turn Afghanistan into the Muslim Brotherhood for you within two years." But the Brothers were afraid to weaken the *da'wa* effort in the Arab world, so the sheikh replied, "Then send me the unemployed ones; we can pay them salaries at our end." But in the end nothing came of it.[164]

Abdallah Azzam was not the only one to try in vain to persuade the Muslim Brotherhood to become more involved. Mustafa Hamid said he met with Mustafa Mashhur in Peshawar in 1984 with the same objective.[165] "My words made the man angry," Hamid said, "he believed the involvement of Ikhwan Muslimin in military action in Afghanistan would turn Arab governments against them."[166]

Some sources have suggested that relations between Azzam and the Jordanian Muslim Brotherhood soured to the point of his exclusion. Rougier says Azzam was suspended in 1984 following his disagreement with the leaders of the Jordanian Brotherhood.[167] Similarly, Jamal Isma'il said, "His relationship with Islamic movement in Jordan in particular ... was a little bit tense, because he was so popular with the youngsters ... The leadership of the Ikhwan in Jordan feared that he would deprive them of their younger members, so they froze his membership in Jordan."[168] Abd al-Mun'im Abu al-Futuh, the former leader of the Egyptian Muslim Brotherhood, said that Azzam "never contacted the Brotherhood after he stopped working with it and none of them helped him in Peshawar".[169] However, while the Jordanian

Brothers may have kept Azzam at arm's length in the 1980s, he was probably not formally excluded. Azzam described himself as a Muslim Brother to the very end, and the Jordanian Brotherhood organized large commemorative events in Amman after his assassination, as we shall see in Chapter 15.

In addition to asking the Brotherhood to send personnel, Azzam also tried hard to get Islamic scholars to come and join him in Afghanistan. One of his earliest articles in *al-Jihad* magazine was "An Open Letter to the Scholars," which called on them to get involved in the war effort.[170] From the start he had sensed his colleagues' reluctance; for example, in March 1983, at a conference in Islamabad, Azzam offered to take some of the other Arab scholars to Peshawar and give them a quick tour, but they all politely declined.[171] In the early and mid-1980s he wrote personal letters to several senior clerics in the Middle East urging them to join him.[172] He also asked friends to ask their friends; for example, in 1986 he wrote a letter to his former assistant Abu Akram in Amman asking him to persuade Ahmad Nawfal to come to Peshawar.[173] Of the senior Brotherhood clerics in the Middle East, only the Yemeni Abd al-Majid al-Zindani came and settled for a while, but only at the end of the 1980s. Azzam eventually resigned himself to working alone.

Still, a large number of senior Muslim Brothers from the Middle East visited Peshawar at one point or another during the 1980s. For example, the Jordanian Muslim Brotherhood leader Abd al-Rahman Khalifa "came and visited the training camps and used different weapons, concluding his visit by saying that he would ask the general guide [in Cairo] for permission to return to the land of jihad and settle there, but his many duties prevented him from carrying out this idea."[174] Similarly, Azzam's old friend Ahmad Nawfal came to Peshawar in the summer of 1986, although he did not stay either.[175] Other visitors included, in rough chronological order, Ahmad al-Malt, Abu Badr al-Mutawwa', Yusuf Azm, Mustafa Mashhur, Muhammad Mahmud Sawwaf, Yusuf al-Qaradawi, Zaynab al-Ghazzali, Hasan al-Turabi, Abd al-Mun'im Abu al-Futuh, Muhammad Hamid Abu al-Nasr, Hasan Ayyub, Adnan Sa'd al-Din, Ahmad Mahlawi, Kamil al-Sharif, Ali al-Hawamida, and Rachid Ghannouchi.[176] Most of these people connected with Azzam in Peshawar, and several of them gave interviews to *al-Jihad* magazine, as we shall see in the next chapter. In early 1988 even Muhammad Hamid Abu al-Nasr, the supreme guide of the

Muslim Brotherhood, gave an interview from Cairo to the jihadi magazine *al-Bunyan al-Marsus*.[177] In addition, the Brotherhood had representatives permanently based in Pakistan, such as Ahmad al-Assal and Kamal al-Helbawy, both of whom interacted regularly with Azzam.[178]

In the late 1980s Azzam quarreled with the Brotherhood again over training camps in Afghanistan. According to Noman Benothman, the Brotherhood at one point tried to get Azzam to close Khaldan, one of the Services Bureau's two main training camps. The reason was reportedly that the training there involved explosives, and this worried some governments in the Gulf on which the Brotherhood depended for funding. Benothman says that in 1988 Kamal al-Helbawy relayed a message from Mustafa Mashhur and Muhammad Hamid Abu al-Nasr in Cairo to the effect that "you are still a member of the Ikhwan and you need to shut down Khaldan." Azzam refused to comply, arguing that "this camp is built with money of the *umma*; it's *waqf* [an endowment of Islam]."[179] Similarly, in 1989 Azzam briefly set up a camp to train Palestinians with a view to sending them back to join Hamas, as we shall see in Chapter 15. Again the Brotherhood protested, but this time Azzam agreed to close it down, because the request came from Hamas itself.[180] Kamal al-Helbawy later denied any such conflicts, saying he met with Azzam regularly in this period and that they had a good working relationship.[181]

Azzam also worked with Pakistani Islamists, although not as closely as with Arabs and Afghans. He was in contact with all three main branches of the Pakistani Islamist movement that were involved in the Afghan jihad – the Jamaat-e Islami, the Deobandis, and the Ahl-e Hadith. Azzam's first contacts were with the Jamaat-e Islami, a group that had longstanding links to the Muslim Brotherhood and was well represented at the International Islamic University.[182] Jamaat-e Islami had a strong presence on the political and charitable scene in Peshawar. Azzam knew its leader, Mian Tufayl Muhammad, and was in regular touch with other figures such as Khurshid Ahmed and Qazi Hussein Ahmed throughout the war.[183] *Al-Jihad* magazine also featured interviews with Jamaat-e Islami leaders such as Qazi Hussein Ahmed and articles about the group's humanitarian efforts in Peshawar.[184] "In Pakistan," Azzam once wrote, "there is no [Islamist] group that stands sincerely behind the Afghan jihad, except the Jamaat-e Islami headed by Mawdudi's successor Tufayl Muhammad."[185] As far as we know,

Azzam never met Jamaat-e Islami's founder Abu al-A'la Mawdudi (1903–1979) himself. Some writers have suggested that Azzam was influenced by the Pakistani thinker, but Azzam does not cite him much, and it is difficult to trace any specific aspect of his ideology to Mawdudi.[186]

Azzam was also peripherally in touch with Pakistani Deobandis, who were represented on the Afghan battlefield with the group Harakat al-Jihad al-Islami. The group was founded in the early 1980s by three students from the Dar al-Ulum seminary in Karachi for the purpose of recruiting Pakistani fighters to Afghanistan.[187] In the course of the 1980s it recruited up to 4,000 people from Deobandi madrasas in Pakistan – mostly Pakistanis but also some Bangladeshis and a few South East Asians.[188] One of the Pakistani recruits, Mohammad Rafi Usmani, later wrote a book about his experience. He mentions that "I had opportunities of meeting [Abdallah Azzam] frequently during the jihad."[189] Usmani also cites Azzam's book *Signs of the Merciful* in several places, suggesting that Azzam had a certain Pakistani readership.[190] Azzam likely met Usmani and other Pakistani Deobandis through Jalaluddin Haqqani, who was in close touch with this group. Haqqani also put Azzam in touch with Sami' al-Haqq, the director of the Dar al-Ulum Haqqania in Akora Khattak. Al-Haqq says he met Azzam several times and was very impressed by him.[191] After Azzam's assassination in 1989, Deobandi militants issued a statement of condolence under the name Ansar al-Mujahidin.[192]

Azzam was also in contact with members of the Salafi-oriented Ahl-e Hadith movement in Pakistan. This movement, whose center of gravity was in the Lahore area, had old ties to the Saudi religious establishment.[193] Small groups of Pakistani Ahl-e Hadith activists fought in Afghanistan from around 1984, but it was mainly after the founding of the Markaz al-Da'wa wa'l-Irshad (MDI) in 1987 that substantial numbers – at least several hundred – joined the war. The main founder of the MDI, Hafiz Saeed, had got to know Abdallah Azzam in Islamabad in the early 1980s and had studied the Qur'an with him there.[194] It is not clear how they met, but it probably helped that Saeed spoke Arabic and had taught at King Saud University in Riyadh in the late 1970s. When Hafiz Saeed founded the MDI, he appears to have involved Abdallah Azzam in some way. This has led Azzam to be presented in several works on Pakistani Islamism as a co-founder of the MDI.[195] However, new research suggests that Azzam's role was more peripheral; he was just one of between fifteen and twenty people involved, and he likely only had an advisory role.[196] In late 1987 a group of MDI recruits trained under Abu Burhan al-Suri in a camp in the border areas (possibly Sada), suggesting that Azzam initially put Services Bureau training infrastructure at the disposal of the MDI. Later, however, the MDI established its own camps in Paktia and Kunar provinces. As we shall see in Chapter 13, the MDI was the Pakistani group that interacted the most with Arabs in the 1980s, but their interlocutors were mainly Salafi Arabs such as Jamil al-Rahman in Kunar and not Azzam's Services Bureau. In any case, Azzam had nothing to do with the MDI's more famous armed wing, Lashkar-e Tayyiba, which only emerged in the early 1990s.[197]

Azzam was also in touch with the Tablighi Jamaat movement in Pakistan, even though they were not involved in the Afghan jihad. He reportedly used to visit the large Tabligh convention in Raiwand south of Lahore every year, and would bring a small group of Arabs with him to "build trust between the Afghan Arabs and the Tablighis."[198] Even though Azzam had criticized the Tabligh in his 1978 book *The Islamic Call*, the proselytizer in him respected and took an interest in the movement. On the whole, he did not collaborate very closely with Pakistani Islamists, but he was in touch with many as a result of his extensive networking activity. This said, there is a need for more research on the role of Pakistani Islamists in the Afghan jihad.

As we have seen, Azzam spent the first few years in Pakistan trying to support the Afghan jihad politically, with varying success. He failed to unite the Afghans or to bring the Muslim Brotherhood on board, but he succeeded in enlisting the help of Islamic charities and in building decent relations with the Saudi and Pakistani governments, which were crucial to his subsequent activities. We have also seen that Azzam's clerical background was unusual in the Afghan Arab community, and that this gave him a level of access and a degree of clout that few others in that community enjoyed. By 1984, however, he had started to grow weary of mediating between Afghans and impatient to see more things done. It was time to take matters into his own hands.

9 Manager

"The young Arab keeps his head down and his mouth shut and stays for a week or two and returns disappointed about the jihad and the Mujahidin." Thus Abdallah Azzam described the situation for foreign fighters in Peshawar in the early 1980s.[1] He had noticed a steady increase in Arab volunteer arrivals in 1983–1984, and it frustrated him to see their enthusiasm going to waste. In the summer of 1984 he decided to set up the Services Bureau (Maktab al-Khidamat), an organization devoted to hosting Arab volunteers and putting them to good use in the Afghan jihad. The establishment of the Services Bureau would turn out to be a game-changer for the mobilization of Arabs to Afghanistan.

This chapter looks in depth at the Services Bureau: its history, organization, activities, and internal problems. It focuses on the Bureau's activities in Pakistan and Afghanistan; its international infrastructure will be dealt with in the next chapter. We will see that the Services Bureau owed its existence to funding from Usama Bin Ladin, that it had a much broader portfolio than just foreign-fighter training, and that it was riddled with internal conflicts from the start. The problems were partly due to Azzam's weaknesses as a manager, for he was a conflict-shy idealist who was unable to handle the disagreements that inevitably emerged when people of many different backgrounds and aspirations came together. Still, the Services Bureau played a central role in bringing Arab volunteers to the Afghan jihad in the 1980s.

Foundation

The idea of an organization for Arab volunteers had grown in Azzam's mind during the winter of 1983–1984 from a triple frustration. First, his mediation efforts seemed increasingly pointless as the Afghan Mujahidin just kept on quarreling. Second, more and more Arabs turned up in Peshawar, only to turn around and go home because there was nothing for them to do. Third, most Islamic NGOs operated only in the Peshawar area, and not inside Afghanistan.[2] Azzam thus began to think that it might be a better use of his time build an organization that could use the Arabs to offer support to the Mujahidin inside and outside Afghanistan. As he later wrote:

> I found myself in 1984 unable to reconcile Hekmatyar and Sayyaf as I had hoped ... Then the Arabs, who were eager for jihad, began to return depressed and discouraged from the jihad. Because, if they came to the Union, then they were questioned about their brothers' position toward the Union. If they came to the party of Hekmatyar, then they were questioned about Sheikh Sayyaf monopolizing the funds. If they encountered Sheikh Rabbani, then they were questioned about Hekmatyar, Sayyaf, and the need for the fronts ... All these things made me think of going into Afghanistan, finding a haven [*mahdan*] for the incoming Arabs far from these negative influences, a quarantine station [*mahjar sihhi*] far from the sources of rumors ... this was the idea behind the Services Bureau.[3]

Azzam's idea was to have an organization that could host the Arab volunteers and put them to good use in the Afghan jihad, while keeping them neutral to intra-Mujahidin politics. As Azzam conceived it, the Services Bureau had a dual mission: "to serve the [Afghan] Mujahidin ... and to be a starting point for Arabs in the service of Afghans."[4] However, the Afghans' interests would come first; Azzam always insisted that the "Services" in "Services Bureau" referred to the support the Arabs would provide to the Afghans, not to the practical support the Arabs received from the Bureau. Moreover, Azzam wanted the Services Bureau to work in a variety of domains, including logistics, education, and medical support. He did not envisage it as a purely military organization limited to recruiting and equipping foreign fighters for combat.

The catalyst for Azzam's organization-building ambitions appears to have been the so-called Badr project that he helped launch in early 1984. The Badr project was an attempt to foster cooperation between Afghan Mujahidin parties by having their cadres train together.[5] In late 1983 or early 1984 Azzam had been approached by a Saudi businessman named Salih Kamil who wanted him set up a new camp to train Mujahidin cadres from all the parties. The instructions were quite specific: name the facility Badr and have exactly 313 trainees, to echo the number of

Muslim fighters in the historical battle of Badr.[6] Azzam consulted with Sayyaf, who offered to host the camp in his newly opened training facility near the village of Pabbi, some forty-five minutes east of Peshawar.[7] Sayyaf later recalled:

We had there camp of refugees ... also we had a camp beside this camp for the gathering of the Mujahidin in the winter time when they were coming back from the fronts; about 15,000–17,000 were staying in the winter time there. For getting training to some of them, Badr project was established. Some people from the Mujahidin were brought there to be trained, and for the purpose of training others by them.[8]

In February 1984 the Badr camp opened, and "300 leaders from all the parties" came to train for two weeks under the leadership of Sayyaf's deputy Muhammad Yasir.[9] This first batch of trainees were called the Akfan Brigade, from the Arabic word for burial blankets. The course was then repeated a second time, under the name the Bayt al-Maqdis (Jerusalem) Brigade.[10] Azzam was directly involved in every aspect of the Badr project, from planning to execution, and Muhammad Yasir later called him the camp's spiritual guide.[11] The Badr project did not have the intended effect; instead, it only highlighted the tensions between the parties. According to Abdallah Anas, the problems were worse in the Badr camp than in the top-level negotiations, because factionalism was stronger among the cadres than among the top leaders. Azzam's experience was not unique; Pakistani intelligence also found the Afghan Mujahidin notoriously unwilling to train or receive instruction with members of parties other than their own.[12]

However, the Badr project had an important side effect, which was to bring the Arabs in Peshawar closer together. In early 1984 Azzam knew that there were a few dozen Arabs lingering in Peshawar keen to join the jihad, but with no opportunities to train, so he invited them to enter the Badr course alongside the Afghans. The first four were reportedly Mahir Shalbak (Abu Hamza), Abu al-Hasan al-Maqdisi, Abdallah Anas, and Isam al-Din al-Libi. Azzam later said, "We handed over those four persons to Badr camp. Thus the march began with these four."[13] A few more Arabs joined over the subsequent weeks, bringing the total number to approximately fifteen or twenty.[14] The Badr project helped foster an *esprit de corps* among the Arabs, and it created a social network that Azzam would draw upon when founding the Services Bureau.

Let us pause here for a moment to assess a competing claim about the Services Bureau's origins. In a book published in 2015 – in a chapter titled "The Real Origins of Maktab al-Khidamat" – Mustafa Hamid claimed that he had proposed the setting up of a very similar organization before Azzam did. He says the idea emerged after the battle of Urgun in 1983, when the Mujahidin ran out of ammunition and could not get more because supplies were allocated according to political agreement rather than military need.[15] He says it convinced him that Arabs should play a more direct role in the distribution of aid, and prompted him to write two memos about the need for an Arab-run organization to supervise aid distribution. The proposal was not adopted, but Hamid goes far toward suggesting that Azzam stole the idea and used it to set up the Services Bureau:

> In 1984 Haqqani was going to the Hajj and he said, "Write something for me to show them what we need." So this was the paper I gave him. Haqqani did not take the first part of the paper because I had written about why the jihad was in need of repair. My paper took a strong stand against the parties and their inefficiency ... Haqqani thought the first part might cause further divisions, so he only took the second part, which outlined the solutions ... My solution was that an Arab committee supervise aid and supplies, with members stationed inside Afghanistan and also in Peshawar ... My other solutions involved arranging for the training of Afghans to increase their effectiveness ... another of my suggestions was for doctors to go inside Afghanistan. The Western doctors went inside Afghanistan, but the Arab doctors did not; it was very shameful ... I also wrote about the need for a big media and education effort ... so another of my points was to organize this and send people inside Afghanistan to gather the information, photos, films and other materials that could be distributed all over the world to news agencies to give a real and reliable picture of the jihad. Haqqani took [the document] to the Hajj and it reached Azzam and [Usama Bin Ladin]. They agreed on it, and then they took it to Sayyaf as the leader of the Afghan Union; they went to him and said, "this is our project" and sought his approval.[16]

It is difficult to know what to do with this claim. No other sources corroborate it, and Hamid has not presented the memo he said he wrote. Moreover, it is difficult to see why Azzam would not have credited Hamid if he knowingly got the idea for the Services Bureau from him. Azzam and Hamid were not enemies at the time, and Azzam usually gave credit where it was due. The most charitable interpretation of Hamid's claim is that both men had a similar idea around the same time. Perhaps Hamid's memo helped Azzam along in his own thinking by reassuring him that others also saw the need for such an organization. But Hamid's claim of outright intellectual theft does not hold in the absence of corroborating evidence. In any case, it was Azzam who went ahead and set up the organization.

The main hurdle to begin with was funding. Azzam did not have any money of his own, and existing donor streams were directed to the Afghan Mujahidin. Fortunately, a "jihadi venture capitalist" had turned up in Peshawar that spring, and his name was Usama Bin Ladin. The son of Saudi Arabia's most successful construction magnate, the twenty-seven-year-old had access to substantial resources. On top of savings, Bin Ladin received an annual family stipend in this period of around $200,000.[17] This was in addition to the money he could raise from his wealthy family and friends in the kingdom. Here was a man who could easily put cash on the table for a cause he believed in.

Bin Ladin was no stranger to Azzam. As we saw in Chapter 5, the two had met in America in 1978 as well as in Saudi Arabia when Azzam lived there. Moreover, Azzam had been a guest at Bin Ladin's house in Jeddah several times in 1982 and 1983.[18] As Azzam later recalled, "I used to visit him at his house in Jeddah whenever I used to go for Hajj or Umrah ... The first time he invited me to his house was in Ramadan [i.e. July 1982]."[19] One of Bin Ladin's Saudi friends at the time, Jamal Khalifa, also recalled Azzam's visits:

Osama invited me to his house in al Aziziyyah. He has a building there, he was twenty-five, twenty-six, he's already married a couple of times. He told me that Abdallah Azzam [was coming]. I knew Abdullah Azzam from his books. He's a very good writer and he's really educated so I was really very eager to hear him when he started to talk about Afghanistan.[20]

Azzam brought his sons along on some of the visits and they would all go on excursions together. Hudhayfa Azzam says that in 1984,

bin Ladin took us to his farm forty kilometres from Jeddah. We used to go there for hunting, whatever we find in the desert ... We're brothers in Islam and we were very close to him. We used to stay in his house in Wadi Bisha street in al-Aziziyya District in Jeddah. He had a building with four flats for the three wives and one for the guest.[21]

According to Hudhayfa Azzam, Bin Ladin also once visited the Azzam family in Amman in the summer of 1984.[22]

Bin Ladin was no newcomer to the Afghan jihad either. He had been going to Pakistan regularly since 1979 to give money to the Afghan Mujahidin via Jamaat-e Islami, the Pakistani branch of the Muslim Brotherhood. As he later said:

> In 1979, I remember that I heard from the media, while in Jeddah, that Russian forces had entered Afghanistan. This news saddened me greatly, and it strengthened my determination to come to the Mujahidin brothers here in Pakistan. So I spent about two weeks preparing myself and collecting some funds from my stepbrothers and brothers. We had a brother and friend who was studying in Karachi, the brother of Abdallah al-Jafri. So my stepbrother, Mahrus, and I came there, we came to Karachi. Delivering donations at that time was through Jamaat-e Islami. Sheikh Abu A'la al-Mawdudi – may God have mercy on him – was still present, but he was sick, so it was his deputy, Tufayl Muhammad, who took the responsibility of giving the donations to the Mujahidin ... We met Mr. Tufayl in Lahore, in Mansura, and, by God's grace, we gave him some donations, and we continued doing so without any physical support. It was only financial support because the stance of Islamic countries on Afghanistan had not yet been announced. In the kingdom too, the general atmosphere was one of caution around this issue because we were not familiar with jihad or armed support, so we went and returned secretly. There were many excuses for those who stayed behind, even though their reticence was in good faith. So unfortunately – and I emphasize unfortunately – we continued like this until 1984.[23]

We do not know how many trips to Pakistan Bin Ladin made in the 1979–1983 period, but we know that in the beginning he only went to Lahore, and that at some point he also started going to Islamabad, where he would visit Azzam. Abdallah Anas recalls meeting Usama Bin Ladin for the first time in Azzam's home in Islamabad at the start of 1984, at which time Bin Ladin was known only as a donor:

> I asked sheikh Abdallah, "The Saudi brother we just met, why isn't he coming to Peshawar?" He said, "He is not coming to Peshawar. He just comes from time to time, to visit me in Islamabad, for a day or half a day, and he returns to Jeddah by plane the same day. Perhaps some benefactors will donate money, and he will bring it to give to the orphans or to the Mujahidin or something like that." I understood that he was not able to devote himself full time to the jihad.[24]

Bin Ladin appears not to have set foot in Peshawar in the first four years of the war. He later said it was because Saudi authorities – and his mother – had advised him against it.[25] Later Bin Ladin expressed embarrassment over his late arrival:

Until April 1984, the fear of physical participation remained before me in various ways, and those discouraging [me] had many reasons. However, their discouragement was in good faith, as they were not accustomed to this atmosphere in the Islamic world. Unfortunately, we continued in this situation, and I am very sorry to say it did so until April 1984 when we entered the camps of fighting and jihad in [Afghanistan] for the first time.[26]

It was Abdallah Azzam who, in early 1984, convinced Bin Ladin to go to Peshawar and on to the border areas. Azzam later said, "Brother Usama Bin Ladin came to Islamabad in 1984 bringing aid, and he was nervous about going to Peshawar, as some wise people advised him against it ... I told him: Do not listen to anyone and go to Jaji as Sheikh Sayyaf is there."[27] The visit became a turning point in Bin Ladin's involvement in the Afghan jihad.

I was very, very surprised by the poor situation in terms of weapons, roads, trenches, everything ... I asked forgiveness from God Almighty as I felt I had committed a sin by listening to some brothers, sheikhs, and loved ones, and not going inside because I was afraid that I would cause an embarrassment in terms of security. I felt that this delay by four years could not be atoned for except through martyrdom in the cause of God.[28]

According to Azzam,

Brother Usama came back from Jaji very moved by the jihad and began to give it all his efforts. It was Ramadan [June 1984] so he collected approximately $5 to 10 million – I do not remember exactly now – and he returned to Sheikh Sayyaf and handed it over to him for the Union.[29]

Thus in the summer of 1984 Usama Bin Ladin was an easy fundraising target. When Azzam presented his plan to him, "[Bin Ladin] became enthusiastic and made an agreement to pay some of the costs of the Office of Arab Mujahidin in Afghanistan."[30] According to Jamal Isma'il, Bin Ladin "agreed to finance the presence of fifty or sixty Arab families, anyone who was chosen by Sheikh Abdallah Azzam."[31] Having found a financial backer, Azzam now needed Sayyaf's formal permission for the Services Bureau to operate in Peshawar and Afghanistan. Azzam decided to convene a meeting in Mecca during the Hajj (late August or early September 1984) between himself, Sayyaf, and Bin Ladin:

We made Hajj that year and we sat with Sheikh Sayyaf, and brother Usama said, "I am responsible for every Arab who comes: accommodation, a ticket, pocket money, and support for the family. From he leaves his country and until he returns." With Sheikh Sayyaf, we determined the allowance of the Arab brother and his wife, what was enough for his house, and so on. The idea was in my mind, but God Almighty sent the brother Abu Abdallah to support it financially.[32]

Bin Ladin later recalled:

I mentioned to Sheikh Sayyaf in the presence of Sheikh Abdallah Azzam that the number of Arabs was gradually increasing, and [I said we would like it] if you – as the emir of the Mujahidin and President of the Union – permit us to establish an office or a house where we can receive these Arab brothers and benefit from their potential. So he permitted us to do so. Indeed, we established the office immediately after Hajj and the work went on from there.[33]

In mid-September 1984 Azzam began the practical work of setting up the Services Bureau. He was joined by a group of around ten Arabs who had been in Pakistan for a while. Several of them had been involved in the Badr project earlier that year.[34] They included Abu Akram, Mahir Shalbak (Abu Hamza), Abu al-Hasan al-Maqdisi, Abdallah Anas, Isam al-Din al-Libi (Abu Mu'adh), Abu Hudhayfa, and Abu Ammar.[35] Azzam later said, "God be praised, we began with less than ten people; the Services Bureau, we started it with less than ten young men, and now in Afghanistan the youth are all over the place and have a big role."[36]

The most important of these pioneers was Mahmud Khawaja (Abu Akram), a Palestinian-Jordanian friend and former neighbour of Azzam's from Amman.[37] He was older and more experienced than the others, having spent several years in the 1970s as a trainer for Fatah and as the head of Fatah's medical corps in Syria and Lebanon.[38] He had moved to Pakistan in 1983, probably as a result of Azzam's encouragement, and the two became close. According to Abdallah Anas, "Abu Akram was tagged onto Abdallah Azzam, like his shadow. He was his administrator, bodyguard, cook, driver, advisor – he was everything to Sheikh Abdallah."[39] Abu Akram was the Services

Bureau's first executive director until he decided to return to Jordan for family reasons in late 1985, to Azzam's great disappointment.[40] Azzam and Abu Akram stayed in touch by mail afterward; in one letter, Azzam writes, "How fondly I remember your driving the white car between Islamabad and Peshawar."[41] Incidentally, it was Abu Akram who had come up with the name "Services Bureau."[42]

A network factor was behind the early recruitment to the Services Bureau. At least fifteen of the early members were Palestinians or Jordanians, and several had known Azzam in Amman. Abu Akram, Abu al-Hasan al-Maqdisi, Abu Hudhayfa, and Abu Ammar were all Jordanians of Palestinian background, and Mahir Shalbak was Palestinian. At least six other Jordanians (possibly of Palestinian background) came in 1984: Abu Dawud, Abu Sayyaf, Abu Umran, Abu Zayd, a certain Usama, and someone named Ziyad. In addition, Azzam would soon be joined by no less than four of his nephews from Jordan; Jamal Azzam (Abu Harith), Mahmud Azzam (Abu Adil), Ahmad Azzam (Abu Ibada), and Abu Abdallah (real name not known).[43] Azzam later said of the early members of the Bureau: "They were our neighbors, relatives, and graduates of Jordan University, and some of them went to the same mosque which we used to attend."[44] Another recurring profile in the Bureau's early membership was Palestinian students in Pakistan.[45] The abovementioned Abu Hudhayfa and Abu Ammar had both studied in Pakistan before. Abu Dawud and Jamal Isma'il were both enrolled at Peshawar University, and a recruit named Munqidh had been studying in Lahore.[46] Later, the Services Bureau's membership would diversify considerably in terms of the nationalities represented. Still it would remain almost exclusively Arab, with the exception of some Afghan translators, such as Vahid Mojdeh.[47]

In the very beginning, when the Services Bureau lacked a physical office, Azzam and his comrades would meet in the building of the Muslim Student Union at Peshawar University. Known as Bayt al-Muslimin, it was located in Tahkal, a neighbourhood just east of the university.[48] However, the people in charge of the student union did not like having jihad volunteers around, so they limited access to students only, effectively kicking Azzam and his friends out.[49] Therefore, when Usama Bin Ladin next came to Peshawar, probably around November 1984, he rented a house for them to use as a headquarters.[50]

They named the house Bayt Abu Hamza (Abu Hamza's House) after a man named Abu Hamza who had just been killed inside Afghanistan while on a mission for the Services Bureau.[51] The building would serve as headquarters for the Services Bureau throughout the war. Here was Azzam's office, the editorial office of *al-Jihad* magazine, and rooms for incoming volunteers. Bayt Abu Hamza was located at 61 Syed Jamal-ud-din Afghani Road in University Town just south of Peshawar University campus.[52] University Town was an affluent area popular with expatriates of all nationalities, because it had villas. Across the street was the Saudi Red Crescent and right next door to the east was Hekmatyar's Peshawar residence.[53] There were also Western NGOs; right opposite, for example, was the office of the Christian charity Union Aid. Bayt Abu Hamza itself was a small building with a reception area, a kitchen, three toilets, and four or five rooms, some used as offices and some as bedrooms. It also had a walled garden where a tarpaulin could be set up to create extra rooms. Outside the gate were two Suzuki cars for picking up volunteers. The facility could accommodate about forty men "if we packed them right," as Abdallah Anas later wrote.[54]

This was not enough for the growing inflow of Arabs, and new guest houses would soon be added to the property portfolio. In early 1985 the Bureau rented another house, named Bayt Abu Uthman, after a man who had been killed together with Abu Hamza the previous autumn.[55] Bayt Abu Uthman was used mainly to host visiting donors and other VIPs.[56] Later that year Usama Bin Ladin sponsored the setting up of yet another guest house named Bayt al-Ansar (House of the Supporters) located some 400 meters down the street to the west of Bayt Abu Hamza.[57] Still later, they set up a guest house named Bayt al-Shuhada' (House of the Martyrs) in a neighborhood called Hayatabad.[58] Yet more properties were added later, and at its peak around 1988 the Services Bureau operated seven guest houses around Peshawar.[59]

Organization

The leader (*amir*) of the Services Bureau was Azzam himself. As the founder and the most senior religious authority among the Arabs, he remained the Bureau's undisputed leader until his death in November 1989. His name would become almost synonymous with the organization; in fact, on Bureau stationery Azzam's name was printed right below that of the organization, practically as part of the logo.⁶⁰ As a leader, Azzam was friendly and well liked. His speaking skills made him a particularly good motivator. "[He] has this reputation to push people," a former subordinate said. "That's what he did with Osama later. He sees what talent you have, journalist or organizer or fighter [and lets you use it]."⁶¹ He was also a relatively hands-off leader who stayed out of day-to-day operations to focus on larger issues.

Daily management was left to an executive director (*mudir*), who was also deputy leader. The first director was the able Abu Akram, but he left in late 1985 and would turn out to be difficult to replace. He was succeeded by an interim director called Abu Hudhayfa al-Urduni, before Abu Hajir al-Iraqi (aka Mamduh Mahmud Salim) took over in early 1986.⁶² Abu Hajir only lasted six months, and passed the office back to Abu Hudhayfa al-Urduni.⁶³ He was replaced in 1988 by Tamim al-Adnani, who held the position until he died while on a speaking tour in America in October 1989.⁶⁴ As we shall see in Chapter 15, the Services Bureau would undergo a serious leadership crisis in late 1989 after Azzam and al-Adnani died within weeks of one another.

The executive director reported to two committees, the Bureau Committee (*lajnat al-maktab*) and a Consultative Council (*majlis al-shura*). Both entities were boards of sorts, but the Bureau Committee seems to have dealt with management oversight, while the Consultative Council dealt with strategic and theological issues. According to Wa'il Julaydan, the Bureau Committee consisted, in the mid-1980s, of Abdallah Azzam "whoever was his deputy and three other brothers. It was limited to these five or six persons."⁶⁵ The Consultative Council was larger; in 1986 it consisted of Usama Bin Ladin, Wa'il Julaydan, Abu al-Bara', Abu Hudhayfa al-Urduni, Nur al-Din, Abu Dawud al-Urduni, Abu Mu'adh al-Sharkasi, and Abu Hajir al-Iraqi.⁶⁶ In early 1986 it was reportedly expanded to include as many as fifteen members.⁶⁷

Although Bin Ladin was represented on the Consultative Council he was not a very active member in the Bureau. His role was to provide funding, and although he was probably consulted for major expenditures, he was not very deeply involved with day-to-day management. His jihad experience and knowledge of the situation in Peshawar was limited compared with the other members, because he was not based in the city. Between 1984 and 1986 Bin Ladin continued to live in Saudi Arabia, and only came to Pakistan for visits. According to Wa'il Julaydan, "Abu Abdallah would come and go. He was only responsible for funding. When he would come to Peshawar, he would go for a few days to the front and come back."[68] Bin Ladin would eventually come to live in Peshawar full time, but only after he had begun to withdraw from the Services Bureau.

At the next level down was a range committees responsible for specific activities such as transportation and education. The number of committees grew over time, reportedly reaching a total of twenty in the late 1980s.[69] The sources I reviewed allowed me to identify nine of them: the Reception Committee, the Education Committee, the Scholars Committee, the Orphans and Widows Committee, the Medical Committee, the Transportation Committee, the Technical Committee, the Military Committee, and the Media Committee (more on each of these below).

The size of the Services Bureau at any one time depended on how one counted. Core staff were in the dozens, but the number of loosely affiliated people could be substantially larger, because the majority of Arabs who came to Peshawar passed through the Services Bureau. Moreover, many of the projects were temporary, and Arabs in the Peshawar area could be brought in to work on them for a limited period of time. It was not uncommon for Arabs to switch between spending time in camps or at fronts inside Afghanistan and working for the Bureau in Peshawar or somewhere else. In early 1986, for example, there were some seventy Arabs affiliated with the Services Bureau, but only half of them were in Peshawar; the rest were in the field.[70]

Most of the Bureau's activities took place in and around Peshawar, but in 1985 Azzam set up a satellite office in Quetta in southwestern Pakistan.[71] It was long headed by an Egyptian named Abu Khabab al-Masri, who appears to have been succeeded around 1988 by a certain Muhammad Yusuf al-Libi, and then after that by Abu Hamza al-Urduni.[72] Abu Khabab was described as the *amir* of the Arabs of Qandahar and the correspondent of *al-Jihad* magazine for the south.[73] The Quetta office was set up because the city had a very large Afghan refugee population, and the Services Bureau was involved in the setting up of a hospital there together with the Saudi Red Crescent. Another factor was the proximity to the Mujahidin fronts in Qandahar, which needed logistical support. Representatives of the

Services Bureau would travel to the Qandahar area to deliver supplies to Afghan fighters there.[74] The Afghan Mujahidin commander Abdul Salam Zaeef writes in his memoirs that he was given a tractor from an Arab-funded organization headed by Abu Khabab.[75] In the late 1980s dozens of Arabs also went into Afghanistan to fight on the Qandahar front; one of them was Abu Ja'far al-Qandahari, who later wrote a detailed book about his experiences.[76] When Azzam died in 1989, a certain Abu Ayyub would go to Peshawar to give a speech on behalf of "the Arab Brothers in the Western region."[77]

Financially speaking, the Services Bureau was a small operation compared with some of the other Arab charities and NGOs in Peshawar. While the latter handled multi-million-dollar budgets, the Services Bureau subsisted at around $200,000–$300,000 per year in the 1980s.[78] Everything came from private donations. The single largest contributor, especially in the first few years, was Usama Bin Ladin, who provided a steady cash flow of several thousand dollars per month (the precise amount is disputed), in addition to extra funding for ad hoc projects.[79] However, the organization worked hard to expand its donor base.[80] The main fundraiser, or, as Abdallah Anas put it, "the engine that kept it running with funds," was Wa'il Julaydan (Abu al-Hasan al-Madani). Julaydan was an old friend of Bin Ladin's from Saudi Arabia who had gone to study in Tucson, Arizona, in the early 1980s. After meeting Azzam on one of the latter's speaking tours in America, he started coming to Peshawar in 1984, and eventually settled there permanently. According to Anas, "Julaidan was a force of nature in Peshawar. It was incredible what he could do, he travelled to Saudi Arabia and spoke to worshippers in the mosques and collected donations in the millions."[81] Julaydan did not only fundraise for the Services Bureau, because, as we saw in the previous chapter, he also served as the director of the Saudi Red Crescent in Peshawar, but his dual role was a major asset for the Bureau.

Activities

Azzam and his men handled a wide portfolio of activities. The Services Bureau was never a purely military organization or recruitment outfit, but rather a militarized charity with projects in multiple domains. As we shall see in Chapter 12, Azzam had a holistic view of the war effort and believed that education, medical care, and logistics were as important as fighting. When asked in the late 1980s about what the Services Bureau had contributed to the jihad, he offered a list of thirteen achievements which give a sense of the range and scale of the Bureau's activities:

1. It helped move the issue of the Islamic jihad in Afghanistan to a global Islamic issue.
2. It helped make the jihad issue known through *al-Jihad* magazine, *Luhayb al-Ma'raka*, books, and publications.
3. In the domain of education and instruction: the establishment of educational courses for leaders, the opening of schools inside the trenches; so far approximately 250 schools have been opened, and the establishment of an educational center in the land of battle, the opening of a Qur'an course under artillery bombardment, and the printing of books; in 1988, 400,000 copies were printed, and most of them were sent to schools inside Afghanistan.
4. Fanning the flame of battle and increasing its burning by introducing Islamic hawks who flapped their wings and soared in their quest for the highest paradise ...
5. Raising the morale of Afghan Mujahidin brothers.
6. Addressing the great issue in jihad: the provision of convoys, dispatching them, and equipping the fronts. The transportation department in the Bureau supervised the sending of 20,130 caravans carrying everything the Mujahidin need in terms of ammunition, food, clothes, and mattresses. This work was very substantial and helped fuel the battle. This work cost hundreds of millions of rupis, and it was supported by many of the Islamic foundations.
7. Melting of jihadi efforts in the Islamic crucible; the Arab ones and Afghan ones.
8. Caring for the war victims and the wounded by establishing five hospitals inside Afghanistan: in Jaji, Tokhar, Faryab, Ghazni, and Panjshir, in addition to the Mecca Hospital, the Central Laboratory, and the Natural Medicine Clinic. These institutions were a solid rock before the Crusader army and a thorn in its side. And the Benevolence Committee contributed the lion's share.
9. Stopping the surging flow of emigration; by paying scientists and leaders who were in the running lava [of refugees].
10. Helping the children of martyrs by opening a department for orphans and widows inside Afghanistan and building homes for orphans.
11. Waking the interest of Muslims around the world in going out to stand by this blessed jihad and supporting this Muslim *umma* from this despair and chasm.

12. Equipping the fighters and looking after their families.
13. Forming a committee of scholars to issue fatwas, spark interest, and correct flawed opinions.[82]

We see here that military activities were only a small part of what the Services Bureau did; in fact, of these thirteen achievements, only one (number 7) was about putting foreign fighters on the battlefield. Notice also the absence of a logic to his list – the military, the medical, the educational, and other efforts are all mixed up – showing the extent to which he saw them as intertwined. Still, it is possible to sort the Bureau's activities into categories, and we shall look now at six of the main ones: reception, fact-finding, education, aid, logistics, and publishing. The Bureau's straightforward military activities will be examined separately in Chapter 12.

Reception

One of the key tasks from the beginning was to host incoming war volunteers. The Bureau provided new arrivals with a first port of call, offered them food and accommodation for an initial period, and gave options for what to do next. For this the Bureau had a dedicated Reception Committee, which was initially run by a certain Abu Dujana al-Misri and his deputy, Abu Usayd al-Suri.[83] It included a "check-in department" (*qism al-amanat*), responsible for the initial reception, keeping people's belongings, and helping out with Pakistani visas. It was long led by a friendly Palestinian-American named Abd al-Quddus (aka Abu Faruq).[84] Bayt Abu Hamza and Bayt al-Ansar also served as rest and recuperation facilities between deployments. The Bureau tried to keep track of the volunteers, but this was like herding cats. As one source said, "We started to register new recruits to Afghanistan and their location in the provinces, as the brothers got used to non-compliance in this regard. A recruit would be dispatched to Baghlan and we would meet him in Herat, for instance."[85]

The influx of guests was initially slow but the numbers increased from 1985 onward as word of Bayt al-Ansar spread to Islamist communities around the world. With time the reception service became more streamlined. A Saudi named Hasan al-Surayhi described his second trip to Peshawar in 1987 as follows: "I found out that conditions in Peshawar airport were different from the first time. This time I saw individuals greeting and welcoming the seekers of jihad. They were facilitating their entry and providing them with transport buses. [Leading this effort] was Abdallah Azzam."[86]

A contributing factor to the increase was *al-Jihad* magazine, which provided prospective recruits with travel information. It advertised the existence of the Services Bureau, complete with the phone number for Bayt al-Ansar (41501) as well as a postal box address. The street address was never provided, presumably for security reasons, but people could call the number upon arrival in Peshawar and be met by a Services Bureau representative. Several of the books published by Abdallah Azzam in the late 1980s also included contact details for the Services Bureau. In Chapter 13 we will see what it was like to arrive as a new volunteer.

The Services Bureau also catered for those who stayed longer. It helped them find apartments of their own in Peshawar and to bring their families if they had them. One source notes, "Let us not forget the wonderful work the sheikh did to comfort the Arab *mujahidin* in the land of jihad by helping to bring their wives and children so they could be together."[87] The Bureau even set up a school for the children of Afghan Arabs, called the Ansar School, which covered all ages from primary to high school.[88] To direct the school, Azzam recruited a Jordanian woman who had studied with him in Amman and was married to a volunteer fighter.[89]

Azzam even worked to get the school accredited in Arab countries so that the children could reintegrate more easily in their home country upon their return:

> In the beginning they applied the Jordanian curriculum without official accreditation from Jordan. But the lack of official recognition made some worry about the fate and future of their children, so the sheikh worked hard to obtain accreditation for the school from Saudi Arabia and Jordan. In the end he obtained Jordan's approval, but Saudi Arabia refused to recognize this school. The Jordanian curriculum was taught in the school, despite the families worrying, for security reasons, that the security agencies might discover their names. Finally the sheikh was able to obtain accreditation from the Yemeni institutes

for this school, and with it the application of the curriculum of these institutes.[90]

In December 1987 *al-Jihad* magazine included a long article about the Ansar School, complete with a picture of the entrance gate and facsimiles of the letters of accreditation from Yemeni Ministry of Education.[91] The letters said the school was accredited from the start of the academic year 1987–1988, which suggests that Azzam founded the school around 1986. We find another description of the school in the biography of Rabiah Hutchinson, whose children attended the school in the early 1990s:

[Azzam] had founded the Al Ansar school in Peshawar for the offspring of the Afghan Arabs. His school taught a mixture of secular and religious subjects and the children were taught to memorize the Quran from kindergarten. However, Sheikh Azzam opposed rote memorization; with every Quranic verse they memorized the children would also learn its origin and meaning, the hadith that explain it and the laws that derive from it. [After his death] his school was being administered by his wife.[92]

Fact-finding

The Bureau also gathered political intelligence on Afghanistan. By 1984 Azzam had come to suspect that the information he was getting from the Afghan parties was unreliable and that he needed independent sources so as to make better decisions. "It's one of our aims to get deep information about what is happening inside Afghanistan," Abdallah Anas later said.[93]

One of the first things Azzam did after setting up the Services Bureau was therefore to send a fact-finding mission into Afghanistan. In late 1984 he asked Sayyaf for permission to send a delegation across the border, and recruited a group of young Arabs in Peshawar for this purpose. The mission would consist of four groups or "caravans," each heading to a different part of the country: one to Sholgara near Mazar-e Sharif in the north, one to Herat in the west, one to Zabul in the east, and one to Parwan in central Afghanistan. Each delegation was made up of three or four Arabs accompanied by a few dozen Afghan guides and helpers.[94] The expedition was a very risky undertaking. It was midwinter, and Russian helicopters and fighter planes patrolled the skies.

As Anas later remarked, "It wasn't like taking the Eurostar from London to Paris where you sit down and have internet; no, this journey took forty days. People died from cold, from disease. You could die at any moment, from air bombardment, from ambush or something else."[95] Many of the Arabs on this mission did in fact perish. The delegation heading west – which included the abovementioned Abu Hamza and Abu Uthman – was wiped out in a Russian helicopter raid before they could reach Herat, while those heading to Zabul and Parwan were killed in ambushes inside Afghanistan. Only the Mazar-e Sharif delegation made it safely back.

Even though the overall outcome was tragic, the survivors brought home crucial new insights that came to change Azzam's understanding of the war. On his return, Anas drafted a long travel report, the gist of which was that Sayyaf did not have much of a presence on the ground inside Afghanistan. From Wardak and up, Anas insisted, almost everyone was either Jamiat-e Islami or Hizb-e Islami. Anas thus advised Azzam to reconsider his sole reliance on Sayyaf. As we saw in Chapter 8, Azzam would heed this advice and start seeing the situation more from Hekmatyar and Rabbani's perspective.

Anas also recommended that the Services Bureau send "a cadre of people who can go to Afghanistan and serve as liaisons to facilitate the provision of assistance." Azzam agreed, and suggested that Anas himself go back into Afghanistan to fill this role. On Anas's second trip in mid-1985 he brought two doctors to Mazar-e Sharif before going to Panjshir to meet Ahmed Shah Massoud, whom he liked so much that he stayed for several months.[96] On his third journey, in the spring of 1986, Anas brought a whole delegation of about thirty Arabs from the Services Bureau to Panjshir. (Abu Ubayda al-Banshiri, whom we will meet in Chapter 12 as a key figure in the formation of al-Qaida, earned his nickname from that trip.) Later Anas would spend even more time in Panjshir, becoming very close with Massoud. Incidentally, these expeditions did not go unnoticed. In late 1985, in one of the very first Western press reports to highlight the presence of Arabs in Afghanistan, the French journalist Alain Chevalérias wrote:

Since last winter, representatives of the Muslim Brotherhood have roamed the Afghan countryside. With their fanatical message, they are trying to drive a wedge between the resistance and its original ally, the European public opinion. They visit villages looking for the locals who understand Arabic and liberally hand out money to whoever wants to listen to their propaganda. One of their more pernicious themes is their accusation that European doctors have come to undermine Islam. Thus far, the so-called "Arabs" were only seen around the party of a certain Sayyaf, an obscure guerrilla leader based in Pakistan ... The Arab project is already having an effect. Rabbani ... has recently decided to not allow female doctors in the medical teams.[97]

From mid-1985 onward the Services Bureau regularly sent Arabs on shorter fact-finding trips into various parts of Afghanistan. According to Abu Hajir al-Iraqi, "[The Bureau] began to give recorders and cameras to those who traveled to the interior in order to meet the leaders there, to take some photos from the fronts, and to return with a wealth of information that could help to distribute aid."[98] Starting in October 1985, *al-Jihad* magazine included an increasing number of field reports from these envoys, who were presented as "correspondents" of the magazine. Judging from these reports, the Services Bureau had, at any one time in the late 1980s, a network of between five and ten correspondents inside Afghanistan, including in the far south, west, and north. Thus in 1985–1986 we hear from "Abu Ayyub al-Tayyib" in Qandahar, "a correspondent" in Herat, "Mansur Banzarti" in Balkh, "Abu Qutayba" in Badakhshan, "Abu Bakr" in Panjshir, "Abu al-Adib" in Kunar, "Abd al-Samad" in Nangarhar, "Abu Shu'ayb" in Baghlan, "Abu al-Bara'" in Farkhar, and from "Abu Husayn" and "Maysara al-Faransi" in Lugar.[99]

The Services Bureau also closely monitored the local and international press for coverage of the political and military situation in Afghanistan. They used this material to produce detailed reports about the latest developments for their two magazines *al-Jihad* and *Luhayb al-Ma'raka*. Ahmad Zaidan later wrote that *Luhayb al-Ma'raka* "depended [on] translation of Pakistani paper clippings, Al Bunyan news service, A.M.R.C., Mujahideen news Agencies like Midia and ANA, in addition to Radio Pakistan, Kabul monitoring and Arab eye witness accounts of places in Afghanistan, who belonged to the Services Office."[100] In other words, the Services Bureau ran a veritable all-source intelligence operation during the war.

This information-gathering reflected a broader intellectual interest, within the Afghan Arab community, for empirically founded military analysis. The Afghan jihad was the birthplace of the genre of jihadi literature that later became known as "jihadi strategic studies," that is, writings that apply evidence-based reasoning to speak to *how* jihad should be waged.[101] This genre is interesting because its tone is measured and scientific and very different from the religious argumentation of most other jihadi texts. *Al-Jihad* magazine published a large number of articles in this genre from 1985 onward, several of them written by the Syrian ex-officer Adnan Ibrahim. They ranged from scoresheets of losses on either side in the Afghanistan war, via detailed descriptions of Soviet weaponry and battlefield tactics, analyses of the strategic situation in Afghanistan, analyses of historical military campaigns such as the Afghan fight against the British in the nineteenth century, articles about general military topics such as propaganda or land warfare, to analyses of conflicts other than Afghanistan, such as Lebanon or the Philippines.[102] One article (about the armies of the Warsaw Pact) notes that "knowing the enemies of the *umma* and keeping up with the latest and most important news about them is a fundamental duty."[103] Another interesting article from 1988 makes the case for critical analysis of the history of Islamist rebellions, a type of analysis that would proliferate in the jihadi movement from the early 1990s onward.[104]

Education

Azzam considered that the main role of Arabs should be in the domain of education.[105] The Services Bureau therefore had an Education Committee which worked hard to promote what they saw as proper religious knowledge in Pakistan and Afghanistan. It was led initially by a Saudi named Jamal Khalifa (aka Abu al-Bara') and his two deputies, Abu Mu'adh al-Sharkasi and Abu Rida al-Suri (aka Muhammad Lu'ay Bayazid). They were in charge of education inside Afghanistan and in Pakistan respectively. In late August 1986 Khalifa left, and al-Sharkasi took over as committee director.[106] At some point in 1987 the committee appears to have been officially disbanded and its activities and personnel transferred to something called the Islamic Assistance Foundation (Mu'assasat al-'Awn al-Islami). This was an entity that Azzam helped set up to make it easier to obtain the official Pakistani permissions necessary to operate in the education sector.[107]

One of the Bureau's first educational activities was to support the University of Da'wa and Jihad in Peshawar. Established by Abd Rabb al-Rasul Sayyaf in early 1985 in the Jalozai refugee camp just south of

Pabbi, the university sought to offer advanced training in religion and vocational subjects to Afghan refugees in Peshawar.[108] According to Sayyaf, Azzam "encouraged the university very strongly" and taught there on and off throughout the 1980s.[109] The university was also showcased in several articles in *al-Jihad* magazine.[110]

Starting around 1985, the Education Committee initiated a variety of projects for Afghan children both inside Afghanistan and in the refugee camps. Over the next few years they would work on at least four different types of projects. One was the setting up of two preacher training schools, called Ansar Institutes (Ma'ahid al-Ansar), in Peshawar and Quetta.[111] The idea was to "train the trainers" by bringing in Arab religious instructors to teach Afghan preachers. Another activity consisted of sending Arab preachers directly to schools inside Afghanistan. Azzam wanted to do this on a large scale, but he was never able to recruit as many as he had hoped. He was very proud of the ones who did go, such as an Iraqi named Abu 'Asim (aka Muhammad Uthman):

My meeting with him was over a year and a half ago. I saw light shining from his face. He had blonde hair and a constant smile. He was calm when he spoke, and would only speak the small words that were necessary … Ramadan began, and the youth began to gather to pray Tarawih behind him, and it was as if you were listening to the Qur'an fresh, as if it were just revealed. When Ramadan was half over, Abu 'Asim bid Peshawar farewell for the caravan that was traveling towards Panjshir … Thus, Abu 'Asim began his blessed struggle, and Ahmad Shah began to set him up to for educational, spiritual, nurturing seminars teaching the Qur'an to the commanders who were in the area, and from the best of the Mujahidin. Over the course of a year, he had taught and encouraged over 200 commanders and soldiers the recitation of the Qur'an, fasting on Mondays and Thursdays, and praying at night. 'Abd al-Wahid – one of the Arab brothers in Badkhshan – said to me: "I heard an Afghan youth reciting the Qur'an correctly, accurately pronouncing each letter, and I asked him which Arabic university he had graduated from. So, he replied: 'I graduated from the university of Abu 'Asim al-'Iraqi!'"[112]

A third strategy was to help build schools in Afghanistan. The Services Bureau itself claimed that it had enabled the construction of between 250 and 400 Afghan schools.[113] The fourth initiative was the development of an entire new curriculum in Islamic Studies for Afghan schoolchildren. Around 1986–1987 the Bureau put together a working group led by an Egyptian named Fathi al-Rifa'i which brought together representatives of all seven major Mujahidin parties to work out a new curriculum.[114] The group reportedly succeeded, and even produced a new primary-school book, which was printed in large quantities – 400,000 copies according to Azzam himself – and distributed to Afghan schools.[115] The accuracy of all these numbers is difficult to verify, but the scale of the alleged contributions is not inconceivable given that the Services Bureau collaborated with larger Islamic charities on several projects.

In the late 1980s the Services Bureau also ran an ideological training center of sorts for Afghan Mujahidin commanders in Mehtarlam. Abu Ja'far al-Qandahari writes:

When I returned to Peshawar I talked to Sheikh Abdullah Azzam and told him what was on my mind. He reassured me and gave me confidence by saying: "How can you leave while we desperately need people like you?" He wanted me to work as a correspondent for *al-Jihad* magazine, and I told him I would not be good at it because during the battles I was completely absorbed and could not do anything else. He said: "I will send you to Mehtarlam and you will have all the battles you want for as long as you like." The main goal behind sending me there was for me to join a group of Arabs affiliated with the sheikh who had established a training center for the Afghan Mujahidin and especially the prominent leaders and fighters. The center did not train in the use of arms or in tactics. We could call it a center for ideological guidance to provide the Mujahidin with an Islamic education and teach them the principles of loyalty and obedience while raising their political awareness and clarifying the Islamic system as a comprehensive system for life and the rule. The *amir* of this center was a young Egyptian aided by a number of Algerians who were all in Peshawar at the time getting supplies, books, and tapes. I joined them and we started a long journey from Peshawar to Mehtarlam.[116]

Aid

The Services Bureau also provided various forms of humanitarian aid to the Afghan Mujahidin and their dependents. It had a Widows and Orphans Committee that took care of families of fallen *mujahidin*, and it had a Medical Committee that sought to improve healthcare for Afghan fighters and refugees. This is part of the reason why many Islamists in Peshawar at the time saw the Services Bureau more as a charity than a paramilitary organization.[117] Jamal Isma'il, for example, said the "Services Office by '87, '88 it was becoming more of an NGO. They were having a printing press in Peshawar. They were helping with orphans and schools, mosques and dispensaries."[118]

The Orphans and Widows Committee helped build and operate orphanages both in Peshawar and in Afghanistan.[119] It notably established the al-Medina al-Munawwara orphanage in Peshawar in early 1987.[120] It also distributed food and other supplies to the widows of fallen Afghan *mujahidin* and to Peshawar-based widows of Arab volunteers. Mustafa Badi (Abu Ibrahim al-Yamani) describes how he and a Palestinian named Abu Hamza were personally tasked by Abdallah Azzam in 1987 to travel around Afghan camps and register the names of children of fallen Afghan *mujahidin* for the Orphans Committee.[121]

The Medical Committee engaged in two main types of activities: setting up medical facilities and recruiting doctors for service on the frontlines in Afghanistan. By the end of the 1980s the Services Bureau claimed to have established four main facilities. One was the Mecca Surgical Hospital in Quetta, which was later handed over to the Saudi Relief Committee.[122] The second was a medical laboratory in the province of Sarhad, which served "all the Islamic hospitals responsible for treating the refugees and Mujahidin."[123] By early 1988 it claimed to be conducting over 6,000 tests each month.[124] The third was a rehabilitation clinic (described in one source as a "natural medicine clinic") for wounded *mujahidin*. It was set up in partnership with the Saudi Relief Committee and later handed over to the Saudi Red Crescent.[125] It served "Afghans who had completed their natural convalescence and were coming to prevent disability in their limbs or get a prosthetic replacement."[126] In 1988 the clinic reportedly received 220 patients a day.[127] The fourth was a care center for disabled fighters which helped the severely wounded transition from hospitals to the care of relatives inside Afghanistan.[128]

As we saw in the previous chapter, Azzam lamented the low number of Muslim medical personnel in Afghanistan and the superior presence of Western aid organizations. To improve the situation, the Services Bureau launched two initiatives. One was a medical training program inside Afghanistan called the Medical Challenge Project, which aimed to teach selected Afghans basic medical skills.[129] After getting it up and running, the Bureau then handed it over to the Benevolence Committee

(Lajnat al-Birr), a Saudi-run charity. One of the men Azzam put to work with the Benevolence Committee at this time was reportedly Khalid Sheikh Muhammad, the future mastermind of the 9/11 attacks.[130] The other initiative was an effort to recruit Arab doctors and male nurses to work inside Afghanistan.[131] This appears to have been less successful, but as we saw in the previous chapter, they recruited at least one doctor in 1985 to chase the French Médecins Sans Frontières from Mazar-e Sharif.

Logistics

One of the flagship activities of the Services Bureau, especially in the early years, was to assist the Afghan Mujahidin with military logistics. In the spring and summer of 1985 Azzam had watched with frustration how weapons and equipment accumulated on the Pakistani side of the border because the Mujahidin parties were too disorganized to sort out the transportation. Azzam later said:

By dissolving the Union around May 1985, a problem transpired in sending the fee for arms and ammunition to the interior, because the Union had previously been responsible for this task. May, June, and August passed – the most important period for jihad – and the Mujahidin were waiting in their winter camps in Peshawar. So I asked them, "What is the problem?" They answered, "We do not have the money to transport our weapons, luggage, and ammunition."[132]

Azzam concluded that for the resources to reach the battlefield he needed to circumvent the party leaders and bring in the goods himself: "Therefore, we started sending the money with our brethren straight to the fronts. This way the aid operations were centralized in our hands."[133] The Bureau established a separate Transportation Committee (*lajnat al-tarhil*) for shipping equipment and personnel into Afghanistan.[134] To lead it, Azzam assigned Wa'il Julaydan.[135]

Thus from late 1985 onward the Services Bureau mounted large numbers of convoys – or "caravans," as they called them – into Afghanistan. Each carried some combination of weapons, equipment, food, money, and personnel. The Bureau's own numbers should be taken with a pinch of salt, but Azzam claimed that the Transportation Committee had organized no less than 20,130 caravans in the course of the second half of the 1980s.[136] Abu Hajir al-Iraqi said that the Services

Bureau "transported tens of thousands of *mujahidin* to the interior."[137] Transportation came to be seen by the Services Bureau itself as one of its most important contributions to the war effort.[138]

The Services Bureau also had a Technical Committee (*al-lajna al-fanniyya*) which provided military engineering services to the Mujahidin. The Technical Committee was further divided into a maintenance division, led around the same time by Abu Hajir al-Iraqi, and a design division (for developing new products) headed by a US-trained electrical engineer named Abd al-Haqq al-Jaza'iri.[139] The Technical Committee repaired and designed telecommunications equipment, landmines, and other gadgets, and it trained Afghan *mujahidin* to do the same.[140] However, the Services Bureau's contribution in the engineering field was limited by the lack of skilled personnel. The Bureau did have access to some high-caliber individuals, however. One was Isam al-Ridi, an Egyptian who had worked as a flight instructor in the USA. In early 1983 al-Ridi went to Pakistan after meeting Azzam at a conference. On arrival he stayed at Azzam's house in Islamabad, and then Azzam took him to see Sayyaf, who took him on as an international logistics officer. He would spend the next eighteen months based in Peshawar and traveling the world to purchase equipment for Sayyaf's fighters. He went to the USA, UK, Japan, Kuwait, and Saudi Arabia, purchasing things such as range finders, night-vision goggles, night-vision scopes, and even scuba-diving equipment.[141]

Publishing

One of the most visible aspects of the Bureau's work was publishing. Its efforts in this domain were shaped by a twin objective: first, to raise awareness about the Afghan jihad among Muslims abroad; and second, to spread Islamist ideas among the Afghans. To achieve this they distributed Islamist literature to the Afghan Mujahidin, and they produced several Arabic-language magazines, and even some films. Each of these activities got going at different times and differed in scale, but by the late 1980s the Services Bureau seems to have had four different foundations (*mu'assasat*) dedicated to information work: one for printing educational materials for the *mujahidin*, one for translating Islamist literature from Arabic into local languages, one for audiovisual productions, and a fourth for Arabic-language magazines.[142]

The Bureau's most successful publication by far was *al-Jihad* magazine (see below), but this was not their only magazine. In 1988 Azzam also launched *Luhayb al-Ma'raka* (The Flame of Battle), a weekly newsletter intended for fighters in the field.[143] Edited by his nephew Mahmud Azzam (Abu Adil), it was a more rudimentary production: just a few pages of black-and-white text on stenciled paper.[144] The magazine appears to have been discontinued in 1990 after seventy-nine issues. In 1989 the Bureau added another publication to its portfolio, namely, the jihadi women's magazine *Dhat al-Nitaqayn* (She of the Two Waistbands) (see Chapter 13).[145]

From 1985 to 1987 the Services Bureau also had an audiovisual department called MAJ, an acronym for Mirror of the Afghan Jihad (*mirayat al-jihad al-afghani*).[146] It was supervised by a person named Abu Imran (aka Hudhayfa), and who "made a continuous effort to organize the arrival of images and jihadi clips from inside Afghanistan."[147] The MAJ produced at least nine video films and three audio cassettes with jihadi hymns, all of which were available for sale by mail order.[148] The films were available in Arabic, English, French, Urdu, and Pashto. It also sold "jihadi postcards by packets of thirty," a book-length illustrated history of the Afghan jihad, and large posters with pictures from Afghanistan. These audiovisual products appear not to have had a very wide distribution, at least not compared to the Services Bureau's flagship publication.

al-Jihad Magazine

The Services Bureau's greatest success on the propaganda front was *al-Jihad*, a monthly Arabic-language magazine that, at its peak, was distributed in around fifty countries in as many as 50,000 copies. Launched in December 1984, it would keep going for over a hundred issues before closing down in early 1995.[149]

Azzam did not start *al-Jihad* from scratch. Instead, he took over and renamed an existing newsletter, *al-Mujahid*, which had been produced since 1982 by students at the University of Peshawar. *Al-Mujahid* was a weekly four-page bulletin on stenciled paper that conveyed news from the Afghan battlefield in Arabic based on reports from the Mujahidin parties.[150] Jamal Isma'il, who worked on the newsletter, explains how Azzam got involved:

When Abdallah Azzam came to know about it, he supported the idea. He was supporting and he was advocating it and even giving it more publicity. And he was each time visiting Peshawar giving us some new addresses; send it to this center, send it to this center; because he was in contact with many centers, many groups here and there. In late '84, there were students, problems in the university, for Arab students, for the Pakistani students' organizations. For us, the [Student] Union was in trouble, because of, none of us was ready to give so much time ... The offices of the Afghan Mujahidin groups sometimes it was a little bit far, we didn't have transportation, we don't have enough time for this, and the students union decided to stop it. Sheikh Abdallah Azzam at that time, in December 1984, he decided to establish [the Services Bureau]. When he came to know that the newsletter has been stopped, he said, Okay, I'll carry on with this newsletter ... [But we said] ... this name is reserved for us, for student's union. You cannot use it ... And he said, okay, I'll name it *al-Jihad* instead of *al-Mujahid*. And his magazine started from that point.[151]

Al-Jihad started small. In the beginning there were just three people in a small room: Azzam the chief editor, Imad al-Abid the executive editor, and Ahmad Abd al-Futuh the typist. Imad al-Abid (aka Abu Anas) was a Jordanian Palestinian who had studied in Saudi Arabia and arrived in Peshawar in the autumn of 1984.[152] He would serve as executive editor for over five years. Ahmad Abd al-Futuh was an Egyptian with some typing experience. Little by little the editorial staff expanded. Over the next few years they were joined by a Tunisian, a Saudi-educated Syrian named al-Shawwaf, an Egyptian named Isam Abd al-Hakim, and by a certain Salah Hassan.[153] In 1986 Ahmad Zaidan joined; he was a Syrian student at the University of Peshawar who would go on become a famous al-Jazeera reporter.[154] The abovementioned Jamal Isma'il joined in 1988, and he too would later become a well-known mainstream journalist. At the time, though, none of the staff had professional publishing experience. Aside from a few Afghan translators such as Vahid Mojdeh, all the staff were Arabs. *Al-Jihad* also relied heavily on external contributors. Some contributed on a regular basis, such as Adnan Ibrahim, a Syrian former army major who covered military–strategic affairs. Others provided material on an ad hoc basis. Mustafa Hamid, for example, says he occasionally wrote for *al-Jihad* under a pen name.[155] Indeed, many articles in *al-Jihad* were written pseudonymously, sometimes to protect the author, and sometimes to make the magazine seem better staffed. Abdallah Azzam often wrote articles pseudonymously; his main nom de plume was "Abu Muhammad," especially for martyrdom biographies, but he also used "Sadiq Amin" and "Hassan Abd al-Rahman."[156] Azzam's role was mainly to produce the editorial for every issue and to make major decisions; otherwise Imad al-Abid ran the show. Busy as he was, Azzam sometimes had to be chased down for his submission:

These [editorials] were written after strong suggestions and comments to me by Abu Adil [Mahmud Azzam]; sometimes he would come to me when I was next to my mother's hospital bed, reminding me that the next issue needs your input; at other times when I was at the front, and yet other times he stalked me by phone and fax on my travels, and the editorial would arrive Thursday evening and the issue had to go out on Friday morning.[157]

The production process also evolved. The first three issues were printed in Peshawar, but in March 1985 they moved production to Lahore to get color prints.[158] In late 1988 production was moved to a Karachi press which used computers.[159] The publishing frequency evolved through trial and error: The first three issues were monthlies; then the fourth to the seventeenth were bimonthlies, after which it switched back to being a monthly.[160] The magazine followed a steep improvement curve in terms of production quality. The first issue, published on 28 December 1984, was all black and white, twenty pages, with a plain front cover with "al-Jihad" in hand-drawn Arabic letters. By the third issue, which was thirty-six pages, the front-cover design was visibly improved, with colors and a new logo, although the inside was still black and white. The magazine eventually stabilized at forty-eight pages and with color pictures throughout.

Azzam later said that the magazine was initially seen by some in the community as extravagant. Some fighters in the field said the money would have been better used on supplies. Some conservatives in the Gulf thought it was too lavishly produced: "Why all these colour photographs?" they complained. But Azzam was able to convince critics that the magazine brought in ten times more money than it cost to produce. "If someone reads the story of a martyr or a victorious battle, they might pay a million riyals or fifty thousand dollars, and this keeps the magazine running for months."[161]

A typical issue of *al-Jihad* had a range of different types of articles; always an Azzam editorial and a substantial news section, often a sermon-like theological article and a military–political analysis, and sometimes an interview with a prominent military commander, Mujahidin party leader, or religious scholar. Issue 9 (July 1985) introduced a regular article series titled "With the Martyrs," in which Arabs who had fallen in combat were presented with a brief biography and a picture where available. All issues included poetry, earlier issues showed political cartoons, and from issue 13 there was a women's column and a "letters from the readers" section. From issue 30 there was usually also a book-review section that summarized various books on jihad or Islamic history. *Al-Jihad* also included advertisements, typically for magazine subscriptions, charity projects, books by Abdallah Azzam, or audiovisual products. Aside from a brief experiment with an English supplement in issues 17 and 18, the magazine was always in Arabic. It included a lot of photographs, many of them extremely graphic. No image was too strong for the magazine, not even pictures of infants with faces melted from severe burns or with half the head missing above the nose.[162]

The magazine also included interviews with prominent international Islamist figures, especially Muslim Brotherhood leaders from the Arab world. Whenever a prominent Brotherhood figure was passing through Peshawar, Azzam made sure to get an interview. Among the people featured in the magazine were Yusuf al-Qaradawi (issue 5), Zaynab al-Ghazzali (issue 14), Abd al-Majid al-Zindani (issue 21), Hasan al-Turabi (issue 37), Hasan Ayyub (issue 40), Adnan Sa'd al-Din (issue 42), Qazi Hussein Ahmed (issue 45), Muhammad Mahmud Sawwaf (issue 51), Ahmad al-Mahlawi (issue 51), Rachid Ghannouchi (issue 59), and Mustafa Mashhur (issue 62). In addition, the magazine published written statements from prominent clerics such as Abd al-Aziz Bin Baz, Ahmad al-Qattan, Abu Bakr al-Jaza'iri, and Ahmad al-Khalili (the mufti of Oman). This was in addition to interviews with prominent Afghan Mujahidin leaders such as Sayyaf, Hekmatyar, Gailani, and Haqqani.

In March 1986 *al-Jihad* featured an interview with none other than Yusuf Islam, better known as the British singer–songwriter Cat Stevens.[163] After his conversion in 1977 Stevens had devoted himself to Islamic philanthropy, and in early 1986 he was in Peshawar to inspect the Afghan refugee situation with a view to involving his charity, Muslim Aid. Interestingly, the interview marked the beginning of an extended period of cooperation between Cat Stevens and Abdallah Azzam. A year later, in March 1987, *al-Jihad* published a full-page advertisement for Muslim Aid, saying that Cat Stevens had visited Peshawar several times and that his charity was now officially registered in Peshawar and collaborated with the Muslim World League, the Saudi Red Crescent, and the Services Bureau's own Ansar Institute (*ma'had al-ansar al-'alami*).[164] Moreover, in September 1987 *al-Jihad* started advertising a tape recording with jihadi *anashid* (hymns) by Cat Stevens, produced and sold by Mirror of the Afghan Jihad, the Services Bureau's own audiovisual department (see Illustration 11).[165] It is unclear how long the cooperation continued, but Azzam was certainly the first jihadi leader to enlist a Western pop star in his propaganda effort. Muslim Aid appears not to have been involved in military activities, but Cat Stevens cannot have been oblivious to Azzam's hardline reputation and the Services Bureau's paramilitary work at this time.

Al-Jihad magazine was financed primarily from the coffers of the Services Bureau.[166] At one point a group of Saudi merchants reportedly tried to finance the magazine directly, but Azzam declined for fear of losing editorial control.[167] Store sales and subscriptions also provided some income. The subscription cost was $20 per year in Asia and Africa, $25 per year for the rest of the world, and $35 per year for governments and institutions. However, according to Zaidan, "most of the circulation depended on agents [i.e. store sales] rather than individual subscription."[168] Occasionally wealthy donors would pay a larger sum for multiple copies to be distributed for free.

The distribution of the magazine increased rapidly. In an interview in mid-1989, Imad al-Abid provided detailed production numbers. He said the first issue had been printed in 1,000 copies, and that by the tenth issue (August 1985) they were up to 5,000 copies. From issue 20 (July 1986) to 40 (March 1988) it stabilized at 15,000 due to production capacity limitations and lack of permission to distribute in key markets. Issues 31 and 32 (June and July 1987) with martyrs from Jaji had print runs of 35,000 and 50,000 copies because Usama Bin Ladin paid to have extra copies produced. After issue 40 it printed in 35,000–38,000 copies.[169] After 1990 numbers fell drastically: "After the invasion of Kuwait," Ahmad Zaidan says, "we were publishing 8,000 or sometimes 5,000 copies."[170]

Al-Jihad had a remarkable international reach for its time. Azzam built a global distribution network through a combination of outreach and incoming offers. In the beginning he actively solicited Islamic centers abroad, but as the magazine became known, prospective distributors came to him.[171] By February 1987, page 3 of the magazine listed the following twenty distribution points:[172]

- Jordan: Amman, Maktabat al-Risala al-Haditha, PO Box 1100
- Emirates: Dubai Maktabat Dubai li'l-Tawzi', PO Box 1529
- Saudi Arabia: Eastern Province, Maktabat Dar Ibn Qayyim, PO Box 1865; Medina Maktabat al-Ulum wa'l-Hukm, PO Box 688
- Norway: Islamic Centre, Youngs gate 7, Oslo
- Sweden: Islamiska forbunden, Högbergsgatan 59, S11638 Stockholm
- Germany: Islamic Centre Wallner st 1–3/8, München
- Austria: M. Elbiery,/Lindeng 1–72/1070 Wien
- Switzerland: Centre Islamique, 10 Place Delagave 1003 Lausanne, Switzerland
- Italy: U.S.M. I/C-P 13161 Roma
- Paris: Groupement islamique, Cité de l'avenir, 121 Bd Menilmontant, 75011 Paris
- Spain: Centra Islamica, P.O. Box 12315, Madrid/C/Alanso CANO 3.
- Belgium: SELOMEX/Box P.O. 1403, Brussels
- Holland: Muslims Inf Centre, Becklaan 207–2562 AE The Hague
- United Kingdom: London Islamic Inf. Centre, 233 Seven Sisters road, London N4 2DA
- Denmark: Aziz Alwaly, Scandiagade 58, 4 rv/2450 kph
- Athens: M. T. Ghozlan, P.O. Box 64004 Zografou 15701 Athens
- Turkey: P.K. 269/AKSARAY/Istanbul
- Canada: 3210 GOYER 27 Montreal, QC, Canada H35 1HR; SHERBROOKE University B-225 Sherbrooke QC CANADA 1R 2RI; P. O. Box no. 7442 Trois Rivers QC Canada C56 5LC
- USA: Islamic Centre Tucson 1627/ St St Tucson AZ 85719
- Germany: Mainzes Landstrasse 176 6000 Frankfurt A.M.

In late 1988 the magazine listed no less than forty-nine countries with cover prices in local currencies: Afghanistan, Algeria, Argentina, Austria, Bahrain, Bangladesh, Belgium, Brazil, Canada, Cyprus, Denmark, Egypt, France, Germany, Greece, Hong Kong, India, Indonesia, Iran, Iraq, Italy, Japan, Jordan, Kenya, Kuwait, Lebanon, Libya, Malaysia, Morocco, Nigeria, Oman, Pakistan, Philippines, Portugal, Qatar, Saudi Arabia, Singapore, South Africa, Spain, Sudan, Sweden, Syria, Tanzania, Thailand, Tunisia, Turkey, UAE, UK, and USA.[173]

Al-Jihad quickly gained an international and active readership. Starting from issue 7 (June 1985) it devoted a special section to letters to the editor. Readers would submit political and theological reflections, suggestions for the magazine, poetry, and the like. By the summer of 1986 the magazine had received letters from Mauritania, Morocco, Algeria, Tunisia, Egypt, Ghana, Sudan, Lebanon, Turkey, Jordan, Iran, Kuwait, Qatar, UAE, Saudi Arabia, Yemen, Pakistan, India, Philippines, and Indonesia, as well as from France, West Germany, UK, Ireland, Norway, Sweden, Italy, Yugoslavia, Cyprus, USA, Canada, Puerto Rico, Australia, and Taiwan. Azzam later said, "In terms of distribution, Saudi Arabia was our biggest market, but Algeria, Saudi Arabia, and America sent the most letters. We get several thousand letters from them."[174]

Al-Jihad was far from being the only magazine published out of Peshawar. As we saw in Chapter 7, the Afghan Mujahidin produced dozens of magazines in Arabic, English, French, and other languages. As such, *al-Jihad* was only one voice in a choir of jihad-related propaganda coming out of Peshawar. The main competitor to *al-Jihad* in the mid-1980s was *al-Bunyan al-Marsus*, which was launched in July 1985 by Sayyaf's Ittihad Party. At its peak, it printed in almost as many copies as *al-Jihad*, but it was not as widely distributed outside the Gulf.[175] The editor of *al-Bunyan* was an Egyptian named Muhand al-Shar'a, and Sayyaf himself wrote the lead article in every issue. The content was quite similar to that of *al-Jihad*, because the two editorial groups knew each other and frequented the same circles.[176] Some people wrote for both magazines, and *al-Bunyan* published at least one article by Azzam and a review of his book *Defense of Muslim Lands*.[177] In 1989 *al-Bunyan* published an interview with Azzam to mark the fifth anniversary of *al-Jihad* magazine, the headline being "*al-Bunyan* in a brotherly meeting with its comrade *al-Jihad*."[178] *Al-Bunyan*, which probably had more money at its disposal, was even more lavishly produced than *al-Jihad*, with state-of-the-art color and paper quality, but there was somewhat less original content. *Al-Bunyan* was widely considered as the "little brother" of the two magazines. It also came out less often; four to six issues per year versus *al-Jihad*'s twelve.

Al-Jihad magazine was a resounding success as far as branding, recruitment, and fundraising was concerned. It is difficult to quantify its effect, but judging by the many letters to the editor and the references to the magazine in fighter autobiographies, there is little question that it inspired a good number of Arabs to go to Afghanistan. It also remains one of the most widely distributed international jihadi magazines of all time.

Problems

From the start, the Services Bureau was marred by internal disagreements. There were several underlying reasons for this. One had to do with personnel: The Bureau's members came from many different countries and social backgrounds, bringing with them diverging opinions about how things ought to be done. Moreover, their comings and goings were unpredictable, and key staff could suddenly disappear. Besides, the level of education and professional experience among the recruits was generally low, so many were less than competent at their assigned tasks. A second reason was its ambiguous mission. It was never clear, even to insiders, whether the Services Bureau was a military organization, a logistics organization, a charity, or something else. People thus arrived with different expectations, and the organization would inevitably disappoint some of them. A third reason was that Azzam was not a particularly good manager. Some of the traits for which he was praised in other contexts – such as his reluctance to speak badly of people, his tendency to forgive, and his insistence on keeping a semblance of unity – became a liability when faced with real incompetence and serious internal friction.[179] He was notoriously conflict-shy, preferring to ignore incompetence and leaving tough practical decisions to his deputies.

The sources speak of a wide range of problems, from small frustrations to serious crises. The Egyptian militant Osama Rushdi later said the Services Bureau "had a lot of bureaucracy problems; the administration was not good, and projects were not completed."[180] In the first year or so of its existence, the Services Bureau saw much rumbling in the ranks. As Basil Muhammad noted:

The general administration of the committees and the [Services] Bureau, however, did not have the full chance to take form and to stabilize ... Dr. Abdallah Azzam was still commuting between Peshawar and Islamabad ... Usama Bin Ladin was still traveling between the Kingdom and Pakistan, between Pakistan and Afghanistan, without any stability or regularity. Inside the administration of the Services Bureau and the Shura Council, the situation was always apprehensive and agitated; disagreements would erupt and fade away, only to reemerge ... The majority of the committed and pious recruits were not sufficiently experienced ... in the administrative and organizational domain.[181]

Similarly, in mid-1985:

Abu Hasan and Abu Rida, these two zealous young men from America, discovered that chaos reigned among the Arabs there, and that order and discipline was the exception. "The brothers came," Abu Rida narrates, "and found no one to meet them. One of them would enter the Bureau not knowing where to go. Is there training? Will he go to the fronts? He did not know! This was approximately six months after the establishment of the Services Bureau."[182]

Abu Hajir al-Iraqi also noted that "in the early period of my arrival – in late October 1985, when hearing about feelings of despair and complaints here and there – I would avoid them and concentrate more on my work," but eventually he could not ignore the "rise in complaints."[183] Middle managers, for example, complained that new recruits did not inform them about their whereabouts:

Abu Dujana al-Masri, may God have mercy on him, and Abu al-Sa'id al-Suri organized the attendance of the brothers and taught them the system. The majority of the brothers, however, rejected it! Abu Dujana had organized an exit and return register at the Services Bureau, and put it on the door. Yet, some brothers became annoyed. In the field "going where," they wrote "I don't know"! In the field "time of return," they wrote "God willing"!! Abd al-Mannan, may God have mercy on him, would explode in anger and shout: "This is Masonic!" So the brothers were not following the system.[184]

Lower-level members, for their part, complained of being deployed in the field to perform difficult tasks with little guidance. One such envoy, Yahya Sanyur, expressed his frustration to his boss Abu al-Hasan al-Madani in a letter dated 19 September 1985:

- Some of caravan owners are cursing us and some want to clash with us. What should we do?
- We are driving alone in the car, brother Amin, brother Din Mohammad and I, knowing that the road has become more dangerous than before after a mine exploded on the Fath road, blowing up a car in front of us.

- Everyone here demands money, such as Mr. Gharib and Mr. Umar, so what do I tell them? I always tell them that I need a document from Abu al-Hasan.
- In Fath, there is no guard around the safe. However, the room in which the safe is placed is now for us and is always kept locked.
- The tent is in a critical situation because of the great number of people visiting it on the pretext that they have camels, horses, and donkeys that they want to lease. Most important is the problem of the bank, which is only cashing out with a written notice three days in advance. Please provide us a letter [for the bank] as soon as possible.[185]

Others complained of insufficient pay. Once, in the late 1980s, Azzam was confronted by a volunteer who said, "Sheikh Abdallah ... you did not give me enough money to bring my wife, and because of you my wife has divorced me. The leader of the jihad is supposed to give the *mujahidin* money to bring their wives."[186]

There were also problems inside *al-Jihad* magazine. According to Ahmad Zaidan, the editorial work was "without planning. There was no follow up on the departments. There was lack of financial administration ... The people who ran the magazine did not follow the rules and principles of professional journalism ... the material was weak, lacked depth."[187] In 1989, according to Zaidan, there was a veritable mutiny inside the editorial committee:

In the 56th issue, the editorial staff tendered their resignations, because of its unrealistic articles and for not deriving news from the sources. But some of them, went back, except I and another. Dr. Azzam convinced them back and allowed them to include in every issue a letter criticizing the situation and discussing Afghanistan from their own differing point of view.[188]

Others disagreed on larger issues, such as how to allocate donations. Isam al-Ridi, a US-based Egyptian, became so frustrated that he left Peshawar; he disliked the Services Bureau's subservience to the donors regarding how their money should be spent. In a poorly veiled criticism of Bin Ladin's influence, he said:

I was one of the people invited to special meetings with Sheik Abdallah to organize the work of the Arabs and the visitors in Peshawar, and things of, you know, important nature to Afghans, how are we helping them, including donations and things. One of the main sticking issue was that I was totally opposing the fact that any rich individual who comes to Afghanistan would control the decision making. I think they have, you know, pure, I mean pure feeling to the code, but I don't think he have the experience to be involved in the day-to-day running of the business in Afghanistan. I was very much opposed to that and I, my voice was very well heard out, but nobody really acted on it. I have asked other scholars, I've asked other colleagues. I think I was right and I took a stand on that.[189]

Most of the time such frustrations were swept under the carpet, but sometimes they erupted in quarrels and confrontations. Azzam himself spoke of one episode in which "the administration staff had made some mistakes in the office, so they met with Brother Usama [Bin Ladin], and they blamed each other."[190] The situation reached boiling point toward the end of 1985. At some point that autumn, the Services Bureau's first executive director, Abu Akram, unexpectedly packed up and returned to Jordan. It is unclear whether he left because of the internal problems, but his departure made the situation worse. His successor, Abu Hudhayfa al-Urduni, was widely disliked, and toward the end of 1985 the Bureau organized a vote for the executive directorship and the Shura Council "in an attempt to contain the malfunction and correct the approach."[191] They convened a meeting with all the Services Bureau members who were in Peshawar at that time. The meeting turned into a farce, because almost everybody wanted to be on the Shura Council, but nobody wanted to be executive director. Abu Hajir al-Iraqi, who found himself virtually forced to take over the directorship, later offered a blistering account of the meeting:

It was wonderful to see a consensus to create a council of 15 people to be elected from the thirty-five brothers who were present. So I told them: "Glory be to God! 15 out of 35 is nearly half! Imagine that we, for example, give the administration of the entire world to one half of its population to rule over the other!" However, they insisted on that figure. It was even more amazing that the majority of votes went to the brother Abu Muhammad al-Sudani [for director], then to the humble servant [me]! It was a surprise ... What is this? I have not been here for three months even, and I hardly know the scene as I should. Yet, people's concept [of a leader] is that of he who leads their prayers or presides over their sermon. They don't ask: Does he understand this? Does he have experience? ... So when they decided that Abu Muhammad al-Sudani should be the director, he excused himself with Abu

Suhayb from the first meeting. We looked around and asked: Who will replace him? So in the next meeting, we gathered to elect the new director to act on behalf of Sheikh Abdallah in his absence. We began to count the votes ... Then the papers followed successively: Abu Hajir, Abu Hajir ... Abu Hajir. When I read the first piece of paper, I laughed. They asked: Why are you laughing? So I told them: Imagine, one of the brothers wrote my name! I drew the second: What is this? Then the third: I blushed and said: This must be a joke.[192]

Abu Hajir al-Iraqi reluctantly took on the task, but he only lasted six months. "I found myself faced with an immense accumulation of mistakes, starting from the way people were invited to jihad to their treatment [after arrival]."[193] He also admitted that he himself had underestimated the challenges of keeping discipline in the ranks because he had wrongly assumed that people would simply do as they were told:

We tried as hard as we could to deal with the brothers, but I admit that my [personnel] selection was wrong ... I thought of people as I read in the books. That you would tell someone: ... Do this ... so he does ... I thought that just as I was dealing with a switch, by turning it to the right, the light is turned on, and by turning it to the left, it is turned off. In such manner will the people be with me! ... Dealing with the Arabs was the hardest thing.[194]

Abu Hajir later also criticized Azzam for his naïve attitude to management:

It was a surprise to me, upon my arrival, that one of us [i.e. Azzam] had an angelic conception of the Mujahidin ... When he reads that the peak of Islam is jihad in the cause of God, he imagines that all the brothers would have attained that position ... But is there a guarantee for purity of intentions to last? Chaos and the lack of control and accountability of the people will allow the Devil to gradually make the brother forget the purpose for which he came ... Therefore, the valid and correct action was then to make sure that we chose the right place at the right time for the right person to the right project ... There is nothing wrong with that as administration is part of our religion. To characterize chaos as blessing is only a misuse of sanctity to muzzle the voices and justify our mismanagement![195]

In late June 1986 the Services Bureau reached the low point of its history in terms of morale. Having recently returned from the humiliating battle of Jaji (see Chapter 12), members gathered in Peshawar to discuss the resignation of Abu Hajir al-Iraqi. At the meeting, Abu Hajir surprised everyone by proposing nothing less than the *closing down* of the entire Services Bureau:

> I told them: "Brothers, we are doctors now, and between our hands is a wounded, dying man who is breathing his last breath. At this hour, it is not in your interest to discuss with me whether I am correct in my diagnosis or not. Join me hand in hand to cure this dying man, because if you go to prove to me that he is well, then I fear he will die in our hands!" After discussing, they asked me: "So what is the solution?" I told them: "... Dissolution!" Then they asked: "How can you say that?" So I said: "To dissolve this work, we would be in control of a decision, which is better than to let it dissolve itself. We then rearrange our work on sound foundations and a well thought out plan."[196]

The proposition, needless to say, was not adopted. Instead Abu Hajir left, leaving the Services Bureau in the hands of Abu Hudhayfa al-Urduni, whose abysmal tenure in late 1985 had led to Abu Hajir's appointment in the first place.

Abu Hajir al-Iraqi (aka Mamduh Mahmud Salim) would later come to play a central role in the al-Qaida organization. Born in Sudan in 1958 to Iraqi Kurdish parents, he studied electrical engineering in Baghdad before serving as a communications officer in the Iraqi army from 1981 to 1983, when he deserted and fled to Iran before later moving to Pakistan.[197] Widely described as charismatic and strong-willed, Abu Hajir was knowledgeable in religion. He had memorized the Qur'an and was known for his beautiful Qur'an recitation. According to Abdallah Anas, "Azzam had three imams to lead the prayer if he wasn't there. One was Abu Hajir al-Iraqi, the second Abu Ibrahim al-Iraqi, and when neither of them could lead, I would step in." Later, Abu Hajir became a religious authority in al-Qaida and helped develop its justification for attacking the United States.[198]

In 1986 another major issue plagued the Services Bureau, namely the organization's inability to provide training and combat opportunities on a level that would satisfy the most martially minded volunteers. This problem, which led Usama Bin Ladin and several others to break away from the Services Bureau and form the al-Qaida organization, will be dealt with separately in Chapter 13.

Still, the Services Bureau survived, in large part due to its position as the main port of call for incoming foreign fighters. Management also seems to have improved later on, especially after Tamim al-Adnani assumed the executive directorship of the Services Bureau in 1988. On the whole, the Services Bureau played a crucial role in the mobilization of Arabs to Afghanistan. When Azzam observed, in 1989, that "the Bureau helped move the issue from its local existence to a global one," he was not exaggerating.[199] The Services Bureau was by far and away the most important organization in the Afghan jihad as far as recruitment of Arab fighters was concerned. Before its foundation, no entity undertook any form of systematic recruitment of foreign fighters, and in the middle of the 1980s it was the only organization to do so. In short, the Services Bureau was a vital mechanism for turning global Muslim interest in the Afghan jihad into actual fighters on the ground. So far, however, we have mostly described its activities in Pakistan and Afghanistan, while most of the recruiting was being done abroad. As we shall see, Azzam was a better recruiter than manager.

10 | Recruiter

They came from California and Australia, from South Africa and Norway. They came from at least forty different countries, including every single Arab state down to the Comoros Islands. The foreign fighters in 1980s Afghanistan were the most international volunteer force the world had ever seen. This remarkable mobilization did not happen by itself. Abdallah Azzam and the Services Bureau worked hard to reach out to the international Muslim community, and actively recruited in many different countries. But what did their activities consist of? Where exactly did Azzam go in the 1980s and what did he do on his trips?

This chapter examines Abdallah Azzam's international recruitment efforts during the Afghan jihad. It looks in turn at his outreach strategy, his lecture tours, the Services Bureau's foreign infrastructure, and the recruitment efforts of other organizations. At the end it examines the number and backgrounds of the foreign fighters. We will see that Azzam and his comrades engaged in extensive, if somewhat improvised, international outreach. Azzam visited mainly the Gulf and North America, while his deputy Tamim al-Adnani traveled more widely, including to Africa and South America. We will also see that the Services Bureau's most elaborate overseas infrastructure was not in the Middle East, but in the United States.

Strategy

Azzam engaged in international outreach because he believed that a collective Muslim effort was the only way to liberate Afghanistan. He also hoped that an international mobilization could outlive the Afghan conflict and help rid the rest of the Muslim world of oppression. Much of his political energy from 1984 onward therefore went into raising awareness of the Afghan jihad among Muslims around the world.

Azzam was never single-mindedly focused on recruiting foreign fighters. He also sought to solicit donations, recruit preachers, and raise awareness more generally. A good illustration of his broad approach to mobilization is the paper he presented at the World Mosque Conference in the Maldives in early December 1985.[1] He outlined six specific things the *umma* could provide for the Afghan Mujahidin. Interestingly, he prefaced his remarks by saying that the main problem was not a lack of soldiers, but a lack of *preachers*. Afghanistan, he said, was suffering an exodus of Afghan Islamic scholars from Afghanistan to Peshawar, and the flow needed to be reversed, because "the scholars are crucial for the spirit of fighting and self-sacrifice." He then proceeded to list the six action points:

- First, money for food to the Afghan Mujahidin. Back-of-the-envelope calculation – 3 rupees per day per soldier, with half a million men under arms, required approximately 45 million Pakistani rupees per month, i.e. 10 million Saudi riyals or $3 million.
- Second, to incentivize Afghan scholars to return to Afghanistan, one should pay them a monthly salary of 100 riyals per month. Each returning scholar would bring with him at least fifty soldiers and children. So if 1,000 scholars returned to the trenches, there would be 50,000 more *mujahidin*.
- Third, one should pay a salary to Mujahidin commanders so that they will not be tempted to leave the battlefront. If there are some 1,000 commanders and we pay them 500 rupees (100 riyals) a month, this would cost 1.2 million riyals a year.
- Fourth, one should allow motivated Arab volunteers, who are ready to sacrifice and aspire to martyrdom, to reach the battlefield. Arab youth have an important role to play on the battlefield, including (a) education and instruction, (b) lifting morale, (c) unifying various afghan factions (because Arabs are independent), (d) revitalizing the spirit of jihad and martyrdom, (e) solving various problems, (f) bringing aid from outside donors to the battlefronts, and (g) bringing special skills and expertise to the battlefield.
- Fifth, increasing the encouragement of Arabs during their entry to Afghanistan.
- Sixth, enabling larger numbers of Arab preachers who are motivated and who are not engaged in other functions, to join the ranks of the Mujahidin.

Islamic NGOs should pay attention to this fact [and] pay a salary to preachers to go to Afghanistan.[2]

Later, Azzam would stress the foreign-fighter component somewhat more. In July 1986, for example, he declared:

Here we are in the seventh year of the jihad in Aghanistan ... we have found ourselves few in number (of men not money) ... we ask for a small number of students; we would like two brothers from each Islamic center ... God knows and bears witness to the fact that we need men more than anything, regardless of their specialization.[3]

Azzam's outreach work was multifaceted and included at least five key components. One was to produce and disseminate publications in the form of books, magazines, films, and recorded lectures. The second was to reach out directly to people in his existing social network and ask them to contribute. The third was to give media interviews and facilitate media coverage of the cause. The fourth was to personally travel around and give lectures and meet new people. The fifth was to build an organization that could scale up the communication work. He engaged in all these activities in parallel.

At the same time, there was an improvised and opportunistic aspect to his outreach efforts. For example, there does not appear to have been an overall plan behind the sequence of his publications; he wrote the books he felt inspired to write. Similarly, he gave interviews to the journalists who came to him; he did not cold-call newspapers for coverage. Moreover, where he went to speak depended largely on who invited him; he rarely turned up unsolicited. Also, he expanded the Services Bureau in countries where there was already substantial local interest in collaborating, such as the United States, leaving other countries be.

Of the five components, the first – the publications – is described extensively in Chapters 9 and 11. The next two – reaching back to friends and giving interviews – can be covered briefly here. In the early years especially, Azzam contacted many of his friends and family in the Middle East, asking them to come to Pakistan. For example, at one point he reached out to a man named Abu Ahmad who had been with him in the Fedayin camps and had subsequently moved to Saudi Arabia, and "when we asked him to come from Riyadh, he left the material world [al-dunya], left his residency permit, left everything, and he came here to work with us."[4] Similarly, we saw in Chapter 8 how he pleaded with Muslim Brothers in Jordan to send preachers. He also wrote to fellow professors asking them to send students. "Do you have a group of students that you can send at this critical and sensitive time in the history of the *umma*?" he wrote to Sheikh Abu Bakr al-Jaza'iri at the University of Medina in June 1989.[5]

We also know that Azzam gave many media interviews, especially in the late 1980s. He was often interviewed in connection with his lecture tours, and some journalists also sought him out in Peshawar.[6] On at least one occasion, in Kuwait in 1989, he gave a press conference.[7] In his writings, Azzam encouraged Arab journalists to cover the Afghan jihad, and when Arab journalists came to Peshawar he would facilitate meetings and field trips. The Saudi journalist Jamal Khashoggi, who visited Peshawar several times in 1988 and 1989, said that Azzam took him to meet Rabbani and Sayyaf and that Azzam invited him to join him on a trip to northern Afghanistan in September 1988.[8]

As for the last two components of Azzam's outreach – his lecture tours and his international organization-building – they were so extensive as to require more in-depth examination.

Lecture Tours

Azzam traveled extensively throughout the 1980s to lecture about the Afghan jihad. As we saw in Chapter 5, he had been on the international conference trail since the 1970s, but Afghanistan made him something of an Islamist rock star. He made intercontinental trips right from his first year in Pakistan (1982), but the schedule was not particularly hectic until 1988 and 1989, when he really did travel a lot.[9]

Most of Azzam's trips were to the Gulf, and by far the most frequent destination was Saudi Arabia. Every year he went to Mecca for Hajj, and in most years he did Umra, the optional "small pilgrimage," during Ramadan. He often took part in the Muslim World League's events in Mecca during Hajj. He gave numerous talks, both in the Hijaz, the Najd, and the Eastern Province. In Jeddah he often spoke at the Shu'aybi mosque and at least once at the *Ukaz* newspaper.[10] In Riyadh he lectured at the World Muslim Youth Association, the Muslim World League office, and in the al-Manhal hotel in the central Ulayya district.[11] He also gave at least one lecture at the King Faisal Foundation in Riyadh. He drew large crowds; Jamal Khashoggi recalled attending a Friday sermon by Azzam in a Jeddah mosque and having to pray in the street outside.[12] Azzam also raised substantial sums of money from Saudi donors, although we lack precise numbers. According to an apocryphal story, businessmen in Riyadh refused to pay *zakat* (the religious income tax) the regular way in 1989, saying they wanted to give it straight to Abdallah Azzam himself.[13] In any case, Azzam enjoyed considerable freedom of operation in the kingdom, at least until 1989, when he started facing some restrictions (see Chapter 14). He would later say that "the Saudi government and its people were with the Afghan jihad from about 1983, as the only Arab state that worked with Pakistan to support the Afghan jihad."[14]

He also went several times to Kuwait, which had a strong Muslim Brotherhood branch and several charities providing support to Afghan refugees. Ahmad al-Qattan said he first met Azzam in the Islah mosque in Kuwait in 1981.[15] On his trips to Kuwait Azzam also met with an old friend from the Fedayin camps, Isma'il al-Shatti, who had become editor of *al-Mujtama'* magazine. In late 1989 Azzam spent a whole week in Kuwait, giving several lectures and a big press conference.

The first three summers after moving to Pakistan – that is, in 1982, 1983, and 1984 – Azzam also went to Jordan to see friends and family and give lectures.[16] On those trips he would stop in Saudi Arabia for Umra on the way.[17] He had kept his house in Amman, so he was able to host visitors and talk to them about what he was up to in Peshawar. Someone who visited Azzam's house in the summer of 1984 later said it was full of young people all day.[18] One of these young people was Abu Mus'ab al-Suri, the Syrian militant who later became a well-known jihadi military strategist.[19] In the early 1980s al-Suri was in exile in Amman, having previously joined the Combatant Vanguard, a militant wing of the Syrian Muslim Brotherhood. After 1984 Azzam was denied entry to Jordan as well, and he would never return to Amman again.[20] Entry bans probably explain why he did not visit any other Arab countries aside from the Gulf and Jordan in this period. He appears to have been prohibited from entering most of the Arab republics in the 1980s, notably Algeria, Libya, Egypt, Syria, and Iraq.[21] He never went to Turkey either, probably for the same reason.

Azzam faced no such restrictions in the West, so he traveled there widely, especially in the United States. He went to the USA practically every year for the annual conference of the Muslim Arab Youth Association (MAYA), and he usually gave many other lectures while he was there. In one audiotape, Azzam "recounts stories of his trips to

Detroit, Kansas City, Los Angeles, and dozens of other American cities between 1979–89."[22] A US-based Palestinian named Jalal Abualrub reportedly "helped Azzam visit more than 50 US cities, spreading the word about the Afghan jihad and raising funds."[23] By the end of the 1980s Azzam had reportedly visited about half of America's fifty-two states.[24] For reasons that are not clear he went less often to Europe than to the USA. Perhaps there was less demand for his lectures among student societies there, and perhaps the visa situation was a disincentive (a tour of Europe required multiple visas). Still, we know that he visited Britain, Germany, and Spain at least once in this period, and possibly other countries too (see below).

Azzam also lectured in South Asia. He attended several Islamic conferences in Pakistan, both in Islamabad, Lahore, and Karachi.[25] And as we saw earlier, he once went to the Maldives for a conference. He may also have visited Bangladesh, but appears not to have visited Indonesia or Malaysia.[26]

When Azzam went somewhere, he rarely gave just one talk. He usually had a very hectic schedule, as on this trip to Qatar in 1989:

He came to Doha on Tuesday 28 [March] 1989, and Sheikh Tamim al-Adnani and a number of scholars and a group of youth received him at the airport. We did not spend many days there ... the day he arrived, he gave a lecture in the Umar Ibn Khattab mosque, and then Wednesday evening he gave a lecture in Abu Bakr al-Siddiq mosque, and in the morning of the Thursday he gave a lecture in the mosque of the Religious Institute. And then Thursday morning in the Qatar Club, and the title was "The road from Kabul to Jerusalem," and then Friday prayer in the Ishaq mosque. And he gave a lecture after the Friday prayer in the same mosque, and another in the Wakra mosque after the afternoon prayer. In the evening of 1 April he left Doha for the Emirates. All of his trips were like this.[27]

Azzam also used these trips to network with prominent Islamist figures. When he went to Germany in the mid- to late 1980s he took a day off to go and see Isam al-Attar in Aachen. "He didn't give a lecture, it was just a private visit. He spent a whole day here. We ate together, prayed together, talked hadith together," al-Attar later said.[28]

We do not know Azzam's full travel history in the 1980s, but we can reconstruct parts of it by aggregating information from different sources. The following is a chronological list of all the dateable trips for which I found a source.

1981
- December: Possibly to the USA for a MAYA conference in Springfield, Illinois.[29]

1982
- July: To Jordan for family visits and lectures.[30]
- Late September: To Saudi Arabia for Hajj.[31]
- December: To the USA for the MAYA conference in Fort Worth, Texas, and possibly other US locations.[32]

1983
- July: To Jordan for family visits and lectures.[33]
- Mid-September: To Saudi Arabia for Hajj.
- December: To the USA for the MAYA conference in St. Louis, Missouri, and possibly other US locations.[34]

1984
- July: To Jordan for family visits and lectures.[35]
- Early September: To Saudi Arabia for Hajj.
- December: To the USA probably for the MAYA conference (location unknown), and possibly other US cities.[36]

1985
- Late August: To Saudi Arabia for Hajj.
- December: To the Maldives for the World Mosque Conference.[37]
- Unspecified month: To the UK for a lecture at a Muslim student conference.[38]
- Unspecified month: to the Islamic University of Medina, Saudi Arabia.[39]

1986
- Mid-August: To Saudi Arabia for Hajj.

1987
- Early August: To Saudi Arabia for Hajj.[40]
- December: To the USA for the MAYA conference (city unknown).[41] He also spoke in al-Faruq mosque in Brooklyn, at al-Salam mosque in Jersey City, and likely in other US locations.[42]

1988
- May: To the USA for a lecture on 5 May at a MAYA conference (city unknown).[43]
- Late July: To Saudi Arabia for Hajj.
- Around 2 November: Unspecified destination "outside of Pakistan"[44]

- December: To the USA for the MAYA conference at the convention center in Oklahoma City. On this trip he also spoke at a mosque in Fort Worth, Texas.[45]
- Unspecified month: To Saudi Arabia for a lecture in the Qasim region and in Jeddah.[46]
- Unspecified month: To the USA for lectures in Seattle, Kansas, Brooklyn, somewhere in California, and possibly other US locations.[47]

1989
- March/April: To Qatar and the UAE for multiple lectures.[48]
- Mid-July: To Saudi Arabia for Hajj.[49]
- Late October: To Kuwait for a week-long visit to participate in the meetings of the World General Association of Islamic Charity Boards. He also gave several lectures.[50]
- 8 November: To Lahore for a lecture at a large conference.[51]
- Unspecified month: To Saudi Arabia for a lecture at the King Faisal Foundation for Research and Islamic Studies in Riyadh.[52]

In addition to these dateable trips we know that he went to Spain and Germany at some point in the 1980s.[53] He may also have visited France, Italy, and Greece.[54]

Azzam was no underground preacher; he usually spoke in large lecture theatres or mosque prayer halls. His talks were usually widely advertised, and he could draw big crowds. One video from Saudi Arabia in the late 1980s shows Azzam speaking in a very large mosque to an audience of probably more than a thousand people.[55] The MAYA conferences in the USA drew similar-sized audiences. If we include his lectures in major mosques in the Gulf and in Jordan, then the total number of people who attended a talk by Azzam in the 1980s is probably over ten thousand.

Azzam quickly acquired a reputation as a powerful speaker. Years of *da'wa* work had taught him how to capture a crowd with great storytelling and verbal imagery. He made creative use of objects, sometimes bringing a blood-stained piece of clothing worn by a fallen Afghan Arab to his presentations abroad.[56] He spoke with clarity and energy, impressing audiences with his detailed knowledge of Afghan history and politics, and by reeling off long passages from the Qur'an and the Hadith from memory. Dressed in Afghan clothes, typically sporting the pakol hat, he often lectured standing up (he used to say, "It is bad to talk about jihad when we are sitting down and relaxing").[57] Even on a bad day he could spellbind audiences and make them cry; as one listener noted, "I attended the gathering and the sheikh looked tired and depressed. But as usual, his speech inflamed all those around him with enthusiasm. Next to me, there was a young Afghan man whose eyes were in tears."[58] Indeed, his sermons often made people cry; an Afghan Arab recalled, "He used to come from Islamabad to Peshawar and make us weep on Thursdays and Fridays."[59]

As an illustration of Azzam at work, we can take a closer look at one of his conference appearances in the United States. In December 1983 he went to St. Louis, Missouri, for the MAYA annual convention. That year 5,000 people gathered for what conference spokesman Ahmad Saifuddin told local media would only feature "scholars who lecture about life. The convention does not deal with politics or international affairs."[60] That, as we shall see, was not quite accurate. We happen to have the testimony of a certain Muhammad Siddiqi who attended the conference and who ended up going to Afghanistan soon afterward. The testimony is worth quoting at length:

I got to know Sheikh Abdallah in 1983 when I was a student in America and God guided me. I was following the articles of Sheikh Ahmad al-Qattan on Afghanistan, and I was thrilled by his articles. My big problem was that I wanted to go there. We were close to the Christmas holiday, and the custom of the brothers in the Muslim Arab Youth Association was to have a big conference during this vacation. I had questions on jihad, and one of the brothers told me you can go to the conference and ask about what you want. When we arrived at the conference I discovered that Sheikh Abdallah Azzam [was speaking]. It was the first time I would meet the sheikh. His talk at the conference was about the Afghan jihad, and by God he was a flame of enthusiasm. God knows that his speech captivated our hearts. He mentioned that jihad is an individual duty and brought evidence ... Many scholars were sitting at the conference ... most of them said [jihad] is not *fard 'ayn* and differed with him in this opinion ... I saw how the youth flocked around the sheikh, and his words had credibility, because he was a man who said something and then acted on it. In the late afternoon after 3 p.m. there were meetings and lessons with each sheikh in a separate room, fourteen or fifteen sheikhs altogether. In most of the rooms you would find a small number of people, but in Abdallah Azzam and Ahmad al-Qattan's rooms you could barely find space for a needle. He said, "Come closer, come closer," and they gathered around him. I found that the sheikh had many traits that set him apart from the rest of the sheikhs, not least his youthful spirit, which attracted the young. He spoke in the mindset of young people, about the problems of young people, and about things that interest young people ... God knows that these six days at the conference were the most beautiful days in my life.[61]

In his lectures abroad, Azzam spoke largely about the same things that he wrote about: the Afghan jihad, Palestine, or general religious themes such as the virtues of jihad and the importance of Islamic education. To get a sense of a typical lecture we can look at the one he gave in Germany in the late 1980s.[62] He opened by describing the status of the conflict as favorable to the Mujahidin and by relating stories of miracles from Afghanistan. He then listed four things that people should do. The first is to give money. Azzam said it costs 10 German marks to feed a *mujahid* for a month, and there are 500,000 *mujahidin*, so feeding all Afghan *mujahidin* costs 5 million marks. Given that there are 2 million Muslims in Germany, it would cost each of them only 2.5 marks to feed all *mujahidin* for a month. The second is for Muslim medical doctors to go to Afghanistan. Here he guilt-tripped them, saying, "If a French girl can spend four years inside Afghanistan on the Russian border serving the Mujahidin [then you Muslim men should be able to go there too.]" The third is for religious teachers to go to Afghanistan. "We offer them a salary," he said, "salary from clean [*halal*] money". He then added,

The least the jihad wants from you is that you follow its news. We publish a monthly magazine in Arabic called *al-Jihad* magazine. And there's another monthly magazine called *al-Bunyan al-Marsus* ... We want you to give two hours to the jihad by reading the news about those who write history with their blood. We write this magazine in blood, and you read it sitting down in your chairs. Will you not give it two hours?!

The fourth thing is for Arab youth to come to Afghanistan and train. "We thus ask you, Arab youth, to come to us. Because, my brothers, our primary battle is the battle for Palestine; our primary battle is the battle for al-Aqsa, this is what the [Afghan] Mujahidin leaders have declared."

In the question-and-answer session one person asked: "How can I get to Afghanistan? Is it possible to join a front and teach the children of the *mujahidin*?" "Yes," Azzam replied,

and we welcome you. If you don't have a ticket, then the ticket is on us, as is our food, drink, accommodation, training, your rounds, to the very end from the moment you depart from Germany till you leave us after a year or two, to join God or your country. None of this will cost you a single dirham. And if the Islamic Center you come from is able to pay for your ticket and your expenses, then praise be to God, Lord of the two worlds ... How do you proceed? You go to the Pakistani embassy and ask for a visa, and normally they give it to you if you are not from one of the countries neighboring Israel ... If you are Jordanian, Palestinian, Syrian, God help you, but try once, twice, three times, and if you don't succeed, take a plane without the visa but tell us that you are coming, on which flight and which day. We have some people who can receive you at the airport and will try to get you in one way or another. That's it. Our telephone numbers in Peshawar: country code Pakistan (0092) city code Peshawar (521), and then you call. We will send you the book *Join the Caravan* which has the telephone numbers and how to reach us. In any case, when you reach Peshawar, just ask: "Where are the Arabs?" Only, before you come, let us know by telephone, let us know by telephone or by letter (Peshawar telephone 40973 or 40437). Call us and we will try to get you out. But try to come with a visa if you can, try to go with any company that will take you without a visa, get to Islamabad – it has to be Islamabad, not Karachi, because we have some people who might get you in. And if you can't make it, at least donate 10 marks at the end of each month, and stop by ten Turks or ten students and collect from each 10 marks, 100 marks to give to the Mujahidin.[63]

Another key message in his recruitment talks in the West was to say that Muslims should not live in the West because it exposed them to sinful things and benefited the Jews who run the global capitalist system. In his lecture in Seattle in 1988, he said:

You want to enter an American enterprise, who give you five hundred or a thousand dollars and you work for them? Everything of you pours into [pockets of] Jewish industrialists, into their financial factories and into their banking houses which they have. All of our blood, all of our sweat, our whole life pours now into the usurious banks of the Jews ... do you want to get a piece of paper of a Jewish-American university? How much you have paid and endeavours undertaken until you get the paper after five years. If you were only to work one fourth of what you have invested for this paper for Islam, to aid Islam.[64]

There is little question that Azzam's lectures had an impact. Dozens of individuals have explicitly mentioned them as a key inspiration for the decision to go to Afghanistan. For example, there is the case of Abu Bakr al-Zayla'i, a Somali who later became a top leader in al-Shabaab, who "attended one of 'Abdullah 'Azzām's lectures in Virginia which inspired him to participate in jihad, thus he told him about his desire to go to Afghanistan and he accompanied him back to Afghanistan, leaving everything behind in 1987."[65] Another example is that of Abd al-Aziz al-Dawsary, who heard Azzam speak in Jeddah in 1984:

I was one of those who heard about Jihad in Afghanistan when it started . . . but was hesitant about [it] . . . One of those who came to our land (presumably Saudi Arabia) was sheikh Dr. Abdallah Azzam – may his soul rest in peace – I heard him rallying the youth to come forth and (join him) to go to Afghanistan . . . I decided to go and check the matter for myself.[66]

There was also El Sayyid Nosair (the man who murdered Rabbi Meir Kahane in New York in 1990), who heard Azzam speak in the al-Salam mosque in Jersey City in 1987. His son later wrote:

My father meets Azzam at the mosque and returns home transformed. His whole life has acted upon him; here, at last, is *his* chance to act and make a clear and irrefutable demonstration of his devotion to Allah. He and the men from the mosque start meeting in our apartment, talking loudly, ecstatically, about supporting the jihad in Afghanistan.[67]

Nosair ended up going to Afghanistan, and in 1988 he accompanied Abdallah Azzam on the latter's trip to the USA.[68]

Yet another example is the British-Egyptian Mustafa Kamal Mustafa, better known as Abu Hamza al-Masri, the radical, hook-handed imam of Finsbury Park mosque in north London in the late 1990s. After becoming interested in political Islam in the mid-1980s he traveled to Mecca for Hajj in 1987, where he met Abdallah Azzam. According to his biographer, the meeting "would change the course and thinking of his life."[69] Abu Hamza did not go to Afghanistan at this point, but on his return to Britain he told a friend he had met Azzam and that "he was a great man who represented the future of Islam." Later, in the 1990s, Abu Hamza went to Afghanistan, where he lost an eye and both hands in an accident during explosives training, before returning to the UK.

By 1988 the demand for information about the Afghan jihad was so high that Azzam began delegating some of the requests to his deputy, Tamim al-Adnani. For example, when he was invited to a conference in San Francisco in 1989, he replied, "I cannot attend it, for I have work to do here. I will send you Sheikh Tameem instead."[70] Al-Adnani became such an influential fundraiser for the Services Bureau in the late 1980s that his story merits special attention.

Tamim al-Adnani was a Palestinian who served as the Services Bureau's executive director in 1988 and 1989.[71] He was the son of the famous Palestinian poet Muhammad al-Adnani and the grandson of a former governor of Jerusalem. Born in 1942, he was raised in Aleppo in Syria, and studied economics in Cairo in the early 1960s. There he met the Syrian Islamist Marwan Hadid, and became his student and assistant.[72] Religious, al-Adnani turned down the option of a banking career, and instead became an English teacher in Jenin in Palestine. He was actually in Jenin in the mid-1960s when Azzam was active in the Muslim Brotherhood there, but the two never met at the time. Tired of supporting a family on a low salary, al-Adnani moved to Saudi Arabia in the late 1960s or early 1970s to take up a highly paid job in a British airplane company. By the early 1980s he was working at the Dhahran airbase in the Eastern Province, where he became the imam of the mosque on the base.[73]

Al-Adnani took an early interest in the Afghan jihad; in the summer of 1982 he went to visit Abdallah Azzam in Amman, and emerged enthusiastic.[74] Back in Dhahran he began fundraising for the Mujahidin, and in the summer of 1983 he reportedly went to deliver some $50,000 to Sayyaf in Peshawar. The next year he went again, this time bringing $275,000 and also paying a visit to the training camps on the Afghan border. He also started recording and distributing speeches about Afghanistan in the kingdom, becoming an important early advocate there for the Afghan jihad. Wa'il Julaydan later said, "His cassettes spread like a light in darkness, like fire in the woods."[75] These activities eventually got him expelled from Saudi Arabia to Qatar in late 1985.[76] He kept going to Afghanistan, and in 1988 he settled permanently in Peshawar, and soon became the executive director of the Services Bureau.

The corpulent al-Adnani was a charismatic public speaker with a self-deprecating sense of humor and fluent English. "If any of you drops out of the jihad, I will sit on you," the 130-kilogram man used to tell the Mujahidin leaders. He quickly became very popular on the speaking circuit; Azzam later complained that "women from the Islamic World have been phoning my house and saying, 'Where is Sheikh Tameem Al-Adnani? We want to speak to him. We have heard his cassettes and we want to tell him that we want to come to the Jihad.'"[77] On another occasion, "a brother phoned Afghanistan from Sweden saying, 'Where is Sheikh Abdullah Azzam? I want to speak to him because he promised to send us Sheikh Tameem Al-Adnani to deliver some lectures here in Sweden.' He was in so much demand that while he was in the middle of one event, he would be required for the next."[78]

Al-Adnani traveled widely in the Middle East, and he was renowned for his ability to raise funds in the form of jewelry from wealthy women:

> He used to gather gold from women to give to the Mujahideen. Once he collected some gold in Jordan and put it in a bag ... Sheikh Tameem wanted to bring this gold to Peshawar. He went from Jordan to Saudi Arabia by car, and at the Saudi Arabian border they search everything, for fear of any type of smuggling, especially drugs ... Naturally, this also happened to Sheikh Tameem: the whole of the car, even inside the tyres, were searched; everything, that is, except the one bag that contained the gold! He took it from Saudi Arabia to Qatar, and then to Peshawar, where he gave it to the Mujahideen![79]

Azzam also recalled,

> Another time we were together in the United Arab Emirates. There Allah – the Mighty and Majestic – made the hearts of the people accept his words fully. His speeches used to reach the hearts very quickly. He would say to the women, "I will make dua (supplication), and I will tell the Mujahideen to make dua, for every sister who contributes her jewellery to them." Thus, through approximately three lectures that he gave only for women, he gathered about 4 kg of gold earrings, bracelets, and the like![80]

Al-Adnani also traveled extensively in North America. His first trip on behalf of the Services Bureau was in April 1988, when he traveled to several different states and to Canada to lecture about the Afghan jihad. We know he was in Lawrence, Kansas on 19 April 1988, because he recorded a ninety-minute video interview in English with the Islamic center there.[81] His second trip was in December 1988, when he went on a one-month speaking tour, visiting twenty-two different American states in twenty-one days before spending five days in Canada.[82] His trip was coordinated by a Nebraska-based man named Usama Uthman.

In the summer of 1989 Tamim al-Adnani embarked on a veritable world tour which would be his last journey. First he went to Nigeria to inaugurate an exhibition on the Afghan jihad. He was interviewed widely in Nigerian media, including on television.[83] From Nigeria he flew to Egypt, where he spent a day in Alexandria giving a lecture about the Afghan jihad in the al-Mahlawi mosque. The next day he flew to Yemen, where he gave a number of lectures before returning to Qatar prematurely to get treatment for malaria. After a few weeks he headed to the United States for an extensive speaking tour in mosques and Islamic centers across the country. While in the USA he received an invitation from the Saudi ambassador in Venezuela, a certain Sheikh Bakr Khamis, to come and speak to the Muslim community there. He went, only to receive a lukewarm reception among the PLO-sympathizing Palestinians in the audience.[84] From Venezuela he went to San Francisco for a large Islamic conference, and from there to a number of other states. However, all the travel became too much for al-Adnani, who was overweight and had a heart condition. On 18 October 1989 he died from a heart attack on the way to a speaking venue in Orlando, Florida.[85]

Foreign Branches

Azzam also sought to build an international network of contacts that could represent the Services Bureau abroad. He succeeded in building a loose network of contacts, but he failed in setting up anything resembling a global organization or franchise. In fact, as we shall see, the only country in which the Bureau had something we can call an official branch was the United States.

In the Arab world, the Services Bureau faced political restrictions that prevented the setting up of formal branches. Even in Saudi Arabia there were no Services Bureau offices in the strict sense of the word.[86] What Azzam did instead in these countries was to rely on informal networks. Typically he would encourage people who had already made it to Peshawar to go home and recruit and fundraise on the Bureau's behalf. The sources contain multiple examples of this "reachback" mechanism. A prominent one is that of Usama Bin Ladin, who recruited dozens of friends and acquaintances from Jeddah and Medina to Afghanistan between 1984 and 1986.[87] Ad hoc recruiters such as Bin Ladin could in turn task their new recruits with reaching back to their friends, thus extending the informal recruitment network. Bin Ladin, for example, "asked Brother Abu Hanifa to travel to the Hijaz and recruit some good young people and bring them with him.

I told him, 'you go and you come back with twenty brothers or more.' The Brothers were laughing from my optimism ... But thank God, our brother left for 24 days and came back with 24 men."[88] Over time, as more people went to Afghanistan and came back again, Afghan Arab alumni networks could be relied upon to fundraise and recruit. Thus the Services Bureau's informal recruitment networks grew without anyone acting formally as its agent or official representative.

The United States was a different matter. There the Services Bureau would end up having at least one official branch as well as multiple affiliated offices. As we have seen, Azzam first visited the USA in 1978, and he spoke regularly at the annual conferences of MAYA from at least 1982 onward. From early 1984 people started coming from the USA to work with the Services Bureau in Peshawar. In 1984–1985 Azzam used these people to spread information about the Afghan jihad and facilitate the distribution of *al-Jihad* magazine in the USA.[89] By September 1985 Azzam had reached an agreement with the Islamic Cultural Center in Tucson, Arizona, to distribute *al-Jihad* magazine in America.

An important development occurred in 1986 or 1987 when a group of Arabs at the al-Faruq mosque in Brooklyn established something called the al-Kifah Refugee Center.[90] According to a later *New York Times* article, al-Kifah "started out as a desk in Al Farooq Mosque around 1986 and then moved into a small apartment in a building a few doors away at 566 Atlantic Avenue, above what is now a perfume factory, with just enough room for a desk, a few chairs, a phone and a fax machine."[91] Al-Kifah raised funds in the name of the Afghan jihad and used it to send people to Peshawar. In the autumn of 1987 it was officially registered as a charity. In December 1987, during Azzam's December visit to the MAYA conference, its representatives contacted Azzam and proposed that al-Kifah serve as a bridgehead for the Services Bureau in the United States, which Azzam gladly accepted.

In early 1988 Azzam published an article in *al-Jihad* magazine in which he describes his recent meetings with pro-jihad activists in the USA. The article starts by commending "the brothers" for their many initiatives to collect money for Afghanistan (such as producing T-shirts with "Help free Afghanistan" and having a van drive around the state to collect donations). Then Azzam highlights the al-Faruq mosque in Brooklyn:

I was also pleased that [the brothers in the al-Faruq mosque] have themselves opened a Bureau to serve the Afghan jihad [*maktab li-khadamat al-jihad al-*

afghani] and appointed a lawyer and gotten him a government license, and started coordinating trips to Afghanistan, paying for their tickets and sorting out the visa for them from the embassy in New York. So far we have received seven delegations without it costing us a dirham. I have opened an account in my name in Brooklyn, and the account number is: 016714446, Independence Saving Bank, and may God bless whoever wants to send or transfer money to it; and whoever wants to send a check, he may send it to this address: Maktab al-Khadamat in Brooklyn (552 Atlantic Ave, Brooklyn NY; tel. 718-797-0207). Write my name on the check: "Dr. Abdallah Azzam." Finally I thank the brothers who coordinated my visits and who accompanied me on my travels … especially Hisham Yusuf, Muhammad Tawba, Muhammad Balata, Abd al-Razzaq al-Aradi, Abdallah al-Shaybani, Muhammad Awaynat, Abd al-[illegible] al-Amriki.[92]

Later, both al-Kifah itself and US counterterrorism analysts would claim that Azzam founded al-Kifah.[93] However, there is no evidence that Azzam took that initiative. As his remarks suggest, al-Kifah came to him, not the other way around.

Once the formal link was established, however, al-Kifah effectively served as the US branch of the Services Bureau. It recruited and fundraised on the Bureau's behalf and distributed *al-Jihad* magazine in substantial numbers across the country.[94] It organized lecture tours for Azzam and Tamim al-Adnani in multiple US cities in 1988 and 1989. It also organized screenings of videotaped lectures by Azzam and propaganda films from Afghanistan at mosques in the greater New York area.[95] Azzam's charisma and ascetic lifestyle made a big impression on the young men who hosted him. One of them later wrote:

He would come to us after several trips, exhausted, carrying in his hand a small bag and wearing Afghan clothes. He would wait in the airports, sometimes for hours, until a brother came and picked him up. He did not like to sleep in hotels, he would sleep wherever the circumstances allowed, usually on the floor in our homes. He ate what we ate, only less. When we slept, he would get up to pray at night. He embarrassed us with his humility, his politeness, and his asceticism. If he opened his small bag, you would find just a simple change of clothes, some papers, a Qur'an, and dry bread.[96]

Al-Kifah presented itself as a charity, but its activities were more nefarious. Not only did it recruit and send people to Afghanistan, its members also trained with weapons in the USA. The *New York Times* wrote:

The prospective guerrillas were sent off [to Afghanistan] in groups of three or four. Instructed to pay their own way, they bought $500 and $600 one-way tickets to Peshawar, according to a Brooklyn immigrant who helped with the arrangements. The office provided help with visas and contacts at the other end of the journey. Before they went, the recruits received training in using rifles, assault weapons and handguns. One recruit was El Sayyid A. Nosair, later convicted of assault and weapons possession in connection with the 1990 assassination of Rabbi Meir Kahane, the Jewish militant. Court papers showed that he received weapons training during the summer of 1989 at the High Rock Shooting Range in Naugatuck, Conn.[97]

Al-Kifah also expanded its organizational presence inside the United States by establishing new offices in other cities. These satellites were not really "branches" in the sense of entities controlled by the Services Bureau, but rather affiliated offices or contact points. According to *The 9/11 Commission Report*, al-Kifah would acquire offices in Atlanta, Boston, Chicago, Pittsburgh, and Tucson.[98] The wider network of contact points was even larger. Abdallah Anas later said, "Most of [the copies of *al-Jihad* magazine] go to the United States because we had fifty-two [distribution] centers in the United States. The main office was in Brooklyn, [also] Phoenix, Boston, Chicago, Tucson, Minnesota, Washington DC and Washington State."[99] In October 1988 *al-Jihad* magazine published a "Call from the Offices of the Jihad in America" listing a number of things people in the USA could do to contribute.[100] At the bottom it lists phone numbers of offices in the USA that people could call for more information: New York, Chicago, Washington DC, New Mexico, Boston, Pennsylvania. There was even a hotline people could call to hear a recording with the latest news from Afghanistan: 312–778-2444 (a Chicago-based number).

The Services Bureau's operations in the United States yielded many recruits. J. M. Berger estimates that a minimum of 150 American citizens and residents fought in Afghanistan in the 1980s, noting that "the reality is probably much higher."[101] Indeed, given the size of the Services Bureau infrastructure in the USA it would be somewhat surprising – and a low "return on investment" for Azzam – if the number was only 150. However, more important than the total number of the recruits is the *quality* of some of the personnel enlisted in this period. Several of the most prominent figures in the Afghan Arab community, and later in al-Qaida – such as Ali Mohamed, Muhammad Bayazid, Wa'il Julaydan, and Wadih El Hage – were recruited from the USA.[102]

All these activities happened without interference from, and largely under the radar of, domestic US authorities.[103] A Freedom of Information Act (FOIA) request about Azzam to the Federal Bureau of Investigation (FBI) yielded nothing except documents from a small investigation in 1989.[104] Early that year the FBI's Dallas office learned of a seventeen-year-old high school student from Fort Worth, Texas, who "had been recruited by Abdula Azzam" to go to Afghanistan. In March the office asked FBI headquarters "to advise Dallas of any background information available regarding recruitment activity of the Islamic Jihad or Mujahadeen [sic] in the United States." In May headquarters wrote back saying, "Searches of Bureau indices revealed no information indicating that captioned subjects, the Islamic Jihad, or the Mujahadeen was involved in the recruitment of mercenaries to fight in Afghanistan." It nevertheless instructed Dallas to "pursue captioned investigation as a neutrality matter," i.e., as a possible violation of the US Neutrality Act. This investigation uncovered some background information about Azzam and some details about his trip to the MAYA conference in Oklahoma City in December 1988. When the high school student returned in September, he was interviewed by FBI agents, but denied any involvement in military activity and any contact with Azzam; he said he had gone on his own initiative with his own money for religious reasons. On 20 November 1989 the Department of Justice closed the investigation, noting that "even though it appeared that several Muslim followers had been induced to travel to Afghanistan to participate in the military action in that country, this will not be considered as mercenary recruiting, since they did not sign any documents nor did it appear that they were recruited to go to Afghanistan to fight."

Interestingly, on the other side of the Atlantic there was nothing like the al-Kifah network. In Europe there were several distribution points for *al-Jihad* magazine, and Azzam visited on several occasions, but the Services Bureau did not have formal offices as it did in the USA. This is surprising given that Europe had a larger Muslim population and would have a vibrant jihadi scene in the 1990s.[105] Moreover, political freedoms did not differ, and Afghan Mujahidin parties operated extensively in Europe in the 1980s. One possible explanation for the lack of a Services Bureau infrastructure may have been practical hurdles, such as the multitude of languages and the need for a separate visa for each country. Another hypothesis is that it was easier for the Services Bureau to expand in America because the Muslim Brotherhood was more active there than in Europe.[106] In the 1980s the Muslim Students' Association (MSA), the Muslim Arab Youth Association (MAYA), and the Islamic Society of North America (ISNA) were strongly influenced by the Muslim Brotherhood and enjoyed close links to religious networks and economic benefactors in the Arab world.[107] In the late 1980s in particular, overseas Ikhwan members were heavily represented among speakers at MAYA and ISNA conferences.[108] Azzam thus found himself more often in America – able to inspire and recruit more local helpers – than in Europe.

None of this is to say that Arab Afghan recruitment did not occur in Europe, only that it was less structured than in America. There is plenty of evidence of ad hoc recruitment efforts in Europe beyond Azzam's lectures. For example, when Abdallah Anas went to Spain for two weeks in 1986 to meet his parents, he used the opportunity to speak about the Afghan jihad at the Islamic Center in Madrid, where he was staying.[109] He notably met with a group of Syrian Islamists which included the abovementioned Abu Mus'ab al-Suri, who was now living in Spain. Al-Suri and his friends quizzed Anas about the practicalities of joining the Afghan jihad, and they ended up going to Afghanistan in July the following year.

Competing Structures

It would be inaccurate to suggest that all the foreign fighters in Afghanistan came because of Azzam and the Services Bureau. Several other organizations also maintained an international outreach infrastructure and contributed to the overall mobilization.

For one, many actors disseminated information about the Afghanistan war without necessarily recruiting foreign fighters. As we saw in Chapter 7, Brotherhood magazines wrote extensively about Afghanistan, and Afghan Mujahidin parties engaged in outreach throughout the 1980s in the form of magazines, films, and lecture tours. We know that some people were inspired to go to Afghanistan by Mujahidin propaganda. Abu Ja'far al-Qandahari recalls his reaction on seeing Sayyaf's deputy Muhammad Yasir in Afghanistan:

I said to myself: "My God, Muhammad Yasir, I know him, he is the reason why I came here." The man came to Egypt to the Doctors' Syndicate to stage a massive conference where I was able to see for the first time videos of the jihad and Mujahidin in Afghanistan. He also showed us hundreds of pictures of disfigured children and women and the Soviet military arsenal burned to the ground. This was what pushed me to come to Afghanistan. Yasir had also distributed pamphlets from Sayyaf requesting our help and assistance. The letter said: "If the jihad does not need men, men do need jihad."[110]

We also know that some people were inspired by the writings of other scholars such as the Kuwaiti Muslim Brotherhood preacher Ahmad al-Qattan. Al-Qattan later wrote:

I met [Azzam] last year, and he told me, "My brother, I love you by God, dearly and greatly, and my love for you increases each year." I said "Why?" He said, "I have more and more esteem for your recordings." I said, "How?" He said, "I asked a brother in al-Ma'sada what had brought him to the jihad, and he said 'I heard a recording by Ahmad al-Qattan calling for people to join the jihad, and I was influenced by it and I went to fight.'"[111]

In addition, other militant groups ran independent recruitment pipelines. That was notably the case with the Egyptian Islamic Jihad (Tanzim al-Jihad) and the Egyptian Islamic Group (al-Jama'a al-Islamiyya) in the late 1980s. These organizations had been largely absent from the Peshawar scene in the first half of the war because many of their members were in prison. When repression in Egypt eased, these groups found Peshawar to be a practical safe haven. Egyptian Islamic Jihad (EIJ) developed a presence from 1986 after Ayman al-Zawahiri came, and the Egyptian Islamic Group (EIG) grew from 1987 with the arrival of leaders such as Muhammad Shawki al-Islambuli, Ali Abd al-Fattah, and Rifa'i Ahmad Taha. Their spiritual leader, Sheikh Umar Abd al-Rahman, visited Peshawar at least twice; once in 1988 and the second time in June 1990.[112] We know that both of these organizations recruited at least a small number of Egyptians to the Afghan jihad. In his insider account of life in EIG in the 1980s, Khalid al-Berry mentions "Mahmud, the youth who was sent at the end of the eighties, when he was seventeen, to Afghanistan and was killed there."[113] Al-Berry describes recruitment events in Egypt organized by EIG: "In the summer of 1987, I started going to movies shown by the Jama'a, at the Jam'iya Shar'iya mosque. There were pictures of children disfigured during the war against the Muslims in Afghanistan that would have wrung tears from a stone, while the rallying songs in the background stirred up one's anger."[114]

EIJ seems to have had the more elaborate structure, with representatives in Saudi Arabia who coordinated paid recruitment agents in Egypt. Muhammad Salah describes a recruitment pipeline from Cairo to Mecca to Peshawar with a certain Abdallah al-Muharib (aka Abu Shahida) as the key middleman. Salah quotes one recruit as saying that Abu Shahida

> sent $4,000 [to Egypt] to spend on sending young men for jihad in Afghanistan ... I seized the opportunity and traveled to Saudi Arabia for Umra ... I met Abu Shahida and we talked about traveling to Afghanistan and my ability to send some people. He gave me addresses in Pakistan to give to people who would travel ... I returned from Saudi Arabia [to Egypt], and sent Abdallah al-Sayyid, his brother Muhammad al-Sayyid, the engineer Majdi Abd al-Maqsud ... and my neighbor Ahmad Abu Sari'i ... I traveled to Saudi Arabia [again] and met Abu Ubayda ... We agreed on my return to Egypt and to convince and send members to Afghanistan ... They gave me money, $2000 as I recall, as a first payment. I resided in the apartment in al-Aziziyya for three days [with other Egyptians] I returned to Egypt and stepped up the recruitment work.[115]

Also in the late 1980s, Saudi Arabia saw the emergence of a separate recruitment infrastructure designed to channel young people to Jamil al-Rahman's Afghan Salafi group Jama'at al-Da'wa. As we shall see in Chapter 14, it enjoyed the semi-official blessing of the Salafi clerical establishment, which preferred to see Saudi youth join a proper Salafi group rather than the Muslim Brotherhood-leaning Services Bureau.

Exactly how much each of these actors contributed to the overall mobilization is difficult to say. We lack hard data on how many people were recruited in each pipeline. Moreover, the outreach efforts all occurred in parallel, so that for a given volunteer it was not always clear which voice or influence inspired the trip to Peshawar. As one author described the situation in Algeria:

> The name of this country invaded by the Soviet Union featured incessantly in the sermons in mosques. Video cassettes were distributed, showing the destruction and suffering of an oppressed people. Cassettes of the martyr Abdallah Azzam were imported in large quantities. Algerian students at the Islamic universities of Medina and Umm al-Qura played an important role in inspiring Algerians to go to Afghanistan.[116]

Khalid As'ad describes a similar atmosphere in certain Egyptian mosques in the late 1980s:

> The eloquent preachers in the mosques contributed to igniting a flame of mad zeal among the young Egyptian men to what was happening in Afghanistan. I remember one of them, called Shaykh Hamdi ... was preaching in one of the mosques on Egypt and Sudan Street. He was an extremely eloquent orator. His

sermons caused bodies to tremble and hairs to stand on end. He told the worshipers about the atrocities the communist Red Army was committing in Afghanistan and the blessings and miracles that were being achieved for the Afghan Mujahidin.[117]

Even though we cannot specify the respective recruitment contributions of these different actors, the available evidence strongly suggests that Azzam and the Services Bureau made the largest contribution. In the available travel accounts of Afghan Arabs in the 1980s, Azzam's name – or that of people in his network or of *al-Jihad* magazine – features more frequently than all other sources of inspiration. Moreover, most of the competing structures operated in geographically confined areas, while the Bureau had a wider reach. Strick van Linschoten and Kuehn also note that Azzam was "the central figure around whom most Afghan Arabs tended to coalesce during the 1980s."[118] Alastair Crooke, a former British official in Pakistan in the 1980s, estimated that around 2,000–3,000 people passed through the Services Bureau up to 1989.[119] This amounts to roughly half of the best estimate for the total number of Afghan Arabs in this period (see below). Azzam, in other words, was not alone in the foreign-fighter recruitment field, but he was the most important player.

Recruits

How many foreign fighters ended up going to Afghanistan, and what backgrounds did they have? As we shall see, lack of good data makes it very hard to answer these questions, but this section will make a modest attempt.

My best estimate for the total number of Arabs involved in the Afghan jihad between 1979 and 1992 is around 7,000 (see Table 10.1). This number is based on a collection of all numerical observations of Afghan Arabs I could find in primary and secondary sources while researching this book.[120] The estimate includes people in non-combat roles and people who made brief visits. For the period 1979–1989 the number may be around 4,000. To these must be added an unknown number of volunteers from Pakistan, Bangladesh, Indonesia, and other Asian countries. Assuming they numbered around 3,000 – and I am guessing here – then the total number of foreign fighters in the Afghan jihad from 1979 to 1992 may have been around 10,000. If the bulk of "Afghan Asians" arrived in the early 1990s, as some sources suggest, then the number of foreign fighters of all backgrounds in the 1980s may have been around 5,000.[121]

Table 10.1 *Author's Best Estimate of the Number of Foreign Fighters in 1980s Afghanistan*

	1979–1989	1979–1992
Arabs only	4,000	7,000
All foreign fighters	5,000	10,000

The numerical observations in the sources also allow us to reconstruct the rough chronological evolution of the size of the Afghan Arab community over time (see Figure 10.1). These numbers suggest that the vast majority of Afghan Arabs went in the second half of the 1980s and that the years 1986–1987 may be considered the tipping point of the mobilization. This tallies with available anecdotal assessments. Abdallah Anas, for example, recalls returning to Peshawar from Panjshir in early 1986 to find that "the number of young Arabs had increased by far. The city abounded with them."[122] Similarly, Basil Muhammad wrote that in mid-1986 "Peshawar was witnessing new development on the level of the Arab presence." Anthony Davis noted that "by 1987 the war had begun to attract significant numbers," and Edwards observed that "between 1984, when I left Peshawar ... and 1986, when I returned ... the biggest change I noted was the conspicuous presence of Arabs in Peshawar."[123] Figure 10.1 also suggests a striking chronological correlation between the founding of the Services Bureau (in late 1984) and the beginning of the rise in the number of Arab volunteers.

Unfortunately, lack of data prevents us from saying very much about the characteristics of the Afghan Arab population in the 1980s. Some observers have ventured descriptions of the composition of the Afghan Arabs, but most of these are quite vague and appear to be based on anecdotes. For example, Abdallah Anas described recruits as follows:

We had the three categories of recruits: people who did not speak Arabic, from Malaysia, Indonesia, India, Burma, the Philippines. Normally they were really poor. The other kind of people came from the non-Gulf area. Algeria, Egypt, Morocco, people normally between middle class and a little bit poor. The wealthy people were from the Gulf area, Kuwait, Emirates, Saudi. Most of the mujahideen were Saudi ... Some of the Saudis used to come and go as a trip, as a holiday.[124]

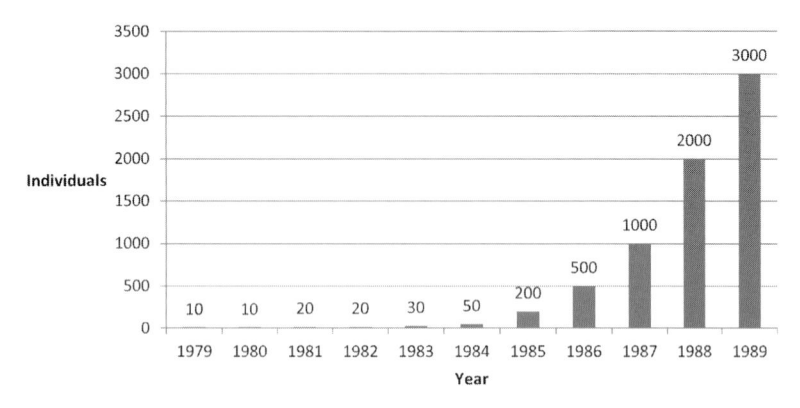

Figure 10.1 Approximate number of Arabs present in Peshawar and Afghanistan, 1979–1989

The closest thing to an existing dataset is the various compilations of martyrdom biographies, but only a fraction of the Arabs died in battle, and we do not know whether this sample is representative of all fighters.[125]

Creating a new dataset is difficult because only a small proportion of the Afghan Arabs feature by name in written sources, and even fewer are described in any detail. Early in my research I attempted to build a dataset of Afghan Arabs by extracting names and biographical information from martyr biographies, war memoirs, and other primary sources.[126] However, it proved difficult due to the nature of the sources. I quickly arrived at some 150 names, and with a few months' more effort I could bring it up to around 250. However, by then I had exhausted the most information-dense sources, and the "further out" I went in the corpus of sources, the fewer the names and the less biographical information on average about each new name. Bringing the list up to something like 500 names would require a prohibitively large time investment, and finding 1,000 would be practically impossible. And even then, the sample would be non-representative and have a lot of missing values, so I discontinued the effort.

For what it is worth, we can make four very broad observations about the Afghan Arab population based on my proto-sample of 250 Afghan Arabs and a reading of the primary sources. First, the vast majority of Afghan Arabs appear to have been young men between their late teens and late thirties. There were some women, children, and elderly, but they were almost all dependents of a fighting-age *mujahid*.

Second, the Afghan jihad drew recruits from dozens of different countries, but some nationalities seem to feature more prominently in the sources than others, notably Saudis, Egyptians, Algerians, Syrians, Jordanians, and Iraqis.[127] However, virtually every country in the Middle East, North Africa, and Muslim Asia was represented, including Turkey but possibly excluding Iran and Israel.[128] From the West there were sizable contingents from the USA, the UK, and France, in addition to smaller numbers from other European countries, Canada, and Australia. Although we lack good data, it seems that more people went from the USA than from any other Western country. Most European countries did not produce many fighters; for example, Isam al-Attar, who was a prominent preacher in Aachen throughout the 1980s, says he does not remember hearing about any Arabs going from Germany to Afghanistan.[129] There is anecdotal evidence of a small number of Western converts, both black and white.[130] Some sub-Saharan African countries were also represented with smaller numbers.[131] However, it is not possible to establish a precise cross-country distribution.

Third, the Afghan Arabs seem to have included many students and relatively few people with established professional careers. One of Azzam's biographers noted that "most of the brothers around the sheikh in the field of jihad did not have diplomas."[132] Students seem to be the most frequent status category, but then again most recruits were young, and there were many students in the Muslim world at this time. There is anecdotal evidence of recruits from a broad range of socio-economic backgrounds, from the unemployed to the super-wealthy, but without good data on the distribution of socio-economic backgrounds we cannot say how the Afghan Arabs compared with Arab youth in general.

Finally, we see a broad range of declared motivations for going to Afghanistan. Some emphasize theological arguments, such as the perceived religious duty to fight or the promise of paradise. Others stress the political dimension of the conflict, such as the unacceptable infidel occupation of Muslim land or the severe humanitarian suffering of the Afghan people. Yet others mention proximate social or psychological reasons for going, such as a desire for adventure or inspiration from a friend or relative who also went. Some Afghan Arabs went primarily in search of a safe haven, escaping repression in their home countries. This was notably the case with a number of Egyptians, such as Ayman al-Zawahiri, who left Egypt in 1986 to avoid getting imprisoned again. Similarly, the al-Jama'a al-Islamiyya activist Ali Abd al-Fattah and his wife Amani Faruq fled Egypt for Afghanistan in 1988 after discovering that the security services were after them.[133] Not everyone left with the intention of going to Afghanistan. Abu Ubayda al-Banshiri, for example, had gone to Saudi Arabia in 1981 for work, and only later decided to go from there to Afghanistan.[134] Another Egyptian, Muhammad Abd al-Rahim al-Sharqawi, found himself stranded in Saudi Arabia after going there for pilgrimage and learning that his friends back in Egypt had started being rounded up by police.[135]

As we have seen, Abdallah Azzam and his colleagues in the Services Bureau engaged in extensive international outreach to muster support for the Afghan jihad. Their efforts can be evaluated in at least two ways. In one sense it was an uneven, partially improvised effort that should dispel any attempt to cast Azzam as a radical mastermind or the Services Bureau as an elite organization with global reach. The reality was clearly much messier. From another perspective, the effort was a remarkably far-reaching for its time and impressively ambitious. It reveals a man who saw the world as his oyster and truly believed he could rally many of the world's Muslims behind his cause. But what exactly was that cause?

1 Abdallah Azzam's native village, al-Sila al-Harithiyya, in 2008. View from the southeast, with the road from Jenin in the foreground.

2 Abdallah Azzam as a young schoolteacher, around 1961.

الدكتور عبد الله عزام
مـــدرس

3 Abdallah Azzam as a teacher in Amman, around 1968.

4 Abdallah Azzam and his children in Cairo, around 1972.

5 Cover of Abdallah Azzam's book *The Red Cancer*, published 1980.

6 Azzam lecturing at the University of Da'wa and Jihad, around 1985.

7 Azzam relaxing during a visit to an Afghan Mujahidin camp, early 1980s.

8 Azzam writing, location unknown, mid-1980s.

9 Cover of the first edition of Abdallah Azzam's book *The Defense of Muslim Lands*, published in Peshawar in March 1985.

10 Cover of *al-Jihad* magazine in March 1986. Cat Stevens in the picture below on the left.

11 Advertisement for propaganda materials in *al-Jihad* magazine, September 1987. Among the products on offer is a cassette tape containing "*Anashid* of jihad by the British Muslim preacher Yusuf Islam [Cat Stevens]."

12 Facsimile of *al-Jihad* magazine report on the al-Sada camp in August 1986.

13 Abdallah Azzam, Tamim al-Adnani, Gulbuddin Hekmatyar, and Abd Rabb al-Rasul Sayyaf at Jaji in May 1987.

14 Abdallah Azzam in Afghanistan in the mid-1980s.

15 Abdallah Azzam (middle) with Ahmed Shah Massoud (second from left), Azzam's son Ibrahim (far left), and Azzam's aide and driver Abu Harith (far right). Fifth man unidentified.

16 Ahmed Shah Massoud, Burhanuddin Rabbani, and Abdallah Azzam inspecting Massoud's troops in the Panjshir valley, September 1988.

17 Abdallah Azzam speaking about Palestine in the Muslim Student Union Centre in Islamabad during the "Solidarity week with global movements of liberation," November 1985.

18 Abdallah Azzam and Rachid Ghannouchi in Peshawar in 1989.

19 Abdallah Azzam and his father Yusuf Azzam in Peshawar, around 1988.

20 The wreck of Abdallah Azzam's car after the assassination on 24 November 1989.

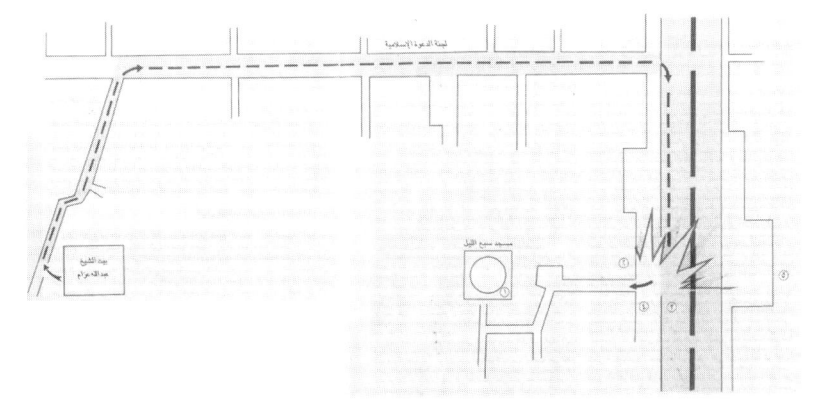

21 Drawing from *al-Bunyan al-Marsus* magazine of the area around the site of Abdallah Azzam's assassination in Peshawar on 24 November 1989. Azzam's house on the left; the Sab'al-Layl mosque on the right.

22 Abd Rabb al-Rasul Sayyaf grieving before the dead body of Abdallah Azzam in Pabbi on the evening of the day of his assassination.

23 Pro-al-Qaida photo montage from around 2011 showing Abdallah Azzam (far right) alongside (from left) Usama Bin Ladin, Abu Yahya al-Libi, Abu Musʿab al-Zarqawi, and Ayman al-Zawahiri.

24 The author and Hudhayfa Azzam in Amman, July 2018.

11 | Ideologue

"O Sheikh," a young Arab exclaimed upon arrival in Peshawar, "I have come here only after having read your book."[1] An Islamist writer later commented, "The Afghan Arabs'... numbers increased tenfold, and all the brothers had come based on the fatwa of the sheikh."[2] Another added, "Two things mobilized Muslim public opinion to Afghanistan: The [book on] miracles and the fatwas on jihad in Afghanistan."[3] Statements such as these suggest that Azzam's ideas had a major effect on the mobilization of foreign fighters to Afghanistan. But what exactly were these ideas, and why were so many people swayed by them? What sort of things did he write about, and where does he fit in the intellectual history of the jihadi movement?

This chapter will look at Azzam's ideological production in the Afghanistan years. It first describes elements of his ethics, then his writings on miracles and martyrs, his foreign-fighter doctrine, his strategic vision, his views on Muslim regimes, his views on the West, and his views on tactics. We will see that he made two particularly important contributions to jihadi thought: a foreign-fighter doctrine and a martyrology for Sunni jihadism. We will also see that he was very anti-Western, but did not advocate international terrorist tactics, although his commitment to clean warfare may have been somewhat overstated.

The chapter only offers a cursory overview of his main ideas; he wrote so much that it is difficult to cover everything. As we saw in Chapter 6, Azzam had already published several books before joining the Afghan jihad, but it was nothing compared to his production in the Afghanistan years. From 1982 to 1989 he published nine books and well over a hundred articles in magazines such as *al-Jihad*, *Luhayb al-Ma'raka*, and *al-Mujtama'*.[4] This is in addition to hundreds of recorded lectures and many unpublished works that came out after he died. It was in this period that he wrote his most famous works, such as *Signs of the Merciful in the Afghan Jihad* (1983), *The Defense of Muslim Lands*

(1985), and *Join the Caravan* (1987), which established him as one of the most prominent jihadi writers of all time. The majority of his works in this period relate to the Afghanistan war, but he also addressed other topics.

Azzam remained productive through good writing habits. He typically wrote in the morning after the dawn prayer, and he started every writing session with the same set of invocations and prayers.[5] "Whenever he sat down to write, his wife said, "He would perform ablution and pray two *rak'as* ... and invite God to inspire him. Only then would he begin to write."[6] At home he used a typewriter, and on the road he always carried a notebook and a red, green, and blue ballpoint pen for taking notes.[7] Azzam wrote mostly like an Islamic cleric, that is, in elevated language and with copious citations from scripture. However, some of his works were more accessible and became bestsellers as a result. He usually had his manuscripts printed first on a press in Peshawar, and then by an Islamist publisher named Maktabat al-Risala in Amman, after which they were picked up and reprinted by Muslim Brotherhood-linked publishers in other countries. This is why his most popular books exist in a bewildering number of editions and why it is impossible to know how many copies he sold. In any case, he appears to have made very little money from book sales due to the unregulated nature of the book market in the region.

Azzam's work contains inconsistencies and contradictions. For example, in *Defense of Muslim Lands* he says that women can go for jihad without permission from anybody, while in *Join the Caravan* he says they need a male chaperon. In *Proper Conduct and Rulings in Jihad* he says that Muslim fighters should not target enemy women and children, only to note later that Communist women must always be killed. In one lecture he says that you cannot break the law in countries where you have a visa; in another that it is permissible to kill supporters of Israel in the United States. Similarly, in some texts the Jews are presented as the Muslims' worst enemy, in others it is America, and in yet others it is Britain. There are probably several reasons for these inconsistencies. On some issues, he may simply have changed his opinion. On others, he adapted his position to the context about which he was speaking, not realizing or caring that it contradicted previous statements. He could also get carried away and exaggerate, for rhetorical effect, whichever point or argument he was making. All this can sometimes make it difficult to say what Azzam's opinion was on a given topic, but it also helps explain why his legacy is so contested, as we shall see in Chapter 16.

Guiding Ethics

Before delving into specifics, it is useful to reflect on the broader features of his worldview. Like everyone else, Azzam was guided by a set of moral intuitions, many of which, such as his respect for the divine and his belief in afterlife rewards, sprang from his religious conviction. However, he also had other, less intuitive ones, four of which are particularly useful for understanding his other opinions and decisions in the 1980s.

The first was his appreciation for intellectual independence. Azzam believed that ideas should, within limits, be evaluated on their merit rather than their reputation, and he was open to mixing ideas from different intellectual traditions. This is why he is not easily categorized as either a Muslim Brother or a Salafi. On the one hand, he self-described as a Muslim Brother, venerated Hasan al-Banna and Sayyid Qutb, and used Qutbist terminology such as *hakimiyya* (sovereignty) and *jahiliyya* (age of ignorance).[8] On the other, he also self-described as a Salafi, quoted Ibn Taymiyya, and expanded on terms associated with Salafism such as *tawhid* (oneness of God) and *al-wala' wa'l-bara'* (loyalty and disavowal).[9] This syncretism led Abu Qatada to write that "the sheikh represented an advanced and high-level jurisprudence that one might call 'contemporary Salafism' ... His jurisprudence cannot be classified as Salafi or *madhhabi*; rather, he selected [his approach] according to the circumstances."[10] There are even Sufi influences in Azzam's work, as we shall see later. His son-in-law Abdallah Anas wrote, "We were not Sufis but we believed in the science of purification of the heart, and we were not Salafis but we did not oppose their ideas."[11] According to Anas, Azzam also borrowed from the Tabligh when designing the religious instruction program in the training camps in Afghanistan.[12]

Azzam's general attitude was not to adopt a position because his own ideological clan already held it, but rather to go to the sources and make up his own mind. The same attitude made Azzam open to working with people from different Islamist groups and currents. In his early years he carefully toed the Muslim Brotherhood party line, but in the

Ideologue 291

1980s he denounced factionalism. For example, in September 1986 he told a group of followers:

Just because you are part of a particular group doesn't mean that you are better than other people. Just because you read a particular book doesn't mean that you are better than other people. There is some good with the Ikhwan, and there is some good with the Tabligh, and there is some good with the Salafiyyah; every one of them has a portion of the good, so, try – if you are able – to collect all of the good from these groups.[13]

A second feature of Azzam's worldview in the 1980s was his pan-Islamism. Azzam saw the *umma* – the community of believers – as the paramount social category, and he worked hard to promote unity and solidarity among Muslims. He believed that internal division was the main source of Muslim weakness, and he was critical of all forms of nationalism, sectarianism, ethnic politics, and tribalism that might divide the Muslim nation.[14] He was a "macro-nationalist" in the sense that he talked about the *umma* in much the same way that other ethno-nationalists talk about their respective in-groups, namely, as bound by blood relations, as having a physical homeland, and as being threatened by hostile outside actors.[15] When describing the threats to the *umma*, Azzam spoke of land usurped, civilians massacred, women raped, and holy places desecrated. In so doing, he illustrated what Laleh Khalili described as "the continuities between nationalist and Islamist discourses in the Middle East and their intimate family resemblance."[16] Azzam's pan-Islamism helps explain many of his other opinions, such as his advocacy of foreign fighting, his yearning for a new Caliphate, and his relative friendliness toward Shiites.[17]

A third element of Azzam's ethics was his belief in the benefits of religious education. He saw it not only necessary, but also as largely *sufficient* to the success and well-being of Muslims. He had an untechnocratic view of education, seeing no great need for Muslims to get vocational training. If a Muslim had pure faith and proper religious education, God would help him succeed in his endeavors. Here Azzam differed markedly from the Muslim Brotherhood, which for decades had encouraged its members to study technical–vocational subjects. Azzam saw this as misguided:

The manner of tarbiyah [education] is wrong. The [Islamic groups] ended up sending their youth ... one to medical school, another to study engineering, another to study pharmacy ... [But] who will look in the Book of Allah? Who will derive rulings from it with which to solve the problems of our reality? So, you find that the leadership of the various Islamic groups are not from the scholars ... You find that the leader of an Islamic group is either a doctor, or an engineer, or a pharmacist, etc. Such people do not have much knowledge of the Shari'ah. As a result, you find them constantly making mistakes.[18]

Azzam's preference for religious over technical education manifested itself also in his approach to warfare. He believed that religious education of soldiers was crucial to military success, so he reserved a large part of the curriculum in the training camps to religious topics. This led Mustafa Hamid to remark about the Sada camp that "what Azzam created was a mosque, not a training camp."[19]

Azzam's emphasis on religious education was also informed by his sense that Islamic culture was under threat from secularism and other ideologies. The problem with educating only doctors and engineers was that these technical professions exercised no cultural influence on the world:

Philosophy, psychology, history, social sciences, economics, politics ... are the subjects that change mentalities. As for the professor in the college of engineering, what will he change? ... Look at the Jews. The Jews in America and outside of America occupy positions in Eastern studies, Islamic studies, Arabic language studies, history, economics, etc. ... As for us, we want the Muslim doctor, the Muslim lawyer, the Muslim engineer ... We should advise our brothers to study Shari'ah, to study literature, to study Arabic literature, to study history.[20]

Azzam was thus in some sense an Islamic culture warrior; he considered it more important to protect Islamic culture from foreign influences than for Muslim society to advance materially or technologically. This instinct of his produced some striking positions; For example, as we saw in Chapter 8, he forced French doctors out of northern Afghanistan even though it entailed a drastic decrease in healthcare provision in the area. Similarly, he once commended the Afghans for refusing "to let the Americans open schools in Peshawar or in Afghanistan, despite the fact that half a million Afghan pupils [in Peshawar alone] do not have access to education."[21] In other words, no education at all was better than non-Islamic education.

The fourth key element of Azzam's ethics was the value he placed on practice and activism. In his view, a good Muslim needed to practice or perform his Islam in the physical world, not just study it academically.

Interestingly, he sought to theorize and popularize this idea by linking it to the theological concept of *tawhid*, "the oneness of God," a central term in Salafi doctrine.[22] He introduced a new notion that he called the "*tawhid* of action" (*al-tawhid al-'amali*), which he argued was as important to observe as the other variants of *tawhid*.[23] "[*Tawhid*] cannot be understood just by reading some words in some books," he argued.[24] By practice Azzam meant all things that, in his view, Islam requires Muslims to perform in the material world, such as the observance of rituals, proper Islamic manners and conduct, and the spreading of Islam.

The ultimate form of practice was jihad, by which he meant warfare. Azzam was completely unapologetic about the militaristic side of the Islamic tradition. He firmly dismissed the notion that jihad means a spiritual endeavor against the believer's sinful inclinations. This, he argued, was an innovation based on "false, fabricated" Hadith propagated by people who wish to weaken Islam.[25] Not afraid to associate Islam with violence, he wrote that "this religion came by the sword, was established by the sword, stays by the sword, and will be lost if the sword is lost."[26] To drive the point home, he often used explicit language, saying things like "the tree of this religion ... cannot be watered except with blood" and "the monuments of glory can only be built on skulls and limbs."[27] Azzam's unabashed militarism was relatively new within the Islamist movement. Earlier ideologues such as Hasan al-Banna, Abu al-A'la Mawdudi, and Sayyid Qutb had spoken of jihad as combat, but in less explicit terms.[28] As such, Azzam marks the beginning of the disappearance of apologetics about jihad in the Islamist movement, a trend that would be taken to extremes by subsequent jihadi groups.

To Azzam, jihad was not only a religious duty, but also a fast track to salvation. "While living in Afghanistan," he wrote, "I have realized that Tawhid cannot penetrate into the soul of the human being, nor will it intensify and strengthen, the way it does in the fields of Jihad."[29] He described jihad as "the most excellent form of worship" and cited Hadith to the effect that "a month of *ribat* [frontline guard duty] is better than a thousand days with nights spent in prayer and daytime in fasting" and "an hour of fighting in the name of God is better than sixty years of prayer."[30] Azzam went a long way toward describing jihad as an end in itself. A common phrase among the Afghan Arabs became "the Afghan jihad does not need us. We need the Afghan jihad."[31] He effectively articulated a new conception of the ideal Muslim, a kind of *homo jihadicus* for whom warfare is integral to his way of life. Azzam's ideal Muslim has pure faith, sound religious education, good manners, and wages jihad as much as possible.

Azzam's ethics thus included an implicit value hierarchy of activities in which warfare is better than other forms of religious activism, which is better than religious education, which is better than secular education. Azzam judged other Muslims on this metric; for example, he did not care what diplomas his daughter's suitors held so long as they were doing something for Islam. Similarly, he said that businessmen who come to Pakistan to donate money to the Mujahidin are better Muslims than students who come to Pakistan for religious study "and who wait for months for their thesis defence without bothering to spend a week among the *mujahidin*."[32] Moreover, one of the reasons he cut the Afghans slack with regard to what he considered unorthodox Islamic practices (see Chapter 13) was that they were fighting. Jihad, in other words, trumped everything. What, then, did Azzam have to say about the Afghan jihad?

Miraculous War

Azzam's first reports from Afghanistan were neither about the political situation nor about the need for foreign fighters. Instead, they were about divine intervention, which he said was occurring at a high frequency on the battlefield. Throughout the 1980s Azzam would write extensively about the supernatural dimension of jihad in a way that few if any modern Islamist writers had done before him. The theme captured people's imagination and suggested that the Afghan jihad was favored by God and therefore worth supporting. Azzam's writings on miracles (*karamat*) and martyrdom laid the foundations for the Sunni jihadi martyrdom culture that is still with us today.

Azzam's writings on the supernatural involved two different but closely linked themes, namely, miracles that happen in connection with battle, and miracles triggered by a martyr's death. In the first few years he wrote mostly about the former. His very first Afghanistan-related article, published in May 1982, relayed extraordinary stories from inside Afghanistan.[33] It told of armies of white-clad angels on horseback chasing the enemy, birds intercepting Russian bombs mid-air to protect the *mujahidin*, and vipers that leave the *mujahidin* alone but bite the Russians. In one story a Russian soldier tried to destroy a copy of the Qur'an by throwing it under the belt of a tank, only to see the tank explode as a result. In another, 350 *mujahidin* held out against 5,000 Russian soldiers and 40 airplanes, losing only 40 men while killing 3,364 Russians. Azzam's article generated a lot of feedback from readers, prompting him to expand the article into a book. In late 1983 he published *Signs of the Merciful in the Afghan Jihad*, his first book on Afghanistan. It contained an even longer catalogue of battlefield miracles; here were *mujahidin* downing Russian fighter planes with pebbles or merely through prayer, ghost armies helping outnumbered fighters, and animals giving advance warning of bombing raids. There were also stories of mysterious things happening to the bodies of fallen soldiers: their blood smelling of musk, their bodies not decomposing at all, and rays of light emanating from their graves.

Azzam insisted that these stories were not his inventions, but rather witness reports from Afghan fighters on the ground. To convince readers, he provided a source for each story, just as a Hadith specialist provides the chain of transmission for stories about the Prophet. Azzam spent much time talking to Afghan *mujahidin* the early 1980s, so there is little reason to doubt that he mainly conveyed what he heard; however, he may also have contributed to the mythology by soliciting such stories from his interlocutors and by embellishing them in his writings. In any case, Azzam himself seemed to firmly believe the stories to be true. For him, the occurrence of miracles was above all evidence that God was on the side of the Mujahidin, and that the intentions of the Mujahidin were pure. "There is no doubt," he wrote, "that the Afghan Mujahidin have realized victories that the human mind cannot explain, and we find no convincing explanation for these victories except that God almighty is directing the battle with his hand and watches over it with his eye."[34] Moreover, Azzam claimed to observe an inverse relationship between military strength and miracles: "In the beginning of this jihad, the victories and the miracles were many, because of the devotion and sincerity to God, but no Muslim paid attention to them. When the Afghan cause became famous and the aid came, the victories and miracles became less frequent."[35]

In retrospect, miracles was a clever choice of topic, because it attracted readers' attention at a time when many other things were happening in the Middle East. A straightforward situation report from Central Asia might not have cut it for an Arab readership just months after the Sadat assassination and the Hama massacre. Miracles, on the other hand, was an unusual topic even in Islamist magazines. Moreover, the miracle reports conveyed a broader point, namely that the Afghan jihad enjoyed divine favor and was therefore worth paying attention to. What seemed like an esoteric topic was in reality a powerful tool for recruitment and fundraising. *Signs of the Merciful* struck a chord with young Islamists across the Middle East. It became an immediate bestseller and was eventually published in multiple editions in many countries.[36] By several accounts it was the single most influential book in terms of inspiring Arabs to go to Afghanistan in the 1980s.[37] It became one of the great classics of jihadi literature, and the title has been borrowed for books about miracles in other conflicts.[38]

From the mid-1980s, the emphasis in Azzam's writing on miracles shifted from battlefield stories to martyrs. He had already talked about martyrs in *Signs of the Merciful*, but as years went by he spoke more and more about the topic. In March 1985 Azzam published his first martyrdom biography in *al-Jihad* magazine (issue 3), the first in a long series of such biographies written under the pen name "Abu Muhammad."[39] Azzam did not invent the martyrdom biography – death notices had been published in Islamist magazines for years. Nor was he the only one who wrote them in the late 1980s – other jihadi magazines also published similar texts. However, Azzam helped develop the genre by writing more elaborate texts with more references to miracles.[40] The martyrdom biographies were short hagiographies describing the life of the deceased – usually an Afghan Arab – and the circumstances of his death, often including one or more stories about a miracle observed in connection with his death. They were highly stylized and hagiographic – most presented the individual as a humble and sincere believer who was liked by all and who had been yearning for martyrdom, only to finally achieve it in an act of bravery.

Martyrdom became a major theme in Azzam's discourse in the late 1980s. He wrote many articles about the benefits and miracles of martyrdom, and the topic was mentioned in most of his other books and lectures. For example, here is from one of Azzam's lectures in the late 1980s:

It is not strange that you see the light that had filled his heart begin to emanate from his grave towards the sky and returning, as witnessed by someone who is with you, and to which an Afghan testified to as well ... It is not strange that we see the corpse of Sa'd ar-Rashud eighteen hours after his martyrdom trembling at the sound of the Qur'an ... It is not strange that we smell the scent of Yahya from a distance of over five hundred meters, and that the hospital that handled his pure corpse smelled of musk for an entire week afterwards ... It is not strange that we still hear the sound of takbir coming from the grave of 'Abdullah al-Ghamidi ... It is not strange that you smell the clothes of 'Abd ar-Rahman al-Banna – Hamdi al-Banna – and they are still with us in this library four months after his martyrdom, and his hat and personal items emanate a sweet scent.[41]

By all accounts, Azzam's writings about martyrdom had significant appeal. Many Afghan Arabs said they had come to Afghanistan because they wanted to become martyrs, and some fighters took extreme risks on the battlefield in the hope of reaching the hereafter. Azzam himself said that stories of martyrs often moved the crowds to which he lectured, and the letters section of *al-Jihad* magazine filled up with correspondence about martyrs and martyrdom. By all accounts, the rewards of martyrdom that Azzam and others described became important incentives for many Afghan Arabs to volunteer for war. As Nasir al-Bahri noted,

I always had [Azzam's] books and tapes with me. In them, he speaks of paradise, the glory of jihad, the afterlife, as the great manifestations of the Almighty. His stories invoke the mysterious power of the mujahid, who does not feel the pain of his injuries when he falls a martyr. His words are echoed by the stories of the jihadis who tell us their miracles when they return to Jeddah.[42]

Although battlefield miracles and martyrdom miracles were part of the Islamic tradition, no Sunni Islamist had developed the topic in the same way that Azzam did. Besides, while many of the specific types of miracles mentioned by Azzam – such as a martyr's blood smelling of musk – were mentioned in earlier sources, others, such as downing of airplanes with pebbles, were entirely new. This raises the question where Azzam got the inspiration from. Most likely it was a combination of at least three impulses.

The first was a local Afghan narrative tradition about miracles.[43] David Edwards has described in detail how the Afghan Mujahidin had developed a distinct discourse on martyrs and miracles by the time Azzam arrived.[44] This phenomenon may have reflected the Sufi influences on Afghan religious culture. As a mystical tradition, Sufism is oriented toward connections between the real world and the divine, and it has a tradition of attributing supernatural powers to Sufi saints. Indeed, Azzam himself said he first heard about the *karamat* in Afghanistan in a lecture by Sayyaf's aide Muhammad Yasir in Mecca during Hajj in 1981, and that the topic kept coming up in his conversations with Afghan *mujahidin*.[45]

There are also non-Afghan precedents for a narrative tradition about miracles and martyrs. The concepts have deep roots in the Islamic tradition and had crept up in conflict situations earlier in the twentieth century. For example, miracle stories had reportedly proliferated in the Pakistani military during the Indo-Pakistani war of 1965, and the same happened in the Egyptian military during the 1973 Arab–Israeli war.[46] In the late 1960s the Fedayin movement initiated the now widespread practice of glorifying fallen Palestinian fighters as martyrs on photographic posters in the street.[47]

There is some evidence that Azzam himself had taken an interest in these topics as early as the 1960s. As we saw in Chapter 3, he had lectured in Zarqa in 1969 about his fellow Fedayin falling as martyrs and their blood smelling of musk. He had even brought the bloodstained handkerchief of a dead friend to prove the point. This suggests that he had been aware of the classical Islamic literature on martyrdom from an early stage, and that he was predisposed to taking an interest in the topic when he came to Peshawar and heard all the stories from the Afghan *mujahidin*.

Azzam's writings about miracles and martyrdom were not uncontroversial. They raised two main types of objections: that the stories were implausible, and that they were inspired by Sufism. As early as August 1982 Azzam wrote an article titled "Some of the Secularist and Leftist Comments on the Miracles of the Mujahidin," in which he addressed common critiques and complaints about the article he had published three months previously.[48] His main response was to say that those who doubt the reports must have weak faith, an argument not unlike that of the tailors in the fairy tale *The Emperor's New Clothes*. However, many still doubted the veracity of Azzam's stories, even inside the Afghan Arab community. For example, Nabil Na'im, a former leader of the Egyptian Islamic Jihad, later described Azzam's book as "mostly myths. We used to read it and laugh," while the Saudi cleric Siraj al-Zahrani said that these stories were "just fairy tales they used to tickle the emotions of the youth."[49] Others said that Azzam had bought the stories, pointing to his practice of paying his Afghan sources a small amount of money, a so-called *ikramiyya* (honorific present), for sharing their miracle stories.[50]

For his fellow Islamists, the other problematic aspect about Azzam's writings about miracles and martyrdom was that they were clearly inspired by Sufism. For one, Azzam cites Sufi authors for key points in his texts on these topics.[51] For another, there are clear similarities between the way Azzam describes martyrs and the way Sufis refer to their saints (*awlia'*).[52] He portrays them as close to God, as having divine grace (*baraka*) and as triggering miracles (*karamat*). As Meir Hatina notes, "terms [such] as awlia', baraka, and karamat ... bear a strong sufi connotation and had the potential to challenge the key concept of the unity of God."[53] Azzam was never openly accused of Sufism by other Islamists, but he probably realized that this was theologically dangerous territory. Hatina has shown that Azzam employed several strategies to preempt or guard against accusations of Sufism: He denounced other manifestation of Sufism; he argued that miracles were part of mainstream Islam and not just Sufism; he emphasized that miracles were confined to the battlefield; he highlighted the proper (non-Sufi) behavior of the martyrs, and he provided examples of miracles from early Islamic history.[54]

Azzam was neither the first not the last Sunni radical to have dabbled with Sufi ideas without admitting it. Sayyid Qutb did it in *In the Shade of the Qur'an*, and recent research on jihadi cultural practices shows that even groups such as al-Qaida and Islamic State have embraced weeping and other practices previously associated with Sufism and Shiite Islam.[55] As Hatina notes, these tendencies reveal "the complex and ambivalent Salafi stance regarding Islamic mysticism in modern times."[56]

Azzam played a major role in the development of a contemporary Sunni discourse on martyrdom.[57] Prior to the Afghanistan war, modern Sunni jihadi groups did not write much about martyrdom, although they typically described their fallen comrades as martyrs. After Afghanistan, on the other hand, martyrdom became a major theme in the jihadi literature.[58] None of this is to say that Azzam was not only interested in the supernatural – he also wanted to help win the war in Afghanistan.

A Duty for All

Azzam's main message during the 1980s – and the one with the largest historical repercussions – was that all Muslims worldwide needed to go and fight in Afghanistan. His 1984 fatwa to this effect was the first elaborate Islamic legal argument for foreign fighting in the modern era, and it inspired war volunteering not just to Afghanistan, but also to many other conflicts in the following decades. The fatwa also contained within it an idea with more far-reaching consequences, namely that Muslims should defy all authorities that try to prevent them from waging jihad.

The foreign-fighter doctrine developed gradually in Azzam's mind, and it was not widely publicized until 1985. Before that, he issued an escalating series of requests for external support. The first came in an October 1982 article in *al-Mujtama'* magazine, where he urged rich families in the Arab oil states to donate one dinner's worth of money per month to the Afghan jihad.[59] Then, in April 1983, he published a more elaborate list of requests, including a call for doctors and journalists to come to Afghanistan:

1. That all religious universities and institutes organize an "Afghan jihad victory week" to "collect money and send the money with a person or a group of people to Peshawar to give it to the president of the Union, Sheikh Sayyaf."
2. That every Islamic newspaper have a special section on the Afghan jihad.
3. That every Muslim family set aside the equivalent of one day's expenditures every month for the Afghan jihad.
4. To organize study trips to Peshawar to see the Afghan jihad.
5. That doctors set aside one month per year to live among the Mujahidin.
6. That the Islamic newspapers send at least one correspondent to the fronts and that those with filmmaking skills come and make films about the jihad.
7. That the Muslim states allow the Afghan Mujahidin to open offices to make their cause known and collect donations for the jihad.
8. Anybody who wants to transfer money can use the Bayt al-Tamwil al-Kuwayti and write "Afghan jihad" on the check. The account number is 1920/1.[60]

In his next article, in August 1983, he ramped up the rhetoric by guilt-tripping donors more and asking for a wider range of professionals to join the jihad: "The jihad is in need of people with expertise and technical ability; they need Muslim journalists, Muslim doctors,

Muslim engineers (especially in electricity, chemistry, and electronics). [And they need] scholar-educators who can live with them and teach them matters of religion."[61]

In early 1984 Azzam published his first formal fatwa on jihad in Afghanistan – at the back of a new edition of his book *Signs of the Merciful* – and his ruling was that jihad is optional except for Afghans, their immediate neighbors, and skilled professionals:

Summary of the ruling on jihad in Afghanistan

1) *Fard 'ayn* by one's person and by money: On the entire people of Afghanistan and anyone who resides within 88 kilometers of the Afghan border, be it in Pakistan, Iran, or elsewhere.
2) *Fard 'ayn* by support: By weapons, food, money, facilitating border crossings for Muslims all over the world and entry visas.
3) *Fard 'ayn* by one's person: on the rest of the Muslims who have expertise needed by the jihad, such as preachers, imams, engineers, doctors, military personnel, speakers, cameramen, journalists, and writers.
4) As for the rest of the Muslims, jihad is *fard 'ayn* on them in their countries to establish God's Shari'a and to expel the infidels. He who cannot wage jihad with his person in his country, and who has the opportunity to go to Afghanistan, the individual obligation remains his right.[62]

Then, at some point in the spring or summer of 1984, Azzam judged the international response too slow and decided to declare jihad in Afghanistan an obligation for all Muslims. He composed a text that he took with him to Mecca for Hajj in late August 1984. (This was the same trip on which he agreed with Sayyaf and Bin Ladin to set up the Services Bureau; see Chapter 9.) He spent a few days chasing down scholar friends of his – such as Sa'id Hawa and Abdallah al-Alwan – and got them to sign a written endorsement.[63] He then arranged with Sayyaf that he would read out the new fatwa right after Sayyaf's speech at the General Enlightenment Center in Mina.[64] Thus in early September 1984 Azzam ascended the podium before a large group of Islamic scholars and declared:

My brothers: Peace be upon you, and God's mercy and his blessings. I shall not take much of your time ... bear with me five minutes before I turn it over to the Commander of the Mujahidin [Sayyaf] to answer questions. First of all, brothers, for those who don't know me, my name is Abdallah Azzam. My brothers, to repeat what the Commander of the Mujahidin said regarding jihad today by one's person and money... listen once again... jihad by one's person and money is now an individual obligation on every Muslim everywhere on Earth... My brothers, the *ulama* have ruled with consensus that if a small piece of Muslim land is infringed upon, the jihad becomes an individual obligation on the people of that location... And if the people of that country are too few, fall short, are idle, or sit still, then the individual obligation extends to those near them, and if those sit still, are insufficient, fall short or are idle, then the duty extends to the next ones and so on and so forth until the obligation until it covers the whole earth. This issue is agreed upon by all the Hadith specialists, the Qur'an commentators, the jurists, the predecessors, and the successors... Before the Commander of the Mujahidin I repeat, based on the three years I have spent with them, that the Mujahidin are in need of money, in need of men, in need of energy, in need of capabilities, and the sin increases as the need for capabilities increases. Have you heard, Muslims? If the [duty of] jihad is individual, the father does not [give] permission to the child, nor the husband to the wife, nor the master to the slave nor the creditor to the debtor. This is not my decision, but that of the four imams, the scholars of Hadith, the Qur'an commentators, jurists, the predecessors and the successors since this religion first was revealed... Peace be upon you, and God's mercy and his blessings.[65]

And just like that, Azzam's new foreign-fighter doctrine was born. He subsequently elaborated the argument, first in an article in *al-Mujtama'* magazine and then in his famous book *The Defense of Muslim Lands: The Most Important of Individual Duties*, published in March 1985.[66] He later included reformulations of the fatwa in other books such as *Join the Caravan* and *Jihad of Muslim People*, but the basic argument was the same, and it was highly influential.

Azzam's fatwa was not a radical innovation – only an incremental one – but that is why many were swayed by it. Put very simply, Azzam combined two existing but previously unconnected ideas. The first was the age-old and uncontested Islamic legal principle that occupation of Muslim land triggers a duty to repel the invaders through jihad.[67] The second idea was the argument developed by militant Islamists in the 1970s that the duty of jihad is universal and not subject to approval by any one nation-state.[68] Before Azzam's fatwa these two ideas existed side by side, each connected to another chain of ideas. The notion that non-Muslim invasion of Muslim land triggers defensive jihad was orthodoxy, but in the modern orthodox view it was the prerogative of individual nation-states to decide whether or not their citizens should participate in the jihad. Meanwhile, the radical Islamists who in the 1970s and early 1980s rejected official authority were advocating jihad for the purpose of toppling regimes, not to defend against invaders. Azzam mixed and matched, saying that jihad is indeed for the defence of territory, but governments have no say in who should participate.

By declaring liberation of territory as the main objective of jihad, Azzam effectively moved radical Islamist discourse on jihad closer to orthodoxy. This is probably one of the reasons why his message resonated the way it did. If the Afghan jihad attracted many more recruits than had any of the revolutionary groups in the 1960s and 1970s, it was because fighting infidel invaders was theologically much less controversial than rebelling against Muslim rulers. In addition, the wave of pan-Islamist sentiment that washed over the Middle East in the 1980s strongly favored Azzam's call to resist foreign occupation.

Vis-à-vis orthodox jihad jurisprudence, on the other hand, Azzam's message represented a move toward radicalism. In Islamic law the responsibility to wage jihad is typically assigned using the concepts of *fard 'ayn* (individual obligation) and *fard kifaya* (collective obligation).[69] According to classical jurists, jihad is in principle only an individual obligation for the population touched by the invasion; for everyone else it is a collective obligation, meaning that it is optional and subject to a range of restrictions.[70] However, if the locals are too weak to defend themselves, the individual duty can extend outward in concentric circles to their neighbors and, if necessary, to all the world's Muslims. In the late twentieth century, however, most mainstream modern clerics exonerated outsiders from the responsibility to fight. They would say, for example, that there is a jihad in Palestine, and outsiders can fight there, but only Palestinians are under an individual obligation to fight.[71] Azzam, however, took a different view. For him, the very existence of an occupation somewhere was evidence that the locals were unable to defend themselves, and hence the individual obligation should extend to all the world's Muslims immediately. He effectively dismissed the distinction between *fard 'ayn* and *fard kifaya*, saying that "there is no difference between *fard 'ayn* and *fard kifaya* before sufficiency [*kifaya*] is attained."[72] In so doing, Azzam excluded national religious authorities entirely from the process of deciding whether citizens should fight. Instead he said that when a Muslim territory is occupied, Muslims should come to its rescue regardless of what their respective local authorities say. In 1986 he wrote, "Know that the emir has no power over you to prevent you from jihad, or to seduce you to abandon jihad by propagating *da'wa*, and keep you away from the battlefield where men are made. Never ask for anyone's permission to do jihad."[73]

Azzam's ruling represented a challenge to political and religious authority, and was therefore quite controversial. Azzam himself said, "Some were angry, some were pleased, some reproved. Our brothers scolded us and sent a storm in our face, saying 'You are urging the youth to rebel against us.'"[74] The most tangible evidence of opposition was the "great number of fathers and brothers who came to bring their sons back from the land of jihad."[75] In one story,

An elderly woman came from Jordan to search for her son in the jihad. She came to [Azzam's] house, and the enemies had fueled her anger against the sheikh, who was the reason why her son had gone for jihad ... She said furiously, "Where is my son? What have you done with him? What makes you think you have the right to do this?"[76]

There was also opposition from other religious scholars, the majority of whom agreed that the Afghan war was a legitimate jihad, but disagreed that it was *fard 'ayn* for all Muslims.[77] When Tamim al-Adnani said, "Not all *ulama* view it that way," it was an understatement.[78] Azzam's fatwa notably faced opposition from members of the so-called Sahwa movement in Saudi Arabia represented by scholars such as Salman al-Awda, Safar al-Hawali, and Muhammad al-Munajjid.[79] These Saudi sheikhs mustered two main counterarguments; the first was that the Islam practiced in Afghanistan was theologically suspect due to its Sufi influences. The other was that the Afghan jihad served US interests, and Muslims should be wary of fighting on the same side as the Americans. The most outspoken of these critics was Safar al-Hawali, who dedicated a long lecture to Azzam's Afghanistan fatwa.[80]

Azzam also faced skepticism from the Muslim Brotherhood, whose objections were somewhat different from those of the Saudi Sahwa clerics. The Sudanese Brother Hasan al-Turabi notably argued that it was both impractical and unwise for all the world's Islamists to assemble in one place; it would detract from the many other causes around the world and leave the Islamists vulnerable to enemy repression. Here is al-Turabi speaking to Azzam in an interview published in *al-Jihad* magazine:

Turabi: It is wise that Islam be established all over the world, not that all of it be concentrated in one place, for it will then be easier to eradicate ... it is better to distribute the pressure across the world, this is my view ... I don't want us to withdraw from all the arenas and assemble in one place, for then all the eggs will be in one basket. ...

Azzam: Is it not possible to gather the Islamic forces now in one framework, as Salah al-Din al-Ayyubi did, for example?

Turabi: First of all, it was the region that got together for Salah al-Din, then whoever could follow him did, but we know that the situation in the world today, and there is much suffering, and Islam is challenged in many different areas ... today we are spread out all over the world and I do not consider it wise that we assemble.[81]

Azzam also argued with Pakistani Islamists over the *fard 'ayn* fatwa. The Afghan Mujahidin leader Muhammad Yasir wrote, "On our trip to Karachi, I was in another meeting with [Azzam], and a debate erupted between him and Taqi Uthmani, the mufti of Jamaat-e Islami. This sheikh was denouncing the notion that the jihad is *fard 'ayn*. He said it is not *fard 'ayn*, it is *fard kifaya*."[82]

Most other clerics chose a more diplomatic approach than al-Hawali and al-Turabi, which was to neither endorse nor criticize Azzam's fatwa. Rather than say explicitly whether participation is *fard 'ayn* or *fard kifaya* for outsiders, they would say things that could be interpreted both ways. That was notably the approach of the Saudi Grand Mufi Abd al-Aziz Bin Baz, who said, "Helping and aiding our fighting and exiled Afghan brothers is an individual duty on Muslims today, financially and physically or one of the two according to one's capability."[83] At first glance this looks similar to Azzam's position, but look again and it is clear that Bin Baz says fighting is optional.[84]

Azzam was probably the first trained *'alim* to articulate an elaborate legal argument for jihad as an individual obligation for all in the modern era. However, there are some indications that other scholars had made similar rulings for previous conflicts in the 1970s, although without articulating it in writing and without publicizing it. For example, Mustafa Hamid says that in the late 1970s Sheikh Ahmad Bin Abd al-Aziz Mubarak, head of the Shari'a court in Abu Dhabi, "issued a fatwa ruling that jihad [in Lebanon] on the side of the

Palestinians and against the Jews was now an individual duty on every Muslim" and that Sheikh Abd al-Badi' Saqr, a Muslim Brother in Qatar, privately told Hamid the same.[85] However, neither published their fatwa, and Hamid says Mubarak backtracked following a meeting with other clerics in the UAE. Another small precursor was a remark by the Afghan Mujahidin commander Jalaluddin Haqqani, who said in 1980, "There is a tendency in most of the Islamic countries which wish to help us to present aid and food as a kind of jihad ... This, however, does not absolve the Muslim of the duty to offer himself for the jihad."[86] Vahid Brown and Don Rassler argue that "clearly Haqqani, not Azzam, was the innovator [regarding jihad as an individual duty], and it is even possible that Jalaluddin's views on this issue influenced those of Azzam, as the two were very close."[87] However, this is probably overstating Haqqani's ideological contribution. For one, the notion that jihad might be an individual obligation for non-residents of a conflict zone was not new even in 1980, as we just saw. For another, Haqqani's contribution was just a sentence, not a full legal argument. Third, if Azzam lifted the idea straight from Haqqani, Azzam would presumably have published his fatwa soon after they met in 1982, not two-and-a-half years later.

Azzam's "privatization" of jihad was a tremendously significant idea, perhaps more than he himself realized. By telling Muslims to ignore all authorities and join the jihad, he helped open a Pandora's box of militancy that could not be controlled, precisely because it was reared on rejection of authority. Interestingly, and fatally for his historical legacy, Azzam never proposed an alternative governance structure for the people who came from abroad to join the jihad. He seems to have expected that they would all melt into the local insurgency and obey its *amir*. It never occurred to him that the local leader might be weak, that there might be several competing leaders, or that the foreign fighters might be unruly. It would not take long, however, before Azzam felt the consequences of his own idea. Many Afghan Arabs refused to submit to the authority of either Sayyaf or Azzam, and instead went their own ways in a multitude of factions. Azzam could do little to prevent it, because he had not put in place any governance mechanisms for the war volunteers. This fundamental authority problem would later contribute to the radicalization of the jihadi movement.

Tactical Restraint

Azzam wrote extensively on the jurisprudence of military tactics in jihad. It is clear that he sought to restrain and regulate the violence deployed in the Afghan war, and broadly speaking he held more moderate views on tactics than the jihadi movement as we know it today. At the same time, his commitment to "lean and clean jihad" should not be overstated.

Azzam demonstrated a concern for the observance of Islamic laws of war by writing and lecturing about them in several places. As early as February 1985, in issue 3 of *al-Jihad* magazine, he introduced an article series titled "The Jurisprudence of Jihad," which addressed various issues relating to the laws of war.[88] It dealt with things such as the killing of women, children, and the elderly, the treatment of prisoners and spies, the management of spoils, and collateral damage.[89] In 1987 he also published a book titled *Proper Conduct and Rulings in Jihad* which presented key excerpts from the classical legal literature on jihad accompanied by comments from Azzam.[90] He also discussed proper conduct in war in recorded lectures, several of which were later transcribed and compiled into books such as *Illustrating the Virtues of Jihad to God's Servants, Declaring Jihad, Jihadi Questions and Answers*, and *The Crime of Killing a Muslim Soul*.[91]

The fact that Azzam wrote about the laws of war at all suggests a desire to limit violent excesses. Treatises on this topic are quite rare in the jihadi literature, and few if any jihadi magazines after *al-Jihad* have had a column dedicated to this topic. Groups such as al-Qaida and Islamic State occasionally discuss the legitimacy of certain tactics, but mostly to justify the ones that they have already adopted.

Overall, Azzam seems to have favoured conventional paramilitary tactics against enemy combatants in confined theaters of war. Because classical jihad jurisprudence reflects, for the most part, a concern for proportionality and discrimination in the use of violence, Azzam ends up expressing similar concerns. For example, he states explicitly that "it is not allowed to kill non-combatants: [such as] children, women ... priests and monks."[92] He also ruled against taking Communist women as slaves or concubines because then the enemy would do the same to Muslim women. Azzam neither preached nor practiced international terrorism of the kind that secular Palestinian groups had used before him and jihadi groups would use after him. He did not actively prescribe or condone out-of-area attacks on Soviet targets outside Afghanistan, deliberate mass-casualty attacks on civilians, or suicide bombings. He did embrace the term terrorism (*irhab*) by saying things like "We are terrorists. Every Muslim needs to be a terrorist. Terrorism is a duty written in the Book and the Sunna."[93] Such statements were a reference to the Qur'anic verse 8:60 ("Make ready for them whatever force and strings of horses you can, to *terrify* [my emphasis] thereby the enemy of God"). However, they must be understood as a rhetorical posture against the Western labeling of Islamist militants as terrorists, not as an endorsement of the tactics that we commonly associate with terrorism.

Azzam almost certainly disapproved of the most blatant forms of international terrorism, such as hijackings and the bombing of civilians. He is admittedly not on the record as explicitly discussing many such tactics, but we do have some comments by close associates of his, such as Tamim al-Adnani. In a 1988 interview al-Adnani said:

I notice that some people here [in America] misunderstand the word *mujahidin*. They have bad information or bad understanding to that word. They think *mujahidin* are people who attack people or hijack planes, aircraft like those who hijack the Kuwaiti aircraft; we are against this completely – this is not jihad. This is nonsense. Jihad is fighting for the sake of Allah to protect our religion. We make jihad against those who prevent us from performing our religion ...[94]

This is the character of Islam. We do not touch women, we do not touch girls. Those who are doing hijackings, it's completely against Islam ...

All of [the Mujahidin leaders] are against hijackings. As Muslims, these hijackings, is not fair at all; you are killing innocent people, like these two Kuwaitis who were killed. What was their crime? Why? It is because they were Kuwaitis you kill them? ... This is not Islam, this is against Islam. Don't kill innocent people. Go and fight those who are fighting you ... go and fight the men. Don't kill innocent people who are not fighting, civilians, doing nothing. This is not fair. This is not accepted in our religion ... only we do fight those who are fighting us.[95]

However, Azzam was not quite the proponent of tactical restraint and ethical warfare that some of his moderate supporters have sought to present him as. Whenever the classical sources are ambiguous or contradictory on the legality of a particular tactic, Azzam usually endorsed the more radical interpretation. For example, in *Proper Conduct and Rulings in Jihad*, he qualifies the ban on killing non-combatants in numerous respects. For example, women may be targeted if they take part in the fighting.[96] And if non-combatants mingle with the combatants or are used as cover, the group as a whole may still be targeted so long as one does not deliberately aim at the non-combatants.[97] Interestingly, Azzam ascribes special status to Communist women in Afghanistan, whom he says must be killed, regardless of whether they are participating in combat or not, and whether they are encountered alone or in a group.[98]

Moreover, Azzam's only frame of reference is Islamic laws of war, not international norms such as those enshrined in the Geneva Conventions. Where the two do not overlap, for example on the neutrality of ambulances and places of worship, Azzam ignores the international legal norms. In fact, we know he personally breached them. As we saw in Chapter 8, he helped organize transportation of military equipment under humanitarian cover and used ambulances to transport fighters. Once, he boasted about training with artillery inside mosques in Afghanistan: "We had a mosque or pergola, and inside the mosque we trained with mortars, we trained with anti-aircraft artillery. I told them, what is greater than this? Inside the mosque. The Zikwiyak, inside the mosque!! Missiles, inside the mosque. A mortar, inside the mosque."[99]

To get a better sense of Azzam's views and their ambiguities, let us take a look at two tactical issues where we know that subsequent jihadi groups have taken a radical view: the targeting of Westerners in the Muslim world, and out-of-theater attacks. As for attacks on Westerners in the Muslim world, it seems clear that Azzam opposed them in the context of his time. In fact, he actively restrained people who wanted to carry out such attacks. His son Hudhayfa later said in an interview that "some in Peshawar (Pakistan) would ask permission from Abdallah Azzam to kill foreigners and reporters with the pretext that they were corruptive. He answered them by saying that, 'You cannot touch anyone of them because the state of Pakistan pledged safety for them.' My father stood as a barrier and prevented them from carrying out such actions."[100] Hudhayfa's claim is corroborated by the transcript of a discussion which emerged during a lecture Azzam gave at the Sada camp in the autumn of 1986:

QUESTIONER ASKS: "Who is the one that determines what the actions are that deem [the Westerner's] blood lawful? Do I determine this? Or do the scholars?"

SHAYKH: "The scholars. The scholars are the ones who determine this ... The issue isn't as simple as you think, and this is what Jama'at at-Takfir wal-Hijrah was afflicted with. This shaykh – their leader, Shukri Mustafa, rahimahullah – began issuing fatawa, and every single one began reading and issuing fatawa declaring the blood of the Muslims lawful ... "

[The brother continues debating, mentioning that the Christians of our times are all muharibin]

SHAYKH: "Who are the Christians that are muharibin?"

BROTHER: "All of the Christians are muharibin."

SHAYKH: "How are they all muharibin?"

BROTHER: "Those who put the covering on their head, and wear the cross."

SHAYKH: "The one who wears the cross is a muharib? The one who wears the cross, this is his belief."

[The brother continues arguing]

SHAYKH: "My brother, do you still consider them muharibin? The muharib is the one who brandishes weapons against the Muslims!" after some more argument): "I will not give a fatwa for this. Look for some other mufti besides myself."[101]

While this particular exchange is clear, Azzam also spoke about the same issue in terms that are slightly more ambiguous:

BROTHER: "However, now, they come to our lands mostly to spread their ideology."

SHAYKH: "My brother, who has brought them into our lands?"

BROTHER: "A disbeliever, like them."

SHAYKH: "OK, excellent. You say to them that the one who has brought you into this land is a disbeliever. Therefore, you cannot be here ... You must warn them, is this not so? Either Islam, or the jizyah, or the sword. Is this not so? So, you must warn them, my brother. Send them a message: 'You are spreading this evil, so, leave this land. Otherwise, you will die.' That's it. After this, kill him. As for coming to kill him while he is secure and under a pact of security, this is not allowed. As for those People of the Book who live with us in our lands, it is not allowed to kill them in our times, unless they initiate fighting with us. It is not allowed, as this will cause great fitnah that will never end, and the rulers will stand on their side, and they will attack the Muslims, and put pressure on the Islamic movement – all for what? Because of you poking out the eye of a Christian in your land, or you killed a Christian, resulting in tens of Muslims being killed in prison as the result of torture ... "

[The brother continues debating]

SHAYKH: "It is not allowed for you to take the wealth of a Christian, at all. It is not allowed to kill the Western Christian in the lands of the Muslims, unless you first issue him a warning, and unless it first becomes clear to you that he is engaging in an act that deems his blood lawful. Understood?"[102]

Here Azzam qualifies the ban on killing Westerners in ways that open the door ever so slightly to such operations. He says that if Westerners "initiate fighting with us" or if they "spread evil" and ignore requests to leave, then they can be killed. The problem with such statements is that they leave room for interpretation of what constitutes "initiating fighting," what constitutes "a warning," and who "they" are. Historically, several radical groups have exploited such ambiguities to legitimize attacks. Some groups have attacked Western civilians in the Muslim world, claiming to be retaliating against the "aggression" of Western governments and claiming that the victims had been warned by the group's previous statements.

Regarding attacks in the West, the evidence is also slightly ambiguous. On the one hand, Azzam is on the record as saying that people who hold visas to Western countries should follow local laws. In 1986 he told an audience of Afghan Arabs at Sada, "If you are given a visa to any country in the world, it is not allowed for you to partake in any action that breaks its laws. This is not allowed, unless this would contradict something from Islam, such as the prayer, fasting, etc. It is not allowed for you to cheat them or take from their wealth."[103] On the other hand, this statement only speaks about ordinary crimes, not acts of war, and Azzam qualifies his admonition to follow local laws by saying "unless this would contradict something from Islam."

Besides, Azzam is not on the record as having explicitly ruled out out-of-theater attacks. The closest thing we have is a claim from his nephew and biographer Mahmud Azzam, who wrote in a 2012 book that Azzam believed that "armed operations against other countries – dispatched from Afghan territories – would backfire on the Afghan Mujahidin."[104] However, in a martyrdom biography from 1989, Azzam mentions that the martyr in question had proposed to carry out an attack in Moscow: "I first met him through a letter he sent to his friends in Peshawar, and from it I understood his ambitions and hopes. He thought about striking Moscow, and he warned against the Russian plots and tricks. I sensed the depth [of his convictions]."[105] Here Azzam says nothing about the proposition other than that it made him sense the depth of his convictions. Incidentally, this passage is the first recorded suggestion of an out-of-theater attack by Afghan Arabs in the 1980s.

More importantly, Azzam is actually on the record as having explicitly condoned attacks inside the United States on Jews and on anyone funding Israel. In 1988 Azzam gave an open lecture in a mosque in California, where the following exchange occurred in the question-and-answer session:

Q: Is it permissible to take revenge on American Jews present in America, given [the Qur'anic verse] "kill them wherever you find them"?
A: Of course it is permissible.
Q: But in America you will face punishment . . . .
A: Someone who is prepared to die, if he is prepared to die, then go ahead. But strictly in terms of permissibility, it is permissible.[106]

Shortly after, he gets a similar question:

Q: A man who donates money to the Jews in Palestine, is it permissible to kill him here [when] it's confirmed that he is donating money?
A: It is permissible. Well, whether he does it or not, this depends on what is beneficial. Does the harm of not doing it now outweigh the benefits? This is for the Muslim youth here to assess. So the answer is, it is permissible, but whether it is possible for us to do it or not is another matter.[107]

In this exchange, Azzam is effectively sanctioning the assassination of civilians on American soil. The statement is noteworthy because it is ahead of its time; in 1988 Sunni jihadi groups had not yet conducted any attacks in the West. It is worth stressing here that Azzam does not appear to have written anything to this effect in his books or articles. It could thus be that the remarks were delivered in affect, and that he got carried away trying to please his Palestinian audience. However, it could also mean that he really held more radical opinions than he

Ideologue 313

expressed in writing. The 1988 statement in California was made less than a year after the outbreak of the Palestinian Intifada, which probably made Azzam more open to radical measures against Israel. However, this only shows that he was susceptible to accepting more controversial tactics if the political situation changed. It follows that his views on other tactics might have changed as well, had he lived into the US-dominated world of the 1990s (more on this in Chapter 16).

Toward the Caliphate

Even though Azzam saw jihad as an objective in its own right, he did have ideas about where the mobilization to Afghanistan might lead. In short, he hoped that the Afghan Mujahidin would win and set up an Islamic state in Afghanistan, which would then be used as a base from which an Islamic army could set out and recapture all of Islam's lost territories and eventually unite them all under a transnational caliphate.

Azzam's starting point was the diagnosis that the Muslim world was in bad shape. Like other pan-Islamists he saw the *umma* as facing an existential external threat on multiple fronts, in addition to suffering crippling internal divisions. In his recruitment calls he often provided long lists of examples of places where Muslims were being persecuted and Muslim territory was being occupied. For example, he blamed Muslims for "not advancing Afghanistan, Palestine, Kashmir, Lebanon, Chad, Eritrea, etc."[108] He would speak of

> the bloody tale of Bukhara, the narrative of mutilated Palestine, and blazing Aden and its enslaved peoples, the sorry stories of Spain, the terrible accounts of Eritrea, sore Bulgaria, the tragedy of Sudan, the devastated remnants of Lebanon, Somalia, Burma, Caucasia and its deep wounds, Uganda, Zanzibar, Indonesia, Nigeria. All these slaughters and tragedies are the best lesson for us.[109]

Azzam had a maximalist view of what constituted Muslim territory, namely, any land where Muslims had been either in a majority or in power. It included not only today's Muslim-majority countries, but also areas ruled by Muslims centuries ago, such as southern Spain and southeastern Europe. It is clear that he hoped for Muslims to reconquer all these territories one day; "Before us," he wrote, "lies Palestine,

Bokhara, Lebanon, Chad, Eritrea, Somalia, Philippines, Burma, South Yemen, Tashkent, and Andalusia."[110]

His recommended short-term response to these problems was an immediate and comprehensive military mobilization to liberate occupied Muslim territories, especially in Afghanistan and Palestine. "The time is ripe," he wrote, "for Muslims to concentrate their efforts after the slaughter and the massacres inflicted on them."[111] This is where his foreign-fighter doctrine came in; the situation was so acute that all the world's Muslims must participate in the resistance effort. Azzam considered Palestine as the highest priority and said that those who can, must fight there. However, he realized that this was unfeasible for most people, so he called on everyone else to go to Afghanistan for now.

Azzam believed that non-Muslims would always conspire against Islam, so he was opposed to any negotiated solution to the Afghanistan war, or indeed any other conflict between Muslims and infidels. "The political solution pursued by America and Russia [in Afghanistan] is wrong and forbidden," he argued. "The experiences of Palestine and elsewhere have taught us that the solution is only through the mouths of the rifles, and that sending the issue to the international fora etc. [is pointless]."[112] Incidentally, this quote is probably the origin of the phrase "jihad and the rifle alone: no negotiations, no conferences, and no dialogues," which is often presented in the English-language literature as Azzam's "slogan," but which he does not seem to have articulated in those exact terms.[113]

In the medium term, Azzam hoped that Afghanistan would become an Islamic state (*dawla islamiyya*) that would be a territorial base for what he considered true Sunni Muslims. Azzam wrote extensively on the Islamic state, more so than most other jihadi ideologues before the rise of the Islamic State organization in the 2010s. While all militant Islamists in the 1980s, 1990s, and 2000s shared the objective of establishing an Islamic state of some kind, most tended merely to pay lip service to the idea without going into specifics about how to implement it or what it might look like. Azzam, by contrast, devoted many articles and lectures to the topic, suggesting that it was a high priority for him.

Azzam had the idea of using Afghanistan as a base very early on. In April 1983 he wrote: "There is now a golden opportunity to establish an Islamic state in Afghanistan. I say it again: It is a golden opportunity now in all the world to establish God's rule on Earth."[114] Then, in August 1983, he wrote:

The time is ripe for us to think about a land that can be a solid base [*qa'ida sulba*] from which the Islamic call can depart and where preachers can find refuge from the hell of the *jahiliyya*. Is the time not ripe for us to think about finding an abode for Islam on whose land God's religion can be represented with its culture, system, people, and laws? ... I see Afghanistan as the best land for this abode now.[115]

Later, in 1988, he would write an article in *al-Jihad* magazine titled "The Solid Base" which received much attention from analysts in the years after 9/11, because it was interpreted by some as an early manifesto for the al-Qaida organization.[116] However, this was a misinterpretation stemming from the fact that the Arabic word for base is *qa'ida*. Azzam was not speaking about an organization, but rather about a territorial base in the literal sense.[117] In 1989 he elaborated on his vision, saying:

What do we want? We want a state that will represent the Muslims in the world as the Iranian state represents the interests of Shiites in the whole world. We want a state that represents the interests of the Sunnis in all the world. We want a state that can give you a passport if you are fleeing because of your religion and creed. We want a state that protects your honor and blood if you seek protection in it, one that does not extradite you to authorities who want to violate your honor and uproot Islam on its territory. We want a state that truly adopts Islam and will be a launching-pad and solid base for jihad on earth. We want a state that launches war on those who fight Islam and keeps peace with those who keep peace with Islam.[118]

In an interview in 1988 Azzam's deputy Tamim al-Adnani also went into some detail about what the Islamic state might look like:

Interviewer: when you talk about an Islamic government ... they jump to the picture of Iran ... how would it be different from Iran?

Adnani: It will be completely different from Iran ... we are not going to do like the Iranians, we are not going to kidnap people or, you know, hijack aircraft and doing these things. ... I am against hijackings as I told you. ...

Interviewer: in the minds of many non-Muslims, when you talk about an Islamic state, you talk about a state that are going to be fighting them, like you hear, many people saying Muslims are going to be condemning the Unites States, attacking, fighting the United States and everybody else around ... they would not allow anybody to live inside, to let any other religions be with them.

Adnani: This is nonsense. Look at our history and you will see the different ... we are against any kind of attacking their liberty or freedom of other religions. Anybody is free to have his own religion under the Islamic flag when we have a Muslim country ... we are not going to attack anyone except those who attack us. If somebody attacks us then we will know how to answer it.[119]

Thus in the short term Azzam seems to have envisaged something similar to Afghanistan under the Taliban, that is, a passport-issuing state that lives alongside other countries and does not extradite Islamist dissidents who seek refuge there.

However, both in this passage and elsewhere Azzam hints at something more expansionist than the Taliban state. He talks about Afghanistan being a "launching-pad [*mantalaq*] for jihad on earth" and he makes clear, as we saw earlier, that he considers much of the Muslim world as being under infidel occupation. It is fairly clear that he hoped the Islamic state in Afghanistan would serve as a base for a new missionary effort and a military reconquest of other lost territories. He appears to have envisaged a type of international Islamic brigade that would march southwest from Afghanistan in the direction of Palestine and add new territory to the Islamic state as it went along. At the same time, he was realistic about the expansion stage, expecting it to take time and involve setbacks. In the meantime, the Islamic state in Afghanistan would serve as an "impregnable fortress where those who undertake missionary activity could seek refuge from the hell of shameful ignorance."[120] Azzam's longer-term objective was thus for the Islamic state in Afghanistan to grow into a transnational caliphate that would encompass all the world's Sunni-majority nation-states.

For the very long term, Azzam was ambiguous about whether he wanted the caliphate to seek world domination. Sometimes he suggested a more limited objective, namely, that jihad would continue "until all the lands that were once Islamic have been liberated."[121] At other times he suggested a maximalist aim. For example, he once approvingly quoted his hero Sayyid Qutb as saying that "protecting the abode of Islam ... is not the final aim; its protection is not the end purpose of the Islamic jihad movement; rather its protection is a means to establish God's kingdom in it and to take it as a base to spread to the whole earth."[122] Like other religious men with missionary zeal, Azzam probably hoped and expected that his religion would eventually be adopted by all of humanity, but he may not have wanted it to happen entirely by military conquest. In any case, he focused more on the short term, and he was convinced that the jihad in Afghanistan was the best way forward. He once recalled a phone conversation with another Islamic cleric who said he was going on vacation to Turkey "to visit the capital of the Caliphate," to which Azzam replied, "why don't you come to Peshawar and see people who are trying to *reestablish* the Caliphate?"[123]

Postponed Revolution

Azzam's desire for an Islamic state stemmed from his conviction that God ordained Muslims to implement Islamic law in their societies. For the same reason, he was critical of governments in the Muslim world that in his view were not Islamic enough – which was most of them. His reorientation of jihad toward non-Muslim invaders did not take away his hostility to secular regimes; he walked and chewed gum at the same time.

For the same reason, it would be reductive to view Azzam merely as a kind of pan-Islamic national liberation activist. He wanted not only the liberation of Muslim territories, but also their Islamization. That is why Azzam did not call off the jihad in Afghanistan when the Soviet Union withdrew in early 1989 – the Afghan Communist regime also needed to go:

> This jihad did not begin against the Russians but against the Afghan rulers themselves, starting with Muhammad Dawud, then Taraqi, then Hafidhullah, and finally Karmal ... If the jihad departs from its basic objective, it will fall and end; if the Mujahidin lose the aim, namely "that God's word be supreme," then the jihad will change into a nationalist fight ... The jihad will lose its sanctity.[124]

Azzam was skeptical of most Arab regimes, albeit to different degrees. He was especially hostile toward the secular Arab republics, such as Egypt, Syria, Iraq, and Libya, which he saw as tyrannical and antireligious. He did not devote large tomes to denouncing these states, perhaps partly for fear of retribution and partly because their unIslamic status was taken for granted in the Islamist movement. However, his writings and lectures are full of side comments and anecdotes that reveal his hostility to them. He sought to portray the regimes as sadistic and debauched by retelling stories of imprisonment and torture of Islamists, for example that of an Egyptian torturer named

Hamza Bassiuni who would tell prisoners crying for God that "If God came here I would put him in a cell."[125] Azzam was less critical of the Gulf states, and he was quite positive, if somewhat apprehensive, about the Saudi regime. He emphasized on several occasions that he had done nothing but praise the Saudi government for its efforts in Afghanistan.

Azzam did attack one Muslim-majority state in book form in the 1980s, namely, Turkey. In 1987 he published a book titled *The Lost Beacon*, which was a hostile biography of Mustafa Kemal Atatürk and a blistering critique of Kemalism.[126] (The beacon in question was the Ottoman Empire, whose fall he had long lamented). Azzam presents Kemal as a traitor who conspired with the Jews to end the Ottoman state and who sold Palestine to the British. Azzam also criticizes Kemal's domestic policies, at one point offering a charge sheet listing twenty-one policies which he considered authoritarian and anti-Islamic. Azzam's interest in Turkey probably came from his fascination with the Ottoman Empire and his view of secularism as a corrosive force. He may also have been inspired by his conversations with Necmettin Erbakan, the founder of the Millî Görüş (National View) movement, who later served briefly as president of Turkey. Erbakan was a personal friend of Azzam's, and they met several times in Pakistan and in Saudi Arabia in the mid-1980s, at a time when Erbakan's movement was banned in Turkey.[127] *The Lost Beacon* earned Azzam many followers among Turkish Islamists, and he was interviewed by Turkish media on at least one occasion.[128] Turkey today is also one of the countries where Azzam is most openly celebrated, as we shall see in Chapter 16.

In many accounts about the Afghan Arabs in Peshawar, Azzam is portrayed as a moderate counterweight to the *takfiri*s, the radical Arabs who labeled other Muslims as infidels for the slightest infraction. However, as we saw in Chapter 6, Azzam certainly also had *takfiri* tendencies. He did not hesitate to declare Muslim rulers as infidels, as in this passage: "Let it be clear from the beginning that a tyrant [*taghut*] is a tyrant whether he is American, Arab, Afghan or Russian, and let it be clear from the start that those who legislate by something other than God's revelation are infidels [*kuffar*], even if they pray, fast and build places of worship."[129] Similarly, he said those regimes that put obstacles in the way of jihadi efforts were un-Islamic: "Banning jihad is *kufr* and leads to expulsion from the *milla*."[130] Being prevented from preparing for jihad, he argued, is "one of the worst forms of oppression."[131]

Moreover, as we saw in Chapter 6, Azzam was very clear and explicit in his view that political leaders who do not implement Islamic law in full are to be considered infidels. For example, he said, "Changing any one of God's rulings is *kufr*," and "as for he who applies man-made laws ... he is an infidel outside the creed [*kafir kharij min al-milla*]. The top ruler in any state, if he applies something other than God's law, he is an infidel outside the creed. The lawmaker or parliament that establishes man-made laws: outside the creed."[132] He was careful not to name too many individuals, but he did say, "Surely you agree that the legislation of someone like Hafiz al-Assad, al-Qadhafi and others like them is the greatest *shirk* that expels them from the community."[133] As for the Afghan Communist regime, Azzam once said that mere sympathies with the Najibullah regime merited excommunication: "He who hopes for Najib to defeat the Mujahidin is not a Muslim under any circumstances."[134]

Azzam, in other words, wanted to see all non-Islamist regimes go, but he nevertheless gave priority, in the short term, to fighting non-Muslim invaders. For him, the liberation of Muslim territory had to precede the toppling of secular governments, because the latter can only be defeated by a jihad movement operating from an external territorial base. Azzam explicitly dismissed the idea of toppling governments from within through military coup: "There are the handful of officers, some of whom may think that it is possible for them to carry out a collective Muslim effort – this is a kind of fantasy or delusion reminiscent of the past. It will be no more than a repetition of the tragedy of Abdel Nasser with the Islamic movement once again."[135] His reluctance was based on a pragmatic assessment that targeting regimes prematurely would harm the Islamist movement. In 1989 he was asked why *al-Jihad* magazine focused mainly on Afghanistan and not on oppressive regimes. He said, "We do not want to enter into a battle with the regimes, which keep a record of every outcry against them. In order for the journal to enter these Arab states, we prefer to concentrate on this issue which everyone agrees on, and around which there is no sensitivity for other regimes."[136]

Azzam's son Hudhayfa later insisted that his father had sought to prevent Afghan Arabs from targeting regimes other than the Afghan one:

Let me state clearly from now that before we started training in Afghanistan we used to swear by the Book of God that we would never use this training and technology against any Arab or Islamic state or against any Arab or

Islamic regime. My father made all trainees promise that they would not use their weapons in this way.[137]

This stance is partly corroborated by Abu Mus'ab al-Suri, who recalled that when he first met Azzam in Peshawar in July 1987, the latter was less than enthusiastic about reviving the Islamist insurgency in Syria, the cause in which al-Suri had been invested in the previous eight years. Azzam said the Syrian jihad had "had its chance; people no longer believed in it and wished to support it."[138] At the same time, Azzam "had not completely ruled out the possibility of a reinvigoration of the Syrian Jihad, if the Syrian jihadis managed to rebuild a group of capable fighters in Afghanistan."[139] Indeed, elsewhere, Azzam let it shine through that he believed that force would one day have to be used against these regimes: "[This religion] will face obstacles ... A religion for the salvation of mankind cannot hold its hands and preach with the tongue when the *jahiliyya* is wielding weapons and blades."[140]

Anti-Westernism

Azzam did not advocate violence against the West the way groups like al-Qaida did in the 1990s, but he regularly expressed very anti-Western views. He was especially critical of the United States and Britain, and his declared hostility increased in the late 1980s. Azzam was not especially more anti-Western than other Afghan Arabs; rather, his views were representative of the mood of the entire community. It is very clear from the writings of Azzam and others that the jihadi movement was extremely hostile to the United States already in the 1980s.

Azzam's writings suggest that his anti-Westernism was rooted in a combination of religious convictions, antipathy to Western culture, and anger over real and perceived Western political meddling in the Muslim world. He repeatedly expressed categorical distrust of Christians and Jews with reference to scripture. He often suggested that Islam and the Judeo-Christian world were in a state of never-ending conflict:

The battle continues between the infidels and the believers ... the people of the book have resentment toward us and our belief ... the people of the book conspire against us ... it is impossible for Jews and Christians to be friendly toward us ... it is impossible for the people of belief and the people of unbelief to meet half-way, however much we present ourselves as open-minded and flexible.[141]

In fact, he argued that Muslims should distrust not only Jews and Christians, but also anyone else who cooperates with them:

So, if you see America or Russia or Britain or the criminals and tyrants in the Islamic world – if you see them pleased with someone, you should doubt this person's Islam and his faith. Understood? This is because Allah has set down a [Qur'anic] rule that does not change, and this rule says: "And the Jews and Christians will never be pleased with you until you follow their way."[142]

Azzam was also skeptical of Western culture, and he looked with disdain at what he saw as the moral corruption and spiritual emptiness of Western societies. For example, in 1986 he said:

The Western society is one that is quite dull, in every sense of the word ... Imagine that in some places a woman will marry another woman, and a man will marry another man! Such evil! [It's] an evil, wasted society! ... They walk around, eating, enjoying themselves, not knowing how to rid themselves of these pains that they are living in. So, they do not find anything but the path of alcohol, the path of drugs. These drugs, such as marijuana, that these Americans use, and heroin, etc. – this heroin costs $1,000 for a gram! A kilogram costs a million dollars! You constantly see them with a needle – a syringe, for their drug use ... They cannot sleep! Constant anxiety, sadness! 54 million Americans – one quarter of the American population – suffers from mental and psychological problems. You see one of them, a millionaire, in the newspapers: "Such-and-such killed themself ... threw himself in front of a train ... put himself underneath a train ... threw himself off of a rooftop ... " – all in order to rid himself of this anxiety and sadness.[143]

For these reasons, Azzam said Muslims should keep their distance from Westerners. He advised young Muslims not to live in the West:

I declare it forbidden for the youth to study in the West, except if they are married. Hear it from me: it is forbidden for a youth to study in the West, unless he is married. Relay on my behalf, even if it is one fatwa: it is not allowed, not allowed, not allowed ... Separation from the disbelievers, and not living with them, is something clearly intended in the Shari'a, and is supported by logic and emotion, as the Prophet said: "I am free of anyone who lives with the disbelievers," and: "Whoever lives with a disbeliever and dies with him, then he is like him." There are many, many *ahadith* to this effect ... four or five about living with the disbelievers. Because of this, the Western life, living between the disbelievers, is a very, very, very difficult life.[144]

He also argued that Muslims should shun Christians living in the Muslim world, and if they found themselves before Christians, they should avoid shaking hands with them.[145] As an example of good conduct, he held up a story he had heard from Muhammad Abd al-Rahman Khalifa, the leader of the Muslim Brotherhood in Jordan:

When I was young, the judge of as-Salt (a town in Jordan) became ill. I was in my sixth year of elementary school, and I decided to go visit him ... I entered to find that the heads of the Christian community had all come to visit him because of his illness. There was the priest of the Orthodox Church, and the Latin Church ... When I entered the room – and I was only a young boy at the time – he said to the head pastor: "Get up and sit over there," and he said to me: "Come, my son, and sit next to me." He then looked to the pastor and said to him: "This is how my religion commands me to behave with you."[146]

Most of the time, though, Azzam's diatribes against the West cited political arguments, typically in the form of examples of Western meddling in Muslim affairs. However, these examples were usually a mixture of real events and conspiracy theories, often with conspiracy theories as the main ingredient. For example, he blamed America for the death, in August 1988, of Pakistani President Zia ul Haqq, even though the latter perished in a plane accident together with the US ambassador to Pakistan.[147] He also implicated the USA in the death of his friend Kamal al-Sananiri in an Egyptian prison in 1981.[148] In a 1986 article in *al-Jihad* magazine titled "The Crusader Wars Continue," the author claimed that the Red Cross was systematically amputating the healthy limbs of Afghan Mujahidin.[149] Meanwhile, he sought to discredit reports that might reflect well on the West, for example by dismissing the news about the Stinger rockets provided by the USA to the Mujahidin in 1986 as "lies designed to mislead public opinion."[150]

The political examples Azzam cited conveyed three main themes. The most prominent was that the West, led by America, was working in various ways to weaken the Afghan Mujahidin. According to Mahmud Azzam, who was a close aide in the late 1980s, Azzam was convinced that the West was trying to weaken Islamist forces in Afghanistan to prevent them from moving on to Palestine. Azzam also said the real reason the USA had become involved in Afghanistan was to destroy them: "[America] thought that it had an opportunity to relieve its resentment from Vietnam and to destroy both of its traditional enemies, namely the communists and the Muslims."[151] Similarly, as early as 1985, Azzam wrote that "there is an international plot to neutralize us and to steal the fruit of our fight" and that "the US wants to have an American Islam which would be controlled by them."[152] Azzam and other Afghan Arabs were particularly incensed by the Geneva accords in 1988 (about ending the Soviet–Afghan war), which they saw as a Russian–American plot to weaken the Mujahidin. Besides, Azzam remarked, the accords had been "coordinated by a Jew."[153]

A second and related theme was that Western media were waging an information war against the Islamist Mujahidin parties and the Afghan Arabs. In August 1989 this was the topic of the month in *al-Jihad* magazine, whose front page carried a picture of the British Crown.[154] Later that autumn Azzam wrote an editorial about the international media campaign against the Mujahidin, citing the Protocols of the Elders of Zion and describing the onslaught as led by the Jews.[155] In another article, he was particularly critical of the British Broadcasting Corporation (BBC), which he said used its Pashto and Farsi service to spread disinformation in Afghanistan intended to weaken the Islamist Mujahidin parties and sow discord between the Afghans and the Arab volunteers.[156]

A third theme was the West's long history of interventions and manipulations in the Middle East. Azzam wrote several articles about the history of Western interference.[157] For example, in April 1989 he wrote an article titled "Britain's role in fighting Islam," which elaborated on the many things that had given the English a "big role in the destruction of Islam and the subjugation of Muslims everywhere."[158] These things included colonizing Palestine and facilitating the Zionist project, bringing down the Ottoman Empire, colonizing and Westernizing Egypt, bringing down Muslim rule in India, bringing Ba'thist rule to Iraq, spreading the cultivation of hashish and opium in Central Asia, bringing Communists to Aden in Yemen, and waging three wars in Afghanistan. In other texts, Azzam also accused the USA of being behind no less than all the military coups in the twentieth-century Muslim world, including in Egypt, Sudan, Iraq, Turkey, Iran, and Pakistan.[159]

The enemy hierarchy in Azzam's worldview in the 1980s was not quite clear. Israel – which he refers to only as "the Jews" – is clearly a very prominent, almost primordial enemy for him. He obviously also has little love for Russia for its actions in Afghanistan. Among the Western countries, his main enemies are the United States and Britain. He devotes the most attention to America, but he ascribes a more manipulative role to Britain, which he calls the "the speckled viper" (*al-haya al-raqta'*) of international politics.[160] In one article he wrote that "British intelligence is the brain of the infidel encampment of the Muslim world while America is its muscle ... America consults with [Britain] in matters pertaining to fighting Islamist movements, suppressing the Islamic awakening, and silencing the voice of the jihadi Intifada in Jerusalem."[161] Other Western countries receive less attention, although he does note that France was "the spirit and mastermind behind American and British colonial intelligence services in general."[162] Some other countries, such as Bulgaria, were criticized for their treatment of their Muslim populations, while yet others, such as the Scandinavian countries and Italy, were cited as examples of moral decay due to their sexual promiscuity and high divorce rates.[163] It is difficult to find in Azzam's writings any positive remarks about any Western country.

Azzam's anti-Westernism is difficult to explain with reference to personal experiences. After all, in Afghanistan Western countries were on the same side as he was, supporting the Afghan jihad with billions of dollars. Moreover, Azzam himself did not have any personal negative experiences with Westerners as far as we know. Unless we consider Israel part of the West, he was not a direct victim of any hostile Western acts in the region, nor did he report any experiences with racism or the like on his travels in Europe and the USA. On the contrary, he and the Services Bureau enjoyed complete freedom to recruit and fundraise in the West, a freedom they did not enjoy anywhere in the Muslim world, with the possible exception of Saudi Arabia.

Azzam's unwillingness to acknowledge the Western support for the Afghan jihad was representative of Islamist attitudes at the time. Martyn Frampton, in his book about the Muslim Brotherhood and the West, noted that, in 1980, some senior Muslim Brothers had attributed the Soviet invasion to the machinations of the West, and that their subsequent views did not change to reflect events on the ground:

American support for the mujahideen appears to have made little impression on the way Brotherhood leaders looked at the United States. Indeed, [former supreme guide] 'Umar al-Tilmisani remarked in his memoirs that Afghanistan was a "victim of the conspiracies of the United States and the Soviets against the Islamic world." He dismissed American criticism of Soviet actions in 1979 as "specks of dust in the eyes," designed to distract from their "real" support for Moscow ... In this way, the general guide contrived to ignore US support for the Mujahideen, in preference for a narrative that stressed ongoing hostility toward Islam.[164]

Interestingly, this attitude was less widespread among Afghan Mujahidin, who occasionally expressed gratitude for the Western support and whose publications featured less anti-Western rhetoric. It seems that it was primarily non-Afghan Islamists who struggled with the cognitive dissonance created by America coming to the Muslims' rescue in Afghanistan.

Even more curiously, Azzam's hostility toward the West *grew* in the late 1980s, just as Western support for the Afghan jihad increased and the Mujahidin were winning on the battlefield. While the West is a minor theme in his early Afghanistan writings, it features prominently in his articles and interviews in 1988 and 1989. For example, in late 1988 Azzam gave an interview to the Islamist magazine *al-Mughtarab*, which the magazine summarized in six bullet points, all of which were about the West:

- The West's attempts to divide the jihad organizations have failed and they are now agreed politically and militarily.
- America killed Zia ul Haq – and this is the evidence.
- The government of Benazir Bhutto is implementing an American plan.
- There is an American plan to get rid of the leaders of jihad, especially Hekmatyar and Sayyaf.
- Britain has adopted the lie of Wahhabism being a source of discord (*fitna*), and the West and the East and the governments of Iran and Kabul have followed it.
- The West fears that the light of jihad will move from Afghanistan to Palestine.[165]

In fact, in some of the Afghan Arab literature of the late 1980s one almost gets the impression that the Afghan Mujahidin were at war with the United States, not Russia. For example, in March 1987 Azzam wrote an editorial in *al-Jihad* magazine titled "The American Attack," in which he denounced US-funded educational projects in Afghanistan as an "ideological Crusader assault," adding:

The American presence in the Afghan field poses no less of a danger than that of the Russians, but perhaps even a greater danger in many respects because the American policy is very complex. It always tries to give preference to the principle of expectation and stability and its machinations depend not on one artery but on hundreds of arteries and veins that feed its black heart. It wears every mask and intervenes in different countries.[166]

Interestingly, the end of the 1980s also saw a noticeable increase in the use of the term "Crusader" in Azzam's writings and in those of other Afghan Arabs.[167] The term had been used by Azzam earlier in the 1980s, and occasionally by other Islamists in the 1970s, but the frequency appears to increase around 1989. In one article Azzam talks about having "repelled the Crusaders" – by which he means the NGO Médecins sans Frontières – from northern Afghanistan in 1985.[168] In another article titled "Jewish–Crusader Malevolence" he says the "Crusader campaigns have intensified" against the Arab presence in Afghanistan.[169] Similarly, in April 1989 *al-Jihad* magazine published a "Statement from the leaders of jihad on the situation of refugees – great Crusader conspiracy to engulf the Afghan people."[170] And in the space of a few months in late 1989, *al-Bunyan al-Marsus* published at least three articles using the term Crusader in the headline.[171] This is interesting because in the jihadi context the use of the term Crusader – which connotes a threat of a more imminent and existential nature than simply "the West" – is usually associated with more aggressively anti-Western attitudes. In the 1990s, when al-Qaida began launching terrorist attacks on US targets, it described its main enemy as the "Crusader–Jewish alliance." It may thus seem that as early as the late 1980s the Afghan Arab community was starting to see the West as representing an imminent military threat to the Muslim world. The ideological groundwork for the anti-Western turn in jihadism was thus already being laid in the 1980s, and Azzam played a part in it.

It is difficult to explain why Afghan Arab anti-Westernism increased in the late 1980s. Perhaps it reflected a realization that America was about to emerge victorious from the Cold War. Perhaps it was a reaction to the increased presence of Westerners in Afghanistan and Pakistan in the late 1980s. Or perhaps it reflected frustration with Western policy toward the Palestinian Intifada, which Azzam and others followed closely. It may also simply have been an ideological trend boosted by rhetorical outbidding inside the radical Islamist movement.

We have seen that Azzam was a very prolific author whose main ideological contribution was an Islamic legal argument for foreign fighting in a modern context. His foreign-fighter doctrine entailed two significant innovations which helped change the course of the jihadi movement. One was to shift the emphasis in jihadi thinking away from revolution toward "*umma* defense." This laid the foundation not just for more foreign-fighter mobilizations in the 1990s and beyond, but also for the emergence of al-Qaida's anti-Western terrorism. Bin Ladin's justification for his war on America was merely an extension of Azzam's idea of *umma* defense. Azzam's second key innovation was to divest governments of the authority to veto their citizens' involvement in jihad. By arguing that under certain political circumstances Muslims should mobilize for war regardless of what their government says, Azzam undermined traditional religious authority and opened the door for a host of radical fringe groups. We have also seen that Azzam helped develop an esoteric strain of jihadi thought centered on miracles and martyrdom. These ideas appealed to the imagination and religious sentiment of many young Muslims, and inspired many to join the jihad in search of wonders and afterlife rewards. The prominence of these ideas in the jihadi movement today is testimony to Azzam's enduring ideological influence. Azzam, in other words, was a highly influential jihadi thinker. As we shall see in the next chapter, his record in the military domain was not quite as stellar.

12 | Mujahid

In the pantheon of jihadi ideologues, Abdallah Azzam is known as the *'alim mujahid* – the jihad-fighting Islamic scholar. It was rare for a religious cleric to take part in paramilitary activities, and Azzam was widely admired for it. But how much of a fighter was he really? And what was his role, if any, in the establishment of the al-Qaida organization?

This chapter examines the military activities of Azzam and the other Arabs in the Afghanistan war. We will see that Azzam was not very forward-leaning in the military domain, and that the Services Bureau's perceived softness led impatient militarists to break away and launch activities of their own. One of these projects, Bin Ladin's al-Ma'sada camp, evolved into the al-Qaida organization in the winter of 1987–1988. Azzam was never involved in al-Qaida, but he did not object to it, and he stayed on decent terms with Bin Ladin till the end. The chapter follows the main stages in the process of separation between the Services Bureau and the militarists, from the early tensions, via the founding of al-Ma'sada, to the emergence of al-Qaida, concluding with an assessment of the Arab military contribution to the war.

Dissatisfied Militarists

Azzam had a reputation as an Islamic warrior-monk who would not only talk the talk but also walk the walk. It was an image he carefully cultivated, for example by wearing Afghan clothes when lecturing abroad, or by making sure *al-Jihad* magazine published photographs of him in combat gear.[1] He repeatedly stressed how much he enjoyed taking part in the jihad and disliked being away. In one lecture he said:

> It is hard for me to move from a land in which weapons are abundant and in use to a land in which there are no weapons ... If I stay away from [the Mujahidin] I feel like I am dying ... Just like the fish cannot survive outside

the water, I and my soul do not feel content unless I am participating in battles. But I come to you today so perhaps I can drag some of you with me to this land.[2]

By casting himself as a fighting scholar, Azzam sought to insert himself in an old tradition of Islamic scholars involved in jihad.[3] Early Islamic history features many scholars who fought on the frontlines, from Abu Ishaq al-Fazari in the eighth century to Ibn Taymiyya in the thirteenth. Azzam did not compare himself to such figures, but his warrior-scholar image earned him respect among many young radicals in the 1980s and after.

Azzam's reputation as a fighter was not undeserved. He often left the office for the field, spending time in training camps such as Sada and al-Ma'sada and visiting frontlines across the Afghan border. He loved talking to fighters, both Arabs and Afghans, about their battlefield experiences.[4] Since his first year in Pakistan he had been in regular contact with Jalaluddin Haqqani, whose forces were constantly fighting government forces in Paktia province.[5] Moreover, he did witness real combat. He was present at several of the most famous battles in Afghan Arab history, such as Zhawar (1986), Jaji (1987), and Jalalabad (1989). *Al-Bunyan al-Marsus* magazine was largely correct in noting that "whenever a big battle was going on, Abdallah Azzam was nearby."[6] His willingness to go into the field earned him the respect of other Arabs. Abu Mus'ab al-Suri, for example, was

particularly impressed by the fact that, unlike the MB commanders whom al-Suri had known and who used to command their troops via telephone, Azzam went to see his men personally and travelled from one frontline to the other and from one outpost to another. This was, in al-Suri's words, "a true leadership".[7]

However, it would be an exaggeration to say that Azzam was very active on the frontlines. For one thing, he did not venture much into Afghanistan, and when he did, it was to the border areas of Jaji, Khost, and Jalalabad. He only made three trips deep into the country; twice to northern Afghanistan in 1988 and 1989, and once to Qandahar province in 1988 or 1989.[8] For another, when he was near the fronts his role was often more that of a preacher than a soldier. As Sayyaf said, "When he went down to a front, he typically recited the Qur'an, gave lessons in *da'wa* and jihad, encouraged the *mujahidin* to stick to religious principles and rulings of Shari'a. He urged them to seek death and described to them the rewards of the martyr."[9]

At the end of the day, Azzam was a scholar at heart. He considered that spiritual preparation was a prerequisite for success in battle, and ultimately more important than skills and equipment. This earned him criticism from more pragmatic Afghan Arabs such as Mustafa Hamid, who later said, "Abdullah Azzam was a traditional Islamic leader: he wanted the Afghans to sit together in one place and be friends, and to recite the Qur'an and pray at night and fast two days every week. He was seeking to encourage them to follow such religious practices and to sit together; not to train them how to fight."[10] Similarly, Ahmad Zaidan, who worked with Azzam on the editorial committee of *al-Jihad* magazine, criticized Azzam for being too preoccupied with religious matters and for shying away from important political developments.[11] Moreover, as we saw in Chapter 9, Azzam had a broad view of war: He saw support activities – such as logistics, medical support, and religious education – as necessary for strategic victory. As a result, he spent much of his time dealing with matters other than purely military–technical ones.

The problem was, not everyone shared Azzam's spiritual and broad view of war. Many incoming volunteers simply wanted to fight; as one former fighter said, "Their minds were full of Sylvester Stallone and visions of paradise."[12] They arrived expecting to be trained and deployed to the frontlines, but often found themselves doing menial tasks or guard duty in quiet locations.[13] A divide soon emerged in the Afghan Arab community between militarists and pragmatists over how much military work the Bureau should be doing. Azzam was never really able to satisfy the more restless segment of the foreign fighters, and this would lead to a split in the organization.

The tension had been there since the start of the war. In 1983 a group of Egyptians around Mustafa Hamid had left Peshawar for the frontlines in search of combat. They had joined Haqqani's forces in Paktia province, where they fought like Afghan Mujahidin. The group, which included Abu Ubayda al-Banshiri, Abu Hafs al-Masri, and a few others, spent months at a time in the field. However, Hamid and his comrades were in a special situation; Hamid had known Haqqani for a long time, and the other Egyptians already had military experience. Other incoming recruits did not have this option, and depended on what the Services Bureau had to offer.

In the Bureau's first two years, in 1985 and 1986, this was not much, for its military activities were limited. As we saw in Chapter 9, the Services Bureau did mostly "soft" support work such as logistics, education, and aid. The Badr training project in Pabbi in early 1984 (see Chapter 9) had been temporary, and did not include much weapons training anyway. In early 1985 the Services Bureau made an agreement with Sayyaf to have Arabs train at a camp called Salman al-Farsi on the road to Kunar. According to Abu Rida al-Suri, some twenty-five Arabs trained there under Afghan supervision in April 1985, but this did not become a regular program.[14]

Things looked set to change in late 1985 when the no-nonsense Abu Hajir al-Iraqi took over as executive director of the Services Bureau. He understood the problem and did his best to beef up the military portfolio, but struggled against the Bureau's dysfunctions. In early 1986 he was able to organize a unit of some twenty to thirty Arabs to go and fight in the Jalalabad area alongside Afghan Mujahidin forces. The group was led by a man named Abu Anis and performed honorably, but it did not last.[15] In the spring of 1986, as we also saw in Chapter 9, Abdallah Anas took a group of some thirty Arabs to Massoud's forces in Panjshir. There they got some combat exposure, notably at the so-called battle of al-Nahrayn. Anas later recounted:

Massoud began distributing the *mujahidin*, about three hundred of them, in addition to the Arab brothers who decide to take part; they were about fifteen Arabs. The rest of the Arabs were not fighters. They were doctors and teachers, so they stayed in the first region and did not join the battle ... Eighteen *mujahidin* fell as martyrs including four Arabs ... Arabs remained for a period of almost one month and a half with Massoud's fighters before they decided to go back to Peshawar.[16]

Other than these ad hoc activities, however, Azzam did not have that much to offer the testosterone-filled youth showing up at Bayt Abu Hamza.

Part of the problem was Azzam's insistence that any Arab military activity should occur under the supervision of the Afghan Mujahidin. He clung firmly to this principle, which made sense in theory. The Afghans were already waging war; surely the Arabs could just join them. In practice, however, the Afghans were not that interested in including Arabs, because the latter were few in number and poorly trained. In the accounts of Arab attempts to join the battlefield, there is a palpable reluctance on the Afghan side. As a result, some Arabs felt excluded, and in 1985 and early 1986 there was mounting dissatisfaction over the lack of fighting opportunities.

One of the most frustrated was Usama Bin Ladin. The young Saudi had initially served only as a financial donor, but after his first visit to the frontlines in 1984 he rapidly developed a taste for war. By 1986, according to Jamal Isma'il, "Osama was spending most of his time on the Afghan frontline with commanders, especially general Jalaluddin Haqqani in Khost."[17] He grew increasingly frustrated with the lack of military activities in the Services Bureau, and he worried for the morale of the Arabs. "I was afraid," he later said, "that some of the brothers might return to their home countries and tell their people that they had stayed here for six months without ever shooting a single gun ... people might conclude that we don't need their support."[18] As the Bureau's main donor, Bin Ladin started to wonder whether his money was being put to good use. In the spring of 1986 he and Abu Hajir al-Iraqi were both of the view that something needed to be done about the training situation for Arabs. Abu Hajir later said Bin Ladin "backed me up in the Consultative Council and the trend he wanted ... he was inspiring me and promising me better results."[19]

Meanwhile, Azzam did not really see any problems. In his view there were plenty of opportunities for interested recruits to get training, as the recent Arab collaborations with Haqqani, Sayyaf, and Massoud had shown. It was not that Azzam was opposed to expanding the Services Bureau's training activities – he went along with most initiatives put before him – it was just not an agenda he pushed actively. He seems to have thought things were fine as they were. He was in for a serious wake-up call in the spring of 1986 at the battle of Zhawar.

Zhawar – also known as Zhawar Kili, Zawara, or Jawar (but not to be confused with Jaji) – was the site of Jalaluddin Haqqani's main base. Located in the south of Khost province right on the Pakistani border, the base was a complex of underground barracks and storage facilities lodged into the hillside for protection against air raids. A French journalist who visited in January 1986 described it as follows:

The camp ... has a stunning number of shelters and underground garages. Both the hospital and the mosque are carved out from the cliffs. In a room inside the rock, there's a screen where the Mujahidin can watch a film of their latest ambush. Further up, Afghan and Pakistani workers are finishing a new hospital, this one for women. In underground workshop, Mujahidin are repairing machine guns. In another, mechanics work on tanks, ten real tanks captured from the Soviets. On the hilltops are numerous and well placed machine guns and artillery, and the fighters have missiles too. The base has been bombed twenty-six times.[20]

Zhawar was strategically important because it offered access to the battlefield while being easy to supply from the Pakistani army base at Miranshah. Zhawar was a showcase for the resistance effort, and a number of foreign VIPs such as US congressman Charlie Wilson would visit the base.[21] Zhawar had been a thorn in the side of Afghan government forces for years, because it had enabled Haqqani to close off the road between Gardez and Khost, forcing the Soviets to resupply the government base in Khost by air.[22]

However, in the spring of 1986 the Russians were able to reopen the road and prepare a major offensive against rebel strongholds in the area.[23] The offensive started in the first week of April, and from 11 to 22 April Zhawar was isolated and under heavy bombardment. Things looked particularly bleak around 20 April, when Haqqani had to withdraw most his forces from the base and seek refuge at Miranshah. At this point, Abdallah Azzam and a group of over sixty Arabs from the Services Bureau turned up at Haqqani's house close to Miranshah airport, intending to help recapture Zhawar. It was the first time in the war that such a large group of Arabs had moved together to enter hostilities. Once in place they appointed Azzam as their *amir* and swore loyalty to him, whereupon Azzam named them "the Brigade of the Strangers" (*katibat al-ghuraba'*).[24] Morale was sky high, and the young men were "longing to enter the front." Azzam himself was so taken by the moment that on 22 April he wrote his will in the presence of Haqqani and other witnesses.[25]

However, because the Arabs were untrained, the Afghans did not let them participate. Azzam and his men were left waiting in Miranshah for the two days it took for Haqqani to retake the base. Usama Bin Ladin later said, "We wanted to move, but they told us: we have sent brothers who are more qualified than you, and who know the situation better, and they are physically fit to find out what the situation is like inside." After a while, two Palestinians, Nur al-Din and Abu Ammar, were allowed to go in, but the rest still had to wait. "We were just sitting there, and we used the time to organize classes for the brothers to absorb the wait," said one frustrated fighter.[26] When the Brigade of the Strangers finally moved in, the battle was practically over. As Bin Ladin recounts:

At last, the order came for us to move. We drove the cars until we reached the last checkpoint in Pakistan, and then we got off. We were approximately sixty men, and we only had one Afghan with us, the driver ... We ascended towards Jihadwal by foot after Abu Amr and Abu Khalid al-Urduni had divided us into groups, and they led the march. Each of the groups had an *amir* assigned. Some took the responsibility for reconnaissance from the right and from the north. Finally, at approximately 10 p.m., we arrived in Jihadwal as night had fallen. In the morning, Hekmatyar arrived and said that the troops had withdrawn from the area and retreated, that your presence here is no longer needed, and may God bless and reward your efforts. So return! Indeed, Sheikh Abdallah Azzam decided to return with us.[27]

The battle of Zhawar was a humiliation. It laid bare the Arabs' lack of training and showed that, when push came to shove, the Afghans did not trust them to perform in the field. Haqqani later said that Arabs made a difference by "raising the morale," but that was hardly a consolation.[28] Incidentally, the near-loss of Zhawar had shaken Haqqani and his Pakistani backers as well; According to former ISI brigadier Mohammad Yousaf, the problems at the Zhawar battle in facing helicopter attacks were a catalyst for the US decision to provide Stinger missiles to the Mujahidin later that year.[29]

Azzam must have sensed the disappointment in his ranks, but he did little to address the underlying problem. For the militarists among the Arabs, however, Zhawar was a watershed. It was final proof that the Services Bureau could not be trusted to provide adequate training. It was notably after Zhawar that Usama Bin Ladin became involved full time in the Afghan jihad; up until then he had resided in Saudi Arabia visiting only for weeks at a time.[30] In late May or early June 1986 Usama Bin Ladin, Abu Hajir, and a few others started discussing training alternatives for the Arabs. They "decided to pick an independent location where we would receive the brothers and train them away from the internal problems at the Services Bureau."[31] After considering a few candidate locations, including Jalalabad and Zhawar, they opted for Sada ("Echo"), a Sayyaf-run training complex southwest of Peshawar on the way to Parachinar.[32]

Bin Ladin's idea was to set up a training section especially for Arabs on the outskirts of Sayyaf's camp.In early June 1986 Bin Ladin, Abu Hajir, and a few others went to Sada and "used our shovels to set up about three tents."[33] They did all this behind Azzam's back, rightly calculating that it would be easier to obtain his forgiveness than his permission. They did not want to secede from the Services Bureau, only to get a test project running without having to involve the entire organization.

A few days later Azzam discovered the tents, and discussion ensued.[34] Azzam was not against the idea of a camp so much as disappointed to have been left out of the loop. After some persuasion he endorsed the project, on condition that it was carried out in cooperation with the Bureau's Military Committee.[35] Abu Hajir was appointed commander and Abu Nur al-Urduni was brought in as a trainer. Azzam's handling of the situation was emblematic of his attitude to new military projects throughout the 1980s: He rarely initiated them, but he usually tolerated them. We would see this pattern again in his dealing with the al-Ma'sada camp and the al-Qaida organization. As time went on he usually embraced such projects, sometimes to the point of retroactively embellishing his initial role in them. For example, when he later described the beginning of Sada, he cast himself as one of the founders, when in fact it had landed in his lap:

The Sada camp was founded in the summer of 1986 after Mr. Sayyaf set up a special camp and school ... Sheikh Sayyaf was the one who offered us a place in the camp, telling us "I have established a camp there, if you'd choose a place in it." So we chose a place, and in Ramadan we launched a training camp in the name of the Services Bureau.[36]

For a while in mid-June everyone seemed satisfied. However, there had been a misunderstanding between Azzam and the militarists. Bin Ladin and Abu Hajir wanted the camp to remain secret until it had the capacity to receive more recruits. Azzam, on the other hand, thought that it was now official, and he started sending recruits there. When the uninvited guests turned up, Abu Hajir's jaw dropped:

One day, I was surprised that two or three cars full of brothers returned from Peshawar. One of them told us, "I brought you the brothers as you requested!" I asked him, "What is this?" He answered, "My brother, you called out to go to war, so we came." I said, "Glory be to God. [But] by God, we have not called on anyone, and we have not sent for you." He asked,

"How?" He then pulled out a note from Sheikh Abdallah mobilizing the married and unmarried, the employed and unemployed, the doctor, teacher, and the engineer, all of them being called for to the battles of Jaji.[37]

Abu Hajir was angry. Azzam had sent them a whole bunch of people with no advance notice and no extra supplies. "Where are our tents?" the guests asked, forcing Abu Hajir to go and ask Sayyaf for help: "We collected his reserve of bread, we even took blankets from his private bedroom!"[38] Bin Ladin and Abu Hajir felt that their project had been compromised, and they again started thinking about moving to another location.[39] At first they tried to set up a new, secret camp elsewhere in Sada, but it too was discovered. This time, with Azzam not around, a more heated argument broke out between Bin Ladin and Bureau loyalists at Sada.[40] "From that moment," Abu Hajir later said, "[Bin Ladin] started to distance himself and take his work in a new direction."[41]

The camp, however, continued to operate, and became the Services Bureau's main training facility. It started small and unsophisticated. A visitor in late June 1986 said that it "consisted of five to six tents, in addition to the mosque tent. There were about fifteen to twenty-five brothers in training."[42] The training became more serious with the arrival of Abu Burhan al-Suri in October 1986. Abu Burhan was a Syrian Muslim Brother and former military officer who brought with him an entirely different level of professionalism.[43] Later he was joined by other competent trainers, such as Abd al-Aziz Ali, the veteran instructor from the Egyptian Muslim Brotherhood, and Ali Mohamed, the US-trained officer who later became a double agent between American intelligence and al-Qaida.[44] Over time, Sada became an important center of military expertise. It offered a range of courses, including in advanced explosives training. It built a library of military science books and produced training manuals in Arabic.[45] The most famous of these was the so-called *Encyclopedia of the Afghan Jihad*, which Ali Mohamed and Abu Burhan compiled in part from US military manuals that Ali Mohamed had stolen during his time in Fort Bragg, North Carolina, in 1986.[46]

Sada's main function was to serve as a boot camp for new recruits. It was the principal first station in the Services Bureau pipeline for Arab volunteers, a system based on Azzam's original idea of spreading Arabs thinly across Afghan Mujahidin units. People would come to Peshawar, go to Sada for training, and from there to the frontlines.[47] The system worked reasonably well; by 1988 Sada-trained Arabs were embedded with Afghan forces in multiple locations across Afghanistan, including as far west as Qandahar. The system remained in place into the early 1990s, and many hundreds of Arabs went through it.

Sada was not the only boot camp to which the Services Bureau sent recruits. Later in the 1980s it also ran a camp named Khaldan in Paktia province near the border southwest of Parachinar, some two hours from Sada.[48] Sada and Khaldan were the main camps run by the Services Bureau in the 1980s; there had been a brief attempt in 1988 to also operate in Hekmatyar's Warsak camp, 30–40 kilometers from Peshawar, but it failed.[49]

The Services Bureau pipeline never became militarily significant, because it leaked. Many recruits were simply not that committed, and returned to their home countries after basic training. Others were *too* committed, felt that Sada was too basic for them, and instead joined one of the more advanced training camps that would emerge outside of the Services Bureau's control. As Azzam later noted, "Young men began to gather around me step by step in Sada, and at the same time young men gathered around Abu Abdallah in al-Ma'sada."[50]

Victory at the Lion's Den

For Bin Ladin and the other militarists, the competence problem laid bare at Zhawar had not been solved at Sada. In a sense, Sada had merely been hijacked by the "softies" in the Bureau, and there was still a need for a new camp. Bin Ladin would spend the early autumn of 1986 searching for a suitable location.

The motivation for Bin Ladin's move away from Azzam has been somewhat misrepresented in the secondary literature. Several accounts say Bin Ladin wanted Arab-only camps and combat units while Azzam wanted mixed units, but this is not quite accurate.[51] The camp Azzam had already agreed to set up at Sada was just for Arabs. Moreover, Azzam had previously approved all-Arab combat units, first in the Abu Anis Group in Jalalabad and then in the Brigade of the Strangers at Zhawar. Bin Ladin, for his part, was happy to have his men fight in close coordination with Sayyaf's forces in the battle of Jaji, as we shall see. Not only that, he was initially also happy to have Afghans – Shiite Afghans, in fact – stay and train in the al-Ma'sada camp.[52] Having ethnically pure combat units cannot have been Bin Ladin's main objective.

Instead, Bin Ladin was looking for higher-quality training. The main problem with Sada and previous initiatives was that they were sausage factories – boot camps with no intake selection and only basic instruction. Bin Ladin wanted something more serious, where Arabs could become such fierce fighters that they would be *respected*. It was, in some sense, a matter of honor; the militarists could not bear to see the Arab volunteers gain a reputation for weakness. Incidentally, that was also probably why Bin Ladin was to seek a location dangerously close to the frontlines; he wanted the Arabs to be seen as brave and competent fighters.

Part of Bin Ladin's motivation was also to get away from the internal problems of the Services Bureau. Years later, in one of the Abbottabad Documents, he wrote:

The relations with Shaykh 'Abdullah were considered the best relationship ever, although the gossip environment, due to several brothers who had joined, had a negative impact. I left them the services office without even joining them in their aptitudes, but maintained good and strong ties with Shaykh 'Abdullah, may God the Almighty have mercy on his soul. I entered Jaji and when we were far from the conflict environment and the gossip, the military work began to launch at a high speed with the grace of Allah the Almighty.[53]

Another misconception about Bin Ladin's actions in this period is that he was being manipulated by clever Egyptians, and really only served as a financier. Mustafa Hamid, for example, says it was Abu Ubayda al-Banshiri who had the idea of setting up a separate camp and who suggested the location.[54] However, this claim is firmly contradicted by Basil Muhammad's better-sourced account.[55] The notion that Bin Ladin played second fiddle to Egyptians will be discussed in more depth below, but suffice to say here that Bin Ladin was almost certainly the driving force behind the move to establish a new Arab camp in late 1986. The documentary evidence shows him leading the process, and much of what we now know about his career and personality suggests that he was a determined entrepreneur, not a pushover.

After leaving Sada in late June 1986, Bin Ladin initially thought of setting up a camp near the southwestern Afghan city of Qandahar. In

July and August 1986 he and his associates made several trips to Baluchistan to explore the possibility of establishing a logistics pipeline across Afghanistan's southern border.[56] He envisaged a supply route stretching from the Indian Ocean (complete with a fish-canning factory as cover) across the Afghan border toward Qandahar, where he would have his training camp. However, he scrapped the plan, citing "some circumstances [that] stood in the way of such intentions."[57]

Meanwhile, in August 1986, he had become involved in a construction project in a place called Arin, a Sayyaf-run Mujahidin base in northern Paktia province.[58] Arin was in a mountainous area called Jaji just across the Afghan border, some 40 kilometers west of the Pakistani city of Parachinar. It was a very strategic location; within a 100 kilometer radius were three key Afghan cities: Jalalabad to the northeast, Kabul to the northwest, and Gardez to the southwest. A well-supplied bridgehead in Jaji could maintain pressure on all three of these government strongholds and supply Mujahidin deeper into the country. Provided with a decent road, Jaji could be easily supplied from the Pakistani army base in Parachinar. Indeed, later in the war, Jaji would become one the two main supply points (together with Zhawar) for the entire Afghanistan war. Brigadier Mohammad Yousaf estimated that up to 60 percent of the ISI's supplies to the Afghan Mujahidin were passing through these two points.[59]

It was on a trip to inspect the construction work at Jaji that Bin Ladin discovered the location for al-Ma'sada. When he went to Arin in September 1986, some of his representatives said they had found an interesting location with a good view of the frontline. Intrigued, Bin Ladin sent them back with a camera, and when he saw the pictures he decided to go explore himself.[60] The place was on the edge of a mountain plateau with the frontline so close it could be seen with the naked eye. The place had not been used by the Afghan Mujahidin because it was too exposed; any activity here was bound to attract enemy airstrikes. In fact, it did not even have an Afghan name, so Bin Ladin later called it "al-Ma'sada" – the Lion's Den – from a well-known seventh century poem by Ka'b bin Malik in which the city of Medina is likened to a Lion's Den.[61] The name signaled that this would be a place where Arabs would have the opportunity to fight like lions, just like the Prophet's companions. In October 1986, having obtained Sayyaf's permission to build, Bin Ladin and four of his associates arrived at the new site.[62] Over the next few weeks they slept in tents at night and did construction work during the day using a bulldozer and drilling equipment. Bin Ladin's idea was to get around the problem of the exposed location by building underground fortifications.

Bin Ladin had launched the project on his own, so over the following months he tried to bring in other experienced fighters, but the response was slow. Mustafa Hamid says:

> They were asking people to come to participate and Abu Khalid al-Masri called us in Miranshah and asked if we would come. Abu Hafs [al-Masri] initially agreed to go – but my friend Abdul Rahman and I said we would think about it. We decided not to go; we worried that everyone was rushing to join them but there was no planning, no strategy and very little organization.[63]

Fortunately for Bin Ladin, a few key figures such as Abu Ubayda al-Banshiri, Abu Hajir al-Iraqi, and Abu Hafs al-Masri reluctantly agreed to join. Al-Banshiri later said he only stayed because he "did not want to let Abu Abdallah down and felt pity towards his brothers ... I felt that most of the people left him at that time."[64] Bin Ladin would remain grateful; some twenty years later he wrote: "With the grace of God, I led the lion's den of Al-Ansar against the Russians ... this was at a time when my group was split and all my colleagues stood against me in Peshawar until Aba 'Ubayda arrived from the north and helped me, May God have mercy on him."[65]

Other early visitors were critical, insisting that the location was too exposed. It was also unusual for Afghan Mujahidin – and unheard of for Afghan Arabs – to try to keep a static frontline position.[66] In November or December 1986, Abu Ubayda al-Banshiri brought a delegation of Arab military experts from Peshawar to al-Ma'sada to get their opinion.[67] It included Abu Khalid al-Masri, Abu Hafs al-Masri, and Abd al-Aziz Ali (aka Abu Usama al-Misri).[68] All were seasoned military men, especially Ali, whose militant career stretched back to the 1940s (see Chapter 3). The latter was very skeptical about Bin Ladin's new project:

> I went to [Usama Bin Ladin] with Sheikh Abdallah Azzam and some of the youth who shared his view on the importance of this work. I saw the place: proximity to the enemy centers, surrounding mountains, a limited number of young people, some of them untrained, excavations, sites, cars, compressors, and a decent workshop! I saw that it was very easy to attack the place and eradicate it so I told him, "My brother, this is advice from God Almighty, this

place is only suitable for ... fighters with a high level of experience. Even then, this site is very dangerous, and it is likely that they will pay dearly. If you must [stay], leave only two or three men, and not 200" ... I could not understand how millions of dollars or rupees could be thrown in there. It looked as if someone was throwing his money into dust.[69]

Tough discussions followed, for Bin Ladin was not prepared to abandon the camp.[70] The experts agreed to reconsider, and reportedly retreated to Islamabad for an in-depth discussion.[71] Then, "after three days studying from the morning until the evening, they agreed that Ma'sada did not match the expectations."[72]

During this controversy, Azzam was one of Bin Ladin's few supporters. The leader of the Services Bureau was fully informed about the new project; In fact, he had been present at the very moment in September when Bin Ladin first discovered the site for al-Ma'sada. Bin Ladin's reconnaissance team had, on its return, "found Sheikh Abdallah Azzam and Abu Abdallah having lunch in front of the Arin area. We showed them the photos and told them what we saw."[73] Azzam had not been part of the initial team that set up al-Ma'sada in October, but he came to visit in November as one of the first senior Arabs.

I found Abu Abdallah working in the snow in an isolated area with a group of young men whose number was not more than ten. I was afraid that a helicopter would descend down on them, arrest them, and take them to Kabul, so I told the brothers who gathered with me in Sada: "It is neither Islamic – by God – nor manly to leave this brother alone, so let us go to him." I took the brothers, we went to Ma'sada, and we sat down together.[74]

Azzam was thus cooperating with Bin Ladin on the al-Ma'sada project from the start. "We agreed to coordinate with Abu Abdallah from the very first moment," Azzam later said. "We did not want him to feel alone or despair and causing him to go back to his country."[75] Bin Ladin, for his part, said he was "very anxious ... to continue coordination and cooperation [with the Services Bureau] under all circumstances."[76]

To be sure, Azzam was not overly enthusiastic. He later said, "We were not happy about gathering the Arab youth there, and we considered it a great risk as the place needed a whole battalion to protect it."[77] According to one Arab fighter, "Abdullah Azzam thought some of the cave building and road construction was a waste of money ... why spend so much on one elaborate place right on the border, practically in Pakistan?"[78] Still, in the initial debate over the suitability of al-Ma'sada, Azzam defended Bin Ladin. He thought the latter should be allowed to continue so long as not all the Arabs assembled there. According to a source who was there, "Sheikh Abdallah was insisting that [Bin Ladin] and he stayed together, and that preparations and training be conducted in his presence. He, may God have mercy on him, kept insisting on this whenever the guests – which were increasing in number – wanted to discuss the danger of the place … In addition, the Services Bureau kept insisting that Sheikh Abdallah leave."[79] However, at the end of those discussions, Azzam yielded to the side that was asking Bin Ladin to close down the camp. Azzam was likely swayed by his old Fedayin instructor Ali, whose military experience was hard to argue against.[80]

However, Bin Ladin was able to wriggle out of the demand by agreeing with the Services Bureau on three principles. The first was to evacuate the camp until the most important security measures had been implemented.[81] This concession satisfied Ali, who later said, "The man listened to me and ordered the evacuation of the location. He ordered them to evacuate the men first and then the cars."[82] The second was that al-Ma'sada would be an integrated part of the Services Bureau's training system. There would be a division of tasks between Sada and al-Ma'sada whereby recruits would get basic training at Sada and advanced instruction at al-Ma'sada.[83] The third principle was that al-Ma'sada would not have more than twenty Arab trainees at any one time, to reduce the risk of heavy losses in case of an enemy attack.[84] To kick-start the new arrangement, Bin Ladin had all recruits who lacked basic training transferred to Sada: "He assigned brothers Shafiq and Azmaray to write the list of the untrained brothers. So only about seventeen brothers remained in al-Ma'sada at the beginning of January."[85] Around the same time, some recruits went the other way; according to Abu Burhan, "the first group that got its training in Sada and was then sent to Ma'sada was in the beginning of 1987."[86]

However, as the months went by, the al-Ma'sada crew broke the agreed-upon principles with increasing frequency. Trainees started going straight to al-Ma'sada without passing through Sada. The number of Arabs at al-Ma'sada soon exceeded twenty again. Afghans at al-Ma'sada were thrown out to make room for more Arabs.[87] When people in the Services Bureau complained, Bin Ladin shrugged, pointing to his frequent trips to Saudi Arabia and saying he could not control everything while he was away. In reality, he had probably long since decided he was going to do as he pleased at al-Ma'sada. Abdallah Azzam saw what was happening, but there was not very much he could do. He later noted with resignation:

> the march [of Bin Ladin's group] went to Ma'sada, and the other to Sada. Although we agreed with Abu Abdallah one, two, and three times that the number should not exceed twenty people, the brother wanted to expand the work. He wanted to mobilize the Arabs, he wanted to resist the Russians, and there were a number of projects in his mind. Indeed, Abu Abdallah's enthusiasm, with the money in his hands, enabled him to do as he wanted.[88]

By mid-February 1987 al-Ma'sada was up and running as a training camp, with Abu Ubayda as commander and Abu Hajir as chief instructor. Later they recruited additional trainers such as Abu Hafs al-Masri and Abu Khalid al-Masri. Abu Hajir al-Iraqi was the former executive director of the Services Bureau we met in Chapter 9. Abu Ubayda al-Banshiri (aka Ali Amin Ali al-Rashidi, b. 1950) was a former Egyptian police officer who had been dismissed from his job and briefly arrested in 1981 for his Islamist connections.[89] In 1983 he went to Jeddah to seek work, but decided after a while to go to Peshawar for jihad. From 1984 to 1986 he spent much time with Mustafa Hamid on Haqqani's fronts in Paktia, and in mid-1986 he spent several months with Massoud's forces in Panjshir, hence his nickname. Abu Hafs al-Masri (aka Muhammad Atif, aka Subhi Abu Sittah, b. 1944) was another Egyptian who probably also worked as a policeman in the early 1980s before moving to Peshawar around 1983, after which he too joined Mustafa Hamid and Haqqani in Paktia.[90] Abu Khalid al-Masri's background and real identity are not known, but he is described by Basil Muhammad as "having military experience."[91]

By late February there were thirty-five Arabs at al-Ma'sada, and in April they were seventy. When they were not training or on guard duty, the recruits took part in construction work. That winter they dug a series of large caves, six in all, to serve as living quarters and storage facilities. The caves were at several hundred meters' distance from one another, and together they formed an elongated, crescent-shaped cluster. Each cave had its own name and was considered a camp within the camp. There was "Medina," "Ta'if," "Badr," "Zikwiyak," "The

Gate" (*al-bawwaba*), and the "Command Room" (*ghurfat al-qiyada*).[92] A veritable community was forming.[93]

A curious and little-known part of jihadi history is that Shiites played an important role in the establishment of al-Ma'sada. The Jaji area was under Sayyaf's control, but Sayyaf's forces included Afghan Shiites. The site of al-Ma'sada happened to be on the territory of Abd al-Sami', one of Sayyaf's Shiite commanders. It was his men who showed Bin Ladin the location that autumn of 1986: "I went with Shafiq, Abd al-Awwal, and the group of Abd al-Sami' the Shiite, who guided us to the place of the current al-Ma'sada."[94] Moreover, when Bin Ladin began construction work at al-Ma'sada, he enlisted the help of some of Abd al-Sami''s men, all Shiites. In fact, Afghan Shiite Mujahidin stayed in al-Ma'sada next to the Arab fighters for several months in the winter of 1986–1987. When Bin Ladin asked the Afghans to leave around March 1987, it was primarily to make space for more Arab recruits. Given the jihadi movement's extreme hostility to Shiites in later decades, there is no small irony in the fact that Shiites helped build the cradle of al-Qaida.

The relaxed attitude to Shiism was not unique to Bin Ladin and his men. Many Afghan Arabs in the 1980s did not mind Shiites. As we saw in Chapters 5 and 11, Abdallah Azzam himself had been intrigued by the Iranian revolution, and never expressed particularly anti-Shiite views. Similarly, Abdallah Anas later said that he and his friends were happy to meet Shiites on their travels inside Afghanistan. In fact, Anas and his Arab companions enjoyed Shiite *anashid* (religious hymns) and read Iranian Islamist magazines:

On the trip up north, we were influenced by the Iranian revolution. We liked the slogans and the *anashid* coming out of Iran ... One of the *anashid* that influenced me, even though it was in Farsi, I have memorized it: "Allahu Akbar, allahu akbar, la illaha illa allah, la illlaha illa allah, Iran iran, iran khunu margo ossiyan." This hymn, I heard it more than thirty or forty times. We didn't understand the lyrics, but knew it was [an Iranian] revolutionary hymn. We would [also] go, Ya'qub and I, to get *al-Shahid* magazine, which was printed in Iran.[95]

This is not to say that the Arab Afghans were all hand-holding ecumenists. In the late 1980s anti-Shiite attitudes appear to have become more widespread among the Arabs, probably reflecting the growing influence of Salafism or anti-Iranian rhetoric from Saudi

Arabia. The end of the decade saw a growing number of Saudi volunteers and substantial Saudi support to the Salafi Mujahidin commander Jamil al-Rahman, which did little to promote cross-sectarian understanding. Bin Ladin himself seems to have grown somewhat more anti-Shiite in those years, for we know that he gave speeches in 1989 and 1993 describing Iran as a threat to Islam.[96]

The Arabs at al-Ma'sada would grow more hardline over time. The establishment of al-Ma'sada initiated a self-reinforcing process of separation between the pragmatists in the Services Bureau and the militarists around Bin Ladin. Al-Ma'sada attracted people who were more militaristically inclined, and it bonded them through training and shared combat experiences, while keeping them apart from the pragmatists in Peshawar. The result was a tightly knit community with a more martial culture than that of the Services Bureau. At the core of this network were Bin Ladin himself, Abu Ubayda al-Banshiri (the commander of al-Ma'sada), Abu Hajir al-Iraqi (the chief educator), Abu Hafs al-Masri, Abu Khalid al-Masri, Abu al-Rida al-Suri, and Abu Mahmud al-Suri. These men would go on to found al-Qaida, but only after they had proved themselves on the battlefield.

The Ma'sada project would produce an event of great importance to the history of the Afghan Arabs, namely the battle of Jaji in the spring of 1987. This was the only Arab military exploit of note during the Afghanistan war, and it had a considerable effect on morale and recruitment. The battle of Jaji was really several combat episodes stretching over a period of almost two months. Put simply, there were two main sets of incidents: an initial one in mid-April 1987, referred to in the primary sources as the "battle of Sha'ban" or "the Badr operation," and a second one in late May and early June called the "battle of Ramadan." The second was the more dramatic, and is the one most have in mind when they speak of the battle of Jaji. The whole series of events was a direct consequence of the establishment of al-Ma'sada, because it was Bin Ladin's men who provoked it.

Al-Ma'sada gathered the most combat-hungry of all the Arab volunteers, so the trainees were keen to get on the battlefield. Bin Ladin later said, "All along, the brothers were pushing for a fight with the enemy and I was only trying to let them stay there for some time and dig some tunnels."[97] Bin Ladin held back because most of the recruits had not finished training. In late March the most impatient of them slipped out while Bin Ladin was away, hoping to engage the enemy, but they were caught red-handed when he returned earlier than planned.[98]

Bin Ladin realized that he could not hold back his men for much longer, so in early April 1987 he decided to "allow them to conduct some minor military operations so that they would relieve some of their over-enthusiasm."[99] In preparation, he intensified the training and asked for reinforcements from Sada, bringing the number from 70 to 120.[100] It was the largest Arab-majority combat unit assembled thus far in the Afghan war. In the evening on Friday 17 April they launched what Bin Ladin called "the first military operation for the Arab Mujahidin."[101] They called it the "Badr operation," and it consisted of a straightforward assault on a small Afghan army outpost called Umm al-Khanadiq (Mother of Trenches).[102] About half of the force of 120 took part in the assault.

Abdallah Azzam was one of them. He had come up to Ma'sada the day before, not wanting to miss a rare event such as this. He spent the night with the soldiers, and on the Friday morning he gave a speech to the whole group "encouraging them to stand firm, wage jihad, and have pure intentions."[103] As Abu Hajir recalled it, "Abdallah Azzam delivered a good sermon that included quotations from the book *Lesson of the Prophet on Raids, Jihad, and Emigration*. It was a beautiful sermon."[104] When the battle started, Azzam took part. Tamim al-Adnani later said: "We were five on that *hown* [mortar]: I, Abu Hamza al-Amriki, Abd al-Aziz al-Turkistani, and two others ... we fired over a hundred rounds on the enemy and most of them hit the target ... even Sheikh Abdallah Azzam was with us, and he took part in the firing of the *hown*."[105] This passage is a rare – perhaps the only – primary source reference to Azzam firing a weapon in battle. Most other accounts that place him in a battle either do not specify what he did or say that he had a non-combat role. The battle of Sha'ban may well have been the only time in the entire Afghanistan war when Azzam fired a weapon in combat.

The operation lasted only one evening, and did not achieve much. The Arabs initially made some headway, but had to retreat when they came under heavy artillery fire. They lost one man, while a few sustained injuries. Still, the operation was perceived as a relative success and geared the fighters for more.[106] Over the next month they prepared for retaliation from the enemy side, working on their fortifications and adding a backup defence position. They carried out several smaller attacks, which only showed that the Arabs still had a long way to go. In one instance, a team fired too early, botching the operation, because the two teams had set zero hour at different times.[107] In another, a set of code words had not been shared, so one platoon leader did not understand what the other was talking about.[108]

About a month later, the Communist forces struck back as anticipated. Alerted to the threat from al-Ma'sada, Russian and Afghan government forces launched a major cleanup operation using cluster bombs, helicopter gunships, heavy artillery, and Special Forces. The assault began with air bombardment around 22 May and continued till around 9 June. The battle of Ramadan went through several stages, and included many dramatic moments which we shall not repeat here because they are so meticulously described in other sources.[109] Suffice to say that the Arabs were able to ward off the attack, thus scoring what came to be seen as a heroic victory. The highlight was an episode on 29 May – also referred to as the "battle of 1 Shawwal" – when a group of around twenty-five Arabs and a few Afghans fought it out against a much larger group of Russian commandos inside al-Ma'sada. The jihadis displayed real courage, but they were also lucky. At one point there were only nine defenders left, but the Russians did not realize, and failed to take advantage of the situation before the reinforcements arrived. Besides, the Arabs, who numbered about eighty in the battle as a whole, were supported by a substantial Afghan force. This was reflected in the casualty figures; the Arabs lost thirteen or fourteen men while Sayyaf's men lost around seventy. Still, it was a landmark achievement for the Arabs, who until then had not made much of a mark on the battlefield.

Azzam was also present at this part of the battle of Jaji. After the April attack he appears to have returned to Peshawar, but he returned in late May when the situation heated up again. Azzam recalls arriving at Sayyaf's base in Arin after the air raids had started:

I entered the Jaji camp during the battle. I was fasting and the sun was about to set in the horizon, so about sixty of us gathered in one of the caves and the fighter jets attacked. Only one 1,000-kilogram bomb, which could penetrate seven meters deep into the rock, was sufficient to kill everyone in the cave. In the soil, I could see with my own eyes a spring force its way above the surface as a result of the explosion. I had a few dates in my pocket that I felt with my hands and I took them out waiting for the call to prayer. The orders came for us to disband, and the missiles began to shower us from every direction ... so we threw ourselves on the mountainside waiting for the missile with which we would bid life goodbye, and I could not in two hours finish the dates that were in my hands![110]

This time Azzam did not take part in the fighting. Instead, he was part of a command group that kept a safe distance from the hostilities. At times they were "following the battle from a very high mountain in Ma'sada," at others they were "gathered at the rear line."[111] The stay-behind group consisted of Sayyaf, Azzam, Bin Ladin, Tamim al-Adnani, and a certain Abu al-Hasan (perhaps Wa'il Julaydan). Of these, only Bin Ladin ventured periodically into the field because he "insisted on participating."[112] We know that Azzam was an influential voice within this command group because his name features prominently on the code sheet that the Arabs used for communication at al-Ma'sada. The sheet included preset terms for frequently used words, including nine names ranked by seniority, and Azzam is listed as number two, after Sayyaf and before Bin Ladin.[113]

In the midst of the Jaji battle, a disagreement arose in the command room between Sayyaf and Bin Ladin's men. The Arabs found themselves outnumbered in al-Ma'sada and asked for Arab reinforcements, but Sayyaf instead wanted them to withdraw and let Afghan fighters finish the job. Abu Hafs al-Masri recounts his version of what happened:

> In the center of Mr. Sayyaf were approximately a hundred Arabs in the caves ... When I entered the group, I found Dr. Abdallah Azzam. May God reward him, for he bestowed me with great honor on that day. Sheikh Sayyaf was there, as were Sheikh Tamim al-Adnani and Abu Abdallah. They first asked me for a report on the situation, so I sat down to explain to them and present a general conception ... When we finished, I found them making every attempt to withdraw the Arabs from the place ... Mr. Sayyaf, however, told me: "There are now groups of Afghans armed and ready waiting outside, and you will work with them." I replied, "Sheikh, this kind of work requires people who fully understand [one another], and I cannot understand the Afghans. All I ask of you is to allow us two groups of Arabs only, each consisting of fifteen people, with freedom of movement in the area." He asked: "Is it not enough with one group of ten?" ... After discussions and negotiations, they agreed on a group of fifteen people, and another group as backup, which was Abu Abdallah's proposal.[114]

Faced with this unpleasant dispute between friends, Azzam sided with Sayyaf, to Abu Hafs's great disappointment: "I also found that Dr. Abdallah [Azzam] insisted on that, I don't know why!!"[115] Azzam's stance should have been no surprise, however, because he had always insisted that Afghans should be in command. However, it disappointed Bin Ladin's men and convinced them of the need for more independence from the Afghans. Fortunately for everyone, the Arabs and the Afghans won the Jaji battle, so the episode could be swept under the carpet for now.

The victory at Jaji sent a wave of euphoria through the Afghan Arab community. According to one account, "feelings couldn't be captured into words. Victory songs were chanted in all dialects, and eyes were in tears over the lost martyrs."[116] Jihadi media covered it extensively, sparing no hyperbole.[117] Bin Ladin himself proudly declared having "inflicted a crushing defeat on the Russians."[118] Word of the battle spread as far as mainstream Arab media such as *al-Sharq al-Awsat* and *al-Majalla*.[119] It was even covered in the American military magazine *Soldier of Fortune*.[120]

The battle of Jaji finally gave the Arabs something to be proud of. At last they were taken seriously as fighters by the Afghans. Abu al-Hasan al-Madani later said that "for the first time, we found Shaikh Sayyaf treating the Arab brothers as he treated the Afghans."[121] In *al-Jihad* magazine, Abdallah Azzam published a veritable catalogue of compliments and praise from Afghans and Pakistanis about the Arab performance in Jaji, and an even longer list is included in Basil Muhammad's book about the Afghan Arabs.[122] Of course, all the hyperbole and back-patting only highlighted the extent to which the Arabs had felt militarily inferior up to this point.

The event had a substantial effect on recruitment. A 1989 article in *al-Jihad* magazine noted that "after the victorious battle of Ma'sada in 1987, the youths started coming in waves. The number of young Arabs arriving in Afghanistan was getting much bigger."[123] Moreover, al-Ma'sada became, if not a site of pilgrimage, then at least a jihadi tourist destination, as many incoming volunteers asked to see the place they had read about. "They all wanted [to see] al-Ma'sada in particular, they wanted to see a specific room or a location!!" Basil Muhammad wrote.[124]

The battle also raised the status of the people involved, not least Usama Bin Ladin. "That's when everybody started to know about

Osama," one of his companions noted.[125] In May 1988, when the Saudi journalist Jamal Khashoggi published his article series on al-Ma'sada in *al-Majalla* and in *Arab News*, Bin Ladin became something of a poster boy for the Afghan Arabs. Jaji also made heroes of other men, especially Abu Ubayda al-Banshiri and Abu Hafs al-Masri, who had been commanders on the ground and who were among the last nine fighters holed up in al-Ma'sada on 29 May.[126] The success at Jaji gave the militarists great tailwind. The high-risk al-Ma'sada project had paid off, and demonstrated that if only the Arabs could get some serious training, they could achieve great things.

al-Qaida: The Jihadi Special Force

When Bin Ladin first put the shovel in the ground at al-Ma'sada in October 1986, he unknowingly started a process that would lead to the formation of al-Qaida, the world's most famous terrorist organization. As we shall see, al-Ma'sada produced a group of people who believed in the creation of an elite jihadi fighting force and did their best to make it happen.

Much has been written about al-Qaida over the years, but the group's early history remains poorly elucidated.[127] The body of primary sources is complex, ambiguous, and not easily accessible. Put simply, there are two main sets of sources on al-Qaida's formation. One is written and verbal testimonies from insiders, which were mostly recorded years after the group's formation and by people who were not part of the inner core.[128] (We do not have detailed descriptions of al-Qaida's formation by key players such as Usama Bin Ladin and Abu Hafs al-Masri.) The other is the set of internal documents known as the Tareekh Osama and Tareekh Musadat collections.[129] They contain scanned copies of documents from the circle around Bin Ladin going all the way back to 1987. They were discovered by Bosnian police in 2002 in the Sarajevo office of the Benevolence International Foundation, an Islamic charity with longstanding links to Bin Ladin. Their existence became known in the early 2000s during the trial of Enaam Arnaout, but the original documents did not become publicly available until 2016 when the researcher Michael S. Smith II posted them on his blog *Inside the Jihad*. In the meantime, a few writers such as Lawrence Wright, Peter Bergen, and J. M. Berger had obtained exclusive access to the documents and described some of them, notably the so-called founding memos of al-Qaida, in their books.[130] However, large portions of the collection have yet to be studied academically, and some of the key documents appear to have been misinterpreted, as we shall see below.

My reading of the sources suggests that the emergence of al-Qaida was the outcome of three factors. The underlying driver was the demand among some of the Afghan Arabs for high-quality military training. This demand increased in the mid-1980s as the overall number of Arabs rose. The failure of the "moderate center" in the Afghan Arab community (Azzam) to cater for this demand led a resourceful militarist (Bin Ladin) to set up a facility (al-Ma'sada) for the specially interested. Other militarists and risk-seekers then self-selected into the new camp, forming a group of similarly minded individuals.

The second factor was the victory in the battle of Jaji, which motivated the leaders at al-Ma'sada to expand their operations. Not only did Jaji convince Bin Ladin, Abu Ubayda, and other Ma'sada cadres that they were doing something right; it also created an incentive to preserve and harness the experience and team spirit generated during the battle.

The third factor was the practical process of running the al-Ma'sada camp, which created a proto-organization that lent itself to subsequent formalization. This is the most important factor for understanding why al-Qaida emerged when and with the people it did. Building and running a camp like al-Ma'sada requires the execution of a variety of tasks, from procuring food and supplies via cooking and emptying latrines to carrying out construction work and military training. This necessitates a minimum of organization in the form of division of labour, hierarchy of command, and record-keeping. As it happens, many of the internal documents from al-Ma'sada in the first half of 1987 have survived, complete with shopping lists, travel orders, weapons registries, and many other records. They clearly show the contours of a proto-bureaucracy in the making. In addition, we know that Bin Ladin had already set up a separate recruitment pipeline from Saudi Arabia directly to al-Ma'sada in November 1986, and that he independently asked journalists to come write about the camp.[131] Thus even though Bin Ladin did not found al-Ma'sada with the intention of creating a new organization, the process of running the camp created organizational structures which lent themselves to further formalization.

The name "al-Qaida" (the Base) appears to have first emerged as a nickname for the al-Ma'sada camp and then become shorthand for "the people associated with the Base," meaning the people who had spent time at al-Ma'sada and supported the idea of improving training. It is easy to see how one might go from the notion of "the people associated with the Base" to that of "the group of people associated with the base."

Precisely when al-Qaida was founded is not clear. Until recently, it was believed that the group emerged in August 1988, because the Tareekh Osama collection contains documents that can be interpreted that way. Three documents in particular have received attention. The first, which we can call the "11 August Document," consists of notes from a meeting on 11 August 1988 between Abu Rida al-Suri and an unspecified "Sheikh."[132] The agenda is "the shaping of the new military work," specifically a three-tier training system consisting of "a general camp, a special camp, [and] a base [qa'ida]."[133] A sentence at the end of the document reads, "initial estimation, after six months at the base [khilal 6 shuhur li'l-qa'ida], 314 brothers will be trained and ready."[134] Second is what we may call the "17 August Document," which is a summary of three meetings held on 17, 18, and 21 August 1988.[135] Here fourteen people – including Abu Burhan al-Suri, Abu Hajir al-Iraqi, and Abu Ubayda al-Banshiri, but excluding Bin Ladin and Azzam – met to discuss various worries and complaints about the Services Bureau and the Afghan jihad.[136] The word al-Qaida is not mentioned, but the general tone is critical of the Services Bureau. The third exhibit – henceforth the "20 August Document" – is from a series of meetings around 20 August 1988 in which nine senior Afghan Arabs, including Bin Ladin but exluding Azzam, discussed the training system for Arab volunteers.[137] It notably says:

The military work was suggested to be divided into two parts, according to duration:

- Limited (defined) duration: they will go to Sada and get trained and distributed on the Afghan battlefronts under the supervision of the military council.

- Open (long) duration: they will enter a trial camp and the best brothers among them will be chosen, in preparation to enter the military base [al-qa'ida al-'askariyya].

The abovementioned base [al-qa'ida] is basically an organized Islamic faction [fasila munazzama islamiyya] whose goal is to raise the word of God to make his religion victorious.

Then, on the back page, a passage added later reads "The work with the base [al-qaʿida] began on 10 September 1988 with a group of 15 brothers."[138] Several authors have viewed these documents as the "founding minutes of al-Qaida" and dated the group's establishment to 20 August 1988.[139]

However, this appears to be a misinterpretation, as Mustafa Hamid and Leah Farrall have also argued.[140] For one, the content of the three documents is not what one might expect from the record of a constituent assembly. The language is vague, at times almost cryptic, and the tone of the recorded discussion is polemic rather than unified and enthusiastic. The 11 August Document records a back-and-forth between someone who wants a new military approach and someone who defends the status quo; the 17 August Document is a litany of complaints against the Services Bureau, while the 20 August Document details how the new training camp will fit with the existing training infrastructure such as the Sada camp. For another, the attendees were not those one might expect to see in an internal al-Qaida meeting. Alongside undisputable al-Qaida figures such as Abu Ubayda al-Banshiri and Abu Hajir al-Iraqi we find people such as Abu Burhan al-Suri and Tamim al-Adnani, who were deeply involved with the Services Bureau at the time, and whose subsequent links with al-Qaida are unclear.

A more plausible interpretation of the three documents is therefore that they record meetings in which representatives of an *already existing* al-Qaida organization unveiled their new plans to representatives of the Services Bureau so as to get their approval and coordinate their activities with them. This would explain why the unnamed sheikh in the 11 August meeting – who was most likely Tamim al-Adnani (more on this below) – comes across as so defensive of the status quo. It also would explain the presence of Abu Burhan and Tamim al-Adnani in the latter meetings.

This interpretation is strengthened by two other sources which suggest that al-Qaida had been founded *before* the August 1988 meeting. One is the testimony of Mustafa Hamid, who says the group had been founded in the autumn of 1987. The other is Madani al-Tayyib, who told Lawrence Wright that he had joined al-Qaida on 17 May 1988, leading Wright to note that "the organizational meeting on August 11 only brought to the surface what was already covertly under way."[141] On balance, then, al-Qaida appears to have been founded earlier than previously believed, although it is not possible to specify a foundation date. Early 1988 seems a good bet, but any time between August 1987 and July 1988 is conceivable.

We do not know exactly who the founding members of al-Qaida were, but there is a cluster of people who feature in early sources and recur in subsequent ones. Usama Bin Ladin appears to have served as the nominal leader from the start. Abu Ubayda al-Banshiri was also a key figure, possibly the driving force behind the move to formalize the organization. Jamal al-Fadl also highlights Abu Ayyub al-Iraqi and says it was Abu Ayyub and Abu Ubayda who had pushed to establish the group.[142] Several others, such as Abu Hafs al-Masri, Abu Khalid al-Masri, and Abu Hajir al-Iraqi, can also be assumed to have been part from the beginning because they were prominent figures at al-Ma'sada in early 1987 and reappear in later lists of al-Qaida members.

Abdallah Azzam has often been described as a "co-founder of al-Qaida," but this is almost certainly inaccurate. In fact, there is no evidence to suggest that he was anything more than an observer during the emergence of the new group. The confusion about Azzam's relationship with al-Qaida has two origins. The first is the article titled "al-qa'ida al-sulba" (the Solid Base) which Azzam wrote in *al-Jihad* magazine in April 1988.[143] Some analysts have interpreted this article as a concept paper for an al-Qaida organization, but it is not. The article merely says Afghanistan is the territorial base on which the Islamist movement must establish itself before it can make further conquests.[144] The second source of confusion has been the Tareekh Osama documents. Lawrence Wright and others have suggested that Azzam attended or even initiated the first of the August 1988 meetings which, in their interpretation, led to the foundation of al-Qaida.[145] However, as we have seen, these meetings were probably not about the founding of al-Qaida in the first place. Moreover, the evidence for Azzam's presence there is slim, as he is not mentioned explicitly as an attendee in any of the three key Tareekh Osama documents.[146] The only possibility is that he was the unidentified sheikh in the 11 August Document (see above), but the document refers to Azzam in the third person, as if he is someone other than the sheikh attending the meeting.[147] More likely, the sheikh in question was Tamim al-Adnani, the executive director of the Services Bureau. Al-Tamimi was regularly described as a sheikh at the time, and as the executive director he would have been a natural interlocutor for Abu Rida on a military matter such as this.[148] In any case, the sheikh in the 11 August meeting expressed skepticism of the proposal to establish a new specialized camp, so even if it was Azzam, it would not implicate him. Moreover, Azzam is not described as an al-Qaida member in other relevant primary sources from this period, and he never mentioned the organization in his own writings or speeches. In short, Azzam was neither a co-founder nor a member of al-Qaida.

No organogram from al-Qaida's early years appears to have survived either. The closest thing is the testimony of Jamal al-Fadl from 2001, which says that al-Qaida by late 1989 or early 1990 was organized with a general leader (Bin Ladin), a general commander (Abu Ayyub), a twelve-member Shura Council, and four committees: a Military Committee, a Money and Business Committee, a Fatwa Committee, and a Media Committee.[149] He names a total of twenty-five people in the various committees, including several old hands from al-Ma'sada, notably Abu Ubayda (leader of the Military Committee), Abu Hafs (Military Committee), and Abu Hajir (Fatwa Committee). He also includes people who were not at al-Ma'sada and who may have joined a little later, notably "Dr. Fadl" (Sayyid Imam al-Sharif) and "Dr. Abd al-Mu'izz" (probably Ayman al-Zawahiri). However, al-Fadl gave his testimony years after the events, so he may have been describing the organization as it looked in the early 1990s rather than in 1989. The same anachronism problem plagues the entire early historiography of al-Qaida. A number of sources depict a highly structured organization, but most of them are undated and may well be from the early 1990s. This is notably the case with some of the so-called Harmony documents, which were captured by the US military at undisclosed locations around 2002 and later published by the Combating Terrorism Center at West Point.[150] For example, the document known as "al-Qaida's Bylaws" has no datable information except that it talks about salaries in Pakistani rupees, which means it predates 1993.[151] Similarly, the Harmony documents known as "Interior Organization" and "al-Qaida Goals and Structure" describe a very elaborate organization, but are also undatable and were written on a computer (computers were rare in 1980s Peshawar).[152] The same applies to other sources; for example, Lawrence Wright, citing oral testimonies, writes that al-Qaida had its own villa in Peshawar and published a newspaper titled *Nashrat al-Akhbar*, but these reports probably pertain to the early 1990s.[153] The point is, we know very little for certain about what al-Qaida was doing in the first year or two of its existence.

What does seem clear is that al-Qaida had no clear political objective or designated geographical operating area at this time. It was not until the mid-1990s that the group would stake out a clear strategy in the form of war against America. In fact, internal al-Qaida documents from the early 1990s say very little about politics; they reveal an organization single-mindedly focused on military self-improvement. "Was there a particular target that the jihad was directed at during that time?" Jamal al-Fadl was asked in the East Africa Bombings trial. "Not that time," he replied.[154] The political vagueness may have reflected a relative lack of interest in politics, but perhaps also an inability to agree internally on a specific strategy.[155]

The group's main objective in the first years was more limited, namely, to create a cadre of elite Arab fighters through rigid personnel selection and advanced training.[156] In many ways, early al-Qaida resembled a special force in conventional militaries, in the sense that they were relatively apolitical and primarily concerned with producing great soldiers. And like Western Special Forces, al-Qaida would later move between conflict zones to "train the trainers" and carry out particularly difficult operations. Training is therefore the best documented part of al-Qaida's early activities. We know, for example, that Bin Ladin and his men kept the al-Ma'sada camp until at least the spring of 1988, and probably longer. The Tareekh Musadat collection contains al-Ma'sada's personnel archive from May 1988, which lists around ninety recruits.[157] The autobiography of Abu Ja'far al-Qandahari also describes the hard training he went through at al-Ma'sada in 1988.[158] Al-Ma'sada may have served as a "farmer team" of sorts; a place where recruits went for initial training and where the best were selected for more advanced courses in other places. Jamal al-Fadl, for example, was at al-Ma'sada in May 1988 before joining al-Qaida in 1989. The precise composition, location, and evolution of al-Qaida's training camp infrastructure outside of al-Ma'sada in these early years is not clear. We know that Bin Ladin sent a team to Nangarhar in late 1988 and early 1989 to scout for new camp locations.[159] We also know that, starting in 1989, they set up a string of camps in the Khost area named Jihadwal, al-Faruq, Siddiq, and Khalid bin al-Walid.[160] In the early 1990s they appear also to have established three camps in the Jalalabad area named Badr al-Kubra, Badr al-Sughra, and Abu Shahid al-Qatari.[161]

Multiple sources describe al-Qaida training in al-Faruq in Khost in 1989. According to Nasir al-Bahri, who served as bodyguard to Bin Ladin in the 1990s, "Bin Ladin ... established a new and more advanced training camp that was tantamount to a military college. It was called Al-Faruq Camp or the Al-Faruq Military College. [It] bypassed the 45-day period of quick training on weapons that was in force in the Sada camp."[162] Jamal al-Fadl says he attended a meeting in al-Faruq camp in Khost in 1989 where the agenda was the establishment of a new group to be called al-Qaida. Fadl said that Abu Ayyub al-Iraqi "bring a lot of papers and he give each person three and he say read and we make lecture and we talk about what we want to do." The papers included "the rules you have to make if you agree about everything in the paper, you have to make *bayat*." Also present at the meeting, according to al-Fadl, were Abu Ayyub al-Iraqi, his brother Yasin, Abu Ubayda al-Banshiri, Abu Faraj al-Yamani, Ayman al-Zawahiri, Sayyid Imam al-Sharif (Dr. Fadl), Abu Burhan al-Suri, Abu Hafs al-Masri, Abu Mus'ab al-Sa'udi, and a certain Izz al-Din.[163] Similarly, Lawrence Wright says, citing Abdallah Anas, that al-Qaida "held its first recruitment meeting in the Farouk camp near Khost, Afghanistan, shortly after the debacle in Jalalabad," that is, in the spring of 1989.[164]

Selecting the best appears to have a key concern for al-Qaida from the start. Abu Ja'far al-Qandahari mentions an al-Qaida delegation coming to visit Arabs in Qandahar around 1989 to scout for recruits.[165] He also describes an al-Qaida recruitment process in 1989 in which candidates filled out application forms with information about their background, experience, and ambitions, before undergoing practical tests. In the end, only three out of fifty candidates were accepted. Al-Qaida, in other words, was never intended to be a mass movement, but rather a small jihadi special force.

Al-Qaida leaders also showed a strong interest in urban warfare and terrorist tactics, suggesting that they envisaged operations outside of the battlefields of Afghanistan. The best evidence of this is the *Encyclopaedia of Jihad*, whose redaction began in the late 1980s, and which includes instructions for a wide range of non-conventional tactics, including assassination, abduction, remotely detonated bombs, and poisoning.[166] It notably includes a reconnaissance case study on one of the Afghan Arab safe houses in Peshawar (probably Bayt al-

Ansar), written in the spring of 1989, which reflects on "Acts of Sabotage that can be Carried Out in the Hostel", including

1) Poisoning the drinking water inside the house through the water tanks that are on top of depot 1 and through the refrigerators ...
2) It is possible to plant bombs everywhere ...
3) It is possible to enter a car bomb, because they allow the entry of cars with heavy loads. It is possible to use this point and get in a car loaded with explosives ...
4) It is possible to wire the buses of the hostel, where they would explode at a specific speed or at a specific time.[167]

These scenarios are putative, and no such operations are known to have been carried out by Afghan Arabs in the 1980s. However, they show that some of the Arabs in Peshawar were contemplating non-conventional tactics at least as early as 1989.

Bin Ladin and his comrades kept a strict veil of secrecy around the organization. The name al-Qaida is absent from all the main Arab accounts about the Afghan Arabs written in the early 1990s, including Basil Muhammad's *Pages from the Record of the Arab Supporters in Afghanistan*. Several former Afghan Arabs say they were unaware of an al-Qaida organization in 1988–1989, and some say they never heard of it until 9/11. Rather than proving that al-Qaida is a post-9/11 Western construction, as some have suggested, this absence reflects the deliberate strategy of its leaders not to build a brand around the name.[168] This is supported by the fact that the name "al-Qaida" was virtually never used in public statements by the group itself prior to the 9/11 attacks. However, a number of sources recorded in the late 1980s and the early 1990s – not least the 20 August Document – clearly show that an organization by that name existed.[169]

Many have argued that Egyptians played an important role in the emergence of al-Qaida. Hasan al-Surayhi, for example, said that "the idea of al Qaeda is an Egyptian one by the Islamic Jihad group led by Abu-Ubaidah al Banjshiri and Abu-Hafs."[170] In fact, we can speak of a whole narrative theme – that of the "evil Egyptians" – that runs through much of the secondary literature. Put simply, the narrative is that Egyptians were the real brains behind al-Qaida, that they radicalized and manipulated Bin Ladin, and that they hated Azzam so much that they may have ordered his assassination. The central villains in the story are Ayman al-Zawahiri and Sayyid Imam al-Sharif (Dr. Fadl), leading figures in Egyptian Islamic Jihad. Here, as in all compelling scripts, there are elements of both truth and exaggeration. In the following I will look at the first two parts of the narrative – the Egyptian role in al-Qaida and the Egyptian radicalization of Bin Ladin – leaving the relationship between the Egyptians and Azzam to Chapter 14.

The Egyptian role in the formation of al-Qaida was smaller than the standard narrative suggests. On the one hand, some Egyptians, especially Abu Ubayda al-Banshiri and Abu Hafs al-Masri, were undoubtedly in the core group of people who established al-Qaida. It is probably also true that a certain number of experienced Egyptian militants were drawn early to al-Qaida for the training opportunities it provided. Some of them seem to have brought vital military expertise; Nasir al-Bahri said the al-Faruq camp was only established "after the arrival of many members of the Egyptian Islamic Group (EIG) and Egyptian Islamic Jihad (EIJ) who were qualified militarily."[171] On the other hand, the Egyptians were far from alone. The Iraqi Abu Ayyub and the Saudi Bin Ladin held the two top positions and were central to the enterprise. Of the twenty-five names listed on Jamal al-Fadl's organizational chart of early al-Qaida, only six were identifiably Egyptian. By comparison, at least five were Saudis. Besides, it is not clear that all Egyptians in al-Qaida saw themselves as part of an Egyptian collective. Abu Ubayda al-Banshiri and Abu Hafs al-Masri invested themselves so fully in the al-Qaida project that it would be misleading to see them as undercover agents for al-Jihad.

Moreover, attention may have been given to the wrong Egyptians. Judging by the documentary evidence, Ayman al-Zawahiri and Dr. Fadl were less prominent figures in the Afghan Arab community than the secondary literature suggests. As a matter of fact, there is almost no trace of them in the written sources from the late 1980s and early 1990s. In reviewing Basil Muhammad's *Pages from the Record of the Arab Supporters in Afghanistan* and the Tareekh Osama and Tareekh Musadat collections, I found only a few references to Dr. Fadl and none to Ayman al-Zawahiri. Judging by these sources, Ayman al-Zawahiri and Dr. Fadl were not central figures in the Afghan Arab community at all in the 1980s. It is only in the oral testimonies collected after 9/11 that these two are depicted as key players in Peshawar. And even there, they are described as relative latecomers to al-Qaida; crucially, they are not reported to have been in al-Ma'sada in 1987 with the other founding fathers of the organization.

Furthermore, Usama Bin Ladin was probably not manipulated by Egyptians quite to the extent suggested in the literature. Some sources come close to portraying him as a victim of brainwashing. In Wright's influential *The Looming Tower*, Isam Diraz, an Egyptian filmmaker who visited al-Mas'ada in February 1988, says he "soon came to notice how the Egyptians formed a barrier around the curiously passive Saudi, who rarely ventured an opinion of his own, preferring to solicit the opinions of others in his company ... whenever [Diraz] tried to speak confidentially to Bin Laden, the Egyptians would surround the Saudi and drag him into another room."[172] However, little if anything else in Bin Ladin's biography suggests that he was this gullible. Throughout his life he went his own ways and took bold decisions. He had defied family instructions not to go to Peshawar in 1984, set up al-Ma'sada against good advice in 1986, and would declare war on the United States in 1996 when many other jihadis said it was madness.[173] In the late 1980s he was an educated man, over thirty years old, and accustomed to being courted for his money. It is highly unlikely that he was a passive victim of manipulation.

Of course, Bin Ladin may well have been influenced by others. One of Azzam's biographers later wrote, "Some overenthusiastic youth entered the line between [Bin Ladin] and Sheikh Abdallah, and they started pushing in the direction of [the former's] operational independence."[174] However, if Bin Ladin was influenced by Egyptians, it was probably more by people such as Abu Ubayda and Abu Hafs than by Ayman al-Zawahiri and Dr. Fadl. Bin Ladin and al-Zawahiri had little in common at this time. First, Bin Ladin was a militarist who respected experienced fighters; Al-Zawahiri, by contrast, is not known to have spent any time on the fronts or the training camps prior to 1989.[175] He did have a history in the Egyptian Islamic Jihad, but not really as a military operator. Second, Bin Ladin had a Muslim Brotherhood background, while al-Zawahiri came from Salafi circles (see Chapter 14). Third, Bin Ladin was by all accounts more of a pan-Islamist than a revolutionary at this time, while al-Zawahiri was at war with the Egyptian government.[176] Last but not least, al-Zawahiri had no formal religious credentials and was famously uncharismatic. On the whole, there are few good reasons why al-Zawahiri would have had great sway over Bin Ladin in the 1980s.

Why, then, has the "evil Egyptian" narrative been so pervasive? Michael Scheuer has suggested that it stems from an effort by Saudi Arabia and members of the Azzam family to whitewash Bin Ladin and Azzam.[177] There may well be something to this. Blaming the Egyptian radicals makes both Azzam and Bin Ladin (and, by extension, Saudi Arabia) look better in the history books. It is noteworthy that most of the testimonies suggesting Egyptian manipulation were offered after 9/11, when the incentives to shape the historical narrative about the al-Qaida would have been the strongest. However, to speak of a conspiracy would be going too far. Western authors and journalists may also have overdramatized the intrigues in Peshawar in their urge to tell a good story. Besides, there is a kernel of truth to it; there really was bad blood between Abdallah Azzam and some of the Egyptians, as we will see in Chapter 14. Still, al-Qaida arose for reasons other than Egyptian manipulation. The fundamental driver was the quest, among a minority of Afghan Arabs, for military expertise and status. Al-Qaida emerged to meet this demand, and Bin Ladin played an active and central part in it.

Bin Ladin's involvement with al-Qaida led him to drift somewhat apart from Azzam in the late 1980s. As Abdallah Anas later said:

The second part of [our relationship with] Osama is when he started in '86 to take distance from Abdallah Azzam, but not in a rude way, or in an unacceptable [way]. Externally [the relationship] seemed very fine. Very, very few people [knew otherwise], no more than five to six people ... In that period, Sheikh Abdallah did continue his policy without consulting Osama and Osama continued on his own way ... Our relationship as a friend continued, but our relationship as a colleague of work completely stopped.[178]

Jamal Isma'il also said, "Osama was not having any involvement in the Services Office since late '87 or maybe early '88. In '88 his financial support for Services Office was stopped by mutual understanding between him and Abdallah Azzam."[179] However, the enmity between Bin Ladin and Azzam should not be overstated. Despite spending less time together, the two remained on cordial personal terms until Azzam's death.

More important, Azzam was not a very active opponent of the al-Qaida project as he knew it at the time. He was neither a member nor an enemy of al-Qaida, but rather a passive spectator to its emergence. It is not clear whether he knew the full extent of al-Qaida's activities and ambitions, but he must have been aware of the group's existence, because his right-hand man Tamim al-Adnani was present at the 20 August 1988 meeting in which al-Qaida was described as an "organized Islamic faction." However, there was no reason why Azzam should be fiercely opposed to it, because the al-Qaida project was quite compatible with his plans for the Afghan Arabs. Bin Ladin and his comrades were not proposing to create a massive Arab army or to conduct international terrorist attacks, but rather to train elite fighters in special camps. Bin Ladin was happy to let most recruits go to Sada and be distributed on the Afghan battlefronts just as Azzam and the Services Bureau wanted. All al-Qaida wanted was an option on the most talented fighters. Moreover, as we saw with the establishment of al-Ma'sada, Azzam was conflict-shy and generally tolerant of the activities of other Afghan Arabs, especially Bin Ladin. As Kuehn, Farrall, and Strick van Linschoten have noted, "Azzam would often choose not to voice his differences or let others continue for the sake of unity, even when he disagreed with their programs."[180] Azzam did grumble in private about Bin Ladin going his own way, but there is no evidence of him openly criticizing or condemning al-Qaida.

On the contrary, there was a degree of practical cooperation and dialogue between al-Qaida and the Services Bureau in 1988 and 1989. Tamim al-Adnani, the executive director of the Services Bureau, is recorded as having participated in several meetings with known al-Qaida figures in this period. Bayt Abu Hamza, the Services Bureau's guest house, continued to serve as the main entry point and guest house for many Arabs, including those who trained at al-Ma'sada and ended up in al-Qaida.[181] Besides, the tone between the two communities remained respectful. When Tamim al-Adnani died, Abu Hafs al-Masri, one of the core al-Qaida members, wrote a glowing obituary.[182]

In fact, Azzam was so keen to maintain cooperation with Usama Bin Ladin and his men that in late 1988 he proposed having bin Ladin appointed leader of all the Arabs. According to Abdallah Anas, Azzam gathered the original founders of the Services Bureau and told them to go to Usama's house and "organize an election of sorts where Osama becomes the emir."[183] Azzam saw this as a way both to maintain unity in Arab ranks and to make the Services Bureau more palatable to the Saudi government. The Tareekh Osama collection contains a number of documents that appear to stem from this unification attempt. One of the charts show Bin Ladin as the *amir* and Abdallah Azzam as one of four deputies.[184] However, for reasons that remain unclear, these plans never left the drawing-board, and Azzam stayed on as *amir* of the Services Bureau. From early 1989 there were no prospects of unification, and al-Qaida and the Services Bureau increasingly went their separate ways.

This became clear at the battle of Jalalabad in the spring of 1989, when Bin Ladin and the men around him threw themselves head-on, while Azzam observed from the sidelines.[185] Jalalabad was the last of the three big battles that defined the military history of the Afghan Arabs. Unlike the Zhawar and Jaji battles, which were footnotes in the history of the war, Jalalabad was a battle of geopolitical proportions. It was pushed for by Benazir Bhutto and planned at the highest echelons of the Pakistani government, with significant input by the CIA.[186] The objective was to allow for a transfer of the newly formed Afghan interim government – and the rest of the Mujahidin in exile – from Peshawar to Jalalabad, and thereby hasten the downfall of the Kabul government. Starting in March 1989, a force of 5,000–7,000 Mujahidin, mostly Hekmatyar's and Sayyaf's men, were sent to besiege the city and prepare for a conventional assault.[187] Several hundred Arabs also participated.

However, the offensive proved an unmitigated disaster.[188] After some initial progress, the attack stalled and for two months the Mujahidin made no headway while taking severe casualties. On the open plains around the city the attackers were left vulnerable to artillery, helicopters, and SCUD missiles from Kabul. Some 3,000 Mujahidin – half of the attacking force – were killed. The operation ended in July with Jalalabad firmly in the hands of the Najibullah government. According to Kiessling, "today, Jalalabad stands as a huge blunder on the part of the ISI and is considered a blemish on Hamid Gul's military career."[189] In fact, Gul was fired by Bhutto in June 1989 over Jalalabad. For the Arabs, who lost over eighty men, it was a traumatizing event and the undisputed low point in the Afghan jihad. As Azzam later wrote, "the land of Jalalabad swallowed one lion after another."[190] *Al-Jihad* magazine noted quietly in its July/August issue of 1989: "The hot fights started in Jalalabad; And Abu Abdallah took charge of the closest front lines to the enemy and started attacking ... the Arab mujahideen lost eighty and more than one hundred were injured."[191] For the rest of 1989, the martyr sections in *al-Jihad* magazine were 5–10 pages long, packed with biographies of the dead from Jalalabad.

The defeat in Jalalabad undermined the authority of leaders such as Usama Bin Ladin, accelerating the fragmentation of the Afghan Arab community.[192] According to Mustafa Hamid, the defeat led several Arab factions to start operating on their own, outside the framework of both the Services Bureau and al-Qaida.[193] From mid-1989 onward, the number of training camps increased significantly, creating large, decentralized clusters of camps in the border areas, especially in Khost and around Jalalabad. According to Hamid and Farrall, the factions who had camps in the Jalalabad area around 1989–1990 included EIJ, EIG, a group of Algerians, the Saudi fighter Ibn Khattab, and the Indonesian group Jemaah Islamiyya.[194] From this cluster of camps emerged a new and highly militaristic subculture which Hamid calls the "Jalalabad School of Jihad," made up of young people who "operate without leadership, political vision, or strategic planning, and do not care about the consequences of their actions. [They were] led by new and inexperienced young people who were extremist in their thinking and behaviour and refused the historical leadership of [Usama Bin Ladin] and Abdallah Azzam. They wanted action."[195] This development arguably represented the continuation of the same trend that had produced al-Ma'sada and al-Qaida a few years earlier, namely a tendency toward increasing militarism and disrespect for authority. The trend was a product of the fact that foreign fighting attracts action-minded individuals and also that there was no mechanism for controlling the volunteers upon arrival. Azzam's charismatic authority was not enough to hold it all together.

The Arab Contribution

The Soviet withdrawal from Afghanistan in February 1989 was a morale boost of historical proportions for the jihadi movement. In the eyes of the Afghan Arabs, the Mujahidin had defeated a superpower against all odds, and the Arabs had helped them do it. This conviction provided the movement with a self-confidence and a political momentum that would last for years. But how much of a military contribution did the Arab volunteers really make?

The Arabs themselves certainly believed they had made an impact. Abu Ja'far al-Qandahari, for example, said, "One of the main reasons behind the Russian retreat and defeat was the bravery and heroism showed by the Arab recruits."[196] Azzam himself was a little less bombastic, but still argued that the Arabs had made a substantial contribution. In a lecture titled "The influence of the Arab *mujahid* on the Afghan jihad," Azzam could not point to tangible military contributions, but said the Arabs were important because they brought religious knowledge and inspired the Afghan Mujahidin through heroic acts of self-sacrifice.[197] In another article he wrote, "[The Arabs] are like salt in the food; the Afghan Mujahidin are the food and the Arabs are the salt."[198]

In reality, the Arab role in evicting the Soviet Union was minuscule. It suffices to look at the numbers. The Afghan Mujahidin counted between 175,000 and 250,000 men, while the number of Arabs who arrived before the announcement of the Soviet withdrawal (February 1988) was at most 2,000.[199] The Arabs were thus 1 percent of the fighting force at most, and that is being generous, because only a minority of those 2,000 Arabs ever fought.[200] Abdallah Anas says only 300 people were permanently fighting in Afghanistan, and a former British intelligence officer put the number at 300–400.[201] When we look at casualty figures, the contrast is even starker. Afghan Mujahidin deaths from 1979 through 1987 were in the order of 50,000–100,000.[202] The number of Arabs killed in the same period was approximately fifty, that is, at most 0.06 percent of the combat deaths on the resistance side.[203] If we include civilians, an estimated 875,000 Afghans lost their lives between 1978 and 1987 as a consequence of the war.[204] To be sure, if we include the years 1988 and 1989, then the total number of Afghan Arabs rises to 7,000 and number of Arab deaths to around 150, but in this last phase the war was already won. Thus the claim that Afghan Arabs helped liberate Afghanistan borders on the preposterous. Some Arabs recognized this; Abdallah Anas later noted that "the truth requires that we admit that the Arabs ... played a minor role; they were a drop in the ocean compared with the effort of the Afghans."[205]

We may add that the Arab military contribution was limited geographically to a small sliver of eastern Afghanistan, mainly in modern-day Khowst, Paktia, and Lugar provinces and to a lesser extent in Kabul, Nangarhar, and Kunar. There were a few exceptions, such as the small Arab contingent in Qandahar in the late 1980s and the even smaller number in the Panjshir valley. Eastern Afghanistan was admittedly a strategically important theater which saw much fighting because of the supply lines from Pakistan. Still, the Afghanistan war was fought across the country, most of which did not see many Arab combatants.

Theoretically, the Arabs could have made a qualitative difference larger than their numbers suggest, but they did not. Most of the volunteers arrived with little or no prior military training. Many were physically unfit, especially those coming from the Gulf countries, where there was neither military conscription nor a sports culture. And only a few Arabs were sufficiently committed to stay for extended periods of time. As Musa al-Qarni later noted, "The Arabs, many of them or actually most of them who came to carry out jihad, were not fond of military discipline. They were disorganized. Some came and stayed for one week only. They would join an operation, fire their weapons, storm a position and then return. Some stayed for a month or two and so on".[206] Similarly, Strick van Linschoten and Kuehn found that the Afghan view of the Arab contribution was at best mixed: "Some mujahideen from southern Afghanistan point out that the Arabs for most of the 1980s did not know the lay of the land, did not speak the language, and had no feel for local customs."[207] When Commander Abdul Haq was interviewed in *al-Jihad* magazine in 1989 about the contribution of the Arabs, he said diplomatically, "It is impossible to generalize about the Arabs in Afghanistan; some are fulfilling their duty of jihad with us, while others have played an unconstructive role."[208] To be sure, some Afghans, especially those who worked most closely with the Arabs, such as Sayyaf and Haqqani, had positive things to say.[209] Strick van Linschoten and Kuehn also mention that "a prominent mujahideen commander in Eastern Afghanistan ... valued the Afghan Arabs highly and thought they made an impact."[210] However, the list of Afghan commanders praising the Arab contribution is short. The Pakistanis were similarly unimpressed. For example, Muhammad Yousaf, the former head of ISI's Afghan bureau, made no mention of Arabs at all in his 1992 book *Afghanistan: The Bear Trap*.

It is possible that the foreign volunteers boosted Mujahidin morale by displaying fighting spirit and by showing Afghans that outsiders cared. However, this effect would have been small and limited to the few Afghans who had direct contact with the foreigners. In subsequent foreign-fighter destinations in the 2000s and 2010s, foreign fighters made a military difference through their overrepresentation among suicide bombers.[211] However, suicide bombings were not used by

Sunni militants in the 1980s, so the Afghan Arabs did not have this tool at their disposal to make a mark.

This brings us to an upside, if we can call it that, of the limited Arab contribution to the war, namely, that the Afghan Arabs did not radicalize the tactics of the local insurgents the same way foreign fighters would do in later conflicts.[212] Contrary to what has sometimes been claimed, there are relatively few reports of Afghan Arabs committing atrocities during the 1980s.[213] Of course, the sources might underreport such incidents, but this seems unlikely given that foreign fighters in later conflicts were happy to display their violent excesses.[214] In the 1980s at least some Afghan Arabs took pride in their relatively clean methods; Abdallah Anas, for example, has insisted that he and his comrades never mistreated Russian prisoners.[215] This restraint may have been partly a result of Abdallah Azzam's insistence on teaching the rules of war to incoming recruits. The few reported atrocities by Arabs occurred at the end of the 1980s, when more people bypassed the Services Bureau and Azzam's influence.[216]

Whatever dirty tactics other Arabs engaged in, the Afghan Mujahidin were likely already using, and worse. Braithwaite says local insurgents sometimes "wiped out 'collaborators' and 'spies' inside Afghanistan, sometimes with their families, sometimes whole villages."[217] In the early 1980s Afghan Mujahidin placed bombs at civilian targets in Kabul, such as the Radio Afghanistan building, the Communist Party office at Kabul University, and bus stops frequented by Soviet advisors.[218] Summary executions of prisoners were also common; according to al-Qandahari, "If the battle cost the Mujahidin martyrs, they would kill as many detainees."[219] Most detainees were executed by shooting, but some were buried alive or decapitated.[220] Torture was not routine, but it did occur, and it could be horrific.[221] According to Braithwaite, "One minor mujahedin leader boasted that he had made a practice of half-skinning Russian prisoners ... and leaving them alive, surrounded by booby traps, to catch the Soviet rescue teams."[222] Another captive was castrated, pulled through a village by a rope attached to a big ring through his nose, and only then executed.[223] Transnational jihadis, in other words, are not always more brutal than their local hosts.

We have seen that the Arab military presence in Afghanistan remained very limited until 1987. It expanded then because Bin Ladin and other impatient volunteers forced their way to the battlefield against the wishes of risk-averse Afghan Arabs and Afghan Mujahidin commanders. Abdallah Azzam, always more preacher than soldier, did little to facilitate serious Arab participation in the war, although he rarely opposed initiatives from others. This attitude of passive tolerance also characterized his relationship with the al-Qaida organization, which emerged from late 1987 onward as an attempt to build an elite Arab fighting force.

Later in the 1980s, Arab military contribution grew in scale to a peak in 1989 of several hundred men under arms in various parts of eastern Afghanistan and in Qandahar. For all the mythology around the battle exploits of the Afghan Arabs, they made a small contribution to the overall war effort. In sum, Azzam was a minor contributor to a military effort that was a footnote to the war as a whole.

In the late 1980s Azzam became even less involved in military work. With al-Qaida emerging and a Services Bureau camp already in place in Sada, Azzam probably felt there was not a whole lot more he needed to do. Meanwhile, the political situation in the late 1980s left much for him to think about: The Soviets were pulling out from Afghanistan, tensions were rising between Hekmatyar and Massoud, Pakistani President Zia ul Haqq died in a plane crash, and the Palestinian Intifada was raging. In this turbulent time, he chose to concentrate on his intellectual and political work and let others do the fighting. His life was busy enough as it was.

13 Resident

Signs of war were visible everywhere in Peshawar. Men on crutches and children with stumps of legs and arms hobble through the bazaar, sprayed with mud by Japanese Pajero jeeps containing Afghan commanders and their bodyguards en route to negotiate some lucrative arms deal. Suzuki vans packed with mujaheddin yelling "Allah-o-Akbar" ... race along the Khyber road to the battlefront, ignoring the constant scream of ambulance sirens bringing back the maimed ... Frequent bomb blasts rock the city – apparently the work of agents from KHAD, the Afghan secret police ... Merchants from far-off republics ... hawk carpets and lapis outside the gates of Deans Hotel, in the fading British glory of which Churchill once stayed and where I had made my temporary home.[1]

This depiction of Peshawar in early 1989 by the British journalist Christina Lamb shows that the city had become a political Klondike. It was a place at the edge of the world where people could come, forget their past, and delve into the fog of war. For radical Islamists, it was a unique situation; at no previous point in the twentieth century had militants from around the world been able to assemble and operate as they pleased almost without government interference. They used the opportunity to form the first jihadi colony in the modern history of the Muslim world. What was life like inside this community? What did Azzam do when he was not traveling or in the field? And what was it like being an ordinary foreign fighter?

This chapter describes daily life among the Afghan Arabs in the heyday of the war. It portrays a community that was fluid and fragmented, but nonetheless bound together by a sense of mission and historical significance; one in which young men moved between the mundaneness of Peshawar and the horrors and magic of the battlefield. It was a place in which women, equally enthused with pioneering spirit, waged jihad through writing, charity work, and teaching. The six-part chapter looks in turn at Abdallah Azzam's personal situation, the

Afghan Arab community, the role of Arab women, Arab relations with Afghans, the individual foreign fighter experience, and the jihadi culture which developed at this time.

Azzam's Best Years

The second half of the 1980s was a good period in Azzam's life. He was now fully invested in jihad, largely in control of his own situation, and at the peak of his fame. During the first five years in Pakistan he had only been a part-time *mujahid*, dividing his time between Islamabad, where his house and job were, and Peshawar, where the action was. In the spring of 1986, however, he left the International Islamic University and moved permanently to Peshawar to focus all his efforts on the war.[2] No more three-hour commutes and no more grading. He found a house a few hundred meters north of Bayt Abu Hamza, near the Khyber teaching hospital, and brought his family up from Islamabad a few weeks later.[3] In 1988 the family moved to another house a few kilometers northeast of University Town, on Arbab Road right behind the Sab' al-Layl mosque.

Even though he was now in his late forties, he had lost nothing of his energetic demeanor. Aside from his salt-and-pepper beard, receding hairline, and weaker eyesight, he was in very good shape.[4] Well-built from constant activity and lean from ascetic habits, Azzam had what one Afghan leader described as "an extremely good physique, like the Pathans."[5] At about 1.75 meters, he was taller than average, and his posture was that of a younger man.[6] He was always well groomed, and according to a former assistant, he "did not wear the same clothes regularly. He always changed his appearance. Sometimes he wore an Afghan turban, at other times a Palestinian *keffieh*. You could notice this by watching his Friday sermons or his videotaped lectures; he always changed his dress."[7]

Azzam's daily life was marked by religious rituals and habits. He got up in the middle of every night to pray the optional night prayer.[8] He fasted every other day.[9] He uttered invocations for ordinary activities such as eating, going to the bathroom, or getting into a car. Like others in the movement, Azzam frequently shed religious tears. One fighter recalls hearing him "giving a sermon while crying heavily" at the Badr camp in 1984.[10] Abdallah Anas said Azzam was "an angel," who would be "worshipping all night, crying and fasting."[11] Another source says Azzam

used to weep during the evening and afternoon prayers. If he found a brother with a good recitation, he would put him at the front in prayer, and say, "I want to hear from you." By God, there was not a single time he did not weep. Sometimes I prayed behind him and he wept and I wept; It was always like this, praise be to God.[12]

Another of his biographers wrote:

And his tears fell when he lauded the martyrs after their burial. He would stand on the grave of each martyr and say a few inflamed words full of enthusiasm and compassion, and it was almost never without tears. We saw them as a mark of distinction falling on his beard, like drops of dew fall on twigs. We saw his beard wet with tears.[13]

Azzam also signaled his piety by dress and accessories. He almost always wore either military dress, Afghan clothes, or Arab dress. He said he always carried three things: water for ablution, a siwak stick, and the Qur'an.[14] This brought him once into a discussion with a friend about whether you can bring the Qur'an with you into the toilet.[15] He also boasted that he never used a toothbrush, only the siwak stick.[16]

Azzam was a workaholic and a utility maximizer who would not spend a minute on anything or anybody if he did not think it helped the cause. For the same reason, he had no hobbies, did not watch films, and read no fiction. He slept only three to four hours per night, topping it up with five-minute naps in the car throughout the day.[17] He also spent little time at home. When he was not at Bayt Abu Hamza, he was meeting people elsewhere in Peshawar. When he was not in Peshawar, he was on the Afghan border or abroad giving lectures. He sometimes went away for long periods of time, such as in the autumn of 1986, when he spent several months at the Sada camp. Once his wife Samira was asked about his whereabouts, to which she replied, "I don't know anything about him; ask the brothers, they know more than me."[18] When he was at home, he could be absent-minded. Once, after returning from a trip to Panjshir to meet Ahmed Shah Massoud, he showed a video of the meeting to his wife, who remarked, "Why do you never smile like that with us in Peshawar"?[19]

As the most senior religious authority in the Afghan Arab community, Azzam spent much of this time preaching and teaching. He taught periodically at the University of Daʿwa and Jihad in Pabbi and at Peshawar University.[20] He also lectured in the training camps, especially at Sada. In the autumn of 1986, for example, when Azzam was in "exile" in Sada due to Pakistani police harassment (see next chapter), he gave a fifty-hour lecture series which was recorded and later distributed under the title "In the Shade of Surat al-Tawba." Azzam also served as imam and preacher in the Sabʿ al-Layl ("Nightly Predator") mosque on Arbab Road, where most of the Afghan Arabs prayed.[21] The mosque, which was named after a fallen Yemeni fighter who carried this nickname, was established around 1986 to cater for the rapidly growing Arab community.[22] It was quite large; there could be up to 2,000 people at Friday prayer.[23] Azzam was practically an in-house imam, because he lived just a block away from the mosque. Unless he was out of town, Azzam would lead Friday prayer there every week and deliver a sermon in Arabic. His speeches were long, and often improvised. One of his younger followers was so intrigued by the question of how Azzam prepared that he did an experiment whereby he stayed with him around all Thursday evening, slept over at his house, and followed him all Friday morning. Only in the car on the way to the mosque did Azzam take out a piece of paper and start scribbling down keywords.[24]

Despite all the absences, he was, at heart, a caring family man who did not take his wife for granted. In his will, which he wrote in the midst of the battle of Zhawar in April 1986, he addressed Samira:

> To you my wife: I have so much to say to you, Umm Muhammad, may God reward you on my behalf and on behalf of Muslims. You were patient with me and you stood by me through thick and thin with patience and courage. From you I got the support I needed to carry on this jihad. I let you assume the responsibility of the house in 1969, when we had three small children, and you were living in one small room with no kitchen and no utilities. When the family became larger, the children grew up and our guests increased in number, you tolerated this and much more for God and my sake. I pray that God will reward you on my behalf. Had it not been for your patience, I would never have been able to bear this burden alone. You are a content wife who does not care for material things, and you never complained about having too little of it. You were never extravagant when we have had some wealth . . . I pray to Allah that he unites us in paradise as he united us in life.[25]

At this time Abdallah and Samira had eight children, including a toddler (Musʿab, b. 1984). By 1986 he also had at least two grandchildren, Hasan and Yahya, by his daughters Fatima and Wafa, both of whom lived in the Rahat Abad area of Peshawar.[26] Azzam married off his daughters young, and preferably to devout men involved in Islamic activism.[27] His first son-in-law was Abu al-Hasan al-Maqdisi, a Palestinian-Jordanian civil engineer and Muslim Brother who had studied under Azzam in Amman. He married Fatima in Amman in 1980 and moved to Pakistan to take part in the jihad shortly after Azzam himself.[28] His second son-in-law was Abu Yahya, a Jordanian computer engineer who had also studied under Azzam in Amman and who had been among the first Arabs in Peshawar. He was allowed to marry Wafa around 1984 only after he had proven himself on the battlefield inside Afghanistan.[29] The third was Abdallah Anas, one of Azzam's most trusted associates, who married Sumayya in 1990.

Meanwhile, he groomed his boys to be fighters. He regularly brought them to training camps, and he sent them off for military training on their own. His son Hudhayfa later said, "We used to accompany him to the battlefronts, and even my brother Mus'ab learned to use a revolver when he was only three years old."[30] Hudhayfa says that he and his older brother Muhammad went to Sada for training each year from 1984 through 1987, and that they also attended the Khaldan and Ya'qubi camps.[31] In 1986 they stayed for a whole six months in Sada. Hudhayfa has also said he accompanied his father at the battle of Jaji in 1987.[32] The sons also helped out with logistics at the Services Bureau, such as going to the airport to pick up newly arrived volunteers.[33] And in June 1988 the sixteen-year old Hudhayfa Azzam made his debut as a writer with a short article in *al-Jihad* magazine.[34]

Several members of the extended Azzam family in Jordan and Palestine joined Abdallah in Peshawar. Several cousins and nephews came to join him, so that by the late 1980s the Azzam clan in Peshawar counted at least twenty, perhaps over thirty, children included. Azzam chose his personal assistants from among his relatives. Most important was his nephew Mahmud Azzam, who served as his personal assistant, but another nephew, Jamal Azzam (Abu Harith), also worked as a driver.

Some time around 1987, even Azzam's parents moved to Peshawar. Both in their late eighties, they had left al-Sila al-Harithiyya to experience the jihad and be with their family.[35] A picture from the late 1980s shows Azzam and his father sitting next to one another in front of a bookshelf and behind a large copy of the Qur'an (see Illustration 19). Both are wearing bright white thawbs, no shoes, and white skullcaps.[36] Both look serious, but there is an ever-so-slight smile on Azzam's face. Azzam almost never smiled in photographs, so perhaps he was happy or proud to have his father by his side. His mother Zakiya was in poor health, however, and she died on 7 December 1988 after a lengthy spell in Peshawar University Hospital.[37] Azzam spent much time with her in the hospital, and was affected by her passing. As his nephew later wrote:

> When we entered the hospital, he burst out crying. So I told him: Sheikh, I was expecting you to raise our morale; if you are in this state, what about us? It seems that these words found their way to the sheikh's heart and affected him, and he stopped crying. Then I moved the body to the sheikh's house so he could continue saying his farewells behind closed doors and continue weeping away from the gaze of others and empty himself of the sorrow, sadness, and pain he felt over his mother's passing.[38]

The next day, Azzam's mother was buried in the martyr's cemetery in Pabbi.[39] The funeral was reportedly attended by thousands of people, and Abd Rabb al-Rasul Sayyaf gave a speech.[40] Azzam wrote a short obituary about his mother in the newsletter *Luhayb al-Ma'raka*, and he would later dedicate the book *In the Heat of Battle* to her.[41] Azzam's father was in good shape for his age. He met with the Afghan Mujahidin leaders and accompanied his son to Sada for shooting practice.[42] In late 1989 he went to Palestine to visit relatives, and was away when his son was assassinated. He returned to Peshawar, however, and passed away there on 16 November 1990.[43] He too was buried at Pabbi.

After leaving the International Islamic University in Islamabad (IIUI), Azzam's main source of income appears to have been the Muslim World League (MWL). His closest personal assistant Abu Harith has insisted that Azzam received a salary from the MWL from the time he left the IIUI until his death. Abu Harith says the MWL paid him to be an "education supervisor for the Afghans" (*mushrif tarbawi 'ala al-afghan*).[44] This is corroborated by the records from the so-called al-Tahaddi dispute in December 1988 (see below), where Azzam is referred to as an "employee of the Muslim World League."[45] This appears to have been a pro forma position, because as far as we know, Azzam did not organize many activities, if any at all, in the name of the MWL in the late 1980s. It seems that Azzam's friends in the MWL, who included its director general, Umar Nasif, simply created the position for Azzam to support him financially.

His MWL salary was probably not very large, because he led a materially modest life in Peshawar. According to one source, Azzam left behind debts of $25,000 when he died in November 1989.[46] He was not pleased when, one day, he discovered that his wife had bought new cushions for their reception room:

> One day, I came home to find new sponge cushions with matching sheets. When I saw them, I lost my mind. I said, "By God, women have no religion. This must go" ... I said, "It must leave the house. It cannot remain in the house," and I spoke such words to my wife that she was going to pass out ... I said, "Where did this gift come from?" She said, "Why does it matter to you? Your guests are here day and night, coming in and out, and I wash the sheets of these mattresses and change them. I change them everyday because the cotton in these Pakistani sheets gets stuck in the creases of the cushions. I am tired, and I found some gold that I had, which I then spent on this to make things a bit easier for me." I said to her, "While the Mujahidin are dying of hunger?" She said, "I donated a third of the value to the Mujahidin." I said, "Even then, it cannot remain." Honestly, my chest becomes tight every time I come home and see them.[47]

The issue was not always that he could not afford things, but that he wanted to live modestly. He once boasted that he had bought the cheapest chocolates in the store for his eldest daughter's engagement party.[48] On another occasion, his son Hudhayfa bought a cheap car on his own initiative, thinking his father would approve because it did not cost more than the trolley they already had. However, his father asked him to return it, saying he wanted his sons to walk to school and to be like common people.[49] Similarly, according to one of his biographers:

> It was in the sheikh's nature to not accept invitations from his brothers, especially when he was traveling and touring in other countries, but he did not like to see money spent on material things, so he would say to anyone who invited him that they should work out the cost of his meal and give the equivalent to the *mujahidin*, "then I will pay you a short visit in your house and we'll have a cup of tea."[50]

In his own home, however, Azzam had a reputation for hospitality. He had always practiced an open-door policy, and as his fame grew, so did the number of visitors. His neighbor in Peshawar said, "Not a day passed without there being guests in his house," while a friend said that the "house was like a hotel, in every room there were guests, night and day. Every time we asked for the family in the house, we found them busy catering for their guests."[51] Abdallah Anas says that when he arrived in Pakistan in late 1983 or early 1984, Azzam received him in his home and struck Anas as very kind and lacking in ulterior motives. "I felt genuinely at home," Anas said, adding: "It did not feel like he was trying to recruit you to a particular group or organization. Many others said the same, that he was genuine, had integrity, didn't want people to swear loyalty to him, to be his follower, be in his party or anything like that – he only wanted you to be close to God."[52]

The guests who frequented Azzam's house in the late 1980s were a mixture of Afghan Arabs, Afghan Mujahidin leaders, and foreign visitors. Azzam knew many of the Arabs based in Peshawar, and would have dealings with his Services Bureau staff on a daily basis. Azzam was in regular touch with several Afghan Mujahidin leaders and commanders, especially Sayyaf, but also, especially in the later years, Hekmatyar. Azzam also had contact with Pakistani Islamists in the Jamiat-e Islami and in Jamiat Ulema-e Islam.[53] As the war progressed, more visitors came from the Middle East, and Azzam was happy to host.

Azzam was easy to connect with; he could be serious and intense when talking about religious matters, but he also knew how to relax. One journalist who knew him said, "Azzam was always smiling a lot; he was not a gloomy person."[54] Isam al-Attar also said that when Azzam visited him in Aachen, "we laughed a lot together. Abdallah Azzam was more cheerful than his image."[55] Azzam also made it a habit to visit sick and wounded Arab fighters near the frontlines, which earned him much goodwill in the community. Mustafa Badi recalls being sick with malaria and lying half-conscious on a bed in Jaji in 1987 when Azzam and Sayyaf paid him a visit:

> I loved this Palestinian sheikh and I could not find anything to say to express my love for him as I lay on the bed in a very bad condition. I said to myself, "What can I present to this sheikh to express my love and appreciation for him?" When he came close to my bed, I grasped his hand hard to pull myself up ... He put his hand on mine and said, "Don't worry, no need to get up." I said, "But I would like to get up a little." I searched with my hand under the bed, took out my rifle and told him, "Sheikh, I don't have anything to offer you other than this weapon, which is very dear to me; I took it as booty from one of the Russian soldiers. I would like you to have it." It was an emotional,

wonderful moment and the sheikh could not hold himself together. He wept and we wept with him, and Sayyaf too. Even the Afghan patients who did not understand Arabic were taken by the moment.[56]

As we also saw in Chapters 4 and 7, Azzam had a way of connecting with young people, and he liked to spend time with foot soldiers. For example, in early 1984, when he organized the Badr project in Pabbi,

[Azzam] stayed with us in the Badr camp ... We were waiting impatiently for the sheikh, and I remember how we were squeezed into the small room in the Badr brigade. We were there: I, Sheikh Abdallah, Sheikh Sayyaf, Muhammad Yasir, Ahmad Shah ... and a group of Afghan leaders. When night came, Sheikh Sayyaf said, "Why don't you come and sleep at my house?" but Sheikh Abdallah said, "No, I'm sleeping with the young guys." He was like this; he liked to be with the youth, to sit with them, eat with them, sleep with them.[57]

Azzam had many friends, but few really close ones. The people who saw him the most in this period were probably his two nephews Abu Harith and Abu Adil (Mahmud Azzam) who were his driver and assistant respectively. Azzam was also close to Tamim al-Adnani, the executive director of the Services Bureau from 1988 (see Chapter 11). When al-Adnani died of a heart attack in Orlando, Florida in October 1989, Azzam wrote, "It was as though my right hand was cut off. The news of his death struck on my heart like a thunderbolt, for nobody could take the place of Sheikh Tameem."[58] In early November 1989 Azzam also wrote a book titled *The Lofty Mountain* which eulogized al-Adnani.[59]

Azzam's lifestyle changed somewhat toward the end of the decade as he withdrew from operations and devoted more time to writing and lecturing. He spent less time in the camps and more in his office and on the road. By 1989 he was more of a scholar and diplomat than an operator. He no doubt enjoyed his role as the grand old man of the Afghan Arabs, who had now become quite numerous.

Fragmented Community

If you came to Peshawar in the late 1980s, you probably would not notice the Arabs at all unless you went looking for them. The community was too small: Peshawar was a city of a million people, and the Arabs never exceeded 3,000 at any one time. They were also spread out across Peshawar, the border areas, battlefronts inside Afghanistan, and the southern Pakistani city of Quetta. Peshawar was the main hub, but even here Arabs lived in different areas. There was never an Arab ghetto in Peshawar, although areas such as University Town, Hayatabad, and Pabbi had a higher concentration of Arabs.[60] In these areas one might, toward the end of the 1980s, see shop signs in Arabic, find Arab newspapers for sale, and spot the odd foreign fighter in the street.[61] Other than that, the Arab presence was not conspicuous.

The community was also fragmented, especially toward the end of the decade. In 1985 there was really only the Services Bureau with its one guest house, Bayt Abu Hamza. By 1989 there were multiple factions and organizations, some of which had their own guest houses.[62] The Egyptians had a guest house named Dar al-Salam (the House of Peace), and Jamil al-Rahman's Jama'at al-Da'wa group had another house for Arabs.[63] It is still unclear exactly how many guest houses were in operation at any one time, but Hudhayfa Azzam says there were five to six guest houses in 1988–1989, and that the number increased to around eight in 1990.[64]

National and ethnic divisions also prevailed despite all the talk of Muslim unity. Linguistic and social similarities no doubt nudged countrymen and people from similar regions toward one another, a common dynamic in most diasporas. Volunteers clustered by country backgrounds, leading to talk of national contingents, such as "the Algerians," "the Egyptians," and "the Saudis." The clustering became more pronounced toward the end of the decade when the number of volunteers increased and more national contingents acquired critical mass.

Still, the intra-Arab divisions were smaller than those separating Arab and non-Arab volunteers. The foreign-fighter community included substantial numbers of non-Arab foreign fighters: white and African-American converts from the West; Turks and Central Asians, South East Asians, and South Asians. Out of the non-Arab groups, it seems that Turks and non-Arab converts from the West were better integrated with the Arabs, perhaps because they were too few to have camps of their own and because they were more likely to have had Arab friends in their home countries. By contrast, there seems to have been less interaction with South Asian and South East Asian foreign fighters. This said, there was a certain amount of interaction, because everybody rubbed shoulders in Peshawar, and because some camps and combat units were open to recruits from all nationalities. Al-Qandahari, for example, says that in Torkham in 1989 there was something "called the

Arab front although the place was filled with Indonesians, Malaysians, Filipinos, Turks, and American (black) Muslim fighters. But ... the majority was Arab and had come from Saudi Arabia, Egypt, Algeria and Yemen."[65] Al-Qandahari also mentions an Indian named Abu Taha al-Hindi who commanded an Arab unit in Qandahar.[66]

The Afghan Arab community was a transient one, because most fighters came only for a few weeks or months. They were typically pupils or students who came during the summer break and circulated within the safe-house and training-camp system. Only a minority were in it for the long haul. These residents started in the guest houses but later moved on to flats of their own. They also brought their wives from home (or started a new family if they did not have one), and sent their children to the Ansar School, the Services Bureau-run school for Arab children. The long-term volunteers formed a community inside the community and developed close ties to one another. While the visitors were mostly young men, the residents were a more diverse crowd, not least because they included women.

Active Women

Even though they have not received much attention in the literature thus far, women were an integral and important part of the Afghan Arab community. In the early years they were few and far between; as late as 1984, Azzam said, "There were no [Arab] women in Pakistan except those in my family and in [the families of] Abu Akram, Abu Tariq, Abu Hudhayfa, and Abu Amir al-Urduni."[67] But as more families moved to Peshawar, their numbers increased steadily, reaching perhaps several hundred by the end of the decade. There were women of all ages; in addition to Azzam's mother, there was, for example, Fatima Umm Faisal al-Makkiyya, a seventy-year old woman from Mecca who, after reading Azzam's book *Signs of the Merciful*, insisted on accompanying her son to Peshawar so she too could take part in the jihad.[68] She worked with widows and orphans there a good while, and when her son Faisal tried to get her to go home, she refused until they obtained a fatwa from Abdallah Azzam saying that it was okay.

Practically all Arab women were there as dependents of male volunteers, but that did not make them passive housekeepers. Many women were involved in various kinds of support activities for the jihad on top of their home duties. They were not allowed to fight or train, but they worked in charities, schools, or hospitals, and saw themselves as taking part in the broader jihad effort. Some had leadership positions in the charity sector; the wife of Ahmad Sa'id Khadr, for example, ran a motherhood and childhood center in Peshawar.[69] Others, such as Umm Siddiq, organized handicraft exhibitions to raise funds for the Mujahidin.[70] A number of women were also involved in writing and publishing, as we shall see below.[71] A few also entered Afghanistan, staying in local villages and camps close to their fighting husbands. For example, the wife of the Saudi fighter Abu Abd al-Aziz accompanied her husband to the battle of Jalalabad, and she later went with him to Bosnia.[72]

This relative emancipation was not new; rather, it reflected the connection of many Afghan Arabs to the Muslim Brotherhood, which had a decades-old culture of female participation. It was represented most forcefully by Zaynab al-Ghazzali, who established the Muslim Ladies' Association in Egypt as early as 1936 and worked for the next fifty years as an activist and writer.[73] Her book *Days from my Life* (1986), which details her ordeals in prison in the 1960s, is a classic of Islamist literature. Thus by the 1980s there was a long tradition of women writing for Islamist magazines and taking part in various kinds of social work to promote religion. This was true also in Afghanistan; as early as 1960 there had been an Islamist magazine for women in Kabul titled *Khawahar-e Shahid* (the Martyr's Sister).[74]

It helped that Abdallah Azzam himself was something of an Islamist feminist. He encouraged his own wife and daughters to educate themselves and be active in the community, and he discussed his work with them. This was not a given; some Arabs in Peshawar, especially the Salafi-leaning ones, kept their women in total seclusion.[75] By contrast, Azzam's wife Samira worked in the charities of the Services Bureau throughout the late 1980s, assisting Afghan refugees and delivering aid to hospitals.[76] She taught religion to Afghan and Arab women, and probably also to children in the Ansar School. She helped set up the women's magazine *al-Mu'minat* (the Women Believers) in 1987, and likely also contributed pseudonymously to *al-Jihad* magazine.[77] Samira lacked formal education, but it is clear from her later interviews that she was an articulate woman with strong convictions.

Azzam also called on other women to participate. In June 1985 he published a "Letter to our Mujahid Sisters" in *al-Jihad* magazine, listing five ways in which women outside Pakistan could support the Afghan jihad. They could (1) cultivate their own faith, (2) goad their husbands, sons, and brothers to fight, (3) reassure hesitant husbands that it is okay to leave for jihad, (4) donate money for the cause, and (5) "support media jihad through this magazine and other channels ... the magazine invites you to write and welcomes it."[78] By the following issue, *al-Jihad* had published its first letter from a woman writer, "the *mujahid* sister Umm Sayf."[79]

In November 1985 (issue 13), Azzam introduced a women's section in *al-Jihad* magazine called "Women Mujahidin Corner" (*rukn al-mujahidat*), which ran for the rest of the magazine's history. Usually two or three pages long, and toward the end of the magazine, the section contained articles by in-house female editorial staff as well as letters from women readers around the world. For example, in January 1986 the Women Mujahidin Corner included letters from women in America, France, Kuwait, Saudi Arabia, and Oman. The section editor from 1985 to 1989 was a certain Umm Mu'adh, who had been a student of Azzam's in Amman.[80] Other staff writers included A'ida Muhajir and Ahlam. Other magazines had similar columns; *al-Bunyan al-Marsus*, for example, had a section called "The Mujahid Family" (*al-usra al-mujahida*) with letters from women readers and articles by contributors such as Umm Sayf, Umm Siddiq, Umm Suhayb, and Umm al-Nur.[81] Some women such as Umm Sayf and A'ida Muhajir wrote for both *al-Jihad* and *al-Bunyan al-Marsus*. A'ida Muhajir was the most prolific female writer overall; unfortunately, as with all the others, her real identity is not known.

The content of the women's section both resembled and differed from the rest of the magazine. Women wrote about the need to fight hard in Afghanistan and about the duty for Muslims around the world to support the war effort.[82] They also wrote poetry and statements of support for the Arab fighters, just as the men did. However, a distinct, major theme in the Women Mujahidin Corner was stories of women in early Islamic history who had played a part in jihad, either by offering logistical support or urging their sons to fight. Several of the contributions also dealt with the role of Muslim women in general, and of spouses of fighters in particular. Most advocated traditional gender roles and sought to distance themselves from Western notions of female emancipation, which they saw as a form of cultural imperialism. For example, in issue 18, Ahlam wrote that "it is indeed the age of women's liberation; liberation from the noose of *jahiliyya* and allowing her in every way to practice her correct role in building the Muslim generation."[83] However, some women were more gung-ho, and expressed a desire to fight. One writer used the pen name Khawla bint al-Azwar – a famous female warrior from the Prophet's time – and lamented, "I only wish I could give my life and my spirit as a gift to this pure land as a martyr. But I am a girl and not able to do anything."[84] Similarly, a young girl (*tifla*) named Bayan Kharabsha wrote, "How I hope to grow up quickly so I can join you and be a martyr together with you to revitalize Islam."[85]

In 1989 Azzam also launched an entire women's magazine titled *Dhat al-Nitaqayn* (She of the Two Waistbands). The title was a reference to the historical figure Asma bint Abu Bakr, who earned the name after cutting her waistband in half to help carry provisions to the Prophet Muhammad during the *hijra* (emigration) from Mecca to Medina. Azzam wrote that she "served the most noble of refugees in this religion" and was thus an appropriate symbol for the women in Peshawar who were helping Afghan refugees.[86] The bimonthly magazine was not widely distributed, however, and it appears to have ceased publication in 1991.[87]

When Zaynab al-Ghazzali herself visited Peshawar in November 1985, Abdallah Azzam published a three-page interview with her in *al-Jihad* magazine.[88] The two figures, who knew each other from Azzam's time in Egypt in the early 1970s, talked at length about the Afghan jihad and the role of women in jihad. At one point Azzam asked, "Many Muslim girls write to us asking whether Afghan women can participate in the jihad. Do you support this?" She said, "I support it with all my heart and body. Muslim women participated in the jihad of the Prophet, carrying water for the army and bags of bandages to treat their wounds. She carried weapons to fight for God's Prophet at Uhud, and she carried weapons in every location as she was carrying water and emergency equipment." At the same time, Ghazzali underlined that in peacetime "the Muslim woman ... should return to the family ... and enable her husband to work outside the home, for that is his nature, and housework is her nature."

Azzam also held a relatively liberal view on the role of women in jihad.[89] He notably declared that when jihad is an individual obligation (*fard 'ayn*), as in the case of Afghanistan and Palestine, it applies to women as much as to men. In such situations, "the son may go out without the permission of his father, the debtor without the permission of the creditor, the woman without the permission of her husband, and the slave without the permission of his master."[90] At one point he said that in the specific context of the Afghanistan conflict, "Arab women may not fight because until now, Afghan women are not participating in the fighting," suggesting that his view on women fighting was contingent on prevailing norms in the conflict zone.[91]

In later statements Azzam backtracked a little, and said that women did need a male chaperon (*mahram*) if they wanted to travel for jihad. In one lecture he said:

> The participation of women in jihad is stated in the Shari'a, but we cannot escape complying with the legal conditions such as the need for the presence of a mahram, no mixing of the sexes, guarding against temptation, the woman must be neither young nor beautiful, [the condition] of covering the face in the presence of men or when they carry out an urgent task that could not be carried out by men. The participation of women in jihad occurred during the time of the Messenger of God, but only in rare circumstances and by older women – except in the case of 'Aisha for she is a special case by virtue of her [unique relationship] with the Messenger of God. It is therefore possible for women to serve behind the lines [of the battlefield], carrying out such tasks as cooking, nursing and similar womanly activities. Opening the door [to women to participate in jihad] amounts to a great evil.[92]

Azzam thus had an ambiguous position on women's participation in jihad, but that ambiguity made him somewhat more of a liberal than other jihadi ideologues at the time. Sayyid Imam al-Sharif (Dr. Fadl), for example, was more categorical in his opposition.[93] Azzam may therefore have been something of a door-opener for female involvement in jihad.

In recent years some women have used Azzam to justify attacks and foreign-fighter trips. For example, after stabbing British MP Stephen Timms in London in 2010, Roshonara Choudhry said in her police interrogation:

Q: And what changed... what made you get those strong feelings that you've obviously got now?
A: When I realised that I have an obligation to defend the people of Iraq and to fight on their side, that's when it changed my mind and also just like the

death tolls and the civilian, like casualties and the pictures from the prisons.

Q: OK, can you pinpoint the time when that changed or was it a gradual ... was there one particular incident?

A: Like, erm, after like listening to the lectures, I realised by obligation but I didn't wanna like fight myself and just thought other people should fight, like men, but then I found out that even women are supposed to fight as well so I thought I should join in.

Q: Where did you find that out from?

A: A YouTube video by Sheikh Abdullah Azzam.

Q: And what was he saying?

A: He was saying that when a Muslim land is attacked it becomes obligatory on every man, woman and child and even slave to go out and fight and defend the land.[94]

Similarly, in 2013, when two Somali-Norwegian girls left Oslo to join Islamic State in Syria, they sent a digital copy of *Defense of Muslim Lands* to their father to legitimize their decision.[95] Thus, whether Azzam intended it or not, his writings have been interpreted by some women as legitimizing their participation in combat.

We should not, however, overstate the emancipation of the Afghan Arab women. For one, those women who wanted to contribute were confined to the softest support activities. For another, their writings were not taken as seriously as those of the men. Very few of the contributions by women became feature articles in *al-Jihad* magazine; most were published in the women's section.[96] Moreover, the community was socially very conservative: Most Afghan Arab women wore the *niqab* (face veil), social life was gender segregated, and when women worked, they did so mostly with other women. As a result, many Afghan Arab men never interacted with women at all during their time in Pakistan and Afghanistan. At the same time, polygamy was not uncommon. Sometimes a woman would join her husband in Peshawar, only to find that he had taken a second wife. For example, an Egyptian named Muhammad al-Sharkawi went to Pakistan, and "soon, he had married a Pakistani woman and started a family. He sent for his Egyptian wife and two sons, who moved in with him in Peshawar."[97]

We get a realistic account of the journey to jihad from a woman's perspective in the testimony of Hafsa Rashwan, the wife of Abu Ubayda al-Banshiri:

It all began in 1983 about two months after we were married when we were in a bad financial situation. After he was discharged from the police, my husband started working as a construction laborer. He began thinking of leaving and we did and left for Saudi Arabia where we stayed for one month in Jeddah in a house belonging to Usamah Bin-Ladin. We then left for Medina and stayed for ten days ... Then, my husband thought of leaving for Pakistan and we were helped by someone whose name I do not recall exactly but I think it was al-Kardisi. This man brought us a work contract and permit to work in one of the relief agencies ... When we arrived in Pakistan, there was a car waiting for us that took us from Islamabad to Peshawar ... Many people used to drop by the house where we lived and I did not know them all. However, they were mujahidin from Egypt and some other Arab countries. They all had code names and concealed their real names ... We moved from our house to collective housing devoted to the families of the Arab mujahidin in the area of Hayatabad ... Other mujahidin and their families lived with us in the same building, such as Abu-Talhah and his family, Abu-Hafs and his family, and Shawqi Salamah, also known as Abu-Islam, and his wife ... We stayed in Hayatabad from 1990 until the end of 1992 when I was taken by surprise by him telling me that we will be leaving for Yemen. He did not tell me why he was leaving or anything about the trip. However, I found out some things from the wives of the other mujahidin I used to sit with, such as Um-Talhah, Um-Jihad, and others. I learned a lot about my husband's activities but he never told me anything. He refused to discuss such matters and would get angry with me, saying women are not supposed to know anything about jihad affairs.[98]

Life as a woman in the Afghan Arab community was decidedly unglamorous, but just as the men survived the hardships of war through companionship, so the women in Peshawar forged strong bonds with each other. The process of coming to terms with a rough life is captured well in the story of the Australian convert Rabiah Hutchinson:

[She] landed in Peshawar in August 1990 accompanied by her five youngest children ... they were greeted in Peshawar by a man who introduced himself as Abu Ubeidah, who was apparently a representative of the Maktab al-Khadamat ... [he] drove [them] to the new suburb of Hayatabad on Peshawar's outskirts, where MAK had a guesthouse and where many of the Afghan Arabs had made their homes ... "I was put in this house and left. We were told, don't go outside, it's dangerous," Rabiah remembers. "We could hear automatic gunfire and we'd go out at night on the roof and you could see explosions. Everyone had guns, you could hear the gunshots it was so exciting!" The excitement evaporated when the children fell violently ill from dysentery, which left them with uncontrollable diarrhoea and vomiting. It was the middle of summer with temperatures in the high thirties, sauna-like humidity and an air-conditioning system that worked if and when the sporadic power supply flickered into life. After a few days, Abu Ubeidah came back, with a surprise announcement. "Now you're here, you have to get married ... you can't stay here by yourself." Left to her own devices, Rabiah's first resort was to pray for guidance ... Next, she got dressed in her black abaya and hijab and covered her face with the Arab-style black veil, the niqab, which was customary attire for many Afghan-Arabs. Then she ventured up onto the flat roof of their house to survey the scene beyond its 3-metre-high mudbrick walls. The children were sick, I was stranded and alone, and I thought, what am I gonna do?[99]

Soon after, Hutchinson and her children moved to Pabbi, 20 kilometers east of Peshawar, where many foreign families lived. Her daughter Rahma, eight at the time, later recalled:

It was three streets made of poor mud houses on dirt roads, all connected to each other by lanes, and situated on each end of the streets was a tent with armed Afghan guards. It was at the time known as the village of the muhajirin (migrants), as many of the families of the mujahidin stayed there. It was summer and 50-degree heat. The ground was extremely dry and if anyone walked on it, it would cause clouds of dust.[100]

At Pabbi, the family of six had half a mudbrick house with a kitchen, a sitting room, and a bedroom. There was no electricity, no television, and no telephone line. The children had to look out for scorpions, and there were lots of cockroaches and mosquitoes.[101] Still, Hutchinson enjoyed it, in part because she had meaningful work at the local al-Jihad hospital, and in part because she and her children became part of a tight-knit community. As Hutchinson's biographer Sally Neighbour put it:

The women of Pabbi formed a kind of exclusive society of their own, in which their integral role was only enhanced by their separateness from the men. It was communally based, so that everything was shared; when a new *muhajir* arrived, the *ansar* – the resident Muslims whose duty it is to welcome them – would chip in to donate cooking pots, clothing, bedding, and whatever else they needed. When a woman had a baby the others would draw up a roster to share her cooking, cleaning and washing ... there were no "haves" and "have-nots"; and the dirt and deprivation only intensified the sense that they were part of an exclusive elite, united by their unyielding faith, their disdain for material wealth, and their righteous sense of mission ... It was like a little United Nations of Muslim fundamentalists.[102]

Hutchinson's account suggests that despite the factionalism and intrigues between leaders, there still was, on the ground, a strong sense of community among the foreign jihad volunteers. The connection between them and their Afghan hosts was another matter.

Tensions with Locals

The relationship between Arabs and Afghans in the 1980s jihad was generally good, but somewhat distant, and occasionally complicated.[103] On the one hand, there was mutual admiration and respect. Arab leaders such as Azzam regularly praised the courage and hospitality of the Afghans, and Afghan commanders often expressed gratitude for the support and sacrifices of the foreign fighters. Leaders on both sides went to great lengths to convey an image of unity.

At the grassroots level, too, people mostly got along. Afghans, it was often said, treated Arabs with particular respect because they viewed them as descendants of the Prophet.[104] Al-Qandahari mentions Khalid, an Afghan commander in Jalalabad, who "loved the Arabs dearly."[105] Abdallah Anas described the reception given to three Arabs who reached northern Afghanistan in 1985:

> This was the first event of its kind in Mazar-i-Sharif. When the Arabs arrived, it was as if a miracle had happened which shook the whole area! All the people of Mazar left their homes in excitement and walked for days in the snow to meet these people. Even a very old man, carrying a stick which he leant on in his right hand, and his grandson in his left hand, went to meet them. He wanted to show the Arabs to his grandson, because he himself was never before blessed with seeing an Arab.[106]

However, there was limited social interaction between Arabs and Afghans. It was the norm for Arabs to fight alongside Afghan Mujahidin in the field, but they rarely socialized with them in their spare time. Al-Qandahari writes that in Torkham in 1989, "we headed to the Arabs' post where the men had their own weapons and ammunition and were almost completely independent from the Afghans. They never even sat with an Afghan except during the battles."[107]

Deeper integration was rare, although a few Arabs forged strong friendships with Afghans. Abdallah Anas, for example, developed close links with Massoud and his men, spending a total of several years with them in the Panjshir valley. A small number of Arab men married Afghan women, but few if any Arab women married Afghan men. Al-Qandahari mentions the case of an Egyptian who was promised the daughter of an Afghan in Qandahar in 1989.[108] Some Arabs and Afghans also learned each other's languages. It was more common for Afghans to learn Arabic than the other way around, presumably because Islam recommends learning Arabic. Qandahari wrote that "the Afghans [in my unit] spent most of their time with us trying to learn Arabic, and they were very friendly people."[109] A few Arabs spoke Dari or Pashto. Abdallah Anas learned Dari during his time in Afghanistan, while a certain Abu Yusuf al-Filastini "spoke perfect Pashto."[110] A small number of Arabs went further:

Asad al-Rahman al-Jaza'iri was with us at Abd al-Raziq's post and had become a real Qandahari, speaking Pashto very fluently. His Pashto was even better than his Arabic, but he also wore their clothes and had gained their manners. He would enter the city as any other Qandahari, thus crossing the Communist checkpoints with no one ever finding out that he was in fact an Arab. I think that he even forgot that he was an Arab.[111]

However, below the surface the relationship was not always rosy. There are many examples of communication problems and tense situations between Arabs and Afghans during the war. One problem was language. Sometimes it could be a source of comedy, such as when an Algerian man boasted about his wife's couscous and almost caused a shootout because the word for couscous was "identical to an Afghani slang term that refers to a woman's genitalia."[112] More often, the language barrier simply prevented cooperation and socialization between Arabs and their hosts.

Another problem was lack of trust. This manifested itself in several different ways. Some Arabs, including Azzam himself, had a somewhat paternalistic attitude to the Afghans; he saw their leaders as notoriously quarrelsome and prone to telling half-truths about each other. "Arabs should not believe what an Afghan says of another Afghan, because they are mired in factionalism," he would tell other Arabs.[113] At the same time, some of the Arabs felt that the Afghans did not take them seriously as a fighting force and denied them the combat opportunities they yearned for. On some occasions Arabs felt that the Afghans actively undermined them during combat. In the battle of Jaji, as we saw in the previous chapter, some of Bin Ladin's men accused Sayyaf of seeking to undermine the Arab effort.

Conversely, some Afghans questioned the sincerity of the Arabs' commitment to the cause and accused them of vanity or other less noble motives. Ali Jalali and Lester Grau, who interviewed over a hundred Afghan Mujahidin field commanders, noted that "the overall impression of the Arab Mujahideen, gathered from our interviews, is that they were prima donnas who were more interested in taking videos than fighting."[114] They told unflattering anecdotes; one Afghan said, "We had a few Arabs in our base at the time [June 1987]. They were there for jihad credit and to see the fighting. 'If you are Muslims, help us collect the wounded,' we would tell them. They would refuse."[115] Another Afghan said that in the autumn of 1987 "We had some Arabs who were with us for jihad credit. They had a video camera and all they wanted to do was to take videos. They were of no value to us."[116] The distrust was largest between the Arabs and the non-Islamist Afghan Mujahidin; the so-called traditionalist parties of Gailani, Mujaddidi, and Muhammadi were skeptical of the Arab presence.[117]

A third source of tension was theology. Arabs and Afghans came from different Islamic legal traditions and had different views on what was considered appropriate ritual practice. For example, as Hanafis, the Afghans prayed differently from the Arabs, who were mostly Shafi'is and Hanbalis.[118] Afghans also had a somewhat more liberal view on rituals, and did things that the Arabs, especially those from the Gulf, considered inappropriate, such as wearing amulets, worshiping graves, and dancing. These differences would not have been a problem were it not for the fact that many Arabs were influenced by Salafism and saw it as their religious duty to correct the Afghans' behavior. According to Abu Ja'far al-Qandahari, "as soon as an Arab joined one of the posts, he would thus start analyzing and issuing bans until the Afghans learned the expressions 'this is prohibited', 'this is an innovation', 'this is apostasy.'"[119] Abdallah Azzam complained that "[the Arabs] accuse [the Afghans] of polytheism at the mere sight of amulets or flags on graves."[120] This interventionist attitude could cause bad blood between Arabs and Afghans, not least at the foot soldier level. In one instance,

One of the short-sighted Arab brothers noticed an amulet hanging on the neck of one of the Afghan *mujahidin* and he grabbed it with his hand thinking this was the best way to do *da'wa*, but the *mujahid* grabbed his hand and said, "What do you want?" "This is *shirk*!!" he said. The Afghan *mujahid* replied, "My sheikh made this amulet for me." The Arab did not relent but tried to take it away by force, saying, "This is *shirk* and you have to take it off," so the Afghan stepped back and said, "*You* are the polytheist," loaded the gun and wanted to shoot the Arab, but fortunately some brothers intervened.[121]

In another instance, a Salafi Arab doctor working in a hospital in Wardak received a gravely wounded Afghan fighter, but refused to treat him until he had removed the amulet from around his neck.[122] The request incensed the man's comrades, who ended up chasing the doctor from the hospital. In yet another episode, sparks flared when a team of Arab and Afghan fighters found a damaged Qur'an in a bombed house, whereupon the Arabs insisted on burning the remains of the Qur'an, which the Hanbali school instructs them to do in such cases. The Afghans, by contrast, viewed burning the Qur'an as blasphemy and protested vehemently.[123] Funerary rites were another contentious issue. Here is what happened after the death of a certain Abu Salih al-Yamani in near Qandahar in 1988:

When we arrived at the graveyard, there were many Afghans who had come to bid the martyr farewell and pray on his body. However, the Arabs would not allow it and a blind strife almost erupted between the two groups ... the Arabs started blaming the Afghans for the things they put on the graves, seeing how the latter placed on the tomb of the martyr a flag that distinguished it from the other tombs. Luckily, an Afghan sheikh contained the situation and talked to the Arabs in perfect Arabic, telling them that the Hanafi sect imposed the prayer on the martyr, "so if you do not want to pray on him, let the Afghans do it to put an end to strife." Indeed, the Afghans performed their funerary prayer while the Arabs stepped aside in anger saying that victory was delayed by these unbearable decadent practices.[124]

Quarrels over ritual became so numerous that some Mujahidin leaders began imploring the Arabs to respect Afghan customs. Once, Burhanuddin Rabbani reportedly gave an emotional speech in which he told the story of a school in Peshawar which experienced a veritable riot in response to the Salafi instruction of the Arabs. According to Rabbani, one of the pupils had said with tears in his eyes: "My father was killed in the jihad in defense of the Hanafi sect and I will never betray my father."[125]

Not all the Arabs were equally intolerant. As noted in Chapter 8, Abdallah Azzam was a vocal advocate of respecting Afghan practices:

> If you want to wage jihad and perform this duty in the land of jihad, then you have to deal with the Afghans in the correct way; which means you pray like the Afghans, the Hanafi way ... either you hold on to [your version of] these external details and leave the duty of jihad, or you respect the Hanafi school or jurisprudence and execute this great duty.[126]

Azzam also defended the Afghans against the objections of senior Arab scholars. Abdallah Anas recalls a discussion between Saudi Grand Mufti Abd al-Aziz Bin Baz and Abdallah Azzam over how to deal with Afghan prayer customs, in which Azzam took the more liberal, pragmatic position.[127] In his view, the Afghans should be given time to change their ways gradually. Azzam even introduced cultural-sensitivity training in the training camps for Arabs: "When the sheikh set up educational camps ... he insisted on having cultural quizzes at the end of each course, and they included questions about the Afghan social situation, and the main one was the important question 'What is Abu Hanifa's view on amulets?'"[128] In mid-1989 Azzam also published a list of twelve rules for Arabs to follow while they were inside Afghanistan:

1) Make sure not to take sides among the Afghans.
2) Do not criticize the Hanafi *madhhab* in front of Afghans.
3) Do not eat food in front of them without giving them some of it or eat it in secret.
4) Do not believe what the Afghans say when they discuss disagreements between them.
5) Do not disagree in front of the Afghans; it will lessen your standing.
6) Show complete obedience to the Arab commander in your province. ...
7) Pray according to the Hanafi *madhhab*, and do likewise with purification. ...
8) If they ask you about your *madhhab*, be truthful about your being a Shafi'i or otherwise; do not lie to them.

9) Seek to mend differences between people and try to extinguish the fire of discord [*fitna*].
10) Establish a Qur'an study house, however small, in every front you find yourselves in.
11) Divide the aid between all the organizations, and make sure that those who are closer to the enemy or stronger militarily get a larger share according to their needs.
12) Visit all the fronts in every organization, and do not stay with a single organization, so as to avoid tensions between the organizations, and so that the Arabs do not become a separate group or party.[129]

Sometimes, even Azzam was frustrated with the Afghan level of religious knowledge. Muhammad Yasir says that once, in the Badr camp in early 1984,

> he prayed the morning prayer with us, and he read Surat al-Sajida in the first *rak'a*. It was the first time the Mujahidin had prayed to this sura, so the worshipers behind him thought he had done three *rak'a*s and they turned around and left the prayer, saying this Arab sheikh prayed the morning prayer with three *rak'a*s. When he was done, he got up and preached; he was very angry about it, and he was angry with me and angry with the scholars in the group. He said, "You have failed to provide this people its due rights; you have not given them a proper religious education."[130]

This, however, was a rare loss of composure from Azzam. He generally chose to overlook the Afghans' shortcomings. He once admitted, "Yes I know there are all these issues, but this cause is the Muslims' best hope, so I focus on their positive traits."[131]

Many Arabs shared Azzam's pragmatism and adapted to local custom. "We [therefore] decided to perform their prayer, earn their trust, and not to address any topic of dispute," one Arab later wrote.[132] In his memoir, Abu Ja'far al-Qandahari describes Afghan rituals in positive terms:

> The Afghans also performed other rituals which carried great meanings, despite the condemnation of some. They wrapped a Qur'an in a turban, two of them carried the turban from both ends with the Qur'an inside of it before the post's exit, and the Afghans stood in one long queue passing one by one beneath the Qur'an and putting on the ground all that they were carrying in terms of money and belongings except for their arms and

ammunition in reference to the fact that they relinquished the worldly things for Allah. This was a beautiful message.[133]

Al-Qandahari also mentions an Arab commander named Abu Sulayman who joined in an Afghan war dance rather than condemn it:

> During these great fights which entailed massive losses, the Afghans prepared themselves with different means to raise their morale. Among the latter methods was one in which they gathered, held hands, and performed the dance of war which revolved around determination and solidarity. However, many of the Arabs condemned that and *amir* Abu Sulayman urged them to participate instead. He thus headed toward the Afghans, stood in the circle, and performed the war dance. If only there were more scholars like you O Abu Sulayman.[134]

Vahid Mojdeh, an Afghan who worked for the Services Bureau, also said,

> Arabs did not have any problems in Khost, Paktiya, Paktika, Nuristan … because sometimes the people of these areas would go to Arab world for business or other purposes. They observed how they were praying, how they were performing their duties, Islamic obligations. And also, in Nuristan there was a Hizb-e-Islami commander, Mawlawi Jamil al-Rahman. He was a Salafi, he also understands how they were praying, so they did not have problems with these guys. But with others, they had somehow conflicts.[135]

In fact, some Arabs were also frustrated with the Arab Salafis' intolerance. Abdallah al-Rumi, a correspondent for *al-Jihad* magazine, used to hide his camera when he met new groups of Arabs "because he was afraid that the Arab Salafis would object to him using it."[136]

Sometimes the cultural chauvinism went in the other direction. According to Jean-Christophe Notin, the Afghans considered the Saudis in particular to be badly behaved Bedouins, because they eat with the whole hand as opposed to with only the last few phalanxes.[137] Toilet habits were another point of controversy:

> Qari Ibrahim was sent to engineer Bashir following an incident I heard of once in Shakamesh, one thing he reproves. The issue is, Afghans disparage a man who urinates while standing. It is a disdained habit indeed, but Afghans consider it as very loathsome. Among engineer Bashir's men was a French Algerian who was not, unfortunately, up to the mission. So engineer Bashir exclaimed: "You go to Massoud and send me people who urinate while standing!"[138]

Afghans were also skeptical of blood donations:

> After meeting with Sheikh Yunus Khalis, Abu Dharr al-Libi came to ask us to donate blood because there was a shortage at the hospital and many were wounded. Most of the Arabs went with him and before we reached the hospital he took us to a restaurant and ordered us kabab and juice. This became the object of jokes. In the hospital, the Afghans were looking at us donating blood with panic and surprise since this Bedouin population had naïve ideas about blood and its importance at the level of one's health. They thought that whoever donated his blood remained weak for the rest of his life and unable to approach his wife. Moreover the ignorant sheikhs prohibited the donation of blood because they believed this established familial ties since they thought that sperm was created from blood![139]

On a few rare occasions, tensions between Arabs and Afghans deteriorated to outright hostility. One such situation emerged in Qandahar in 1989:

> While the Khosh Ab battle was at its fiercest, an extremely dangerous thing occurred. A large council including all the scholars of Qandahar gathered and issued a statement saying that the Arabs were Wahhabis and infidels. The statement also ordered each leader to get rid of the Arabs with him or to oust them ... The commanders, however, refused to relinquish the Arabs, although it was not easy to disregard the calls of the scholars, while party leaders at the highest levels acted to extinguish this strife. Hekmatyar came in person to see what was happening and wanted to build a post just for the Arabs. But Abu Khabib rejected the idea since he was afraid that the Qandaharis would attack the post, considering it a Wahhabi one. The leaders of Hizb-e Islami thus pledged to protect the Arabs and Hekmatyar set a meeting for the scholars of Qandahar who were loyal to the parties so that they would issue a statement contradicting the previous one. Despite that, Abu Khabib was concerned about the Arabs and decided to distance them from the province until the situation calmed down. Most of the Arabs headed to different provinces while others returned home.[140]

Such standoffs were the exception, however. Most of the time the foreign fighters got along just fine with their local hosts. As Darryl Li has argued, the widespread view of Arabs as puritan hardliners and Afghans as Sufi-oriented pragmatists is a severe oversimplification.[141] Afghans could be intolerant, Arabs could be accommodating, and there was a good amount of cultural cross-pollination between the two communities.

The Arab relationship with "the other locals" – the Pakistanis – was more distant than complicated. Even though most of the Arabs were based in Pakistan, there was limited interaction with Pakistanis. The Pakistanis were the largest non-Arab foreign-fighter contingent in Afghanistan, numbering somewhere in the low thousands, most of whom fought in the late 1980s.[142] However, because they were so many, they had their own training infrastructure, and the language barrier complicated interaction with Arabs. For example, in the late 1980s the Pakistani organization Markaz al-Da'wa wa'l-Irshad had at least two training camps for Pakistanis in Afghanistan; one in Paktia called Muaskar-e Taiba and another in Kunar called Muaskar-e Aqsa.[143] Mustafa Hamid also mentions two Pakistani camps in Khost in 1989–1990 called Salman al-Farsi and Badr.[144] In the Arab sources there are references to Pakistanis, but they are strikingly few considering the size of the Pakistani contingent.[145]

The Pakistani sources suggest that the degree of interaction with Arabs varied by ideological orientation. The Deobandi fighters rarely crossed paths with Arabs. The 350-page autobiography of Mufti Mohammad Rafi Usmani, a Pakistani member of Harakat al-Jihad al-Islami who fought in Afghanistan in the late 1980s, contains just two brief references to encounters with Arabs. In 1988 he took part in a battle in a unit comprised of sixty mostly Afghan *mujahidin*, and "there also was in this unit an Arab mujahid, Abu al-Harith."[146] At another point Usmani found himself on a battlefront with "a hundred and twenty mujahideen ... Ten of them were Arabs, Twenty from Philippines and Malaysia, many from Bangla Desh and a majority from Pakistan."[147]

The Brotherhood-linked Jamaat-e Islami seems to have had much to do with senior Arabs in Peshawar, but less to do with Arab fighters in Afghanistan. As we saw in Chapters 7 and 8, Kamal al-Sananiri was hosted in Peshawar by Jamaat-e Islami in 1980, and Azzam was in touch with the group throughout the 1980s. Curiously, however, there is little evidence, in either the Arab or Pakistani sources, of interaction between Jamaat-e Islami fighters and Arabs. This is despite the group having, according to Syed Shahzad, a camp called Badr in Khost which "in the early 1980s ... came under the command of Bakht Zameen Khan, who organized a network of thousands of Pakistani volunteers to fight against Soviet forces in Afghanistan."[148] This discrepancy is hard to explain. It could be that I have missed important Pakistani sources; but if not, then either the Jamaat-e Islami fighters were fewer than Shahzad suggests, or they chose, for unknown reasons, to avoid Arabs.[149]

The Salafi-oriented Pakistanis sent by the Markaz al-Da'wa wa'l-Irshad (MDI) had more to do with the Arabs in the field. The autobiography of Amir Hamza, who went to Afghanistan with the MDI in August 1987, mentions at least eighteen Arabs by name.[150] He notably describes training in a camp in Paktika in late 1987 under Abu Burhan al-Suri, Abu Faris al-Suri, and Abu al-Bara' al-Yamani.[151] Hamza says the camp had recruits from 36 different countries, including 60–70 Saudis and 350 Filipinos. Later he describes joining Jamil al-Rahman's forces in Kunar where he encountered yet more Arabs. He highlights three Saudis who worked regularly with MDI in Kunar, namely, Abu Abd al-Rahman, Abu Abd al-Aziz, and Ahmad Sa'd al-Ghamidi.[152] Hamza also mentions Usama Bin Ladin and describes meeting two of Bin Ladin's commanders named Abu Sufyan and Shafqat.[153] Throughout, Hamza speaks very highly of the Arabs and their contribution to the war. Hamza's account suggests that the Pakistanis in MDI interacted more with Salafi Arabs in Kunar than with the Arabs in the Services Bureau and al-Qaida.

On the whole, most Afghan Arabs did not spend much time with Pakistani foreign fighters. The Afghan Arab community was generally quite inward-looking and self-sufficient vis-à-vis both Pakistanis and Afghans. Azzam's vision of a multinational Muslim army in perfect harmony never materialized. However, this did not matter much for individual Afghan Arabs.

Otherworldly Experience

What was it like to be a foreign fighter in 1980s Afghanistan? Fortunately, we have many detailed first-person accounts to shed light on the matter.[154] Each person's experience was different, so it is difficult to generalize, but three themes recur: the thrills and hardships of military life, the pleasures of companionship, and the sense of religious purpose.

The typical trajectory of a new Arab volunteer was roughly as follows. After arriving at Peshawar airport or bus station, he would call the Services Bureau or some other prior contact and be taken to one of the guest houses for Arab volunteers. These were ordinary houses at various locations around Peshawar which in layout and atmosphere resembled youth hostels, with bunk beds or mattresses in communal bedrooms and a constant stream of people moving in and out. At this point he would choose a *kunya*, or *nom de guerre*, and cease using his real name. Kunyas were created on the model Abu + *[name]* + *[place adjective]*, for example Abu Muhammad al-Iraqi or Abu Hafs al-Amriki. Here is an extract from the memoir of Abu Ja'far al-Qandahari, an Egyptian who came to Peshawar in 1988. He had flown from Cairo to Karachi and on to Islamabad, from where he took a minibus to Peshawar:

Finally, after four long hours on the road, I arrived to Peshawar. I was very exhausted and had only one telephone number in my pocket. I performed the evening prayer in one of the mosques ... I called the number in my possession from one of the stores and the man on the other end of the phone gave me an address to meet him at ... I gave the address to a driver and was finally able to arrive at Bayt al-Ansar. The tenants all came here from all Muslim countries to support their Afghan brothers in their fight ... The house we were at offered food and shelter to all the newcomers and sent them to the training camps. Then it would receive them again before sending them to the different fronts. Other *mujahidin* would visit the house for rest or to take a break. Many came to write down speeches or send letters and contact their families via telephone.[155]

After a few days of settling in, most recruits would be taken to the border areas for ten to fifteen days of basic training at one of the Afghan Mujahidin camps, typically at Sayyaf's Sada camp.[156] We get a sense of life at Sada from an article in *al-Jihad* magazine from August 1986 that showcases the newly opened camp.[157] The article says the curriculum includes weapons practice, physical exercise, martial arts training, lectures on religious topics, and more. The feature includes several pictures, including one of Azzam giving a lecture and another of recruits receiving martial arts training, accompanied by the caption "the physically strong believer is better than the weak believer."

After basic training, trajectories diverged; many returned home, some stayed on for more advanced instruction, others sought out combat opportunities inside Afghanistan, while yet others got involved in support activities in and around Peshawar. Many did all of the above at different stages. We find an account of a fairly typical trajectory in the court testimony of Jamal al-Fadl, who went to Pakistan in 1988. Al-Fadl describes a hectic series of trips back and forth between the border areas and Peshawar and the various types of military training he received along the way.

Q. Once you arrived, once you got to the airport at Peshawar Pakistan, what did you do?
A. We went to the hotel for two days and somebody come, he give us a little lecture about what going inside the war and about jihad and about the rule ... He tell us about the rule, if you go inside what you have to do, and what going on inside Afghanistan. And you have to go inside the guesthouse first to put all your stuff. And when you go to the guesthouse, you go to take your passport, your documents, your money and save it for you as you're going to tell you more about the rule when you go inside.
Q. So did you actually take your documents, your passport and your money and give them to someone?
A. Yes. We went after that, we went to the guesthouse and we give them – each one, he gives them his stuff and they put it in envelope and they give you nickname ... Nickname mean when you go for training or you go inside Afghanistan you not going to use your true name, you going to use a nickname for that and you choose your nickname ...
Q. [Then] Where did you go?
A. We went to Khalid Ibn Walid camp ... We went to Khalid Ibn Walid camp with other brother and the camp is for training, for training new people ... I got training for legal weapons regular weapons ... Like small, the personal small gun and Kalashnikov [and] RPG ... When we finish our training [45 days later] the emir of the camp, Abu Shaheed al-Falastini, he say you have to go inside [Afghanistan] because your training is finished and the people need you.
Q. So where did you go ... ?
A. We went to Areen guesthouse. It's like guesthouse before you go inside the war. ... after that we go to Jaji in front line.
Q. When you went to Jaji, the front line, did you help out fighting in and around the front in Afghanistan?
A. Yes, I went with Izzeldine al Saudi group.
Q. For how long did you spend with the Izzeldine al Saudi group?
A. Around two weeks.

Q. How much time in total do you recall spending at the front at or about that time?
A. Around two months ... After that, me and other brother, we went back to Peshawar ... to Bait al Ansar ... Bait al Ansar, for people when they came back from inside the fight, they go over there and they got dressed. If someone he got hit, he go to clinic, if someone he wants to check, he go to clinic. Someone he wants to buy something from the market, he go before they give you another order ...
Q. And where did you go next?
A. I went to near Kabul in Afghanistan ...
Q. Where did you go after that? Did you ever go back to another camp?
A. Yes. When we finished in Chakary our time, we went back to the guesthouse in Peshawar, and after that they tell us to go to [another] camp in Afghanistan.[158]

For many recruits, this was the first encounter with military life. They came from protected civilian lives and suddenly found themselves in strenuous training programs and bloody battles. Many seem to have found it thrilling and exhilarating. Abdallah Anas, for examples, describes the emotional rush of finding himself in the field.[159] However, it was no walk in the park. It was a life of physical exhaustion, little sleep, simple food, and extreme temperatures. Medical support was almost non-existent, so getting injured involved extended pain, risk of infections, and possibly slow death. As the Pakistani brigadier Mohammad Yousaf wrote, "the time between being hit and receiving qualified medical attention is more often measured in days, rather than minutes. Amputations without anaesthetics were commonplace, using a knife, or even an axe, to chop off a mangled foot or leg. Many died of shock."[160] A Saudi fighter named Amin described the problem of finding treatment after injuring his leg severely in a car accident near Parachinar in Pakistan:

"They ... put me in the car while I was still hallucinating ... Then they dropped me off at the Jihad hospital in Parachinar ... an Egyptian doctor came ... and began to treat me quickly. He tried his best to stop the bleeding, and he couldn't. He said: Then there is only one way left. He began to clean the wound and sew it. At that moment, the Pakistani intelligence arrived ... The area is [a] military area and very sensitive. So they came immediately and began to talk at the door. Quickly, the doctor told me: pretend to have passed out ... He put me in the ambulance and got on board, may God bless him. And we headed to Peshawar." Amin continues: "All attempts to stop the bleeding failed ... and we did not arrive in Peshawar until 11 at night ... the accident took place at 10 or 10:30 in the morning. And there, at Badr hospital – and that was the only hospital available to the Arabs then – there they received me – and did first aid on me first and then took me to the operations room.[161]

Similarly, J. M. Berger recounts the ordeal of Clement Hampton-El (aka Abdullah Rashid), a US convert who traveled to Afghanistan in 1988:

Rashid's trip to the front lines was fraught with problems. First he was stricken with malaria and spent long days lying in bed. When he recovered ... he ventured onto the battlefield ... and promptly stepped on a land mine ... It took eighteen hours for Rashid's fellow combatants to get him to a medical facility ... "They carried us by stretcher for a while, first on their backs, then on stretchers, then on mules,' Rashid said. "Nobody ever immobilized my leg. All the way there, for 14 hours, just flop, flop, flop, flop. Blood comin' in and out in and out. I was yelling and screaming."[162]

Others got serious diseases. The Yemeni fighter Mustafa Badi contracted malaria while in the al-Ma'sada camp and had to be brought back to Peshawar, an ordeal so traumatic that he devoted an entire chapter to it in his memoirs.[163]

And even if you personally escaped harm, you were likely to witness horrific scenes up close: your friends dying, your comrades suffering grotesque injuries, and enemy soldiers in terrible condition. This is not to mention the shock, fear, and confusion of finding oneself under heavy bombardment or assault. Abu Ja'far al-Qandahari described seeing his friend Akrama al-Jaza'iri shot in the head in 1989:

It was a horrid sight since his back was lying on the wall and his head was wide open. His brain was intact and in its place but the bones of his head above the eyebrows were non-existent ... The tragedy was that he was still alive and stayed alive for a few hours. I saw blood flowing from his head as though it was a fire hose ... I tried to pull him out from this dammed room but he was a heavy giant. I tried to push him while maintaining his head in an upward position so that his brains would not fall out.[164]

Abdallah Anas described a Russian air raid on one of Massoud's camps in 1985:

A shower of rockets started pouring down on us like rain in the bottom of the hole. In less than five minutes, we suffered the loss of more than ten men.

Blood and body parts splashed over the rocks that turned blood red. An unimaginable sight ... Rockets hit us in the middle. We did not know where to bury the martyrs. The region is not earthy so we could [not] dig in the ground and lay them to rest. It was all rocks. We gathered the bodies in one spot and placed rocks over them.[165]

Al-Qandahari also admitted to being frightened by the things he saw:

I thought of myself as being very courageous and I was never afraid of anything. I was not really afraid of death maybe because I was so far away from the battlefield, the blood, the body parts and the danger. But when you see death with your own eyes and when you are permanently in danger, you cannot help but fear death. Maybe it was a lack of faith on my part, since Abu Dujana for example wished for death and Abu Mu'adh was praying all day long to get killed. I tried to be like them but I could not.[166]

Perhaps because of these intense experiences, the fighters developed a strong sense of community. It is clear from the accounts that life in the training camps and trenches was marked by an atmosphere of companionship and camaraderie. There was lightheartedness and humor: Fighters told funny stories, gave each other nicknames, and played practical jokes on each other. There was friendly teasing, as in the following joke about Tamim al-Adnani's weight: "Shaykh Tamim weighs about 140 kilograms, and that's why whenever the shaykh gets mad at someone, he says: 'I will sit on you', that's it! And what that means is, that he is going to kill you!"[167] By all accounts, the atmosphere among the men in the field was positive and optimistic.

At the same time, there is an undertone of emotional detachment in several of the autobiographies. For all the kind words about friendship, several fighters come across as somewhat fatalist about their comrades dying, moving on to another camp, or otherwise disappearing from their lives. It is almost as if friends are replaceable; if you lose one, there will be another, and besides, the one you lost is in heaven anyway. This could be a feature of their writing, but more likely it reflects a way of coping with the reality that friends often disappeared.

The foreign-fighter experience was also a spiritual one. Many Afghan Arabs seem to have found their time in the field to be religiously intense. This is not surprising, given that the volunteers were religious men who had come precisely because they viewed the war as divinely sanctioned. However, it is perhaps not obvious, especially to secular readers, just how all-pervasive and intense the religious sentiment was in the Afghan Arab community.

For one thing, life in the community was structured around religious rituals and activities. Practically everyone prayed all the five daily prayers, fasted extensively, regularly read the Qur'an and other religious literature, and generally followed conservative moral codes. For example, we can read of a Saudi fighter named Khalid Qablan, who

> would choose to stand guard from midnight to 1:00 a.m., then he would stay up in prayer until the Fajr. He would make the adhan for Fajr, then pray. After that, he would begin his adhkar. He would fast every Monday and Thursday – continuously –the White Days (the 13th, 14th, 15th day of each month), and the six days of Shawwal. They also said that on the night before Friday – and it was the final night of his life – he stood guard from midnight to 1:00 a.m., stayed up in prayer until the Fajr, made the adhan for Fajr, prayed, made his morning adhkar, then we moved to the location of the battle for that day. On the way there, he recited [surat] "al-Kahf," and increased in his invoking of peace and blessings upon the Prophet.[168]

For another, religious issues dominated conversations. It was common to discuss theology and tell stories from the early history of Islam. A prominent topic was martyrdom and paradise. They talked at length about the many wonderful things that awaited the fallen in the afterlife. Martyrdom was a major preoccupation for the Afghan Arabs, and it was something that many of them ostensibly yearned for.[169] It was common to volunteer for highly risky operations and to express sadness or even weep if you survived them. In fact, we probably underestimate the degree to which the Afghan Arabs were preoccupied by martyrdom, because those who sought it the most did not survive. The people who lived to write books were the more pragmatically minded individuals who did not go out of their way to die.

As we saw in Chapter 11, Abdallah Azzam had contributed greatly to this martyrology with his writings. He relayed stories about dead fighters smiling, smelling of musk, not decomposing for months, and projecting beams of light from their graves into the air. These stories caught the imagination of the volunteers, and became a conversation topic in the field. Al-Qandahari, for example, writes:

> Then, surprisingly, I was able to smell a beautiful scent coming out of him, it was that of musk. I am sure of that. Abu Suleiman was sitting next to me and I wanted to make sure that my senses were right so I turned toward him and

even before asking my question he smiled at me and said: "Yes that is the smell of musk." In the past, I had seen many martyrs but never smelled this lovely odor.[170]

Another big topic of conversation was dreams and visions. The foreign fighters believed, as do most religious Muslims, that God may convey messages to the believer through dreams.[171] Dreams can notably contain hints about what will happen in the future, or injunctions about what to do, and jihadis are afraid to miss these messages. The Afghan Arabs therefore spent a lot of time discussing and interpreting their dreams and visions. Most of the dream accounts were interpreted in relation to martyrdom. For example, "Asadallah had [a] vision predicting his martyrdom. After the interpretation reached, he had more visions. The next day, he saw himself walking while followed by four brides. One of the Mujahidin had a much more exciting vision since he saw him driving a bus filled with brides."[172] In another account:

I noticed [Sayyaf al-Masri] wanted to follow Assadullah by any means, and he started to have martyrdom visions almost every day. He once dreamt he was trapped in a destroyed house like the ones surrounding us and trying to exit it. Whenever he climbed through a window, or broke through a door, he found himself still standing in the rubble, until he opened one door and reached a magnificent garden with green trees that were too wonderful to describe. I thus heralded his martyrdom and his rise to heaven and his joy was indescribable.[173]

Similarly:

When I was in the post of Abdul Razeq the second, I had a dream about a giant which threw away all the *mujahidin* who tried to ride him. When I succeeded, he tried to throw me off by all means possible but I remained steadfast on his back, at which point he turned his head and bit off my left foot. This caused me a pain I will never forget since it was real pain that made me yell while I was dreaming and fall on the ground. When I woke up, I realized I was going to encounter great harm and related the vision to my companions.[174]

According to the Islamic dream tradition, dreams do not necessarily mean what they literally convey; they need to be interpreted, and some individuals are said to be better at interpreting dreams than others. In the Afghan Arab community there were certain people who had a reputation for being good dream interpreters, and were often called upon to make sense of dreams. The ability was considered an innate gift and not something you could study for. Abu Ja'far al-Qandahari was one such person: "I thank God who taught me how to interpret dreams."[175]

Many Arab Afghans also believed in *jinn* (genies), spiritual beings believed to occasionally possess a person or an object. For example, at one point during the battle of Jaji, Usama Bin Ladin suspected that Tamim al-Adnani had been possessed by a *jinn*, because he "began to pull at his beard and his hair and cry and scream" over the decision to temporarily retreat.[176] Flagg Miller describes an interesting audiotape from July 1989 featuring a "genie talking with Arabs in Afghanistan."[177] It is a conversation between a voice purporting to be a genie by the name Abdallah and around seven Arab fighters. The men ask the "genie" various questions about what genies can do and whether they can harm humans, and it willingly replies. It is unclear whether the conversation is deliberately staged or whether the participants believed they were interacting with a real genie.

On the whole, the Afghan jihad experience was otherworldly compared with the ordinary lives most fighters left behind. It involved extended isolation in landscapes that were literally moon-like, as well as intense emotional and spiritual experiences. It was a place where supernatural events could happen at any moment and where paradise was just a grenade's throw away. For young men raised in the suburbs of Algiers or Cairo, it must have been a special, not to say magical, experience. One former fighter later described it as a "bubble," and said "we lived in our own world."[178] Perhaps for this reason, many Arab volunteers liked it so much they never looked back. One Abu Asim al-Iraqi "was engaged, but he phoned his fiancée and told her to marry someone else, as he was not coming back. 'Here is my life, and here I will die,' he said."[179] Another fighter named Sa'ud "spent about a year and eight months in jihad until he could no longer remember what his children's faces looked like. He used to say, 'It's God's mercy on me that I can no longer remember the faces so that I don't miss them.'"[180]

But behind this façade of enthusiasm was probably also a good deal of sadness and homesickness. The emotional strain of the foreign-fighter experience is palpable in the many letters from fighters to their families – and vice versa – that were published in *al-Jihad* magazine. In one letter, titled "Letter to my Son," an Afghan Arab on the frontlines addresses his only child, saying he recently saw him in a dream, misses him very much, and looks forward to be united with him in heaven.[181] We can also read other letters titled "Letter from a Murabit to his Son," "Letter from a Mujahid to his Wife," "Letter from a Muhajir to his Mother."[182] Similar letters went in the other direction, as in the "Letter from the Wife of a Mujahid," the "Letter from a Wife to her Husband," and the "Letter from the Wife of a Martyr to her Mujahid Brother."[183] In addition to these public statements, we can assume that many private messages also went between homesick fighters and their loved ones. It was possible to send messages by regular mail to some of the fronts; an Egyptian fighter in Qandahar "received a letter from his village carrying the address: Quetta – Qandahar – Malajat front – Muhammad Ayub Agha post – Assadallah al-Masri."[184] Let us also not forget that these testimonies are from the people who chose to stay. The majority of Arab volunteers did not stay very long, and for some of them emotional pressures may have affected the decision to leave. Foreign fighting was not for everyone.

Jihadi Culture

The Afghan Arab community also developed a distinct new lifestyle, with its own music, poetry, iconography, sartorial style, and social practices. This "jihadi culture" would outlive Afghanistan, spread to radical Islamist groups around the world, and survive – albeit in modified form – to this day. The jihadi culture that emerged in the 1980s did not come from nowhere; each of its constituent elements was rooted in older traditions. However, it was in 1980s Afghanistan that these various elements were combined into the medley that we associate today with jihadi culture.

The lifestyle reflected their understanding of how a good *mujahid* should behave. This understanding was in turn informed largely by their reading of how the Prophet Muhammad and his companions had lived during their military campaigns in the seventh century. The Afghan Arabs had a romantic vision of the *mujahid* as a brave, chivalrous, ascetic soldier of God. Their culture reflected this backward-looking worldview, and thus included old artistic genres such as poetry and *anashid*, often in archaic forms. Moreover, jihadi culture encouraged expressions of emotion and artistic sensitivity, making it "softer" than some other military cultures. Where modern Western militaries tell soldiers to be hard and stoic, jihadi culture encourages fighters to show feelings and enjoy art. This is best illustrated with the jihadi appreciation for weeping; rather than being associated with weakness and femininity, male weeping was appreciated by Afghan Arabs as a sign of devotion.

The Arab jihadi culture differed somewhat from the culture of the Afghan Mujahidin. As we saw above, the Afghans engaged in things like dance and music with drums that the more conservative Arabs did not approve of. Still, there was a degree of overlap and mutual inspiration between the two communities; many Arabs, for example, enjoyed songs in Pashto and Dari, and vice versa.

Arabs also differed among themselves over which cultural expressions were appropriate. Those who came from a Salafi background were notably skeptical of the use of images and music, and advised that such elements be kept to a minimum. Thus *al-Jihad* magazine, which was run mostly by people with a Muslim Brotherhood background, made much more liberal use of photographs than did Jamil al-Rahman's *al-Mujahid*, which was by and for Salafis. Similarly, Salafis at the time warned against excessive use of *anashid*, on the grounds that they could distract from more important religious activities. These debates show that the jihadi aesthetic has undergone a process of liberalization, because today jihadi propaganda is highly audiovisual and the permissibility of images and *anashid* is taken for granted.

One of the main elements of the jihadi culture that emerged in the 1980s was *anashid, a capella* hymns with religious lyrics. *Anashid* are an old Islamic cultural expression with roots in pre-Islamic times, and to this day are enjoyed by many Muslims. Since the 1960s and 1970s, however, Islamists have produced *anashid* with political lyrics, and the Afghanistan war inspired numerous *anashid* about jihad. Jihadi *anashid* were very popular among the Afghan Arabs. Abdallah Anas later said, "You know, the *anashid*, they had an influence, the jihadi *anashid*, *anashid* of the Islamic awakening, Abu Ratib and others, Abu al-Jud."[185] The Afghan Arabs would sing or listen to *anashid* in many different settings: in the guest houses, in the camps, and on the frontlines. For example, during the battle of Zhawar in 1986, while the Arabs were waiting in Miranshah, "they all swore allegiance to [Azzam] amidst emotional Islamic *anashid* [*anashid islamiyya hamasiyya*]".[186] Some fighters became known as talented singers; for example, *al-Jihad* magazine at one point paid tribute to a fallen Afghan Arab described as the "*nashid*-singer of Ta'if."[187] Afghan Arab leaders promoted the genre; as we saw in Chapter 9, the Services Bureau's audiovisual department sold cassette tapes with jihadi *anashid*.

Another prominent element of jihadi culture was poetry. Poetry is also an age-old feature of mainstream Arab culture which in the 1980s was used by Islamists to glorify jihad. Afghan Arabs recited poetry in a variety of contexts. A former trainee at the al-Ma'sada camp recalled "the Syrian Abu Hasan, a lawyer in his late sixties and a great poet whose verses motivated the whole camp and set hearts on fire. He used to write great songs for the young men to sing when training started in Ramadan."[188] The very first issue of *al-Jihad* magazine included a substantial poetry section, and there was poetry in practically every subsequent issue, sometimes over three or four pages. In the course of the war, many hundreds of poems were written about the Afghan jihad, both by fighters and by observers in the Arab world.[189] Abdallah Azzam himself was very well versed in poetry. Most of his texts and speeches are sprinkled with verse. According to Vahid Mojdeh, an Afghan who worked closely with the Services Bureau, "Azzam knew by heart an endless treasury of Arab epic poems and exactly how to use them in provoking the sentiments of Arab youths. It was the magic of his speech that brought thousands of young Arabs to Afghanistan for jihad."[190]

Jihadi culture had many other components, for it was an entire lifestyle. Many Afghan Arabs wore Afghan dress when they returned to their home countries or moved to other conflict zones such as Bosnia and Algeria, as a way of displaying their jihadi pedigree. The 1980s also saw the beginnings of a specifically jihadi iconography in the magazines that were produced in Peshawar. The period also saw the first jihadi videos and the emergence of a cinematographic tradition with recognizable themes and techniques.

Leaders in the Afghan Arab community seem to have actively promoted the development and consumption of jihadi culture. For example, the article in *al-Jihad* magazine on the Sada camp highlighted the non-military dimension of camp life, saying that it involves "sitting before a jihadi film in the evening, or singing Islamic *anashid* which make the heart pulsate," "practicing the *sunna* of fasting and drawing from its benefits," and "following the prophetic instructions from [when] one wakes up in the morning till one goes to bed at night."[191] Similarly, an internal al-Qaida document from the late 1980s recommended the purchase of poetry books and equipment to record *anashid*, saying these were necessary to "raise the intellectual level of the *mujahidin*."[192] Leaders thus appear to have understood the significance of jihadi culture for building morale, commitment, and cohesion among recruits.

The Afghan Arab community in the 1980s was the original jihadi foreign-fighter colony. Later, there would be many other such communities: in Bosnia, Chechnya, Iraq, Syria, and elsewhere. These communities would share many of the features of Peshawar in the late 1980s. This was partly because there was personnel overlap – many Afghan Arabs moved on to new conflicts – and partly because the new communities sought to emulate the Afghan Arab experience.

Subsequent foreign-fighter colonies would experience many of the same challenges as the Afghan Arabs, such as internal factionalism, friction with the locals, and the radicalization of some volunteers. These problems are likely inherent to foreign fighting. Multinational contingents of volunteers are vulnerable to factionalization because people come from different backgrounds. They are also prone to quarreling with locals, because they come from other cultures and are more ideologically motivated, on average, than the locals. Foreign fighters self-select to a conflict zone based on ideological commitment, while local rebels are often drawn into the war by other factors. Local rebels also have more vested interests in the conflict zone – in the form of property, family members, and the like – which presumably makes them more pragmatic than the foreigners on average. Problems such as these have haunted most Islamist foreign-fighter communities since Afghanistan.

For Azzam personally, the late 1980s were his golden years. Almost everything was going his way: Volunteers and donations were flowing into Peshawar, his books were selling in ever-increasing numbers, and he received more speaking invitations than he could handle. He was the undisputed spiritual leader of the Afghan Arabs and an influential figure in intra-Mujahidin politics. By 1988 Azzam had his own stationery, suggesting he had become a veritable brand.[193] However, as we shall see, fame often comes at a price.

14 | *Enemy*

"He always refused to have bodyguards," Azzam's wife remarked in an interview years after his death.[1] But why would he need bodyguards? Who posed a threat to him and why? In this chapter we will look at the contentious side of Azzam's activities to discover that he was accumulating enemies in the late 1980s. He faced hostility from five main sides: The Pakistani government was concerned about the Afghan Arabs' military activities, the Saudi Salafi establishment disliked Azzam's Muslim Brotherhood orientation, the revolutionaries in Peshawar found him too moderate, the allies of Hekmatyar disliked his rapprochement with Massoud, and the Israelis became alert to his involvement with the Palestinian Intifada. The chapter discusses each of these challenges in turn.

As we have seen in previous chapters, Azzam was no stranger to controversy and disagreement. Aside from his long history of confronting Israel, the Arab left, and Arab governments, he was used to quarreling with other Islamists. In the 1970s he had been declared an infidel by a follower of Shukri Mustafa in Egypt, fallen out with the Syrian Salafi scholar Nasir al-Din al-Albani, and caused commotion with his book *The Islamic Call*. In the early 1980s he had argued with the "doves" in the Jordanian Muslim Brotherhood both before and after leaving Amman. Later he faced criticism of his foreign-fighter fatwa from mainstream clerics as well as dissent in the Services Bureau over how to train recruits. None of this, however, compared with the pressures he would face in the late 1980s.

Pakistani Unease

One opponent was the Pakistani government. From the mid-1980s onward, Islamabad was concerned that the foreign-fighter community in Peshawar might become unruly. Islamabad did not mind a few Arab volunteers on its territory so long as they did not interfere with

Pakistan's strategic game in Afghanistan.[2] The Pakistanis also realized that they needed to act as reasonably good hosts to Arab visitors because the latter brought a lot of donor money. However, as the number of Arab fighters increased in the mid-1980s, Pakistani security services became more apprehensive.

The Arabs, meanwhile, saw the Pakistani state as reasonably friendly, but ideologically uncommitted – and thus untrustworthy. Azzam himself complained that there was little interest in Pakistan for the jihad in Afghanistan. Only the Pakistani military fully supported it, he argued; the civilian government did not really care. Arabs suspected that the Pakistani government was involved in the jihad more out of self-interest than genuine pan-Islamic zeal. They were also disappointed by the constraints, however superficial, that the Pakistanis placed on the foreign volunteers, such as the visa requirement, the nominal ban on crossing the border into Afghanistan, and the official ban on Arabs carrying arms in Peshawar. Still, relations were fine, if not cordial, during most of the war.

The exception was in 1986, when the Pakistani government temporarily interrupted the running of the Services Bureau. As we have seen, this was the year when the foreign fighters really began growing in number and becoming more involved in military activities. Uncomfortable with this development, Pakistani security services made the Services Bureau aware that it was being watched. In 1986, according to Usama Bin Ladin, the Arabs in Peshawar faced "continuous inconveniences" from Pakistani authorities – probably a reference to raids and detentions for questioning – so much so that the Services Bureau decided to close its main guest house for a while.[3] Another Afghan Arab said that in early 1986 "orders were issued that no Arab was to be present in the Bureau, and that those who wished to stay had to do so at the Bayt al-Maqdis camp in Pabbi."[4]

During this time, Pakistani authorities also tried to make Abdallah Azzam leave the country. As he later explained, "the Pakistani government put pressure on me through some Arab governments and asked me to depart from Pakistan and to leave the jihad."[5] Rather than expel him forcibly, they asked his employers to recall him. In early 1986, likely on Pakistan's request, King Abd al-Aziz University declined to renew the contract for Azzam's position at the International Islamic University in Islamabad. As Mahmud Azzam recounts:

In early 1986 Azzam returned to Saudi Arabia to renew his yearly contract with King Abd al-Aziz University in Jeddah. He was surprised to find that the university administration did not agree to renew his contract; instead it wanted him to return to teach [in Jeddah], and this led to him leaving the university. When Dr. Umar Abdallah Nasif, the general secretary of the Muslim World League, heard about his leaving the university, he suggested he could represent the MWL in Pakistan and Afghanistan. But [Azzam] refused outright, saying, "I don't want to hold an official position that might constrain me." So instead he agreed to be an "educational supervisor" without any official bindings.[6]

When Azzam found a lifeline in the Muslim World League, the Pakistani ambassador to Saudi Arabia reportedly asked MWL General Secretary Nasif to call Azzam home.[7] Nasif went to Pakistan and asked Azzam to return to Saudi Arabia for six months until things had calmed down. Azzam refused, suspecting – probably rightly – that it would be a one-way trip. According to Mahmud Azzam, Nasif said, "We worry that they might kill you, sheikh! The Muslim World League has a university in Niger; why don't you go there? Here is a jihad and there is a jihad." But Azzam was adamant, saying, "I will only leave the land of jihad in one of three ways: either I'm killed in Pakistan, or I'm killed in Afghanistan, or the Pakistani government puts me in chains and sends me out of the country."[8]

Fearing arrest and deportation, Azzam went into hiding in the early autumn of 1986.[9] He fled first to Pabbi and then to Sada, where he would stay for about two months. Muhammad Yasir later wrote:

When we learned that the order had been issued for his arrest and expulsion from Pakistan, he left the Bureau. I remember the days when he was living in secret in Sayyaf's house in Pabbi, then he went secretly to Sada, and he stayed in exile in Sada. The exile was a blessing because he was able to write and finish some publications.[10]

His nephew later wrote:

Everybody remembers the year [1986], when the world turned against him to imprison him, and the international intelligence services were searching for him. The Pakistani government cracked down on the line that the sheikh was pursuing. The Pakistani officials told us, "We are under much pressure and we have been very patient, but we cannot sever our links with other states. So the sheikh must stop training Arabs and sending them to the battlefronts and calling the youth to jihad."[11]

Eventually, in late 1986, the pressure lifted and Azzam was able to move back to Peshawar. It is not clear what caused the Pakistani change of mind. According to one account, it was none other than Zaynab al-Ghazzali, the grand old lady of the Egyptian Muslim Brotherhood, who persuaded Pakistani president Zia ul Haq to leave Azzam alone. Mahmud Azzam writes:

In this period Zia ul Haq was still president of Pakistan, and he was a Muslim who held Zaynab al-Ghazzali in great respect for her strong stance during Abdel Nasser's repression ... Then the news came that Hajja Zaynab al-Ghazzali was going to Pakistan to meet with Sheikh Abdallah Azzam during one of the most intense periods of surveillance and pressure on him on the part of the Pakistani government ... she heard that the sheikh was being chased from place to place by the Pakistani government, and she decided to raise [the issue] with Zia ul Haq when he came to greet her at the airport. He said, "How can I serve you my lady?" and she replied, "Look after my son." "Do you have a son in Pakistan that I do not know about?" "Yes, Abdallah Azzam." After this the surveillance and the chasing stopped for good.[12]

The story may be apocryphal, but Azzam and al-Ghazzali did know each other, and we know she visited Pakistan in the autumn of 1986.[13] Either way, Azzam himself was convinced the Pakistani government had been after him. He later hinted at this, saying, "No power on earth can exert ... pressure on me, even Pakistan ... for if they come after me I will just go into Afghanistan."[14]

Although there were no major run-ins after 1986, relations remained tense. In late 1987, according to Bin Ladin, trainees heading to the al-Ma'sada camp faced more and more problems on the roads leading to the camp; they had started to dress like Afghans and learn some words in Pashto to evade detection from Pakistani police, who "had orders to harass Arabs and prevent them from traveling."[15] Moreover, after the Geneva accords in April 1988, Azzam and other Afghan Arabs expressed loud criticism of the Pakistani government. Under the Geneva accords, Russia and Afghanistan agreed with the USA and Pakistan on a scheduled Soviet withdrawal in exchange for the closing of the Afghanistan–Pakistan border and an end to Pakistani support for the Mujahidin. Both the Afghan Mujahidin and the Afghan Arabs were very critical of the accords, because the Mujahidin had been excluded from the talks and because the plan threatened to undermine the effort to topple the Communist regime in Kabul. In May 1988 Azzam wrote an article in *al-Jihad* magazine openly criticizing Zia ul Haq:

"The Mujahidin have been fighting for eight years and have not tired or faltered; but we have tired without doing anything"!? These frank words the Pakistani President Zia ul Haq uttered at the event referred to in the last issue of *al-Jihad* magazine. He thereby expressed the truth about his weakness and the weakness of his government by signing the Geneva accords.[16]

In the same issue, *al-Jihad* editor Isam Abd al-Hakim wrote an article titled "Camp Geneva Accords" – a clear reference to the 1978 Camp David accords between Egypt and Israel, widely viewed by Islamists as an act of treason by Egyptian president Anwar Sadat.[17] Subsequent issues of *al-Jihad* included other, thinly veiled jabs at the Pakistani government. For example, the October 1989 issue included a report about Nasrat Bhutto, the mother of Benazir Bhutto, attending an event in Karachi with representatives of the Afghan Communist government, something most Islamists would consider unacceptable.[18] Another article in the December 1989 issue bore the title "Bhutto's Government Draws Problems to Pakistan by Leaving the Previous Policy toward Afghanistan."[19] It is also noteworthy that *al-Jihad* magazine paid relatively little attention to Zia ul Haq's death in August 1988, while other magazines such as *al-Bunyan al-Marsus* covered it extensively.[20]

Saudi Concerns

Azzam also faced opposition from Salafi circles in Saudi Arabia, who saw him – as they did most Muslim Brothers – as too critical of regimes and too liberal on ritual issues. As we saw in Chapter 11, many Saudi scholars were critical of Azzam's fatwa about jihad in Afghanistan being an individual obligation. But their skepticism ran deeper, and had to do with Azzam's general approach to ritual practices and politics.

As we have seen, Azzam was willing to cut the Afghans slack for their saint-worship, use of amulets, and the like. These were practices which hard-core Salafis considered deviant and not to be tolerated under any circumstances. For example, in a lecture titled "Discussion on Afghanistan" from the late 1980s, the Saudi cleric Rabi' bin Hadi al-Madkhali criticized Azzam, saying, "Abdallah

Azzam and others from the Ikhwan are prepared to live with the *rawafidh* [Shiites], with the *khawarij*, with all people of innovation ... he is unable to remain quiet about Salafiyya but he is able to stay quiet on *al-rafd* [Shiism], on *ahl al-hulul* [Sufis] and *wihdat al-wujud* [the Sufi idea of unity of existence], about everything."[21] In addition, Azzam talked freely about politics and openly criticized Arab governments, to the horror of Saudi Salafis, who considered that Muslims should obey authority and leave politics to the ruler. Thus for the Saudi establishment Azzam was a potentially bad influence on youth who went to fight in Afghanistan. He seems to have been aware of this, and reportedly once told Abdallah Anas privately:

The Saudi authorities are not pleased that I am leading the Arabs in Afghanistan ... All the money that comes for orphans and widows and schools comes from Saudi Arabia. They are unhappy to see the young Saudis being organized under my leadership. They fear they will become a part of the Muslim Brotherhood ... [but] I am a Palestinian. They have no way of stopping me.[22]

In addition, the Saudi security establishment had practical reasons to worry about the foreign-fighter flow to Peshawar. A senior French DGSE official who visited his counterparts in Riyadh in the late 1980s later said, "The Saudis were already devoting a big chunk of their resources to that issue [of radical Arabs traveling to Afghanistan]. It was clearly a big concern for them."[23] Prince Turki al-Faisal, head of Saudi foreign intelligence at the time, later said, "General intelligence service followed [Azzam] but not as much as the Mabahith [domestic intelligence]."[24]

There is evidence from quite early on that Saudi officialdom was not quite as supportive of Azzam's efforts as has sometimes been claimed. In June 1986 *al-Jihad* magazine printed a facsimile of a letter from the Saudi Ministry of Information responding to a request from Azzam dated 18 February 1986 for permission to sell *al-Jihad* in stores in Saudi Arabia.[25] In the letter, the Ministry asked for copies of the three latest issues in order to process the request, suggesting that it was not rubber-stamped. The slight delay probably did not make much of a difference, however, because, judging by the many letters to the editor from Saudis, *al-Jihad* had already been widely available in the kingdom for some time.

At some point in the late 1980s the Saudi government began trying to steer volunteers away from Azzam's Services Bureau and promote their own alternative host group. According to Bernard Rougier, "At the end of 1986, the Saudis encouraged the creation of new guest houses (madafat) for Arab volunteers, which competed with and weakened the Services Bureau."[26] The main alternative promoted by the Saudis was the Salafi group Jama'at al-Da'wa ila al-Qur'an wa'l-Sunna in Kunar province. Jama'at al-Da'wa (for short) had been set up in the mid-1980s by Jamil al-Rahman, an Afghan Islamist who had broken with Hekmatyar's Hizb-e-Islami.[27] It preached a Salafi-inspired Islam, and in 1990 it would declare an Islamic emirate which violently enforced the ban on grave worship and other local practices considered by Salafis as heretical.[28] Official Saudi clerics much preferred Jama'at al-Da'wa over other groups in Peshawar, and offered it substantial support from around 1988 onward.[29] Not only did it receive money and weaponry from Saudi intelligence; it was also promoted by Saudi clerics as the best destination for prospective foreign fighters. The Saudi government also seems to have paid for the distribution of *al-Mujahid*, the group's magazine (launched December 1988), in an attempt to counter the influence of magazines such as *al-Jihad* and *al-Bunyan al-Marsus*. When this author visited King Saud University Library in Riyadh in 2005, it held ten copies of each issue of *al-Mujahid* and only one copy of each issue of *al-Jihad* and *al-Bunyan al-Marsus*. Not surprisingly, a substantial number of Saudi volunteers in the 1988–1992 period joined Jama'at al Da'wa instead of other groups such as the Services Bureau.[30] Jama'at al-Da'wa also offered fighting opportunities, notably at the Asadabad and Jalalabad fronts.[31] Later on, it drew fewer recruits as it became embroiled in a violent dispute with Hekmatyar's Hizb-e Islami for control of parts of Kunar province. On 30 August 1991 Jamil al-Rahman was assassinated by an Egyptian militant named Abdallah al-Rumi, widely believed to have been sent by Hekmatyar.[32]

The effort to divert volunteers away from the Services Bureau raises the question whether the Saudi government in some way encouraged Bin Ladin to set up the al-Ma'sada camp, or even al-Qaida. We know that Bin Ladin was in close contact with Saudi intelligence and performed tasks for them (see Chapter 8). It is almost inconceivable that they did not know about al-Ma'sada and Bin Ladin's drift away from Azzam, so at least they tolerated it. Whether or not they actively supported the al-Ma'sada project is difficult to say based on the available sources. As for al-Qaida, it seems very unlikely that it enjoyed Saudi government support in the early days, because it was a potentially more subversive force than the Services Bureau. If the Saudis discouraged their youth from following Azzam, they were not going to send them into the arms of seasoned revolutionaries such as Ayman al-Zawahiri. The al-Qaida project was also so low profile that Bin Ladin may well have been able to keep it secret from his contacts in Saudi intelligence.

Toward the end of the 1980s, the Saudi government took a variety of steps to limit Azzam's influence in the kingdom. At one stage, Grand Mufti Abd al-Aziz Bin Baz was reportedly fed disinformation in the form of rumors that Azzam was "fighting Sunnis" (*yuharib al-sunna*) in Afghanistan.[33] Azzam reportedly wrote to Bin Baz to counter the accusations, and Bin Baz replied acknowledging that this had been an attempt to "sow discord between the *ulama*."[34] Moreover, around 1989 Saudi security services started obstructing some of Azzam's speaking activities in the kingdom. That summer they canceled at least one of his speeches at the last minute. Azzam was supposed to give a lecture in the King Khalid mosque to over 3,000 attendees, but, hours before the event, security officials ordered him to cancel. One of Azzam's biographers said he was no longer permitted to lecture in Saudi Arabia after this incident.[35]

In the autumn of 1989 Azzam was invited to meet Prince Salman bin Abd al-Aziz, the governor of Riyadh – now the king of Saudi Arabia – at his palace in the capital. Prince Salman was in charge of the official Saudi humanitarian support for Afghanistan, and thus well informed about Azzam's activities.[36] According to the 2004 memoir of a former Afghan Arab named Mustafa Badi, the meeting was tense and confrontational. Here is the story as reportedly told by Azzam to Mustafa Badi just weeks after the meeting happened:

After some days and many meetings and lectures on the Afghan jihad, Sheikh NN called me one night and said, "I will come and pick you up now, because you have been invited to one of the big businessmen of Riyadh." I said, "That's what I'm here for. I'll wait for you." Then someone came and took me in his American car. We rushed through the streets of Riyadh until we came to a lane; he brought me into the garden of a great palace, then we entered the palace, and I found myself in the reception room of none other than Prince Salman, the governor of Riyadh province. Everybody in the room got up, and I passed by and greeted everyone until I got to Prince Salman, who got up and greeted me coldly. "You are Palestinian," he said, "you have not done anything close to the things that the Kingdom of Saudi Arabia has done for the Afghan Mujahidin. So why do you incite the Arab youth against the kingdom?" He went on, and I stood before him, listening to his remarks about the Palestinians, and when the prince had finished, I wanted to end this unblessed meeting. I took out my residency permit from my pocket and said, "Listen, your majesty, what binds me to your government is this piece of paper" – and I threw it on the table – "and you can issue a royal decree canceling it and bring me to the airport directly, for I will never tolerate being [falsely] accused by anyone, whoever the person is." After Salman heard my reply and saw my position, he said, "Sheikh, you have misunderstood me; I only meant to ask a question, because news have reached us suggesting that you are inciting the Arab youth against the kingdom. That is why I asked you." I said, "You know, your majesty, that in almost all my lectures and sermons I mention the Saudi kingdom's supportive stance toward the Afghan jihad, both that of the government and that of the people. Most of my sermons and lectures are recorded, and I can send you the complete collection from the Services Bureau in Peshawar so you can hear for yourself if you wish."[37]

This account, if accurate, would suggest that relations between Azzam and the Saudi regime had become really quite tense by the autumn of 1989.

The problem is that another source– Azzam's son Hudhayfa – has offered a very different account of what happened in the meeting. In March 2018, Hudhayfa disputed Badi's account as false, saying his father had told him that the meeting was amicable, and that Prince Salman had kissed Azzam's head at the end as a blessing and sign of appreciation.[38] The truth may be somewhere in the middle. Badi's account is clearly exaggerated; even a person as outspoken as Azzam would probably not dare to address a Saudi royal quite in such terms. At the same time, it is not clear why Badi would invent intrigue where there was none, so there could well be a kernel of truth to the story. The meeting could have been amicable *and* included a polite exchange about rumors that Azzam was promoting anti-Saudi views. That such rumors circulated in parts of the Saudi government system seems plausible given all the other indications of Saudi unease about Azzam. In any case, Azzam's reception in a royal palace was testimony to his influence and reputation.

Revolutionary Hostility

While some saw Azzam as too politically radical, others considered him too moderate. In the late 1980s Azzam's most outspoken critics in Peshawar were the revolutionaries, the Arab militants whose priority was the toppling of Arab regimes. Often referred to by their opponents as *takfiri*s for their tendency to label other Muslims as infidels, these uncompromising activists were generally hostile to pragmatists such as Azzam.[39]

The revolutionaries were a mixed bunch. For one, they differed in their degree of organization: some were members of groups such as Egyptian Islamic Jihad while others, such as Abu Muhammad al-Maqdisi, were unaffiliated. For another, they were preoccupied with different Arab regimes, and thus they often clustered by national background.[40] They were also not equally uncompromising. There was, for example, an important difference between the Egyptian Islamic Jihad and the Egyptian Islamic Group (al-Jama'a al-Islamiyya), with the former being more hardline than the latter.[41] As we shall see below, most of Azzam's problems were with EIJ leaders such as Ayman al-Zawahiri, not with the EIG. Azzam was notably good friends with the latter's spiritual leader, Umar Abd al-Rahman ("the blind sheikh"), an al-Azhar alumnus like himself.[42] Abd al-Rahman spent at least two extended periods in Peshawar in the late 1980s, during which he frequented Azzam and even received a subsistence stipend from the Services Bureau.[43] *Al-Bunyan al-Marsus* once published a picture of Azzam kissing Abd al-Rahman's head.[44] When Azzam died, Umar Abd al-Rahman issued a statement from Egypt on behalf of the Egyptian Islamic Group, and when Umar Abd al-Rahman moved to America in 1990, the Services Bureau paid his airfare.[45] Abd al-Rahman and Azzam did not see eye to eye on military strategy, but they were both relative pragmatists who agreed to disagree.

Broadly speaking, the revolutionaries were of the view that the main problem in the Muslim world was not the external threat from non-Muslim aggressors, but rather the internal threat from un-Islamic regimes and other bad Muslims. Many revolutionaries had a Salafi background: Ayman al-Zawahiri, for example, was a veteran member of the Egyptian Salafi scene; he had never been a member of the Egyptian Muslim Brotherhood.[46] However, they were not Salafis of the pro-Saudi variety. Most were skeptical of the Saudi government, and some, like Abu Muhammad al-Maqdisi, were outspoken critics of the regime in Riyadh.[47] Many revolutionaries had come to Pakistan more for the refuge and the recruitment opportunities than for the chance to help liberate Afghanistan, and as a result they spent more time in Peshawar than on the battlefronts.[48] Al-Maqdisi, for example, visited Sada briefly, but he never engaged in combat, while al-Zawahiri is not recorded as having visited the border areas before 1989.[49]

The number of revolutionaries in Peshawar increased markedly from the mid-1980s onward, when the city's reputation as a safe haven was growing. A number of subsequently famous revolutionaries arrived at this time, including Ayman al-Zawahiri, Sayyid Imam al-Sharif (Dr. Fadl), Rifa'i Taha, Abu Muhammad al-Maqdisi, Umar Abd al-Rahman, Qari Sa'id, and Abu Mus'ab al-Suri. They also produced influential new writings such as Sayyid Imam al-Sharif's book *The Pillar of Military Preparation* (1988) and Abu Muhammad al-Maqdisi's *The Community of Abraham* (1984) and *The Blatant Proof of the Infidel Nature of the Saudi State* (1989).[50] Subsequent books such as al-Zawahiri's *The Bitter Harvest: The Muslim Brothers in Sixty Years* (ca. 1991) and Abu Mus'ab al-Suri's *The Jihadi Revolution in Syria: Hopes and Pains* (ca. 1991), both written in Peshawar, further raised the prominence of this jihadi current.[51]

As their numbers increased, the atmosphere of the Afghan Arab community changed from one of unity and inclusiveness to one of fragmentation and mutual suspicion. As Abdallah Anas later wrote:

> I was shocked at what I saw in Peshawar in 1988. I felt that the Services Office was no longer the sole custodian of Arab affairs there. The Bayt al-Ansar had been established, and I sensed a sort of insolence among the Arabs towards Sheikh Abdallah Azzam. He no longer had that absolute authority that he used to possess at the start of the jihad. Arab guest houses proliferated and their numbers grew. I noticed that the Arab scene in Peshawar had changed ... The sheikh did not hide his dislike for the actions of some of our good brothers who were starting to follow dictates different than those of the sheikh concerning Arab involvement [in the war].[52]

For Azzam this was bad news. He found himself criticized with growing frequency by other radicals in Peshawar. They reproached him for his tolerance of Hanafi religious practices, his insistence on working with Afghans, his support for the relatively liberal Ahmed Shah

Massoud, his willingness to work with Gulf states, and more. Kamal al-Helbawy said, "Before [Azzam] was killed there were many statements and leaflets distributed in Peshawar saying he is not a good Muslim."[53] The new atmosphere frustrated Azzam: "I don't know what some people are doing here in Peshawar," he reportedly complained. "They are talking against the mujahideen. They have only one point, to create fitna between me and these volunteers."[54] He was notably unhappy that Usama Bin Ladin seemed to spend more and more time with the revolutionaries. "What is Osama doing gathering these people around him in Peshawar?" he grumbled.[55]

It takes two to tango, however, and the revolutionaries saw things differently. In their view, Muslim Brotherhood figures like Azzam exercised a suffocating ideological hegemony in Peshawar and were preventing Salafis from voicing their opinion. As Abu Muhammad al-Maqdisi later wrote:

> I went [to Afghanistan] numerous times; a month, a month and a half at a time, and sometimes six consecutive months . . . I went to Peshawar, and one of the first people I met there was Sheikh Abu Walid al-Ansari . . . and with him was Dr. Ahmad al-Jaza'iri, who is now imprisoned in Algeria. They had washed their hands of the Afghan fighting parties . . . they had collected lots of documentation on these parties . . . so when I arrived, I learned what I needed to know about these parties, and I did not need to experience it myself . . . I published *The Creed of Abraham* and had it distributed in Peshawar. I also copied and distributed chapters from *The Glittering Pearls* [*al-durar al-sanniya*] – on jihad and on apostasy. So the call for *tawhid* began to spread among the ranks of the young men in Peshawar . . . remember that a lot of books were circulating, by all kinds of groups . . . even the poems of Shukri Mustafa were printed . . . I went to Bayt al-Ansar, as people did, and signed up for Sada . . . So I arrived, and my brothers had warned me: don't expect to be able to denounce every sinful thing that you see, especially things that have to do with *tawhid*, *shirk*, that you might see among the Afghans. If you try to denounce them, you will be stopped and maybe thrown out of the camp. So I found their reports to be true, all talk about controversial issues was forbidden. Then I met a group of students of Badi' al-Din al-Sindi, who was in Mecca, with whom Juhayman and others studied etc. . . . They were frustrated with not being able to talk about these matters, and they suffered from the Ikhwani hostility to Salafists.[56]

The revolutionaries mostly criticized Azzam behind his back, but they also engaged in overt provocation. Years later, Abu Muhammad al-Maqdisi described his own run-in with Azzam:

One night, after the afternoon prayer, the sheikh began talking about these controversial issues which were forbidden ... and he would denounce the people who cared about Tawhid and who denounced *shirk* among the Afghans. At the same time he prevented others from discussing and talking about this. And there were lots of people, and some of them revered him to the point of imitation. And his style was to always underscore points by saying "understood?", this was his teaching style ... and I was on the second and third row, and I don't remember exactly where I cut him off, but I remember that he was talking about *taqlid* and the need to avoid talking about *shirk* and denouncing it among the Afghans, and that we have to be patient with them, etc. ... I got up and said, "No. Not understood." This may have been the first time anyone did this to [the] sheikh ... there had been almost nobody before him in the Levant more learned, with the possible exception of Marwan Hadid. In this period there was nobody as prominent and beloved among the youth as Sheikh Abdallah Azzam. I respected him for this, but I could not keep quiet on this type of matter ... and Sada went quiet ... and in the small window where it was quiet, in this electrified atmosphere I quickly summarized my concerns ... then there was more and more uproar, people said this is a Russian agent, and Abu al-Burhan came and took the microphone and asked everyone to leave the mosque ... They never spoke to me about it or brought it up again.[57]

In an interview with this author in 2018 Abu Muhammad al-Maqdisi confirmed the episode, and added that this was his only personal encounter with Azzam, as the two frequented different circles in both Jordan and Peshawar.[58] Al-Maqdisi insisted that they had not been involved in polemics after this incident, and he described Azzam diplomatically as "one of the best people to come out of the Muslim Brotherhood."

Azzam's main detractors were a small group of hardliners consisting of people such as Ayman al-Zawahiri, Sayyid al-Imam al-Sharif (Dr. Fadl), Ridwan Nammus (Abu Firas al-Suri), and Ahmad al-Jaza'iri.[59] Ayman al-Zawahiri was a doctor and leading member of the Egyptian Islamic Jihad who had arrived in Peshawar in 1986 after a stint working in Saudi Arabia.[60] He worked in the Kuwaiti Red Crescent hospital together with Sayyid Imam al-Sharif, another doctor and senior member of EIJ.[61] Ridwan Nammus was a former Syrian military officer who had fought against the Assad regime in the early 1980s and came to Peshawar later in the decade.[62] Ahmad al-Jaza'iri was an Algerian Salafi and doctor who had joined the Afghan jihad in the early 1980s.[63] Al-Zawahiri and Dr. Fadl appear to have been the leading figures among the hardliners.

Their hostility to Azzam stemmed partly from their dislike for the Muslim Brotherhood and partly from their view of Azzam as a rival for Usama Bin Ladin's resources. According to Osama Rushdi,

> Ayman had a severe conflict with Dr. Abdullah Azzam. He called him an agent of America, an agent of Saudi Arabia. I have spoken to Dr al Zawahiri many times. [He said to us] "why do you have a good relationship with Dr. Azzam?" ... The bad chemistry [between Bin Ladin and Azzam] began because the Maktab al-Khadamat had a lot of bureaucracy problems ... Ayman al-Zawahiri [was frustrated about this]. He made a lot of [noise] about it and pushed bin Laden to be not happy with this [situation]. [Zawahiri told him], "Spend your money yourself, [do] not give it to Abdallah Azzam." ... Al Zawahiri [tried to maneuver] Bin Laden away from Dr. Azzam.[64]

In October 1988 the tensions between Azzam and the hardliners came to the surface in the form of a bitter financial dispute. In July 1987 Azzam and Wa'il Julaydan had embarked on a joint charitable project called al-Tahaddi ("Challenge") with an Egyptian-Canadian named Ahmad Sa'id Khadr (aka Abd al-Rahman al-Kanadi).[65] Khadr was put in charge of it, but his alleged mismanagement led its main sponsor, the Islamic Benevolence Committee, to withhold funding.[66] By the early autumn of 1988 al-Tahaddi had a severe deficit, and Azzam and Julaydan started to get cold feet. To limit their liability, Julaydan requested a meeting with Khadr on 19 October to specify their respective roles and responsibilities in writing and to establish a steering committee. They produced a project bill which Khadr signed, without noticing that it gave the steering committee the power to replace administrative personnel. About a week later the committee, with Azzam as president, demanded Khadr's resignation. Khadr refused, and went on a pre-planned trip to Canada on 29 October.

Azzam and Julaydan were now convinced that Khadr was taking steps to secure the remaining assets. In the evening of 2 November 1988 the Azzam team – we do not know who exactly – broke into Khadr's office in Peshawar and seized all the documents they could find.[67] They also emptied the project's storage facility and moved the contents to a Saudi Red Crescent warehouse. They also got the Habib Bank in Peshawar to freeze al-Tahaddi's accounts. Azzam's men then trawled through Khadr's documents and found what they considered evidence that Khadr was trying to hijack the project and that he had suspicious contacts with Western organizations. They then produced a statement dismissing Khadr from the leadership of the project and listing his alleged infractions. The statement was faxed to all of al-Tahaddi's partners in Peshawar and abroad (reportedly to Saudi Arabia, Kuwait, Yemen, Sudan, Canada, the USA, and Sweden). Khadr later claimed that Azzam's men also threatened him with jail and a beating if he returned to Peshawar, and that they promised to use *al-Jihad* magazine to defame any party that collaborated with him from then on.

When Khadr returned to Peshawar later in November, he was not happy. He refused to step down as leader of al-Tahaddi, demanded all the materials back, and accused Azzam of theft and slander. He mobilized his allies in Peshawar, but Azzam and Julaydan did not budge. Khadr then "asked for arbitration ... beginning on 26 November 1988, in the form of phone calls, hand-delivered messages, mediation of the leaders of the Mujahideen such as Sheikh Rabbani, Sheikh Sayyaf, Engineer Hekmatyar, and Sheikh Yunus Khalis," and finally sent a delegation to negotiate.[68] In mid-December Azzam and Julaydan agreed to have the matter resolved in an ad hoc Islamic legal proceeding led by a mutually agreed-upon adjudication committee. After some preliminary meetings, the main session was held on 26 December from 9 a.m. to 9 p.m. This is what later became known as "the trial of Azzam."

In some of the existing literature, the proceedings are described as very dramatic. In Lawrence Wright's rendering, which relies primarily on testimonies of Azzam's close friends Abdallah Anas and Wa'il Julaydan, Azzam was nearly sentenced to death or to public mutilation in a ramshackle Shari'a court mounted by the hardliners.[69] Similarly, Michelle Shephard, who also relied on Abdallah Anas's testimony, says that Azzam was tried in absentia and found guilty, but a jury of elders "agreed to spare his life."[70]

However, Azzam's life was most likely never on the line. We now have the written records from the proceeding, and they offer a very different picture.[71] First, it was a very small affair; only four people were present: the two adjudicators, Dr. Fadl and Abu Hajir al-Iraqi, Khadr himself, and Wa'il Julaydan.[72] Second, the adjudication committee was not uniformly hostile to Azzam; Abu Hajir was a friend of Azzam's and was probably in the committee on the latter's request. Third, the jury's written deliberation was nuanced, and although it ruled mostly in Khadr's favor, it also faulted him on some counts, such as making bank transfers without a second signature. More importantly, the decision nowhere mentions physical punishment; it merely rules that Khadr should be reinstated as director of al-Tahaddi and that Azzam and Julaydan should return all of Khadr's private possessions. It also declares Khadr innocent of conspiring with Western agencies, and asks that al-Tahaddi's partners be informed of the acquittal. The language of the verdict is cautious, and it concludes diplomatically that "distrust and defamation without circumspection and clarification have all played a major part in developing this dispute and escalating it."[73]

It is also clear that Azzam was no innocent victim in the affair. Khadr had good reason to complain about having his office broken into and being defamed in a public statement. Moreover, as far as we know, Azzam and Julaydan did not comply with all the rulings of the verdict. They probably returned Khadr's private possessions, but appear not to have returned the other goods or issued a retraction statement.

Azzam's failure to respect the outcome of the arbitration annoyed Dr. Fadl. Many years later, Dr. Fadl, then in prison in Egypt, published a book titled *Rationalizing Jihad in Egypt and the World* in which he recanted his old jihadi positions and reflected on his life in the jihadi movement. At one point he talks about the al-Tahaddi trial as an example of the un-Islamic practices of the Afghan Arabs. He says Azzam disrespected Islamic law by ignoring the committee's ruling:

God willed that I be a mediator between the parties made up of the famous proselytizers, and when truth become unavoidable, they fled from it and [refused] to comply with what was required of him. So I said, by God, God will not bless us with an Islamic rule until the day that we are satisfied with God's will amongst us.[74]

Ayman al-Zawahiri later expressed a third view of the trial. In 2008 he wrote a book titled *The Exoneration*, criticizing Dr. Fadl's recantation point by point. He notably took Dr. Fadl to task for giving an unfair description of Azzam's behaviour in the al-Tahaddi dispute:

The story of the incident which [Dr. Fadl] referred to is that the two martyrs Abu Abdal-Rahman Al-Kanadi [Ahmad Khadr] and Shaykh Abdullah Azzam ... were involved in a combined rescue effort. Then, a disagreement developed between them and they decided to resort to [external] mediation. They chose two mediators one of whom was [Dr. Fadl]. I did not witness the mediation, but [Dr. Fadl] said to me: "The result came out for the benefit of Abu Abd-al-Rahman Al-Kanadi against shaykh Abdullah Azzam ... Shaykh

Abdullah – according to [Dr. Fadl] – fled from the application of the judgment. I did not hear the story from shaykh Abdullah Azzam nor from shaykh Abu Abd-al-Rahman Al-Kanadi, may God have mercy upon them both. The important thing is that [Dr. Fadl] considered Shaykh Abdullah Azzam's fleeing from what was ruled against him as rejection of the ruling of Shari'ah. Imagine that! . . . Perhaps shaykh [Abdallah Azzam] had a point of view. We did not ask him neither did we hear from him; we only knew him as the spiritual, worshipping, devout, godly, pious scholar who was one of the people of determination and patience and who upheld this religion to the fullest extent.[75]

All this suggests that Abdallah Anas and Wa'il Julaydan have offered a somewhat inaccurate description of the al-Tahaddi dispute in their testimonies to Lawrence Wright and Michelle Shephard. A good-faith interpretation is that they perceived it at the time as more dramatic than it was. A more critical view is that this is part of a pattern by which Azzam loyalists have sought to cast the Egyptians in Peshawar as more nefarious and hostile to Azzam than they really were. As we saw in Chapter 12, the same "Evil Egyptian" narrative has presented Bin Ladin as a passive victim of Egyptian manipulation, when the circumstantial evidence suggests otherwise.

Something similar appears to be going on with the Azzam family's claim that some of the Egyptians considered Azzam an infidel. Hudhayfa Azzam later said, "[The Egyptians] would refuse to let him lead them during prayers in the mosque. They split the Arabs into two camps, Abdallah Azzam used to pray at a mosque called Sab' al-Layl, while the Egyptians would perform the Friday prayers at the Kuwaiti Red Crescent's mosque in Peshawar."[76] Azzam's wife said in an interview in 2006 that Ayman al-Zawahiri refused to pray behind Abdallah Azzam, thus effectively declaring him an infidel.[77] Abdallah Anas has made the same claim.[78] However, in 2008 al-Zawahiri himself flatly denied the allegation:

As for . . . my declaring Shaykh Abdullah Azzam an unbeliever and that I wouldn't pray behind him, it is a statement which is the complete opposite of the truth, and I remind the virtuous sister Umm Muhammad [Azzam's wife] (may Allah protect her) that my wife . . . used to go with my permission to attend her lessons and meetings.[79]

Moreover, as we shall see in Chapter 16, there are no known statements by al-Zawahiri criticizing Azzam; on the contrary, al-Zawahiri has praised Azzam lavishly in later years. Even if we assume that al-Zawahiri changed his pitch on Azzam for opportunistic reasons, his reply to Azzam's wife raises the question whether she may have made wrong assumptions about al-Zawahiri's opinions at the time. It is possible, for example, that al-Zawahiri disliked Azzam and preferred to pray in a different mosque without necessarily considering Azzam an infidel. Even Dr. Fadl may not have been as anti-Azzam as previously assumed. In *The Exoneration*, al-Zawahiri criticizes Dr. Fadl's disparaging comments about Azzam in *Rationalizing Jihad*, pointing out that his old friend had not previously been this hostile:

> This was not his original opinion of Shaykh Abdallah Azzam ... [Dr. Fadl] once wrote a treatise defending [Azzam's book *The Defense of Muslim Lands*] after Shaykh Abdullah Azzam was martyred. He made that defense in response to Shaykh Safar Al-Hawali's comment on it. He called his treatise "A Comment on A Comment." He then asked me to deliver a copy of the treatise to Shaykh Azzam's disciples and inform them that it was a tribute from Al-Jihad Organization to the martyr.[80]

Even though the al-Tahaddi dispute was only about money, the episode was significant. It turned an internal disagreement into a public confrontation, and this must have been humiliating and aggravating to Azzam, who strove for consensus in the community.

Anti-Massoud Sentiment

Another controversy in the late 1980s was Azzam's support for Ahmed Shah Massoud, which earned him the distrust of not only Massoud's enemy Gulbuddin Hekmatyar, but also of the Pakistani ISI and of some Arabs. Massoud was Rabbani's long-time military commander in the Panjshir valley, but he was so militarily successful and popular that, by the late 1980s, he was a contestant for political leadership in a post-Communist Afghanistan. This put him at odds with Hekmatyar, who had similar aspirations and was Pakistan's principal client among the Mujahidin.[81] Massoud was controversial in Islamist circles because of his relative pragmatism. In 1983, for example, he had agreed to a truce with Communist forces, drawing the ire of other Mujahidin leaders and the ISI.[82] He was also French-educated and friendly to Westerners, which led some to accuse him of being an agent.[83] It did not help that Massoud was based in Panjshir and never around to defend himself against rumors and accusations in Peshawar.

In 1988 and 1989, as the Russians pulled out from Afghanistan and the Mujahidin looked set to seize power, tensions between Massoud and Hekmatyar escalated to the point of armed clashes. Later, in the early 1990s, the conflict would escalate further, becoming a full-fledged civil war. Azzam saw this coming. He worried that gains made in the jihad might be lost if the infighting among the Afghan Mujahidin continued. In one of his last lectures, he told an audience of Afghans that "if you lose the opportunity of Afghanistan, you will wait half a century or a century before you get another opportunity." In the same lecture he warned against factionalism, saying, "You will suffer what the Palestinians suffered."[84]

Azzam worked hard to bring about a rapprochement between Massoud and Hekmatyar.[85] As part of this effort, he decided to travel into Afghanistan in early September 1988 to speak to Massoud. The two had exchanged letters in 1985, but had never met in person.[86] Together with Burhanuddin Rabbani and a small group of aides, Azzam walked across the Hindu Kush for the two weeks it took to reach the Panjshir valley. They also visited other locations in northeast Afghanistan to meet with commanders and get a sense of the situation. It was Azzam's first proper journey deep into Afghanistan, and he later wrote a book about it titled *A Month among Giants*.[87] (The book was never published, reportedly because all the presses in Peshawar were controlled by Hekmatyar and Sayyaf, who did not want to promote a pro-Massoud publication.[88]) Azzam spent several weeks with Massoud, and like many others who met the Tajik commander, he was charmed and impressed. Toward the end of his visit, he told Massoud:

I want to tell you that I went through three stages in my relationship with you. In the first, I hated you and campaigned against you, as I was reliant on information from your competitors who say that you are a French agent and that you do this and that. I wrote against you a small letter which I sent to Beirut for publishing, but God willed that the letter be lost when the brother who was carrying it suffered an accident. This was the first stage in which I was your enemy. The second stage is when we learned the truth about you, neither lies nor praise, when our brother Nur al-Din (one of the Arabs sent to Massoud) visited you and told us about you. As for the third stage, it is the stage in which I loved and respected you and worked to help you. This stage started after Abdullah Anas came to us after visiting you. Consider us now your friends, and all that was said about you, we will disregard as lies and rumors.[89]

Azzam returned to Peshawar even more convinced of the need to bring Massoud and Hekmatyar together. For this to happen, Azzam needed to convince a lot of people in Peshawar that Massoud was trustworthy, which was difficult given all the rumors propagated by Hekmatyar and his supporters. Wa'il Julaydan later said that Azzam "continued to talk good about Massoud, writing books about Massoud, giving speeches about Massoud. [saying] 'Massoud is the hope of the whole nation.'"[90] In the spring of 1989 Azzam also tried to organize "an Arab religious group numbering about two hundred whose mission was to travel around Afghanistan using Islamic principles to mediate a peace between Hekmatyar and Massoud."[91] However, this jihadi peace corps never materialized.

Although Azzam liked both Massoud and Hekmatyar and just wanted them to get along, he quickly earned a reputation for being pro-Massoud. This almost certainly irritated the Pakistani ISI, who distrusted the non-Pashtun, pro-Western Massoud and did not want to see any rapprochement between the two rivals. Hekmatyar himself was also displeased about Azzam's "bromance" with Massoud, but he was probably not among those most upset. Hekmatyar and Azzam were good friends, and Hekmatyar likely knew that Azzam was a sincere person who had the best interests of the Mujahidin in mind.

The harshest response came from pro-Hekmatyar elements among the Arabs. Most Arabs were suspicious of Massoud, but a group of Egyptians, Algerians, and Yemenis were particularly hostile. Usama Bin Ladin was also anti-Massoud, but not among the most aggressive.[92] According to Abdallah Anas, the main critic was an Algerian named Qari Sa'id, who had previously traveled with Abdallah Anas to Panjshir, but after some time with Massoud had joined Hekmatyar's forces instead.[93] Sa'id reportedly bore a grudge against Massoud for a reprimand during his time in Panjshir.[94] Some time in 1988 the anti-Massoudists issued a communiqué signed by some twenty Arabs detailing Massoud's various sins. It made its rounds in Peshawar, and was followed by a trial-like meeting in which a committee of senior Arabs were to decide whether he had broken Islamic law.[95] The result was inconclusive, but the anti-Massoud sentiment prevailed. According to Musa al-Qarni, "All the Arabs in the city [were] against Masud ... The only exception was Shaykh Abdallah Azzam."[96]

Some observers have suggested, not without reason, that the criticism of Massoud was also an indirect way of targeting Azzam. Osama Rushdi later said, "That was the negative thing that Ayman used against Dr. Abdullah Azzam: The good relationship between Abdullah Azzam and Massoud. Because [al-Zawahiri] described Massoud in this period as an agent for the French ... And [they said] Abdullah Azzam is a liar when he said Massoud is a good man."[97]

Still, the peace process continued, but it hit a rough patch in mid-1989, when some of Hekmatyar's men killed thirty-six Massoud-linked commanders in Farkhar in Takhar province, on 9 July 1989.[98] The incident led to the collapse of the transitional Mujahidin government and prompted retaliations against Hekmatyar's forces by Massoud's men. Right after the Farkhar massacre, Azzam decided to travel into Afghanistan again to meet with Massoud and persuade him not to retaliate.[99] He appears to have been able to get Massoud to withhold immediate retaliation, but hostilities soon picked up again.

However, Azzam did not give up. In November 1989 he worked with a committee of prominent Muslim Brothers to secure an agreement between Rabbani (Massoud's superior) and Hekmatyar.[100] The process went well, and an agreement was finalized on 23 November 1989.[101] Late that evening Azzam and the other committee members went to Rabbani's house to get his signature. Rabbani later said:

I heard a knock on my door in the middle of the night – I was asleep – and I went out and found the martyred sheikh and a group of brothers, and they asked me to sign this paper, and I signed it without reading it. He said, we have an appointment with you in Islamabad tomorrow.[102]

The reason Azzam was in such a rush was that he wanted to announce the agreement the next day in his Friday sermon in Sab' al-Layl mosque.[103] The plan was then for the key actors to go to Islamabad on the Friday afternoon and present the deal to the other Mujahidin leaders. However, as we shall see in the next chapter, things would not work out that way at all.

Israeli Suspicions

In the last two years of his life, Azzam re-invested himself in the Palestinian struggle. The outbreak of the First Intifada in December 1987 put Palestine back in the news and gave Azzam hope that the resistance might finally be led by Islamists. In June 1988 he wrote an article about "the blessed jihadi intifada," saying, "Hearing the stories have shaken me to the core, for I never thought these events would unfold so very quickly and in this wonderful way."[104] He was particularly pleased to hear that youth in his own village, al-Sila al-Harithiyya, were taking action; in the same article he proudly related anecdotes from al-Sila about youth throwing Molotov cocktails and sending burning car tires against Israeli soldiers.

Azzam began to write much more about Palestine. Starting with issue 43, he introduced a regular column in *al-Jihad* magazine titled "From One Heart to Another," which was specifically devoted to his homeland. In May 1989 he completed the book *Hamas: Historical Roots and Charter*, which was a history of the Islamist resistance in Palestine, from the late nineteenth century to the present. He also wrote a booklet called *Memoirs of Palestine* about his own experiences as a Palestinian activist in the 1950s, 1960s, and 1970s. He also talked more about Palestine in his lectures and sermons, often speaking of Afghanistan and Palestine in the same talk. In 1988 and 1989 he used his talks on Afghanistan to raise funds for Hamas, both in the Middle East and in the West. For example, at the MAYA conference in Oklahoma in December 1988 he spoke about Palestine and called for donations to Hamas, which reportedly resulted in a spontaneous collection of money and gold from the audience.[105]

Azzam was also in direct contact with Hamas representatives and sympathizers in the Territories. According to one biographer, he was "in constant touch with the Palestinian resistance movement represented by Hamas through the Muslim Students' Association [in the United States], and they were providing him with news of the jihad."[106] It is not clear whether Azzam ever met Hamas' spiritual leader Ahmad Yasin, but they likely communicated occasionally in the 1980s, and they certainly knew of one another. Azzam praised Yasin publicly on several occasions.[107] At one point, at an Islamic conference in Oklahoma City in December 1988, Azzam declared, "Now I would like to turn to the paralyzed man who educated an entire generation that stood against the Jews with these stones: Ahmad Yasin – greetings from this podium. The man moves an entire generation, although he himself cannot move."[108]

Some have suggested that Azzam wrote the Hamas charter, because the text is included at the end of his book on Hamas. His wife has also said he wrote it, although in another interview she said that Hamas "contacted him to write the introduction and edit the document."[109]

However, it is very unlikely that he contributed substantially, if at all, to the charter. Neither Azzam himself, Azzam's main biographers, nor senior Hamas officials ever said that he wrote it. People who worked closely with him in the late 1980s, such as Abu Harith (his driver) and Jamal Isma'il, have insisted that he did not.[110] Most likely he simply included it in the book for the reader's information; this made sense because the charter (dated 18 August 1988) was less than a year old when the book came out.

What Azzam did do was to call on Palestinians to come and train in Pakistan and Afghanistan with a view to redeploying in the Territories. "Sons of Palestine," he said in one lecture, "you have an opportunity to train on every type of weapon [in Afghanistan], this is a golden opportunity, do not miss it."[111] In another lecture he said, "Send me a hundred Palestinians; I will insert them into training and education courses and then send them to real battles inside Afghanistan. Twenty of them will be martyred, twenty of them will be obstructed, and there will be sixty left for you to take and distribute in the mountains of Nablus, Jerusalem, Hebron, and Gaza."[112] Azzam saw the Afghan camps as a potential game-changer for the Palestinian struggle, offering the strategic depth that the resistance so sorely lacked. He was very optimistic about this strategy, writing in 1989 that 2,000 *mujahidin* could destroy Israel if there was a way to get them to the battlefield.[113]

Dozens of young Palestinians, perhaps over a hundred, heeded his call and went to Pakistan. Many came from the diaspora, but some also traveled from the Territories. According to Jamal Isma'il, those who left from inside Palestine would typically go to Saudi Arabia for pilgrimage and on from there to Pakistan.[114] Azzam took a particular interest in Palestinian recruits, and according to one biographer, "he participated in [the training of Palestinians] himself."[115] He was particularly interested in those who had the paperwork to re-enter. According to Jarrar, "[Azzam] trained the youth who had the permission and were able to go to Palestine, and sent them back after training and advised them to stay in Palestine and join the *mujahidin* there."[116] In September 1989 Azzam even tried to set up a training camp specifically for Palestinians. Jamal Isma'il later said:

Azzam announced the formation of "Hamas brigades" in Afghanistan. And he announced that we will have training camp to support Hamas. And in his speeches he talked about this and he called for Hamas supporters, especially those who are living, or can't get inside Palestine either West Bank or Gaza to come and get training and go back, but that camp it was closed within one month due to some logistical problem with Hamas leadership; they did not allow him to use their name; they said all our struggle is inside Palestine and we don't want to have any accusation from any country that you are doing training here. We want all our stuff or all of our supporters to fight or to train there, inside Palestine. They requested him to close that camp, and it was closed. It was near Jalalabad.[117]

This report, if true, further suggests that it was primarily Azzam, not the Hamas leadership, who wanted Palestinians to train in Afghanistan. It also suggests that Hamas understood from the beginning that "going international" the way the PLO had done was politically risky. Azzam was no doubt frustrated at Hamas's attitude; Once again, a Muslim Brotherhood branch in the Middle East had refused to support his international activities.

Some of the "Afghan Palestinians" did end up returning and plotting attacks in the Territories. For example, a Palestinian named Ibrahim Abdallah Abd al-Rahman (aka Abu Jandal), who had gone to Afghanistan in 1987, was arrested by Israeli police on his return in 1991. He later said that Azzam had "asked him to go to Palestine for jihad."[118] Another example is Nazir al-Tamimi, a Hamas member who killed a Jewish settler near Ramallah in 1993, having previously been to Afghanistan.[119] There appear to have been several more cases of returnee attacks where the identity of the perpetrators is unknown.[120] An Afghan Arab named Muhammad Siddiqi said:

Some of [the Arabs who trained in Afghanistan] have conducted operations inside the Occupied Territories in Palestine ... He whom they followed in a plane was also here with us. And he who was killed in Cyprus. And the brother who did the nice operation called "Operation Buraq" and who killed ten Israeli officers and soldiers ... And then the brother who tried to enter the compound of Ministries with the veiled sister and whose plan was discovered moments before he entered.[121]

Similarly, Azzam himself proudly noted in a lecture in 1988 that he had read in newspapers about two Palestinian Afghanistan veterans attacking a car in Tel Aviv.[122] There was also at least one case of a non-Palestinian Afghan Arab carrying out an attack on an Israeli target. In 1989 the Jordanian former officer Darar al-Shishani was killed in an attack on an Israeli border patrol just inside the Israeli–Jordanian border. Al-Shishani had trained in Afghanistan and was featured in *al-Jihad* magazine after his death.[123]

A key question is whether the Afghan Palestinians brought military skills that made a difference to Hamas's capabilities. Azzam's wife suggested as much when she said, "The first generation of the military wing of the al-Qassam [Brigades] was trained by him."[124] There appears to be a kernel of truth to this claim; a martyr biography on the Hamas website mentioned a certain Izz al-Din Subhi al-Shaykh Khalil, who "travelled from the Gaza strip in 1986 to the UAE and on to Pakistan and Afghanistan. There he got to know Sheikh Abdallah Azzam. He returned in 1990 to found the Qassam brigades."[125] Another Afghanistan veteran who later joined Hamas was Ibrahim Abd al-Karim Bani Awda, who, after his Jordanian military service in 1989 had "moved [to Afghanistan] to increase his military expertise and to meet with his first teacher Sheikh Abdallah Azzam."[126] It is also possible that some explosives expertise entered the Palestinian Territories from Afghanistan; one of Azzam's Islamist biographers wrote that Azzam "trained the youth from Palestine in the production of explosives" and that "after the training they returned and entered the occupied land."[127] Elements of Afghan Arab jihadi culture certainly seeped back to Palestine in this period, with returnees from Afghanistan wearing the Afghan pakol hat and people in the Territories humming *anashid* from Afghanistan.[128] Moreover, Azzam's writings on Afghanistan were very popular in Palestine, to the point where several were reprinted there in substantial numbers.[129] However, Azzam's influence on the Intifada should not be exaggerated. Attacks perpetrated by Afghan veterans represent a tiny proportion of all Palestinian operations in this period, and the military skills imported from Afghan camps were not game-changing. Moreover, the Hamas leadership did not adopt Azzam's internationalist worldview, preferring instead a local strategy.

Several of Azzam's friends and supporters have said that his activities made the Israelis want to kill him. Jamal Isma'il, for example, says that "when they discovered that these [incidents in the Territories] were all linked to Abdallah Azzam, they started thinking about assassinating him."[130] Another biographer claimed that "someone came and warned Azzam that the Israeli newspapers had started mentioning his name a lot."[131] However, these are speculations. We do not know for sure how closely Israelis really followed the Afghan trail generally, or Azzam specifically. There is little evidence of Israeli services harassing him or his family at this time, let alone attempting to kill him.

Israeli sources diverge regarding how early they learned about Azzam's role, and how closely they followed him. The late jihadism scholar and former Shin Bet analyst Reuven Paz told this author, "There are Israeli documents on Azzam from at least the 1970s."[132] However, Shaul Shay, a former Israeli military intelligence official, doubts this, saying that the Muslim Brotherhood in Jordan would not have been a collection target in the 1970s.[133] In addition, several Israeli sources insist that Azzam did not come to their attention until the late 1980s, and even then only as a peripheral figure. Shlomo Shpiro dates the discovery to 1987:

In late 1987, during the early stages of the first Palestinian Intifada (uprising), officers of Israel's General Security Service, the Shabak, began to see the name "bin Laden" appearing in documents captured from Palestinian terrorists in the West Bank and Gaza. Investigations revealed that the man in question was a rich Saudi working closely with the radical Palestinian cleric Abdullah Azam, who was recruiting volunteers in Arab countries to fight with the mujahedeen against the Soviets in Afghanistan.[134]

Yonathan Fighel, an IDF colonel-turned-academic who was military governor of Tulkarm from 1987 to 1989 and of Jenin from 1991 to 1993, says he first came across Azzam's name in 1988:

In one of the [mosque] searches in the Tulkarm vicinity we found a lot of material, and something struck my eye: a copy of *al-difa' 'an aradi al-muslimin*. I remember thinking, "Who the hell is Abdallah Azzam?" At that time we did not really know what was going on in Afghanistan. I didn't understand what I was seeing ... But then I forgot about it until we discovered it again in Hebron in 2002.[135]

However, all the Israeli sources interviewed for this book insist that Azzam was not high up on the Israeli intelligence radar in the late 1980s.[136] Shaul Shay says he never heard of Azzam during his twenty-five years in military intelligence. Fighel says Azzam was not a topic of concern in Israeli intelligence circles until after 9/11: "I don't know how much the Shin Bet knew, but I had a lot of meetings with Shin Bet [in the 1990s] and I don't recall any discussions about Arab Afghans or al-Qaida."[137] Of course, it is difficult to specify exactly what an intelligence apparatus like Israel's knew and when they knew it, because even truthful former insiders might not have the full picture. However, it is entirely possible that he was in the archives, but not considered an important collection target, for Israel had many other fish to fry at that time.

We have seen that Azzam had many critics and opponents in the late 1980s. Some were on the inside of the Afghan Arab community, especially among the revolutionaries, who saw him as too moderate and pragmatic. Others were on the outside, in the form of governments who found his activities subversive. We have also seen that Azzam mostly did not initiate or provoke these polemics; rather, they were reactions to strategies that Azzam was following for other reasons. With the Pakistanis, the Saudis, and the Arab revolutionaries, he tried his best to deescalate the situation and not provoke his foes unnecessarily. The exception is his involvement with the Palestinian Intifada, which drew unnecessary attention from the Israelis.

However, none of these controversies was particularly intense. The Pakistanis were apprehensive of the Afghan Arabs, but mostly let Azzam be after 1986. The Saudis worked against him mainly by promoting his competitors. The revolutionaries disliked Azzam, but the so-called trial of Azzam was never about a death sentence. Hekmatyar was less upset than the Afghan Arabs about Azzam's rapprochement with Massoud. And we do not even know if the Israelis were doing more than compiling an intelligence file on him. It was far from clear that events would take such a dramatic turn toward the end of 1989.

15 | Martyr

When the last piece of metal fell on the ground, there was half a second of quiet before people crowded around the wreck. It was clear that Muhammad and Ibrahim had died instantly, but Abdallah Azzam was still breathing. He was taken out of the car and brought straight to the Hayat Shahid hospital, where he perished not long after.[1] In the late afternoon the three bodies were taken to the martyrs' cemetery in Pabbi, where a crowd of thousands had assembled to pay their respects. By the end of the evening of that Friday, 24 November 1989, Abdallah Azzam and his two sons were resting in the ground. What had just happened? Who would want to kill the spiritual leader of the Afghan Arabs? And why now, at the *end* of the war?

This chapter looks at the assassination of Abdallah Azzam, the biggest murder mystery in the history of jihadism. We will examine, in turn, the political atmosphere of late 1989 Peshawar, the details of the operation, the potential perpetrators, and the effects of Azzam's death on the Afghan Arab community. The jury is still out on who killed Azzam, but the complexity of the operation points to a government agency, and the choice of time and place suggests that the perpetrator wanted to send a message to all the Arabs in Peshawar. Azzam's disappearance would send the Services Bureau into rapid decline and contribute to the fragmentation, radicalization, and eventual dispersion of the Afghan Arabs.

Quiet Autumn

In the autumn of 1989 things were calming down in Peshawar. Intra-Arab disputes were less intense than in the previous year, and relations between Hekmatyar and Massoud were slowly improving. Many Arabs were packing up; Usama Bin Ladin, for example, moved back to Saudi Arabia in October. For those who stayed, there were still problems to deal with, but the situation was less tense than it had been the previous year. It was quiet enough for Azzam and his deputy Tamim al-Adnani to go abroad on lengthy trips; al-Adnani to Africa and America and Azzam to the Gulf. As far as Azzam was concerned, the most dramatic event this autumn was al-Adnani's unexpected death in America in October, but aside from this, he went about his business largely as usual.

At the same time, Peshawar had never been a particularly safe place. Bombings and assassinations were so commonplace that in 1987 *al-Jihad* magazine published an article defiantly but revealingly titled "Peshawar Will Not be Another Beirut."[2] In the late 1980s the city saw dozens if not hundreds of bomb attacks per year.[3] The Arabs had also experienced security incidents; for example, in August 1989 unknown perpetrators burned down the house of Adnan Ibrahim, a Syrian who used to cover military affairs for *al-Jihad* magazine.[4] Azzam's friend Wa'il Julaydan reportedly received threats in 1989.[5] There was always a chance of meeting a violent death in Peshawar, but again, the risk did not appear particularly more acute at the end of 1989 than in preceding years.

Azzam was aware that he might become the target of an assassination. Several sources later said he had been warned through various channels of some kind of plot in the making.[6] Some Arabs had started taking security precautions; Bin Ladin later said, "A plot was concocted to assassinate all. We were very careful not to be together all the time. I often asked the shaykh, may God have mercy on his soul, to stay away from Peshawar [and stay] in Sada due to the increasing plots."[7] One of the Arab fighters offered to make Azzam a bulletproof vest, but he refused.[8] In 1988 and 1989 Azzam also had an Afghan bodyguard provided by Rabbani – because Arabs were not allowed to carry weapons in Peshawar – but this bodyguard was not with him all the time.[9] Jamal Khashoggi said that when Azzam was in a car, he would usually sit in the back seat with one person on either side as protection.[10]

Moreover, there had been two specific incidents in the preceding months that had raised concern about a threat to Azzam's life. The first, which may have been a coincidence, was the reported finding of a bomb on a Saudia Airlines plane that Azzam had been due to take on his last trip to the kingdom.[11] The second, decidedly not a coincidence, was the discovery, in late October or early November 1989, of an explosive device inside the Sab' al-Layl mosque. According to the November issue of *al-Jihad*, published before Azzam's assassination, the bomb was found "under the wooden minbar from which Dr Abdallah Azzam preaches."[12] The device reportedly contained 2 kilograms of explosives, and was defused by a Pakistani ordnance expert. The mosque administrators reportedly increased security and notified Azzam, but he took no special protective measures. He had a fatalist view on the situation, and it would cost him his life.

Complex Operation

The assassination took place at 12:20 p.m. on Friday 24 November 1989.[13] As described in the prologue, Azzam was driving with his two sons Muhammad and Ibrahim to the Sab' al-Layl mosque when a roadside bomb exploded under their car. The blast occurred near the crossing of the Great Trunk Road and Arbab Road, on the south side of Great Trunk Road. The bomb was concealed under a small bridge that took cars over a ditch between the main road and the mosque parking lot (see Illustration 21). It actually consisted of two devices, one on each side of the bridge, containing an estimated total of 20 kilograms of explosives.[14] They were connected by a wire that continued along the ditch until it came up from an opening 20–30 meters further west. We do not know where the wire then led or what it was connected to.

The operational details suggest a highly capable perpetrator. Constructing a bomb and getting it to detonate under a specific car in motion requires considerable expertise. Moreover, it took strong operational security at all stages of the process. First, the perpetrator must have been able to place the bomb undetected in a highly trafficked location. Next, the perpetrator must have had have eyes on the target as it approached the bridge. The device must have been detonated remotely and manually – as opposed to by a pressure mechanism or a timer – because there was other traffic on the same bridge around the same time. Finally, those involved had to be able to get away from the blast site without attracting attention. The operation could go wrong in several ways: the operator might get caught placing the bomb; the device might fail to detonate and the police would discover it; or the operators on site might not be able to extract themselves undetected after the blast. Capture would likely entail arrest and interrogation for the individual, and political embarrassment for the organization behind him.

Azzam's assassins must also have wanted to create a spectacle, because there were simpler and quieter ways of killing him. A drive-by shooting from a motorcycle or a bomb outside his house would have done the trick. The choice of place (the main Arab mosque), time (Friday prayer), and weapon (bomb) clearly suggests a desire to attract attention and send a message. Somebody wanted to scare the Arabs in Peshawar. But who?

Many Candidates

There has been much speculation about who killed Azzam, but so far nobody has mustered sufficient evidence to identify the perpetrator. At least nine theories have been proposed. This section will evaluate each by assessing their capabilities and motivations for an operation of this kind. The candidates are presented in increasing order of likelihood according to this author's assessment.

Usama Bin Ladin

Some sources have suggested that Bin Ladin orchestrated Azzam's assassination as part of their alleged feud over the leadership and strategic direction of the Afghan Arabs.[15] This is a highly unlikely hypothesis, because we know that Bin Ladin liked and respected Azzam until the end. It is also unclear what Bin Ladin would have gained from killing him. As explained in the previous chapter, al-Qaida and the Services Bureau were not so much competitors as complementary organizations catering for different segments of the Afghan Arab community.[16] Besides, Bin Ladin had left Peshawar in October 1989, and had already started setting his sights on other conflict zones such as Yemen.[17] Moreover, the normative barrier was high; Azzam was a highly respected figure, and there was no culture of internecine killing among Arab jihadis at this time. The reputational downside to such a plot would have been devastating. As Ahmad Zaidan put it, "if he be exposed, he would be finished, really."[18]

In a 1998 interview, Bin Ladin was directly confronted with the accusation that he ordered Azzam's assassination. He replied:

As for this accusation, I think that it is being promoted today by the Jews, Americans, and some of their agents. However, this is not worth a response. It is illogical for a person to chop off his head while the one who was in the field knows the extent of the strong relationship between me and Shaykh 'Abdallah 'Azzam. This accusation is silly and baseless. There was no competition [between me and him]. Shaykh 'Abdallah's field was that of call [*da'wa*] and instigation, while we were on the (Baktia) mountains in the interior. He sent us young people as well as directives. We did what he ordered us. We pray that God will accept him and his two sons, Muhammad and Ibrahim, as martyrs, and to compensate the nation by giving it one who can carry out the duty he used to perform.[19]

Saudi Intelligence

A few sources have pointed to Saudi intelligence on the basis that the Saudi government may have seen Azzam as a radicalizing influence on the foreign fighters and as an obstacle to Saudi control over Arabs in Peshawar. However, Riyadh arguably lacked both the capability and the motivation. The Saudi General Intelligence Directorate did not have a history of targeted assassinations abroad, and it is doubtful that it had the ability to carry out an operation like this under the radar of the Pakistani services. Besides, it is not clear why the Saudi government would have wanted to take such a drastic step. Some Saudi officials may have seen Azzam as a rabble-rouser, but they did not consider him an outright security threat to the kingdom. Besides, there were other, more fiercely anti-Saudi activists around at the time such as Abu Muhammad al-Maqdisi and the militant Saudi Shiite group Hizballah al-Hijaz, and even they were not targeted with assassination.

Jordanian Intelligence

Some have also suspected the Jordanian government in light of Azzam's history of criticizing the regime and of training Jordanian militants. In the book about the Jordanian al-Qaida operative Humam al-Balawi, Joby Warrick writes that during al-Balawi's time in Jordanian custody in the late 2000s, intelligence officials boasted of being behind Azzam's assassination.[20] In Joby Warrick's retelling, al-Balawi's handler "said flatly that Azzam's death too had been the work of the Mukhabarat. He even offered the name of the assassin: bin Zeid's own boss, Ali Burjak, the 'Red Devil'."[21] A claim this specific deserves to be taken seriously, but on balance it seems implausible. The Jordanian General Intelligence Directorate probably did have the capability for an operation like this, but it is harder to see what their motivation would have been. Jordan at that time did not have a problem with jihadi violence, and Azzam was not inciting recruits against the Jordanian government. If they worried about people going to Afghanistan, it did not make sense to kill Azzam at the end of the war. Besides, Amman does not have a track record of assassinating Islamist leaders; on the contrary, several radical and influential ideologues such as Abu Muhammad al-Maqdisi and Abu Qatada have been allowed to operate in Jordan. A somewhat less implausible scenario is that Jordan did it at the request of an important ally such as the USA, but it is not clear why the CIA would turn to a Middle Eastern service for help with an operation in South Asia.

US Intelligence

Not surprisingly, many have suggested that the CIA did it on its own. This is one of the most common views among Azzam's sympathizers, including his immediate family.[22] They believe the USA killed Azzam to prevent him from uniting the Islamist Mujahidin, and they view the assassination as one in a series of CIA operations in Pakistan, including the plane crash that killed President Zia ul Haq in August 1988.

The CIA unquestionably had the capability for an operation such as this, but it is doubtful whether Azzam was important enough to justify the risks involved. On the one hand, Azzam could well have been perceived as a potential threat to US interests. He wrote anti-American articles in *al-Jihad* magazine, he was responsible for the recruitment of many Muslim Americans to the Afghan jihad, and he had declared it legitimate to kill Jews on American soil. Many Westerners in Afghanistan, including CIA operatives, had had run-ins with hostile Arabs. Moreover, Steve Coll has argued that the late 1980s saw attempts inside the Reagan administration to adopt more aggressive counterterrorism operations and get around the Ford-era executive order banning political assassination.[23]

On the other hand, the USA cannot have been that concerned with Azzam if it let him travel freely to America throughout the 1980s, and even use a bank account there. Besides, precisely because Azzam came regularly to the USA, it would have been easier to just arrest him there if they wanted him out of circulation. Moreover, America had many enemies at this time, and Azzam was not among the most prominent ones. Last but not least, the Soviet withdrawal from Afghanistan in February 1989 had reduced the region's strategic importance to the United States. It is unlikely the USA would have invested in such a high-risk operation in a region where it saw no future.

Israeli Intelligence

Another oft-cited suspect is the Israeli Mossad.[24] Usama Bin Ladin, for example, later said, "It is believed that Israel, together with some of its Arab agents, were the ones who assassinated the shaykh."[25] Of course, the Mossad is often the default scapegoat for bad things that happen in the Muslim world, but in this particular case we cannot dismiss the suggestion off hand. Mossad was a highly capable service with a long history of assassinating Palestinian militants abroad.[26] Although the Mossad had no known history of major operations in Pakistan, it had a good relationship with Indian intelligence, which could have helped with an operation like this.[27]

On the motivation side, it is reasonable to think that the ongoing Palestinian Intifada and the prospect of a rising Hamas may have made Israeli services jittery. As we saw in the previous chapter, Azzam had helped train Palestinians in Afghanistan for attacks in Israel. An argument could thus be made that Azzam had Israeli blood on his hands and that he was a strategic asset for Hamas. However, Azzam and the Afghan Arabs would have been a small concern compared with the many other threats Israel was facing at this time, from Hamas in the Territories, via the old PLO groups, to Iran and Hizballah. The Mossad was notably bent on tracking down Imad Mughniyeh, the senior Hizballah operative linked to a series of bombings and kidnappings in the 1980s.[28] Moreover, Mossad was a relatively small intelligence service, and an operation in Peshawar would have been resource-intensive. In 2018 the Israeli journalist Ronen Bergman published a 750-page book about the history of Israel's targeted assassinations. He put the number of such operations at 2,400 (the vast majority in the Territories during the Second Intifada) and described many controversial operations in detail. He mentions Azzam briefly (in connection with another case) but says nothing to suggest that the Israelis killed him.[29] All in all the Mossad seems a rather unlikely candidate.

Ayman al-Zawahiri

One of the most widely endorsed theories implicates Ayman al-Zawahiri, either alone or in an alliance with Gulbuddin Hekmatyar.[30] The Zawahiri hypothesis is notably supported by several former Afghan Arabs who cite Zawahiri's well-known hostility to Azzam. Hasan al-Surayhi, for example, said, "I doubt bin Laden was involved in Azzam's assassination. I suspect the Egyptians because the killing of Azzam coincided with the idea of establishing the al Qaeda organization."[31] Osama Rushdi has said that "Two days before Dr. Azzam [was assassinated] I am in conversation with al Zawahiri [for] two hours, and trying to change his mind, but he was very angry. But before [Azzam was] dead he [was saying Azzam] is a spy."[32] Al-Zawahiri's motivation, the theory goes, was that Azzam stood in the way of further Egyptian influence on Bin Ladin and access to his money. Azzam was also an ideological competitor to the more revolutionary-minded Egyptians; getting him out of the way would make it easier to win supporters for the Egyptian approach.

However, killing Azzam would have been an extreme breach of the norms that prevailed in the Afghan Arab community at the time. There was virtually no precedent for Arab jihadists assassinating each other, and certainly not for killing respected clerics. Even if Zawahiri had personally lacked the qualms to do it, the political cost in the event of a botched operation would have been extremely high.

Moreover, it is not clear that Zawahiri had the capability to carry out an operation of this complexity. To be sure, some of his men had bomb-making expertise, al-Qaida's camps included explosives training, and parts of the *Encyclopedia of Jihad* were devoted to remotely detonated devices.[33] However, as far as we know, this expertise was not deployed outside of the training camps in this period (with the possible exception of plots in Israel), so the Arabs did not have much experience of operating in complex urban environments. We cannot rule out the possibility, but on balance it seems unlikely.

Hekmatyar

Another frequently mentioned suspect is Gulbuddin Hekmatyar, the leader of the Afghan Mujahidin party Hezb-e Islami.[34] Many fingers have been pointed at Hekmatyar, because he had a reputation for liquidating enemies and because he was the archenemy of Ahmed Shah Massoud, Azzam's newfound friend in 1988–1989. Prince Turki al-Faisal, the head of Saudi foreign intelligence at the time, later said Azzam's assassin was "definitely Hekmatyar, because Abdallah Azzam was championing other Mujahidin leaders."[35]

Many who suspect Hekmatyar point to his supposedly ruthless character. The Saudi journalist Jamal Khashoggi said:

[Hekmatyar is] an arrogant, self-obsessed person. I think Hekmatyar had a secret organization to eliminate his enemies. Hekmatyar was obsessed with the concept that he is the legitimate leader of the Afghan jihad movement because he is the one who started jihad in the '70s. From an early time some of the secret assassinations which took place against certain Afghan mujahideen were done by Hekmatyar.[36]

Similarly, Gilles Dorronsoro wrote that "political assassination, justified by takfir, was a vital part of the political culture of Hezb-i Islami."[37] Kurt Lohbeck wrote that "Gulbuddin ... ordered the execution of several mujahaddin commanders, some on the streets of Peshawar."[38] In 1988, the killing of the royalist Professor Sayd Bahouddin Majrooh was widely interpreted as Hekmatyar's work.[39] Moreover, in the autumn of 1988 the US special envoy to Afghanistan Ed McWilliams toured the tribal areas and found that:

As the Soviets withdrew, Gulbuddin Hekmatyar – backed by officers in ISI's Afghan bureau, operatives from the Muslim Brotherhood's Jamaat-e-Islami, officers from Saudi intelligence, and Arab volunteers from a dozen countries – was moving systematically to wipe out rivals in the Afghan resistance ... Hekmatyar and his kingpin commanders were serially kidnapping and murdering mujahedin royalists, intellectuals, rival party commanders – anyone who threatened strong alternative leadership.[40]

As we have seen, Hekmatyar later became famous for sending an Egyptian operative to kill the Salafi Mujahidin leader Jamil al-Rahman.[41]

The question is what Hekmatyar's motivation might have been. Some say he bore an old grudge against Azzam for supporting Sayyaf in the first half of the war. According to Mustafa Hamid, Hekmatyar made death threats against Azzam as early as 1986:

[In mid-1986] Azzam sought protection and refuge in Sayyaf's territory after Hekmatyar made strong threats against him. Hekmatyar was angry with

Azzam because he thought Azzam was making propaganda in favour of Sayyaf and financial support of his activities. Burhanuddin Rabbani too was angry with Azzam, but unlike Hekmatyar, he did not resort to death threats. Both Hekmatyar and Rabbani were angry that Azzam was giving too much money to Sayyaf and not supporting their organization with anything. Hekmatyar said, "I am going to kill him [Azzam]; he damaged our work, he took our money."[42]

Others have highlighted Azzam's rapprochement with Massoud as a possible motivation. Tomsen notably relates an anecdote about Hekmatyar allegedly threatening to kill Azzam if he published his pro-Massoud book *A Month among Giants*:

> Soon after Azzam returned to Peshawar, Hekmatyar requested that he come alone to his office. Abu Tahla [sic], Azzam's Kuwaiti assistant, accompanied him to the meeting. Hekmatyar personally barred Tahla from entering his office. When Azzam emerged from Hekmatyar's office, Tahla noted he had an angry look on his face. When Tahla asked him what happened in the meeting, Azzam curtly responded, "I received a warning. If this book is published, I will receive a bullet."[43]

As we saw in the previous chapter, Azzam was involved in a process of negotiations between Rabbani and Hekmatyar in late 1989, one that was completed the night before the assassination. According to Jamal Khashoggi, Hekmatyar perceived this negotiation as an investigation into the Farkhar massacre in July, and he expected the inquiry to conclude with criticism of Hizb-e Islami over the Farkhar incident.[44] Khashoggi suggested that Hekmatyar was so unhappy with Azzam's role in this "investigation" that he may have decided to eliminate him.[45]

The case is far from clear-cut, however. For one thing, Hekmatyar's reputation for evil was probably exaggerated. CIA station chief in Islamabad Milt Bearden later wrote that "the KGB had a special disinformation team tasked with sowing discord among the Peshawar Seven, and Gulbuddin Hekmatyar, as Pakistan's favourite, was its central target … USSR spread rumours about Hekmatyar as a cool murderer willing to execute people with his own hands and to have fellow mujahidin leaders killed."[46] Steve Coll also writes that "the KGB also ran 'false bands' of mujahidin across Afghanistan, paying them to attack genuine rebel groups in an attempt to sow dissension."[47]

For another, Hekmatyar and Azzam were much better friends than Hamid and Tomsen's accounts suggest. According to Abdallah Anas,

"Sheikh Abdullah Azzam was very highly respected ... by the Mujahidin leaders, including Hekmatyar."[48] Abu Harith, Azzam's driver and assistant in the late 1980s, said Azzam liked Hekmatyar the best of all the Mujahidin leaders.[49] Ahmad Zaidan, who worked closely with Azzam on *al-Jihad* magazine, said Hekmatyar was one of Azzam's three closest friends in Peshawar in the late 1980s.[50] Hekmatyar himself said, "I accompanied him on many journeys into Afghanistan, long journeys, and I knew in detail the sheikh's sensibilities and aspirations. I accompanied him to Nangarhar, Lugar, Paktia, and Kunar, and on the most recent long trip, and one learns to know one's friend the best on such trips, I sensed his strong determination and commitment to the leadership."[51] Of all the Mujahidin leaders, Hekmatyar was the most frequently interviewed in *al-Jihad* magazine, and the last interview with him was published in October 1989.[52] And for what it is worth, we know that Hekmatyar attended the celebration of Abdallah Anas's engagement to Azzam's daughter Sumayya at Bayt al-Ansar in early December 1988.[53] Finally, both Hekmatyar himself and other senior Hezb-e Islami leaders eulogized Azzam extensively in speeches and statements after the assassination.[54] If Hekmatyar was behind the assassination, he did a very good job of covering it up.

Afghan Intelligence

Several observers have suspected the KhAD (Khadamat-e Ittila'at-e Dawlati), the intelligence service of the Afghan Communist regime.[55] KhAD certainly had the capability. It was trained and equipped by Soviet advisors, and it had carried out numerous attacks not just inside Afghanistan but also in Peshawar. ISI brigadier Mohammad Yousaf wrote that "Pakistan had been swamped with KhAD agents bent on undermining the government by a terror campaign of bombing civilians."[56] The American journalist Kurt Lohbeck, who lived in Peshawar for several years in the 1980s, writes that, from 1987, "Terrorist bombings became commonplace in Peshawar and other border spots, during which hundreds of Pakistani and Afghan refugees were killed. KGB and KhAD terrorist groups were responsible."[57] The Egyptian filmmaker Isam Diraz has said that KhAD also went after Arabs in Pakistan, citing the example of a Saudi named Yahya Mansur who reportedly was assassinated in Parachinar in 1986 while carrying money to refugee camps on the border.[58] The Afghan Communist regime had several reasons to assassinate Azzam, the most obvious being to avenge and deter Arab military involvement in the war. Another might be to prevent the rapprochement between Hekmatyar and Massoud, which, if realized, would have made for a stronger adversary. A third one may have been to eliminate a moderate voice in the Arab community so that the Arabs would radicalize and delegitimize themselves and their Afghan partners. The main argument against KhAD involvement is the timing. They must have known about Azzam for a long time, which raises the question why they would have waited till late 1989 to eliminate him.

Pakistani Intelligence

The final candidate is the Pakistani Inter-Services Intelligence (ISI). Several informed observers have raised this possibility. For example, Vahid Mojdeh, an Afghan who worked for the Services Bureau, says that on the day before the assassination he saw unusual road work being done around the Sab' al-Layl mosque:

On that day that ... it was quite interesting also, sophisticated, that when Azzam was killed, on that particular day when I came out from, in the area of Arbab road in Peshawar, PDA [Peshawar Development Authority] members came to clean the area, this side or this side were not clean just the middle part of that one which has, you know, vast materials and all these things, so they were cleaning only the middle part. There was a small bridge. When the car came to the street ... After returning to the office I told my colleagues that the PDA is very efficient now, they are cleaning our areas and these things. But it was Thursday. And on Friday, under that bridge a mine was set, and then, Abdullah Azzam and his two sons were killed in that explosion.[59]

The Pakistani investigation of the incident also appears to have been half-hearted, although it is difficult to know whether this was due to ill will or incompetence. To be sure, the incident was formally investigated. The person in charge of the investigation, a police officer named Iskandar Khan, visited the Services Bureau and was interviewed several times by *al-Jihad* magazine.[60] He said police interviewed the shopkeepers near the blast site and that they had taken "some people" in for questioning, but otherwise he was reluctant to provide details. However, there seems to have been no in-depth forensic investigation, and Arab eyewitnesses reportedly said the blast site was hosed clean by the end of the afternoon of the attack.[61] In the end nothing came of the investigation and nobody was ever charged. It is clear from the coverage in *al-Jihad* magazine that Azzam's supporters felt Pakistani police were dragging their feet. For example, in February 1990 *al-Jihad* noted that "Police colonel Iskandar Khan denied the accusation directed at Pakistani authorities of lack of serious interest in the investigation."[62] In April 1990 Khan said, "We have no witnesses or evidence pointing to involvement of 'official Pakistani' agencies in this incident."[63]

Of all the candidates, Pakistani intelligence is the one with the highest capability. For one thing, it would have been operating on home turf without having to worry about police detection. For another, the ISI had extensive experience with assassinations and bombings, notably against Soviet targets in Kabul.[64] According to Brigadier Mohammad Yousaf, the ISI trained "car bombing squads" and gave them explosives to attack Russian officers and soldiers in Kabul.[65] Steve Coll also notes that the CIA provided the ISI with "many tons of C-4 plastic explosives for sabotage operations during this period," and that "after 1985 the CIA also supplied electronic timing and detonation devices that made it easier to set off explosions from a remote location."[66]

The ISI had two conceivable motives to liquidate Azzam. One was to prevent a rapprochement between Hekmatyar and Massoud. The other and more likely one was to intimidate the Arab community to make them leave. The Pakistani government had never been pleased with the Arab foreign-fighter presence, and now that the jihad was over, they may have liked them to start packing up. The proliferation of Arab training camps in 1989 may have worried both Pakistan and its international partners. Moreover, as we saw in the previous chapter, Azzam and other Arabs had started to openly criticize the Pakistani government in 1988 after its signing of the Geneva accords. Vahid Mojdeh has said that "After Zia ul Haq was killed [on 17 August 1988], the pressure increased on the Arabs from the Pakistan government ... it was evident from the [Azzam assassination] that this was a big plan, made against Arabs. Either they should be killed or sent out of the country."[67] We know that other prominent Afghan Arabs were pressured to leave not long after the Azzam assassination; Abu Burhan al-Suri, for example, "departed to Sudan following Pakistani threats against him."[68] And the spring of 1992 saw a heavy Pakistani crackdown on Arabs in Peshawar. The Azzam assassination may have been the opening salvo in a concerted intimidation campaign.

The main argument against the ISI hypothesis is that Azzam was not important enough. They had bigger fish to fry, and a bomb assassination could have unforeseeable consequences. Moreover, Pakistan arguably had other ways to make the Arabs leave, such as arrests and deportations. Hein Kiessling, a German military advisor who worked closely with the ISI in the 1980s and 1990s, expressed skepticism of an ISI role in the assassination: "There is no hint that ISI was involved in killing Azzam – but of course they knew who the culprits were."[69] Asked in a follow-up question whether ISI involvement was inconceivable, he wrote, "'inconceivable' of course not, but I don't see a special interest on the ISI's side at that time. I think it was an Arab hand behind it." On balance, the ISI is one of the stronger candidates on this list, but doubts remain.

Unfortunately, based on what we know today, we cannot say who killed Azzam. The two most likely candidates are arguably ISI and KhAD, because only they had the capacity and motivation to mount an attack of such complexity against a target of such limited international importance. If forced to put money on one candidate, this author would reluctantly say the ISI, because the timing (the end of the Afghan jihad) made more sense for the Pakistanis and it was easier for them to do. However, this is just a guess, and we cannot firmly rule out any one of these nine candidates, except perhaps Bin Ladin. The frustrating reality is that we may never know the answer. We can only hope for a sudden breakthrough in the form of a key witness who decides to tell all or declassified intelligence documents with revelatory information.[70]

Sad Aftermath

Azzam's assassination caused a major stir in Peshawar and beyond. The burial on the evening of his assassination was a major public event, and thousands of people flocked to Pabbi in the course of the afternoon. Most Arabs in Peshawar were there, as were all the Mujahidin leaders except Hekmatyar (who was traveling and did not make it back in time for the funeral). Abd Rabb al-Rasul Sayyaf, Burhanuddin Rabbani, and Fathi al-Rifa'i gave passionate eulogies, as did Azzam's nephews Fayiz and Ahmad.[71] The bodies, faces uncovered, were carried on stretchers through the crowd. Martyrs are buried as they are, so Azzam wore the same clothes he had put on in the morning. Somewhere along the way, his bloodstained jacket was taken off and handed to his family as a memento.

Azzam was of course widely viewed as a martyr, and before long he became the object of the same types of miracle stories that he himself had chronicled so often for others.[72] Witnesses would say that his dead body had smelled of musk, more strongly so than those of his sons. They also said that while his sons' bodies were badly mutilated, his body was intact.[73] His face was supposedly smiling, and he reportedly had a small wound on the forehead where the prayer mark normally is. Some said his body had been found kneeling down as if in prayer. However, news reports said that Azzam was found in the car and that he did not die on the spot (he died either on the way to the hospital or in the hospital a few hours later).[74] Dream accounts also proliferated. Several of Azzam's friends claimed to have been forewarned in their dreams about what was about to happen. Azzam's nephew and biographer Mahmud Azzam, for example, writes that, a few weeks before the assassination, his wife told him about a vision she had about someone putting a revolver in one of the corners in the mosque.[75] Mahmud Azzam says he told Azzam about it and that in the following weeks Azzam would occasionally ask Mahmud if his wife had had any dreams recently. After the assassination, several others claimed to have had dreams which they now understood to be forewarnings.[76] Sayyaf, for example, said he had dreamt the night before that both his hands had been cut off.[77] Others said they had seen Azzam and the Prophet Muhammad in the same dream; as Meir Hatina relates:

> One of his followers related that before 'Azzam's death he dreamt that he and his friends were seated around the Shaykh when the door suddenly opened and a man with an impressive bearing, a well-tended beard and a pleasant scent entered the room, blessing all present. No one replied, except for 'Azzam, who took him by the hand, led him outside and closed the door. In another dream, after 'Azzam's martyrdom, a disciple of 'Azzam saw him in a crowd, which honoured him with a feast in heaven – one of 'Azzam's most joyous moments. The Prophet and a group of sahaba [companions] approached, welcoming him. Sweets were then distributed to all.[78]

The mourning continued in Peshawar for days. The Afghan Mujahidin organized a three-day event at the headquarters of the Mujahidin government featuring numerous speakers.[79] They included the four Mujahidin leaders Sayyaf, Rabbani, Hekmatyar, and Yunus

Khalis, several of their deputies, such as Muhammad Yasir (Sayyaf), Sadiq Jakri (Rabbani), Abd al-Rahim Khanjani (Hekmatyar), in addition to an envoy from Ahmed Shah Massoud. Leading Afghan Arabs such as Abd al-Majid al-Zindani and Musa al-Qarni also spoke, as did representatives of the Muslim Brotherhood such as Ahmad al-Assal. From the Pakistani side, Qazi Hussein Ahmed spoke on behalf of Jamaat-e Islami, and an envoy spoke for the Committee of the Ulama of Pakistan in Islamabad. Azzam's former employer, the International Islamic University in Islamabad, also sent an envoy, as did the student unions at the IIUI and the University of Da'wa and Jihad. Later the Pakistani Student Union issued a statement of condolence.[80]

The following weeks would reveal the true extent of Azzam's status and network. There was a massive outpouring of sympathy from outside Pakistan. Abdallah Anas said:

> You can't imagine [the reactions to Azzam's murder]. We used to receive calls from everywhere in the world, people are just calling and crying, because they can't speak. Ladies and gents. From Palestine, from the United States, from Algeria, from Saudi, from everywhere, and three, four telephone lines, twenty-four hours for more than one month, people calling and crying. It's without exaggeration, an earthquake.[81]

The reactions went far beyond phone calls. Inside Afghanistan, "students of the sheikh" among the Mujahidin mounted an "Abdallah Azzam operation" in his honor by firing twenty-seven Saqr 20 and Saqr 30 missiles from Paghman toward the presidential palace in Kabul.[82] A picture published in *al-Bunyan al-Marsus* shows one of the missiles ready to launch, with the phrase "Martyrs Abdallah Azzam and Tamim al-Adnani operation" written in white paint along the black metal case.[83] In Jordan, the Muslim Brotherhood organized a three-day memorial event at the Islamic Center Association (the organization's headquarters). A parallel event for women was held at the house of his cousin Ahmad Muhammad Azzam (Abu Muhammad Atta).[84] The memorial event included speeches by the Jordanian Brotherhood leader Muhammad Khalifa and several other leading figures. From Cairo came a statement from Muhammad Hamid Abu Nasr, the supreme guide of the Muslim Brotherhood.[85] According to one witness there were large crowds on the streets leading to the house.[86] Even the Jordanian Crown Prince Hassan paid a visit to convey condolences from the royal family.[87] Elsewhere across the Middle East there were similar events; in Kuwait the Muslim

Brotherhood organized a commemorative event at the Islah Association headquarters, attended by "numerous Islamic personalities."[88] In Palestine Hamas reportedly declared a general strike in both the West Bank and Gaza on 27 December 1989 to mark Azzam's assassination.[89]

The following weeks also saw the publication of a large number of eulogies and obituaries by senior Islamist figures such as Rachid Ghannouchi, Abd al-Rahman Abd al-Khaliq, and many others. The obituaries appeared not only in Islamist magazines, but also in mainstream national newspapers such as *al-Ukaz* and *al-Ra'i* and in pan-Arab newspapers such as *al-Sharq al-Awsat*. Later, many of these statements were collected in a 650-page book titled *Through Contemporary Eyes*. The list of people who lauded Azzam reads like a veritable who's who of Islamism in the Middle East and South Asia at the time.

For at least two years after the assassination there were annual memorial conferences and events in various places. In October 1991, for example, the Muslim Student's Union in the Ayn al-Hilweh refugee camp in Lebanon organized screenings of a tribute video about Azzam's life in the camp's mosques and Qur'an schools.[90] In November 1991 Pakistani scholars and Afghan Arabs held a conference in Islamabad about the life of Azzam.[91] The Azzam family's home in Pakistan also became a veritable site of pilgrimage for people wishing to pay homage to the late sheikh. In 1990, for example, Ahmed Shah Massoud, who had been inside Afghanistan at the time of the funeral, came to dine with the Azzam family in Peshawar.[92]

Azzam's death had a profound effect on the Afghan Arab community. There was a change of atmosphere; a sense of gravity reportedly weighed on Peshawar as people mourned Azzam's passing and reflected on the implications. People were also fearful of more attacks, and started praying in different mosques across Peshawar to mitigate risk.[93] To the extent that a community of militants can lose its innocence, that is what happened with the Arab Afghans after the Azzam assassination.

Within months, the Services Bureau fell into disarray. While finding a new executive director to replace Tamim al-Adnani was relatively easy (it fell to Abdallah Anas), agreeing on a new *amir* was another matter.[94] The first choice was Abd al-Majid al-Zindani, but he turned down the offer because he wanted to return to Yemen.[95] Instead, al-Zindani suggested Muhammad Yusuf Abbas (Abu Qasim), a relative newcomer to Peshawar, but someone with apparently solid Islamist credentials. Abbas was a Palestinian religious teacher who had known Azzam at Damascus University in the mid-1960s and had worked for many years in Saudi Arabia before coming to Pakistan in mid-1989. However, Azzam's relatives in the Bureau wanted another candidate, the late sheikh's nephew Fayiz Azzam. With a doctorate in Islamic Law, he also had religious credentials, but having arrived in September 1989 he was even more of a newcomer than Abbas. In the end, Abbas was appointed, but he proved to be an authoritarian and divisive leader.[96] He ended up firing several individuals, while others, such as the longtime editor of *al-Jihad* magazine Imad Ahmed, packed up and left.[97] There was also a political disagreement; Jamal Isma'il said the family faction accused Abbas of being too pro-Saudi: "he is so lenient toward Saudi and he is implementing Saudi government's agenda."[98] The problems split the organization: The family faction went one way, Abbas and his allies the other. Isma'il said, "They have taken some parts, he has taken some other part, departments, the magazine it was with him, he got the support of some NGOs, and they got the support of other NGOs."[99]

At some point the Azzam faction tried to find another director. They approached Ahmad Nawfal, whom they believed to be "closest in thinking" to Abdallah Azzam.[100] Nawfal was ready to move to Peshawar to take over the post, but the University of Jordan would not grant him leave, and he was not prepared to permanently leave his job.[101] Mahmud Azzam then went to Amman and approached Sheikh Abu al-Mun'im Abu Zant, who also politely refused. In the end no replacement was found, so the Bureau continued, divided, but under the nominal leadership of Muhammad Abbas. The conflict reached an apex in August 1991 when someone, presumably from the Azzam camp, distributed a fake press release saying that Abbas had left the Services Bureau and that Hussain Azzam had taken over. Abbas was furious, and had to publish an embarrassing retraction in the following issue of *al-Jihad*.[102] Abbas stayed in Peshawar until at least 1994, when he returned to Saudi Arabia, from where he was later expelled to Yemen.[103]

The Services Bureau survived for several more years, albeit in depleted form. The basic structure remained in place, but one by one the projects ended. Contact with the branches in the United States continued through 1990 – with Abdallah Anas making at least two speaking tours on behalf of the Bureau that year – but it faded after infighting in the US jihadi community led to the death of Mustafa Shalabi, the Bureau's main local representative, in early 1991.[104] In 1992 Abdallah Anas traveled to Croatia and Albania to assess whether to set up a Services Bureau branch for the Bosnia conflict, but the plans never materialized.[105] The guest houses in Peshawar operated until 1992, when Pakistani authorities cracked down on the Arab presence. The readership of *al-Jihad* also kept declining. From around 1994, according to Isma'il, "they were not having any activity, except getting funds for the orphans, running one educational institute, and the magazine." In early 1995 the Services Bureau closed down.[106]

The decline was not all due to Azzam's disappearance or Abbas's mismanagement. For one thing, the Gulf war in 1990–1991 drew attention away from Afghanistan and caused a split between Gulf governments and Islamists because the latter criticized Saudi Arabia for hosting US troops. According to Jamal Isma'il, the funds to the Services Bureau declined by 90 percent after the Gulf war.[107] For another, the capture of Kabul by Mujahidin forces in the spring of 1992 changed the Afghanistan war from an anti-Communist struggle to an intra-Afghan civil war, making it ideologically less appealing to many Islamists. Meanwhile, other crises such as the civil war in Algeria and the jihad in Bosnia took Muslim attention and funds away from Afghanistan. Still, the Bureau would have been better equipped to deal with these challenges with Azzam at the helm.

Aside from weakening the Services Bureau, Azzam's death affected the Afghan Arab community as a whole by depriving it of a unifying figure and religious authority. Mustafa Hamid said Azzam had a certain restraining influence on hot-headed Afghan Arabs: "Abdallah Azzam could not control all of them, but he could control a good number of them. After he died, many of those who were under his influence went to other groups, or fell under the influence of the takfiris."[108] This, in turn, sped up the process of fragmentation of the Afghan Arab community as well as the radicalization of parts of it. As Abdallah Anas noted:

I reached Peshawar [from Panjshir] and found it in a sorry state because of the absence of Sheikh Abdullah Azzam. Hekmatyar summarized the truth when he said: "I started seeing Arabs in Peshawar move around like orphans without a father" ... At that time, I started feeling like a stranger in Peshawar. The region was living in a state of mourning for the sheikh but this did not prevent me from noticing that it was no longer this spiritual base in which most inhabitants were dedicated to supporting the Afghan cause. The factions proliferated and new guest houses appeared, some with *takfiri* thought. New guest houses were founded by people whose only concern was to incite against the Afghan jihad under the pretext that they were blasphemers and heretics.[109]

The fragmentation problem was made worse by an increase in the number of opportunistic Arab volunteers in the 1990–1992 period. As Jamal Khashoggi noted:

Radicalism came to Afghanistan after '89 when the Afghan cause became a popular cause ... Afghanistan became so popular so everybody began to go there; independent Muslims and radical Muslims; people who were a drug addict a couple of months ago and then they're sober, and now they are like a newborn Christian. And I remember us making jokes about those people, like I remember this Belgian Muslim who came to Afghanistan and six months before he was a bouncer at one of the bars there. So after '89, floodgates open to Afghanistan of all kind of Arab adventurists and that's when radicalism starts creeping in.[110]

It did not help that other senior figures such as Abd al-Majid al-Zindani also left Peshawar, leaving the Arab community with fewer pragmatic voices. All this helped the growth of what Mustafa Hamid called the "Jalalabad School of jihad," meaning a culture of hot-headed, unstrategic military action.

The development coincided with the involvement of several returnees from Afghanistan in the nascent insurgencies in Egypt and Algeria, which gave the Afghan Arabs a bad reputation. As Darryl Li noted, "it was in this period that the term 'Afghan Arab' emerged in some parts of the Arabic-language media, denoting a sort of monstrous cultural hybrid, a nightmarish inversion of the relatively benign image of pan-Islamist solidarity that was nurtured during the anti-Soviet war."[111] Whether the "Afghan" Algerians and Egyptians really were more brutal than their fellow rebels who had not been to Afghanistan is unclear, but that became their reputation, and by 1992 the Afghan Arabs were seen as a security threat by many governments.

This was part of the backdrop when Pakistan in 1992 decided to crack down hard on the Arabs in Peshawar. After the fall of

Najibullah's Communist government to Mujahidin forces in April that year, Pakistani authorities arrested and deported many Afghan Arabs, prompting yet others to pack up and leave. An Egyptian volunteer named Zakariya Bashir later said:

I attempted to obtain a Hajj visa, but the Saudi embassy in Pakistan asked for the approval of the Egyptian ambassador. However, the Egyptian embassy refused, and I realized that going to Egypt meant my arrest because I heard that all those returning from Afghanistan were being arrested. We read that anti-terrorism laws punished anyone fighting for another country. I started thinking of going elsewhere to work. The situation in Pakistan was getting harder; they were arresting all the Arabs and deporting them, and Egypt was making treaties with other countries to turn in anyone proven to have lived in Pakistan. I stayed in Peshawar for four extra months and waited to go to Yemen ... Later on, I knew that Egypt pressured Pakistan to deport Egyptians working there, or at least to fire them. The hunt began in earnest in Pakistan. I was dismissed from my job, so I started looking for any possible way out and anywhere to travel. I decided to go to the one place available, to Sudan.[112]

The Pakistani clampdown in early 1992 is widely considered as the end of the Afghan jihad for the Arab volunteers. By the autumn of 1992 the Arab community in Peshawar was decimated, and by 1993–1994 it was, according to Kamal al-Helbawy, "a gloomy, dreary place."[113] A few hundred Arabs stayed, but after Egyptian Islamic Jihad bombed the Egyptian embassy in Islamabad in November 1995 the Pakistanis tightened the screw even further.[114]

As a result, the Arabs dispersed in different directions depending on their preferences and opportunities. Put simply, the Afghan Arab community split into four main pieces. One group simply demobilized and went home. This was the case with many Saudis, Jordanians, and others from countries that did not systematically arrest returnees. A second group continued their foreign-fighter careers in new conflict zones such as Tajikistan, Bosnia, the Philippines, or Chechnya. A third category, especially Algerians and Egyptians, went down the revolutionary track, hoping to topple their respective governments. Some of them made it home to fight, but most opted for safe havens such as Yemen and Sudan (for the Egyptians) and Europe (for the Algerians). The fourth category were the people in al-Qaida, who followed Bin Ladin to Sudan and later back to Afghanistan, where they would develop their strategy to attack the USA. Thus three distinct types of activists emerged from the Afghan

Arab community: the foreign fighters, the revolutionaries, and the global jihadists.[115]

Most of Azzam's own family stayed in Pakistan for the first half of the 1990s, where they helped keep the Services Bureau and *al-Jihad* magazine running. His immediate family – his widow and six surviving children – moved to Islamabad about a year after the assassination. The Azzam "clan" in Pakistan in the early 1990s counted around thirty people, including spouses and children.

Azzam's widow Samira took on a more public role than she had in the 1980s. She helped run the al-Ansar School in Peshawar, wrote articles in Islamist magazines, lectured widely, and gave many interviews.[116] During Ramadan 1990 she went to Saudi Arabia, where she was treated like something of a celebrity, speaking to audiences of hundreds of girls in Jeddah and Ta'if.[117] During the Bosnia war she took part in fundraising telethons in Jordan, at one point donating $10,000 to the Bosnian cause and urging others to do the same.[118] Samira Azzam's stature comes out clearly in the testimony of Rabiah Hutchinson, the Australian convert who arrived in Peshawar in the early 1990s:[119]

Rabiah's family received an allowance of US$150 per month. She says it was always paid to her by Umm Mohammed Azzam, the widow of the MAK founder, Abdallah Azzam. Umm Mohammed Azzam was an illustrious character in her own right, admired as a "mother figure" in the jihadist movement in Peshawar where she lived. After her husband's death she took over the administration of a range of humanitarian services in the Afghan refugee camps in Pakistan. She ran ten schools, a nursery and a charity called Darul Khayat – the "house of sewing" – which provided sewing machines, fabric and thread to Afghan war widows so they could earn an income from making clothing. She also ran the girls section of the Al Ansar school in Peshawar, which Rabiah's children attended.[120]

Other family members were even more active. A key figure in 1990s Peshawar was Mahmud Sa'id Azzam (Abu Adil), Abdallah's nephew by his sister Bahja. Abu Adil had joined Azzam as early as 1985 after obtaining a Master's degree in Islamic Studies in Pakistan.[121] He had served as Azzam's secretary and driver for several years and was, together with Abu Harith, the one who knew him the best in the later years. After Azzam's death he established the Martyr Azzam Media Center and led the editing and publishing of Azzam's writings.[122]

Another prominent family member was the abovementioned Fayiz Azzam (Abu Mujahid), Azzam's nephew by his sister Jamila. Although Fayiz did not make *amir* of the Services Bureau, he was heavily involved in its operations in the early 1990s. He traveled to the USA at least once, in 1990, to fundraise for the Bureau and for Hamas.[123] Other family members to stay in Peshawar included Azzam's nephew and former driver Abu Harith, Azzam's cousin Hussain Azzam, and Azzam's nephew Ahmad Sa'id Salih Azzam (aka Abu Ibada al-Ansari, Mahmud's brother).

We happen to have a detailed description of the Azzam family's situation in 1994. That year the American journalist Steven Emerson visited them in Peshawar as part of an investigation on radical Islamism in the United States. His book *American Jihad* (2002) contains several interesting observations from the trip.[124] After meeting with Hudhayfa in Islamabad, the two went together to see the rest of the family in Peshawar.[125] Hudhayfa took Emerson to the Services Bureau where he met a Palestinian staff member named Salih. At the *al-Jihad* head office he met the then editor, a certain Abu Suhayb. Emerson noted:

> The Arab Afghans we met in Peshawar seemed a milder brand. The tougher ones had all left for Sudan and Yemen ... Those who stayed behind were potential settlers. They already had their own infrastructure, with school and community centers. Hamza, Hudaifa's younger brother, for example, did not attend a Pakistani high school. His high school was all Arabic, a product of the Afghan war. The mosque where Azzam had preached ... had also become a school for the Arab community.[126]

He also describes a palpable attitude difference between the Azzam family and Muhammad Abbas:

> The next day Hudaifa showed us the entire jihad organization, including a fairly large compound with ten printing presses. The laborers were all Afghans, the headmen Palestinians ... Hudaifa was not the boss of the show, however. The headman was Muhammad Yusuf Abbas, commonly known as Abu l-Qasim, who was suspicious and angry to find us in his office.[127]

The next day Hudhayfa took Emerson on a drive to the Khyber Pass, after which they attended Friday prayer in Peshawar with about forty Arabs, most from Azzam's organization. After prayer they met with Abu Adil (Mahmud Azzam) at his house:

Hudaifa, Abu Adil and the immediate family were all jovial and lighthearted, in contrast to some of the other fundamentalists we met earlier that day at another mujahid home in Peshawar. They were dour and tense, exuding unrelenting distrust and hostility. They even slept with their Kalashnikovs. We sensed how rudderless the group had become without Azzam. Whenever we brought up the name of another potential leader with Hudaifa, he immediately dismissed him. The others always agreed. Only two names struck a positive chord: Osama bin Laden and Wa'il Jalaidan. Bin Laden was in Khartoum at the time. Jalaidan, another Saudi, was nearby in Islamabad. He had been put in charge of the Pakistan office of the Muslim World League.[128]

In the mid-1990s, as the funds dried up and the Pakistani pressure on Arabs increased, the Azzam family gradually left Peshawar and went in different directions. Umm Muhammad returned, with her younger children, to Amman, where they still reside. In the years after 9/11 she gave a number of high-profile media interviews about her late husband and his relationship with Bin Ladin.[129] Fatima and Wafa lived many years in Riyadh with their former Afghan Arab husbands Abu al-Hasan al-Maqdisi and Abu Yahya, but moved back to Amman around 2016, apparently as a result of pressure from Saudi authorities.

Hudhayfa Azzam had a more eventful career. He initially went down the foreign-fighter route, spending several months in Bosnia in 1994–1995, after which he tried unsuccessfully to enter Chechnya, before returning to Amman in 1996.[130] After the US invasion of Iraq in 2003 he went to Falluja "to convince Muslim scholars to begin the resistance," but became disillusioned with the sectarianism and the extremism of al-Zarqawi and returned to Amman after four months.[131] In the 2000s he ran a private import business while working on a Ph.D. in Arabic literature at the University of Jordan. Hudhayfa, who has his father's charisma and rhetorical gifts, and with flawless English to boot, became something of a spokesperson of the Azzam family in the post-9/11 years. He featured in a number of newspaper interviews and TV documentaries about al-Qaida, always denouncing Bin Ladin and al-Qaida. Still, he was a strong supporter of foreign fighting in clear-cut cases of foreign invasion. In 2006 he said:

If I find the way, I would go today to fight jihad in Iraq because it is compulsory for me as a Muslim. But it can only take place inside the borders of Iraq, you cannot bring it outside. If I saw an American or British man wearing a soldier's uniform inside Iraq I would kill him because that is my obligation. If I found the same soldier over the border in Jordan I wouldn't touch him.[132]

After the outbreak of the Syria war in 2011 he recast his public image into a more mature, sheikh-like figure, and became involved in mediation between rebel factions in Syria. He currently lives in Amman under travel restrictions but participates in the public debate and is active on social media.

Meanwhile, Abdallah Anas and Sumayya Azzam gravitated to the West. In the early 1990s Anas split his time between the Services Bureau in Peshawar and Massoud's forces in Afghanistan, notably taking part in the liberation of Kabul in April 1992. He also reconnected with the Algerian Islamist scene, supporting the Front Islamique du Salut (FIS) throughout the 1990s. After 1993 he sought to leave Pakistan to settle down with his family, and after visiting several candidate countries, including Turkey, Sudan, Yemen, and France, he moved to Britain in November 1995.[133] He has since acquired UK citizenship and has worked variously as a language teacher, writer, and TV journalist. Although a religious man and a long-term supporter of the Muslim Brotherhood, he has become a relatively progressive voice, an outspoken critic of Islamic radicalism, and a supporter of democratization in the Muslim world.[134]

Fayiz and Mahmud Azzam followed yet another path by returning to Palestine around 1996 and reconnecting with the Islamist scene there. Mahmud was imprisoned in Israel in 1997 and only released in 2009, after which he was deported to Gaza due to his involvement in Hamas. Fayiz, meanwhile, moved back to al-Sila al-Harithiyya, where a substantial branch of the Azzam family resides. They remain proud of their link to Abdallah Azzam, and have led efforts to construct two Abdallah Azzam mosques in the area, one in the refugee camp in Jenin and the other in al-Sila.

A few family members stayed longer in Pakistan. Azzam's nephew and former driver Abu Harith worked as a teacher in Peshawar until 1997. Azzam's cousin Hussain Azzam also worked as a teacher, but stayed past 9/11 and got into trouble as a result. In 2002 he was arrested by Pakistani authorities, handed over to the US military, and sent to Guantanamo Bay.[135] He was released in 2004 and now lives in Jordan.

Some eight members of the Azzam family ended their days in Pakistan. His mother had already been buried in Pabbi in 1988, followed by Abdallah and his two sons in 1989. A year later his father joined them. Later, Azzam's niece Umm Faisal, his niece Fatima, and his granddaughter (Muhammad's daughter) also found their final resting place there.[136] Azzam and his family paid a steep price for his joining the Afghan jihad that autumn in 1981.

So did many other Afghan Arabs. Several of the key characters in this book continued their militant activities and died or were imprisoned as a result. Abu Ubayda al-Banshiri drowned in a ferry accident in Lake Victoria in 1996 while on mission for al-Qaida. Abu Hajir al-Iraqi was arrested in Germany in 1998, extradited to the USA, and now serves a life sentence in the Supermax prison in Florence, Colorado. Abu Hafs al-Masri was killed in a US airstrike in Afghanistan in November 2001. Dr. Fadl was arrested in Yemen in late 2001 and later extradited to Egypt, where he is currently imprisoned or under house arrest. Usama Bin Ladin was killed in the Navy Seal raid on his hideout in Abbottabad in May 2011. Ayman al-Zawahiri, now the leader of al-Qaida, is believed to be hiding somewhere in Pakistan. Mustafa Hamid fled to Iran after 9/11 and lived under house arrest there until he returned to Egypt in 2011.

The Afghan Mujahidin leaders we met in this book fared somewhat differently. Ahmed Shah Massoud led the Northern Alliance against the Taliban in the late 1990s and was killed in an al-Qaida suicide bombing two days before 9/11. Jalaluddin Haqqani joined the Taliban in the late 1990s and later fought the US-led coalition in Afghanistan until his death by natural causes around 2015. Gulbuddin Hekmatyar became something of an independent warlord in Afghanistan in the late 1990s and allied with the Taliban in the 2000s. He remained in hiding, mostly in Iran, for twenty years until his return to Kabul in 2017 under a peace deal with the Afghan government. Abd Rabb al-Rasul Sayyaf joined the Northern Alliance in the late 1990s and became a member of the Afghan parliament in the 2000s. He ran unsuccessfully for president in 2014, and continues his political work today as a grand old man of Afghan politics.

Azzam wrote his will in 1986, and was mentally prepared to die in the course of the Afghan jihad. However, it had probably not occurred to him that he would be killed in Peshawar, a few hundred meters from his house. The Azzam assassination was a truly remarkable event, and it is hard to overestimate the trauma it inflicted on the jihadi movement. Azzam was by far the most respected member of the Afghan Arab community; he was their founding father and undisputed spiritual leader. He was also an Islamic scholar, so his murder was the moral equivalent of the killing of a priest.

The incident was historically unprecedented. No jihadi leader had ever been liquidated in such a spectacular and mysterious way. Many jihadi leaders had been killed, of course, but typically either in battle or by execution in government custody. Even in the history of the Islamist movement more broadly, the Azzam assassination stands out as one of the most high-profile cases. It is arguably overshadowed only by the assassination of Hasan al-Banna some forty years earlier; the founder of the Muslim Brotherhood was killed in Cairo by two unknown gunmen in February 1949.

As we have seen, the reasons behind Azzam's assassination continue to elude us, and unless a new key source emerges, we will never know who killed him. In the meantime, the bombing will stand as the jihadi equivalent of the John F. Kennedy assassination: a mysterious loss of a dear figure that became a source of never-ending speculation. Just how dear a figure Azzam was will become clear in the next and final chapter.

16 Icon

Today, only a small sign marks Abdallah Azzam's grave in Pabbi, revealing nothing special about the man who rests there.[1] Go online, and it is a whole different matter. You will find Azzam celebrated on a plethora of websites and social media, in thousands of pictures and photo montages, and in hundreds of videos. But exactly how significant a figure is he? Who celebrates him and why? This final chapter examines Azzam's legacy. The six-part chapter looks in turn at the ways in which he has been celebrated, the range of actors who embrace him, his operational impact, the reasons for his appeal, the contestation over his legacy, and what he might have done if he had lived into the 1990s. We will see that Azzam has enjoyed a remarkably broad popularity, in part because he never had to take sides in the difficult debates that later divided the movement. Which path he would have taken if he had not died is an open question, but it is not inconceivable that he would have moved in a more radical direction.

A Hero's Celebration

If Azzam was famous in life, he became iconic in death. Soon after his assassination he began to be celebrated by Islamists as a heroic figure, a status he enjoys to this day. The jihadi movement has a culture for venerating prominent individuals, and the list of legendary leaders and ideologues has become rather large with time. Still, Azzam stands out as one of the most deeply appreciated figures of them all. To get a sense of the scale of his reputation, we can take a look at the many different ways in which he has been celebrated.

One indicator is the types of epithets used about him. He has been repeatedly referred to in the jihadi literature as "the imam of jihad," "the imam of scholars," and "the spiritual father of the Afghan Arabs." A hagiography from 2009 introduces him as nothing less than "the sheikh of the *mujahidin*, teacher of the proselytizers and reformers, leader of the brave and the heroes and the *mujahidin*, the imam, the model, the hero, the intrepid, the courageous Abdallah Azzam."[2] Some have even considered Azzam a *mujaddid* – renewer – a highly prestigious epithet in the Islamic tradition reserved for the person in a given century who has done the most to revive Islam.[3] In fact, his name has become an epithet in its own right. For example, in the mid-2010s Abdallah al-Muhaysini, a Saudi sheikh fighting in Syria, was referred to by some as "the Abdallah Azzam of Syria."[4]

Azzam has also been repeatedly celebrated and cited by other leading figures in the movement. Usama Bin Ladin, for example, heaped praised on Azzam in the 1990s and the 2000s. For example, in an interview with al-Jazeera in 1999, Bin Ladin said:

Shaykh 'Abdallah 'Azzam, may God have mercy on his soul, is a man worth a nation. After his assassination, Muslim women proved to be unable to give birth to a man like him. The people of jihad who lived that epoch know that Islamic Jihad in Afghanistan has not benefited from anyone as it has from Shaykh 'Abdallah 'Azzam. He instigated the nation from the farthest east to the farthest west. During that blessed jihad, the activities of Shaykh 'Abdallah 'Azzam, may god bless his soul, as well as the activities of our brother mujahidin in Palestine, particularly Hamas, increased. His books, particularly his book *The [Signs] of the Merciful*, began to enter Palestine and instigate the nation for jihad against the Jews. The shaykh proceeded from the narrow, regional, and often city atmosphere that was familiar to Islamists and shaykhs, to the larger Islamic world and began to instigate this Islamic world.[5]

Even Ayman al-Zawahiri, who, as we know, was not close to Azzam, has praised him extensively in later years. In his 2008 book *The Exoneration* al-Zawahiri eulogizes Azzam over six dense pages, describing him as a martyr, a "great *mujahid*," and a "mentor of the age" who "left a great legacy of religious knowledge."[6] Many other jihadi leaders have described him in similar terms. As late as 2015 the jihadi ideologue Abu Qatada al-Filastini wrote a short biography of him.[7]

Azzam also features in a positive light in internal al-Qaida documents, suggesting that the public praise was not just for show. In the audiotape collection seized at Bin Ladin's house in Qandahar in 2001, there were nearly seventy tapes by Azzam.[8] In the so-called Abbottabad documents, which contain Bin Ladin's correspondence from the late 2000s, Azzam is mentioned several times.[9] One of the texts notes, "We have a great example in front of us, Shaykh 'Abdallah 'Azzam, may God have mercy upon him, who spread Mujahid awakening in the Muslim nation as a whole, who united Muslims to perform Jihad for the sake of God."[10]

Another indication of Azzam's prominence is the sheer availability of his writings and recorded lectures. His books were sold openly in Islamist bookshops around the world well into the 2000s, and videotapes of his lectures also circulated widely. Since the mid-1990s his writings and lectures have been widely available on the internet. The online jihadi propaganda repository Minbar al-Tawhid wa'l-Jihad (www.tawhed.ws) held a near-complete collection of his writings throughout the 2000s. In the same period, users on jihadi discussion forums such as al-Falluja and al-Shumukh frequently posted collections of text, audio recordings, and videos featuring Azzam. In the early 2010s social media platforms such as Facebook, Twitter, and YouTube did the same. His texts have been translated and disseminated in several languages other than Arabic, including English, French, German, Urdu, Indonesian, and Turkish, to mention just the most prominent ones. In the late 2010s, as governments and internet companies acted to limit the availability of jihadi propaganda online, Azzam's writings and lectures became somewhat less available, but as of 2019 they were still not difficult to find. As this book goes to press, Azzam's books and lectures are still being posted on jihadi channels on the social media platform Telegram.[11]

In addition, a number of Azzam tribute websites have existed over the years. The most famous was Azzam Publications (www.azzam.com), which will be described in more detail later in this chapter. More recent examples include the Abdallah Azzam Center for Studies and Research (www.azzamcenter.org), which also has a Facebook page and a Twitter account (@Azzam_Center) with over 6,000 followers. This is in addition to several other Facebook pages and Twitter accounts dedicated to republishing Azzam-related materials.

Another manifestation of Azzam's iconic status is the way in which his texts, videos, and photographs have been reworked and mixed into new propaganda products. We have seen this in probably hundreds of videos, from the films about the Bosnian jihad in the mid-1990s to al-Qaida productions in the late 2010s. Similarly, Azzam's picture features in hundreds of digital photo montages from the 2000s and 2010s.

Some montages promote only him and typically include a quotation from one of his texts; others show him alongside other prominent personalities from jihadi history, such as Bin Ladin, Ibn Khattab, or Abu Mus'ab al-Zarqawi. Hamas has featured Azzam in similar montages, but then accompanied by other figures, such as Hasan al-Banna, Izz al-Din al-Qassam, and Ahmad Yasin.[12] Inside both Hamas and the transnational jihadi movement, Azzam's face has a brand value and level of recognizability comparable to that of Che Guevara on the political left. A related phenomenon is the way in which short excerpts of Azzam's texts are treated as "words of wisdom" and reproduced on memes in the digital era. They have also been reproduced on billboards and murals; in Tel Afar in 2015, Islamic State erected at least one billboard featuring a quotation by Abdallah Azzam.[13] Azzam has essentially become a part of jihadi "pop culture."

Azzam has also been eulogized in poetry. The book *The Martyred Imam Abdallah Azzam through Contemporary Eyes* contains almost a hundred pages of poems written in Azzam's honour in the early 1990s.[14] The production continued throughout the 2000s, and as late as 2017 the Saudi Islamist Abd al-Rahman al-Ashmawi – who knew Azzam in the 1980s – wrote a poem to defend Azzam against criticism from liberals.[15]

Azzam is not only big on the internet; he has also lent his name to a number of real-life jihadi organizations and combat units. The first and most significant was the armed wing of Hamas on the West Bank, which in the mid-1990s was called the Martyr Abdallah Azzam Brigades (Kata'ib 'Abdallah 'Azzam). The name was dropped when Hamas merged its armed wings in the West Bank and Gaza under the name Izz al-Din al-Qassam Brigades, after the hero of the Palestinian revolt in the 1930s.[16]

Since then, many groups have called themselves the Abdallah Azzam Brigades. One emerged in Iraq around 2004, but it was short-lived.[17] In Egypt in the mid-2000s, an al-Qaida-linked organization by the same name claimed responsibility for several high-profile attacks on tourist targets in the Sinai and in Cairo.[18] Another, more successful incarnation of the Abdallah Azzam Brigades was the organization founded in Lebanon around 2009 by the Saudi militant Salih al-Qar'awi.[19] The group developed into a regional franchise with subdivisions in nearby countries: The Lebanese branch was called Abdallah Azzam Brigades – Ziyad Jarrah Division, the branch in Gaza Abdallah Azzam Brigades – Marwan

Hadid Division, and the one in Saudi Arabia Abdallah Azzam Brigades – Yusuf al-Uyayri Division. The franchise had its own logo and published many written statements online, but its precise structure and membership has been poorly elucidated. It carried out several large operations across the region – including rocket attacks against Israel in 2009 and 2011 and the bombing of the Iranian embassy in Beirut in 2013. This incarnation of the Abdallah Azzam Brigades was weakened in 2014 after the death of its commander Majid al-Majid, but is still operational. There have also been other organizations named after Azzam, such as the Ahrar al-Sham-affiliated Abdallah Azzam Battalion (Liwa' 'Abdallah 'Azzam) which emerged in Syria in 2014.[20]

Meanwhile, and somewhat confusingly, the name Abdallah Azzam Brigades has also been used as a name of convenience by several other groups and attack teams over the years. In 1998, for example, al-Qaida claimed responsibility for the East Africa embassy bombings in the name of "the Abdallah Azzam Brigades," presumably as a smokescreen to conceal Bin Ladin's involvement.[21] Similarly, in 2005, when al-Qaida in Iraq conducted a triple rocket attack on a US Navy ship in Aqaba in Jordan, it claimed the operation in the name of the Abdallah Azzam Brigades.[22] In Pakistan between 2009 and 2012, several high-profile attacks believed to be the work of the Pakistani Taliban – such as the attack on the Pearl Continental hotel in Peshawar in 2009 – were claimed in the name of the Abdallah Azzam Brigades.[23] The name has also been used by unknown groups, perhaps ad hoc attack teams, to claim operations; this was notably the case with the bomb attack on a Japanese tanker in the Hormuz Strait near Oman in August 2010.[24]

Jihadis have also named training camps and other facilities after Abdallah Azzam. In 2007 and 2008, for example, the Izz al-Din al-Qassam Brigades of Hamas ran an Abdallah Azzam Academy in al-Nuseirat on the Gaza strip.[25] The academy offered four-month training programs featuring religious classes and courses in variety of paramilitary techniques, including the manufacture of improvised explosive devices. The al-Shabaab militia in Somalia appears to have had at least two Abdallah Azzam institutes in the early 2010s: an Abdallah Azzam Military Academy and an Abdallah Azzam Academy for Preachers.[26] In early 2011 and early 2012 they held graduation ceremonies for batches of 130 recruits. Similarly named institutes have been set up by Jabhat al-Nusra in Syria; for example, in 2013, the Jabhat al-Nusra-affiliated group Shari'a Committee of al-Bukamal ran an Abdallah Azzam Institute for Sharia Sciences in the town of al-Bukamal in Syria.[27] Jabhat al-Nusra has also had several Abdallah Azzam training camps in Syria; in May 2016, for example, it uploaded a YouTube video titled "Watch the Graduation of a Jabhat al-Nusra Unit from the Abdallah Azzam Training Camps."[28] Around 2015, Islamic State also named at least one training camp after him near the town of Tabqa in Syria.[29] An American IS recruit named "Mo" has described how, "after three weeks in Camp Farooq, they were moved to Camp Abdullah Azzam (known colloquially as Camp AA)."[30] Other IS branches have followed suit; in 2015 an Islamic State-sympathizing group in Malaysia published a video from an "Abdallah Azzam academy" for primary-school-age children.[31]

It is not just militant groups that have named buildings after him. As of the late 2010s there were at least eleven Abdallah Azzam mosques in the Middle East: four in Gaza, two on the West Bank, two in Jordan, one in Saudi Arabia, one in Yemen, and one in Sudan.[32] This illustrates a point we will return to below, which is that Azzam's appeal reaches far outside jihadi groups and well into the Islamist mainstream. Few if any other radical Islamist figures – not even Bin Ladin or Sayyid Qutb – can boast a similar legacy measured in mosques. Moreover, as late as 2017, local authorities in Istanbul named a street after Abdallah Azzam.[33]

Broad Appeal

A perhaps even more remarkable aspect of Azzam's legacy is the breadth of his appeal. Years of ideological infighting has left different strands of Islamism with different heroes, and most of the people promoted by transnational jihadis are not celebrated by nationalist Islamist militants such as Hamas, and vice versa. Azzam is one of very few figures who is publicly hailed as a hero by both. In fact, as we shall see below, he is admired across virtually the entire spectrum of militant Islamist groups. This is a status he shares only with a few foundational figures in the movement's history, such as Sayyid Qutb.

Azzam's primary fan base is the transnational jihadi movement, or what many scholars refer to as the Salafi jihadi movement. This is a nebula of actors with particularly uncompromising agendas, a transnational outlook, and a willingness to use terrorist tactics. In the 1990s it included groups such as al-Qaida, the Armed Islamic

Group (GIA) in Algeria, and the EIJ and EIG in Egypt. In the 2000s new actors emerged, most notably al-Qaida's regional affiliates such as al-Qaida on the Arabian Peninsula, al-Qaida in Iraq (from 2006 the Islamic State of Iraq), al-Qaida in the Islamic Maghreb, al-Shabaab, and Boko Haram. The 2010s saw yet more entities, most notably the transformation of Islamic State of Iraq into Islamic State with its various "provinces" around the world. To these groups must be added the many foreign fighters who went to various conflict zones in the Muslim world from the 1990s onward. In addition, the Salafi jihadi community has always included substantial numbers of sympathizers who have offered logistical support, helped with propaganda distribution, or simply been consumers of jihadi propaganda.

Abdallah Azzam seems to have been celebrated to different degrees by different types of Salafi jihadi groups. The movement has had divergent strategic priorities, and we can speak of at least three ideal types of Salafi jihadis: the revolutionaries, the global jihadis, and the foreign fighters. Azzam appears to be the least popular, relatively speaking, among the revolutionaries – that is, groups such as the GIA, the EIJ, and EIG, which have primarily fought Muslim regimes. This has to do with Azzam's pan-Islamist outlook which prioritized Islam's external enemies over its internal ones. Azzam has been more popular among the global jihadis, that is, al-Qaida and other groups that prioritize the fight against Islam's external enemies, especially the West, and are happy to use international terrorist tactics. However, he has been the most popular among foreign fighters, people who are uncomfortable with international terrorist tactics and prefer to fight alongside insurgents in confined theaters of war. Azzam is popular here because this is the type of activism that he himself participated in and advocated the most. Within the jihadi movement, Azzam is the foreign-fighter ideologue par excellence.

In recent years Islamic State and its supporters have also appeared less preoccupied with Abdallah Azzam than al-Qaida has been. Islamic State is a hybrid group that has displayed both revolutionary and global jihadist behavior plus a great deal of anti-Shiite sectarianism. If IS is less enthusiastic about Azzam, it is partly because it represents a strategy that Azzam himself never advocated and partly because IS is in competition with al-Qaida, which, for historical reasons, is more closely associated with Azzam. Thus we see that Azzam features somewhat less frequently in IS's publications, and it is less common for new IS supporters to have been reading Azzam than it was for other aspiring jihadis in the past. As Seamus Hughes, a careful observer of jihadism in the United States, noted, "[I] feel like the new-wave ISIS kids don't appreciate the old school guys."[34] Another meticulous observer of jihadi propaganda, Romain Caillet, noted in mid-2017 that "After Usama bin Ladin, Abu Mus'ab al-Zarqawi is clearly the leader of the contemporary jihad, far ahead of Abdallah Azzam."[35]

None of this is to say that the revolutionaries and IS have rejected Azzam; we are only talking about differences in degree. Azzam was respected in the GIA and similar revolutionary groups, and he is respected today in IS. For example, he has been quoted in *Dabiq* magazine and other IS publications, IS had an Abdallah Azzam training camp in Syria, and several IS supporters have promoted Azzam in social media.[36] However, IS's expansion in the mid-2010s appears to have brought about a decrease in Azzam's relative popularity in the transnational jihadi community. In early 2016 Seamus Hughes observed on Twitter: "Something haven't seen in a while in court docs: Abdullah Azzam. Found in Pugh's thumb drive when he got arrested."[37]

Azzam's other main support base has been Hamas in Palestine. Ever since the late 1980s Azzam has been publicly hailed as a hero by Hamas and its supporters. His writings have circulated widely in both the West Bank and Gaza. For example, during the Second Intifada in the early 2000s, Israeli forces "found large numbers of books, essays, videotapes, and audiocassettes, statements by Azzam, and slogans praising him were found in Hamas mosques and institutions and in the homes of Hamas members."[38] His picture and slogans have regularly featured in Hamas propaganda, both on paper and on the internet. Hamas-linked websites regularly post articles about Azzam, often on the anniversary of his assassination. For example, on 26 November 2016, the website www.alqassam.ps ran an article titled "On the 27th Anniversary, Abdallah Azzam is a Flame of Jihad that Cannot be Extinguished," illustrated with large photographs.[39] He also features in the wills of Hamas suicide bombers; for example, Said Hutri, who blew himself up in a nightclub in Tel Aviv in June 2001, wrote: "I say . . . like the martyr before me Abdallah Azzam: 'If preparations [for jihad] are considered terrorism, then we are terrorists, if defending our honor is extremism, then we are extremists, if jihad against our enemies is fundamentalism, then we are fundamentalists.'"[40] Moreover, Azzam is not a radical blast from the past that the leadership is secretly embarrassed about;

he continues to be promoted by top Hamas officials and in its official media. In 2012, for example, Muhammad al-Madhun, then minister of youth, sports, and culture in Isma'il Haniyeh's government, wrote the foreword for Mahmud Azzam's biography of Abdallah Azzam.[41] Similarly, the group's condolence statement after Azzam's assassination is still featured on the Hamas website.[42] Within Hamas, Azzam is often celebrated alongside figures such as Hasan al-Banna, Izz al-Din al-Qassam, Ahmad Yasin, Salah Shehada, and Yahya Ayyash. As late as November 2018, Hamas posted on its website a photo montage with the faces of Abdallah Azzam, Hasan al-Banna, and Ahmad Yasin above the faces of seventeen fallen Hamas operatives.[43] This suggests that Azzam is considered among the three or four most prominent martyrs in the Hamas movement's history.

Within Palestinian society more broadly, however, Azzam is not particularly well known; his popularity appears to be confined to Hamas circles. For example, he is barely mentioned in the "mainstream" historiography on Palestine such as Yezid Sayigh's history of the PLO. Yonathan Fighel, a former IDF colonel who was military governor of Jenin from 1991 and 1993, says he never even heard Abdallah Azzam's name during his time in the area. "I knew al-Sila al-Harithiyya by heart, but the name Abdallah Azzam never came up."[44]

However, that Azzam should be admired in both the Salafi jihadi movement and Hamas is remarkable, because the two communities strongly dislike one another. Hamas criticizes al-Qaida for defaming Muslims with excessive violence, and al-Qaida lambasts Hamas for taking part in elections and recognizing nation-states.[45] No other figure features as prominently in both camps. His position clearly owes much to his Palestinian background and his involvement in the Palestinian struggle.

Azzam's position as a common denominator raises the question of the degree of ideological overlap between Hamas and transnational jihadi groups. In the context of the Palestinian–Israeli conflict, this question has long been sensitive. Since the 9/11 attacks many pro-Israeli commentators have argued that Hamas and al-Qaida have much in common and should be treated similarly by the international community.[46] Meanwhile, pro-Palestinian commentators have drawn a sharp distinction between the two groups, arguing that Hamas has a local nationalist agenda and does not engage in international terrorism.[47] There is more truth to the latter position, because, as we shall see below, Hamas embraces Azzam for different reasons than al-Qaida does. Having said this, we should not underestimate the support for transnational jihadism in the lower ranks of Hamas. For much of the 2000s the Palestinian Territories had the highest levels of popular support for Usama Bin Ladin of any country in the Muslim world, and levels of anti-Americanism have long run high in Hamas-controlled territories.[48] There have also been cases of Hamas members shifting allegiance and joining transnational jihadi groups.[49] Still, the number of such cases is small compared to the overall size of Hamas, and the organization has always distanced itself from transnational jihadi groups.

Azzam is also respected by other militant Islamist groups with more nationally oriented agendas. The Afghan Taliban, for example, has periodically praised Azzam, although not as much as Hamas does. At first sight, it may seem strange that Azzam does not enjoy a higher status among Afghan Islamists, given his history in the country. As one Afghan-Arab author wrote in 1992, "You will not find a single Afghan who does not know Dr. Abdallah Azzam, the sheikh of the Arab Mujahidin and their commander until now and after his martyrdom."[50] However, we must bear in mind that the Taliban only came of age in the mid-1990s, and that the proto-Taliban that existed in the 1980s did not interact much with Azzam.[51] Instead, Azzam was close to Afghans who later became enemies of the Taliban, notably Massoud and Sayyaf. In addition, due to theological and linguistic differences, the Taliban has developed an ideological corpus and pantheon of heroes that is quite separate from that of the Salafi jihadis.[52]

Interestingly, the Taliban's Pakistani offshoot, the Tehrik-e Taliban-e Pakistan (TTP), has promoted Azzam extensively. They have published montages with pictures of and quotations from Azzam, and have named several of their attack teams "Abdallah Azzam brigades."[53] The Pakistani journalist Iqbal Khattak said that once in the mid-2000s he went to meet TTP leader Baytullah Mahsud, and "came back with an Azzam book and two bottles of perfume."[54] The difference between the Afghan and Pakistani Taliban in this matter may reflect the Pakistani Taliban's larger contact surface with Arab militants in recent years. It also reflects general ideological differences between the two groups; the Pakistani Taliban notably attacks Pakistani security forces and has been tied to at least one attack plot in the West, whereas the Afghan Taliban operates strictly in Afghanistan.[55]

Azzam is also held in high esteem in other groups that do not fit neatly into the Salafi jihadi or nationalist Islamist categories, such as Lashkar-e Tayyiba in Pakistan and Harakat Ahrar al-Sham in Syria. Lashkar-e Tayyiba operates primarily in Kashmir and is not usually considered part of the Salafi-jihadi sphere, but it has longstanding connections with Arab militants, has received foreign fighters, and has carried out large-scale attacks in India. As we saw in Chapter 8, Azzam was involved in the founding of Lashkar-e Tayyiba's parent organization, Markaz al-Da'wa wa'l-Irshad, in 1987. Similarly, the Syrian group Harakat Ahrar al-Sham is widely considered more moderate than groups such as Jabhat al-Nusra and Islamic State, and some analysts have described it as representing a "revisionist jihadism" or "post-salafi-jihadism."[56] Azzam has featured in several items of Harakat Ahrar al-Sham propaganda.[57] Moreover, Abdallah Azzam's son Hudhayfa said in 2015 that he considered Ahrar al-Sham as the Syrian group whose ideology was the closest to that of his father.[58]

Azzam is also respected in certain Islamist groups and communities that do not engage in militancy. He is notably quite popular in conservative parts of the Muslim Brotherhood, and he has a long entry in IkhwanWiki, the online encyclopedia of the Muslim Brotherhood. He is particularly well remembered in the Jordanian branch, despite the differences between him and parts of the leadership in the early 1980s. For example, throughout the 1990s the Jordanian Brotherhood magazine *al-Sabil* regularly published articles about Azzam, and as late as 2013 it published a commemorative article about him on its website.[59] In more progressive Brotherhood circles, on the other hand, Azzam is considered controversial. Brigitte Maréchal, who interviewed many Muslim Brotherhood figures in Europe, noted that none of her informants ever talked about Abdallah Azzam. In these circles Azzam is likely considered as too hardline and old school.[60] Still, even those who do not particularly like Azzam seem to prefer to politely ignore rather than disown him.

Azzam has been held in particularly high esteem in Turkey among followers of the Justice and Development Party (AKP) and its predecessor, the Welfare Party. The AKP is considered an ideological relative of the Muslim Brotherhood, and it has a distinct pro-Ottoman worldview that helps explain its appreciation for Abdallah Azzam. As we saw in Chapters 6 and 11, Azzam was nostalgic about the fall of the Ottoman Empire, and he wrote a whole book (*The Lost Beacon*) praising the Ottoman state and denouncing Kemalism. The book, known in Turkey under the title *Kayıp Minare*, earned Azzam a wide following and spawned a large Turkish-language literature on and by Azzam which is still widely available in bookshops across the country.[61] It is no coincidence that the world's perhaps only Abdallah Azzam Street is in Istanbul.

Since his death there has been remarkably little explicit criticism of Azzam in the Islamist community. The only ones to regularly attack Azzam's legacy are the so-called quietist Salafis, also known as Madkhalis, from the name of one of their leading proponents, the Saudi sheikh Rabi' bin Hadi al-Madkhali. The Madkhalis are strongly supported by the Saudi religious establishment and preach an ultraconservative but apolitical form of Salafism. They are hostile to all forms of political activism and regularly criticize not just militant Islamists but also the Muslim Brotherhood. Madkhali has openly criticized Azzam on several occasions, as in this passage from one of his lectures:

Abdullah Azzam is far away as can be from the Salafi Manhaj. He is an extreme [Kharijite]. He would not be satisfied except to make war against the Salafi Manhaj. Abu Ghuddah says, "I'm a Salafi," but he is the greatest enemy of Salafiyya. Abdullah Azzam makes war against al-Albani and defends Abu Ghuddah. He says, "I can teach Tawhid in a moment ... in half an hour ... I can teach Tawhid in half an hour ... Allah is up, and so forth ... That's it, I'm a Muwahhid." And his chief preoccupation was making war on Salafiyya.[62]

These criticisms notwithstanding, Azzam is respected across a remarkably broad spectrum of Islamist actors.

Tangible Impact

Azzam's posthumous influence not only had breadth, it also had depth in the form of operational effects. As we shall see in this section, his writings continued to be widely read, and they have inspired many people to take violent action right up until today.

A first indication of Azzam's impact is the sheer scale of his readership. On most available indicators, Azzam has consistently been among the most widely read jihadi ideologues. In the 1990s his book *Defense of Muslim Lands* was reportedly the bestselling title in Islamist bookshops in Britain.[63] In the collection of audiotapes that was retrieved from an al-Qaida safe house in Afghanistan in 2001, Azzam was the fifth most featured speaker.[64] In 2004 the Saudi government conducted a study in which they asked thousands of twenty- to thirty-year-old Saudi jihadis or jihadi sympathizers about their sources of ideological inspiration. On the question which non-Saudi scholar had influenced them the most, Abdallah Azzam came out on top, followed closely by Abu Muhammad al-Maqdisi.[65] In 2006 the Combating Terrorism Center at West Point analyzed the traffic to the main online repository of jihadi texts, Minbar al-Tawhid wa'l-Jihad, a website run by supporters of Abu Muhammad al-Maqdisi. On the ranking by citation counts, Azzam shared the fifth place after Sayyid Qutb, Ahmed Shakir, Abu Muhammad al-Maqdisi, and Sheikh al-Shinqiti.[66] On the list of the twenty most saved texts on jihad, three were by Azzam: *Defense of Muslim Lands* (seventh place), *Introduction to Emigration and Preparation* (seventeenth), and *Bestowing the Virtues of Jihad on the Believers* (nineteenth).[67] In 2017 Donald Holbrook analyzed the content on the computers of forty-four suspects in ten terrorism cases in the UK between 2004 and 2015. The study found that "Anwar al-Awlaki dominated the list of most popular authors, in both old and new cases, and material by Abdullah Azzam also featured prominently."[68] Azzam's book *Join the Caravan* (in English translation) was notably the second most popular of all the 1,700 documents in the dataset.

Azzam also features on most lists of recommended reading that have circulated in the jihadi community. In 2003, for example, the Saudi al-Qaida member Isa Al Awshan published a book titled *39 Ways to Serve and Participate in Jihad*. It included a list of five key scholars for the aspiring jihadi to read, and Abdallah Azzam featured on top, in front of Yusuf al-Uyayri, Abu Muhammad al-Maqdisi, Abu Qatada al-Filastini, and Abd al-Qadir Abd al-Aziz (Dr. Fadl).[69] Azzam was also represented, with fifty works in "The Mujahid's Bookbag", a document collection published on jihadi forums in 2009.[70] Similarly, a document titled "Course of Islamic Study for Soldiers and Members," found in the Abbottabad documents, lists Azzam's work among "Lectures to be given in all phases," alongside that of Usama Bin Ladin, Abu Mus'ab al-Zarqawi, Abu Yahya al-Libi, Ayman al-Zawahiri, and Abu Mus'ab al-Suri.[71]

We also know that Azzam's texts have been used actively by jihadi organizations and networks to recruit and indoctrinate new members. In the 1990s, for example, Azzam was on the curriculum in al-Qaida's training camps in Afghanistan. According to Omar Nasiri, a former recruit: "We didn't have electricity at Khaldan, of course, so at night everything was lit with gas lamps or candles. And so it surprised me when, several months after my arrival, a television appeared. It emerged one Friday evening, hooked up to a diesel generator. That night we watched a number of speeches delivered by Abdullah Azzam."[72] Similarly, Fadil Harun, a senior al-Qaida operative in East Africa in the 1990s, used to quiz new recruits about their knowledge of Azzam's ideas: "I deliberately sat with the youth belonging to brother Talha al-Sudani, whether they were Somalis or Kenyans, to know the extent of their real understanding of the al-Qaida approach represented in the approach of Sheikh Abdallah Azzam (may God have mercy on him), and not the groups following the approach of abandonment, suspicion and *takfir*."[73]

Last but not least, a substantial number of active militants have invoked Azzam as an inspiration or are known to have read his texts. The following is a short and incomplete list of examples:

- El Sayyid Nosair, who killed Rabbi Meir Kahane in New York City in November 1990, was radicalized by Azzam's assassination. His son later wrote: "It is difficult to convey the effect of the news on my father. Looking back over two decades later, my mother will pinpoint Azzam's murder as the moment she lost her husband forever."[74]
- Mokhtar Belmokhtar, the legendary Algerian jihadist, has said that the killing of Azzam inspired him to go to Afghanistan in 1990.[75]
- Fadil Harun, a senior al-Qaida leader in East Africa in the 1990s, wrote: "My ideology stems from the ideology of Sheikh Abdallah Azzam and Sheikh Usama Bin Ladin."[76]
- David Vallat, a French convert who fought in Bosnia and was part of the network behind the bombings in France in 1995, said he and his friends read Azzam in the mid-1990s.[77]
- John Walker Lindh was reportedly radicalized by reading Azzam's books in English while in Yemen in the late 1990s.[78]
- Abd al-Karim Majati, a Moroccan member of al-Qaida in Saudi Arabia in the early 2000s, reportedly had been influenced by two sheikhs, Sa'd al-Burayk and Abdallah Azzam, "who opened new horizons for the issue of jihad."[79]
- Several of the perpetrators of the Madrid bombings of 2004 had downloaded texts by Azzam in the year prior to the attack.[80]

- Mohammed Momin Khawaja, one of the men involved in the "Crevice Plot" in 2004, which involved a series of bomb attacks in the UK, frequently referenced Azzam's writings in his email correspondence and on his blog.[81]
- The "Melbourne Cell" uncovered in the so-called Operation Pendennis in Australia in 2004, had amassed a "vast library" of jihadist literature, which included writings by Abdallah Azzam.[82]
- Abdulla Ahmed Ali, the alleged ringleader of the 2006 "Airliner Plot" in Britain, had a copy of Azzam's book *The Lofty Mountain* under his baby son's cot at the time of his arrest.[83]
- Erich Breininger, a German al-Qaida recruit in Waziristan in the late 2000s, wrote in his biography that he was heavily influenced by Azzam.[84]
- Roshonara Choudhry, who stabbed British MP Stephen Timms in 2010, cited Abdallah Azzam as a key inspiration (see Chapter 13).
- Dzhokhar Tsarnaev, who together with his brother carried out the Boston Marathon bombing in 2013, had Azzam texts on his computer.[85]
- A Frenchman named Yassine who went to Syria as a foreign fighter in 2013 had read Azzam texts online in the years prior to his departure.[86]
- Two Norwegian-Somali teenage girls who left Oslo to join IS in Syria sent a digital copy of Azzam's book *Defense of Muslim Lands* to their father to justify their decision (see Chapter 13).
- Mohammed Ahmed, a British foreign fighter in Syria told a fellow militant in an email around 2013 that he had been inspired by Azzam.[87]
- Junaid Hussain, a British IS fighter, quoted Azzam when he was asked in a Skype interview in 2014 why he had gone to Syria.[88]
- Khadar Hassan Khalib, a Canadian who joined IS in 2014, had quoted Azzam on social media.[89]
- Akram Musleh, an American who made five failed attempts to join IS in Syria in the mid-2010s, had a journal containing Azzam quotations.[90]
- Tairod Pugh, an American who was convicted of trying to join ISIS in Syria, reportedly had on his thumb drive "works by Abdullah Azzam ... including *The Defence of Muslim Lands* ... and *Join the Caravan*."[91]

- The Kouachi brothers, who carried out the attack on *Charlie Hebdo* magazine in Paris in January 2015, had texts by Azzam in their apartment at the time of the attack.[92]

Similarly, a study of forty-two cases of individuals in the USA charged in connection with Islamic State in the mid-2010s found that the majority "reference al-Qaeda ideologues – Anwar al-Awlaki, Osama bin Laden, and Abdullah Azzam" in addition to Islamic State ones.[93]

Generally speaking, it seems that Azzam has had more influence on prospective foreign fighters than on perpetrators of international terrorist attacks. However, as the list above shows, a substantial number of people have found inspiration in Azzam's texts for attacks on civilians in the West. Moreover, foreign fighting is often a step toward becoming involved in international attacks. By providing that initial push into foreign fighting for so many people, Azzam's writings have indirectly fueled international terrorist activity by jihadis.

Common Denominator

What explains the breadth of Azzam's popularity? To use terminology from retailing, the answer is part marketing and part quality of the product. Azzam's writings have been very actively promoted by jihadi media entrepreneurs, and they have caught on because they are sufficiently vague on strategy to be relevant to a broad range of groups.

Azzam's message did not spread naturally and spontaneously, but rather through the hard work of dedicated propagandists. In the 1990s, Azzam's writings became subject to a documentation and dissemination effort that was completely unprecedented in the history of the jihadi movement. In this period a veritable industry emerged around the promotion of Azzam's legacy, one that made him the first international jihadi celebrity. In this early period, three actors played a key role in building Azzam's reputation.

The first was Azzam's nephew Mahmud Azzam, who set up the Martyr Azzam Media Center in Peshawar in 1990.[94] Mahmud Azzam had access to his uncle's vast personal archive, and took on the mammoth task of making all of his texts and lectures available to the public. Over the next decade, he and his team of assistants processed and published most of Azzam's ideological corpus. They printed his unpublished manuscripts, compiled his articles, letters, and lecture notes into book-sized collections, and transcribed and published his recorded lectures. The Center's *magnum opus* was the 4,000-page *Encyclopedia of the Relics of the Legacy of the Brave Martyred Imam Abdallah Azzam* (1997), a collection of all the Azzam material in their hands. They also compiled hagiographic material about Azzam, and published at least one biography. The work of the Martyr Azzam Media Center was crucial to Azzam's subsequent fame, because it made available many unpublished texts that would otherwise have lingered in Azzam's private archive, and because it canonized his corpus, making it much easier for subsequent propagandists to digitize and disseminate it on the internet.

The second key actor was Khalil bin Sa'id al-Dik (aka Abu A'id al-Filastini, aka Joseph Adams), a dual US–Jordanian citizen and computer scientist who digitized many of Azzam's texts in the late 1990s.[95] Many jihadism researchers will be familiar with the Word files containing Azzam's texts on the website Minbar al-Tawhid wa'l-Jihad; these were al-Dik's work. Al-Dik was a Jordanian of Palestinian origin who had studied computer science in Los Angeles in the early 1980s and who had met Azzam in the United States before going to Peshawar for the Afghan jihad.[96] He later fought in Bosnia before moving to Peshawar some time in the second half of the 1990s. Here he linked up with Mahmud Azzam and started the work of digitizing the collection of the Martyr Azzam Media Center. Al-Dik's effort was vital, because it allowed for the dissemination of Azzam's texts online, notably on Minbar al-Tawhid wa'l-Jihad, right at the time when the jihadi internet began to grow.

The third main contributor to the Azzam industry in the 1990s was Babar Ahmed, a British-Pakistani computer engineer from south London who founded the website Azzam Publications (www.azzam.com) in 1996. Azzam Publications translated and disseminated several of Azzam's books in English, thus introducing Azzam and his message to the non-Arabic-speaking world. In the late 1990s and early 2000s it was the most prominent of all jihadi websites in English, and one of the most frequently visited jihadi sites in any language. Ahmed had fought in both Bosnia and Chechnya.[97] He had first learned about Azzam from Afghan Arab veterans in Bosnia.[98] In early 1996 he and his friends produced an audiocassette honoring martyred foreign fighters in Bosnia and distributed it under the label "Azzam recordings." The same spring, they printed and sold an English translation of Azzam's Last Will as well as *Join the Caravan* under the publishing label Azzam Publications. In late February 1997 they set up a website to advertise these and other products for sale by mail order, and over time the website grew to become a major resource for jihadi propaganda products in English. The size of its readership grew massively from late 1999 onward after the site began to provide news from the war in Chechnya. At this time the website had a regular daily readership of "hundreds of thousands," but on peak days it could reportedly attract between 1 and 5 million page visits, though these numbers must be taken with a pinch of salt.[99] It was closed down in late July 2002, and Babar Ahmed was arrested in late 2003.[100] Ahmed later said, "We made him a superstar. No-one knew him in the English-speaking world before we told the world about him."[101]

In the 2000s, the distribution of Azzam material became a more decentralized affair as more people became involved in freelance jihadi media work and new entities such as Tibyan Publications translated more of Azzam's texts. However, these later efforts would not have been possible without the pioneering work of Mahmud Azzam, Khalil al-Dik, and Babar Ahmed.

Of course, availability alone does not explain why Azzam's writings caught on the way they did. There must also be something about Azzam or his message that make his works interesting to so many people. Here we can propose at least three candidate explanations. One is the scale of his social network. As we have seen in this book, Azzam knew a great many people in different parts of the world and in different parts of the Islamist community. It could be that he became widely respected because a broad range of people had the chance to meet him. His social network was likely much larger than that of subsequent radical ideologues because he had greater freedom of movement. He traveled relatively freely around the world, and had access to mainstream podiums in the countries he visited. By contrast, most radical ideologues after him have been either confined to operating clandestinely, stuck in a conflict zone, or barred from speaking at large conferences.

A second explanation is that Azzam had certain personal characteristics – or rather, the posthumous image of him had certain characteristics – that appealed to a broad range of people. One such trait is his perceived political courage. Many of Azzam's admirers highlight the fact that he was a scholar who spoke truth to power. This trait likely had particular appeal in the 1990s and 2000s, when other scholars were seen as serving the interests of governments rather than standing up for religious principles. For example, Babar Ahmed, who discovered Azzam in the early 1990s, said, "There was a lot of talk about sell-out scholars. In the midst of all this we find Azzam. We said, 'Hey, look at this guy, here's a scholar who put his money where his mouth is.' We were fascinated and inspired by this guy. In this world where everyone is selling out, there's this guy."[102] Another trait often highlighted in the eulogies is that he was a martyr for the cause. By making the ultimate sacrifice, Azzam demonstrated his commitment to the struggle. His death was all the more symbolic given how much he himself had spoken about martyrdom; it made him, as Meir Hatina aptly put it, a "supermartyr."[103] His death also added to the general perception of Azzam as a man who not only talked the talk, but walked the walk. Besides, the spectacular way in which he died likely suggested to sympathetic audiences that he must have done something really important to merit such attention from Islam's enemies. Yet another appealing characteristic may have been his engaging style of speaking and writing. Although he was no longer around to give lectures, there were hundreds of video-recorded lectures in circulation to give new audiences a sense of his charisma. Babar Ahmed, who only knew Azzam from his videotaped speeches and books, said, "You could feel his heart and soul was in his speeches, in what he was writing."[104] The personal qualities with which Azzam became associated – political courage, self-sacrifice, and charisma – were traits that had appeal across ideological faultlines inside the Islamist movement.

The third and perhaps most compelling explanation for Azzam's broad popularity is that the content of his message lent itself to being a common denominator across groups with different agendas. Azzam spoke about things that were relevant to many militant groups, such as the obligation to fight and the value of martyrdom, all the while staying vague on the practical application of these injunctions. His message was vague in the sense that it did not go very far in specifying *how* each of these positions should be implemented in practice, such as where to fight first, or which methods to use in the fight. Adding to the broad applicability of Azzam's message was his pan-Islamist worldview: He talked about the need to liberate all Muslim lands, and he mentioned by name a broad range of geographical areas, which presumably made his message relevant to a wider audience than if he had been championing a single conflict. This combination of relevance and vagueness made Azzam appeal to many and offend few.

Azzam was able to strike this balance of relevance and vagueness because he died early. From the 1990s onward the Islamist movement would see many vicious debates over strategy and tactics, much more so than in the 1980s. It also saw the introduction of strategies – such as attacking the West – and tactics – such as suicide bombings – that had not really been on the table for Sunni groups in the 1980s (although Shiite groups such as Hizballah had used them). As a result, the radical Islamist landscape fragmented, and the different parts of the movement went their separate ways. Azzam had the fortune to disappear from the scene before these polemics, and hence he is not on the record as having taken a clear stance in any of them. This enabled him to become "all things to all jihadists," a person whose generic message could be invoked by subsequent activists to legitimize very different strategies. Much as Karl Marx's writings inspired leftist militancy of many different kinds in the twentieth century, so Azzam's message has been used to justify several different forms of rebellion, from the "nationalist" jihad of Hamas, via the revolutionary violence of the GIA, via the ambulant guerrilla warfare of the foreign fighters, to the international terrorism of al-Qaida and Islamic State.

Azzam, in other words, holds something of a centrist position in the landscape of Islamist clerics and ideologues. This position can even be quantified through automated text analysis; in his book *Deadly Clerics*, Richard Nielsen uses a statistical model to assign a "jihad score" to the textual corpus of various clerics, and Azzam turns up smack in the middle, between al-Qaida figures such as Usama Bin Ladin on one end of the spectrum and establishment *ulama* such as Abd al-Aziz Bin Baz on the other.[105] However, the best evidence of the ambiguity in Azzam's message is the widespread disagreement over what he really wanted.

Contested Legacy

One of the most fascinating aspects of Azzam's legacy is the intensity with which it has been contested. Ever since the early 1990s different parts of the Islamist movement have sought to define what Azzam really stood for and to portray themselves as his true successors. As Hudhayfa Azzam noted in 2006, "You could say there is a war going on between my father's ideology and that of al-Qaeda. They are trying to use my father's name to justify and market their ideology."[106]

At stake, of course, is the power and legitimacy that comes with having a theological heavyweight such as Azzam on one's side. Whichever group wins the contest can expect to attract more supporters. For some participants in the debate, such as Azzam's family and close friends, their personal well-being are also at stake. Whether Azzam is seen as an international terrorist or a freedom fighter matters for how they will be treated by the public and by governments. For example, Abdallah Anas said he wrote his short memoir *Birth of the Arab Afghans* as soon as he could after 9/11 because he genuinely feared he might get swept up in the War on Terror if governments made wrong assumptions about his past connections to Azzam and Bin Ladin.[107]

Broadly speaking, the debate features four ideal type positions on what Azzam represented. One is that he was the ultimate jihadist who would have supported jihad in all its forms, including al-Qaida's international operations, the GIA's fight against the Algerian regime, and Islamic State's attempt to build a caliphate. This appears to be the view of many revolutionary jihadis and modern-day Islamic State supporters. A second position is that Azzam was a global jihadist in the making who would have endorsed al-Qaida's international terrorism campaign against the West, but not the most bloody revolutionary campaigns such as that of the GIA in Algeria. This is the view of al-Qaida and its affiliates and supporters. As the al-Qaida leader Fadil Harun noted, "The ideology of Sheikh Usama Bin Ladin ... stems from the ideology of Sheikh Abdallah Azzam, who is our imam and was never a *takfiri*."[108] The third claim is that Azzam was the archetypal foreign fighter (or classical jihadist) who would gladly have joined any of the main foreign-fighter destinations in the 1990s and 2000s, such as Bosnia, Chechnya, or Iraq, but not al-Qaida's global jihad. Supporters of this view have often themselves been foreign fighters and see Azzam as closer to a figure such as Ibn Khattab in Chechnya than to Usama Bin Ladin.[109] A fourth position is that Azzam was really a Palestinian Islamic freedom fighter who only operated in Afghanistan because he had no other choice, and who would have returned to the Palestinian theater at the earliest opportunity. This is essentially the view of Hamas.

We can simplify this picture further and say that the debate over Azzam's legacy has really been between two broad interpretations: one radical, the other moderate. The first sees Azzam as an advocate of transnational militancy with few tactical restrictions. The other views him as a representative of more localized and restrained warfare. In a crude sense, the debate is about whether Azzam was a terrorist or a freedom fighter.

The "radicals" see Azzam as a transnational jihadist with anti-Western views, and consider the militancy of al-Qaida as a natural extension of his ideas. A good illustration of this interpretation appears in a booklet titled "Jihad in Pakistan" recovered from Bin Ladin's hideout in Abbottabad in 2011:

He (Shaykh 'Azzam) repeatedly stated, during the days of Jihad against the Russians, that the Afghan Jihad in reality is a preparation for Jihad against America and Israel, and that the first step to evicting the Jews from Palestine is anchoring Jihad in Afghanistan. His eyes were not distracted from the real enemy of the Muslim nation, even when he was fighting the Russians. After him, Shaykh Usama – May God protect him – carried the banner of global Jihad, and he announced in 1996 the targeting of American interests throughout the whole world. By this, he transformed the Mujahid focus from their fragmented and branching objectives to the great oppressor, and he made their (Mujahidin) interest revolve on the roots of the new infidel world order. He (UBL) and Jihad leaders continue to reiterate that the liberation of Palestine and the establishment of God's law there are among the main objectives of Mujahidin. This is to ensure that the Muslim nation does not forget its Zionist enemy; may God reward them with the most beneficial rewards.[110]

A more elaborate version of this argument was published in an al-Qaida magazine in April 2019, when a certain Khattab al-Hashimi responded to an Egyptian academic study published a month earlier which had argued that Bin Ladin's strategy had represented a break with Azzam's ideology.[111] Al-Hashimi disagreed, arguing that Bin Ladin and Azzam represented exactly the same tradition, and that they only appeared different because they operated in different time periods and had different roles. Just as Yahya Ayyash and Ahmad Yasin had different roles in Hamas, so Bin Ladin and Azzam had different functions in the jihadi movement, but it did not mean they represented different movements.

The "moderates," on the other hand, firmly reject the notion that Azzam would have supported al-Qaida's international terrorism, let alone the extreme violence of Islamic State. For example, Azzam's wife said in 2006:

If Abdallah Azzam were alive, they [al-Qaida] would not have been able to override him, for they considered him a legal authority ... Bin Ladin does not have legal knowledge ... and al-Zawahiri is a medical doctor ... Azzam wanted a focused aim, and he disapproved of tactical dispersals such as carrying out bombings here and there. Azzam would send back Palestinian youth who came to Afghanistan and who had the papers to enter Palestine. If the sheikh had been able to fight in Palestine he would not have gone to Afghanistan. All these bombings, including the *fitna* of 11 September, are diversions from the objective ... Bin Ladin fell into error when he built a state within the state of Sudan ... He separated himself from the people [*al-nas*]. Abdallah Azzam never liked to isolate himself from people.[112]

Another good example is that of Babar Ahmed, the founder of Azzam Publications, who said in 2017:

I want to reclaim his legacy. Dirt has been thrown on him. The guy was a hero, no doubt about that. He was very knowledgeable; he related what was in the Islamic texts about jihad. The *fatawa* about killing women and children and such started in the 1990s. Had he been around, he could have stopped it. He was untouchable. I don't like the term "jihadi." It creates an equivalence between the heroes of Afghanistan and Bosnia on one hand and the IS people today who kill, torture, and rape in the name of jihad on the other. For 1,400 years of rich Islamic history and heritage jihad has always meant one thing, now these innovators come along and say something else ... there was a time when jihad was not burning people in cages. All the bad stuff started in 91–92.[113]

As Ahmed's language suggests, emotions have run high in the debate over Azzam's legacy. Azzam's moderate supporters have sometimes expressed frustration over what they see as an unfair association of Azzam with international terrorism. The American researcher Chris Heffelfinger recalled giving a lecture about the Salafi jihadi movement, only to find himself confronted by the former Afghan foreign minister Najibullah Lafraie, who felt insulted that Heffelfinger had associated Azzam with Bin Ladin and al-Qaida.[114] Lafraie viewed Azzam as a national hero and liberator of the Afghan people, not as an international terrorist.

An interesting dimension of the legacy struggle is the way in which Azzam sometimes has been "weaponized" in polemics between moderate and radical Islamists on other issues. For example, in 2015, during the height of the controversy around Islamic State's taking Iraqi Yazidi women as sex slaves, their opponents circulated a meme on social media with Azzam's picture and a quotation from him condemning the taking of concubines during war.[115]

The moderates confront a double challenge, because the radical interpretation of Azzam's legacy is held not only by al-Qaida-style jihadists, but also by liberals. Many Muslim liberals view Azzam as an extremist and a reactionary, and are happy to denounce him as such. This dynamic produced an interesting debacle in February 2017, when an article in the Saudi newspaper *Ukaz* referred to Azzam in passing as a "destructive terrorist" [*irhabi hallak*].[116] Azzam supporters responded by publishing several articles in other Gulf newspapers criticizing *Ukaz* and contending that Azzam had nothing to do with the terrorism of al-Qaida.[117] On Twitter, Azzam supporters created a hashtag called "The midgets dare to attack Azzam" to denigrate the critics.[118] This only provoked more Azzam criticism, notably from the Arab left. For example, the prominent leftist writer As'ad AbuKhalil wrote on his blog:

We in the Arab left, have long hated 'Abdullah 'Azzam, who traveled the world (at the behest of the US and Saudi Arabia) to recruit Jihadi terrorists to fight against the communists in Afghanistan in the 1970s and 1980s … 'Abdullah 'Azzam was a reactionary terrorist, and idol of Bin Laden. There is a campaign among supporters of Gulf regimes to support 'Abdullah 'Azzam, the reactionary anti-communist terrorist who inspired and recruited Bin Laden to the lousy Mujahidin cause in Afghanistan.[119]

Still, Azzam's supporters cared more about the criticism from *Ukaz*, a leading government-controlled Saudi newspaper, because to them it represented a glaring act of hypocrisy in light of the official Saudi support for the Afghan Mujahidin in the 1980s. To prove the point, one of the anti-*Ukaz* newspaper stories included pictures from 1980s Saudi Arabia showing billboards encouraging support for the Afghan jihad.[120] Several people also retweeted a message by Hudhayfa Azzam from 2016, in which he described his father's meeting back in the 1980s with Prince Salman, now the king of Saudi Arabia.[121]

A similar debate emerged in Jordan in early 2018, when Zuleikha Abu Risha, a liberal Member of Parliament, criticized the Shari'a faculty at Jordan University for naming a prayer hall after Abdallah Azzam.[122] In a comment to a Facebook post announcing the opening of the prayer hall, she wrote, "The Shari'a Faculty is an island belonging to Al-Qaeda and ISIS." The same day, the dean of the faculty posted a message on the university website defending Azzam and condemning Abu Risha, while several conservative MPs called for legal action to be taken against her. Bassam al-Amush, a former minister and ambassador, wrote an article praising Azzam and denouncing Abu Risha. In response, she doubled down, posting a series of Facebook posts reiterating her criticism and describing Azzam as an "al-Qaida founder and member." In a follow-up interview, she also referred to Azzam as an "ideological terrorist" and an "extremist." Public criticism of Azzam has been rare in Jordan due to his relative popularity there, so the incident was noteworthy and may reflect receding support for the Muslim Brotherhood.[123]

In the background of these intra-Muslim polemics there has been a debate among Western academics over how much of a radical Azzam was. Some writers have viewed him as a global jihadist and described him as either the mastermind, a co-founder, or an ideological forefather of al-Qaida. Others have stressed his differences with al-Qaida and argued that he should be understood as a more moderate figure. The former view was more widespread in the early 2000s, but subsequent historical research has lent more support to the latter position, notably by showing that he was not a founder of al-Qaida. Today there is arguably consensus among the best-informed analysts that Azzam in his lifetime never called for international terrorism of the al-Qaida type. A much more complicated and interesting question is whether he might have done so if he had not been killed.

Counterfactuals

What would Azzam have done if he had lived into the 1990s? Precisely because his message was so ambiguous and his legacy so contested, this question is very difficult to answer. In fact, not even Azzam's closest family can agree. His wife said in 2006 that he would have joined Hamas: "Hamas is the continuation of Sheikh Abdallah Azzam's line, and the leaders of Hamas themselves have said that their victory is Abdallah Azzam's victory."[124] Azzam's son Hudhayfa has said his father would have considered the jihads in Palestine, Bosnia, Chechnya, and Iraq as duty on all Muslims, suggesting that he might have gone to one or more of these places.[125] Azzam's son-in-law Abdallah Anas, for his part, guesses that Azzam would have stayed in Pakistan and tried to unite the Afghan Mujahidin.[126]

There is no doubt that the Azzam of 1989 would not have endorsed the 9/11 attacks, because in his lifetime he never advocated jihad against the West, international terrorist tactics, or even suicide bombings. The real question is whether he could have *evolved* into a person who would have endorsed such tactics. We must bear in mind that in the late 1980s nobody had proposed global jihad against the West, not even Bin Ladin himself. Imagine that Bin Ladin had also died in 1989, and that we had to judge his potential for anti-American terrorism based on his views at the time; we would have to conclude that it was low, yet history proved otherwise. It follows that we cannot rule out the possibility of similar changes of opinion in Azzam. After all, his own views evolved in his lifetime. Had he died in 1979, we could not have known that he would become a prominent advocate of foreign fighting and martyrdom. History is full of radical Islamists changing their opinions.

A case can be made that Azzam was actually quite well disposed to going further down the line of transnational militancy. For one thing, his commitment to norms of restraint in warfare was arguably not as strong as his moderate supporters have argued. As we saw in Chapter 10, Azzam leaned to the "open-minded side" when discussing certain controversial tactics; for example, he endorsed bombings with a high risk of collateral damage and the unconditional execution of women Communists. For another, his commitment to the norm against out-of-theater operations was probably also weaker than many have assumed. Azzam was, after all, one of the strongest proponents of transnationalism of his time. Not only was he the one who articulated the foreign-fighter doctrine, he was also one of very few to publicly condone attacks on certain categories of civilians in the United States (see Chapter 11). Moreover, Azzam was very hostile to the West, as we saw in Chapters 6 and 11. All his writings, from his BA thesis in the 1960s to his last editorials, reflect enmity to the West in general and to the United States and Britain in particular.

Given the international political climate of the 1990s it is not difficult to imagine Azzam becoming even more anti-American. The 1990s saw the emergence of a US-led world order, which made it easier to blame the USA for the suffering of Muslims. Azzam would not have taken lightly to the deployment of US troops in Saudi Arabia in the autumn of 1990, because he had already written, long before Bin Ladin did, about the need to keep the Arabian Peninsula free of non-Muslims. As early as

1985 he wrote an article in *al-Jihad* magazine titled "The Responsibility of Arabs before God" listing several religious–political priorities for Arab Muslims. The last one was "to make sure to cleanse the Peninsula, for the Prophet said on his deathbed 'expel the polytheists from the Arabian Peninsula' and 'expel the Jews and Christians from the Arabian Peninsula.'"[127] The same *ahadith* became central to Bin Ladin's case for war against the United States in the mid-1990s. Moreover, as we saw in Chapter 8, Azzam once referred to the French doctors in Mazar-e Sharif as "Crusaders" and took pride in chasing them away: "We stood before the Crusaders and made them retreat from inside Afghanistan."[128] If he saw Médecins sans Frontières in northern Afghanistan as an intrusion, he would not have welcomed the 82nd Airborne in the Land of the Two Holy Mosques.

For the sake of argument, we can compose a fictional vignette in which Azzam goes global. It might run as follows:

In 1989 the USSR withdraws from Afghanistan. Bin Ladin goes home, but Azzam stays in Peshawar to help the Mujahidin. Meanwhile, the US deployment in Saudi Arabia in 1990 enrages Islamists across the region. Bin Ladin begins his campaign to have the Saudi government expel the Americans, but ends up a dissident in the Sudan. Azzam, meanwhile, writes a book or two about the US-led conspiracy to weaken Muslims. The books criticize Saudi Arabia and other Gulf states for colluding with the USA, making Azzam *persona non grata* in the kingdom. In 1992 Pakistan kicks the Arabs out of Peshawar, and Azzam has few other places to go than the Sudan, where Bin Ladin warmly receives him. Azzam continues to write about international politics, especially Afghanistan, Palestine, and Bosnia, while being peripherally involved in al-Qaida in the Sudan. Starting in 1993, Abu Hajir al-Iraqi tries to persuade Bin Ladin and others in Khartoum that they must declare jihad on the US forces occupying the Arabian Peninsula, but for several years Azzam objects. In 1996, after the Qana massacre in Lebanon, Azzam has had enough and decides to endorse Abu Hajir's proposal. In his view, Palestine can never be liberated as long as the United States does as it pleases in the region, supplying Israel with weapons and supporting secular dictators. He concludes that Jerusalem can only be liberated by coercing the USA to withdraw from the Middle East, just as the Soviet Union was pushed out of Afghanistan. In late 1996 he moves back to Afghanistan together with the rest of al-Qaida, where he becomes member of the Shura Council. He reluctantly endorses the 1998 East Africa embassy operation and the 2000 *USS Cole* operation, but he dissuades Bin Ladin from carrying out the "planes operation" in the United States. In 2004, however, the Bush administration authorizes an invasion of Iraq to topple Saddam Hussein, after which Azzam gives his blessing to a major attack on the American homeland.

This scenario is entirely hypothetical, but it illustrates that the idea of Azzam going global is not completely far-fetched. None of this is to say that he would necessarily have radicalized in the 1990s, only that it is conceivable.

Realistically, going global is but one of at least five different pathways he could have taken. The first and arguably most likely is to have stayed in Peshawar, at least until the liberation of Kabul. He would likely have continued to support the Afghan Mujahidin's political efforts while writing about other issues and becoming something of a grand old man of jihad. He would have supported Hamas, called on Muslims to fight in Bosnia and Chechnya, and remained on decent terms with Bin Ladin and al-Qaida, but without approving of the latter's international activities.

The second most likely pathway would probably be a move to Saudi Arabia, like his two eldest daughters and their husbands. Saudi Arabia became somewhat less hospitable to radical Islamists in the 1990s, but Azzam probably would have been allowed to settle there if he had stayed out of domestic Saudi politics and kept Usama Bin Ladin at arm's length. Conceivably he could have served as a preacher and teacher while writing about jihad fronts abroad. However, he probably would have run into trouble with the government in the late 1990s and early 2000s, depending on his connections with al-Qaida.

A third scenario would be a return to Jordan, where he had a house and many friends.[129] From there he might have supported Hamas in various ways, for example through fundraising in the Gulf, political writing, and education. He would have been a semi-independent figure, because the Jordanian Brotherhood would likely not have given him a position of responsibility. He would have been a radicalizing influence on Hamas, welcoming its turn to suicide bombings, and opposing ceasefires and participation in elections.[130] The main obstacle in this scenario would have been the Jordanian government, which might not have allowed him to move back. And if they had, they might not have tolerated his inevitably loud objections to the 1994 peace agreement with Israel.

The fourth scenario involves a move to one of the other foreign-fighter fronts in the 1990s such as Bosnia and Chechnya, and becoming one of the leaders of the Arab contingent there. Such a trajectory would have been entirely in line with his views, but difficult to combine with family responsibilities. Moreover, Azzam in his fifties might have been more interested in destinations where he could play a political or ideological role, whereas Bosnia and Chechnya offered mainly fighting opportunities.

The fifth and least likely scenario is that Azzam would have joined al-Qaida and gone down the global jihad route. This would have required him to change his view on out-of-area operations and mass-casualty operations against civilians, as well as to accept a life as a hunted man. This outcome would have been unlikely, but again, not inconceivable.

How would Azzam have viewed the rise of the Islamic State organization (IS) in the mid-2010s? The answer is less obvious than it might seem. On the one hand, he would almost certainly have been very critical of IS's brutality and the youthful arrogance of its members. On the other hand, establishing an Islamic state appears to have been a more urgent priority for Azzam than it was for Bin Ladin and other al-Qaida leaders in the 1990s and 2000s. Faced with a choice between an organization specializing in international terrorist attacks (al-Qaida) and an organization with specific plans to establish a caliphate (IS), Azzam would at least have had to think twice. Most likely he would have chosen neither, but there are some eerie similarities between Azzam's concrete plans to establish an Islamic state and IS's brazen attempts to do the same twenty-five years later. It is clear from IS's rapid ascent that it tapped into a genuine desire in the jihadi movement for an Islamic state, even though they botched the implementation with their violent excesses.

Another question is whether Azzam might have prevented the jihadi movement from going global and ultraviolent in the 1990s. Many of those who view him as a moderate seem to believe so. Usama Bin Ladin's son Umar, for example, wrote that "Abdallah Azzam's assassination in 1989 was a tragedy, for he often calmed the violence brewing in radical believers."[131] However, it is far from clear that Azzam would have made such a big difference. For one thing, he already had problems restraining the radical elements among the Afghan Arabs in his lifetime. For another, the jihadi movement in the 1990s was dispersed across many different parts of the world, which would have made it difficult for Azzam to wield his influence in all nooks and crannies of the community. Finally, even though Azzam himself was not around in the 1990s, his writings and recorded lectures were, and they did not prevent the radicalization of the movement. He might have reduced the number of people who joined the more radical parts of the movement, or he might have delayed certain tactical or strategic shifts. However, to say that he could have prevented them from occurring altogether is overestimating his influence. In fact, one could argue the opposite and say that, if Azzam had been around in the 1990s, even more people would have become foreign fighters in places like Bosnia, Chechnya, and Afghanistan. This, in turn, would have created a larger pool from which the new, more radical currents of the movement could draw recruits.

In any case, Abdallah Azzam became a legend in the Islamist movement. Not only is he a hero to many militant Islamist groups, he is also mainstream enough to have had mosques and streets named after him. His writings have influenced generations of militants, including perpetrators of international terrorist attacks, and continue to do so today. The debates over what he represented will likely also continue: he left enough ambiguity in his writings to fuel competing interpretations for many years to come. In some sense, this is the ultimate testimony to his historical importance, for nobody would bother contesting the legacy of an insignificant man.

Conclusion

Jihadism went global because of local repression. That is the bottom line of this long and complex story. The inability of Arab countries to include Islamists in national politics produced a class of activists who in the 1970s began looking to the international stage for operating space. In the 1980s some of these pan-Islamists gave the notion of Islamic solidarity a military interpretation, and started calling for Muslims to fight in each other's wars. They were helped by a host of other factors – including oil money, technology, and geopolitics – but they would not have embarked on their mission in the first place if they had not been excluded from local politics. Thus the main roots of jihadi transnationalism lie in the domestic and regional politics of the postwar Middle East.

Abdallah Azzam's personal trajectory illustrates this dynamic. When Israel occupied his home village in 1967, Azzam judged local resistance unfeasible and fled to Jordan. After he and other Palestinians tried to fight Israel from Jordan in 1969–1970 the Jordanian government stopped them, killing many in the process. When Azzam went to Egypt to study in 1971 he came into direct contact with the victims of Nasser's brutal repression of the Muslim Brotherhood. Later in the 1970s Azzam came under government scrutiny for his outspoken views, and in 1980 he was fired from his position at Jordan University and encouraged to leave Jordan. He then found a job in Saudi Arabia, but he had no stake or future in Saudi politics and his family did not feel welcome there. Instead, he connected with pan-Islamists in the Hijaz and looked for a new cause abroad. He ended up going to Pakistan, where he played an outsize role in mobilizing Arabs to the Afghan jihad, although there, too, he had to hide from Pakistani police for a while. We still do not know who killed him, but it was probably a government that sought to intimidate the Afghan Arabs. Had he survived, he would most likely have become a Peshawar-based grand old man of jihadism, supportive of Hamas and sympathetic to al-Qaida. Azzam's itinerant life was largely a result of regimes not tolerating his activism and forcing him to move from place to place.

At the same time, this is not simply a story of repression and escape. In the following, I pull together the story's many threads by addressing five key questions: Why did the Arabs go to Afghanistan? How important was Azzam to the mobilization? What shaped his trajectory and personality? How responsible is he for the radicalism that came after him? And what was the role of governments in the emergence of the Afghan Arab movement?

Why the Arabs Went

This question has both a superficial and a deeper answer. At a basic level, the mobilization was enabled by the presence, in the early 1980s, of three necessary conditions. One was a *motivation* – in the form of an Islamic foreign-fighter doctrine adapted to the modern world – that made participation in faraway conflicts compelling and legitimate. Prior to the Afghanistan war, such a doctrine did not really exist. Abdallah Azzam's writings made many non-Afghans see fighting in Afghanistan as an inescapable religious duty.

A second necessary condition was the existence of *organizers* who disseminated the foreign-fighter doctrine and facilitated travel to Pakistan. In the mid-1980s a particularly well-resourced cadre of organizers emerged in the form of the Peshawar-based Services Bureau. This organization helped scale up the Afghan Arab mobilization by spreading recruitment propaganda, recruiting face to face in many different countries, and accommodating new recruits in Peshawar. Later, other facilitator networks followed, making the Afghan jihad a relatively accessible war zone for young Muslims around the world.

The third condition was the *low constraints* on foreign-fighter activism. Most governments – be it in the Arab world, the West, or in Pakistan – did little to stop recruits from going or to limit organizers from operating. Policies toward foreign fighters varied across countries, from light countermeasures in the Arab republics to light encouragement in the Gulf countries, but on average there was indifference. This was in contrast to most previous and subsequent conflicts in the Muslim world, where states did much to prevent foreign Islamists from intervening.

The deeper issue is why these three conditions were present in the early 1980s. An important part of the answer is that the late 1970s had seen the rise of pan-Islamists, a new type of activists who sought to promote Muslim solidarity and cooperation. From their base in the Hijaz region in Saudi Arabia, they had spent years promoting a Muslim victim narrative and building a global network of Islamic NGOs. Their efforts paved the way for the Afghan Arab mobilization in two ways: first, their rhetoric about the *umma* under assault made Muslim audiences more receptive to Azzam's foreign-fighter doctrine, because the latter was only a military extension of the call for Muslim solidarity. Second, the pan-Islamist NGO networks became crucial vehicles for the organizers behind the foreign-fighter recruitment to Afghanistan. Several of the first movers among the Afghan Arabs, including Azzam himself, came to Pakistan through pan-Islamist NGOs and exploited them for their operations. The rise of pan-Islamism thus goes a long way toward explaining both why Azzam's foreign-fighter doctrine resonated and why the facilitation networks emerged so quickly. Pan-Islamism also partially explains why Muslim governments did little to constrain foreign fighting. In much of the Middle East, pan-Islamist sentiment was so strong in this period that crackdowns on foreign fighting were politically costly.

We must, of course, dig deeper, to a third level down, and ask why Hijazi pan-Islamism emerged where and when it did. Put simply, it was because this corner of Saudi Arabia had in the 1960s and 1970s become a safe haven for persecuted Islamists from across the Arab world. There they enjoyed not only relative freedom of association, but also access to Saudi oil money, so long as they avoided domestic politics. This incentivized activists to build a political movement that would operate primarily in the international domain. It also suited Arab governments to have Islamists talk more about Muslim plights abroad than about malgovernance at home. Thus emerged a soft pan-Islamist movement which paved the way for more hardline expressions of Muslim solidarity, such as fighting in each other's wars. The rise of pan-Islamism was helped by additional developments, such as advances in communications technology and rising oil wealth. In the 1970s and 1980s it became possible to move news, resources, and people across the Muslim world much faster and more cheaply than before. Finally there was the oil price increase of 1973, which in subsequent years made large amounts of money available to the international Islamic organizations.

The identification of the pan-Islamist movement as a precursor to the foreign-fighter phenomenon is an important insight, because it provides the missing link between the inward-looking forms of Islamism of the 1950s and 1960s and the outward-oriented ones of the 1980s and 1990s. The existing literature had not adequately explained why the Islamist movement went from fighting only Arab regimes to also fighting infidel invaders. This explanation offers what social scientists would call the microfoundations of the transnationalization. It shows that, rather than being simply a mood swing or opinion shift, the growth of pan-Islamism was the result of strategic action in response to changes in material incentives in 1970s Saudi Arabia.

These findings allow us to downplay two common explanations sometimes encountered in the literature. One is the notion that sheer outrage over the Soviet invasion of Afghanistan caused the inflow of war volunteers. In reality, there was no spontaneous mobilization in the early years; only in 1984 did the number of Arab volunteers exceed a hundred. Another misconception is that Western and Arab governments engineered the Afghan Arab mobilization to weaken the Soviet Union and get rid of Arab Islamists. This theory conflates the Afghan Mujahidin with the Afghan Arabs and assumes that because governments supported the former, they also promoted the latter. However, the evidence shows that the Afghan Arab mobilization was led overwhelmingly by non-state actors and that the main role of governments was simply not to obstruct it. The oft-mentioned example of the subsidized plane tickets from Saudi Arabia to Pakistan was a policy that existed only briefly in the late 1980s and was probably a populist response to – and not a cause of – the high interest in the Afghan jihad among Saudi youth. Besides, if governments really had organized the Afghan Arabs, we probably would have seen them enter the conflict earlier, and in much larger numbers.

All this tells us at least two important things about transnational activism in general. One is that foreign-fighter movements can emerge for reasons unrelated to the host insurgency. David Malet has argued that foreign-fighter mobilizations usually happen when local rebels call for external support and get a response from members of a shared ideological community abroad.[1] However, in the Afghanistan case the Mujahidin did not really call for volunteers; it was rather the

Arab fighters who came knocking on their door. In other words, the Afghan Arab mobilization was driven more by supply than by demand. Sidney Tarrow has proposed that transnational activism often emerges in response to changes in political opportunity structures, and he described six ideal type processes of transnational contention (global framing, internalization, diffusion, scale shift, externalization, and coalition).[2] Of these, the globalization of jihad is closest to scale shift, and Tarrow in fact discusses the Afghan jihad over several pages, arguing that Cold War geopolitics were crucial. He says the USA, Saudi Arabia, and Pakistan "produced the major opportunity for the shift in scale of political Islamism" and goes a long way toward suggesting that the scale shift was directly facilitated by alleged US training of Afghan Arabs.[3] However, as we have seen, the pan-Islamist movement had momentum before the Soviet invasion, and the foreign powers supported the Afghan Mujahidin, not the foreigners.

What, then, are these other reasons if not some feature of the host conflict? It would seem that an important scope condition for the emergence of large foreign-fighter movements is government backing of transnational solidarity activism. It was the Saudi government's tacit support for soft pan-Islamism in the 1970s that allowed the pan-Islamist movement to take the proportions it did. This support was rooted in the Saudi government's self-image as the center of the Muslim world, and had little to do with the politics of Afghanistan. We see something similar in the other large foreign-fighter movement of the twentieth century: the International Brigades in the Spanish civil war in the late 1930s. There, the Comintern played a key role in the recruitment of foreign fighters to Spain, an effort motivated by the ideal of solidarity between the oppressed working classes of the world.[4] Similarly, in the recent Syria war, a key reason for the large number of foreign fighters was the widespread international support for the anti-Assad rebels in the early stages of the war, which placed few barriers in the way of foreign volunteers.[5] A degree of government support thus appears to be a necessary condition for the emergence of large-scale foreign-fighter movements.

The second insight of relevance to broader debates is that transnational movements can take on a life of their own, independently of the politics that created them. Several scholars have argued that transnational activism often emerges in response to domestic pressures, as appears to have been the case with the Islamists from the 1960s to the 1980s. However, most existing models view the ensuing transnationalism as a temporary and instrumental way to affect politics in the country of origin. In these models, transnational activists are really domestic activists in exile. For example, in Margaret Keck and Kathryn Sikkink's "boomerang model," non-state actors, faced with repression at home, seek out allies abroad with a view to achieving domestic political change.[6] Similarly, in Idean Salehyan's work, rebels seek mobilization opportunities abroad when they are unable to challenge the state on its own turf, and much of what they subsequently do is oriented toward the insurgency's homeland.[7] The jihadi foreign-fighter movement, by contrast, took on a qualitatively new agenda and largely lost touch with the domestic struggles from which it emerged. It true that some foreign fighters had political ambitions in their home countries, which they pursued after the Afghan jihad. However, many others became preoccupied with what they saw as the defense of the Muslim nation, and for all practical purposes abandoned domestic politics. Our story thus follows Keck and Sikkink half the way; domestic repression may indeed create transnational activists, but the boomerang need not come back.

What Azzam Contributed

Azzam did not initiate the Arab involvement in Afghanistan, but he increased it. His role was particularly important in the middle stage of the war, from 1983 to 1987, when the Afghan Arabs went from being a fringe phenomenon of dozens of individuals to becoming a self-sustaining movement of thousands. Without Azzam, the Afghan Arab mobilization would likely have stayed in the hundreds or low thousands instead of the seven thousand or so that we think ended up going. The answer to the question "how important" can thus almost be quantified: Azzam's effort was several thousand volunteers' worth.

Azzam contributed in three main ways. One was by establishing an organization to facilitate foreign-fighter recruitment at a time when no such structure existed. The Services Bureau played a crucial role in recruitment, because it provided prospective recruits with travel information, financial support, and a promise of assistance on arrival – all of which lowered the barrier for participation. The Bureau also produced *al-Jihad* magazine, which was by far the most widely distributed Arabic-language magazine about the war. A variant of the Services

Bureau might have emerged without Azzam, but it would probably have become neither as influential nor as long-lived, because he had a rare set of qualifications and skills, as we shall see below.

Azzam's second main contribution was his international lecture tours. He gave hundreds of lectures about the Afghan jihad, primarily in the Gulf, in the United States, and in Pakistan. His international footprint was exceptionally large; if we exclude the Afghan Mujahidin leaders themselves, then nobody came close to giving as many recruitment lectures in as many countries as Azzam did. Moreover, he recruited people such as Usama Bin Ladin and Tamim al-Adnani, who went on to become influential recruiters themselves.

The third key contribution was to articulate a new recruitment message. Azzam was the first religious scholar to present an elaborate modern Islamic legal argument for foreign fighting as an individual religious duty. The originality of the argument is evident from the controversy and resistance it provoked at the time. To be sure, given the pan-Islamic mood of the 1980s, another ideologue might have come up with a similar argument if Azzam had not. However, it would likely have taken longer, because no other Arab clerics got involved in the Afghan jihad until the end of the war. Even though Azzam may not have been indispensable to the emergence of an Islamist foreign-fighter doctrine, he articulated it in time for it to influence substantial numbers of volunteers. There is little question that his doctrine helped persuade many recruits. The books in which it appeared sold thousands of copies, and many volunteers have said that they were swayed by Azzam's writings. Morever, he also developed other original propaganda themes, such as his writings about miracles, which became a big hit among young Islamists. Azzam also churned out a remarkable quantity of texts and lectures about the Afghanistan war, probably more so than any other Arab writer.

But why did other people respect Azzam and heed his word? He was not a particularly good manager, nor was he a skilled military man. He did, however, have a rare mixture of other attributes that made him a good transnational entrepreneur. At the personal level he had charisma and a rare ability to connect with the young. As a Palestinian refugee, he embodied the suffering of the Muslim nation. As a veteran Muslim Brother, he had impeccable Islamist credentials and a vast network of international contacts. As a former guerrilla fighter, he could not be accused of being an armchair intellectual. As an itinerant activist, he was a citizen of the Islamic world well placed to call on others to embrace pan-Islamism. Most important, however, was his training as a religious scholar. This gave him social status and authority, as well as the ability to formulate compelling legal opinions.

What Azzam's admirers seem to have appreciated most of all is that he was a scholar who dared speak his mind and take part in jihad. To many young people he was, to put it crudely, a cleric with balls. In more academic parlance, and in the words of Haroro Ingram, "the potency of Azzam's charismatic appeal is rooted in this inextricable merger of words and action."[8] This, incidentally, tells us something about the status of *ulama* in Islamist circles in the 1980s. They were still held in high esteem, but mainstream scholars were increasingly seen as politically subservient. After all, praising Azzam for his integrity was an implicit way of criticizing others for spinelessness. Clerical authority had started to diminish decades earlier, and the trend would only continue into the 1990s and beyond.[9] The jihadi movement would eventually make do with laymen and undistinguished theology students as their ideologues. Azzam was one of the last accomplished *ulama* to be involved with the movement.

But how can we be sure that Azzam really was that influential? It is important to stress-test a claim like this, lest we succumb to confirmation bias or indulge in great man theory.[10] There are at least three strong indications that Azzam really did make a difference. One is the chronological correlation between his personal recruitment efforts and the influx of Arab fighters to Afghanistan. Azzam stepped up his efforts around 1984 by publishing his foreign-fighter fatwa and founding the Services Bureau. The next two years saw a sharp increase in the flow of war volunteers. Moreover, if we look at how and through whom the volunteers of 1985–1986 were recruited, we see that a substantial number were recruited by Services Bureau-affiliated individuals or people said they were inspired by Azzam's ideas.

Second, even if we look closely for other early movers, we do not find anyone whose contribution comes close to that of Azzam. This book has identified several actors who played a role in the early stages of the Arab involvement. One was the Afghan commander Jalaluddin Haqqani, who appealed for foreign fighters as early as 1980, who received many of the earliest volunteers, and who gave early interviews to international media. Another was Kamal al-Sananiri, the veteran Egyptian Islamist who went to Peshawar in 1981, who recruited Azzam in Mecca the same year, and who might have become a central figure in the Afghan Arab community had he not died in an Egyptian prison that autumn. Yet another was the Egyptian Mustafa Hamid, who was among the very first to go, who covered the jihad in the early years as a journalist, and who, by his own account, tried to establish a Services Bureau-type organization before Azzam did. However, while all of these figures helped bring *some* Arabs to Afghanistan in the early 1980s, neither can claim responsibility for recruiting or inspiring particularly large numbers. Each of them had something that Azzam had – Haqqani the idea to bring Arabs, Sananiri the Muslim Brotherhood network, and Hamid the idea of establishing a Services Bureau – but none had all of Azzam's attributes.

Third, in a counterfactual scenario without Azzam, it is difficult to see how the Arab mobilization might have taken the proportions it did. For most of the war Azzam was the only Arab religious scholar to be based in Peshawar, so if we take him out of the equation we are left with a purely lay Afghan Arab community which would likely have struggled to mount a comparable recruitment operation. Had a lay person come up with the same ideas as Azzam, they would have been taken less seriously. Similarly, lay activists such as Usama Bin Ladin would not have had access to the same types of high-level platforms as a senior religious scholar like Azzam. Besides, the Afghan Arabs would have lacked a natural intermediary between the Arab volunteers and the Afghan Mujahidin, which in turn would have limited their ability to establish reception and training infrastructure for Arabs.

What Shaped Azzam

Azzam's career was, like everyone else's, shaped by a combination of personal traits, social forces, and coincidences. The personal portrait that emerges in this book is that of an idealistic and serious individual with strengths and flaws like any other human being. Deeply religious and conservative, he followed his convictions at high cost both to himself and his family. He was a war romantic who idealized life in jihad, but he was too bookish to be a committed soldier, and too conflict-shy to be a good leader. He was energetic, determined, and disciplined, very much living up to the name Azzam: "very resolved." These traits made him highly productive, but also stern and blunt at times. Humble in day-to-day interactions, he was chauvinistic on behalf of Islamic culture, and could get quite pompous on a podium. A captivating speaker, he was prone to hyperbole to make a point, and white lies to embellish a story. His views changed over time, and he could offer partly contradictory views depending on the context in which he was speaking. In short, Azzam was a more complex character than the super-Muslim of the hagiographies.

Azzam's trajectory was partly steered by political events. Most important was the establishment and expansion of Israel, which cost his family land in 1948, pushed Azzam himself into exile in 1967, and remained for him a humiliating reminder of Muslim geopolitical impotence. Even in his earliest writings we see a nostalgia for the Ottoman regional order and a lack of trust in the region's new nation-states. The Six Day War sent Azzam into statelessness; had the war not happened, he would likely have lived a quiet life as a religious teacher or judge in the Jenin area. His Palestinian background was key to his identity, and the prospect of liberating his homeland motivated him greatly throughout his life. The conflict had the second-order effect of drawing him into bitter intra-Arab disputes over how to confront Israel. His own feuds with Palestinian leftists and disappointment with Jordan's crackdown on the Fedayin left him frustrated and disillusioned. Last but not least, Azzam's career took a fateful turn in 1980 when the Jordanian government effectively exiled him for his political opinions, setting him on course toward Afghanistan. Azzam thus became part of a long list of Palestinians prominently involved in transnational jihadism, which has rightly led some to speak of a "Palestine effect" on the jihadi movement.[11]

However, Azzam was not simply a product of occupation and authoritarianism. His choices were also informed by the religious ideology of the Muslim Brotherhood. He had been socialized into the organization from a very young age, and his core worldview was shaped by the Brotherhood's ideas, especially those of Sayyid Qutb. Azzam was no liberal democrat; he wanted Muslims to be more conservative, and their societies to be governed exclusively by Islamic law. He saw nation-states in the Muslim world as corrupt and artificial entities that should first be Islamized and later merged into a pan-Islamic caliphate. He viewed Western culture as morally corrupt, and he judged individuals by their religion, categorically distrusting Jews, Christians, and atheists. He viewed Islamic history as a constant struggle between Islam and other religious groups, especially the Jews. Deeply anti-Semitic, he blamed Jews not only for the occupation of

Palestine, but also for many other things, including the fall of the Ottoman Empire and the spread of socialism and secularism. Many of his life decisions were informed by ideology; for example, he chose to criticize the Jordanian regime because he viewed its policies as un-Islamic, and he chose to fight in Afghanistan because he felt a religious solidarity with Afghan Muslims, and because he believed God would punish him if he did not.

Azzam's trajectory was also shaped by the transnational network of contacts he accumulated in the Muslim Brotherhood. It was through the Brotherhood that he became involved with the Fedayin in the late 1960s, and it was through them that he got his Ph.D. scholarship to Cairo and later a job at the University of Jordan. Much of his international travel in the late 1970s and early 1980s was for Brotherhood-linked events, and it was through Brotherhood contacts that he found a job in Saudi Arabia after being fired from the University of Jordan. Azzam's encounter with Kamal al-Sananiri in Jeddah in the spring of 1981 – which set him on course for Pakistan – was a feature of his longstanding Egyptian connections. The Muslim Brotherhood thus both inspired and facilitated Azzam's drift toward transnationalism.

Azzam's Historical Responsibility

To what extent is Azzam responsible for the Islamist extremism of the 1990s and beyond? A charitable interpretation of his historical role is that he merely mobilized for the liberation of Afghanistan and that he advocated jihad with clean tactics, so he cannot be held accountable for the violent excesses of later groups. However, we cannot judge a person's historical responsibility by his or her intentions alone. There are several reasons to take a more critical view of Azzam's historical legacy.

For one, he helped create the Afghan Arab movement, from which al-Qaida and other radical groups emerged. Whatever one thinks about the ideological connection between Azzam and his radical successors, the reality is that he helped start their militant careers. If he had not succeeded so well with the Afghan Arab mobilization, the jihadi movement would have been smaller.

For another, he articulated a foreign-fighter doctrine that outlived the Afghanistan war. His writings inspired volunteers to join other war zones, such as Bosnia, Chechnya, and Iraq, and some of those individuals moved on to more radical forms of militancy. A strong argument can now be made that radicalization is a problem inherent to Islamist foreign-fighter mobilizations.[12] The experience of war, the religious indoctrination, and the lack of governance mechanisms likely combine to make some of the fighters prone to more norm-breaking forms of violence. By helping create a foreign-fighter movement, Azzam ensured a steady supply of recruits to the main arenas from which more radical groups drew their members.

Third, the foreign-fighter doctrine arguably paved the way, in ideological terms, for al-Qaida's international terrorism strategy. Azzam propagated militarized pan-Islamism, a worldview in which the *umma* is under assault on multiple fronts by non-Muslims, and in which Muslims must fight together to survive. This worldview involved a reordering of the enemy hierarchy for the Islamist movement; rather than trying to topple corrupt Muslim regimes, Muslims should concentrate on fighting non-Muslim powers. Usama Bin Ladin's call for a terrorism campaign against the West arguably represents a natural extension of Azzam's foreign-fighter doctrine. When Bin Ladin began advocating strikes against US targets in the late 1990s, he used rhetoric very similar to that of Azzam in the 1980s: The *umma* is under attack on multiple fronts, Muslim women and children are dying at the hands of non-Muslims, and we must defend ourselves. The main difference between Azzam and Bin Ladin was the prescribed solution; while Azzam called on people to go and fight in those areas where Muslims were under attack, Bin Ladin said Muslims had the right to also attack the occupying powers in other parts of the world.

Fourth, Azzam's promotion of a Sunni martyrdom culture in the 1980s arguably prepared the ground for the adoption of suicide bombings by Sunni groups such as Hamas and al-Qaida in the 1990s. Azzam wrote extensively about the benefits of martyrdom, and he celebrated fallen Arabs in *al-Jihad* magazine and in his talks. The culture of self-sacrifice that he helped create likely made it easier to present suicide bombings as heroic acts of resistance. Of course, another important factor behind the Sunni adoption of suicide tactics in the 1990s was the actual use of suicide bombings by Shiite groups such as Hizballah in the 1980s.

Azzam's fifth and most destructive contribution was to undermine established authority in questions to do with jihad. A key premise of his foreign-fighter doctrine was that governments have no right to stop citizens from joining a legitimate jihad. At the same time, he did not offer any alternative short-term mechanism to control the military force that would accumulate during a transnational jihad mobilization. The result was a movement that could not be governed, because there was no consensus on who should lead. Azzam no doubt had good intentions; he wanted to wrest military authority from corrupt regimes, and he believed, very naïvely, that a fighting force generated by popular mobilization would self-organize. In practice, however, the Afghan Arabs faced significant coordination problems from the start, and things only went downhill from there. Divested of authority figures, the movement had no mechanism for arbitrating between alternative strategies and tactics. When people disagreed, they simply parted and pursued their preferred strategies in separate factions. Over time, more and more brutal groups would emerge, and there was little that religious authorities could do about it, because the radicals would not listen. For the same reasons, it is unlikely that Azzam would have been able to prevent the radicalization of the jihadi movement if he had lived. After all, he was unable to do anything about the radicalization that occurred right before his eyes in Peshawar in the late 1980s.

Besides, it is not entirely clear that Azzam would have *wanted* to rein in all the radicals, because his commitment to clean warfare may not have been quite as strong as some of his supporters have suggested. For one, when he discussed specific tactics mentioned in the classical sources, he tended to lean to the more hardline of the available interpretations. For another, he explicitly approved of at least one type of out-of-theater operations, namely the assassination of Jews in the United States. He is also not on the record as having issued many explicit bans or reprimands for wrongful use of violence; if he had been, he would probably not be so widely respected in the radical parts of the movement today. One might also argue that the reason Azzam did not advocate terrorist tactics in the Afghan context is that there was no need for them. It was a conflict with large conventional battlefronts and few relevant out-of-area targets. In the 1990s, by contrast, the conflicts in which jihadi groups found themselves were more asymmetrical, increasing the temptation to use terrorist tactics. Had he lived into the 1990s, Azzam would very likely have supported Hamas's use of suicide bombings. It is also not inconceivable that, under the right circumstances, he might have condoned a strategy of attacking US targets, at least in the Muslim world. That he never did in his lifetime means little, because, at the time, nobody else had either, not even Usama Bin Ladin. The bottom line is that Azzam does bear a certain responsibility for the jihadi violence that spread after his death.

The Role of Governments

Governments are also to blame for the internationalization of jihadism, but not quite to the extent that is often argued, and not quite for the same reasons. This book has shown that, generally speaking, the jihadi movement staked out its own course based more on ideological convictions than on government manipulation. Still, the policies of both Muslim and Western countries contributed to the globalization of jihad in several ways.

For one, several Arab countries used excessive force against their Islamist dissidents from the 1950s to the 1980s. This pushed existing leaders onto the international stage and created grievances that mobilized new activists. To be sure, Islamists were not always easy to include in the political process, because hardliners among them often rejected fundamental features of the existing system. Besides, these regimes' authoritarian policies reflected dysfunctions inherited from the colonial period. Still, countries such as Egypt and Syria often chose confrontation or repression when alternative strategies were available.

Second, Saudi Arabia and other Gulf countries went too far in their promotion of populist pan-Islamism in the 1970s and 1980s. They effectively paid for the rise of the pan-Islamist movement by funding the international Islamic organizations. Had Saudi Arabia not funded organizations such as the Muslim World League and given them such freedom, then the pan-Islamist victim narrative would not have been so influential, nor the transnational networks so large. This, in turn, would likely have reduced the resonance of foreign-fighter recruitment calls, and limited the ability of organizers such as Azzam to exploit charities and educational programs for military purposes. The book has provided ample evidence that government-supported organizations and charities contributed to the military effort in Afghanistan. The most striking exhibit is the fact that Azzam himself subsisted on Saudi money during his entire time in Pakistan – first from King Abd al-Aziz University and then from the Muslim World League.

A third culprit is of course the Soviet Union. By intervening militarily in Afghanistan, propping up the Communist dictatorship, and practicing brutal counterinsurgency, Moscow created a major symbol of Muslim suffering. Without a Soviet occupation, Afghanistan would probably have seen further conflict and instability, but it would have been an intra-Afghan war, one that could less easily have been cast as a non-Muslim occupation of Muslim land and thus as a clear-cut case of jihad. An intra-Afghan conflict between Islamists and Communists might still have attracted foreign fighters, but their numbers would have been smaller.

Fourth, the main sponsors of the Afghan Mujahidin – the United States, Saudi Arabia, and Pakistan – are to blame for allowing foreign fighters to operate virtually freely in Pakistan and Afghanistan as well as in their own societies. We have seen that Western intelligence services did not actively support Arab volunteers, but they also did little to stop them. This is somewhat understandable, because the Arabs were marginal players in the war, and there was no precedent for foreign fighters becoming international terrorists. Still, there were plenty of warning signs for those who cared to look, for example in the fierce anti-Westernism of the Arab volunteers and in the terrorist tactics used by jihadis in Egypt and Syria in preceding years. It was naïve to think that the foreign-fighter influx into Afghanistan would not have international repercussions.

Fifth and finally, most international actors abandoned Afghanistan to its fate after the Soviet withdrawal.[13] This left the country unstable and vulnerable to takeover by the Taliban, who in turn hosted al-Qaida in the late 1990s. It also left the West open to the accusation that its support for the Afghan jihad had been entirely self-serving. While it is true that winning the Cold War was the primary motivation for the Western governments' involvement, it was not the whole story. Some politicians and many NGO activists had also supported the Afghan people because they saw it as a victim of injustice and humanitarian suffering. This aspect of the contribution was quickly forgotten in the 1990s because Afghanistan was largely left to its own devices.

This brings us to an oft-ignored aspect about West's role in the Afghan jihad, namely, that, at the end of the day, it helped liberate a Muslim country from non-Muslim occupation. Not only that: the USA gladly supported the most hardline Islamist wing of the Afghan Mujahidin, helped Pakistan distribute Qur'ans in Central Asia, and let

Afghan Mujahidin operate freely on American soil. Besides, in no country did Azzam and the Services Bureau enjoy more political freedom to fundraise and recruit than in the United States. Yet in the Islamist victim narrative that developed from the late 1980s onward, Western countries are cast as vicious Islamophobes bent on killing and humiliating Muslims. Gone is any trace of recognition for the support that the West lent to the Afghan resistance. This goes to show that historical realities can be twisted to the unrecognizable in ideologically motivated narratives.

If radical Islamists never recognized the US support for the Afghan jihad, it is because they were very anti-American to begin with. We have seen how Azzam disparaged Western society in his Bachelor's thesis – echoing Sayyid Qutb's writings about America a decade earlier. In the late 1970s, the front pages of *al-Mujtama'* magazine printed warnings of Crusader aggression alongside pictures of American flags and stars of David. Throughout the 1980s, Azzam and other Afghan Arabs made their anti-Westernism crystal clear both in their writings and their actions on the ground. In fact, their hostility increased in the late 1980s when the Western support for the Mujahidin was at its peak. These attitudes had deep and complex roots. Real historical grievances – not least colonial oppression and Western support for Israel – are obviously an important part of the story, but the Islamists' own prejudices and selective interpretation of history clearly also played a part. This strengthens the argument that the jihadi movement internationalized primarily for reasons internal to the Muslim world.

The phenomenon that Abdallah Azzam helped create has become the preeminent rebel movement of the post-Cold War era. Its offshoots have perpetrated spectacular acts of violence, caused unrest in multiple regions, and drawn major powers into quagmires. It has proved more resilient than most other rebel movements, largely because of its exceptionally transnational character. Transnationalism has provided flexibility and redundancy, allowing the movement to survive the loss of individual leaders and organizations. At the time of writing, the jihadi movement is at a crossroads following the rise and fall of the Islamic State organization. There is no saying where the Caravan is heading next, but it is a fair bet that it will keep moving well into the twenty-first century.

Note on Sources

Availability

The book is accompanied by a website, www.azzambook.net, which will contain links to most primary and secondary sources cited in the book. For this reason, some of the references exclude URLs and other cumbersome citation elements.

Many items cited in the book come from the online text repository Minbar al-Tawhid wa'l-Jihad (www.tawhed.ws). The site closed down in 2015, but as of August 2019 it could still be accessed through Internet Archive's Wayback Machine (https://web.archive.org). For some Azzam books, I sometimes cite page numbers from the Word file version that was available on the Minbar al-Tawhid wa'l-Jihad website as opposed to the original printed version of the book. This is indicated with the phrase "Minbar version."

"Tareekh Osama" and "Tareekh Musadat" refer to document collections available at Michael S. Smith II, 'al-Qa'ida Archives: Tareekh Osama & Tareekh al-Musadat', Downrange Blog, 9 December 2016, https://insidethejihad.com/2016/12/al-qaida-archives-tareekh-osama-tareekh-al-musadat/ (accessed 11 April 2018).

Jihadi magazines such as *al-Jihad* and *al-Bunyan al-Marsus* are available at the Jihadi Document Repository at Oslo University (www.hf.uio.no/ikos/english/research/jihadi-document-repository/index.html).

Interviews

I interviewed the following: Mariam Abou Zahab, Abu Suhayb, Babar Ahmed, Roy Allison, Börje Almqvist, Abdallah Anas, Frank Anderson, Zafar Ishaq Ansari, Isam al-Attar, Fayiz Azzam, Hudhayfa Azzam, Jamal Azzam (Abu Harith), Jihan Bakeer, Peter Bergen, Noman

Benothman, Alain Chevalérias, Charles Cogan, Steve Coll, Larry Crandall, Alastair Crooke, Yusuf al-Dayni, Mishari al-Dhaydi, Gilles Dorronsoro, Charles Dunbar, Gunnar Ekberg, Muhammad Fahim, Prince Turki al-Faisal, Mahmud Faruqi, Yonathan Fighel, Ibrahim Gharaybeh, Basim Ghozlan, Abd al-Rahman al-Hadlaq, Hasan Abu Hanieh, Sami' al-Haqq, Kamal al-Helbawy, Aqil Hussain, Muhammad Zaki Hussain, Jamal Isma'il, Mulla Izzat, Eli Karmon, Jamal Khashoggi, Iqbal Khattak, Hein G. Kiessling, Fahim Kohdamani, Tahir Mansuri, Abu Muhammad al-Maqdisi, Avishai Margalit, Abdallah Abu Nabah, Ahmad Nawfal, Reuven Paz, Khalid Rahman, Olivier Roy, Ahmed Rashid, Salim Safi, Marc Sageman, Saud al-Sarhan, Muhammad Sawalha, Abd Rabb al-Rasul Sayyaf, Yusuf Shah, Marwan Shahadeh, Shaul Shay, Rachel Simon, Peter Tomsen, Tariq Tell, Thomas Twetten, Abdallah al-Yahya, Rahimullah Yusufzai, Atiq-uz-Zafar, and Ahmad Zaydan. The interviews were conducted in Aachen, Amman, Cambridge (MA), Hertzlia, Falls Church (VA), Islamabad, Jeddah, Jenin, Kabul, London, Oslo, Paris, Peshawar, Princeton (NJ), Riyadh, al-Sila al-Harithiyya, and Washington (DC). A few interviews were done by phone or by email.

Overview of Abdallah Azzam's Works

Azzam's ideological corpus is unwieldy, because it is spread over different formats and has been subject to extensive posthumous editing and unregulated distribution. The following is a tentative bibliography of his longer works in Arabic based on my trawling of libraries, bookshops, and the internet over many years. The overview does not include individual articles, recorded lectures, or translated works (although it does include edited compilations of articles and lecture transcripts). The list is divided into three sections: student works, books published in his lifetime, and posthumously distributed works. The first two sections are probably accurate, because I have seen the actual printed copies or photographs of the books on the list. The list of posthumously distributed works is less authoritative because the distribution has been so decentralized. I rely here on the two main compilations of Azzam's works, namely the book *Encyclopedia of the Relics* and the digital collection on Minbar al-Tawhid wa'l-Jihad, taking the former as a baseline.[1] I list all the items in these collections minus the approximately 175 free-standing lecture transcriptions in the *Encyclopedia*. The reader may encounter texts online whose titles are not in this overview; often these are repackaged extracts of works listed below.[2] Datable items are arranged in chronological order, the rest alphabetically.

Student Works

- 'inhilal al-zawaj fi'l-fiqh wa'l-qanun' [Marriage Dissolution in Islamic Jurisprudence and Civil Law], 1967 (BA thesis).
- 'dalalat al-kitab wa'l-sunna 'ala al-ahkam' [The Implications of the Book and the Sunna for Legal Rulings], 1973 (Ph.D. thesis).

Books Published in his Lifetime

- *al-'aqida wa atharuha fi bina' al-jil* [The Creed and its Effect on Building the Generation], 1975.
- *al-da'wa al-islamiyya* [The Islamic Call], ca. 1978 (under the pseudonym Sadiq Amin).
- *al-saratan al-ahmar* [The Red Cancer], 1980.
- *al-islam wa mustaqbal al-bashariyya* [Islam and the Future of Mankind], ca. 1980.
- *ayat al-rahman fi jihad al-afghan* [Signs of the Merciful in the Afghan Jihad], 1983.
- *al-difa' 'an aradi al-muslimin: ahamm furud al-a'yan* [The Defense of Muslim Lands: The Most Important of Individual Duties], 1985.
- *'ibar wa basa'ir li'l-jihad fi'l-'asr al-hadir* [Lessons and Insights on Jihad in the Current Age], 1986.
- *fi'l-jihad adab wa ahkam* [Proper Conduct and Rulings in Jihad], 1986.
- *al-manara al-mafquda* [The Lost Beacon], 1987.
- *ilhaq bi'l-qafila* [Join the Caravan], 1987.
- *jihad sha'b muslim* [Jihad of a Muslim People], 1988.
- *hamas: al-judhur al-tarikhiyya wa'l-mithaq* [Hamas: Historical Roots and Charter], 1989.
- *kalimat min khatt al-nar al-awwal* [Words from the First Line of Fire], 1989.

Posthumously Distributed Works

- *wathiqa ila al-ikhwan al-muslimun fi'l urdun* [Document to the Muslim Brotherhood in Jordan], ca. 1980.
- *nazarat wa adwa' 'ala al-qawmiyya al-'arabiyya* [Views and Elucidations on Arab Nationalism], ca. 1981.*[3]
- *wasiyat al-'abd al-faqir ila allah ta'ala 'abdallah bin yusuf 'azzam* [The Will of God's Poor Servant Abdallah Yusuf Azzam], 1986.*
- *fi zilal surat al-tawba* [In the Shade of Surat al-Tawba], 1986.*
- *basha'ir al-nasr* [Tidings of Victory], 1987.*
- *shahr bayna al-'amaliqa* [A Month among the Giants], 1989.*
- *fi'l-ta'amur al-'alami* [On the Global Conspiracy], 1989.*
- *fi khidamm al-ma'raka* [In the Heat of Battle], 1989.*

- *al-tawd al-shamikh* [The Lofty Mountain], 1989.
- *adhkhar al-sabah wa'l-masa'* [Morning and Evening Supplications], n.d.*
- *'amlaq al-fikr al-islami (al-shahid sayyid qutb)* [A Giant of Islamic Thought (The Martyr Sayyid Qutb)], n.d.
- *as'ila wa ajwiba hawla fiqh al-jihad* [Questions and Answers on the Jurisprudence of Jihad], n.d.*[4]
- *al-dhaba'ih wa'l-luhum al-mustawrada* [Slaughter and Imported Meats], n.d.*
- *dhikrayat filastin* [Memories of Palestine], n.d.*
- *fi'l-hijra wa'l-i'dad* [On Emigration and Preparation], n.d*[5]
- *fi'l-jihad fiqh wa'l-ijtihad* [There is Jurisprudence and Interpretation in Jihad], n.d.
- *fi'l-sira 'ibra* [The Prophet's Biography Contains a Lesson], n.d.*
- *hadir al-'alam al-islami* [The Current Muslim World], n.d.*
- *hadm al-khilafa wa bina'uha* [The Destruction of the Caliphate and its Construction], n.d.
- *hatta la tudi' filastin ila al-abad* [So that Palestine is not Lost Forever], n.d.
- *hukm al-'amal fi'l-jama'a* [The Ruling on Operating in Groups], n.d.*
- *al-ijra'at wa'l-murafa'at* [The Jurisprudence of Legal Measures and Procedures], n.d.*[6]
- *i'lan al-jihad* [Declaring Jihad], n.d.*
- *ithaf al-'ibad bi-fada'il al-jihad* [Illustrating the Virtues of Jihad to God's Servants], n.d.*
- *jarimat qatl al-nafs al-muslima* [The Crime of Killing a Muslim Soul], n.d.*
- *khatt al-tahawwul al-tarikhi* [The Historical Line of Transition], n.d.*
- *mabahith fi'l-salah* [Investigations into Prayer], n.d.*
- *al-ma'thurat bi-thawbiha al-jadid* [The *Ma'thurat* in New Garb], n.d.
- *muhawalat 'ala tariq al-dawla al-islamiyya* [Attempts along the Road to the Islamic State], n.d.
- *nazariyyat al-'aqd wa'l-kaffala* [Theory of Contract and Sponsorship], n.d.*[7]
- *al-nihaya wa'l-khalasa* [The End and the Summary], n.d.**
- *al-qawa'id al-fiqhiyya* [Rules of Jurisprudence], n.d.*
- *qisas wa ahdath* [Stories and Events], n.d.*
- *sa'adat al-bashariyya* [The Happiness of Mankind], n.d.*

- *tahdhib sharh al-'aqida al-tahawiyya* [Refining Explanation of Tahawi Creed], n.d.
- *al-tarbiya al-jihadiyya wa'l-bina'* [Jihadi Education and Edification], n.d.**
- *tujjar al-hurub* [War Merchants], n.d.**
- *'ushshaq al-hur* [Those who Love of The Virgins of Paradise], n.d.

* Also in Minbar al-Tawhid wa'l-Jihad.
** Only in Minbar al-Tawhid wa'l-Jihad as a separate item. May be extract from lecture included in the Encyclopaedia.

1. *mawsu'at al-dhakha'ir al-'izam fima uthira 'an al-imam al-humam al-shahid 'abdallah 'azzam* [Encyclopedia of the Relics of the Legacy of the Brave Martyred Imam Abdallah Azzam] (Peshawar: Markaz al-Shahid Azzam al-I'lami, 1997), available at https://archive.org/details/zakhaer3ozma (accessed 1 February 2016).
2. This is notably the case of many English-language texts attributed to Azzam. For example, the pdf booklet *The Tawhed of Action* from Tibyan Publications is a (suboptimally) translated extract of *fi zilal surat al-tawba*.
3. The Minbar version title is *al-qawmiyya al-'arabiyya* [Arab Nationalism].
4. The Minbar version title is *al-as'ila wa'l-ajwiba al-jihadiyya* [Jihadi Questions and Answers].
5. The Minbar version title is *al-hijra wa'l-i'dad* [Emigration and Preparation].
6. The Minbar version title is *fiqh al-ijra'at wa'l-murafa'at* [The Jurisprudence of Legal Measures and Procedures].
7. The Minbar version title is *al-kaffala* [Sponsorship].

Notes

Introduction

1. In this book Islamism is defined as activism of any kind justified with primary reference to Islam, while jihadism is used as a synonym for violent Sunni Islamism. Definitions of both Islamism and jihadism are contested; for in-depth treatments see, for example, Richard C. Martin and Abbas Barzegar, eds., *Islamism: Contested Perspectives on Political Islam* (Stanford: Stanford University Press, 2009); and Mark Sedgwick, 'Jihadism, Narrow and Wide: The Dangers of Loose Use of an Important Term', *Perspectives on Terrorism* 9, no. 2 (2015): 34–41. I describe as transnational or international those groups that involve activists from different countries and engage in cross-border activities. By foreign fighting I mean privately organized, ideologically motivated involvement in foreign insurgencies. For a more elaborate definition see Thomas Hegghammer, 'The Rise of Muslim Foreign Fighters: Islam and the Globalization of Jihad', *International Security* 35, no. 3 (2010): 53–94, pp. 57–59.
2. Brynjar Lia, *Architect of Global Jihad: The Life of al-Qaeda Strategist Abu Musʻab al-Suri* (London: Hurst, 2007), p. 90.
3. In the Western literature the terms "Afghan Arabs" and "Arab Afghans" are used in roughly equal measure, but "Afghan Arabs" is more logical, because these men were Arabs who had been "Afghanized" by their involvement. Another reason to use "Afghan Arabs" for the foreign fighters is that there is actually an ethnic group in Afghanistan that identifies as Arab, claiming heritage from previous Arab migrations into Afghanistan: see Thomas J. Barfield, *The Central Asian Arabs of Afghanistan: Pastoral Nomadism in Transition* (Austin: University of Texas Press, 1981). In this book I use the term Afghan Arabs somewhat loosely to describe foreign fighters recruited through Arab-run networks. Certain categories of non-Arab foreign fighters, such as Turks, Kurds, sub-Saharan Africans, and Western converts are included in the term because they usually joined through such networks. Excluded, however,

are foreign fighters from Asian countries such as Pakistan, India, Bangladesh, Malaysia, Indonesia and the Philippines.
4. Kepel writes, "Three arms of the Saudi administration (the intelligence services ... the ad hoc support committee and the Muslim world league) formed the main channels of transmission [of Arab aid]. But in order for aid to reach those for whom it was intended ... trustworthy agents were needed on the spot. Thus, Arab volunteers were recruited to make the journey to the Pakistani-Afghan arena": Gilles Kepel, *Jihad: The Trail of Political Islam* (Cambridge, MA: Belknap, 2002), p. 144. Mandaville writes, "The emergence of the global jihad movement can only be explained within the context of late cold war geopolitics ... soon a number of radical Arab Islamists whose efforts had previously been confined to resistance against states and occupiers in their home countries began to find their way to Afghanistan to join the struggle": Peter Mandaville, *Global Political Islam* (London: Routledge, 2007), p. 241.
5. Gerges writes, "[The jihadis] went to Afghanistan to find a 'secure base' to train and conduct military operations against renegade rulers back home, not to wage jihad globally": Fawaz Gerges, *The Far Enemy: Why Jihad Went Global* (New York: Cambridge University Press, 2005), p. 12. Rougier writes, "Unable to fight for Palestine or topple their regimes, many volunteers sought, in the beginning of the 1980s, a substitution front on the Indian subcontinent": Bernard Rougier, 'Le jihad en Afghanistan et l'émergence du salafisme-jihadisme', in *Qu'est-ce que le salafisme?*, ed. Bernard Rougier (Paris: Presses Universitaires de France, 2008), 65–86, p. 66.
6. See, for example, Lawrence Wright, *The Looming Tower: Al Qaeda and the Road to 9/11* (New York: Knopf, 2006), pp. 95–98.
7. Yahya al-Awadh, *afghanistan: tahaddiyat al-jihad al-akbar* [Afghanistan: The Challenges of the Great Jihad] (Doha: Dar al-Sharq, 1992), p. 68; Tawfiq Yusuf al-Wa'i, *mawsu'at shuhada' al-haraka al-islamiyya* [Encyclopaedia of the Martyrs of the Islamic Movement] (Cairo: Dar al-Tawzi' wa'l-Nashr al-Islamiyya, 2006), p. 223.
8. Muhammad Haniff Hassan, *The Father of Jihad: 'Abd Allah 'Azzam's Jihad Ideas and Implications to National Security* (London: Imperial College Press, 2014). The book was based on Hassan's Ph.D. thesis: Muhammad Haniff Hassan, 'Jihad ideas of "Abd Allah" Azzam and their implications for national security' (Nanyang Technological University, 2012). In addition, Asaf Maliach wrote a Ph.D. thesis on Azzam in Hebrew, but it has not been translated: Asaf Maliach, 'Abdallah Azzam and the Ideological Origins of Usama Bin Ladin's Worldwide Islamic Terrorism' [in Hebrew], Ph.D. dissertation (Bar-Ilan University, 2006).

9. Andrew McGregor, '"Jihad and the Rifle Alone": 'Abdullah 'Azzam and the Islamist Revolution', *Journal of Conflict Studies* 23, no. 2 (2003) 92–113; Thomas Hegghamer, 'Abdallah Azzam: l'imam du jihad', in *al-Qaida dans le texte*, ed. Gilles Kepel et al. (Paris: Presses Universitaires de France, 2005), 115–138; John C. M. Calvert, 'The Striving Shaykh: Abdallah Azzam and the Revival of Jihad', *Journal of Religion and Society* – Supplement Series (2007): 83–102; Youssef Aboul-Enein, *The Late Sheikh Abdullah Azzam's Books* (3 parts) (West Point, NY: Combating Terrorism Center, 2007); Camilla Holte Wiig, 'Forpliktet til kamp: En studie av Abdullah Azzams fiendebilde og krigslegitimering' [Bound to Fight: A Study of Abdallah Azzam's Enemy Picture and Legitimation for War], MA thesis (University of Oslo, 2007); Asaf Maliach, 'Abdullah Azzam, al-Qaeda, and Hamas: Concepts of Jihad and Istishhad', *Military and Strategic Affairs* 2, no. 2 (2010): 79–93; Sebastian Schnelle, 'Abdullah Azzam, Ideologue of Jihad: Freedom Fighter or Terrorist?', *Journal of Church and State* 54, no. 4 (1 December 2012): 625–647; Thomas Hegghamer, 'Abdallah Azzam and Palestine', *Die Welt des Islams* 53, no. 3–4 (2013): 353–387; and Jed Lea-Henry, 'The Life and Death of Abdullah Azzam', *Middle East Policy* 25, no. 1 (2018): 64–79.
10. Steven Emerson, 'Abdullah Assam: The Man before Osama Bin Laden', *Journal of Counterterrorism and Security International* (1998), www.iacsp.com/itobli3.html (accessed 11 April 2009); Jonathan Fighel, 'Sheikh Abdullah Azzam: Bin Laden's Spiritual Mentor', International Institute for Counter-Terrorism (27 September 2001), http://212.150.54.123/articles/articledet.cfm?articleid=388 (accessed 17 May 2013); Chris Suellentrop, 'Abdullah Azzam: The Godfather of Jihad', Slate.com (16 April 2002); and Bruce Riedel, 'The 9/11 Attacks' Spiritual Father', *The Daily Beast* (11 September 2011), www.thedailybeast.com/articles/2011/09/11/abdullah-azzam-spiritual-father-of-9-11-attacks-ideas-live-on.html.
11. A. Jefferson Kilpatrick, *Sayyid Qutb: A Selective Annotated Bibliography of Dissertations and Theses*, annotated ed. ([Scotts Valley, CA]: CreateSpace Independent Publishing Platform, 2015); William Shepard, *Sayyid Qutb: Oxford Bibliographies Online Research Guide* ([New York]: Oxford University Press, 2010).
12. Peter Tomsen, *The Wars of Afghanistan: Messianic Terrorism, Tribal Conflicts, and the Failures of Great Powers* (New York: PublicAffairs, 2011); Alex Strick van Linschoten and Felix Kuehn, *An Enemy we Created: The Myth of the Taliban–al Qaeda Merger in Afghanistan* (Oxford: Oxford University Press, 2012); Vahid Brown and Don Rassler, *Fountainhead of Jihad: The Haqqani Nexus, 1973–2012*

(Oxford: Oxford University Press, 2013); Mustafa Hamid and Leah Farrall, *The Arabs at War in Afghanistan* (London: Hurst, 2015); Anne Stenersen, *al-Qaida in Afghanistan* (Cambridge: Cambridge University Press, 2017).

13. Husni Adham Jarrar, *al-shahid 'abdallah 'azzam: rajul da'wa wa-madrasat jihad* [The Martyr Abdallah Azzam: Man of Da'wa and School of Jihad] (Amman: Dar al-Diya, 1990); Bashir Abu Rumman and Abdallah Sa'id, *al-'alim wa'l-mujahid wa'l-shahid al-shaykh 'abdallah 'azzam* [The Scholar, Mujahid, Martyr and Sheikh Abdallah Azzam] (Amman: Dar al-Bashir, 1990); Muhammad Abdallah Amir, *al-shaykh al-mujahid 'abdallah 'azzam: al-rajul alladhi tarjama al-aqwal ila af'al* [The Mujahid Sheikh Abdallah Azzam: The Man who Translated Words into Deeds], 1st ed. (Kuwait: Maktabat Dar al-Bayan, 1990); Ahmad Sa'id Azzam, *min manaqib al-imam al-shahid 'abdallah 'azzam* [Character Traits of the Martyred Imam Abdallah Azzam] (Peshawar: unknown publisher, 1990); Abu Mujahid, *al-shahid 'abdallah 'azzam bayna al-milad wa'l-istishhad* [The Martyr Abdallah Azzam from Birth to Martyrdom] (Peshawar: Markaz al-Shahid Azzam al-I'lami, 1991); Adnan al-Nahawi, *'abdallah 'azzam: ahdath wa mawaqif* [Abdallah Azzam: Events and Positions] (Riyadh: Dar al-Nahawi, 1994); Mahmud Sa'id Azzam, *al-duktur al-shahid 'abdallah yusuf 'azzam: shaykhi alladhi 'ariftu* [The Martyred Doctor Abdallah Yusuf Azzam: My Shaykh as I Knew him] (Gaza: Mu'assasat Ibda' li'l-Abhath wa'l-Dirasat wa'l-Tadrib, 2012). There is yet another book that I was unable to locate, namely, Hasan Khalil Hasan (or Hussain), *al-shahid 'abdallah 'azzam mujahidan fi filastin wa Afghanistan* [The Martyr Abdallah Azzam Striving in Palestine and Afghanistan] (unknown place, publisher, and year).

14. *fi 'uyun mu'asira: al-imam al-shahid 'abdallah 'azzam* [Through Contemporary Eyes: The Martyred Imam Abdallah Azzam] (Peshawar: Markaz al-Shahid Azzam al-I'lami, 1997).

15. See, for example, Abdallah Bin Omar, 'The Striving Sheikh: Abdullah Azzam', *Nida'ul Islam*, July 1996; 'Sheikh Abdullah Azzam', n.d., www.azzam.com/html/storiesabdullahazzam.htm (accessed 17 September 2001); 'Abdallah Azzam' (www.ikhwan.net/wiki [accessed 30 January 2018], n.d.); al-Wa'i, *mawsu'at al-shuhada'*, part 1, pp. 222–230; Umar al-Haddushi, 'nubdha mukhtasira 'an hayat mujaddid al-jihad al-shaykh al-imam 'abdallah 'azzam' [Short Presentation of the Life of the Reviver of Jihad, the Sheikh and Imam Abdallah Azzam] (Shabakat al-Tahaddi al-Islami [posted on http://al-faloja1.com/vb/showthread.php?t=93030, 19 November 2009], n.d.); and 'al-'alim al-mujahid wa al-shaykh al-shahid 'abdallah 'azzam' [The Scholar, Mujahid and Martyr Shaykh Abdallah Azzam], *Iyha'at Jihadiyya* no. 1 (July 2015), pp. 21–23.

16. See, for example, Iyad Abd al-Hamid Aql, 'ma'alim al-tarbiya al-jihadiyya fi dhaw' kitabat al-shaykh 'abdallah 'azzam' [Principles of Jihadi Education in Light of the Writings of Sheikh Abdallah Azzam], Master's thesis (Islamic University in Gaza, 2008); Manal Abd al-Karim Hasan Aziz, "abdallah 'azzam wa juhuduhu fi nashr al-'aqida al-islamiyya' [Abdallah Azzam and his Efforts to Spread the Islamic Doctrine], Master's thesis (Islamic University in Gaza, 2012); and Sa'id Sha'ban Khalil al-Dahshan, 'juhud al-duktur 'abdallah 'azzam fi nashr al-da'wa al-islamiyya' [Doctor Abdallah Azzam's Efforts in Propagating the Islamic Call], Master's thesis (Islamic University in Gaza, 2013).
17. Basil Muhammad, *safahat min sijill al-ansar al-'arab fi afghanistan* [*Pages from the Record of the Arab Supporters in Afghanistan*], 2nd ed. (Riyadh: Lajnat al-Birr al-Islamiyya, 1991). Basil Muhammad was a pseudonym of the Saudi Islamist philanthropist Adel Batterjee; see *The 9/11 Commission Report* (New York: W. W. Norton & Co., 2004), p. 467. Although ideologically favorable to the Afghan Arabs, the book is reliable partly because it draws on numerous interviews with key players conducted in Peshawar in the late 1980s, and partly because the author does not shy away from describing the community's internal problems.
18. Azzam evoked the term "caravan" first in March 1985, when he introduced an article series in *al-Jihad* magazine titled 'min qafilat al-shuhada" [From the Caravan of Martyrs]: see *al-Jihad* no. 4 (March 1985), p. 36. The expression "join the caravan" (*ilhaq bi'l-qafila*) appears to be Azzam's invention. There seems to be no clear precedent for it in the Qur'an or the Hadith: email correspondence with Michael Cook, 22 October 2015. David B. Edwards says he saw the Pashto term *shahidan-u caravan* (caravan of martyrs) in an Afghan Mujahidin journal "in the wake of the Soviet invasion of Afghanistan," so it is conceivable that Azzam first heard it from Afghans: David B. Edwards, *Caravan of Martyrs: Sacrifice and Suicide Bombing in Afghanistan* (Oakland: University of California Press, 2017), Kindle edition, location 140.

Palestinian

The sources for the prologue are *fi 'uyun mu'asira*, pp. 10, 128–137; Abu Rumman and Sa'id, *al-'alim*, pp. 13 and 110; Azzam, *al-duktur al-shahid*, p. 71.

1. Azzam's date of birth appears in his application for admission to the Kadoorie Agricultural School dated 7 May 1957: unpublished document

in author's possession. In Arabic sources the village name is spelled variously as al-Sila al-Harithiyya and Silat al-Harithiyya. *Al-sila* means "the brook," and *al-Harithiyya* refers to the Banu Haritha tribal confederation, which controlled the land centuries ago: 'ta'arruf 'ala al-sila al-harithiyya' [Getting to know al-Sila al-Harithiyya], http://a6fal.7olm.org/t50-topic (posted 25 December 2009; accessed 28 January 2016).

2. 'lamha 'an al-sila al-harithiyya' [A Glance at al-Sila al-Harithiyya], http://selahartiah.blogspot.no/p/blog-page_3241.html, n.d. (accessed 29 January 2016). Sami Hadawi, *Village Statistics 1945: A Classification of Land and Area Ownership in Palestine* (Beirut: Palestine Liberation Organization Research Center, 1970), p. 55.
3. They bear no known link to the prestigious Egyptian Azzam family to which Ayman al-Zawahiri belongs.
4. Author's interview with Fayiz Azzam, al-Sila al-Harithiyya, 4 May 2008.
5. "ashirat al-shawahina' [The al-Shawahina Tribe], http://selahartiah.blogspot.no/2010/12/blog-post_6786.html (posted 23 December 2010, accessed 28 January 2016). The clan got its name from a person named Shahin, who had moved to Sila from Arura near Ramallah a number of generations earlier.
6. Jarrar, *al-shahid*, p. 16; Abu Mujahid, *al-shahid*, p. 1 (Minbar version).
7. When Abdallah applied to college in 1957, he gave his father's occupation as farmer (*muzari'*): unpublished document in author's possession.
8. Azzam provided the size of his father's land holding in his 1957 application to Kadoorie: unpublished document in author's possession.
9. His father later said, "In the second semester he went to the headmaster saying, 'my family cannot pay the fee, I want to apologize for it.' When the headmaster looked at his record and saw that he had top grades, he promised to discuss the matter with officials in the Education Ministry in Amman. Indeed the fees were waived thanks to [Abdallah's] hard effort": *fi 'uyun mu'asira*, p. 425. I happen to have the overdue notice which the school sent to Azzam's father in February 1958. It was for 15JD for the spring semester: unpublished document in author's possession.
10. Azzam was in fact his parents' ninth child, but four had died in infancy: photograph of Azzam family tree, taken by the author in Fayiz Azzam's home on 4 May 2008.
11. al-Dahshan, 'juhud al-duktur', p. 32; photograph of Azzam family tree, taken by the author in Fayiz Azzam's home on 4 May 2008.

12. Itzhak Arnon and Michael Raviv, *From Fellah to Farmer: A Study on Change in Arab Villages* (Rehovot: Settlement Study Centre, 1980), pp. 14–15.
13. Eugene Rogan, *The Arabs: A History*, 2nd ed. (London: Penguin, 2012), pp. 56–59.
14. Abdallah Azzam, *hamas: al-judhur al-tarikhiyya wa'l-mithaq* [Hamas: Historical Roots and Charter] (Amman: unknown publisher, 1990), p. 43.
15. Beshara Doumani, *Rediscovering Palestine: Merchants and Peasants in Jabal Nablus, 1700–1900* (Berkeley: University of California Press, 1995), pp. 17–18.
16. Benny Morris, *1948: A History of the First Arab–Israeli War* (New Haven: Yale University Press, 2008), p. 386.
17. Jarrar, *al shahid*, p. 15.
18. Azzam, *hamas*, p. 43.
19. Jarrar, *al-shahid*, p. 15.
20. *fi 'uyun mu'asira*, p. 425.
21. Ibid.
22. Jarrar, *al-shahid*, p. 52.
23. Morris, *1948*, p. 407.
24. Ibid., p. 136; Walid Khalidi, *All that Remains: The Palestinian Villages Occupied and Depopulated by Israel in 1948* (Washington, DC: Institute for Palestine Studies, 1992), pp. 331–341.
25. Morris, *1948*, pp. 248–250.
26. Ibid., p. 250. Azzam later boasted that the Iraqi forces in Jenin "killed 1,000 Jews and wounded 600," a blatant exaggeration: Azzam, *hamas*, p. 33.
27. Azzam, *hamas*, p. 38.
28. Ibid. Al-Sila probably adhered to the collective system of land-sharing that was common in Palestinian villages in the region at the time; under this system, land belonged to the village as a whole and households were allotted crop shares according to family size: Ilan Pappe, *The Ethnic Cleansing of Palestine* (Oxford: Oneworld, 2007), p. 105.
29. Azzam, *hamas*, p. 43.
30. Pappe, *Ethnic Cleansing*, esp. pp. 133 ff. and 200 ff.
31. Jarrar, *al-shahid*, pp. 16 and 20–21.
32. Khalidi, *All that Remains*, p. 583.
33. Jarrar, *al-shahid*, p. 20.
34. *fi 'uyun mu'asira*, pp. 368–369. In 1946, when Abdallah Awatila married, the four-year-old Abdallah Azzam had attended the wedding with his father.
35. *al-Bunyan al-Marsus* no. 30 (February 1990), p. 12.

36. Azzam, *hamas*, p. 44.
37. Ibid., p. 43.
38. Yasir Abu Hilala, *awwal al-afghan al-arab* [The First Afghan Arab], 2009, https://archive.org/details/biographyofazzam, at 11'00" (accessed 17 February 2009).
39. In late January 1948 the Army of Salvation's training center at the Qatana base in Syria reportedly included 1,100 Iraqis, 700 Palestinians, 100 Egyptians, 40 Jordanians, 40 Yugoslavs, and 1,800 Syrians: Joshua Landis, 'Syria and the Palestine War: Fighting King 'Abdullah's "Greater Syria Plan"', in *The War for Palestine*, ed. Eugene L. Rogan and Avi Shlaim (Cambridge: Cambridge University Press, 2007), 176–203, p. 195; Matthew Hughes, 'Collusion across the Litani? Lebanon and the 1948 War', in *The War for Palestine*, ed. Eugene Rogan and Avi Shlaim (Cambridge: Cambridge University Press, 2007), 204–227, p. 214.
40. David Malet, *Foreign Fighters: Transnational Identity in Civil Conflicts* (New York: Oxford University Press, 2013), p. 135.
41. Seth J. Frantzman and Jovan Ćulibrk, 'Strange Bedfellows: The Bosnians and Yugoslav Volunteers in the 1948 War in Israel/Palestine', *Istorija 20. veka*, no. 1 (2009): 189–200, p. 190.
42. Haim Levenberg, *Military Preparations of the Arab Community in Palestine 1945–1948* (London: Frank Cass, 1993), p. 190; Landis, 'Syria and the Palestine War', p. 191; Avraham Sela, 'State, Society and Transnational Networks: The Cases of Arab Volunteers in the Palestine War (1947–48) and the "Afghan Arabs"', Department of International Relations, Hebrew University of Jerusalem, 2005, p. 19.
43. Hughes, 'Collusion across the Litani?', p. 217.
44. Avi Shlaim, 'Israel and the Arab coalition in 1948', in *The War for Palestine*, ed. Eugene L. Rogan and Avi Shlaim (Cambridge: Cambridge University Press, 2007), 79–103, pp. 85–86; Landis, 'Syria and the Palestine War', pp. 194 and 205 (note 59); Sela, 'State, Society and Transnational Networks', p. 19.
45. Levenberg, *Military Preparations*, p. 193. Estimated annual national income per capita in the region ranged from £P15 (East Bank in 1948) via £P40 (Syria in 1950) to £P53 (Palestine in 1948): see Yezid Sayigh, *Armed Struggle and the Search for State: The Palestinian National Movement 1949–1993* (Oxford: Oxford University Press, 1997), p. 274.
46. From video of interview with Turkish journalist dated 3 March 1989, reproduced in Abu Hilala, *awwal al-afghan al-'arab*, at 11'05" ff.
47. Numbers are uncertain, but there were reportedly some 400 Muslim Brothers from Syria and a few hundred Egyptians: Johannes Reissner, *Ideologie und Politik der Muslimbruder Syriens: Von den Wahlen 1947 bis zum Verbot unter Adib as-Sisakli 1952* (Freiburg: Klaus

Schwartz, 1980), p. 247; Thomas Mayer, 'The Military Force of Islam: The Society of the Muslim Brethren and the Palestine Question, 1945–1948', in *Zionism and Arabism in Palestine and Israel*, ed. Elie Kedourie and Sylvia G. Haim (London: Frank Cass, 1982): 100–117, p. 108.

48. Abd al-Fattah M. El Awaisi, *The Muslim Brothers and the Palestine Question, 1928–47* (London: I. B. Tauris, 1998), pp. 148 ff.; Brynjar Lia, *The Society of the Muslim Brothers in Egypt: The Rise of an Islamic Mass Movement, 1928–1942* (Reading: Ithaca, 1998), pp. 235–247. Some have suggested that Egyptian MB volunteers fought in Palestine during the revolt: see James Jankowski, 'Egyptian Responses to the Palestine Problem in the Interwar Period', *International Journal of Middle East Studies* 12 (1980): 1–38, p. 13. Others convincingly dispute this claim: see Israel Gershoni, 'The Muslim Brothers and the Arab Revolt in Palestine', *Middle Eastern Studies* 22 (1986): 367–397, p. 384.
49. Mayer, 'The Military Force of Islam'; Reissner, *Ideologie und Politik*, pp. 238–259.
50. Levenberg, *Military Preparations*, p. 178. Mayer also describes the Egyptian Brotherhood contribution as insignificant: Mayer, 'The Military Force of Islam', p. 108.
51. From video of interview with Turkish journalist dated 3 March 1989, reproduced in Abu Hilala, *awwal al-afghan al-'arab*, at 11'05" ff.
52. Azzam's application for admission to Kadoorie was dated 7 May 1957: unpublished document in author's possession; Jarrar, *al-shahid*.
53. Anita Shapira, *Yigal Allon, Native Son: A Biography* (Philadelphia: University of Pennsylvania Press, 2008), pp. 35–36. The school still exists today: see www.kadoorie.edu.ps/ (accessed 16 March 2012).
54. *fi 'uyun mu'asira*, p. 369.
55. Abu Mujahid, *al-shahid*, p. 2 (Minbar version).
56. Amir, *al-shaykh al-mujahid*.
57. *fi 'uyun mu'asira*, p. 41.
58. Ibid., p. 369.
59. Jarrar, *al-shahid*, p. 19.
60. *fi 'uyun mu'asira*, p. 369.
61. He must have made up his mind by mid-1962, for in August he wrote to Kadoorie requesting his records so that he could apply to Damascus University: unpublished document in author's possession.
62. Jordan University was founded in 1962, but did not have a faculty of Shari'a until 1971: see www.ju.edu.jo (accessed 16 March 2012).
63. Author's interview with Azzam's wife via the intermediary of his son Hudhayfa Azzam, Amman, September 2005.

64. *al-Bunyan al-Marsus* no. 30 (February 1990), p. 12.
65. In 1961 only 24 percent of Palestinian girls aged between fifteen and nineteen were married, while the rate for the age group thirty to thirty-four was 89 percent: Wael R. Ennab, *Population and Demographic Developments in the West Bank and Gaza Strip until 1990* (New York: United Nations Conference on Trade and Development, United Nations, 1994), p. 72.
66. Mohammed Al Shafey, '*Asharq al-Awsat* Interviews Umm Mohammed: The Wife of Bin Laden's Spiritual Mentor', *al-Sharq al-Awsat* English Online, 2005. See also *al-Bunyan al-Marsus* no. 30 (February 1990), p. 12.
67. Azzam, *al-duktur al-shahid*, p. 24.
68. Author's interview with Fayiz Azzam, al-Sila al-Harithiyya, 4 May 2008.
69. Jarrar, *al-shahid*, p. 38; Abu Rumman and Sa'id, *al-'alim*, p. 110; Amir, *al-shaykh al-mujahid*, p. 54.
70. Some sources say he graduated in 1967, but Azzam himself later said in an interview that he graduated in 1966; see *mawsu'at al-dhakha'ir al-'izam fima uthira 'an al-imam al-humam al-shahid 'abdallah 'azzam* [Encyclopedia of the Relics of the Legacy of the Brave Martyred Imam Abdallah Azzam] (Peshawar: Markaz al-Shahid Azzam al-I'lami, 1997), vol. 4, p. 801, https://archive.org/details/zakhaer3ozma (last accessed 1 February 2016).
71. Michael B. Oren, *Six Days of War: June 1967 and the Making of the Modern Middle East* (Oxford: Oxford University Press, 2002), pp. 205 and 219.
72. *fi 'uyun mu'asira*, p. 426.
73. From video of lecture in unidentified location, 16 September 1989, reproduced in Abu Hilala, *awwal al-afghan al-'arab*, at 12'42" ff. See also Azzam, *hamas*, pp. 44–45; Jarrar, *al-shahid*, pp. 21 and 57.
74. Azzam, *al-duktur al-shahid*, p. 28.
75. Amir, *al-shaykh al-mujahid*, p. 55.
76. *al-Bunyan al-Marsus* no. 30 (February 1990), p. 13.
77. It is possible that other forms of intimidation or "migratory encouragement" occurred. According to Benny Morris, "there is some evidence of IDF soldiers going around with loudspeakers ordering West Bankers to leave their homes and cross the Jordan": Benny Morris, *Righteous Victims: A History of the Zionist–Arab Conflict, 1881–2001* (New York: Vintage, 2001), p. 328.

78. Peter Dodd and Halim Barakat, 'Palestinian Refugees of 1967: A Sociological Study', *Muslim World* 60, no. 2 (1970): 123–142, pp. 134–135.
79. Jarrar, *al-shahid*, p. 21.
80. Fouad Ajami, *The Arab Predicament: Arab Political Thought and Practice since 1967* (Cambridge: Cambridge University Press, 1981).
81. The UN estimated that 200,000 people fled during and immediately after the war: Dodd and Barakat, 'Palestinian Refugees of 1967', pp. 123 and 126. Masalha argued that an additional 120,000 people left or were prevented from returning in the second half of 1967: Nur-eldeen Masalha, 'The 1967 Palestinian Exodus', in *The Palestinian Exodus, 1948–1998*, ed. Ghada Karmi and Eugene Cotran (Reading: Ithaca, 1999), 63–110, p. 63.
82. Morris, *1948*, p. 490 (note 28).
83. John K. Cooley, *Green March, Black September: The Story of the Palestinian Arabs* (London: Frank Cass, 1973), pp. 69 ff.
84. Author's interview with Jamal Isma'il, Islamabad, 20 March 2008. Incidentally, a Palestinian relative of Azzam named Mustafa studied in Pakistan in the early 1970s, but he seems not to have been involved in Azzam's Afghanistan-related activities: Azzam, *al-duktur al-shahid*, p. 21.
85. Bruce Hoffman, *Inside Terrorism* (New York: Columbia University Press, 1998), pp. 63–80.
86. See Petter Nesser, 'Abū Qatāda and Palestine', *Die Welt des Islams* 53, no. 3–4 (1 January 2013): 416–448; Joas Wagemakers, 'In Search of "Lions and Hawks": Abū Muḥammad al-Maqdisī's Palestinian Identity', *Die Welt des Islams* 53, no. 3–4 (1 January 2013): 388–415.
87. Abdallah Azzam, 'dhikrayat filastin' [Memories of Palestine] (Minbar al-Tawhid wa'l-Jihad, n.d.), p. 2.
88. For a list see Jarrar, *al-shahid*, pp. 80–81.
89. Ibid., p. 348.
90. Ibid., p. 72.
91. Amir, *al-shaykh al-mujahid*, p. 117.
92. Azzam, 'dhikrayat filastin', p. 1; Abdallah Azzam, *al-difa' 'an aradi al-muslimin: ahamm furud al-a'yan* [The Defense of Muslim Lands: The Most Important of Individual Duties] (Peshawar: Dawa and Jihad University, 1985), p. 15 (Minbar edition).
93. Azzam, 'dhikrayat filastin', p. 1 (Minbar version).
94. Jarrar, *al-shahid*, p. 71.
95. Azzam, 'dhikrayat filastin', p. 1 (Minbar version).
96. Abdallah Azzam, "azima wa tasmim' [Decision and Determination], *al-Jihad* no. 34 (September 1987): 4–7, p. 4.

97. Abu Rumman and Sa'id, *al-'alim*, pp. 85–87; Amir, *al-shaykh al-mujahid*, p. 321.
98. Azzam, 'dhikrayat filastin', p. 5 (Minbar version).
99. Amir, *al-shaykh al-mujahid*, p. 119.
100. Maliach, 'Abdullah Azzam, al-Qaeda, and Hamas', p. 83.
101. Jarrar, *al-shahid*, p. 73.
102. Azzam, *al-duktur al-shahid*, p. 172.
103. Jarrar, *al-shahid*, p. 66.
104. Azzam, 'dhikrayat filastin', p. 1.
105. Abdallah Azzam, 'muhadara fi almania' [Lecture in Germany], in *mawsu'at al-dhakha'ir*, vol. 3, pp. 993–994.
106. Ibid.
107. Abu Umar al-Bilali, 'majallat al-jihad fi 'amiha al-khamis' [*al-Jihad* Magazine in its Fifth Year]', *al-Bunyan al-Marsus* no. 28 (July 1989): 41–43, p. 42.
108. Jarrar, *al-shahid*, p. 23.
109. Erik Skare, a historian of the PIJ, says that in his collection of over sixty martyrdom biographies from the 1980s, not one mentioned training in Afghanistan. To the extent there was foreign training, it took place in Libya and Algeria: email correspondence with Erik Skare, 28 November 2017. Jamal Isma'il has suggested that Azzam may have met Fathi Shqaqi in Cairo in the late 1970s: "When Abdallah Azzam was invited in 1975–76–78 to the annual gathering of the Islamic movement student branch in Egypt, Fathi Shqaqi was also there, and I believe they had met": author's interview with Jamal Isma'il, Islamabad, 20 March 2008. However, Isma'il was not present at this conference and only met Azzam several years later.

Brother

1. Azzam, *al-duktur al-shahid*, p. 146.
2. Ibid., p. 18.
3. 'liqa' zawjat al-shahid 'abdallah 'azzam ma' sahifat al-waqt al-turkiya' [Interview with the Wife of Martyr Abdallah Azzam by the Turkish *Vakit* Newspaper], *Vakit* (date unknown), translated into Arabic and posted on www.al-hesbah.org, 7 March 2006; Al Shafey, '*Asharq al-Awsat* Interviews Umm Mohammed'.
4. Abu Mujahid, *al-shahid*, p. 1 (Minbar edition).
5. Azzam, *al-duktur al-shahid*, p. 18.
6. Ibid., p. 23.
7. Ibid., p. 22.
8. Ibid., p. 72.

9. *fi 'uyun mu'asira*, p. 27.
10. Abdallah Azzam, "ashrun 'aman 'ala al-shahada' [Twenty Years of Martyrdom], *al-Jihad* no. 23 (October 1986): 4–7.
11. Bernard Botiveau, 'La Formation des oulémas en Syrie: la faculté de Sharî'a de l'université de Damas', in *Les Intellectuels et le pouvoir: Syrie, Égypte, Tunisie, Algérie*, ed. Gilbert Delanoe (Cairo: CEDEJ, 1986), 67–87, pp. 70 and 88.
12. Jaques Jomier, 'Programme et orientation des études à la faculté de théologie d'al-Azhar: kulliyat usûl al-dîn', *Revue des études islamiques* no. 44 (1976): 253–272, p. 256.
13. Richard T. Antoun, *Muslim Preacher in the Modern World: A Jordanian Case Study in Comparative Perspective* (Princeton: Princeton University Press, 1989), p. 80.
14. Ibid., p. 88.
15. Amnon Cohen, *Political Parties in the West Bank under the Jordanian Regime, 1949–1967* (Ithaca: Cornell University Press, 1982), p. 162. Cohen's data are reliable because they are based on the original intelligence reports produced by the Jordanian Security Services, whose Jerusalem-based records were captured by Israel in 1967 and made publicly available in the Israel State Archives. An even more detailed description of the Brotherhood on the West Bank is Rachel Simon's chapter in the Hebrew version of Cohen's study: Rachel Simon, 'agudat ha-akhim ha-muslemim (jami'at al-ikhwan al-muslimin)' [The Society of Muslim Brothers], in *miflagot politiot ba-gada ha-ma'aravit* [Political Parties in the West Bank], ed. Amnon Cohen (Jerusalem: Hebrew University, 1980), 274–407.
16. Other sources have provided very different estimates, but usually without offering evidence. Abu-Amr, for example, makes the unreferenced claim that the Brotherhood had over 12,000 active members in Palestine as early as 1947: Ziyad Abu-Amr, *Islamic Fundamentalism in the West Bank and Gaza: Muslim Brotherhood and Islamic Jihad* (Bloomington: Indiana University Press, 1994), p. 3.
17. Cohen, *Political Parties*, p. 55.
18. Jarrar, *al-shahid*, p. 17.
19. Azzam, *al-duktur al-shahid*, p. 154.
20. Cohen, *Political Parties*, p. 158; Richard P. Mitchell, *The Society of the Muslim Brothers* (London: Oxford University Press, 1969), pp. 30–32.
21. Abu-Amr, *Islamic Fundamentalism*, p. 3; Awni Judu' al-Ubaydi, *jama'at al-ikhwan al-muslimun fi'l-urdun wa filastin 1945–1970* [The Muslim Brotherhood in Jordan and Palestine, 1945–1970] (Amman: unknown publisher, 1991), p. 34.

22. Jarrar, *al-shahid*, p. 17.
23. For a good academic treatment of the *da'wa* phenomenon see Egdunas Racius, 'The Multiple Nature of the Islamic Da'wa' (Ph.D. dissertation, University of Helsinki, 2004).
24. Jarrar, *al-shahid*, p. 17.
25. Ibid. Azzam himself said in 1989 that he had been with the Brotherhood for thirty-six years: Azzam, *al-duktur al-shahid*, p. 146. Hudhayfa Azzam said his father had been "influenced by the Muslim Brotherhood since he was 12": 'Abdallah Azzam's Son Says Bin Ladin Driven to Extremism by al-Zawahiri', Al-Arabiyya Television (via FBIS), 2005.
26. Azzam, *al-duktur al-shahid*, p. 16.
27. Abdallah Azzam, 'inhilal al-zawaj fi'l-fiqh wa'l-qanun' [Marriage Dissolution in Islamic Jurisprudence and Civil Law] (BA thesis, Damascus University, 1966), p. 1 (via Minbar al-Tawhid wa'l-Jihad).
28. Abu Mujahid, *al-shahid*, p. 1 (Minbar edition).
29. Jarrar, *al-shahid*, p. 18.
30. Ibid.
31. Ibid.
32. Ibid.
33. Ibid. Azzam's wife says that in this period he was also in close touch with Sa'id Bilal in Nablus, but we know less about their relationship: *al-Bunyan al-Marsus* no. 30 (February 1990), p. 13.
34. al-Ubaydi, *jama'at al-ikhwan*, p. 183.
35. Jarrar, *al-shahid*, p. 19.
36. Ibid., p. 18.
37. Ibid., p. 19.
38. Ibid.
39. Ibid., p. 20.
40. Ibid., p. 27.
41. Simon, 'agudat ha-akhim ha-muslemim'.
42. al-Ubaydi, *jama'at al-ikhwan*, p. 187.
43. Yasir Arafat, for example, was known to be sympathetic to the Brotherhood. He never joined, but in 1950 he trained with a Muslim Brotherhood paramilitary unit in Egypt: see Barry Rubin and Judith Colp Rubin, *Yasir Arafat: A Political Biography* (New York: Oxford University Press, 2003), p. 18.
44. Gilles Kepel, *Muslim Extremism in Egypt* (Berkeley: University of California Press, 1986), pp. 26 ff.; Malika Zeghal, *Gardiens de l'Islam: les oulémas d'al-Azhar dans l'Égypte contemporaine* (Paris: Presses de Sciences-Po, 1996), pp. 102–103.

45. The Syrian Brotherhood suffered repression in the early 1950s and around 1960, but otherwise it was able to operate as a legal political party, in part because it exercised political caution and moderation; see, for example, Raphael Lefèvre, *Ashes of Hama: The Muslim Brotherhood in Syria* (New York: Oxford University Press, 2013), pp. 38–40.
46. Joshua Teitelbaum, 'The Muslim Brotherhood and the "Struggle for Syria", 1947–1958: Between Accommodation and Ideology', *Middle Eastern Studies* 40 (2004): 134–58, p. 153.
47. Bernard Botiveau, *Loi islamique et droit dans les sociétés arabes: mutations des systèmes juridiques du Moyen-Orient* (Paris: Karthala, 1993), p. 186. For the early history of the Syrian Muslim Brotherhood see Hans Günter Lobmeyer, *Opposition und Widerstand in Syrien* (Hamburg: Deutsches Orient-Institut, 1995) and Reissner, *Ideologie und Politik*.
48. Thomas Pierret, *Religion and State in Syria: The Sunni Ulama from Coup to Revolution* (Cambridge: Cambridge University Press, 2013), pp. 36–37.
49. Ibid., p. 37.
50. Botiveau, 'La Formation', p. 77.
51. Pierret, *Religion and State*, p. 37.
52. Botiveau, *Loi islamique*, p. 187.
53. Ibid., pp. 91 and 187.
54. Thomas Pierret, 'Les oulémas syriens aux XXe–XXIe siècles: la tradition comme ressource face aux défis du changement social et de l'autoritarisme', Ph.D. dissertation (Institut d'Études Politiques, Paris, 2009), p. 327.
55. Abdallah Azzam, *fi zilal surat al-tawba* [In the Shade of Surat al-Tawba] (Minbar al-Tawhid wa'l-Jihad, 1986), pp. 92–94 (Minbar edition).
56. For a good account of the Syrian Brotherhood's post-1963 radicalization see Lefèvre, *Ashes of Hama*, pp. 81 ff.
57. For Hadid's biography see Umar F. Abdallah, *The Islamic Struggle in Syria* (Berkeley: Mizan Press, 1983), pp. 104–105 and Lefèvre, *Ashes of Hama*, pp. 98–102. For Hawa's biography see Sa'id Hawwa, *hadhihi tajribati ... wa hadhihi shahadati* [This is my Experience ... and This my Testimony] (Cairo: Dar al-Tawfiq al-Namudhajiyya, 1987); Itzchak Weissmann, 'Sa'id Hawwa: The Making of a Radical Muslim Thinker in Modern Syria', *Middle Eastern Studies* 29 (1993): 601–623; and Brigitte Maréchal, *The Muslim Brothers in Europe: Roots and Discourse* (Leiden: Brill, 2008), pp. 125–126.
58. Lobmeyer, *Opposition und Widerstand in Syrien*, p. 125.
59. Itamar Rabinovich, *Syria under the Ba'th 1963–66: The Army–Party Symbiosis* (Jerusalem: Israel Universities Press, 1972), pp. 109–112;

Thomas Mayer, 'The Islamic Opposition in Syria, 1961–1982', *Orient* 24 (1983): 589–610, p. 593; Olivier Carré and Gerard Michaud, *Les Frères Musulmans: Égypte et Syrie* (Paris: Gallimard, 1983), p. 132.
60. Rabinovich, *Syria under the Ba'th*, p. 143; Lobmeyer, *Opposition und Widerstand in Syrien*, p. 148.
61. Mayer, 'The Islamic Opposition in Syria', p. 593.
62. Email correspondence with Thomas Pierret, 25 April 2018. See also Mayer, 'The Islamic Opposition in Syria', p. 591; Lobmeyer, *Opposition und Widerstand in Syrien*, p. 133; and Hanna Batatu, 'Syria's Muslim Brethren', *MERIP Reports* 12 (1982): 12–20, p. 19. Pierret says the Aleppo branch was somewhat less radical than the Hama branch in the late 1960s and early 1970s, as illustrated by their participation in the elections of 1973.
63. Weissmann, 'Sa'id Hawwa', p. 617; Brynjar Lia, 'The Islamist Uprising in Syria, 1976–82: The History and Legacy of a Failed Revolt', *British Journal of Middle Eastern Studies* 43, no. 4 (8 February 2016): 541–559. Later in the 1980s the Hama and Aleppo branches also parted ways: email correspondence with Thomas Pierret, 25 April 2018.
64. Author's interview with Isam al-Attar, Aachen, 16 December 2009.
65. Weissmann, 'Sa'id Hawwa', p. 615.
66. *al-Jihad* no. 53 (March/April 1989), reproduced in *mawsu'at al-dhakha 'ir*, vol. 1, p. 795.
67. *fi 'uyun mu'asira*, p. 27. Incidentally, Rachid Ghannouchi, the famous Tunisian Muslim Brother and later president of Tunisia, was a student at Damascus University in the year below Azzam, but they did not meet at that time: Azzam Tamimi, *Rachid Ghannouchi: A Democrat within Islamism* (New York: Oxford University Press, 2001), p. 17.
68. Azzam, *fi zilal*, p. 21.
69. Ibid. See also Azzam's eulogy of Hadid in *qahir hafiz al-asad wa'l-nusayriyya fi suria, batal hama Marwan hadid* [The Victor of Hafez al-Assad and the Nusayris in Syria, the Hero of Hama Marwan Hadid], www.youtube.com/watch?v=SPuu1mf-avY (posted 9 January 2011, accessed 29 August 2018).
70. Abdallah Azzam, *The Lofty Mountain* (London: Azzam Publications, n.d.), pp. 24–25.
71. Jarrar, *al-shahid*, p. 20.
72. Azzam, "ashrun 'aman'.
73. Kepel, *Muslim Extremism in Egypt*, pp. 31–35; Omar Ashour, *The De-Radicalization of Jihadists: Transforming Armed Islamist Movements* (London: Routledge, 2009), pp. 74–80.
74. Azzam, "ashrun 'aman'. See also Azzam, *al-duktur al-shahid*, p. 155.
75. Azzam, *al-duktur al-shahid*, p. 153.

76. Abdallah Azzam, 'athar al-namadhij al-hayya 'ala al-nafs wa'l-bashariyya' [The Effect of Living Symbols on Individuals and on Mankind], in *mawsu'at al-dhakha'ir*, vol. 3, p. 1081.
77. Azzam, *al-duktur al-shahid*, p. 154. I have not seen references to such celebrations in other sources.
78. Ibid.
79. Ibid., p. 155.
80. For example, in the 1980s Azzam wrote a book defending Hasan al-Banna against the accusation that one of his best-known works, the collection of invocations known as *al-Ma'thurat*, was based on weak Hadith. "One of the dear brothers brought me *al-Mujtama'* magazine and there was an article by a young Kuwaiti man who said *al-Ma'thurat* is full of fabricated and weak Hadith. I was asked to respond to this man ... [and I did it] despite being extremely busy with serving the Islamic jihad in Afghanistan": Abdallah Azzam, 'al-ma'thurat fi thawbihi al-jadid' [*al-Ma'thurat* in New Garb], in *mawsu'at al-dhakha'ir*, vol. 1, p. 88.
81. *al-Bunyan al-Marsus* no. 30 (February 1990), p. 12.
82. "When I finished high school and studied at university, I was a schoolteacher then, the events of 1965 begun, the Sayyid Qutb events, I began to read Sayyid Qutb": Azzam, 'athar al-namadhij al-hayya', vol. 3, p. 1081.
83. Azzam, *al-duktur al-shahid*, p. 24.
84. For good biographies of Sayyid Qutb see Adnan Musallam, *From Secularism to Jihad: Sayyid Qutb and the Foundations of Radical Islamism* (Westport, CT: Praeger, 2005); John C. M. Calvert, *Sayyid Qutb and the Origins of Radical Islamism* (New York: Columbia University Press, 2009); and James Toth, *Sayyid Qutb: The Life and Legacy of a Radical Islamic Intellectual* (Oxford: Oxford University Press, 2013).
85. For a detailed account of Qutb's experience in Colorado see Wright, *The Looming Tower*, pp. 7–31.
86. See Mitchell, *The Society, passim*; Lia, *The Society of the Muslim Brothers in Egypt*, pp. 178 ff.; Abd al-Azim Ramadan, *al-ikhwan al-muslimun wa'l-tanzim al-sirri* [The Muslim Brotherhood and the Secret Apparatus] (Cairo: Ruz al-Yusif, 1982); Ahmad Adil Kamal, *al-nuqat fawqa al-huruf: al-ikhwan al-muslimun wa'l-tanzim al-khass* [The Points above the Letters: The Muslim Brotherhood and the Special Apparatus] (Cairo: al Zahra li'l I'lam al Arabi, 1989); Mahmud al Sabagh, *haqiqat al-tanzim al-khass* [The Truth about the Secret Apparatus] (Cairo: Dar al-I'tisam, 1989).

87. Ashour, *The De-Radicalization of Jihadists*, pp. 63–89.
88. Sayyid Qutb, *Milestones* (Birmingham: Maktabah Booksellers and Publishers, 2006), pp. 27 and 72, www.kalamullah.com/Books/Milestones%20Special%20Edition.pdf.
89. al-Ubaydi, *jama'at al-ikhwan*, p. 148. Masami Nishino, 'Muhammad Qutb's Islamist Thought: A Missing Link between Sayyid Qutb and al-Qaeda?' *NIDS Journal of Defence and Security* 16 (2015): 113–45.
90. Muhammad Qutb was released on 17 October 1971: Nishino, 'Muhammad Qutb's Islamist Thought', p. 117.
91. Azzam, *hamas*, p. 72.
92. Abdallah Azzam, 'sayyid qutb wa qawl bi-wihdat al-wujud' [Sayyid Qutb and the Unity of Existence], *al-Mujtama'* no. 525 (April 1981).
93. Azzam, "ashrun 'aman'.
94. Abdallah Azzam, *'amlaq al-fikr al-islami (al-shahid sayyid qutb)* [The Giant of Islamic Thought (The Martyr Sayyid Qutb)], in *mawsu'at al-dhakha'ir*, vol. 1, pp. 802–823.
95. Abu Ibada al-Ansari, *mafhum al-hakimiyya fi fikr 'abdallah 'azzam* [The Concept of *Hakimiyya* in the Thought of Abdallah Azzam] (Peshawar: Markaz al-Shahid Azzam al-I'lami, n.d.).
96. Abdallah Anas, *rihlati ma' al-jihad* [My Journey with the Jihad], part 4 (Al-Magharibia Channel, 2015), www.youtube.com/watch?v=w3Dt0egMcLE, at 3'50" (accessed 12 October 2015).

Fighter

1. *mawsu'at al-dhakha'ir*, vol. 4, p. 786.
2. The Arabic term *fida'iyyun* literally means "those who redeem themselves [by sacrificing themselves]."
3. Edgar O'Ballance, *Arab Guerilla Power, 1967–1972* ([Hamden, CT]: Archon Books, 1973), pp. 18–19.
4. Sayigh, *Armed Struggle*, p. 175.
5. Ibid., pp. 178–179; Clinton Bailey, *Jordan's Palestinian Challenge 1948-1983: A Political History* (Boulder: Westview, 1984), p. 37; O'Ballance, *Arab Guerilla Power*, pp. 46–49; Cooley, *Green March, Black September*, pp. 100–102.
6. Sayigh, *Armed Struggle*, p. 181.
7. Ibid., pp. 180–182. On the study trip to Vietnam see Abu Iyad and Eric Rouleau, *My Home, My Land: A Narrative of the Palestinian Struggle* (New York: Times Books, 1981), p. 68. Abu Iyad wrote: "Our visits to military bases and training camps were extremely useful, giving us the opportunity to see how they organized and trained their guerrilla fighters. Many of their methods could be adapted to our own training of Fedayeen."

8. Sayigh, *Armed Struggle*, p. 202.
9. In addition to the Muslim Brotherhood project described here, a separate initiative to mount a religious Fedayin force was launched by Muhammad Amin al-Husayni, the former Mufti of Jerusalem. In early 1969, with help from Fatah, he set up a unit named al-Fath al-Islami which trained briefly in a camp outside Amman before being shut down by the PLO: ibid., p. 226; Zvi Elpeleg, *The Grand Mufti: Haj Amin al-Hussaini, Founder of the Palestinian National Movement* (London: Routledge, 1993), pp. 155–156.
10. See, for example, Cooley, *Green March, Black September*; O'Ballance, *Arab Guerilla Power*; Riad El-Rayyes and Dunia Nahas, *Guerrillas for Palestine* (London: Croom Helm, 1976). As this book went to press, an important new study of the Islamist Fedayin came to the author's attention, but too late to be included in this analysis: Ghassan Muhammad Daw'ar, *qawa'id al-shuyukh: muqawamat al ikhwan al-muslimin didd al-mashru' al-sahyuni* [The Bases of the Sheikhs: The Muslim Brotherhood's Resistance to the Zionist Project] (Beirut: Markaz al-Zaytuni li'l-Dirasat wa'l-Istisharat, 2018).
11. Bailey, *Jordan's Palestinian Challenge*, p. 33; O'Ballance, *Arab Guerilla Power*, p. 60.
12. 'qawa'id al-shuyukh' [The Bases of the Shaykhs], Youtube, n.d., www.youtube.com/watch?v=EN4Ff8JrBkc, at 6'25" (uploaded 12 June 2015, accessed 28 January 2016).
13. Ibrahim Ghusheh, *The Red Minaret: Memoirs of Ibrahim Ghusheh (Ex-Spokesman of Hamas)* (Beirut: al-Zaytouna Centre for Studies and Consultations, 2013), pp. 94–96.
14. Abdallah Abu Izza, *ma' al-haraka al-islamiyya fi'l-duwal al-'arabiyya* [With the Islamic Movement in the Arab States] (Kuwait: Dar al Qalam, 1986), pp. 55 ff. I have not seen other sources corroborating the details of Abu Izza's account.
15. Ibid.
16. Abu Izza says only one Palestinian brother ended up joining the camps, a certain Ibrahim Ashur.
17. Some hardline Jordanian Muslim Brothers opposed the project on the grounds that the camps would be operating under a Fatah banner. Ibrahim Ghusheh and Tahsin Khrais led a hundred-strong faction named the Correction Movement, which sought to mount an independent military effort against Israel. The faction reportedly produced a secret news bulletin and collected some weapons, but it never became operational: Ghusheh, *The Red Minaret*, pp. 94–96.
18. Jarrar, *al-shahid*, p. 58; al-Nahawi, *'abdallah 'azzam*, p. 63.
19. 'qawa'id al-shuyukh', at 6'25".
20. *fi 'uyun mu'asira*, p. 17.

21. Ghusheh, *The Red Minaret*, pp. 94–96.
22. Azzam, *al-duktur al-shahid*, p. 29.
23. Abu Izza, *ma' al-haraka al-islamiyya*, p. 59.
24. Azzam, *hamas*, p. 71. Some sources refer to a fighter as "one of the best instructors in the Aluk camp [*mu'askar al-'aluk*]," but it is not clear whether this is one of the four camps: ibid., p. 73; Jarrar, *al-shahid*, p. 65.
25. See, for example, Azzam, *hamas*, pp. 69ff.
26. Abu Hilala, *awwal al-afghan al-'arab*, at 17'30" ff. In al-Ubaydi's history of the Jordanian Brotherhood we find a slightly different description: "The Muslim Brotherhood had four principal bases, the largest of which was called Jerusalem, and its commander was the sheikh of the martyrs, Dr. Abdallah Azzam. At the time people called the Brotherhood's bases the 'Bases of the Sheikh,' and its centers were taken from Marw, Rafid, Hartha, and Aluk": al-Ubaydi, *jama'at al-ikhwan*, p. 187.
27. Mshari al-Zaydi, 'History of the Jordanian Muslim Brotherhood (Part 1)', *al-Sharq al-Awsat* English Online, 27 December 2005.
28. Jarrar, *al-shahid*, p. 59; Ziyad Abu Ghanima, *al-haraka al-islamiyya wa qadiyat filastin* [The Islamic Movement and the Palestine Issue] (Amman: Dar al-Furqan, 1989), p. 126.
29. Azzam, *hamas*, p. 69; *fi 'uyun mu'asira*, p. 17.
30. Azzam, *hamas*, p. 70.
31. Lia, *Architect of Global Jihad*, pp. 41–42, 72.
32. Ibid., p. 42.
33. al-Wa'i, *mawsu'at shuhada'*, pp. 222–223.
34. Author's interview with Isam al-Attar, Aachen, 16 December 2009.
35. Batatu, 'Syria's Muslim Brethren', p. 19; Lefèvre, *Ashes of Hama*, p. 142. Isam al-Attar says he saw Marwan Hadid there: author's interview with Isam al-Attar, Aachen, 16 December 2009.
36. Al-Attar said that he does not remember meeting Azzam in the camp he visited: author's interview with Isam al-Attar, Aachen, 16 December 2009. If Hadid and Azzam had met in the Fedayin camps, Azzam would probably have mentioned it in his *Memoirs from Palestine*, but he does not.
37. It is possible, but not certain, that Rachid Ghannouchi was also there. He later wrote, "My first meeting with the Palestinian preacher of the world Abdallah Azzam may have been in Jordan during my visit there in 1968." However, he does not explicitly mention visiting the Fedayin camps: Rachid al-Ghannouchi, "abdallah 'azzam namudhaj al-'ulama al-mujahidin' [Abdallah Azzam is a Model of Mujahidin Scholars], *al-Sharq al-Awsat*, 3 December 1989.
38. 'qawa'id al-shuyukh'. All these figures volunteered this information in their obituaries to Abdallah Azzam in 1989; For Nawfal, Anis, and Abd

al-Khaliq see *fi 'uyun mu'asira*, pp. 19, 43, and 196. For al-Yasin see Amir, *al-shaykh al-mujahid*, pp. 169–171; for al-Shatti see ibid., pp. 164–166.

39. *al-Bunyan al-Marsus* no. 30 (February 1990), p. 13.
40. Author's email correspondence with Abdallah Abu Nabah (a pupil at al-Taj in 1967), 26 May 2010.
41. Several of Azzam's Islamist biographers say he joined the armed struggle in 1968, but this is unlikely given that the camps appear to have been set up only in early 1969. Moreover, Azzam himself said he spent "a year and a half in the Palestinian jihad," and he demobilized in September 1970. One source cites Azzam's wife as saying that he had fought his first battle among the Fedayin on 28 May 1968; most likely she or the writer got the year wrong and meant 1969: Abu Rumman and Sa'id, *al-'alim*, p. 85.
42. Azzam, *al-duktur al-shahid*, p. 29. See also Abu Mujahid, *al-shahid*, p. 2 (Minbar edition).
43. 'al-shahidayn ... wa zawjat al-shahid' [The Two Martyrs ... and the Martyr's Wife], *al-Bunyan al-Marsus* no. 30 (February 1990), p. 13.
44. *al-Bunyan al-Marsus* no. 30 (February 1990), p. 14.
45. Abu Mujahid, *al-shahid*, pp. 2–3 (Minbar edition). See also Jarrar, *al-shahid*, p. 59.
46. *fi 'uyun mu'asira*, p. 426.
47. Abu Mujahid, *al-shahid*, p. 3 (Minbar edition).
48. Jarrar, *al-shahid*, pp. 60–61.
49. Dawud Jarrar said, "The first base we established was in the woods of Dibbin, and Azzam was there": ibid., p. 58.
50. Gérard Chaliand, *The Palestinian Resistance* (London: Penguin, 1972), pp. 108–110.
51. Azzam, 'dhikrayat filastin', p. 3.
52. Ghusheh, *The Red Minaret*, pp. 94–96.
53. Abu Hilala, *awwal al-afghan al-'arab*.
54. Chaliand, *The Palestinian Resistance*, pp. 97–98.
55. Ibid., p. 89.
56. Jarrar, *al-shahid*, p. 58.
57. Ghusheh, *The Red Minaret*, pp. 94–96.
58. Jarrar, *al-shahid*, p. 33.
59. *fi 'uyun mu'asira*, p. 203.
60. Ghusheh later wrote: "I recall that I was able to obtain aerial maps of the northern Jordan and Palestine regions. I handed them over to Sheikh Ahmed Nawfal to make use of them in studying the region of the demarcation line with the Israeli enemy in the Golan area": Ghusheh, *The Red Minaret*, pp. 94–96.
61. Azzam, *al-duktur al-shahid*, p. 29.

62. Abu Hilala, *awwal al-afghan al-'arab*, at 18'15".
63. Also referred to in the sources as the battle of "Rotenberg" or "the red belt," for unknown reasons.
64. Azzam, *hamas*, p. 71.
65. Ibid. The attack team included a certain Abu Isma'il, Mahdi al-Idlibi al-Hamawi, Ibrahim bin Billa, and Bilal al-Filastini, in addition to Azzam himself. The team was made up of fighters from different bases, some from the Jerusalem base and some from the Gaza base. Three of them died, including Mahdi al-Idlibi and Bilal al-Maqdisi.
66. Ibid.
67. Ibid., p. 72.
68. Ibid., p. 73; Jarrar, *al-shahid*, p. 65. Ibrahim al-Ghazzi is described in both sources as "one of the founders of Fatah and one of the top trainers in the 'Uluk camp."
69. Azzam, *hamas*, p. 72.
70. *fi 'uyun mu'asira*, p. 17.
71. Azzam, *hamas*, p. 72.
72. Ibid., p. 58.
73. Jarrar, *al-shahid*, p. 26. Muhammad Nur appears to have known Azzam well; he notes that "I also lived with him for a period in Peshawar, Egypt, and Jordan."
74. Ibid., p. 63.
75. *fi 'uyun mu'asira*, pp. 87–88.
76. Abu Izza, *ma' al-haraka al-islamiyya*, p. 59.
77. Bailey, *Jordan's Palestinian Challenge*, p. 61.
78. Azzam, *hamas*, p. 75.
79. Azzam, *al-duktur al-shahid*, p. 30.
80. Abdallah Azzam, *al-saratan al-ahmar* [The Red Cancer], 1st ed. (Amman: Maktabat al-Aqsa, 1980), pp. 38–40.
81. Author's interview with Fayiz Azzam, al-Sila al-Harithiyya, 4 May 2008.
82. Azzam, *hamas*, p. 74.
83. Stefan Aust, *Baader–Meinhof: The Inside Story of the RAF*, trans. Anthea Bell (Oxford: Oxford University Press, 2009), pp. 65–75.
84. Gunnar Ekberg, *De ska ju ändå dö: Tio år i svensk underrättelsetjänst* [They're Going to Die Anyway: Ten Years in Swedish Foreign Intelligence] (Stockholm: Fischer & Company, 2009), pp. 156–167 and 195–213.
85. Azzam, *hamas*, pp. 70–71.
86. Ibid., p. 70.
87. Azzam, *al-duktur al-shahid*, p. 18.
88. Azzam, *hamas*, p. 70.
89. For details on Black September see Paul Thomas Chamberlin, *The Global Offensive: The United States, the Palestine Liberation*

Organization, and the Making of the Post-Cold War Order (New York: Oxford University Press, 2015), pp. 108–141. See also O'Ballance, *Arab Guerilla Power*, p. 137 ff.; and Bailey, *Jordan's Palestinian Challenge*, pp. 49 ff.
90. Jarrar, *al-shahid*, p. 63.
91. al-Zaydi, 'History (Part 1)'.
92. Azzam, *hamas*, pp. 72–73.
93. Azzam, 'dhikrayat filastin', p. 4. See also Azzam, *hamas*, p. 49.
94. Azzam, *hamas*, pp. 49–50.
95. Azzam, 'dhikrayat filastin', p. 4.
96. "When I took over the Ministry of Education, I wanted to fill it with Muslims and give the jobs to Muslims. I first looked to the group that I had been raised in [the Muslim Brotherhood], we brought all the Brothers [we could find], but they only filled a few spaces in the Education Ministry. So we said, go look for all the Tahriris, the Tablighis and the Salafis, etc., but they did not fill one hundredth of what we needed in the Ministry. So we said go look for those who pray, but that was not enough, so we said go look for those who pray on Fridays only, but that didn't suffice either. A ministry in a small country, all the Islamist groups and all those who pray did not fill half its needs, so how do you want to build an Islamic [state] entity?": Azzam, *fi zilal*, p. 89 (Minbar version); see also Azzam, *al-duktur al-shahid*, p. 120.
97. 'Sheikh Abdullah Azzam'; See also Fighel, 'Sheikh Abdullah Azzam'; Azzam, *al-duktur al-shahid*, p. 32.
98. Author's interview with Fayiz Azzam, al-Sila al-Harithiyya, 4 May 2008.

Scholar

1. Abdallah Azzam, 'ya muslimiy al-'alam: intabahu' [Muslims of the World: Pay Attention], *al-Mujtama'* no. 635 (30 August 1983), p. 26.
2. Azzam, *al-duktur al-shahid*, p. 17. A similar anecdote appears in Abu Mujahid, *al-shahid*, p. 1 (Minbar edition).
3. Fayiz Azzam says Abdallah Azzam was very bright in primary school; Mahmud Azzam says he was top of his class in Damascus, and Azzam himself said he was top of his class in his Master's course: author's interview with Fayiz Azzam, al-Sila al-Harithiyya, 4 May 2008; Azzam, *al-duktur al-shahid*, pp. 16 and 31.
4. Jarrar, *al-shahid*, p. 350.
5. Ibid., p. 61.
6. Ibid., p. 27.
7. Ibid., p. 61.
8. Al Shafey, '*Asharq al-Awsat* Interviews Umm Mohammed'.

9. Jarrar, *al-shahid*, p. 34.
10. Ibid., pp. 34–35.
11. '"al-hamdu li'llah rabb al-'alamayn", kanat awwal kalima nataqtu biha ba'd sama'i khabar istishhad zawji wa abna'i' ['Praise be to God' was the First Word I Uttered after Hearing the News of the Martyrdom of my Husband and Sons], *al-Sabil*, 2 December 1997.
12. 'The Words of Abdallah Azzam', n.d., www.scribd.com/doc/5424213 7/The-Words-of-Abdullah-Azzam, p. 62 (accessed 2 May 2011).
13. Abu al-Shaqra' al-Hindukushi, 'min kabul ila baghdad' [From Kabul to Baghdad], 2007, Part 3, http://archive.org/details/fromcaboltobagdad (accessed 2 November 2012).
14. Al Shafey, '*Asharq al-Awsat* Interviews Umm Mohammed'.
15. 'The Words of Abdallah Azzam', pp. 53–54.
16. A Saudi named Abu Abd al-Aziz later wrote, "[Azzam] spent a good year of his life as a teacher in the institute for religious science in Baha": *fi 'uyun mu'asira*, p. 278. See also Abu Rumman and Sa'id, *al-'alim*, pp. 150–151; Amir, *al-shaykh al-mujahid*, p. 55; and Jarrar, *al-shahid*, p. 21.
17. Nabil Mouline, *The Clerics of Islam: Religious Authority and Political Power in Saudi Arabia* (New Haven: Yale University Press, 2014), p. 222.
18. Hawa, *hadhihi tajribati*, p. 95. There is no indication that Hawa and Azzam met in Saudi Arabia.
19. Aziz, "abdallah 'azzam wa juhuduhu', p. 152.
20. Nabil Mouline, 'Enforcing and Reinforcing the State's Islam: The Functioning of the Committee of Senior Scholars', in *Saudi Arabia in Transition: Insights on Social, Political, Economic, and Religious Change*, ed. Bernard Haykel, Thomas Hegghammer, and Stéphane Lacroix (Cambridge: Cambridge University Press, 2015), 48–67, p. 55.
21. The term Salafism is slippery, and has been the source of much confusion and debate among academics. For a good recent analysis see Henri Lauzière, *The Making of Salafism: Islamic Reform in the Twentieth Century* (New York: Columbia University Press, 2015).
22. See, for example, Quintan Wiktorowicz, *The Management of Islamic Activism: Salafis, the Muslim Brotherhood, and State Power in Jordan* (New York: State University of New York Press, 2001).
23. A prominent case of hybridization at the movement level is the Saudi Sahwa movement as described in Lacroix, *Awakening Islam*.
24. *al-Bunyan al-Marsus* no. 30 (February 1990), p. 13. This suggests that he may also have gone to Cairo in 1967 to enroll, although there is no specific evidence of such a trip.
25. Azzam, *al-duktur al-shahid*, p. 31.
26. *fi 'uyun mu'asira*, p. 196; see also Jarrar, *al-shahid*, p. 22.
27. Azzam, *The Lofty Mountain*, p. 23.

28. 'Sheikh Abdullah Azzam'; see also Fighel, 'Sheikh Abdullah Azzam'; Azzam, *al-duktur al-shahid*, p. 32.
29. Abdullah al-Arian, *Answering the Call: Popular Islamic Activism in Sadat's Egypt* (Oxford: Oxford University Press, 2014), pp. 86 ff.
30. Carré and Michaud, *Les Frères*, p. 109.
31. Ibid., p. 110.
32. Ibid., p. 109.
33. Barbara Zollner, *The Muslim Brotherhood: Hasan al-Hudaybi and Ideology* (London: Routledge, 2008).
34. Ashour, *The De-Radicalization of Jihadists*, pp. 80–86.
35. See, for example, Lacroix, *Awakening Islam*, p. 39.
36. Nishino, 'Muhammad Qutb's Islamist Thought', p. 117.
37. Kepel, *Muslim Extremism in Egypt*.
38. Carré and Michaud, *Les Frères*, p. 114.
39. Kepel, *Muslim Extremism in Egypt*, pp. 70 ff.
40. Lawrence Wright, 'The Man behind Bin Laden', *New Yorker*, 16 September 2002.
41. Azzam, *fi zilal*, pp. 92–94.
42. Ibid.
43. Chris Eccel, *Egypt, Islam, and Social Change: al-Azhar in Conflict and Accommodation* (Berlin: Klaus Schwartz, 1984); Zeghal, *Gardiens de l'Islam*; Steven Barraclough, 'al-Azhar: Between the Government and the Islamists', *Middle East Journal* 52 (1998): 236–249.
44. Zohurul Bari, *Re-Emergence of the Muslim Brothers in Egypt* (New Delhi: Lancers Books, 1995), p. 68.
45. Rachel Scott, 'An "Official" Islamic Response to the Egyptian al-Jihad Movement', *Journal of Political Ideologies* 8, no. 1 (2003): 39–61.
46. Saad Eddin Ibrahim, 'Anatomy of Egypt's Militant Islamic Groups: Methodological Notes and Preliminary Findings', *International Journal of Middle East Studies* 12 (1980): 423–453.
47. Zeghal, *Gardiens de l'Islam*, pp. 141 ff.
48. Ibid., p. 128.
49. Ibid., pp. 132 ff.
50. Ibid., p. 133.
51. Ahmed Abdalla, *The Student Movement and National Politics in Egypt, 1928–1973*, 2nd ed. (Cairo: American University in Cairo Press, 2009).
52. Azzam, *hamas*, p. 50.
53. Abdallah Azzam, *dalalat al-kitab wa'l-sunna 'ala al-ahkam: min haythu al-bayan wa'l-ijmal aw al-zuhur wa'l-khafa'* (Jeddah: Dar al-Mujtama', 2001), p. 28.
54. Ibid., pp. 18 and 28.
55. Azzam, *The Lofty Mountain*, p. 24.

56. *fi 'uyun mu'asira*, p. 171.
57. Ibid., pp. 203–204.
58. Ibid., p. 265. It is worth noting that, in the Islamic tradition, the notion of having memorized the Qur'an (or being *hafiz*) does not necessarily mean that a person has the entire text in his head. Memorization programs usually only involve studying, and being tested on, a *section* of the Qur'an at a time. It is usually upon the completion of a sequence of tests, each on a limited part of the book, that a person is declared *hafiz*.
59. John L. Esposito, ed., *The Oxford Dictionary of Islam* (Oxford: Oxford University Press, 2004), p. 329.
60. 'man huwa fadilat al-shaykh 'abd al-ghani 'abd al-khaliq?' [Who is Shaykh Abd al-Ghani Abd al-Khaliq?], n.d., www.ahlalhdeeth.com/vb/showthread.php?t=106337 (accessed 19 April 2009). Ahmad Nawfal described him in glowing terms: "We both had a professor, may God bless his soul, an Egyptian called Abd al-Rahman [*sic*] Abd al-Khaliq, who took particular care of students from Jordan and Palestine, like his own children. And he looked after our group with the utmost compassion. This great kindness had an influence on the personality of the sheikh": Abu Hilala, *awwal al-afghan al-'arab*, at 21'07" ff.
61. Azzam, *al-duktur al-shahid*, p. 151.
62. Ibid., p. 152.
63. The library record of Azzam's thesis in the Jordan University Library says the thesis was printed in 1972, presumably at the very end of the year.
64. Azzam, *al-duktur al-shahid*, p. 32.
65. Azzam, *dalalat*, p. 5.
66. Ibid., p. 12.
67. Ibid., p. 14.
68. Ibid., p. 17.
69. Abu Hilala, *awwal al-afghan al-'arab*, at 21'35" ff.
70. Azzam Tamimi, *Hamas: Unwritten Chapters*, 2nd ed. (London: Hurst, 2009), p. 26.
71. Ibid.
72. *fi 'uyun mu'asira*, pp. 203–204.
73. Peter Tomsen writes that Azzam frequented both Ayman al-Zawahiri and Umar Abd al-Rahman at this time, but the claim is unsourced and I have seen no other evidence: Tomsen, *The Wars of Afghanistan*, p. 193.
74. Sayyaf, who was at al-Azhar from 1971 to 1973, later said, "I did not meet him in that time ... I was in the faculty of Usul al-Din and he was in the faculty of Shari'a, and I was in a dormitory of al-Azhar, and he was living out of the dormitory ... After meeting me, we came to know that we were in the same time in al-Azhar": author's interview with Abd Rabb al-Rasul Sayyaf, Paghman, 8 December 2017.

75. Author's interview with Abu Harith, Amman, 8 May 2008.
76. Abu Hilala, *awwal al-afghan al-'arab*, at 21'35" ff.
77. Amir, *al-shaykh al-mujahid*, p. 165.
78. Jarrar, *al-shahid*, pp. 22–23.
79. 'liqa' zawjat al-shahid'.
80. Abdallah Azzam, 'dhikrayat min sahat al-jihad' [Memories from the Field of Jihad], *al-Bunyan al-Marsus* no. 4 (December 1985): 12–13, p. 13.
81. Amina Qutb, 'risala min amina qutb ila umm muhammad' [Letter from Amina Qutb to Umm Muhammad], in *fi 'uyun mu'asira*, pp. 325–327. The letter was originally published in *al-Mujtama'* magazine in 1990.
82. Azzam, *dalalat*, p. 18.
83. Abdallah Azzam, *al-qawmiyya al-'arabiyya* [Arab Nationalism] (Minbar al-Tawhid wa'l-Jihad, n.d.), pp. 34–35.
84. Abdallah Azzam, *'ibar wa basa'ir li'l-jihad fi'l-'asr al-hadir* [Lessons and Insights on Jihad in the Current Age], 2nd ed. (Amman: Maktabat al-Risala al-Haditha, 1987), p. 108.
85. Jarrar, *al-shahid*, p. 22.
86. Ibid.
87. Abdallah Azzam, 'athar al-namadhij al-hayya 'ala al-nafs wa'l-bashariyya' [The Effect of Living Symbols on Individuals and on Mankind]', in *mawsu'at al-dhakha'ir*, vol. 3, p. 1081.
88. Jarrar, *al-shahid*, p. 23; author's interview with Fayiz Azzam, al-Sila al-Harithiyya, 4 May 2008.
89. 'liqa' zawjat al-shahid'.
90. *fi 'uyun mu'asira*, p. 481.
91. Abu Hilala, *awwal al-afghan al-'arab*, at 23'20" ff.
92. *fi 'uyun mu'asira*, p. 22; Aziz, "abdallah 'azzam wa juhuduhu', p. 153.
93. Jarrar, *al-shahid*, p. 36.
94. Author's interview with Muhammad Sawalha, London, 1 December 2015.
95. Author's interview with Muhammad Sawalha, London, 1 December 2015.
96. Author's interview with Muhammad Sawalha, London, 1 December 2015.
97. Azzam, *al-duktur al-shahid*, p. 247.
98. Jarrar, *al-shahid*, p. 23.
99. Author's interview with Jamal Isma'il, Islamabad, 18 March 2008; author's interview with Muhammad al-Sawalha, London, 1 December 2015. Azzam and Nawfal were very close friends. When the

latter spoke at a memorial event in Amman after Azzam's death, he described him as "my spiritual twin": Azzam, *al-duktur al-shahid*, p. 76.
100. Email correspondence with Jihan Bakeer via her daughter Sumayya Doqa, 10 July 2009.
101. Jarrar, *al-shahid*, p. 32.
102. Azzam, *al-duktur al-shahid*, p. 76; author's interview with Muhammad al-Sawalha, London, 1 December 2015.
103. Azzam, *al-duktur al-shahid*, p. 89.
104. Author's interview with Muhammad Zaki Hussain, Amman, 27 June 2018.
105. Abu Hilala, *awwal al-afghan al-'arab*, at 23'20" ff.
106. Ibid., at 23'20" ff.
107. Ibid., at 23'42" ff.
108. Ibid., at 24'00" ff.
109. *fi 'uyun mu'asira*, p. 168.
110. Jarrar, *al-shahid*, p. 23.
111. *fi 'uyun mu'asira*, p. 253.
112. Kazim Ayish, interviewed in Abu Hilala, *awwal al-afghan al-'arab*, at 22'42" ff.
113. 'UJ's Successive Presidents: Ishaq al-Farhan', http://ju.edu.jo/Lists/SuccesivePresidents/Disp_Form.aspx?ID=4 (accessed 11 September 2018).
114. Abu Hilala, *awwal al-afghan al-'arab*, at 26'00" ff. For example, the martyrdom biography of the late Hamas commander Yusuf al-Sarakji (who died in 2002) highlights his studies with Azzam in Jordan: 'al-rajul alladhi ghayyara majra al-intifada' [The Man who Changed the Course of the Intifada], n.d., www.alqassam.net/arabic/martyrs/details/130 (accessed 7 December 2018).
115. Abu Hilala, *awwal al-afghan al-'arab*, at 24'35" ff.
116. Azzam, *al-duktur al-shahid*, p. 33.
117. Aziz, "abdallah 'azzam wa juhuduhu', p. 166.
118. Jarrar, *al-shahid*, pp. 25–26.
119. 'The Words of Abdallah Azzam', p. 38.
120. Ibid., p. 48.
121. Ibid., pp. 36–37.

Vagabond

1. Abu Rumman and Sa'id, *al-'alim*, p. 152; Amir, *al-shaykh al-mujahid*, p. 57.
2. Sources differ on how the Brotherhood's leadership was structured. According to Ibrahim Gharaybeh, "Brotherhood organizational elections are held every four years on two parallel unconnected levels:

the first is the election of administrative committees for branches and sections, while the second is the election of the 40-member Shoura Council which represents the sections according to the number of members in each section, and who are directly elected by the general electoral college. The Shoura Council itself then elects five extra members to its ranks. The Brotherhood inspector-general is also automatically accorded membership, bringing the total to 46": quoted in 'Jordan's Moslem Brotherhood Braces for In-House Elections', *Mideast Mirror* 12 no. 72 (16 April 1998). J. Millard Burr writes that "the various Jordan Ikhwan al-Muslimun General Associations elect officers every two years. And every four years that body elects the Leadership Council of fifty members (the majlis al-shura). The Council itself elects its own Secretary General (murraqb al-am), his deputy, and an executive committee of seven members": J. Millard Burr, 'Jordan's Muslim Brotherhood: A Short History' (American Center for Democracy, 2014), http://acdemocracy.org/jordans-muslim-brotherhood-a-short-history/ (accessed 1 November 2015).
3. 'Jordan's Moslem Brotherhood Braces for In-House Elections'.
4. Mshari al-Zaydi, 'History of the Jordanian Muslim Brotherhood (Part 2)', *al-Sharq al-Awsat* English Online, 30 December 2005.
5. Juan Jose Escobar Stemmann, 'The Crossroads of Muslim Brothers in Jordan', in *The Muslim Brotherhood: The Organization and Policies of a Global Islamist Movement*, ed. Barry Rubin (London: Palgrave Macmillan, 2010), 57–71, p. 70.
6. al-Zaydi, 'History (Part 2)'. Al-Farhan studied first at the American University in Beirut and later got a Ph.D. in Education from Columbia University.
7. Mohammad Abu Rumman and Hassan Abu Hanieh, *Jordanian Salafism: A Strategy for the "Islamization of Society" and an Ambiguous Relationship with the State* (Amman: Friedrich-Ebert-Stiftung, December 2010), p. 55.
8. Ibid.
9. Ibid., p. 53.
10. Ibid.
11. 'The Words of Abdallah Azzam', p. 59.
12. Lacroix, *Awakening Islam*, pp. 37 ff.
13. Joas Wagemakers, *Salafism in Jordan: Political Islam in a Quietist Community* (Cambridge: Cambridge University Press, 2016), pp. 98–99; Abu Rumman and Abu Hanieh, *Jordanian Salafism*, p. 53.
14. For al-Albani's biography see Jacob Olidort, 'In Defense of Tradition: Muhammad Nasir al-Din al-Albani and the Salafi

Method', Ph.D. dissertation (Princeton University, 2015); and Wagemakers, *Salafism in Jordan*, pp. 100–108.
15. Abu Rumman and Abu Hanieh, *Jordanian Salafism*, p. 54.
16. Stéphane Lacroix, 'Between Revolution and Apoliticism: Nasir al-Din al-Albani and his Impact on the Shaping of Contemporary Salafism', in *Global Salafism: Islam's New Religious Movement*, ed. Roel Meijer (London: Hurst, 2009), 58–80, p. 71.
17. Stéphane Lacroix, 'al-Albani's Revolutionary Approach to Hadith', *ISIM Review* no. 21 (2008): 6–7.
18. Olivier Carré, *Mystique et politique: lecture révolutionnaire du Coran par Sayyid Qutb, Frère Musulman radical* (Paris: Presses de la Fondation Nationale des Sciences Politiques, 1984).
19. Abu Rumman and Abu Hanieh, *Jordanian Salafism*, p. 56.
20. 'The Words of Abdallah Azzam', p. 59.
21. Ibid., pp. 59–60.
22. 'al-Albani about Qutb, Abdullah Azzam and al-Ikhwan al-Muslimun', n.d., www.youtube.com/watch?v=6LYAdAmUqlA&t=190s (accessed 3 February 2018).
23. Ibid.
24. For example, at the MWL conference in Mecca in 1965, the Jordanian delegation included Abd al-Latif Abu Qura and Muhammad Khalifa: Muslim World League, *qararat wa tawsiyat ahamm al-mu'tamarat allati 'aqadatha rabitat al-'alam al-islami mundhu 'am 1381–1412 hijriyya* [The Resolutions and Recommendations of the Most Important Conferences Organized by the Muslim World League, 1962–1992] (Mecca: Muslim World League, 1992), p. 73.
25. The sharpest decline in communication costs occurred from 1940 to 1950, followed by a steady decline from 1950 to 1980, after which prices stabilized: Frances Cairncross, *The Death of Distance: How the Communications Revolution Will Change our Lives* (Cambridge, MA: Harvard Business School Press, 1997), p. 214.
26. Robert Bianchi, *Guests of God: Pilgrimage and Politics in the Islamic World* (Oxford: Oxford University Press, 2004), pp. 49–51.
27. J. M. Berger, *Jihad Joe: Americans Who Go to War in the Name of Islam* (Washington, DC: Potomac, 2011), p. 3.
28. Author's interview with Isam al-Attar, Aachen, 16 December 2009.
29. His student Muhammad al-Hajj says he accompanied Azzam on the Hajj of 1974: *fi 'uyun mu'asira*, p. 41.
30. Abu Rumman and Sa'id, *al-'alim*, p. 33.
31. Author's interview with Fayiz Azzam, al-Sila al-Harithiyya, 4 May 2008.
32. Author's interview with Jamal Isma'il, Islamabad, 18 March 2008.

33. Author's interview with Jamal Isma'il, Islamabad, 18 March 2008.
34. 'Muslim Scholars Visit ITC', *Islamic Teaching Center News* 1, no. 1 (February 1978): 1. I am very grateful to J. M. Berger for sharing this source, which he retrieved from the DePaul University Library. See also Berger, *Jihad Joe*, pp. 7 and 222–223.
35. 'Muslim Scholars Visit ITC'. MSA stands for Muslim Students' Association, NAIT for North American Islamic Trust. ICS is unknown to this author.
36. Email correspondence with Stéphane Lacroix, 7 November 2017. Lacroix writes that al-Funaysan was "a well-known Saudi Muslim Brother and the founder of one of the four big Brotherhood jama'at in the country, the 'Ikhwan al-Funaysan'."
37. 'List of Islamic Society of North America conventions', Wikipedia.org (accessed 11 September 2018).
38. 'Director-General of Islamic Teaching Center Concludes Middle East Tour', *Islamic Teaching Center News* 1, no. 1 (February 1978): 3.
39. Wright, *The Looming Tower*, p. 75.
40. Omar Bin Laden, Najwa Bin Laden, and Jean Sasson, *Growing up Bin Laden: Osama's Wife and Son Take us Inside their Secret World* (New York: St. Martin's Press, 2009), p. 25.
41. Ibid., pp. 35–36.
42. Steve Coll had almost settled it already in a *New Yorker* article, but the evidence of Azzam's trip removes the last bit of doubt: see Steve Coll, 'Osama in America: The Final Answer', *New Yorker*, 30 June 2009.
43. *fi 'uyun mu'asira*, p. 187.
44. al-Ghannouchi, "abdallah 'azzam namudhaj'.
45. Amir, *al-shaykh al-mujahid*, p. 314.
46. Ahmad Mansur, 'al-jihad al-afghani fi marhalat muwajahat al-nifaq' [The Afghan Jihad is in the Stage of Confronting Hypocrisy], *al-Jihad* no. 59 (September 1989): 32–33. In the interview, which was conducted "during his visit recently to the field of jihad," al-Ghannouchi said, among other things, that "the jihadi movement in Afghanistan is among the most important events of the age" while warning that "America bears no less enmity than Russia toward Islam and Muslims." Al-Ghannouchi described his visit to Peshawar in his obituary to Azzam: see al-Ghannouchi, "abdallah 'azzam namudhaj'. A longer version of al-Ghannouchi's obituary was also published in *al-Mujtama'* no. 945: see Amir, *al shaykh al-mujahid*, pp. 311–319.
47. *al-Bunyan al-Marsus* no. 30 (February 1990), p. 22.

48. al-Ghannouchi, "abdallah 'azzam namudhaj'; Amir, *al-shaykh al-mujahid*, pp. 311–319; *al-Bunyan al-Marsus* no. 30 (February 1990), p. 22.
49. Rachid Ghannouchi, *al-hurriyat al-'amma fi'l-dawla al-islamiyya* [Public Freedoms in the Islamic State] (Beirut: Markaz Dirasat al-Wihda al-Arabiyya, 1993), p. 6. I am grateful to Andrew March for pointing me to this reference.
50. *Al-Mujtama'* no. 945, cited in Amir, *al-shaykh al-mujahid*, p. 312.
51. For more on the Brotherhood's views on the Iranian revolution, see Abbas Khamahyar, *iran wa'l-ikhwan al-muslimin: dirasa fi 'awamil al-iltiqa' wa'l-iftiraq* [Iran and the Muslim Brotherhood: A Study of the Causes of Confluence and Divergence] (Beirut: Markaz al-Dirasat al-Istratijiyya wa'l-Buhuth wa'l-Tawthiq, 1997), pp. 228 ff.; Walid M. Abdelnasser, 'Islamic Organizations in Egypt and the Iranian Revolution of 1979: The Experience of the First Few Years', *Arab Studies Quarterly* 19, no. 2 (1997): 25–39; Toby Matthiesen, 'The Iranian Revolution and Sunni Political Islam', in *New Analysis of Shia Politics*, ed. Marc Lynch, POMEPS Studies 28 (Washington, DC: George Washington University Project on Middle East Political Science, 2017), 36–38.
52. Ghusheh, *The Red Minaret*, pp. 118–119.
53. Author's interview with Ahmad Zaidan, Islamabad, 18 March 2008.
54. *al-Bunyan al-Marsus* no. 30 (February 1990), p. 18.
55. Abdallah Azzam, 'tarikh al-haraka al-islamiyya al-'alamiyya' [The History of the Global Islamic Movement], in *mawsu'at al-dhakha'ir*, vol. 3, pp. 1067–1068. I have seen no evidence in the sources that Azzam had contact with Iranians, let alone with Iranian officials.
56. *fi 'uyun mu'asira*, p. 172.
57. Author's interview with Jamal Isma'il, Islamabad, 18 March 2008.
58. Aziz, "abdallah 'azzam wa juhuduhu', pp. 154 and 185.
59. Author's interview with Abdallah Anas, London, 1 December 2015.
60. Author's interview with Hudhayfa Azzam, Amman, 11 September 2006.
61. Author's interview with Fayiz Azzam, al-Sila al-Harithiyya, 4 May 2008.
62. Author's interview with Hudhayfa Azzam, Amman, 11 September 2006.
63. Author's interview with Hudhayfa Azzam, Amman, 11 September 2006.
64. Lia, 'The Islamist Uprising'; Dara Conduit, 'The Syrian Muslim Brotherhood and the Spectacle of Hama', *Middle East Journal* 70, no. 2 (15 April 2016): 211–226. A quick browse through Islamist magazines such as *al-Mujtama'* in the 1980–1982 period shows that the coverage of Afghanistan is there, but only as one of several topics, less prominently covered than Syria.

65. Fayiz said, "afta bi-takfir al-nusayriyyin" – "he gave a fatwa excommunicating the Nusayris [Alawites]": author's interview with Fayiz Azzam, al-Sila al-Harithiyya, 4 May 2008. Such rhetoric was not unheard of in the Brotherhood – the Syrian ideologue Sa'id Hawa notably wrote influential anti-Shiite treatises in the 1980s: see Guido Steinberg, 'Jihadi-Salafism and the Shi'is: Remarks about the Intellectual Roots of anti-Shi'ism', in *Global Salafism: Islam's New Religious Movement*, ed. Roel Meijer (London: Hurst, 2009), 107–125, pp. 118–121.
66. Author's interview with Fayiz Azzam, al-Sila al-Harithiyya, 4 May 2008. Fayiz Azzam also wrote, "A group of Nusayris came to assassinate him. One of them stopped outside a nearby house in Suwailih, but God obscured their thoughts, and they fired to make [Azzam] leave Jordan, after pressure and surveillance": *fi 'uyun mu'asira*, p. 12. When Azzam died, a "representative of the Islamic movement in Syria" mentioned in a statement that "[Azzam] followed the jihad [in Syria]. The Nusayris found out ... and sent some of their guys to Jordan, to his area of residence in Amman, seeking to assassinate him ... Fortunately their plot failed": ibid., p. 81.
67. *fi 'uyun mu'asira*, p. 180.
68. Azzam, *al-duktur al-shahid*, p. 33.
69. Muhammad, *safahat*, pp. 32–33.
70. Several biographical sources, including Azzam himself, mention the caricature episode, but I have not been able to locate the actual drawing. Fayiz Azzam says it was published in *al-Ra'i*, so I had a research assistant in Jordan go through all the issues of *al-Ra'i* from January to October 1980, but without success. Either it was in another newspaper or it was published before 1980.
71. Azzam used the expression *fa qad a'dhara man andhar*, which literally means "he who warns is excused."
72. Azzam, *al-duktur al-shahid*, pp. 33–34.
73. Jarrar, *al-shahid*, p. 27.
74. Muhammad, *safahat*, pp. 32–33.
75. Azzam, 'dhikrayat filastin', p. 5.
76. Author's interview with Tariq Tell, Amman, 15 July 2018. According to Hinnebusch, "the Muslim Brothers were cultivated by the monarchy as a counter to the nationalist left": Raymond Hinnebusch, 'Empire and State Formation: Contrary Tangents in Jordan and Syria', in *Sovereignty after Empire: Comparing the Middle East and Central Asia*, ed. Sally N. Cummings and Raymond Hinnebusch (Edinburgh: Edinburgh University Press, 2011), 263–281, p. 273.

77. Abdallah Azzam, 'wathiqa ila al-ikhwan al-muslimun fi'l urdun' [Document to the Muslim Brotherhood in Jordan], in *mawsu'at al-dhakha'ir*, vol. 1, pp. 999–1006; author's interview with Muhammad Sawalha, London, 1 December 2015.
78. Author's interview with Jamal Isma'il, Islamabad, 18 March 2008.
79. Author's interview with Hasan Abu Hanieh, Amman, 6 November 2015.
80. Azzam, 'wathiqa ila al-ikhwan al-muslimun fi'l urdun'.
81. The document is not dated, but it mentions the Afghanistan conflict and the engagement party of Azzam's eldest daughter, who was born in 1966.
82. Based on interviews in Jordan, Glenn Robinson wrote that "during the early 1980s 'Abdallah 'Azzam and Shaykh Khalifa – both members of the executive council of the Muslim Brotherhood at the time – fought for the leadership of the Brotherhood . . . 'Azzam . . . was openly critical of the regime in Jordan, while Khalifa accepted Hashemite authority. Khalifa ultimately prevailed with help, it is widely believed, from the government, and 'Azzam left to fight in Afghanistan": Glenn E. Robinson, 'Defensive Democratization in Jordan', *International Journal of Middle East Studies* 30 (1998): 387–410, 403. However, Azzam's letter suggests that he was not in a position to really challenge Khalifa.
83. Muhammad, *safahat*, pp. 32–33.
84. Author's interview with Jamal Isma'il, Islamabad, 18 March 2008.
85. *fi 'uyun mu'asira*, p. 489. His wife also said that he had accumulated debts in Jordan and that he could not survive financially without a job: Al Shafey, '*Asharq al-Awsat* Interviews Umm Mohammed'.
86. Author's interview with Jamal Isma'il, Islamabad, 18 March 2008.
87. Author's interview with Jamal Isma'il, Islamabad, 18 March 2008.
88. Author's interview with Jamal Isma'il, Islamabad, 18 March 2008.
89. See T. Cuyler Young, 'Pan-Islamism in the Modern World: Solidarity and Conflict Among Muslim Countries', in *Islam and International Relations*, ed. J. Harris Proctor (London: Pall Mall, 1965), 194–221; J. M. Landau, *The Politics of Pan-Islam: Ideology and Organization* (Oxford: University Press, 1990); and James Piscatori, 'Imagining Pan-Islam', in *Islam and Political Violence: Muslim Diaspora and Radicalism in the West*, ed. Shahram Akbarzadeh and Fethi Mansouri (London: I. B. Tauris, 2007), 27–38.
90. For more on the MWL, see Reinhard Schulze, *Islamischer Internationalismus im 20. Jahrhundert* (London: E. J. Brill, 1990).
91. Naveed S. Sheikh, *The New Politics of Islam* (London: RoutledgeCurzon, 2003).

92. Schulze, *Islamischer Internationalismus*, p. 158; Michael Farquhar, *Circuits of Faith: Migration, Education, and the Wahhabi Mission* (Stanford: Stanford University Press, 2016), p. 97.
93. Courtney Freer, *Rentier Islamism: The Influence of the Muslim Brotherhood in Gulf Monarchies* (New York: Oxford University Press, 2018), chapter 4.
94. *rabitat al-'alam al-islami: 'ashrun 'aman 'ala tariq al-da'wa wa'l-jihad* [The Muslim World League: Twenty Years on the Road of *Da'wa* and Jihad] (Mecca: Muslim World League, 1981), p. 95.
95. Ibid., pp. 4–5. See also Muslim World League, *qararat wa tawsiyat*, pp. 7–8.
96. *rabitat al-'alam al-islami: 'ashrun 'aman*, p. 64.
97. Ibid., pp. 4 and 64.
98. Muslim World League, *qararat wa tawsiyat*, p. 203.
99. A book published in 1992 presented a chronology and summaries of the twenty-two main MWL conferences since 1962. It shows that the MWL's conference circuit really only began in 1974, that it internationalized after 1975, and that it peaked in terms of frequency between 1977 and 1981. The conferences were in Mecca (May 1962), Mecca (April 1965), Mecca (April 1974), Mecca (September 1975), Nouakchott (May 1976), Newark (April 1977), Port of Spain (September 1977), Karachi (July 1978), Mecca (March 1979), Cyprus (June 1979), Kuala Lumpur (January 1980), Mecca (March 1980), Jakarta (September 1980), Mecca (June 1981), Dakar (December 1981), Brazil (September 1985), Freetown (November 1985), Mecca (October 1987), China (December 1987), Trinidad (March 1989), Islamabad (June 1989), and Mecca (September 1990): Muslim World League, *qararat wa tawsiyat*.
100. *rabitat al-'alam al-islami: 'ashrun 'aman*, pp. 10–12.
101. 'MWL Centers & Offices Around the World', https://themwl.org/global/ (accessed 12 September 2018).
102. William Ochsenwald, 'Saudi Arabia and the Islamic Revival', *International Journal of Middle East Studies* 13 (1981): 271–286, p. 281.
103. Samuel Huntington, *The Clash of Civilizations and the Remaking of the World Order* (New York: Touchstone, 1996), p. 207.
104. Muhammad Ali Harakan, 'Duty of Implementing the Resolutions', *Journal of the Muslim World League* (1980): 48–49.
105. *rabitat al-'alam al-islami: 'ashrun 'aman*, p. 1.
106. Ibid., p. 86.
107. Ibid., pp. 88–89.
108. Muslim World League, *qararat wa tawsiyat*, p. 5.
109. Thomas Hegghammer, *Jihad in Saudi Arabia: Violence and Pan-Islamism since 1979* (Cambridge: Cambridge University Press, 2010), p. 16.

110. J. Millard Burr and Robert O. Collins, *Alms for Jihad* (New York: Cambridge University Press, 2006); Abdel-Rahman Ghandour, *Jihad humanitaire: enquête sur les ONG islamiques* (Paris: Flammarion, 2002).
111. Amr Elshobaki, *Les Frères Musulmans des origines à nos jours* (Paris: Karthala, 2009), p. 135.
112. Abdullah al-Arian, 'Commanding the Faithful: Frame Construction in Egyptian Islamist Periodicals, 1976–1981', *Journal of Islamic Studies* 28, no. 3 (September 2017): 341–368, p. 365.
113. Elshobaki, *Les Frères Musulmans*, pp. 133–135. See also Martyn Frampton, *The Muslim Brotherhood and the West: A History of Enmity and Engagement* (Cambridge, MA: Harvard University Press, 2018), chapter 7.
114. Alison Pargeter, *The Muslim Brotherhood: The Burden of Tradition* (London: Saqi, 2010), p. 104.
115. The precise foundation date is unclear. Pargeter and others trace its formal establishment to a document titled 'The Internal Statute' ('al-la'iha al-dakhiliyya') published in July 1982, but, as we shall see below, a statement published in *al-Mujtama'* in November 1981 in connection with Kamal al-Sananiri's death was signed "International Organization." For more on the International Organization, see Husam Tammam, 'al-tanzim al-duwali li'l-ikhwan … al-wa'd wa'l-masira wa'l-mal?' [The Brotherhood's International Organization … its Promise, Path, and Fate?], *al-Hiwar* no. 962 (20 September 2004), www.ahewar.org/debat/show.art.asp?aid=23729 (accessed 13 March 2018); Pargeter, *The Muslim Brotherhood*, pp. 96–132; Abduh Mustafa Dasuqi, *nash'at al-tanzim al-duwali li'l-ikhwan al-muslimin: min al-nash'a hatta al-sab'inat* [The Emergence of the International Organization of the Muslim Brotherhood: From the Emergence to the 1970s] (Cairo: Mu'assasat Iqra' li'l-Nashr wa'l-Tawzi' wa'l-Tarjama, 2013); and Hossam Tamam, 'The International Organization of the Muslim Brotherhood', in *Islamic Movements of Europe: Public Religion and Islamophobia in the Modern World*, ed. Frank Peter and Rafael Ortega (London: I. B. Tauris, 2014), 89–94.
116. Pargeter, *The Muslim Brotherhood*, p. 101.
117. Lacroix, *Awakening Islam*, pp. 44–45. Al-Mubarak, al-Tantawi, and Habannaka were senior Muslim Brotherhood-affiliated clerics who had held a variety of senior religious posts in Syria before emigrating to Saudi Arabia, where they would teach at the university and write religious schoolbooks: Pierret, *Religion and State*, pp. 36, 42, 45. Al-Ghazzali (not to be confused with the medieval thinker of the same name) was one of Egypt's most famous and influential religious clerics

in the twentieth century; he wrote almost a hundred books and taught at al-Azhar before moving to Saudi Arabia. He later moved back to Egypt and became imam of one of Cairo's largest mosques: see, for example, Douglas Jehl, 'Mohammed al-Ghazali, 78, An Egyptian Cleric and Scholar', *New York Times*, 14 March 1996. Sabiq was a senior Egyptian Muslim Brotherhood cleric who knew Hasan al-Banna, fought in Palestine in 1948, and spent time in prison before teaching at al-Azhar and then moving to Saudi Arabia where he later received the King Faisal Prize for his popular book *Fiqh al-Sunna*: Adil Salahi, 'Sayyid Sabiq: The Man who Wrote *Fiqh al-Sunna*', *Arab News*, 22 July 2005.
118. See *al-Jihad* no. 30 (May 1987) pp. 22–27 and *al-Jihad* no. 35 (October 1987), p. 38.
119. Author's interview with Kamal al-Helbawy, London, 23 March 2008.
120. Hudhayfa Azzam says that Bin Ladin later told him that he had seen Azzam give a lecture at King Abd al-Aziz University: author's interview with Hudhayfa Azzam, Amman, 11 September 2006.
121. Abu Jandal al-Azdi, *usama bin ladin: mujaddid al-zaman wa qahir al-amrikan* [Usama Bin Ladin: Renewer of the Century and Victor over the Americans], 2003, www.qa3edoon.com (accessed 5 April 2005) p. 15.
122. In 2017, as part of a large release of documents from the 2011 Abbottabad raid, the US government made available Bin Ladin's personal notebook: see 'November 2017 Release of Abbottabad Compound Material', www.cia.gov/library/abbottabad-compound/index.html (accessed 12 September 2018). There Bin Ladin describes his coming of political/religious age in the 1970s, but it does not mention Azzam: author's correspondence with Hassan Hassan, 5 November 2017.
123. *al-Jihad* no. 56 (June 1989), p. 24.
124. Al Shafey, '*Asharq al-Awsat* Interviews Umm Mohammed'.
125. Thomas Hegghammer and Stéphane Lacroix, *The Meccan Rebellion: The Story of Juhayman al-'Utaybi Revisited* (London: Amal Press, 2011); Yaroslav Trofimov, *The Siege of Mecca: The Forgotten Uprising in Islam's Holiest Shrine and the Birth of al Qaeda*, 1st ed. (New York: Doubleday, 2007).
126. Azzam himself later said, "I served for one semester": Muhammad, *al-ansar*, pp. 32–33.
127. Author's interview with Hudhayfa Azzam, Amman, 11 September 2006.
128. Author's interview with Kamal al-Helbawy, London, 23 March 2008.
129. Abu Hilala, *awwal al-afghan al-'arab*, at 30'15" ff.
130. Ibid., at 30'45" ff.
131. Azzam, 'dhikrayat filastin', p. 5. See also Azzam, *al-duktur al-shahid*, pp. 37–38.

132. Muhammad, *safahat*, pp. 32–33.
133. *al-Jihad* no. 56 (June 1989), p. 24.
134. Author's interview with Jamal Isma'il, Islamabad, 18 March 2008.
135. Abdallah Azzam, 'wathiqa ila al-ikhwan al-muslimun fi'l urdun', in *mawsu'at al-dhakha'ir*, vol. 1, p. 1004.
136. Author's interview with Abd Rabb al-Rasul Sayyaf, Paghman, 8 December 2017.
137. The most detailed biography of al-Sananiri is in al-Wa'i, *mawsu'at shuhada'* (part 1), pp. 212–221. See also Azzam, *al-duktur al-shahid*, pp. 38–39; and Calvert, *Sayyid Qutb*, pp. 274 and 277.
138. *fi 'uyun mu'asira*, p. 372.
139. al-Wa'i, *mawsu'at shuhada'* (part 1), p. 217.
140. *al-Mujtama'*, 11 November 1981, cited in ibid. (part 1), p. 218.
141. Azzam, 'dhikrayat min sahat al-jihad', p. 13. Interestingly, this initial Jeddah meeting is omitted from all the hagiographies that describe al-Sananiri's influence on Azzam. Instead, they mention only the chance encounter in Mecca later that summer (see below); see, for example, Azzam, *al-duktur al-shahid*, p. 37. This is probably a deliberate narrative decision to insinuate that God steered al-Sananiri to Azzam and, by extension, to the Afghan jihad. Azzam himself likely contributed to this narrative by emphasizing the Mecca meeting in his later accounts. That the two first met in Jeddah matters, because it means that the inspiration to go to Afghanistan was not a product of luck, but of the Muslim Brotherhood's political work.
142. *fi 'uyun mu'asira*, p. 44.
143. Abu Hilala, *awwal al-afghan al-'arab*, at 30'20" ff.
144. Ibid.
145. Azzam, *al-duktur al-shahid*, p. 38.
146. Amina Qutb, *rasa'il ila shahid* [Letter to a Martyr] (Amman: Dar al-Furqan, 1985), p. 61.
147. We know the date because Jamal Isma'il says Azzam gave a talk at Peshawar University around 23 September 1981: author's interview with Jamal Isma'il, Islamabad, 18 March 2008.
148. *al-Mujtama'* no 944, in Amir, *al-shaykh al-mujahid*, p. 92.
149. Azzam, *al-duktur al-shahid*, p. 41.
150. Qutb, *rasa'il ila shahid*, p. 64; 'Kamal al-Sananiri', www.ikhwan.net/wiki (accessed 13 March 2009). Azzam's wife later said, "After Sananiri met Sheikh Abdallah Azzam, he headed to Egypt to prepare his family to join the sheikh in Afghanistan. But [President] Sadat – shortly before his assassination – had him arrested. Soon afterward, Egyptian newspapers said he had committed suicide in prison, but the obvious truth is that he was killed under torture": Azzam, *al-duktur al-*

shahid, p. 39. Tal'at Fu'ad Qasim, a prominent member of al-Jama'a al-Islamiyya who was in the same prison at the time, later said he had seen a lifeless, heavily bruised, elderly man being brought back to his cell, a man he later realized was al-Sananiri: Matias Seidelin, *Allahs danske krigere* [Allah's Danish Warriors] (Copenhagen: Politiken forlag, 2012), epub paragraphs 10.50–59.
151. *al-Bunyan al-Marsus* no. 30 (February 1990), p. 8.
152. Abu Hilala, *awwal al-afghan al-'arab*, at 30'20" ff.
153. Abu Hilala, *awwal al-afghan al-'arab*, at 32'50" ff.
154. Sayyaf said they met "at the end of the Hajj rituals," which in 1981 was around 11 October.
155. Author's interview with Abd Rabb al-Rasul Sayyaf, Paghman, 8 December 2017. See also Abu Hilala, *awwal al-afghan al-'arab*, at 34'00" ff.

Writer

1. Originally from Aleppo, Abd al-Rahman al-Sabuni (b. 1929) had studied in Cairo in the late 1950s. He was the brother of the even more prominent Syrian Muslim Brother and medical doctor Hassan al-Sabuni. Abd al-Rahman al-Sabuni later became dean of the Shari'a faculty in Damascus before moving to Dubai to teach at United Arab Emirates University. Author's interview with Isam al-Attar, Aachen, 16 December 2009.
2. Azzam, 'inhilal al-zawaj', p. 11 (Minbar version).
3. Ibid., pp. 12, 16, and 17 (Minbar version).
4. Azzam, *dalalat*, p. 29.
5. It was eventually published in Saudi Arabia in 2001: Ibid.
6. Ibid., pp. 28–29.
7. Ibid., pp. 17–18.
8. Abdallah Azzam, *al-manara al-mafquda* [The Lost Beacon] (Peshawar: unknown publisher, 1987).
9. Abdallah Azzam, *al-'aqida wa atharuha fi bina' al-jil* [The Creed and its Effect on Building the Generation] (Amman: Dar al Aqsa, 1975).
10. Ibid., p. 60 (Minbar version).
11. See, for example, Mitchell, *The Society*, pp. 283–289.
12. Azzam, *al-'aqida*, p. 63 (Minbar version).
13. Ibid.
14. The precise publication date is unclear. The copy I have, and the one in stock at Jordan University library, was published in 1978 by Dar al-Tawzi' in Amman. However, in one of their books Mohammad Abu Rumman and Hasan Abu Hanieh cite a copy of *al-Da'wa* published in

1976 by "Jamʻiyyat ʻUmmal al-Matabi'": see Mohammad Abu Rumman and Hasan Abu Hanieh, *The "Islamic Solution" in Jordan: Islamists, the State, and the Ventures of Democracy and Security* (Amman: Friedrich-Ebert-Stiftung, 2013), p. 458.
15. See, for example, Bernard Rougier, *Everyday Jihad: The Rise of Militant Islam among Palestinians in Lebanon* (Cambridge, MA: Harvard University Press, 2007), p. 80.
16. Author's telephone interview with Jamal Khashoggi, 14 September 2018.
17. Abu Rumman and Abu Hanieh, *The "Islamic Solution"*, pp. 481–482.
18. His wife said in 1990 that "he published a book titled *The Islamic Call* ... under the pseudonym 'Sadiq Amin'": *fi ʻuyun muʻasira*, p. 172. Azzam's daughter Fatima has said that it was the publisher who refused to publish it under his real name: *al-Muslimun*, 15 December 1989, cited in Abu Rumman and Saʻid, *al-ʻalim*, p. 40; Aziz, "abdallah ʻazzam wa juhuduhu', p. 13; Anas, *rihlati maʻ al-jihad*, at 4'10".
19. See, for example, *al-Jihad* no. 29 (April 1987), p. 21 and *al-Jihad* no. 31 (June 1987), p. 37.
20. Abu Rumman and Abu Hanieh, *The "Islamic Solution"*, p. 482.
21. Author's photograph from visit to Jordan University library on 6 November 2015.
22. Author's interview with Jamal Ismaʻil, Islamabad, 18 March 2008.
23. Abdallah Azzam, 'wathiqa ila al-ikhwan al-muslimun fi'l urdun'. The precise expression he used was 'al-kitab alladhi sahamtu fi kitabatihi'.
24. Azzam, *al-saratan al-ahmar*.
25. Author's interview with Jamal Ismaʻil, Islamabad, 18 March 2008.
26. Azzam, *al-saratan al-ahmar*, p. 12 (Minbar version).
27. Ibid.
28. Ibid., p. 14 (Minbar version).
29. Ibid., p. 15.
30. Ibid., p. 16 (Minbar version).
31. Ibid., pp. 21–24 (Minbar version).
32. Ibid., p. 39 (Minbar version).
33. Ibid. (Minbar version).
34. Ibid., p. 40 (Minbar version).
35. Ibid., p. 41 (Minbar version).
36. Ibid. (Minbar version).
37. Ibid. (Minbar version).
38. Ibid., p. 42 (Minbar version).
39. Ibid., pp. 28–29 (Minbar version).

40. Ibid., pp. 42–43 (Minbar version).
41. Azzam, *al-qawmiyya al-'arabiyya* (Minbar version).
42. Ibid., p. 5 (Minbar version).
43. Ibid., pp. 10–11 (Minbar version).
44. Ibid., pp. 27–28 (Minbar version).
45. Ibid., p. 28 (Minbar version).
46. Ibid., pp. 31–33 (Minbar version).
47. Ibid., pp. 34–35 (Minbar version).
48. Ibid., p. 12 (Minbar version).
49. Ibid., p. 37 (Minbar version).
50. Abdallah Azzam, *al-islam wa mustaqbal al-bashariyya* [Islam and the Future of Mankind] (Minbar al-Tawhid wa'l-Jihad, 1980); introduction dated 10 October 1980, p. 2 (Minbar version).
51. Abdallah Azzam, 'al-islam huwa mustaqbal al-bashariyya' [Islam is the Future of Mankind], *al-Mujtama'*, 11 November 1980, p. 26; Abdallah Azzam, 'ma'sat al-fikr al-gharbi' [The Crisis of Western Thought], *al-Mujtama'*, 14 April 1981, p. 26.
52. Azzam, *al-islam wa mustaqbal al-bashariyya*, p. 2 (Minbar version).
53. Ibid. (Minbar version).
54. Imad al-Din Khalil, *fawda al-'alam fi'l-masrah al-gharbi al-mu'asir* [Chaos of the World in Contemporary Western Theater] (Beirut: al-Risala, 1977); Rashid al-Ghannouchi, *nahnu wa'l-gharb* [We and the West] (unknown publisher, n.d.); Rashid al-Ghannouchi, *tariqna ila al-nasr* [Our Road to Victory] (unknown publisher, n.d.). The latter book is also known under the title *tariqna ila al-hadara* [Our Road to Civilization].
55. Azzam, *al-islam wa mustaqbal al-bashariyya*, p. 11 (Minbar version).
56. Ibid., p. 11 (Minbar version).
57. Ibid., p. 23 (Minbar version).
58. Ibid. (Minbar version).
59. Ibid., p. 21 (Minbar version).
60. See, for example, Frampton, *The Muslim Brotherhood and the West*, chapter 7.
61. Nishino, 'Muhammad Qutb's Islamist Thought', p. 121.

Pioneer

1. Muhammad, *safahat*, p. 37.
2. Abu Hilala, *awwal al-afghan al-'arab*, at 34'47" ff.
3. *fi 'uyun mu'asira*, p. 179; author's interview with Ahmad Zaidan, Islamabad, 18 March 2008.
4. Anas, *rihlati ma' al-jihad*, part 3, www.youtube.com/watch?v=8V2Q9I9XaJI (accessed 10 October 2015).

5. Anas, *rihlati ma' al-jihad*, part 3.
6. Author's interview with Abd Rabb al-Rasul Sayyaf, Paghman, 8 December 2017.
7. Author's interview with Jamal Isma'il, Islamabad, 18 March 2008.
8. Azzam, *al-duktur al-shahid*, p. 41.
9. Muhammad, *safahat*, p. 119.
10. Jarrar, *al-shahid*, p. 343.
11. 'History of IIUI', www.iiu.edu.pk/index.php?page_id=30 (accessed 11 February 2016).
12. Author's interview with Atiq-u-Zafar, Islamabad, 20 March 2008.
13. Jamal Malik, 'Islamic Mission and Call: The Case of the International Islamic University, Islamabad', *Islam and Christian–Muslim Relations* 9, no. 1 (1 March 1998): 31–45, p. 33.
14. Author's interview with Atiq-u-Zafar, Islamabad, 20 March 2008.
15. Author's interview with Atiq-u-Zafar, Islamabad, 20 March 2008; author's interview with Khalid Rahman, Islamabad, 20 March 2008; author's interview with Ahmad Zaidan, Islamabad, 18 March 2008.
16. 'Faisal Mosque', Wikipedia.org (accessed 12 February 2016).
17. Author's interview with Mahmud Farooqi, Islamabad, 20 March 2008.
18. Author's interview with Atiq-u-Zafar, Islamabad, 20 March 2008. Some of Azzam's lecture notes have been preserved: see, for example, *mawsu'at al-dhakha'ir*, vol. 1, pp. 570–608. The first page lists Azzam's office address: "Dr. Abdallah Azzam – Islamabad – Faysal Mosque – Islamic University."
19. Author's interview with Atiq-u-Zafar, Islamabad, 20 March 2008.
20. Author's interview with Atiq-u-Zafar, Islamabad, 20 March 2008.
21. Author's interview with Ahmad Zaidan, Islamabad, 18 March 2008. Zaidan, a Syrian (and future al-Jazeera journalist), was a student at IUI from 1983 to 1987.
22. Jarrar, *al-shahid*, p. 343.
23. Anas, *rihlati ma' al-jihad*, part 3.
24. Author's interview with Atiq-u-Zafar, Islamabad, 20 March 2008.
25. See, for example, Abdallah Azzam, 'risala ila al-walid' [Letter to al-Walid], 11 September 1983, in *mawsu'at al-dhakha'ir*, vol. 1, pp. 794–795.
26. One source says that in the late 1980s Azzam was offered the directorship of the Islamic University in Islamabad, which he refused: Jarrar, *al-shahid*, p. 29.
27. Olivier Roy, *Islam and Resistance in Afghanistan*, 2nd ed. (Cambridge: Cambridge University Press, 1990), p. 84.

28. Louis Dupree, 'Afghanistan in 1982: Still no Solution', *Asian Survey* 23, no. 2 (February 1983): 133–142. See also Lester W. Grau, *The Bear Went over the Mountain* (London: Routledge, 2005).
29. Population data from the World Bank (https://data.worldbank.org/country/afghanistan?view=chart [accessed 15 November 2017]).
30. 'Death Tolls for the Major Wars and Atrocities of the Twentieth Century', n.d., http://necrometrics.com/20c1m.htm (accessed 19 February 2016).
31. Simon Wolfgang Fuchs, 'Glossy Global Leadership: Unpacking the Multilingual Religious Thought of the Jihad', in *Afghanistan's Islam: From Conversion to the Taliban*, ed. Nile Green (Oakland: University of California Press, 2017), 189–206, pp. 191 and 194–198.
32. *Journal of the Muslim World League* 6, no. 7 (May 1979), p. 39.
33. Hamid and Farrall, *The Arabs*, p. 34–35.
34. *Journal of the Muslim World League* 6, no. 9 (July 1979), p. 17.
35. Hamid and Farrall, *The Arabs*, p. 30; see also p. 27.
36. Issam Diraz, *malhamat al-mujahidin al-'arab fi afghanistan* [The Epic of the Arab Mujahidin in Afghanistan] (Madinat al-Ashir min Ramadan: Dar al-Tiba'ah wa-l-Nashr al-Islamiyya, 1989), p. 9.
37. Ibid.
38. Ibid.
39. Interview with NN conducted by Alex Strick van Linschoten, Qandahar, 23 August 2009.
40. Hekmatyar's party seems to have had the largest network in the West, while Sayyaf and Khalis were strongest in the Gulf. Rabbani's Jamiat-e Islami was roughly equally well represented in both regions.
41. He notably sent a former madrasa classmate of his, Hanif Shah, to Saudi Arabia for a two-year period, and he dispatched a certain Mawlawi Aziz Khan "and a few other brothers" to the Gulf, where they would be based for five years: Brown and Rassler, *Fountainhead*, p. 63.
42. Ibid.
43. Amir, *al-shaykh al-mujahid*, p. 233.
44. M. Halim Tanwir, *Afghanistan: History, Diplomacy and Journalism*, Kindle (Dartford. Xlibris, 2013), vol. 1.
45. Ibid., vols. 1 and 2. See also D. B. Edwards, 'Print Islam: Media and Religious Revolution in Afghanistan', *Anthropological Quarterly* 68 (July 1995): 171–184.
46. This is only counting those magazines that were linked to an Afghan party or organization, not those run by independent Arabs, such as Azzam's *al-Jihad* magazine. I have also only included magazines that began publishing before 1990.

47. Fuchs, 'Glossy Global Leadership', p. 192.
48. Muzamil later said, "I was in Macca when the Communist coup of 27 April 1978 took place in Kabul, and I heard that Rabbani and other Islamic parties and non-Islamic parties leaders coordinated their work against the regime. This coalition pushed me to publish a newspaper to show our stand." The first eight issues were in Pashto and Dari, and then it changed to Arabic. It was printed in 3–4,000 copies and distributed in the Gulf States free of charge until it disbanded in 1982: Ahmad Muaffaq Zaidan, *The "Afghan Arabs" Media at Jihad* (Islamabad: ABC Printers, 1999), p. 24.
49. Ibid., pp. 33–35.
50. The editor was Abd al-Ahad al-Tarshi, an Afghan who had studied at the Islamic University of Medina. He had approached Rabbani and proposed starting another magazine as a supplement to the Hekmatyar-affiliated *al-Mawqif*. The circulation started with 5,000 copies and rose to 8,000 copies the next year. The magazine later merged with *al-Nafir al-Amm*: ibid., pp. 30–32.
51. Zaidan, *The "Afghan Arabs" Media*, p. 31.
52. *Journal of the Muslim World League* 6, no. 9 (July 1979), p. 17.
53. Video production was happening from at least as early as 1981. In a story from April 1981, an Afghan commander relates how two of his men were missing, since "they had forgotten the 60mm mortar and a video camera and had gone back to retrieve them": Ali Ahmad Jalali and Lester W. Grau, *Afghan Guerrilla Warfare: In the Words of the Mujahideen Fighters* (St. Paul, MN: MBI Publishing, 2001), p. 108.
54. *al-Bunyan al-Marsus* no. 10 (November 1986), p. 13.
55. Jere Van Dyk, *In Afghanistan: An American Odyssey* (New York: Coward-McCann, 1983), p. 55.
56. Olivier Roy, 'The Origins of the Islamist Movement in Afghanistan', *Central Asian Survey* 3 (1984): 117–127; Strick van Linschoten and Kuehn, *An Enemy we Created*, p. 52.
57. For example, a Saudi professor who visited Mujahidin parties in Peshawar in mid-1981 met one Afghan fighter who had learned Arabic in Medina, another who had studied in the Shari'a college of King Abd al-Aziz University in Mecca, and yet another who had graduated in 1979 from the Shari'a college of the University of Medina: Muhammad al-Majdhub, *dhikrayat la tansa ma' al-mujahidin wa'l-muhajirin fi bakistan* [Unforgettable Memories with the Mujahidin and the Emigrants in Pakistan] (Medina: Nadi al-Madina al-Munawwara al-Adabi, 1984), pp. 28 ff. Similarly, Abdallah Azzam recalled meeting an Afghan commander named Muhammad Sadiq Shakwa in 1982 who was a graduate of the Islamic University of Medina: Abdallah Azzam, 'hatta

la nu'idhdh asabi' al-nadam' [So That we Will Not Regret it], *al-Mujtama'* no. 618, 26 April 1983, p. 27.
58. Isam Diraz writes that in mid-1974 Sibghatullah Mujaddidi had been on a visit to Libya, but when news of Dawud's coup emerged, he "headed to Saudi Arabia and contacted the late King Faisal, who proposed that he take a job in the Muslim World League": Diraz, *malhamat*, p. 11.
59. al-Majdhub, *dhikrayat la tansa*, p. 23; author's interview with Jamal Isma'il, Islamabad, 18 March 2008.
60. For example, here is the West Bank Palestinian Jamal Isma'il's explanation for how he ended up in Peshawar: "One of my elder brothers he was killed in Lebanon while he was fighting in the ranks of al-Fath ... in 1976 ... anyone who was killed fighting in the ranks of any Palestinian faction his younger brothers and sisters have the right to get scholarship to study in the universities on the expense of the PLO. And when I finished secondary school I applied through education commission of PLO and they informed me, which country you like, I said I would like to go to Pakistan to be with my brother because that would be less an expenditure for my family and more safer for both of us to live together in one flat or one room": author's interview with Jamal Isma'il, Islamabad, 18 March 2008.
61. Muhammad, *safahat*, p. 46.
62. Van Dyk, *In Afghanistan*, p. 55.
63. Edward Girardet, *Killing the Cranes: A Reporter's Journey through Three Decades of War in Afghanistan* (White River Junction, VT: Chelsea Green Publishing, 2011), p. 249.
64. Zaidan, *The "Afghan Arabs" Media*, p. 9.
65. Al-Rashid came from the position as treasurer at the SRC's central office: Abdallah Azzam, *ayat al-rahman fi jihad al-afghan* [Signs of the Merciful in the Afghan Jihad] (Peshawar: Ittihad Talabat al-Muslimin, 1983), p. 58 (Minbar version).
66. Jasir al-Jasir, 'qissat al-afghan al-sa'udiyyin' [The Story of the Saudi Afghans], *al-Majalla*, 11 May 1996, p. 20.
67. Azzam, 'hatta la nu'idhdh', p. 27.
68. Cited in Peter Bergen, *The Osama bin Laden I Know* (New York: Free Press, 2006), p. 64. See also Muhammad Salah, *waqa'i' sanawat al-jihad: rihlat al-afghan al-'arab* [Realities of the Years of Jihad: The Journey of the Arab Afghans] (Cairo: Khulud, 2001), p. 69.
69. Muslim World League, *qararat wa tawsiyat*, pp. 348–349.
70. Ibid.
71. Ibid., pp. 353–356.
72. Ibid., p. 356.

73. Ibid., p. 364.
74. *rabitat al-'alam al-islami: 'ashrun 'aman.*
75. al-Majdhub, *dhikrayat la tansa.*
76. Ibid., p. 35.
77. Ibid., p. 25.
78. Ibid., p. 27.
79. Ibid., p. 28.
80. Muhammad, *safahat*, p. 39; Ayman al-Zawahiri, 'fursan taht rayat al-nabi' [Knights under the Prophet's Banner], *al-Sharq al-Awsat*, 2 December 2001.
81. Vahid Mojdeh, an Afghan who later worked for Azzam's Services Bureau, afterwards recalled, "There was a conflict between Jamiat and Hizb-e-Islami in Kunar, in the Asmar district, and there was an Arab by the name of Dr. Kamal Sananiri from Egypt, who went to the Asmar district and tried to solve the dispute between these two factions. It was the first time that an Arab went inside the conflict resolution process. It was around 1978 (57 in Afghan year), prior to the Russian invasion": interview with Vahid Mojdeh conducted by Anne Stenersen, Kabul, 18 October 2009.
82. Author's interview with Abd Rabb al-Rasul Sayyaf, Paghman, 8 December 2017.
83. Muhammad, *safahat*, p. 39.
84. Author's interview with Abd Rabb al-Rasul Sayyaf, Paghman, 8 December 2017.
85. Muhammad, *safahat*, p. 39.
86. Anis writes, "A delegation from the Muslim Brotherhood visited the Mujahidin in Afghanistan, and I had the honor of being part of the delegation in 1981. It was led by the Brotherhood martyr and sheikh Muhammad Kamal al-Din al-Sananiri": *fi 'uyun mu'asira*, p. 44.
87. Author's interview with Abd Rabb al-Rasul Sayyaf, Paghman, 8 December 2017.
88. Author's interview with Jamal Isma'il, Islamabad, 18 March 2008.
89. Azzam, 'dhikrayat min sahat al-jihad'; *al-Bunyan al-Marsus* no. 11 (January 1987), pp. 44–45.
90. al-Wa'i, *mawsu'at shuhada'*, p. 224.
91. Muhammad, *safahat*, pp. 52–53. I was only able to find names of fourteen of the seventeen members. Abdallah al-Mutawwa' was spiritual guide of the Kuwaiti Muslim Brothers. Al-Zayid may have been a Muslim Brother, and is considered a moderate Saudi Islamist. He was president of the Islamic University of Medina at the time when Musa al-Qarni was teaching there. Al-Mu'ayyad was close to the

Muslim Brothers. I am grateful to Stéphane Lacroix for the biographical details on the latter three figures.
92. Ibid., pp. 60–61.
93. Ibid., p. 129.
94. *al-Bunyan al-Marsus* no. 7–8 (August 1986), p. 22.
95. Salah, *waqa'i' sanawat al-jihad*, p. 56. According to Abd al-Mun'im Abu al-Futuh, who helped organize this effort, the Brotherhood set up a relief committee under the leadership of the former health minister Sabri Zaki and began recruiting doctors and other medical personnel to go and work in Peshawar. Abu al-Futuh said the work was coordinated with the Egyptian embassy in Islamabad.
96. Author's interview with Noman Benothman, London, 29 September 2010.
97. Gilles Dorronsoro, *Revolution Unending: Afghanistan, 1979 to the Present* (New York: Columbia University Press, 2005), p. 133.
98. Author's interview with Kamal al-Helbawy, London, 23 March 2008. Helbawy's testimony contradicts that of Abd al-Mun'im Abu al-Futuh, the former leader of the Egyptian Muslim Brotherhood, who said that Azzam "never contacted the Brotherhood after he stopped working with it and none of them helped him in Peshawar": Salah, *waqa'i' sanawat al-jihad*, p. 57. However, Abu al-Futuh's statement must be understood as an attempt to distance the Brotherhood from the jihadi movement.
99. Author's interview with Noman Benothman, London, 29 September 2010.
100. 'ma' ikhwanina mujahiday Afghanistan bi'l-suwar' [With our Brothers the Mujahidin in Afghanistan, in Pictures], *al-Mujtama'* 447 (May 1979), p. 12; 'al-thawra al-islamiyya fi afghanistan bayna al-mantalaq wa'l-hadaf' [The Islamic Revolution in Afghanistan: Between Starting Point and Objective]', *al-Mujtama'* 450 (19 June 1979).
101. Muhammad, *safahat*, p. 61–62. In 1989 Azzam was asked whether *al-Jihad* magazine collaborated with outside publications, and he highlighted *al-Mujtama'*, *al-Nur*, *al-Balagh*, and *al-Muslimun*: al-Bilali, 'majallat al-jihad fi 'amiha al khamis', p. 42.
102. Muhammad Qutb, *al-jihad al-afghani wa-dalalatuhu* [The Afghan Jihad and its Proofs] (Jeddah: Mu'assasat al-Madinah li'l-Sihafa wa'l-Tiba'a wa'l-Nashr, 1989).
103. Mustafa Hamid said that "some of its members did participate in the jihad but this was done personally and outside of official guidance": Hamid and Farrall, *The Arabs*, p. 33.
104. Salah, *waqa'i' sanawat al-jihad*, p. 54.
105. Hamid and Farrall, *The Arabs*, p. 78.

106. Abu Walid al-Masri, 'laylat suqut qandahar: al-sumud al-'arabi al-akhir fi'l-waqt al-da'i" [The Night Qandahar Fell: The Last Arab Resistance on Borrowed Time], 2009, p. 19, http://mafa.maktoobblog.com/311555/%D8%AC%D9%85%D9%8A%25 (accessed 26 February 2010).
107. Abu Ja'far al-Misri al-Qandahari, *dhikrayat 'arabi afghani* [Memoirs of an Afghan Arab] (Cairo: Dar al-Shuruq, 2002), p. 123.
108. 'khamas sanawat fi sujun kabul' [Five Years in the Prisons of Kabul], *al-Jihad* no. 46 (September 1988): 16–20. See also the interview with Abd al-Hakim in *al-Bunyan al-Marsus* no. 22–23 (July 1988), pp. 22–29.
109. 'khamas sanawat fi sujun kabul', p. 17; al-Qandahari, *dhikrayat*, p. 232.
110. Van Dyk, *In Afghanistan*, pp. 98–99.
111. Vahid Brown, *Abu'l-Walid al-Masri: A Biographical Sketch* (West Point, NY: Combating Terrorism Center, 2007), www.ctc.usma.edu/v2/wp-content/uploads/2011/06/Abul-Walid.pdf (accessed 19 April 2016).
112. Ibid., p. 3.
113. Saqr was an Egyptian Muslim Brother who had worked as a personal secretary for Hasan al-Banna in the 1940s and who had fled Egypt during the crackdown in 1954. His precise relationship with the Brotherhood in the 1970s is not clear: ibid.
114. Hamid and Farrall, *The Arabs*, p. 26.
115. Brown, *Abu'l-Walid al-Masri*.
116. The sources differ on how many people accompanied Hamid: in one text he says two Egyptians came with him; in another he says "a number of," suggesting more than two. See Hamid and Farrall, *The Arabs*, p. 34–35; and Brown, *Abu'l-Walid al-Masri*.
117. Muhammad, *safahat*, p. 79.
118. Hamid and Farrall, *The Arabs*, pp. 34–35.
119. Muhammad, *safahat*, p. 80.
120. Brown, *Abu'l-Walid al-Masri*, p. 5.
121. Muhammad, *safahat*, pp. 81–82.
122. Ibid., p. 81.
123. Ibid., pp. 81–82.
124. Abdallah Anas and Tam Hussain, *To the Mountains: My Life in Jihad, from Algeria to Afghanistan* (London: Hurst, 2019), pp. 9–22.
125. Anas, *rihlati ma' al-jihad*, part 2.
126. Abdallah Anas, *rihlati ma' al-jihad* [My Journey with the Jihad], part 1 (Al-Magharibia Channel, 2015), www.youtube.com/watch?v=BIYigk0Vu9Y (accessed 10 October 2015), at 20'30". Anas had previously met Azzam very briefly in the Prophet's mosque in Medina in 1981: Anas and Hussain, *To the Mountains*, p. 22.
127. Anas and Hussain, *To the Mountains*, pp. 34–35.

128. Anas, *rihlati ma' al-jihad*, part 1.
129. Anas, *rihlati ma' al-jihad*, part 2.
130. Muhammad, *safahat*, p. 47.
131. A substantial proportion (ten out of thirty-four) of the early travelers were Egyptians, which would seem to suggest something more organized taking place in Cairo in this early period. However, the hypothesis is weakened by the fact that half of them were actually expatriates: Mustafa Hamid and his two friends were living in Abu Dhabi, while Abu Hafs al-Masri and Rajab were based in Yemen.
132. *Ittihad* newspaper, cited in Muhammad, *safahat*, p. 37. At its height in the late 1980s, the Mujahidin may have numbered up to 250,000 men: Milt Bearden and James Risen, *The Main Enemy: The Inside Story of the CIA's Final Showdown with the KGB* (New York: Random House, 2003), p. 240.
133. Hamid and Farrall, *The Arabs*, p. 30.
134. Ibid., p. 39.
135. Ibid., p. 30.
136. Brown and Rassler, *Fountainhead*, pp. 62–63.
137. Muhammad, *safahat*, p. 102.
138. Jean-Pierre Perrin, 'Dans un camp souterrain des moudjahidin', *Gazette de Lausanne*, 14 January 1986.
139. Mohammad Yousaf and Mark Adkin, *Afghanistan: The Bear Trap*, 2nd ed. (Barnsley: Leo Cooper, 2001), p. 167.
140. Commandant Amin Wardak, *Mémoires de guerre* (Paris: Arthaud, 2009), p. 240.
141. Ibid., p. 242.
142. Muhammad, *safahat*, p. 101.
143. Wardak, *Mémoires*, p. 238.
144. Hamid and Farrall, *The Arabs*, p. 56.

Diplomat

1. Jarrar, *al-shahid*, p. 344. Azzam himself also said, "I came to the Afghan jihad with no grey hair, but my head turned all grey from everything I saw. I lived the Afghan jihad in that period day by day with my nerves, heart, emotions, and sensibilities": *al-Jihad* no. 50 (December 1988), p. 4.
2. *fi 'uyun mu'asira*, p. 224.
3. Ibid., p. 73.
4. Yousaf and Adkin, *Afghanistan: The Bear Trap*, p. 39.
5. There is now a substantial literature on the internal politics of the Afghan Mujahidin; for good overviews see David B. Edwards, *Before*

Taliban: Genealogies of the Afghan Jihad (Berkeley: University of California Press, 2002), pp. 225 ff.; and Kevin Bell, *Usama Bin Ladin's "Father Sheikh": Yunus Khalis and the Return of al-Qa'ida's Leadership to Afghanistan* (West Point, NY: Combating Terrorism Center, 2013).

6. Roy, *Islam and Resistance*, p. 120.
7. Bell, *Usama Bin Ladin's "Father Sheikh"*, p. 23.
8. See the maps in Gregory Fremont-Barnes, *The Soviet–Afghan War 1979–89* (Oxford and Long Island City, NY: Osprey Publishing, 2012).
9. Very broadly speaking, Yunus Khalis's main areas were northern Paktika and Nangarhar, Gailani's men were in southern Paktika and eastern Lugar, Mujaddidi was strongest in part of Kunar, while Hekmatyar dominated pockets forming an arc from Baghlan to Nangarhar. Sayyaf held very small pieces of territory in Paktia and near Kabul.
10. According to an apocryphal story, Sayyaf was selected in Ta'if in 1980 after Ahmed Badeeb, the deputy head of Saudi intelligence, locked the bickering Afghan Mujahidin delegation inside Ta'if prison, telling them that he would not let them out until they had agreed upon a spokesperson: Steve Coll, *Ghost Wars: The Secret History of the CIA, Afghanistan and Bin Laden, from the Soviet Invasion to September 10, 2001* (New York: Penguin, 2004), p. 83.
11. Author's interview with Abd Rabb al-Rasul Sayyaf, Paghman, 8 December 2017.
12. Author's interview with Abd Rabb al-Rasul Sayyaf, Paghman, 8 December 2017.
13. Author's interview with Abu Harith, Amman, 8 May 2008; author's interview with Ahmad Zaidan, Islamabad, 18 March 2008.
14. For example, in 1983 Yunus Khalis withdrew from the alliance, describing Sayyaf as "a crook ... who uses the alliances funds to combat other resistance movements inside the country": Muhammad, *safahat*, p. 128.
15. In 1984, for example, clashes between Hekmatyar and Sayyaf units reportedly caused over 400 deaths: ibid., p. 102.
16. Ibid., p. 45.
17. Ibid., pp. 60–61 and 129.
18. Anas, *rihlati ma' al-jihad*, part 9, at 4'20" ff and 9'00" ff.
19. Ibid., around 15'20".
20. *fi 'uyun mu'asira*, p. 73. Azzam and Yasir reconciled a while later, after Yasir had a dream about Azzam being disgusted with him, which prompted Yasir to turn up at Azzam's house in Islamabad one

evening to mend fences: Anas, *rihlati ma' al-jihad*, part 9, at 15'50" ff. When Azzam died in 1989, Yasir would give one of the longest speeches at the memorial service, openly admitting they had often disagreed, but also heaping praise on Azzam: *fi 'uyun mu'asira*, pp. 73–78.
21. Anas, *rihlati ma' al-jihad*, part 9, at 18'30" ff.
22. Azzam, *al-duktur al-shahid*, p. 57.
23. Yousaf and Adkin, *Afghanistan: The Bear Trap*, p. 26; Hein Kiessling, *Faith, Unity, Discipline: The Inter-Service-Intelligence (ISI) of Pakistan* (London: Hurst, 2016), pp. 50–51.
24. Kiessling put the US government's financial contribution at "US$3 billion plus": Kiessling, *Faith*, p. 54. This is consistent with the annual figures provided by Steve Coll (e.g. $470 million in 1986 and $630 million in 1987): Coll, *Ghost Wars*, p. 151. To the US contribution must be added at least a similar amount from the Saudi government, plus contributions from other governments, notably in the Gulf and in Europe. On top of this there was money from private donors.
25. Michael T. Kaufman, 'Mrs. Thatcher Visits Afghans on the Frontier', *New York Times*, 9 October 1981.
26. 'Space Shuttle's Flight Dedicated to Afghans', Reuters, 11 March 1982.
27. 'Reagan Praises Afghan Fighters', Associated Press, 3 February 1983.
28. On Egypt and China's role see John K. Cooley, *Unholy Wars: Afghanistan, America and International Terrorism*, 1st ed. (London: Pluto Press, 1999), chapters 2, 4, and 5; and Yousaf and Adkin, *Afghanistan: The Bear Trap*, p. 83.
29. Cooley writes, "At least half a dozen knowledgeable individuals insisted to the author, without citing proof, that Israel was indeed involved ... what is certain is that of all the members of the anti-Soviet coalition, the Israelis have been the most successful in concealing the details and even the broad traces of a training role": Cooley, *Unholy Wars*, p. 100.
30. Yousaf and Adkin, *Afghanistan: The Bear Trap*, pp. 2 and 27–29; Kiessling, *Faith*, p. 54.
31. Kiessling, *Faith*, pp. 53–54.
32. According to a senior Algerian official, the Algerian government "did nothing to stop the flow of young Algerians toward Pakistan": Mohamed Mokeddem, *Les Afghans algériens: de la Djamaâ à la Qa'ida* (Algiers: Éditions ANEP, 2002), p. 13.
33. For example, when Ayman al-Zawahiri came out of prison in 1985 "he was keen to leave as soon as possible, but was surprised to find his name

on the list of people banned from traveling abroad": Jamal Abd al-Rahim, *ayman al-zawahiri: min qusur al-ma'adi ila kuhuf afghanistan* [Ayman al-Zawahiri: From the Palaces of Maadi to the Caves of Afghanistan] (Cairo: Madbuli al-Saghir, 2006), p. 63. Moreover, as we shall see in Chapter 10, several Egyptian Islamists went to Peshawar to escape further imprisonment at home, and they had to conceal their travel plans by pretending to go to Saudi Arabia for Hajj.

34. According to Jamal Isma'il, the rebate was 75 percent and was introduced in the mid- or late 1980s: Bergen, *The Osama Bin Laden I Know*, p. 41.
35. Author's interview with Abu Suhayb, Jenin, 4 May 2008.
36. Author's interview with Prince Turki al-Faisal, Princeton, 12 November 2009.
37. Author's interview with Prince Turki al-Faisal, Princeton, 12 November 2009.
38. Anas, *rihlati ma' al-jihad*, part 2.
39. Muhammad Yousaf, for example, does not mention Azzam at all in Yousaf and Adkin, *Afghanistan: The Bear Trap*.
40. Muhammad al-Shafi'i, 'Gul, the Godfather of the Taliban, Tells *al-Sharq al-Awsat* that the Tribal Region in Pakistan is Accepting Money and Arms from the Americans', *al-Sharq al-Awsat* Online (via FBIS), 25 April 2009.
41. Even Indian books on the ISI with a strong anti-Pakistani slant do not suggest that Azzam worked closely with the Pakistanis: see, for example, S. K. Datta, *Inside ISI: The Story and Involvement of the ISI in Afghan Jihad, Taliban, al-Qaeda, 9/11, Osama Bin Laden, 26/11 and the Future of al-Qaeda* (New Delhi: Vij Books, 2014).
42. Mustafa Hamid said that "Azzam worked closely and in complete coordination with Abu Mazen, the military advisor at the Saudi embassy in Islamabad. They lived in the same building and the Saudi official was in charge of Saudi intelligence actions in both Afghanistan and Pakistan": al-Masri, 'laylat suqut qandahar', p. 22. Peter Tomsen wrote that "the GID [the Saudi General Intelligence Directorate] coordinated with the ISI and with Abdullah Azzam's Services Bureau in Peshawar during the 1980s": Tomsen, *The Wars of Afghanistan*, p. 248.
43. Azzam once said, "The new Saudi ambassador Tawfiq Khalid Alamdar turned the scales – truly – and he gave an honest image of the Mujahidin to his country, explained the greatness of this jihad to them, and its importance to Saudi Arabia and to the Gulf ... He asked for permission to enter Afghanistan without the knowledge of the Pakistani government, so he disguised himself in Afghan clothes and

operation: ibid., p. 93; Bearden and Risen, *The Main Enemy*, pp. 311–314.
95. Matthew Bolton, 'Goldmine: A Critical Look at the Commercialization of Afghan Demining', research paper (London School of Economics and Political Science: Centre for the Study of Global Governance, 2008), pp. 11–12.
96. Edwards, *Before Taliban*, p. 270.
97. Author's telephone interview with Börje Almqvist, 9 February 2016. The competition got so bad that the Swedes resorted to dirty tactics: "I know it was politically incorrect," Almquist said, "but we tried to negotiate with the landlords by saying that we would leave behind a cleaner property than the Arabs would."
98. The lower estimate is Larry Crandall's: author's interview with Larry Crandall, McLean, VA, 28 May 2009. The higher estimate appears in Helga Baitenmann, 'NGOs and the Afghan War: The Politicisation of Humanitarian Aid', *Third World Quarterly* 12, no. 1 (1 January 1990): 62–85, pp. 62 and 64.
99. One example was Project Boots, "a joint project of the United States Council for World Freedom and the Committee for a Free Afghanistan, [which] included direct aid for rebels, cash for several top commanders, medical supplies, clothing and communications equipment": Van Dyk, *In Afghanistan*, p. 78. Similarly, the organization American Aid for Afghans "delivered medical supplies, winter clothing, blankets, boots and food. It also supported the clandestine Radio Free Kabul with radio transmitters and antennas": John H. Lorentz, 'Afghan Aid: The Role of Private Voluntary Organizations,' *Journal of South Asian and Middle Eastern Studies* 11 (1987): 102–111, p. 106.
100. Christophe de Ponfilly, *Vies clandestines: nos années afghanes* (Paris: Florent Massot, 2001), pp. 233–234.
101. Lohbeck, *Holy War, Unholy Victory*, p. 95.
102. Ibid.
103. Paul Overby, *Holy Blood: An Inside View of the Afghan War* (Westport, CT: Praeger, 1993), p. 3.
104. Thomas Eighmy, 'Remembering USAID's Role in Afghanistan, 1985-1994', *Foreign Service Journal*, December 2007, p. 49.
105. Azzam, 'hatta la nu'idhdh', p. 27.
106. Azzam, *'ibar wa basa'ir*, p. 84.
107. Ibid., p. 86.
108. Ibid., pp. 87–88.
109. *al-Jihad* no. 21 (August 1986), p. 30.
110. Azzam, *'ibar wa basa'ir*, pp. 82–83.

Mainstream, 2001), which later turned out to be a hoax: see Audrey Gillan, 'The Fantasy Life and Lonely Death of the SAS Veteran who Never Was', *The Guardian*, 24 January 2009.
79. Shashank Joshi, 'Assessing Britain's Role in Afghanistan', *Asian Survey* 55, no. 2 (2014): 420–45, p. 422.
80. Author's telephone interview with Alastair Crooke, 23 March 2008.
81. A *New Statesman* article from 2005 notes in passing that MI6 officer Alastair Crooke "got to know some of the militants who would become leaders of al-Qaida," but it is not clear who this referred to: Grey, 'Mint Tea with Terrorists'.
82. Notin, *La Guerre de l'ombre*, pp. 302 and 389–390.
83. Ibid., pp. 302 and 389–390.
84. Ibid., pp. 389–390.
85. In the late 1980s American resources were distributed as follows: 20 percent each to Hekmatyar, Rabbani, and Sayyaf; 15 percent to Khalis; and 25 percent to the three "moderate" parties: author's interview with anonymous former CIA official, 11 November 2018. See also Bearden and Risen, *The Main Enemy*, p. 240; Coll, *Ghost Wars*, pp. 165 and 607; Kurt Lohbeck, *Holy War, Unholy Victory: Eyewitness to the CIA's Secret War in Afghanistan* (Washington, DC: Regnery Gateway, 1993), pp. 9–10; Yousaf and Adkin, *Afghanistan: The Bear Trap*, p. 105.
86. Coll, *Ghost Wars*, p. 165.
87. Ibid., pp. 164–165; Bearden and Risen, *The Main Enemy*, p. 241; Lohbeck, *Holy War, Unholy Victory*, pp. 125–127 and 150.
88. Berger, *Jihad Joe*, pp. 6–7.
89. Joe Stephens and David B. Ottaway, 'From US, the ABC's of Jihad', *Washington Post*, 23 March 2002.
90. Yousaf and Adkin, *Afghanistan: The Bear Trap*, pp. 193 and 195.
91. Abdurraheem Green, 'Abdurraheem Green: "Returning Jihadis Aren't so Bad, I Used to be one"', 5Pillars (blog), 30 October 2014.
92. Cynthia Storer, 'Working with al-Qaeda Documents: An Analyst's View before 9/11', in *Ten Years Later: Insights on al-Qaeda's Past and Future through Captured Records*, ed. Lorry M. Fenner, Mark E. Stout, and Jessica L. Goldings (Washington, DC: Johns Hopkins University Center for Advanced Governmental Studies, 2012), 41–52, p. 41.
93. Bearden and Risen, *The Main Enemy*, p. 366.
94. Lohbeck, *Holy War, Unholy Victory*, p. 92. Lohbeck mentions the example of the mules that were imported from the USA to Afghanistan to help the Mujahidin carry arms, ammunition, and supplies. The project was supervised by USAID but was essentially a CIA

58. According to Mohammad Yousaf, the CIA station had two officers in 1983 and seven in 1987: Yousaf and Adkin, *Afghanistan: The Bear Trap*, pp. 91–92. Larry Crandall says the total number of US citizens who passed through Peshawar in the 1980s was no more than forty: author's interview with Larry Crandall, McLean, VA, 22 May 2009. See also Coll, *Ghost Wars*, pp. 22–23 and 57.
59. Author's interview with anonymous former CIA official, 11 November 2018.
60. Bergen, *The Osama Bin Laden I Know*, pp. 60–61; Coll, *The Bin Ladens*, pp. 87 and 293. See also Panagiotis Dimitrakis, *The Secret War in Afghanistan: The Soviet Union, China and Anglo-American Intelligence in the Afghan War* (London and New York: I. B. Tauris, 2013).
61. Author's interview with anonymous former CIA official, 11 November 2018; Bearden and Risen, *The Main Enemy*, p. 243.
62. Bearden and Risen, *The Main Enemy*.
63. Ibid., pp. 200–201.
64. Coll, *Ghost Wars*, p. 86.
65. Yousaf and Adkin, *Afghanistan: The Bear Trap*, p. 81.
66. Ibid., pp. 115–116.
67. Hamid and Farrall, *The Arabs*, p. 40.
68. FBIS, 'Compilation of Usama bin Ladin Statements, 1994–January 2004' (Foreign Broadcast Information Service, 2004), www.fas.org/irp/world/para/ubl-fbis.pdf, p. 122 (accessed 15 October 2015).
69. From *The International Islamic Resistance Call*, cited in Bergen, *The Osama Bin Laden I Know*, p. 61.
70. Abdallah Anas, *wiladat al-afghan al-'arab* [The Birth of the Afghan Arabs] (London: Saqi, 2002), p. 100.
71. In *Knights under the Prophet's Banner*, cited in Bergen, *The Osama Bin Laden I Know*, p. 61.
72. Azzam, *'ibar wa basa'ir*, p. 77.
73. 'Interview with Sheikh Tameem al Adnani' (Lawrence Islamic Video, 1988), http://archive.org/details/interview-sheikh-tameem-adnani (accessed 2 March 2018).
74. Flagg Miller, *The Audacious Ascetic: What the Bin Laden Tapes Reveal about al-Qaida* (London: Hurst, 2015), pp. 133–134.
75. Coll, *Ghost Wars*, p. 123.
76. Author's interview with anonymous former CIA official, 8 October 2008.
77. Author's interview with Larry Crandall, McLean, VA, 22 May 2009.
78. Mark Curtis, *Secret Affairs: Britain's Collusion with Radical Islam* (London: Serpent's Tail, 2010), pp. 131–149. See also Cooley, *Unholy Wars*, pp. 92 ff. Curtis's account may have been influenced by Tom Carew's book *Jihad! The Secret War in Afghanistan* (London:

entered Afghanistan. This was also asked more than once by his clerk and the director of his office, the brother Muhammad Salim al-Hamud (Abu Mazin), who was a fine man also": Muhammad, *safahat*, p. 89.

44. According to Fawaz Gerges, "the Saudis partially financed sheikh Abdallah Azzam's Services Bureau," while Bernard Rougier writes that "the Services Bureau received money from the emir Salman ... governor of Riyadh": Gerges, *The Far Enemy*, p. 76; Rougier, *Everyday Jihad*, p. 77. However, neither Gerges nor Rougier provides evidence for this assertion.
45. Steve Coll, *The Bin Ladens* (New York: Penguin, 2008), p. 295.
46. Coll, *Ghost Wars*, p. 88.
47. Ibid., pp. 88 and 156–157.
48. Ibid., p. 87. See also Coll, *The Bin Ladens*, pp. 294–296. Lawrence Wright also noted that "Bin Ladin would dutifully report his activities to [Prince] Turki, such as bringing in heavy equipment and engineers to build fortifications": Wright, *The Looming Tower*, p. 104. Abu Mus'ab al-Suri wrote, "Saudi intelligence agencies did have involvement with Bin Laden, and elements of their apparatus did send assistance from Saudi Arabia": *The International Islamic Resistance Call*, cited in Bergen, *The Osama Bin Laden I Know*, p. 61.
49. Azzam, *al-duktur al-shahid*, p. 68.
50. Author's interview with anonymous former CIA officer; author's interview with Steve Coll, Washington, DC, 28 May 2008. See also Milton J. Valencia, 'Accused Al Qaeda Supporter's Defense Rests', *Boston Globe*, 15 December 2011.
51. Author's telephone interview with Alastair Crooke, 23 March 2008. Crooke was identified as a former officer with MI6 in Stephen Grey, 'Mint Tea with Terrorists', *New Statesman*, 11 April 2005.
52. Abdallah Azzam, 'al-tarbiya al-jihadiyya wa'l-bina'' [Jihadi Education and Edification], 1992, pp. 24–25 (Minbar version).
53. Ayman al-Zawahiri, 'Knights under the Prophet's Banner', 2001, https://azelin.files.wordpress.com/2010/11/6759609-knights-under-the-prophet-banner.pdf, p. 11 (accessed 29 January 2018).
54. Cooley, *Unholy Wars*.
55. See, for example, John Pilger, 'What Good Friends Left Behind', *The Guardian*, 20 September 2003; Peter Dale Scott, *The Road to 9/11: Wealth, Empire, and the Future of America* (Berkeley: University of California Press, 2007); Girardet, *Killing the Cranes*.
56. Jack Devine and Vernon Loeb, *Good Hunting: An American Spymaster's Story* (New York: Sarah Crichton Books, 2014), p. 104.
57. Jean-Christophe Notin, *La Guerre de l'ombre des Français en Afghanistan: 1979–2011* (Paris: Fayard, 2011), p. 324.

111. See, for example, *al-Jihad* no. 15 (January 1986), p. 46; *al-Jihad* no. 47 (October 1988), p. 2; *al-Jihad* no. 52 (February 1989), pp. 18–21; and *al-Jihad* no. 58 (August 1989), pp. 24–31.
112. *al-Jihad* no. 15 (January 1986), p. 46. See also *al-Jihad* no. 21 (August 1986), p. 30.
113. Anas, *rihlati ma' al-jihad*, part 8.
114. Azzam, *The Lofty Mountain*, pp. 71–72; Azzam, *'ibar wa basa'ir*, p. 108–109. Al-Farisi was born in Benghazi in 1951 and had trained as a doctor at Qar Yunus University. He had moved to London around 1982 for a postgraduate degree in pediatrics, but he quit his studies to go to Peshawar in 1983: Muhammad, *safahat*, p. 337.
115. Abdallah Azzam, 'maktab khidamat al-mujahidin' [The Services Bureau for the Mujahidin], *al-Jihad* no. 49 (December 1988), p. 3.
116. Jarrar, *al-shahid*, p. 103; Azzam, *'ibar wa basa'ir*, p. 60.
117. Author's interview with Steve Coll, Washington, DC, 28 May 2008; author's interview with Larry Crandall, McLean, VA, 22 May 2009.
118. Abdallah Azzam, 'ayna al-sahafi al-muslim?' [Where is the Muslim Journalist?], *al-Jihad* no. 10 (August 1985): 4–8, pp. 5–6. See also *mawsu'at al-dhakha'ir*, vol. 4, p. 632; Amir, *al-shaykh al-mujahid*, p. 92; Jarrar, *al-shahid*, p. 103.
119. Anthony Davis, 'Foreign Combatants in Afghanistan', *Jane's Intelligence Review* 5 (1993): 327–331.
120. Notin, *La Guerre de l'ombre*, p. 299.
121. Author's interview with Olivier Roy, Salzburg, 5 September 2016.
122. Notin, *La Guerre de l'ombre*, p. 299.
123. Ibid., p. 299.
124. Girardet, *Killing the Cranes*, p. 258.
125. Ibid., p. 258.
126. Bergen, *The Osama Bin Laden I Know*, p. 88.
127. Girardet, *Killing the Cranes*, pp. 259–262 and 271.
128. Ibid., pp. 251–253.
129. Van Dyk, *In Afghanistan*, pp. 98–99.
130. Peregrine Hodson, *Under a Sickle Moon: A Journey through Afghanistan* (New York: Grove Press, 2002).
131. Overby, *Holy Blood*, pp. 90–91.
132. William Dalrymple, 'Nancy Hatch Dupree's Quest to Save Afghanistan's History', *Newsweek*, 12 April 2013, http://newsweekpakistan.com/ill-just-finish-my-chips/.
133. Email correspondence with Peter Tomsen, 22 January 2009.
134. For partial overviews see, for example, Azzam, *'ibar wa basa'ir*, pp. 82–83; Zaidan, *The "Afghan Arabs" Media*, pp. 9–12; Muhammad Tawfiq, *afghanistan al-jariha – afghanistan al-habiba* [Afghanistan the

Wounded – Afghanistan the Beloved] (Riyadh: Mu'assasat al-Jazira, 1990), pp. 127–129.
135. The Saudi Red Crescent (al-Hilal al-Ahmar al-Sa'udi) operated from 1980. The Kuwaiti Red Crescent (al-Hilal al-Ahmar al-Kuwayti) operated from 1981. The Saudi Relief Committee (Lajnat al-Ighatha al-Sa'udiyya) operated from 1983. The Kuwaiti Relief Committee (Lajnat al-Ighatha al-Kuwaytiyya) operated from around 1984. The Islamic Da'wa Committee (Lajnat al-Da'wa al-Islamiyya) was a Kuwaiti organization operating from around 1984. The Islamic Relief Agency (al-Wikala al-Islamiyya li'l-Ighatha) was a Sudanese organization operating from around 1985. Human Concern International (Hay'at al-Ighatha al-Insaniyya al-'Alamiyya) was a Canadian organization operating from around 1985. The Muslim World League (Rabitat al-'Alam al-Islami)/International Islamic Relief Organization was a Saudi organization operating from around 1986. Muslim Aid was Cat Stevens' UK-based charity, which operated from around 1987. The Islamic Benevolence Committee (Lajnat al-Birr al-Islamiyya) was a Saudi charity operating from around 1987. In addition to these ten, there were several smaller or shorter-lived ones, such as the Education Center, the Afghanistan Reconstruction Office, and the Medina Institute. Azzam's Services Bureau was also considered by other Islamists as a charity. Zaidan, *The "Afghan Arabs" Media*, pp. 9–12.
136. Azzam writes that in 1986 the Saudi Relief Committee had a budget of $40 million, while the Kuwaiti Red Crescent had $6 million and the Saudi Red Crescent only $2.7 million: Azzam, *'ibar wa basa'ir*, pp. 82–83.
137. One event was the International Conference on Afghan Education held in Peshawar from 30 October to 2 November 1987: *al-Jihad* no. 37 (December 1987), pp. 14–16. Another was the conference on Afghan reconstruction organized by the Services Bureau in late July or early August 1988: *al-Jihad* no. 45 (August 1988), pp. 14–20.
138. See, for example, *al-Jihad* no. 28 (March 1987), p. 46; *al-Jihad* no. 30 (May 1987), p. 21; *al-Jihad* no. 32 (July 1987), p. 47; *al-Jihad* no. 36 (November 1987), p. 47; *al-Jihad* no. 37 (December 1987), p. 47; *al-Jihad* no. 40 (March 1988), p. 3; and *al-Jihad* no. 47 (October 1988), pp. 30–31.
139. Muhammad, *safahat*, p. 166.
140. In 1989 Nasif wrote, "I knew Sheikh Abdallah Azzam over thirteen years, from when he was a professor at the University of Jordan in Amman": *fi 'uyun mu'asira*, p. 301.
141. Muhammad, *safahat*, p. 193. Later on, Khalifa appears to have been replaced as the MWL representative in Peshawar by a person named

Abd al-Hasan, but the collaboration with Azzam and the Services Bureau continued: Dorronsoro, *Revolution Unending*, p. 133.
142. Muhammad, *safahat*, p. 201.
143. *rabitat al-'alam al-islami: 'ashrun 'aman*, p. 11.
144. Muhammad, *safahat*, p. 193.
145. Ibid., pp. 165 and 193.
146. Jarrar, *al-shahid*, p. 93.
147. Zaidan, *The "Afghan Arabs" Media*, p. 10.
148. Muhammad, *safahat*, pp. 139–140.
149. Miller, *The Audacious Ascetic*, p. 74.
150. Muhammad, *safahat*, p. 87.
151. al-Qandahari, *dhikrayat*, p. 133.
152. Jarrar, *al-shahid*, p. 93.
153. See Tareekh Musadat 29, 29a, 33, 34, 41, 41a, 102, 118, 119, 127, and 436.
154. Azzam, *al-duktur al-shahid*, p. 94; *fi 'uyun mu'asira*, p. 38.
155. Muhammad, *safahat*, p. 227.
156. Ibid., p. 217.
157. Azzam, *al-duktur al-shahid*, p. 152.
158. Abd al-Aziz Bin Baz, 'risala ila aghniya' al-muslimin' [Letter to Wealthy Muslims], *al-Jihad* no. 9 (July 1985): 36–37; Abd al-Aziz Bin Baz, 'al-jihad fi'l-afghan [*sic*] jihad islami yajib "ala jami'" al-muslimin da'muhu wa musanadatuhu' [The Jihad in Afghanistan is an Islamic Jihad and All Muslims Must Support and Assist it], *al-Jihad* no. 22 (September 1986): 24–25; Abd al-Aziz Bin Baz, 'fadl al-jihad fi sabil allah wa'l-musabara fi dhalik' [The Merit of Jihad in God's Path and Perseverance in it], parts 1 and 2, *al-Jihad* no. 42–43 (June 1988): 38–40 and 24–27.
159. 'The Words of Abdallah Azzam', p. 59.
160. Several sources speak of an explicit agreement between the Egyptian Brotherhood and the Egyptian government on this issue: see, for example, Salah, *waqa'i' sanawat al-jihad*, pp. 49–50.
161. Ibid., p. 56; author's interview with Kamal al-Helbawy, London, 23 March 2008.
162. Rougier, *Everyday Jihad*, pp. 83–84.
163. Azzam, *al-duktur al-shahid*, p. 149.
164. Ibid., pp. 149–150.
165. Hamid and Farrall, *The Arabs*, p. 32.
166. Ibid., p. 33.
167. Rougier, *Everyday Jihad*, p. 84.
168. Author's interview with Jamal Isma'il, Islamabad, 20 March 2008.
169. Salah, *waqa'i' sanawat al-jihad*, p. 57.

170. Abdallah Azzam, 'risala maftuha ila al-'ulama' [Open Letter to the Scholars], *al-Jihad* no. 5 (April 1985): 36–37.
171. Azzam, 'ya muslimiy al-'alam' p. 27.
172. Azzam, *al-duktur al-shahid*, pp. 142–143, 161.
173. Abdallah Azzam, 'risala ila abu akram' [Letter to Abu Akram], 8 April 1986, in *mawsu'at al-dhakha'ir*, vol. 1, pp. 793–794.
174. Azzam, *al-duktur al-shahid*, p. 84.
175. Ibid., p. 186.
176. Salah, *waqa'i' sanawat al-jihad*, p. 56; Muhammad, *safahat*, pp. 52–53; *fi 'uyun mu'asira*, pp. 29 and 37; and *al-Jihad* magazine, *passim*.
177. *al-Bunyan al-Marsus* no. 18 (February 1988), pp. 30–32.
178. Ahmad al-Assal later said that he had known Azzam "since he was a student," though it is not clear from where: *fi 'uyun mu'asira*, p. 59. Kamal al-Helbawy knew Azzam from 1981 when they both worked in Saudi Arabia.
179. Author's interview with Noman Benothman, London, 29 September 2010.
180. Author's interview with Noman Benothman, London, 29 September 2010; author's interview with Jamal Isma'il, Islamabad, 20 March 2008.
181. Author's interview with Kamal al-Helbawy, London, 23 March 2008.
182. Author's interview with Atiq-u-Zafar, Islamabad, 20 March 2008; author's interview with Khalid Rahman, Islamabad, 20 March 2008.
183. For example, in February 1988 *al-Jihad* magazine reported from a roundtable organized at the Services Bureau, in which Qazi Hussein Ahmed participated alongside Azzam and several senior Arab Muslim Brothers, including Adib al-Haji, Abd al-Aziz al-Jafri, Muhammad Mahmud Sawwaf, Abd al-Majid al-Zindani, Hasan al-Turabi, and Ali al-Da'i; see *al-Jihad* no. 39 (February 1988), pp. 10–16.
184. See, for example, *al-Jihad* no. 27 (February 1987), pp. 16–22.
185. Azzam, *'ibar wa basa'ir*, p. 75. He made this observation in 1986.
186. Philip Jenkins, 'Clerical Terror: The Roots of Jihad in India', *The New Republic*, 24 December 2008; Farhan Zahid, 'Influences of Abu Ala Maududi on Islamo-Jihadi Thoughts of Abdullah Azzam the Father of Modern Jihad Movement', Centre Français de Recherche sur le Renseignement, Foreign Analysis 33, December 2015.
187. The founders were Irshad Ahmed, Abdus Samad Sial, and Mohammad Akhtar. According to Arif Jamal, the group was initially called Jamiat Ansar-ul-Afghaneen, but changed its name to Harakat al-Jihad al-Islami (HJI) at some point in the early to mid-1980s. HJI is the

mother group of several well-known militant Pakistani Deobandi organizations. Around 1985 it produced a splinter group, the Harakat al-Mujahidin. In 1993 the two merged to form Harakat al-Ansar, which changed its name back to Harakat al-Mujahidin in 1997. In 2000 Masood Azhar split from Harakat al-Mujahidin to form Jaysh-e Muhammad. All these groups operated mainly in Kashmir after the end of the Afghan jihad. See Arif Jamal, *Shadow War: The Untold Story of Jihad in Kashmir* (New York: Melville House, 2009).

188. Arif Jamal, 'The Growth of the Deobandi Jihad in Afghanistan', *Jamestown Terrorism Monitor* 8, no. 2 (14 January 2010).
189. Mufti Mohammad Rafi Usmani, *Jihad in Afghanistan against Communism* (Karachi: Darul-Ishaat, 2003), p. 11.
190. Ibid., pp. 12, 78, 242–244.
191. Author's interview with Sami' al-Haqq, Akora Khattak, 21 March 2008.
192. *fi 'uyun mu'asira*, p. 338.
193. Mariam Abou Zahab, 'Salafism in Pakistan: The Ahl-e Hadith Movement', in *Global Salafism: Islam's New Religious Movement*, ed. Roel Meijer (London: Hurst, 2009), 126–142, p. 133.
194. Mawlana Amir Hamza, *qafilat da'wat jihad* [The Caravan of Da'wa and Jihad] (n.p.: Dar al-Andalus, 2004), p. 97. I am grateful to Saba Imtiaz for sharing the reference and providing the translation.
195. Saeed Shafqat says the MDI was founded in 1987 and that Azzam was one of the three founders alongside Hafiz Saeed and Zafar Iqbal: Saeed Shafqat, 'From Official Islam to Islamism: The Rise of Dawat-ul-Irshad and Lashkar-e-Taiba', in *Pakistan: Nationalism without a Nation*, ed. Christophe Jaffrelot (London: Zed Books, 2002), 131–47, p. 141.
196. Samina Yasmeen, *Jihad and Dawah: Evolving Narratives of Lashkar-e-Taiba and Jamat ud Dawah* (London: Hurst, 2017), p. 47; Stephen Tankel, *Storming the World Stage: The Story of Lashkar-e-Taiba* (Oxford: Oxford University Press, 2011), pp. 20–21. Christine Fair says that the MDI was founded by Saeed and Iqbal and that Azzam "provided assistance": C. Christine Fair, Bruce Hoffman, and Fernando Reinares, 'Leader-Led Jihad in Pakistan: The Case of Lashkar-e-Taiba', in *The Evolution of the Global Terrorist Threat: From 9/11 to Osama bin Laden's Death* (New York: Columbia University Press, 2014), 571–599, p. 576. Fair and Tankel put the date at 1986, but Yasmeen, who has more detailed information, dates the foundation to the spring of 1987. Arif Jamal

says Azzam had nothing to do with the MDI's foundation: Arif Jamal, *Call for Transnational Jihad: Lashkar-e-Taiba 1985–2014*, 1st South Asian ed. (New Delhi: Kautilya, 2015).
197. Fair, Hoffman, and Reinares, 'Leader-Led Jihad in Pakistan', p. 577.
198. Author's interview with Babar Ahmad, London, 31 May 2017.

Manager

1. Muhammad, *safahat*, p. 61.
2. *al-Jihad* no. 49 (December 1988), p. 3.
3. Muhammad, *safahat*, p. 61.
4. Azzam, *al-duktur al-shahid*, p. 42.
5. Mustafa Hamid later wrote, "The immediate objective of the Badr camp was to bring together Afghans from rival fronts within a single programme and highly spiritual atmosphere offered by Azzam's lessons in the hope that hostilities between them would disappear": Hamid and Farrall, *The Arabs*, pp. 81–82.
6. Muhammad, *safahat*, p. 100.
7. Sayyaf had reportedly been given land by the Pakistani government around 1983 to build a training facility in Pabbi: ibid., p. 106.
8. Author's interview with Abd Rabb al-Rasul Sayyaf, Paghman, 8 December 2017.
9. Muhammad, *safahat*, p. 119.
10. *fi 'uyun mu'asira*, p. 74.
11. Ibid.
12. Yousaf and Adkin, *Afghanistan: The Bear Trap*, p. 120.
13. Muhammad, *safahat*, p. 100.
14. Estimates vary slightly. Jarrar said, "The number of Arabs in there at that time ... was no more than nine; two from Saudi Arabia, one from Palestine, one from Egypt, one from Sudan": Jarrar, *al-shahid*, p. 343. Abdallah Anas says that when he and his three other close companions arrived at Badr, they found about a dozen Arabs there already: three or four Syrians, three or four Iraqis, a Kurd (Abu Muhammad), Isam al-Din al-Libi, and then another who had been studying in UK but joined the jihad. These men had arrived in Pakistan a few months earlier: Anas, *rihlati ma' al-jihad*, part 3. Another article says that "all the Arab brothers present at that time, around twenty people, participated": *al-Bunyan al-Marsus* no. 30 (February 1990), p. 8.
15. Hamid and Farrall, *The Arabs*, pp. 66–67.
16. Ibid., pp. 68–70.
17. Coll, *The Bin Ladens*, p. 230. Bin Ladin's savings were probably modest in 1984. It was not until 1989, during a one-time inheritance

distribution from his father's estate, that Usama received approximately $18 million in cash and company stock: ibid., pp. 347–352.
18. Azzam, *al-duktur al-shahid*, pp. 161–162.
19. Azzam, *The Lofty Mountain*, pp. 150 and 152.
20. Bergen, *The Osama Bin Laden I Know*, pp. 27–28.
21. Ibid., p. 26.
22. Author's interview with Hudhayfa Azzam, Amman, 11 September 2006.
23. Muhammad, *safahat*, p. 31.
24. Anas, *rihlati ma' al-jihad*, part 3; Abu Hilala, *awwal al-afghan al-'arab*, at 37'00" ff.
25. Wright, *The Looming Tower*, p. 98.
26. Muhammad, *safahat*, p. 85.
27. Ibid.
28. Ibid.
29. Ibid., p. 88.
30. Azzam, *al-duktur al-shahid*, pp. 161–162.
31. Bergen, *The Osama Bin Laden I Know*, p. 39.
32. Ibid., p. 88.
33. Ibid.
34. Ibid., p. 100.
35. Ibid., pp. 99–100.
36. 'kalimat al-shaykh 'abdallah 'azzam' [Words of Sheikh Abdallah Azzam], *mawsu'at al-dhakha'ir*, vol. 4, p. 1099.
37. Author's interview with Abdallah Anas, London, 27 July 2009.
38. Muhammad, *safahat*, p. 99.
39. Anas, *rihlati ma' al-jihad*, part 3.
40. Muhammad, *safahat*, p. 196. Abu Akram passed away in Amman around 2014: Anas, *rihlati ma' al-jihad*, part 3.
41. Abdallah Azzam, 'risala ila abu akram' [Letter to Abu Akram], 8 April 1986, in *mawsu'at al-dhakha'ir*, vol. 1, pp. 793–794.
42. Jarrar, *al-shahid*, p. 93.
43. Ibid., p. 344.
44. Muhammad, *safahat*, p. 99.
45. Anas says that most of the Arab students in Peshawar were Palestinians, but there were a few from other countries, notably the UAE: Anas, *rihlati ma' al-jihad*, part 4, at 12'50".
46. Muhammad, *safahat*, pp. 101 and 119.
47. Bergen, *The Osama Bin Laden I Know*, p. 40.
48. Muhammad, *safahat*, p. 105.
49. Ibid.
50. Ibid., p. 119.

51. Abu Hamza (Mahir Shalbak) was a Palestinian who had been studying in Sofia in Bulgaria when he decided to join the Afghan jihad in early 1984. He was killed in a helicopter attack in Afghanistan while on the way to Herat as part of a reconnaissance mission for the Services Bureau: Anas and Hussain, *To the Mountains*, p. 149.
52. Notin, *La Guerre de l'ombre*, p. 300.
53. Author's interview with Abdallah Anas, London, 27 July 2009.
54. Anas and Hussain, *To the Mountains*, p. 150.
55. Muhammad, *safahat*, p. 104; Camille Tawil, *Brothers in Arms: The Story of al-Qa'ida and the Arab Jihadists* (London: Saqi, 2011), p. 18. Abu Uthman's real name was Abdallah al-Falkawi.
56. Anas and Hussain, *To the Mountains*, p. 150.
57. Ibid., pp. 183, 189. We know a lot about Bayt al-Ansar, because the authors of the *Encyclopedia of Jihad* used it as a case study for reconnaissance. The *Encyclopedia* includes a long chapter on Bayt al-Ansar, complete with multiple photographs and maps, offering a snapshot of the building in April 1989. *mawsu'at al-jihad* [Encyclopaedia of Jihad] (al-Imara al-Islamiyya fi Afghanistan; Maktab al-Khadamat [1st electronic edition], 2002), pp. 158–258, http://unfulfilledduty.weebly.com/uploads/1/8/5/3/18537222/_1.pdf (accessed 15 February 2018).
58. Author's interview with Abdallah Anas, London, 27 July 2009.
59. Anas and Hussain, *To the Mountains*, p. 150.
60. See documents 109 and 113 in the Tareekh Osama collection.
61. Bergen, *The Osama Bin Laden I know*, p. 29.
62. Muhammad, *safahat*, p. 119.
63. Ibid., p. 196.
64. Zaidan, *The "Afghan Arabs" Media; al-Jihad* no. 43 (June 1988), p. 2.
65. Muhammad, *safahat*, p. 119.
66. Ibid., p. 202.
67. Ibid., p. 196.
68. Ibid., p. 119.
69. Azzam, *al-duktur al-shahid*, p. 42.
70. Ibid., p. 196.
71. Wadih El Hage said he worked for the Services Bureau in Quetta from 1986 onward: USA v Usama bin Laden et al., Southern District of New York, 2001, day 6 (15 February 2001), p. 729. More on the Quetta office in al-Qandahari, *dhikrayat*, p. 53.
72. Ibid., pp. 54 and 181. Abu Khabab may well be the same person as the Abu Khabab al-Masri who served as senior explosives instructor for al-Qaida in Afghanistan in the 1990s and early 2000s. See 'Midhat Mursi al-Sayyid 'Umar: Abu Khabab' (West Point, NY: Combating

Terrorism Center), https://ctc.usma.edu/app/uploads/2011/06/Abu-Khabab.pdf (accessed 1 September 2018).
73. al-Qandahari, *dhikrayat*, p. 185.
74. Ibid., p. 181.
75. Abdul Salam Zaeef, *My Life with the Taliban* (London: Hurst, 2010), p. 35.
76. al-Qandahari, *dhikrayat*.
77. *fi 'uyun mu'asira*, p. 82.
78. According to Basil Muhammad, Azzam "estimated that budget to an annual amount of $300 000, which included the livelihood of the Arab brothers alone so that they would not have to take other money": Muhammad, *safahat*, p. 197.
79. Estimates of Bin Ladin's contribution vary greatly, from $3,000 per month according to Abdallah Anas (Anas and Hussain, *To the Mountains*, p. 150) to $25,000 per month according to Basil Muhammad (Muhammad, *safahat*, p. 198.)
80. Muhammad, *safahat*, p. 197.
81. Anas and Hussain, *To the Mountains*, pp. 166–167.
82. Jarrar, *al-shahid*, pp. 94–95.
83. Abu Dujana eventually left to fight, after which the Reception Committee had a series of different leaders; first Abu Rida, then Abu Usayd al-Suri, and then Abu Du'a al-Yamani: Muhammad, *safahat*, p. 194.
84. Anas and Hussain, *To the Mountains*, p. 158; Mustafa Badi, *afghanistan: ihtilal al-dhakira* [Afghanistan: The Occupation of Memory] (Sanaa: unknown publisher, 2004), p. 132.
85. Muhammad, *safahat*, pp. 194–195.
86. Bergen, *The Osama Bin Laden I know*, p. 52.
87. Azzam, *al-duktur al-shahid*, p. 49.
88. Ibid.
89. She wrote an article praising Azzam after his death: *fi 'uyun mu'asira*, p. 381.
90. Azzam, *al-duktur al-shahid*, p. 50.
91. *al-Jihad* no. 37 (December 1987), p. 9.
92. Sally Neighbour, *The Mother of Mohammed: An Australian Woman's Extraordinary Journey into Jihad* (Philadelphia: University of Pennsylvania Press, 2010), p. 182.
93. Author's interview with Abdallah Anas, London, 28 March 2012.
94. The Herat delegation included Mahir Shalbak, a Palestinian, and Abdallah al-Falkawi, a Kuwaiti. The Mazar e Sharif delegation was led by Abdallah Anas and included a certain Muhammad Amin (aka Dhiya al-Rahman, a Syrian based in Kuwait) and Abu Usayd Izzatyar (a Syrian living in Amman). The names of the Arabs in the other two

delegations are not known. The Mazar-e Sharif delegation traveled with Afghans from Rabbani's Jamiat-e Islami while the Zabul delegation were accompanied by Afghans from Hizb-e Islami (we do not know who the others traveled with). Muhammad, *safahat*, pp. 102–103.
95. Anas, *rihlati ma' al-jihad*, part 5.
96. Anas, *wiladat*, pp. 61–72.
97. Alain Chevalérias, 'L'Afghanistan travaillé par les missionaires intégristes', *Journal de Genève*, 26 November 1985. Later, Chevalérias revealed that the basis for this report was a personal meeting with Abdallah Anas in the north in the spring of 1985: email correspondence with Alain Chevalérias, 13 February 2018.
98. Muhammad, *safahat*, pp. 194–195.
99. See *al-Jihad* nos. 12, 14, 15, 17, 18, 20, 21, and 22. Subsequent issues contain similar reports.
100. Zaidan, *The "Afghan Arabs" Media*, p. 74.
101. Brynjar Lia and Thomas Hegghammer, 'Jihadi Strategic Studies: The Alleged Al Qaida Policy Study Preceding the Madrid Bombings', *Studies in Conflict and Terrorism* 27, no. 5 (2004): 355–375.
102. See, for example, *al-Jihad* no. 18 (May 1986), pp. 24–27 (on the Mg-24 helicopter); *al-Jihad* no. 20 (July 1986), pp. 28–31 (on the Sukhoi airplanes); *al-Jihad* no. 22 (September 1986), pp. 26–28 (on Russian military tactics); *al-Jihad* no. 26 (January 1987), pp. 28–29 (on the use of land in combat); *al-Jihad* no. 30 (April 1987), pp. 28–31 (on Russian combat tactics in mountainous areas).
103. *al-Jihad* no. 19 (June 1986), p. 36.
104. *al-Jihad* no. 43 (June 1988), p. 15.
105. Azzam, *al-duktur al-shahid*, p. 163.
106. Muhammad, *safahat*, p. 201.
107. Ibid., p. 193.
108. In March 1985 *al-Jihad* magazine announced that "the University of Da'wa and Jihad has opened" and that "the teaching has started in the College of Shari'a": *al-Jihad* no. 4 (March 1985), p. 47. Sayyaf later said, "We began it in some tents, and only the faculty of Shari'a. Then the second year we established the faculty of Usul al-Din also. Then we established the faculty of engineering. Then we established the faculty of Agriculture. Finally we established the Medical College": author's interview with Abd Rabb al-Rasul Sayyaf, Paghman, 8 December 2017. The teaching staff included a few Saudi-trained Afghans, teachers from the International Islamic University of Islamabad, and Saudi teachers on loan from the University of Medina. The prominent Saudi cleric Musa al-Qarni notably taught there from

1986 to 1988: Jamil al-Dhiyabi, 'Saudi Academic Recounts Experiences from Afghan War', *al-Hayat* (via Ariana News), 20 March 2006. The University of Da'wa and Jihad became known in the Western press in the 1990s as an "Islamic Sandhurst" after some of its alumni became involved in international terrorism, such as Ramzi Yusuf, who instigated the 1993 World Trade Center bombing in New York: Mary Anne Weaver, 'The Children of the Jihad', *New Yorker*, 12 June 1995. In the late 1990s the university ceased operations in Pabbi and reopened in Kabul, where it exists today as Dawat University.

109. Author's interview with Abd Rabb al-Rasul Sayyaf, Paghman, 8 December 2017.
110. Azzam, *al-duktur al-shahid*, p. 49; 'jami'at al-da'wa wa'l-jihad' [University of Da'wa and Jihad], *al-Jihad* no. 5 (April 1985), pp. 32–35; *al-Jihad* no. 15 (January 1986), pp. 33–37. See also the four-page feature article on the university in *al-Bunyan al-Marsus* no. 10 (November 1986), pp. 34–37.
111. Azzam, *al-duktur al-shahid*, p. 49; Muhammad, *safahat*, p. 193.
112. Abdallah Azzam, *The Scales of Allah*, n.d., www.khilafahbooks.com/the-scales-of-allah-swt-by-shaykh-abdullah-azzam/, p. 18 (accessed 3 December 2016).
113. Azzam, *al-duktur al-shahid*, p. 49.
114. Zaidan, *The "Afghan Arabs" Media*, p. 11.
115. Muhammad, *safahat*, p. 201; Jarrar, *al-shahid*, pp. 94–95.
116. al-Qandahari, *dhikrayat*, pp. 217–218.
117. See, for example, Ahmad Zaidan's overview of Arab charities in Peshawar: Zaidan, *The "Afghan Arabs" Media*, p. 10.
118. Bergen, *The Osama Bin Laden I Know*, p. 63.
119. Azzam, *al-duktur al-shahid*, p. 48.
120. *Mawsu'at al-dhakha'ir*, vol. 3, p. 1133.
121. Badi, *afghanistan: ihtilal al-dhakira*, pp. 132–137.
122. Muhammad, *safahat*, pp. 193–194; Azzam, *al-duktur al-shahid*, p. 49.
123. Muhammad, *safahat*, pp. 193–194; Azzam, *al-duktur al-shahid*, p. 49.
124. Muhammad, *safahat*, p. 201.
125. Ibid., pp. 193–194; Azzam, *al-duktur al-shahid*, p. 49.
126. Muhammad, *safahat*, p. 193.
127. Ibid., p. 201.
128. Ibid., pp. 193–194.
129. Ibid., p. 194.
130. Richard Miniter, *Mastermind: The Many Faces of the 9/11 Architect, Khalid Shaikh Mohammed* (New York: Sentinel, 2011), p. 59.

131. Muhammad, *safahat*, p. 194. *Al-Jihad* no. 33 (August 1987), p. 47 includes a recruitment poster for medics, which says interested doctors can call "Brother Doctor Abu Hasan" for further information.
132. Muhammad, *safahat*, p. 139.
133. Ibid., p. 121.
134. See also Azzam, *al-duktur al-shahid*, p. 49.
135. Muhammad, *safahat*, p. 194.
136. Ibid., p. 142.
137. Ibid., p. 194.
138. Ibid., p. 140.
139. Ibid., pp. 194 and 201.
140. Ibid., pp. 193–194.
141. USA v Usama bin Laden et al., Southern District of New York, 2001, day 5 (14 February 2001), pp. 549–550 and 556–557.
142. Azzam, *al-duktur al-shahid*, p. 48. Some of the books for Afghans produced and distributed by the Services Bureau are showcased in *al-Jihad* no. 17 (March 1986), pp. 24–25. The Bureau had its own printing press, which it used to produce books and posters: al-Bilali, 'majallat al-jihad fi 'amihi al-khamis', p. 42.
143. Azzam, *al-duktur al-shahid*, pp. 43 and 47.
144. Anas and Hussain, *To the Mountains*, p. 153.
145. Zaidan, *The "Afghan Arabs" Media*, pp. 87–88.
146. Muhammad, *safahat*, p. 194. The name Mirror of Afghan Jihad first appears in an advertisement on the back cover of issue 13 of *al-Jihad* (November 1985). Similar advertisements appear intermittently in 1986 and 1987, but then they cease to appear.
147. Ibid., p. 194; author's interview with Ahmad Zaidan, Islamabad, 18 March 2008.
148. *al-Jihad* no. 34 (September 1987), pp. 38–39.
149. The last issue I have seen is number 117, from January/February 1995.
150. *Al-Mujahid* had been established on the initiative of, and with money from, Mustafa Muhammad al-Tahhan, the general secretary of the International Islamic Federation of Students' Organizations (IIFSO), who visited Peshawar in 1982: Zaidan, *The "Afghan Arabs" Media*, pp. 40–41.
151. Author's interview with Jamal Isma'il, Islamabad, 20 March 2008. The first issue of *al-Jihad* magazine only briefly acknowledged the connection, noting on page 3 that "*al-Jihad* magazine is the same as *al-Mujahid* magazine, but in a new form [*qalib*]." The editor, Imad al-Abid, also mentioned the connection in a 1989 interview: al-Bilali, 'majallat al-jihad fi 'amihi al-khamis', p. 43.

152. The sources do not say why al-Abid was chosen, other than that he had "a desire to join the jihad of the pen": Zaidan, *The "Afghan Arabs" Media*, p. 41.
153. Ibid., pp. 41–43 and 46; *al-Jihad* no. 45 (August 1988), p. 15.
154. Author's interview with Ahmad Zaidan, Islamabad, 18 March 2008.
155. Zaidan writes that the long article in issue 19 about the Soviet intervention was written by Hamid: Zaidan, *The "Afghan Arabs" Media*, p. 43.
156. One source noted, "He wrote on martyrs under the name 'Abu Muhammad'": *al-Bunyan al-Marsus* 30 (February 1990), p. 9. In a note to the article 'afghanistan am khurasan?' Azzam's posthumous editors write, "This article was published ... under the name 'Dr. Hassan Abd al-Rahman'": *mawsu'at al-dhakha'ir*, vol. 1, p. 787. For the use of "Sadiq Amin" see *al-Jihad* no. 29 (April 1987), p. 21. For "Abu Muhammad" see, for example, *al-Jihad* no. 12 (October 1985), p. 34 and *al-Jihad* no. 17 (March 1986), p. 12.
157. Azzam, *al-duktur al-shahid*, p. 48.
158. Zaidan, *The "Afghan Arabs" Media*, p. 41.
159. Ibid., p. 40; Bergen, *The Osama Bin Laden I Know*, p. 34.
160. Zaidan, *The "Afghan Arabs" Media*, p. 42.
161. al-Bilali, 'majallat al-jihad fi 'amihi al-khamis', p. 42.
162. See, for example, *al-Jihad* no. 18 (May 1986), p. 2, and *al-Jihad* no. 44 (July 1988), p. 14.
163. 'yusuf islam fi ard al-ribat' [Yusuf Islam in the Land of Ribat], *al-Jihad*, no. 17 (March 1986): 20–22; This was also the first of two issues of *al-Jihad* that included a section in English, consisting mainly of the Cat Stevens interview (p. 44). Presumably the editors had hoped to attract more attention by making the interview available in English. The English supplement was discontinued after issue 18. *Al-Bunyan al-Marsus* also published an interview with Cat Stevens in connection with the same visit: see *al-Bunyan al-Marsus* no. 6 (May 1986), pp. 40–42.
164. See *al-Jihad* no. 28 (March 1987), p. 46 and *al-Jihad* no. 32 (July 1987), p. 47.
165. *al-Jihad* no. 34 (September 1987), pp. 38–39. The recording had actually been advertised first in *al-Bunyan al-Marsus* no. 14 (July 1987), p. 43.
166. Zaidan, *The "Afghan Arabs" Media*, p. 38.
167. Ibid.
168. Ibid., p. 39.
169. al-Bilali, 'majallat al-jihad fi 'amihi al-khamis', p. 43.
170. Author's interview with Ahmad Zaidan, Islamabad, 18 March 2008.

171. For example, issue 11 (p. 44) features a letter from Dr. Ramadan Safar, general secretary of the Islamic Assembly (al-Tajammu' al-Islami) in France, requesting 100 copies for distribution in France.
172. *al-Jihad* no. 27 (February 1987), p. 3.
173. *al-Jihad* no. 48 (October 1988), p. 1.
174. al-Bilali, 'majallat al-jihad fi 'amihi al-khamis', p. 42.
175. *al-Bunyan al-Marsus* was also distributed internationally. Issue 22–23, for example, lists the addresses of distributors in Saudi Arabia, Qatar, Oman, Jordan, Sudan, Kuwait, the UAE, Canada, America, Sweden, West Germany, and the UK. However, this is a smaller network than that of *al-Jihad*, and the letters to the editors in *al-Bunyan al-Marsus* suggest a less international readership.
176. Zaidan, *The "Afghan Arabs" Media*; author's interview with Ahmad Zaidan, Islamabad, 18 March 2008.
177. Azzam, 'dhikrayat min sahat al-jihad' and *al-Bunyan al-Marsus* no. 5 (February 1986), pp. 38–39.
178. al-Bilali, 'majallat al-jihad fi 'amihi al-khamis'.
179. For a hagiographic catalogue of Azzam's personality traits and ethics see Azzam, *min manaqib al-imam*.
180. Bergen, *The Osama Bin Laden I Know*, p. 68.
181. Muhammad, *safahat*, pp. 195–200.
182. Ibid., p. 119.
183. Ibid., p. 196.
184. Ibid., p. 194.
185. Ibid., p. 162.
186. *fi 'uyun mu'asira*, p. 40.
187. Zaidan, *The "Afghan Arabs" Media*, p. 43.
188. Ibid., p. 48.
189. USA v Usama bin Laden et al., Southern District of New York, 2001, day 5 (14 February 2001), pp. 553–554.
190. Muhammad, *safahat*, p. 205.
191. Ibid., pp. 195–200.
192. Ibid.
193. Ibid., p. 195.
194. Ibid., pp. 195–200.
195. Ibid.
196. Ibid.
197. Anonymous, *Through our Enemies' Eyes: Osama Bin Laden, Radical Islam and the Future of America* (Washington, DC: Brassey's, 2002), p. 94.
198. Wright, *The Looming Tower*, p. 170. According to Jamal al-Fadl, it was Abu Hajir who first provided the religious justification inside al-

Qaida for attacking American targets. Al-Fadl says Abu Hajir issued a series of fatwas in Sudan in late 1992 and 1993 justifying attacks on US targets in Somalia and in Saudi Arabia: USA v Usama bin Laden et al., Southern District of New York, 2001, day 2 (6 February 2001), pp. 265–270.
199. Jarrar, *al-shahid*, p. 94.

Recruiter

1. Azzam, *'ibar wa basa'ir*, p. 51.
2. Ibid., pp. 68 ff.
3. *al-Jihad* no. 20 (July 1986), p. 13.
4. 'kalimat al-shaykh 'abdallah 'azzam' [The Words of Sheikh Abdallah Azzam], in *mawsu'at al-dhakha'ir*, vol. 4, p. 1100.
5. 'ila fadilat al-shaykh abu bakr al-jaza'iri' [To his Excellency Sheikh Abu Bakr al-Jaza'iri], 9 June 1989, in *mawsu'at al-dhakha'ir*, vol. 2, pp. 358–359.
6. See, for example, his interviews with *al-Mughtarab* magazine (undated), *al-Ukaz* (undated), and *al-Mawqif* (late 1989): *mawsu'at al-dhakha'ir*, vol. 1, pp. 789–793; ibid., vol. 2, pp. 333–340. See also the collection of interviews in Abdallah Azzam, *al-as'ila wa'l-ajwiba al-jihadiyya* [Jihadi Questions and Answers] (Minbar al-Tawhid wa'l-Jihad, n.d.).
7. Azzam, *al-as'ila wa'l-ajwiba*, pp. 5–23.
8. Author's telephone interview with Jamal Khashoggi, 14 September 2018. Khashoggi said he politely declined the invitation, but instead wrote a series of articles for *al-Muslimun* newspaper about Azzam's trip based on a long interview with him.
9. A former student of Azzam's in Islamabad in 1984–1985 said, "I always found him in class, so he can't have been traveling that much": author's interview with Atiq-u-Zafar, Islamabad, 20 March 2008.
10. *fi 'uyun mu'asira*, p. 85.
11. Author's interview with Abu Suhayb, Jenin, 4 May 2008; Badi, *afghanistan: ihtilal al-dhakira*, p. 197; *fi 'uyun mu'asira*, p. 197.
12. Author's telephone interview with Jamal Khashoggi, 14 September 2018.
13. Badi, *afghanistan: ihtilal al-dhakira*, p. 197.
14. Abu Rumman and Sa'id, *al-'alim*, p. 84.
15. *fi 'uyun mu'asira*, pp. 98 and 101.
16. Author's interview with Hudhayfa Azzam, Amman, 11 September 2006.
17. Author's interview with Jamal Isma'il, Islamabad, 18 March 2008.
18. Author's interview with Hasan Abu Hanieh, Amman, 6 November 2015.
19. Lia, *Architect of Global Jihad*, p. 53.

20. Author's interview with Fayiz Azzam, al-Sila al-Harithiyya, 4 May 2008.
21. Author's interview with Abu Harith, Amman, 8 May 2008.
22. Miller, *The Audacious Ascetic*, p. 86.
23. Shiraz Maher, 'The Future of Unholy War', *Standpoint Magazine*, November 2008.
24. Cooley, *Unholy Wars*, p. 87.
25. Azzam, *The Lofty Mountain*, p. 48; Azzam, 'ya muslimiy al-'alam: intabahu', p. 27.
26. Azzam, *The Lofty Mountain*, p. 48.
27. Jarrar, *al-shahid*, pp. 97–98.
28. Author's interview with Isam al-Attar, Aachen, 16 December 2009.
29. Jamal Khashoggi said he met Abdallah Azzam at a MAYA conference in the early 1980s and that he was fairly certain it was in 1981 in Springfield, Illinois: author's telephone interview with Jamal Khashoggi, 14 September 2018. However, I have not been able to confirm that there was a MAYA conference in Springfield that year.
30. Author's interview with Hudhayfa Azzam, Amman, 11 September 2006.
31. Azzam, *al-duktur al-shahid*, pp. 161–162.
32. USA v Usama bin Laden et al., Southern District of New York, 2001, day 5 (14 February 2001), p. 544.
33. Author's interview with Hudhayfa Azzam, Amman, 11 September 2006.
34. Jarrar, *al-shahid*, pp. 340 and 342.
35. Author's interview with Hudhayfa Azzam, Amman, 11 September 2006; author's interview with Hasan Abu Hanieh, Amman, 6 November 2015.
36. Bergen, *The Osama Bin Laden I Know*, p. 31.
37. Azzam, *'ibar wa basa'ir*, p. 51.
38. Abdallah Azzam, 'mu'tamar al-talaba fi britaniya' [Student Conference in Britain], in *mawsu'at al-dhakha'ir*, vol. 3, pp. 879–887. The document is not dated, but the content of his remarks suggests it was around 1985–1986.
39. *fi 'uyun mu'asira*, p. 283. He gave a lecture there together with Mahmud Ubaydat.
40. Ibid., p. 45.
41. *al-Jihad* no. 39 (February 1988), pp. 40–41.
42. Zak Ebrahim, *The Terrorist's Son: A Story of Choice* (New York: Simon & Schuster, 2014), p. 31.
43. Steven Emerson, 'The Suspect Ties of CAIR Officials, Fundraisers and Trainers' (The Investigative Project, 2008), p. 8.
44. J. M. Berger, ed., *Beatings and Bureaucracy: The Founding Memos of Al Qaeda* (Intelwire Press, 2012), Kindle version, location 764.

45. *mawsu'at al-dhakha'ir*, vol. 3, pp. 906–922; ibid., vol. 2, p. 199. He was on a panel on Palestine with Ahmad al-Qattan and Muhammad Sayyam (Siyam). For the Fort Worth lecture, see 'Neutrality Matter – Afghanistan', FBI Dallas Office, 10 October 1989 (obtained through FOIA request).
46. Salah, *waqa'i' sanawat al-jihad*, p. 157.
47. A video recording titled 'From Kabul to al-Quds' shows Azzam lecturing in Seattle in 1988: video file in author's possession.
48. Jarrar, *al-shahid*, pp. 97–98; Basil Muhammad interviewed Azzam in the UAE on 2 April 1989; Muhammad, *safahat*, p. 34.
49. Azzam, *al-duktur al-shahid*, p. 136.
50. *al-Mujtama'*, no. 944, in Amir, *al-shaykh al-mujahid*, pp. 89–100.
51. *fi 'uyun mu'asira*, p. 236.
52. Abdallah Azzam, 'jihad wa hajat al-umma 'alayhi' [Jihad and the Umma's Need for it], video file in author's possession.
53. Azzam once wrote, "I could never forget my visit to Spain as I was making my way around Grenada and Cordoba": Abdallah Azzam, *The Ruling on Meat Slaughtered in the West*, translation of 2nd ed. (Minbar al-Tawhid wa'l-Jihad, 1989), pp. 4 and 6. Azzam gave at least one lecture in Germany that was recorded, and Isam al-Attar has said that Azzam visited him in Aachen once in the late 1980s. Abdallah Azzam, 'muhadara fi almania' [Lecture in Germany], in *mawsu'at al-dhakha'ir*, vol. 3, pp. 989–994. There is a picture of him in the lecture theatre in Germany in Jarrar, *al-shahid*, p. 99; author's interview with Isam al-Attar, Aachen, 16 December 2009.
54. One source mentions that "he only left the battlefront to attend Islamic conferences in America, France, Britain, and Italy": *fi 'uyun mu'asira*, p. 265. A Jordanian who studied in Greece in the mid-1980s said Azzam was due to speak in Athens at one point, but decided in the last minute to send a representative. The same source says he heard that Azzam had previously visited Greece: author's interview with Basim Ghozlan, Oslo, 30 October 2018.
55. 'al-jihad fi afghanistan' [Jihad in Afghanistan], video file in author's possession.
56. *fi 'uyun mu'asira*, p. 85.
57. Azzam, *al-duktur al-shahid*, p. 92.
58. al-Qandahari, *dhikrayat*, p. 241.
59. *al-Bunyan al-Marsus* no. 30 (February 1990), p. 7.
60. Fred W. Lindecke, '5,000 Muslim Students Spending Holidays at St. Louis Convention', *St. Louis Post*, 25 December 1983.
61. Jarrar, *al-shahid*, pp. 340 and 342.

62. Azzam, 'muhadara fi almania'; see also Azzam, *al-duktur al-shahid*, p. 259.
63. Azzam, 'muhadara fi almania', p. 994.
64. Nico Prucha, 'Abdallah Azzam's Outlook for Jihad in 1988 – "al-Jihad between Kabul and Jerusalem"' (Research Institute for European and American Studies, 2010), p. 5.
65. Abu Bakr al-Zayla'i, 'Verily, I am the Naked Warner' (al-Haqa'iq Media, 1 May 2013), p. 4, http://jihadology.net/2013/05/01/release-from-shaykh-abu-bakr-al-zaylai-an-open-letter-verily-i-am-the-naked-warner/ (accessed 11 November 2015).
66. 'Interview with Sheikh al-Mujahideen Abu Abdel Aziz', *al-Sirat al-Mustaqeem* no. 33 (1994).
67. Ebrahim, *The Terrorist's Son*, pp. 31–32.
68. Miniter, *Mastermind*, pp. 68–69.
69. Sean O'Neill and Daniel McGrory, *The Suicide Factory: Abu Hamza and the Finsbury Park Mosque* (London: HarperCollins, 2006), pp. 14–15.
70. Azzam, *The Lofty Mountain*, p. 53.
71. For biographies of al-Adnani, see ibid. and 'qissat hayat al-mujahid al-shaykh tamim muhammad al-'adnani' [The Story of the Life of the Mujahid Shaykh Tamim al-Adnani], *al-Jihad* no. 62 (December 1989): 24–34. See also 'al-shaykh tamim al-'adnani yatahaddath li'l-jihad' [Sheikh Tamim al-Adnani Speaks to *al-Jihad*], *al-Jihad* no. 32 (July 1987): 35–39.
72. Azzam, *The Lofty Mountain*, pp. 24 ff.
73. Ibid., pp. 22, 24–25, and 28.
74. Ibid., p. 21. Azzam wrote: "I first met him in 1982 when he visited me at my home in Jordan during the summer."
75. Ibid., p. 74.
76. Ibid., p. 39.
77. Ibid., pp. 73–74.
78. Ibid., p. 40.
79. Ibid., pp. 40–41.
80. Ibid., p. 41.
81. In the interview he says this is his first trip to the USA, and he says it is the second day of Ramadan. He also talks about a previous visit to Bulgaria – but it is not clear when or for what purpose that trip was made: 'Interview with Sheikh Tameem al Adnani'.
82. Tamim al-Adnani's speaking schedule in the United States and Canada, December 1988, document in author's possession. I am grateful to Brian Fishman for sharing it.

83. Azzam, *The Lofty Mountain*, pp. 50 ff.
84. Ibid., pp. 52–53.
85. Ibid., p. 54.
86. Some sources have suggested that the Services Bureau ran an organized recruitment operation in Saudi Arabia. Lawrence Wright, for example, writes that "paid agents [in Jeddah] rounded up prospects, pocketing half of the money – typically several hundred dollars – that the recruits received when they signed up": Wright, *The Looming Tower*, p. 97. However, Wright's primary source is actually describing a recruitment operation by the Egyptian Islamic Jihad in the late 1980s, in which a Jeddah-based member is paying another member to recruit in Cairo: see Salah, *waqa'i' sanawat al-jihad*, pp. 80–82. There is no hard evidence that the Services Bureau had an office or a network of recruitment officers in Saudi Arabia. Another source claimed that Bin Ladin ran a recruitment pipeline from Cairo via Jeddah to Peshawar using his father's construction company. He supposedly used the Bin Ladin Group's recruitment office in Cairo to get visas for Egyptian jihadis, whom he then lodged in a guest house in Jeddah before sending them on to Peshawar: Khalid Khalil As'ad, *muqatil min makka: al-qissa al-kamila li-usama bin ladin* [Warrior from Mecca: The Complete Story of Usama bin Ladin] (London: al-I'lam li'l-Nashr, 2000), pp. 29–30. However, this appears to be a false rumor or, at best, something that was done irregularly.
87. Muhammad, *safahat*, p. 85.
88. Ibid., p. 227.
89. For example, when Muhammad Siddique (from the MAYA conference in Missouri mentioned above) went back to the USA in mid-1984 after a stint in Peshawar, Azzam tasked him with spreading the word about his fatwa on the Afghan jihad.
90. The organization was also known as Afghan Refugee Services, Inc. Sources diverge on who exactly started it. One source says al-Kifah was founded by Khalid Abu al-Dhahab and later officially registered by Mustafa Shalabi, Fawaz Damara, and Ali al-Shinawi: Huda Al-Salih, 'How al-Qaeda was Born in a Tiny Office in New York', al-Arabiya English, 14 October 2016, http://ara.tv/px8ak. Some of these questions might be answered in the future with better sources. Steven Emerson writes that he obtained the internal archive of al-Kifah, some 4,000–5,000 documents from before 1993, but these have not been made available: Steven Emerson, *American Jihad: The Terrorists Living among us* (New York: Free Press, 2002), pp. 21–22.
91. Benjamin Weiser, Susan Sachs, and David Kocieniewski, 'US Sees Brooklyn Link to World Terror Network', *New York Times*, 22 October 1998.

92. Abdallah Azzam, 'du'a wa thana' [Supplication and Tribute], *al-Jihad* no. 39 (February 1988): 40–41.
93. For example, an al-Kifah fundraising poster from the mid-1990s read "Al-Kifah Refugee Center is an organization founded by Sh. Abdullah Azzam": see www.investigativeproject.org/documents/751-al-kifah-boston-advertisement.pdf (accessed 4 November 2016).
94. According to Steven Emerson, who cited interviews with *al-Jihad* editors in 1994, over half of the 50,000 copies of *al-Jihad* magazine in 1989 were distributed in America: Steven Emerson, 'Inside the Osama Bin Laden Investigation', *Journal of Counterterrorism and Security International* 5, no. 3(1998): 16–26.
95. Berger, *Jihad Joe*, p. 11.
96. Abottabad document PDF-023412, p. 3 (available at www.cia.gov/library/abbottabad-compound/index_converted_documents.html). The identity of the person behind the quotation is not known.
97. Alison Mitchell, 'After Blast, New Interest in Holy-War Recruits in Brooklyn', *New York Times*, 11 April 1993.
98. *9/11 Commission Report*, p. 58.
99. Bergen, *The Osama Bin Laden I Know*, p. 33.
100. *al-Jihad* no. 47 (October 1988), p. 3.
101. Berger, *Jihad Joe*, p. 8.
102. Ronald Sandee, *America's First al-Qa'ida Fighters* (New York: NEFA Foundation, April 2010).
103. Some writers have argued that Azzam's activities were government orchestrated. John Cooley, for example, claimed that the CIA "used [Azzam] as a recruiter for the Afghanistan jihad in the United States." However, he provides no supporting evidence, and the claim is best considered as a conspiracy theory: Cooley, *Unholy Wars*, p. 202.
104. Documents pertaining to case titled 'Abdula Azzam; Motez (LNU); *REDACTED*; Neutrality matter – Afghanistan; 00: Dallas', Federal Bureau of Investigation, March–November 1989. The FOIA request was submitted by this author in 2008.
105. See, for example, Petter Nesser, *Islamist Terrorism in Europe: A History* (London: Hurst, 2015).
106. According to Lorenzo Vidino, "American-based … Brotherhood networks … have been able to establish a presence that significantly overshadows their European counterparts in terms of organization, funds, and almost monopolistic access to government": Lorenzo Vidino, *The New Muslim Brotherhood in the West* (New York: Columbia University Press, 2010), p. 166.

107. Writing in 1991, Johnson described these organizations as effectively "Ikhwan-controlled": Steve A. Johnson, 'Political Activity of Muslims in America', in *The Muslims of America*, ed. Yvonne Yazbeck Haddad (New York: Oxford University Press, 1991), pp. 111–124, p. 121. See also Alyssa A. Lappen, 'The Muslim Brotherhood in North America', in *The Muslim Brotherhood: The Organization and Policies of a Global Islamist Movement*, ed. Barry Rubin (New York: Palgrave Macmillan, 2010), 161–180.
108. Johnson writes that after Ahmed Zaki, an Egyptian Muslim Brother, became leader of ISNA in 1986, "invited speakers ... included many more overseas members of the Ikhwan than in the past": 'Political Activity of Muslims', p. 122.
109. Lia, *Architect of Global Jihad*, p. 70; Anas and Hussain, *To the Mountains*, p. 225.
110. al-Qandahari, *dhikrayat*, p. 44.
111. *fi 'uyun mu'asira*, p. 101.
112. Salah, *waqa'i' sanawat al-jihad*, pp. 71–72; Caryle Murphy and Steve Coll, 'The Making of an Islamic Symbol: US Spotlight has Elevated Radical Sheik's Status in Muslim World', *Washington Post*, 9 July 1993.
113. Khaled al-Berry, *Life is More Beautiful than Paradise: A Jihadist's Own Story* (Cairo: American University in Cairo Press, 2009), p. 115.
114. Ibid., p. 27.
115. Salah, *waqa'i' sanawat al-jihad*, pp. 80–82.
116. Mokeddem, *Les Afghans algériens*, p. 13.
117. As'ad, *muqatil min makka*, p. 32.
118. Strick van Linschoten and Kuehn, *An Enemy we Created*, p. 52.
119. Author's telephone interview with Alastair Crooke, 23 March 2008.
120. The full details and reasoning behind these estimates are too extensive to include in this book, but are available on the website www.azzambook.net.
121. Davis writes that "the early 1990s were notable too for the growth in the number of Kashmiris and Pakistani Punjabis among the foreign contingent. This development reflected the increasing involvement of Pakistan's Jamaat-i-Islami": Davis, 'Foreign Combatants in Afghanistan', p. 330.
122. Anas, *wiladat*, p. 61.
123. Muhammad, *safahat*, p. 206; Davis, 'Foreign Combatants in Afghanistan'; Edwards, *Before Taliban*, p. 270.
124. Bergen, *The Osama Bin Laden I Know*, pp. 41–42. James Bruce writes that the Arab Afghans included "some 5000 Saudis, 3000 Yemenis, 2000 Egyptians, 2800 Algerians, 400 Tunisians, 370 Iraqis, 200

Libyans, and scores of Jordanians." However, he provides no source for this information, and several of these numbers are implausibly high (such as that for Algeria) or curiously specific (such as that for Iraq): James Bruce, 'Arab Veterans of the Afghan War', *Jane's Intelligence Review* 7, no. 1 (1995): 178–180. See also Davis, 'Foreign Combatants in Afghanistan'.
125. For example, in 1986 the jihadi magazine *al-Bunyan al-Marsus* provided country backgrounds for seventy-nine Arabs who had fallen in battle: *al-Bunyan al-Marsus* 26 (March 1986), pp. 48–51.
126. I had used this method with some success to reconstruct the membership of other jihadi groups. See, for example, Thomas Hegghammer, 'Terrorist Recruitment and Radicalisation in Saudi Arabia', *Middle East Policy* 13, no. 4 (2006): 39–60.
127. Lia, *Architect of Global Jihad*, pp. 73–74.
128. Ferzede Kaya, 'Turks who Fought in Afghanistan', *Turkish Daily News*, 17 October 2001.
129. Author's interview with Isam al-Attar, Aachen, 16 December 2009.
130. Two French journalists encountered a white Frenchman, a former librarian, "who had converted to Islam in 1970, was convinced of jihad as a sacred duty and had only Saudi Arabia as a reference": Notin, *La Guerre de l'ombre*, p. 299.
131. One Afghan Arab noted, "We went to Salman Al Farsi with a large assortment of new brothers, around 20 to 25 brothers from all over. We even had some from South Africa!"; Muhammad, *safahat*, p. 145.
132. *fi 'uyun mu'asira*, p. 477.
133. Seidelin, *Allahs danske krigere*, epub paragraphs 11.1–16.
134. 'Abu 'Ubayda al-Banshiri' (Combating Terrorism Center at West Point, 2008), https://ctc.usma.edu/wp-content/uploads/2011/06/Abu_Ubayda_al-Banshiri.pdf (accessed 24 January 2018).
135. Abigail Hauslohner, 'Friend of Zawahiri: The Tangled Tale of the Mild-Mannered Salafi', *Time*, 11 July 2011.

Ideologue

1. Muhammad, *safahat*, pp. 196–197.
2. Jarrar, *al-shahid*, p. 345.
3. Muhammad, *safahat*, p. 65.
4. Advertisements in *al-Jihad* magazine tell us which nine books were published in his lifetime. These were: *Signs of the Merciful in the Afghan Jihad* (1983), *Defense of Muslim lands* (1985), *Lessons and Insights on Jihad in the Current Age* (1986), *Proper Conduct and Rulings in Jihad* (1986), *The Lost Beacon* (1987), *Join the Caravan*

(1987), *Jihad of a Muslim People* (1988), *Hamas: Historical Roots and Charter* (1989), and *Words from the First Line of Fire* (1989). See *al-Jihad* no. 48 (November 1988), p. 3, and *al-Jihad* no. 58 (August 1989), back page. All the other works circulating online as books are posthumously published manuscripts, article compilations, and transcribed lectures.

5. *al-Bunyan al-Marsus* no. 30 (February 1990), p. 13.
6. Ibid., p. 27.
7. Anas and Hussain, *To the Mountains*, p. 154.
8. al-Ansari, *mafhum*.
9. In *fi zilal surat al-tawba* he said he was influenced by al-Albani, and that "I am Salafi in my belief and thought": 'The Words of Abdallah Azzam', p. 59. On Ibn Taymiyya see e.g. Azzam, *'ibar wa basa'ir*, pp. 22 ff. and 53. On *al wala' wa'l-bara'* see e.g. Abdallah Azzam, 'al-qa'ida al-sulba' [The Solid Base], *al-Jihad* no. 41 (April 1988): 4–6; and *al-Jihad* no. 45 (August 1988), pp. 4–6.
10. Abu Qatada al-Filastini, 'shaykh al-jihad wa 'alam al-din wa'l-shahada 'abdallah 'azzam' [Shaykh of Jihad and Symbol of the Religion and Martyrdom Abdallah Azzam], Justpaste.it, 23 September 2015, p. 5, https://justpaste.it/nxcm (accessed 24 September 2015).
11. Anas and Hussain, *To the Mountains*, p. 148.
12. Ibid., p. 161.
13. From sermon titled 'al-nas asnaf' [People are Different], 26 September 1986: 'The Words of Abdallah Azzam', pp. 6–7.
14. For example, in an article titled 'al-qaba'il wa'l-jihad' [The Tribes and Jihad], Azzam criticized Pashtun tribes in Afghanistan and Pakistan: *al-Jihad* no. 17 (March 1986), pp. 4–7.
15. For example, he said "the blood that runs on the mountains of the Hindu Kush and Kabul is the same blood that runs on the mountains of Nablus and Jerusalem and Hebron and Gaza": Azzam, *al-duktur al-shahid*, p. 173.
16. Laleh Khalili, *Heroes and Martyrs of Palestine: The Politics of National Commemoration* (Cambridge: Cambridge University Press, 2007), p. 26.
17. Azzam was not a complete ecumenist; he usually spoke of Shiites with emotional distance, and he was very critical of the Alawite regime in Syria, but he was nowhere near as hostile to Shiites as many of today's jihadi groups. According to his wife, "He never once declared Shiites as infidels. He opposed the killing of Shiites": Aziz, "abdallah 'azzam wa juhuduhu', p. 30.
18. 'The Words of Abdallah Azzam', pp. 51–52.
19. Hamid and Farrall, *The Arabs*, p. 84.

20. 'The Words of Abdallah Azzam', pp. 51–52.
21. Azzam, *'ibar wa basa'ir*, p. 114. See also Amir, *al-shaykh al-mujahid*, p. 100.
22. Shiraz Maher, *Salafi-Jihadism: The History of an Idea* (Oxford: Oxford University Press, 2016), pp. 158 ff.
23. Abdallah Azzam, *The Tawhid of Action* (Tibyan Publications, n.d.), www.khilafahbooks.com/the-tawhid-of-action-by-imam-abdullah-azzam/ (accessed 3 December 2016).
24. Ibid., p. 5.
25. Abdallah Azzam, *ilhaq bi'l-qafila* [Join the Caravan], Minbar al-Tawhid wa'l-Jihad, 1987, p. 23. Azzam is largely correct regarding the scriptural basis for jihad as a primarily spiritual endeavor. The famous Hadith according to which the Prophet said "We have come back from the lesser jihad to the greater jihad" features in a marginal hadith collection (al-Bayhaqi's *al-Zuhd al-Kabir*) and is considered weak by most senior Muslim scholars past and present.
26. Abdallah Azzam, 'min kabul ila al-quds' [From Kabul to Jerusalem], *al-Jihad* no. 52 (1989): 47.
27. Abdallah Azzam, *'ushshaq al-hur* [Those who Love the Virgins of Paradise], n.d., www.almeshkat.net/book/1242, pp. 7 and 190 (accessed 9 March 2018).
28. Michael Cook, *Ancient Religions, Modern Politics: The Islamic Case in Comparative Perspective* (Princeton: Princeton University Press, 2014), pp. 225–228.
29. Azzam, *The Tawhid of Action*, p. 4.
30. Azzam, *ilhaq bi'l-qafila*, pp. 15 and 21 (Minbar edition); Azzam, *'ibar wa basa'ir*, pp. 27–28.
31. Anthony Hyman, 'Arab Involvement in the Afghan War', *Beirut Review* no. 7 (1994): 73–90, p. 78.
32. Azzam, *'ibar wa basa'ir*, p. 50.
33. Abdallah Azzam, 'ayat wa basha'ir wa karamat fi'l-jihad al-afghani' [Signs, Tidings, and Miracles in the Afghan Jihad], *al-Mujtama'* no. 569 (4 May 1982): 28–30.
34. Azzam, *'ibar wa basa'ir*, p. 60.
35. Ibid., p. 110.
36. As early as January 1985, issue 2 of *al-Jihad* magazine (p. 2) contained an advertisement for the third edition of *Signs of the Merciful*.
37. According to Abdallah Anas, "The majority of those who came had read ... The Signs of the Merciful": Anas and Hussain, *To the Mountains*, p. 156. Basil Muhammad wrote, "I myself heard many brothers who had decided to devote themselves to the Afghan jihad at a young age or to participate in it, who attribute their choice to what

they had read in that book": Muhammad, *safahat*, p. 65. Another Afghan Arab wrote, "*Signs of the Merciful* made hundreds of young Arab men go to Peshawar": *al-Bunyan al-Marsus* no. 30 (February 1990), p. 8.

38. Nasir al-Fahd, 'ayat al-rahman fi "ghazwat sibtimbar"' [Signs of the Merciful in the "September Raid"] (Minbar al-Tawhid wa'l-Jihad, 2002); Diyab Hasan al-Mahdawi, *ayat al-rahman fi filastin walubnan* [Signs of the Merciful in Palestine and Lebanon] (Beirut: Dar al-Mahajja al-Bayda', 2007).
39. After he died, many of them were compiled in to a book titled '*ushshaq al-hur* [Those who Love the Virgins of Paradise].
40. For a catalogue of martyr biographies published in these magazines, see Azzam, '*ushshaq al-hur* and *The Martyrs of Afghanistan* (Azzam Publications, n.d.), www.islamicline.com/islamicbooks/new/current/The_Shuhadaa_of_Afghanistan%28www.islamicline.com%29.pdf (accessed 9 March 2018); and Muhammad Amir Rana and Mubasher Bukhari, *Arabs in Afghan Jihad* (Lahore: Pak Institute for Peace Studies, 2007).
41. Azzam, *The Scales of Allah*, pp. 13–14.
42. Nasser al-Bahri and Georges Malbrunot, *Dans l'ombre de Ben Laden: révélations de son garde du corps repenti* (Paris: Michel Lafon, 2010), p. 23.
43. Pierre Centlivres and Micheline Centlivres-Demont, 'Les martyrs afghans par le texte et l'image (1978–1992)', in *Saints et héros du Moyen-Orient Contemporain. Actes du colloque des 11 et 12 décembre 2000*, ed. Catherine Mayeur-Jaouen (Paris: Maisonneuve et Larose, 2002), 319–333
44. Edwards, *Caravan of Martyrs*.
45. Azzam, *ayat al-rahman* (Minbar edition), p. 13.
46. Abdurrahman Siddiqi, *The Military in Pakistan: Image in Reality* (Lahore: Vanguard Books, 1996), p. 108. I thank Alexander De la Paz for pointing me to this source. Mustafa Menshawy, *State, Memory, and Egypt's Victory in the 1973 War: Ruling by Discourse* (New York: Palgrave Macmillan, 2017), pp. 55 ff.
47. Sayigh, *Armed Struggle*, p. 196.
48. Abdallah Azzam, 'ba'd al-aqlam al-'almaniyya wa yasariyya hawla karamat al-mujahidin' [Some of the Secularist and Leftist Comments on the Miracles of the Mujahidin], *al-Mujtama'* no. 584 (24 August 1982).
49. Alexander De la Paz, 'Miracles, Jihad, and Propaganda' (unpublished draft paper, 2017), p. 18. For more examples of criticism of the miracles see Darryl Li, 'Taking the Place of Martyrs: Afghans and

Arabs under the Banner of Islam', *Arab Studies Journal* 20, no. 1 (2012): 12–39; and Mathias Müller, 'Signs of the Merciful: 'Abdullah 'Azzam (d. 1989) and the Sacralization of History in Jihadist Literature, 1982–2002' (forthcoming in *Journal of Religion and Violence*, 2019).
50. Anas and Hussain, *To the Mountains*, p. 157.
51. Li, 'Taking the Place of Martyrs', p. 22.
52. David B. Cook, 'Contemporary Martyrdom: Ideology and Material Culture', in *Jihadi Culture: The Art and Social Practices of Militant Islamists*, ed. Thomas Hegghammer (Cambridge: Cambridge University Press, 2017), 151–170.
53. Meir Hatina, 'Warrior Saints: 'Abdallah 'Azzam's Reflections on Jihad and Karamat', in *Martyrdom and Sacrifice in Islam: Theological, Political and Social Contexts*, ed. Meir Hatina and Meir Litvak (London: I. B. Tauris, 2017), Kindle version, location 4705.
54. Ibid., Kindle version, location 4723.
55. Thomas Hegghammer, ed., *Jihadi Culture: The Art and Social Practices of Militant Islamists* (Cambridge: Cambridge University Press, 2017).
56. Hatina, 'Warrior Saints', Kindle version, location 4825.
57. Cook, 'Contemporary Martyrdom'.
58. De la Paz, 'Miracles, Jihad, and Propaganda'.
59. Abdallah Azzam, 'al-afghan bayna ta'yid al-rahman wa kunud al-insan' [Afghans between the Support of the Merciful and the Ingratitude of Man], *al-Mujtama*' no. 589 (5 October 1982).
60. Azzam, 'hatta la nu'idhdh', p. 26.
61. Azzam, 'ya muslimiy al-'alam', p. 26.
62. Abdallah Azzam, *ayat al-rahman fi jihad al-afghan* [Signs of the Merciful in the Afghan Jihad], 2nd ed. (Zarqa: Maktabat al-Manar, 1987), pp. 157 and 164–165.
63. In the introduction to *Defense of Muslim Lands*, Azzam writes, "I showed the fatwa in its current status – without the last six questions – to their eminences Shaykh Abdallah Alwan, Sa'id Hawa, Muhammad Najib al-Muta'i, Dr. Hussayn Hamid Hassan, and Umar Sayf. They read it, agreed on it and most of them signed it."
64. Muhammad, *safahat*, p. 93.
65. *mawsu'at al-dhakha'ir*, vol. 4, pp. 1102–1103.
66. Abdallah Azzam, 'jihad al-kafirin fard 'ayn' [Jihad against the Infidels is an Individual Obligation], *al-Mujtama*' no. 686 (9 October 1984), p. 27. We know the publication date of *Defense of Muslim Lands* from an advertisement in *al-Jihad* no. 4 (March 1985), back page.
67. Alfred Morabia, *Le Ğihad dans l'Islam médiéval: le 'combat sacré' des origines au XIIième siècle* (Paris: Albin Michel, 1993), pp. 255 and 259;

Michael Bonner, *Jihad in Islamic History: Doctrines and Practice* (Princeton: Princeton University Press, 2006), p. 10.
68. Johannes Jansen, *The Neglected Duty: The Creed of Sadat's Assassins and Islamic Resurgence in the Middle East* (New York: Macmillan, 1986), pp. 199–200.
69. Nelly Lahoud, 'The Pitfalls of Jihad as an Individual Duty (fard 'ayn)', in *Jihad and its Challenges to International and Domestic Law*, ed. M. Cherif Bassiouni and A. Guellali (The Hague: T.M.C. Asser Press, 2009), 87–106.
70. Azzam, *al-difa'*, *passim*; Morabia, *Ğihad*, pp. 215–216.
71. Scott, 'An "Official" Islamic Response'.
72. Azzam, *al-difa'*, p. 26 (Minbar edition).
73. Abdallah Azzam, 'wasiyat al-'abd al-faqir ila allah ta'ala 'abdallah bin yusuf 'azzam' [The Will of God's Poor Servant Abdallah Yusuf Azzam] (Minbar al-Tawhid wa'l-Jihad, 22 April 1986).
74. Muhammad, *safahat*, p. 89.
75. Azzam, *al-duktur al-shahid*, p. 84.
76. *fi 'uyun mu'asira*, p. 485.
77. Hegghammer, *Jihad in Saudi Arabia*, pp. 28–29.
78. 'al-shaykh tamim al-adnani yatahaddath li'l-jihad', p. 36.
79. Lacroix, *Awakening Islam*, p. 110.
80. Safar al-Hawali, 'mafhum al-jihad' [The Concept of Jihad], 1989, www.alhawali.com (accessed 2 July 2019); Lacroix, *Awakening Islam*, pp. 110–111.
81. Abdallah Azzam, 'al-duktur hasan al-turabi yadli li-jihad bi-tasrihat hamma hawla qadhiyat al-jihad' [Dr. Hasan al-Turabi Presents to *al-Jihad* Important Statements about the Issue of Jihad], *al-Jihad* no. 37 (December 1987): 10–13, pp. 12–13. Kamal al-Helbawy voiced a similar objection to Azzam's fatwa: author's interview with Kamal al-Helbawy, London, 23 March 2008.
82. *fi 'uyun mu'asira*, p. 106.
83. See *al-Jihad* no. 22 (September 1986), p. 25; and Muhammad, *al-ansar*, p. 74.
84. In his introduction to *The Defense of Muslim Lands*, Azzam claims that Bin Baz fully endorsed his book. However, Bin Baz never actually signed an endorsement. Azzam explains that he first presented the argument verbally to Bin Baz, who approved it. When Azzam came back later to have the Grand Mufti sign an endorsement, the latter was unavailable. It is more than likely that Bin Baz deliberately avoided Azzam to evade committing to the latter's position in writing.
85. Muhammad al-Shafi'i, 'tharthara fawqa saqf al-'alam' [Chatter on the World's Rooftop], part III, *al-Sharq al-Awsat*, 28 October 2006.

86. Brown and Rassler, *Fountainhead*, pp. 62–63.
87. Ibid., p. 62.
88. *Al-Jihad* no. 3 (February 1985), pp. 20–21.
89. See, for example, *al-Jihad* no. 17 (March 1986), pp. 30–32; *al-Jihad* no. 18 (April 1986), pp. 30–33; *al-Jihad* no. 20 (June 1986), pp. 34–36; *al-Jihad* no. 29 (April 1987), pp. 36–38; *al-Jihad* no. 36 (November 1987), pp. 4–5; and *al-Jihad* no. 37 (December 1987), pp. 34–36.
90. Abdallah Azzam, *fi'l-jihad adab wa ahkam* [Proper Conduct and Rulings in Jihad] (Peshawar: unknown publisher, 1986).
91. Abdallah Azzam, *ithaf al-'ibad bi-fada'il al-jihad* [Illustrating the Virtues of Jihad to God's Servants] (Minbar al-Tawhid wa'l-Jihad, n.d.); Abdallah Azzam, *i'lan al-jihad* [Declaring Jihad] (Minbar al-Tawhid wa'l-Jihad, n.d.); Abdallah Azzam, *al-as'ila wa'l-ajwiba al-jihadiyya* [Jihadi Questions and Answers] (Minbar al-Tawhid wa'l-Jihad, n.d.); Abdallah Azzam, *jarimat qatl al-nafs al-muslima* [The Crime of Killing a Muslim Soul], (Minbar al-Tawhid wa'l-Jihad, n.d.).
92. Azzam, *fi'l-jihad adab wa ahkam*, p. 5 (Minbar version).
93. Abdallah Azzam, 'bayna al-jihad wa'l-irhab' [Between Jihad and Terrorism], in *mawsu'at al-dhakha'ir*, vol. 4, p. 356. He also wrote, "I will speak clearly without mumbling or stammering: We are terrorists of the enemies of God, but we are humble toward the believers": *al-Jihad* no. 44 (July 1988), p. 4. He is also quoted as saying, "If preparation for jihad is terrorism, then we are terrorists. If defending Muslim honor is extremism, then we are extremists. And if jihad against the enemies is fundamentalism, then we are fundamentalists": Amir, *al-shaykh al-mujahid*, p. 119.
94. 'Interview with Sheikh Tameem al Adnani', around 7'00" ff.
95. Ibid., around 29'45"ff.
96. "There is no need to kill women, on account of their weakness, except if they fight": Azzam, *fi'l-jihad adab wa ahkam*, p. 9 (Minbar version).
97. "Nor [is there need] to kill children or monks on purpose unless they are mixed in with the polytheists": ibid., p. 9.
98. "As for Communist women in Afghanistan, they must be killed, whether they participate in the war or not, and whether as individuals or mixed in, and whether alone or in a group, because they have an ideology and fight against Islam and insult Islam and Muslims": ibid., p. 13.
99. Azzam, 'muhadara fi almania'.
100. '*Asharq al-Awsat* Interviews the Son of Bin Laden's Mentor', *al-Sharq al-Awsat* English Online, 2 September 2005.
101. 'The Words of Abdallah Azzam', pp. 28–31.

102. Ibid.
103. Ibid.
104. Azzam, *al-duktur al-shahid*, p. 164.
105. *al-Jihad* no. 60 (October 1989), p. 41.
106. 'as'ila wa ajwiba masjid kalifurnia' [Questions and Answers from the California Mosque], parts 1 and 2, in *mawsu'at al-dhakha'ir*, vol. 4, p. 844.
107. 'as'ila wa ajwiba masjid kalifurnia', p. 845.
108. Azzam, *al-difa'*, p. 15 (Minbar edition). See also Azzam, *ilhaq bi'l-qafila*, part 2.
109. Azzam, *ilhaq bi'l-qafila*, pp. 21–22 (Minbar version).
110. Abdallah Azzam, *basha'ir al-nasr* [Tidings of Victory] (Minbar al-Tawhid wa'l-Jihad, n.d.), p. 12 (Minbar version).
111. Azzam, 'ya muslimiy al-'alam', p. 26.
112. Amir, *al-shaykh al-mujahid*, p. 117.
113. I have found no trace of this precise formulation in any of Azzam's texts or lectures. The English phrase first appeared in the Australian Islamist magazine *Nida ul Islam* in 1996 and spread to Western literature from there: see Bin Omar, 'The Striving Sheikh'. Another candidate source for the alleged slogan is the phrase "no drawing back, no going back, and no hesitation ever" (*"la manas, la ruju', la taraddud abada"*), which he did say on at least one occasion: Abu Hilala, *awwal al-afghan al-'arab*, at 0'44".
114. Azzam, 'hatta la nu'idhdh', p. 26.
115. Azzam, 'ya muslimiy al-'alam', p. 26.
116. Azzam, 'al-qa'ida al-sulba'; Azzam, 'min kabul ila al-quds'.
117. Darryl Li, 'Lies, Damned Lies and Plagiarizing "Experts"', *Middle East Report* 41, no. 260 (11 September 2011): 5.
118. Azzam, *al-tarbiya*, p. 123.
119. 'Interview with Sheikh Tameem al Adnani', 46'00" ff.
120. Muhammad, *safahat*, p. 66.
121. Jarrar, *al-shahid*, p. 356.
122. Azzam, *'ibar wa basa'ir*, p. 41.
123. Azzam, 'ya muslimiy al-'alam', p. 26.
124. Azzam, *'ibar wa basa'ir*, pp. 109–110.
125. Ibid., p. 40.
126. Azzam, *al-manara al-mafquda*. Azzam had criticized Kemalism in at least one earlier article: see Abdallah Azzam, 'isda' al-haraka al-kamaliyya wa in'ikasatuha 'ala al-'alam al-islami' [The Repercussions of the Kemalist Movement and its Consequences in the Muslim World], *al-Mujtama'* no. 574 (8 June 1982).
127. We do not know when and where Azzam and Erbakan first met, but Abdallah Anas describes the two as "lifelong friends." Erbakan visited

Azzam in Pakistan on at least one occasion, and he also met with Azzam and Bin Ladin in the latter's house in Saudi Arabia during Hajj in 1985: see Anas and Hussain, *To the Mountains*, p. 173, and Anas, *rihlati ma' al-jihad*, part 3. Incidentally, Usama Bin Ladin was a longtime admirer of Erbakan. In Bin Ladin's personal notebook recovered among the Abbottabad documents, the al-Qaida leader, writing in the late 2000s, highlights Erbakan as a major inspiration in the 1970s. He also says he went to Turkey in 1976 for a Muslim Brotherhood conference: Hassan Hassan, 'Bin Laden Journal Reveals he was Shaped by the Muslim Brotherhood', *The National* Online, 2 November 2017.

128. Azzam, *al-as'ila wa'l-ajwiba*, pp. 77–87.
129. Azzam, *'ibar wa basa'ir*, p. 108.
130. Azzam, *al-duktur al-shahid*, p. 177.
131. *al-Jihad* no. 33 (August 1987), p. 4.
132. Azzam, *al-tarbiya*, p. 65; Azzam, *i'lan al-jihad*, pp. 14–15.
133. Azzam, *al-tarbiya*, p. 164.
134. Ibid., p. 209.
135. Azzam, *ilhaq bi'l-qafila*, p. 13.
136. al-Bilali, 'majallat al-jihad fi 'amihi al-khamis', p. 42.
137. '*Asharq al-Awsat* Interviews the Son of Bin Laden's Mentor'.
138. Lia, *Architect of Global Jihad*, p. 72.
139. Ibid., p. 73.
140. Azzam, *'ibar wa basa'ir*, p. 38.
141. Ibid., p. 106.
142. 'The Words of Abdallah Azzam', p. 88.
143. Ibid., p. 17.
144. Ibid.
145. Ibid., p. 7.
146. Ibid.
147. *al-Mujtama'*, 7 November 1989, cited in al-Wa'i, *mawsu'at shuhada'*, p. 227. See also Amir, *al-shaykh al-mujahid*, p. 98.
148. Azzam, 'dhikrayat min sahat al-jihad', p. 13.
149. 'al-hurub al-salibiyya mustamirra' [The Crusader Wars Continue], *al-Jihad* no. 21 (August 1986), pp. 30–32. The article is unsigned, but Azzam either wrote it or made an editorial decision to include it.
150. *al-Jihad* no. 21 (August 1986), p. 30; *al-Jihad* no. 39 (February 1988), p. 32.
151. Azzam, *'ibar wa basa'ir*, p. 107.
152. *al-Jihad* no. 13 (November 1985), p. 7.
153. Amir, *al-shaykh al-mujahid*, p. 96.
154. *al-Jihad* no. 58 (August 1989).

155. *al-Jihad* no. 61 (November 1989), p. 6.
156. Abdallah Azzam, 'dawr britania fi muharabat al-islam' [Britain's Role in Fighting Islam]', *Luhayb al-Ma'raka*, 29 April 1989.
157. See, for example, *al-Jihad* no. 50 (January 1989), p. 47; *al-Jihad* no. 20 (July 1986), pp. 4–7.
158. Azzam, 'dawr britania'.
159. Azzam, *al-duktur al-shahid*, p. 112.
160. Ibid., p. 116.
161. Azzam, 'dawr britania'.
162. Azzam, *al-duktur al-shahid*, p. 116.
163. See, for example, 'The Words of Abdallah Azzam', p. 19.
164. Martyn Frampton, *The Muslim Brotherhood and the West: A History of Enmity and Engagement* (Cambridge, MA: Harvard University Press, 2018), pp. 343 and 461.
165. *Mawsu'at al-dhakha'ir*, vol. 1, pp. 789–790.
166. *al-Jihad* no. 28 (March 1987), p. 3.
167. We also know that in Saudi Arabia around the same time, the scholar Safar al-Hawali began to write about Americans as Crusaders with imperial ambitions in the Gulf: see Mamoun Fandy, *Saudi Arabia and the Politics of Dissent* (New York: Palgrave Macmillan, 2001), pp. 64 ff.
168. Azzam, 'maktab khidamat al-mujahidin', p. 2.
169. Abdallah Azzam, 'al-haqd al-yahudi al-salibi' [Jewish–Crusader Malevolence], *Luhayb al-Ma'raka* no. 47 (23 April 1989), reproduced in *mawsu'at al-dhakha'ir*, vol. 2, pp. 250–252.
170. *al-Jihad* no. 54–55 (April 1989), p. 72.
171. 'al-salibiyyun fi mukhayyam kahi' [The Crusaders in the Kahi Camp], *al-Bunyan al-Marsus* no. 29 (October 1989), p. 42; 'al-salibiyyun wa harbihim al-khaffiyya' [The Crusaders and their Hidden War'], *al-Bunyan al-Marsus* no. 30 (February 1990), pp. 60–61; and 'madha yurid al-salibiyyin?' [What do the Crusaders Want?], *al-Bunyan al-Marsus* no. 31 (April 1990), pp. 44–45.

Mujahid

1. For examples, see the image collection on www.azzambook.net.
2. 'Abdullah Azzam Poem "Bakat 'Ayni – My Eyes Wept"', YouTube, www.youtube.com/watch?v=u0yUiYZiiHzI (accessed 24 January 2018).
3. Bonner, *Jihad in Islamic History*, pp. 97–117; Albrecht Noth, 'Les 'ulama' en qualité de guerriers', in *Saber religioso y poder político en el Islam*, ed. Manuela Marin (Madrid: Agencia Espanola de

Cooperación Internacional, 1994), pp. 175–195; 'karama', in *Encyclopedia of Islam*, second edition.
4. Writing in mid-March 1985, Azzam said, "God was kind to me when I visited the fighters attacked by the Russians. And thank God that the Russians were badly defeated in this battle": Bergen, *The Osama Bin Laden I Know*, p. 42.
5. Haqqani was one of the main informants to Azzam's early writings on battlefield miracles (see Chapter 11). We also know that Azzam was at Haqqani's house on 13 July 1985 when two Afghan planes made an emergency landing in Miranshah: *al-Jihad* no. 10 (August 1985), p. 26.
6. *al-Bunyan al-Marsus* no. 30 (February 1990), p. 9.
7. Lia, *Architect of Global Jihad*, p. 76.
8. *fi 'uyun mu'asira*, p. 299. In 1990 *al-Bunyan al-Marsus* printed a picture of Azzam and his driver Abu Harith taken in Qandahar province: *al-Bunyan al-Marsus* no. 30 (February 1990), p. 15.
9. *fi 'uyun mu'asira*, p. 224.
10. Hamid and Farrall, *The Arabs*, pp. 81–82.
11. Zaidan, *The "Afghan Arabs" Media*, p. 47.
12. Anas and Hussain, *To the Mountains*, p. 155.
13. Ibid., p. 161.
14. Muhammad, *safahat*, p. 112.
15. According to Abu Hajir, "it participated in operations along with the Afghan Mujahidin and with the students of the Religious Institute under the command of the Da'wa Committee. They were successful operations during which nearly eighteen posts were claimed": ibid., p. 200. Issue 16 (February 1986) of *al-Jihad* magazine (pp. 10–11) contains martyrdom biographies of a few Arabs killed in these operations, as well as a description of the events.
16. Anas, *wiladat*, p. 67.
17. Bergen, *The Osama Bin Laden I Know*, p. 47. Mustafa Hamid also suggests that one of the reasons Bin Ladin started his own project was that he spent more time on the front lines in 1984–1985, where he "got to see the real situation," unlike Azzam, who "never travelled to the front": Hamid and Farrall, *The Arabs*, p. 77.
18. Muhammad, *safahat*, p. 261.
19. Ibid., p. 199.
20. Perrin, 'Dans un camp souterrain des moudjahidin'.
21. Yousaf and Adkin, *Afghanistan: The Bear Trap*, p. 62. See also the picture between pages 84 and 85.
22. Ibid., pp. 160–162.
23. Ibid., pp. 166–173; Lester W. Grau and Ali Ahmad Jalali, 'The Campaign for the Caves: The Battles for Zhawar in the Soviet–

Afghan War', *Journal of Slavic Military Studies* 14, no. 3 (2001): 69–92; Wardak, *Mémoires*, p. 238.
24. Muhammad, *safahat*, p. 177; Jarrar, *al-shahid*, p. 87.
25. Azzam, 'wasiyat al-'abd al-faqir'. A facsimile of the handwritten document is available in Abu Rumman and Sa'id, *al-'alim*, pp. 90–102.
26. Muhammad, *safahat*, pp. 177–178.
27. Ibid.
28. Brown and Rassler, *Fountainhead*, pp. 73–74.
29. Yousaf and Adkin, *Afghanistan: The Bear Trap*, p. 182.
30. Azzam had long encouraged Bin Ladin to move permanently to Pakistan; Abdallah Anas recalls a discussion around 1985 in which Azzam chided Bin Ladin for only coming to the region periodically: Anas and Hussain, *To the Mountains*, p. 178.
31. Muhammad, *safahat*, p. 199.
32. In 1984 Sayyaf had moved his military training base from Pabbi east of Peshawar to Sada, because it was closer to the border: Neighbour, *The Mother of Mohammed*, p. 178; Coll, *The Bin Ladens*, p. 255. Abdallah Anas writes that Sayyaf's two camps in Khald and Sada held a total of around 250 Afghan trainees: Anas and Hussain, *To the Mountains*, p. 159. According to Bernard Rougier, Sada at its height accommodated some 400 trainees: Rougier, *Everyday Jihad*, p. 77.
33. Muhammad, *safahat*, p. 200.
34. Ibid.
35. Ibid.
36. Ibid., p. 206. In 1986 Ramadan ended on 9 June. Hamid and Farrall offer a rather different account of Azzam's motivation for founding Sada. They write that Azzam had to flee Peshawar because Hekmatyar was after him, and he established an Arab-only camp at Sada in mid-1986 partly for his own protection: Hamid and Farrall, *The Arabs*, p. 83. This account is not supported by other evidence.
37. Muhammad, *safahat*, p. 200.
38. Ibid.
39. Ibid., pp. 200 and 206.
40. Ibid., p. 200.
41. Ibid.
42. Ibid., p. 211.
43. Ibid.
44. Berger, *Jihad Joe*, pp. 22–32.
45. Muhammad, *safahat*, pp. 194–195.
46. Hamid and Farrall, *The Arabs*, p. 84; Berger, *Jihad Joe*, pp. 24 and 27.
47. For a detailed first-person account of training at Sada in late 1986, see Badi, *afghanistan: ihtilal al-dhakira*, pp. 49–71.

48. Hamid and Farrall, *The Arabs*, p. 132; author's interview with Abdallah Anas, London, 27 July 2009.
49. Hamid and Farrall, *The Arabs*, p. 133; author's interview with Abdallah Anas, London, 27 July 2009.
50. Muhammad, *safahat*, p. 211.
51. Wright, *The Looming Tower*, p. 111; Coll, *Ghost Wars*, p. 157.
52. Bin Ladin was happy to work with Afghan Mujahidin, at least in his early Afghanistan years. For example, before the battle of Sha'ban at al-Ma'sada in April 1987, Bin Ladin insisted that the Arabs coordinate with the Afghan Mujahidin even if they would not participate: Muhammad, *safahat*, p. 264.
53. Usama Bin Ladin, 'Letter on Shura' (Bin Laden's Bookshelf, n.d.), pp. 2–3, www.dni.gov/index.php/features/bin-laden-s-bookshelf?start=1 (accessed 14 February 2018).
54. "Abu Ubaydah was trying to convince Abu Abdallah to use the al-Arin area as a base of guerrilla warfare ... Abu Ubaydah said, 'it is good if we turn this area into a base of guerrilla warfare'": Hamid and Farrall, *The Arabs*, p. 111.
55. Al-Banshiri was in the Panjshir valley when Bin Ladin founded al-Ma'sada. In fact, Muhammad quotes al-Banshiri himself as saying he only reluctantly joined al-Ma'sada in November 1986: Muhammad, *safahat*, p. 236.
56. Basil Muhammad writes that "Abu Abdallah began to scan the region of Baluchistan secretly, and Abu al-Rida, Abu Anis, and Abu Hafs al-Madani accompanied him. Abu Abdallah also got acquainted with people there, had relations with them, and sent some of them for training. Moreover, brother al-Batal told me ... that Abu Abdallah sent him in early July 1986 to Quetta ... Abu Hafs al-Madani, Abu Anis, Abu Ahmad al-Madani, and Najm al-Din accompanied al-Batal from the Eastern Province. At that time the intention was to build al-Ma'sada in Qandahar, but some circumstances stood in the way of such intentions ... Abu Abdallah went on a tour in August 1986 in Baluchistan, accompanied by Abu Qutayba. But he discovered that the security circumstances were not appropriate": ibid., p. 207.
57. Ibid.
58. Ibid., p. 211; Stenersen, *al-Qaida in Afghanistan*, p. 14.
59. Yousaf and Adkin, *Afghanistan: The Bear Trap*, pp. 164–166.
60. The associates, most of whom seem to have been young Saudis, included Usama Azmaray, Shafiq, Amin, Abu Anis, and Abd al-Awwal.
61. Muhammad, *safahat*, p. 241. Bin Ladin later elaborated on the name choice in a speech in Saudi Arabia in 1988: see Miller, *The Audacious Ascetic*, pp. 75–76.

62. The initial "settler group" consisted of five people: Bin Ladin himself, Usama Azmaray, Muhammad al-Mubaraki, a certain Shafiq, and a certain Abu al-Dhahab (aka Nabil): Muhammad, *safahat*, p. 213.
63. Hamid and Farrall, *The Arabs*, p. 95.
64. Muhammad, *safahat*, pp. 234–236.
65. Bin Ladin, 'Letter on Shura', p. 1.
66. Stenersen, *al-Qaida in Afghanistan*, p. 17.
67. Abu Khalid al-Masri later said, "Brother al-Banshiri came to me and told me that Abu Abdallah was doing construction on an advanced location in Jaji which raised much dispute. He asked me to visit that location and give my opinion as a military man": Muhammad, *safahat*, p. 235.
68. Ibid., p. 236. Adnan Ibrahim (aka Abu Sayf), the military correspondent of *al-Jihad* magazine, also came around the same time. Ibid., p. 214–219.
69. Ibid., p. 234.
70. Abu Hafs: "He kept defending his points not from a military point of view but as if he only wanted to gather the Arab brothers and boost the morale of the Afghanis. He wanted them to come in the vanguards": ibid., p. 236.
71. "We made an evaluation committee in Islamabad": ibid. It is not clear why it met in Islamabad.
72. Ibid., p. 237.
73. Ibid., pp. 211–213.
74. Ibid., p. 233.
75. Ibid., p. 234.
76. Ibid., p. 200.
77. Ibid., p. 234.
78. Coll, *Ghost Wars*, p. 157.
79. Muhammad, *safahat*, p. 234.
80. Ibid. Azzam later said, "At that time brother Abd al-Aziz came to us and did not like our situation. He believed we should go back to Sada and focus on training."
81. Ibid., p. 237.
82. Ibid., p. 234.
83. "An agreement was made between Dr. Abdallah and Abu Abdallah that training would be made in Sada, and then they could go to Ma'sada": ibid., p. 238.
84. Azzam said, "We agreed with Abu Abdallah not to increase the number above twenty": ibid., p. 234.
85. Ibid., pp. 234–235.
86. Ibid., p. 238; see also p. 234.
87. Ibid., pp. 250–251.
88. Ibid., p. 234.

89. 'Abu 'Ubayda al-Banshiri'.
90. Abu Hafs' police background is disputed: 'Abu Hafs al-Masri', West Point, NY: Combating Terrorism Center, 2008, https://ctc.usma.edu/wp-content/uploads/2011/06/Abu_Hafs.pdf (accessed 24 January 2018).
91. Muhammad, *safahat*, p. 261. Lawrence Wright suggests that Abu Khalid is the same as Muhammad Shawki al-Islambuli (the brother of Sadat's assassin Khalid al-Islambuli), but this is uncorroborated: Wright, *The Looming Tower*, p. 409.
92. Muhammad, *safahat*, p. 245.
93. For a detailed account of the trip to al-Ma'sada and life there from a foot soldier's point of view, see Badi, *afghanistan: ihtilal al-dhakira*, pp. 82–97.
94. Muhammad, *safahat*, p. 211.
95. Abdallah Anas, *rihlati ma' al-jihad*, part 6 and part 7 at 35'40" ff. Anas later wrote that he had started reading *al-Shahid* magazine in Algeria in the early 1980s, while he was a Muslim Brotherhood member: "[We] would go to the Iranian embassy in Algiers to collect the translated audio-tapes of Khomeini and the revolutionary magazine al-Shahid": Anas and Hussain, *To the Mountains*, p. 51.
96. Miller, *The Audacious Ascetic*, pp. 135, 154, and 392–393.
97. Muhammad, *safahat*, p. 255.
98. Ibid.
99. Ibid., p. 237.
100. Ibid., p. 267.
101. Ibid., p. 264.
102. Ibid., p. 299.
103. Ibid., p. 266.
104. Ibid. It is not clear which book this is referring to. The Arabic title provided is *al-'ibra fima ja' 'an al-nabiy salla allah alayhi wa sallam fi'l-ghazw, al-jihad, wa'l-hijra*.
105. Ibid., pp. 277–278.
106. Ibid., p. 283.
107. Ibid., p. 298.
108. Ibid.
109. See, for example, Muhammad, *safahat*, pp. 303 ff.; Azzam, *The Lofty Mountain*, pp. 77–120; Hamid and Farrall, *The Arabs*, pp. 97–100; Stenersen, *al-Qaida in Afghanistan*, pp. 18–19.
110. Muhammad, *safahat*, p. 280.
111. Ibid.
112. Ibid., pp. 280 and 343.
113. The names are: "Sheikh Sayyaf – Sheikh Azzam – Abu Abdallah – Abu Ubayda – Sheikh Tamim – Azmaray – [illegible] – Doctor Shakir – Abu

Hafs – Abu Khalid." See document 353 in Tareekh Musadat collection. Another code key (document 350) has somewhat different names, but Azzam still in second place between Sayyaf and Bin Ladin.
114. Muhammad, *safahat*, p. 346.
115. Ibid.
116. Ibid., p. 361.
117. See, for example, *al-Jihad* no. 32 (July 1987), pp. 4–11 and 14–16.
118. Jamal Khashoggi, 'Arab Youths Fight Shoulder to Shoulder with Mujahideen', *Arab News*, 4 May 1988.
119. Bergen, *The Osama Bin Laden I Know*, pp. 50 ff.
120. David Isby, 'Four Battles in Afghanistan', *Soldier of Fortune*, April 1988.
121. Bergen, *The Osama Bin Laden I Know*, pp. 317–318.
122. Muhammad, *safahat*, p. 362.
123. *al-Jihad* no. 54–55 (April 1989), p. 38.
124. Muhammad, *safahat*, p. 362.
125. Bergen, *The Osama Bin Laden I Know*, p. 56.
126. Ibid., p. 316.
127. Key works include Wright, *The Looming Tower*, pp. 121–144; Bergen, *The Osama Bin Laden I Know*, pp. 75–81; R. Kim Cragin, 'Early History of al-Qa'ida', *The Historical Journal* 51 (2008): 1047–1067; Peter Bergen and Paul Cruickshank, 'Revisiting the Early Al Qaeda: An Updated Account of its Formative Years', *Studies in Conflict and Terrorism* 35, no. 1 (1 January 2012): 1–36; Hamid and Farrall, *Arabs*, pp. 107 ff.; and Stenersen, *al-Qaida in Afghanistan*, pp. 20–25.
128. Most testimonies were recorded after 9/11, either in the form of interviews conducted by writers such as Lawrence Wright and Peter Bergen, or in the form of memoirs written by former Afghan Arabs. Early testimony collections such as Basil Muhammad's *Pages from the Record of the Arab Supporters in Afghanistan* do not mention al-Qaida at all. The first detailed testimony discussing al-Qaida's early history in detail is that of Jamal al-Fadl from the so-called East Africa bombings trial in New York in early 2001. Al-Fadl, however, had not been part of Bin Ladin's inner circle in the late 1980s.
129. Michael S. Smith II, 'al-Qa'ida Archives: Tareekh Osama and Tareekh al-Musadat', Downrange Blog, 9 December 2016, https://insidethejihad.com/2016/12/al-qaida-archives-tareekh-osama-tareekh-al-musadat/ (accessed 11 April 2018).
130. Wright, *The Looming Tower*, pp. 131–134; Bergen, *The Osama Bin Laden I Know*, pp. 74 ff.; and Berger, *Beatings and Bureaucracy*.
131. First, from November 1986, he went himself: "Abu Abdallah was traveling to Saudi Arabia and met with brothers there and told them about al-Ma'sada, inviting them to come and to convince the others to

come": Muhammad, *safahat*, p. 217. Later he used deputies: "Abu Abdallah asked [Abu Hanifa] to represent the group in Saudi Arabia and to preach about the Lions' Den. Therefore a group of young men departed [from Ta'if in Saudi Arabia for Jaji]": Bergen, *The Osama Bin Laden I Know*, pp. 51 and 58. Jamal Khashoggi said he went to al-Ma'sada in late 1987 or early 1988 on Usama Bin Ladin's personal invitation: author's telephone interview with Jamal Khashoggi, 14 September 2018.

132. Tareekh Osama 122–123.
133. Ibid.
134. Tareekh Osama 122. Some existing English translations say "forming the new military group," but the Arabic original says work (*'amal*), not group.
135. Tareekh Osama 128–135.
136. Ibid. The attendees were: (1) Abu Burhan [al-Suri], (2) Abu Hajir [al-Iraqi], (3) Abu Usama al-Jaza'iri, (4) Amir al-Fath, (5) Yasin al-Iraqi, (6) Abu Ubayda al-Banshiri, (7) Asadallah, (8) Abu Khalid al-Misri, (9) Abu Habib, (10) Abu Abd al-Rahman, (11) Sabir al-Misri, (12) Ibn al-Qayyim, (13) Abu Salim al-Jaza'iri, and (14) Saifullah [al-Maghribi].
137. Tareekh Osama 127–127a. The nine attendees are listed as (1) Sheikh Usama [Bin Ladin], (2) Abu Ubayda al-Banshiri, (3) Abu Burhan [al-Suri], (4) Sheikh Tamim [al-Adnani], (5) Abu Hajir [al-Iraqi], (6) Abu Anas, (7) Abu al-Hasan al-Madani, (8) Abu al-Hassan al-Makki, and (9) Abu Ibrahim.
138. Tareekh Osama 127a.
139. See, for example, Wright, *The Looming Tower*, pp. 131–133; Bergen, *The Osama Bin Laden I Know*, pp. 75–81.
140. Hamid and Farrall, *The Arabs*, pp. 108–111.
141. Wright, *The Looming Tower*, p. 131.
142. USA v Usama bin Laden et al., Southern District of New York, 2001, day 2 (6 February 2001), p. 191.
143. Azzam, 'al-qa'ida al-sulba'.
144. Li, 'Lies, Damned Lies and Plagiarizing "Experts"'. Incidentally, the term "Solid Base" is not Azzam's invention; it comes from Sayyid Qutb's book *In the Shade of the Qur'an*.
145. See, for example, Wright, *The Looming Tower*, pp. 131–133; Bergen, *The Osama Bin Laden I Know*, pp. 75–81.
146. Lawrence Wright's source for placing Azzam in that meeting is the testimony of Wa'il Julaydan, whom he interviewed by intermediary some fifteen years later, and who is not documented as having attended the meeting either: Wright, *The Looming Tower*, p. 402.

147. "Did you [plural] take the opinion of Sheikh Abdullah –> knowing that the Sheikh's military gang has ended": Tareekh Osama 122.
148. Al-Adnani is notably described as a sheikh in the 20 August Document, the only sheikh other than Osama Bin Ladin among the nine attendees: Tareekh Osama 127–127a.
149. USA v. Usama bin Laden et al., Southern District of New York, 2001, day 2 (6 February 2001), p. 205.
150. The Harmony database is the US Department of Defense's registry of documents captured in the early War on Terror. The database is classified, and only parts of it have been released into the public domain. The first Harmony documents were released in 2006: see James J. F. Forest, Jarret Brachman, and Joseph Felter, 'Harmony and Disharmony: Exploiting al-Qaʻida's Organizational Vulnerabilities' (West Point: Combating Terrorism Center, 14 February 2006). The documents can be accessed through the Combating Terrorism Center website (https://ctc.usma.edu/harmony-program/) or the private non-profit website *Captured Document Index* (www.docexdocs.com/docindex.html). Some of the Harmony documents also feature in the declassified collection of documents captured at Bin Ladin's compound in Abbottabad in 2011, currently available at www.dni.gov/index.php/features/bin-laden-s-bookshelf.
151. "Al-Qaida's Structure and Bylaws" (AFGP-2002–600048), available at https://ctc.usma.edu/afgp-2002–600048-orig (accessed 11 April 2018). It exists in a duplicate (AFGP-2002– 600178) available at https://ctc.usma.edu/harmony-program/al-qaidas-structure-and-bylaws-original-language-2/ (accessed 11 April 2018).
152. "Interior Organization" (AFGP-2002–000080), available at https://ctc.usma.edu/harmony-program/interior-organization-original-language-2/ (accessed 11 April 2018); "al-Qaida's Goals and Structure" (AFGP-2002–000078), available at https://ctc.usma.edu/harmony-program/al-qaida-goals-and-structure-original-language-2// (accessed 11 April 2018).
153. Wright, *The Looming Tower*, p. 141.
154. USA v. Usama bin Laden et al., Southern District of New York, 2001, day 2 (6 February 2001), p. 197.
155. Vahid Brown, *Cracks in the Foundation: Leadership Schisms in al-Qaʻida From 1989–2006*, (West Point, NY: Combating Terrorism Center), 2007, p. 22.
156. Stenersen, *al-Qaida in Afghanistan*, pp. 13 ff.
157. 'Connecting the Dots – America's First al Qaeda Fighters' (New York: NEFA Foundation, April 2010).

158. al-Qandahari, *dhikrayat*, pp. 29–30.
159. Stenersen, *al-Qaida in Afghanistan*, p. 22.
160. Hamid and Farrall, *The Arabs*, p. 174; Stenersen, *al-Qaida in Afghanistan*, pp. 26–27.
161. Hamid and Farrall, *The Arabs*, p. 174.
162. 'An Insider's View of al-Qa'ida as Narrated by Abu-Jandal (Nasir al-Bahri), Bin-Ladin's Bodyguard (part 4)', *al-Quds al-Arabi* (via FBIS), 22 March 2005.
163. USA v. Usama bin Laden et al., Southern District of New York, 2001, day 2 (6 February 2001), pp. 190 ff.
164. Wright, *The Looming Tower*, p. 141.
165. al-Qandahari, *dhikrayat*, p. 175.
166. *mawsu'at al-jihad*.
167. Ibid., p. 199.
168. See, for example, Adam Curtis, 'The Power of Nightmares: The Rise of the Politics of Fear' (London: BBC, 2004) [documentary].
169. In addition to the 20 August Document (Tareekh Osama 127–127a) which describes al-Qaida as an "organized Islamic faction" as early as 1988, see the abovementioned Harmony documents "al-Qaida's Structure and Bylaws" (AFGP-2002–600048), "Interior Organization" (AFGP-2002–000080), and "al-Qaida's Goals and Structure" (AFGP-2002–000078). Moreover, in May 1993, Agence France-Presse published a story quoting a Jordanian militant as saying he had been trained by "al-Kaida" in Afghanistan: 'Des Jordaniens rentrés d'Afghanistan inquiètent Amman', Agence France Presse, 28 May 1993. In 1994 Anthony Hyman wrote an article noting that "in Peshawar, the largest Arab organization dedicated to helping the Afghan jihad was Qa'ada, whose director was a Saudi citizen, Usamah bin Laden": Hyman, 'Arab Involvement in the Afghan War', p. 80. Last but not least was Jamal al-Fadl's elaborate testimony about the inner workings of the al-Qaida organization, a testimony made public in February 2001 but offered to US intelligence as early as 1995: Jane Mayer, 'Junior: The Clandestine Life of America's Top Al Qaeda Source,' *The New Yorker*, 11 September 2006.
170. Bergen, *The Osama Bin Laden I Know*, p. 83.
171. 'An Insider's View of al-Qa'ida', p. 19 (English translation from FBIS).
172. Wright, *The Looming Tower*, p. 129.
173. Gerges, *The Far Enemy*, pp. 39, 161–165.
174. Azzam, *al-duktur al-shahid*, p. 162.
175. Abdallah Anas said, "In Peshawar, we didn't count Zawahiri as a *mujahid*. He was just sitting in Peshawar trying to recruit people to fight against Egypt": Bergen, *The Osama Bin Laden I Know*, p. 69.

176. Bin Ladin was critical of secular Arab regimes, but he was not against the Saudi regime in the 1980s, and his only views on record before 1989 relate to pan-Islamist causes such as Afghanistan and Palestine. One source even suggests that Bin Ladin was initially against the Islamist uprising in Egypt in the early 1990s: "The confessions of those accused of religious violence in Egypt confirmed that [Bin Ladin] was still objecting to the operations executed in Egypt because of their high cost and uselessness. However, Bin Laden and Al-Zawaheri's departure from Afghanistan in 1993 to Sudan, reflected the tight relations between them." Salah, *waqa'i' sanawat al-jihad*, p. 74.
177. Michael Scheuer, *Osama Bin Laden* (New York: Oxford University Press, 2011), pp. 8–9.
178. Bergen, *The Osama Bin Laden I Know*, pp. 47–48.
179. Ibid., pp. 62–63.
180. Felix Kuehn, Leah Farrall, and Alex Strick van Linschoten, 'Expert Report – US vs. Talha Ahsan; US vs. Babar Ahmad', April 2014, www.sacc.org.uk/sacc/docs/ba_expert_reports.pdf (accessed 1 March 2018), p. 18.
181. USA v. Usama bin Laden et al., Southern District of New York, 2001, day 2 (6 February 2001), pp. 169 ff.
182. Azzam, *The Lofty Mountain*, p. 65.
183. Anas and Hussain, *To the Mountains*, pp. 194–195. See also Wright, *The Looming Tower*, p. 135.
184. Tareekh Osama 136. See also Tareekh Musadat 2, 3 and 121–126.
185. For details on Bin Ladin's participation in Jalalabad, see Badi, *afghanistan: ihtilal al-dhakira*, pp. 188–194. According to Stenersen, the al Qaida Shura Council was divided on whether to participate, and Bin Ladin represented the faction eager to join: Stenersen, *al-Qaida in Afghanistan*, p. 22. It seems Azzam did not take part in the battle, but he was in the area some of the time; the introduction to his book *Words from the Frontline* says "written near Jalalabad 22 April 1989": *mawsu'at al-dhakha'ir*, vol. 2, p. 221.
186. Christina Lamb, *Waiting for Allah: Pakistan's Struggle for Democracy* (New York: Viking, 1991), pp. 195 ff.
187. Kiessling, *Faith*, pp. 67–68.
188. For a detailed account of the battle, see Yousaf and Adkin, *Afghanistan: The Bear Trap*, pp. 226–232. Azzam was at Jalalabad. He did not fight, but came close to the action. Ali al-Hawamida, a Jordanian Muslim Brother who was visiting Peshawar at the time, says Azzam took him to Afghanistan "to watch Jalalabad. I attended a battle there with him. Three missiles landed in front of us, just fifty meters away. [Azzam] did not lie down, he just stood there, watching

the sky. With us was a group of Yemeni, Saudi, Syrian, Jordanian, and Palestinian mujahidin": *fi 'uyun mu'asira*, p. 37. Yasir al-Umari, a Jordanian Brother and the mayor of Zarqa, said in 1990, "Last summer I was in Peshawar to help organize aid to the Afghan refugees, and on my way I met Abdallah Azzam, who was carrying [*mudajjajan*] weapons with a group of *mujahidin*. I told him, 'I'd like to see you'; he said, 'Come with me to Jalalabad or wait till I come back from the battle'": ibid., p. 89.

189. Kiessling, *Faith*, p. 68.
190. *al-Jihad* no. 59 (September 1989), p. 36.
191. Bergen, *The Osama Bin Laden I Know*, p. 87.
192. Stenersen, *al-Qaida in Afghanistan*, p. 24.
193. Hamid and Farrall, *The Arabs*, pp. 164 ff.
194. Ibid., p. 174.
195. Ibid., p. 170.
196. al-Qandahari, *dhikrayat*, p. 37.
197. Abdallah Azzam, 'athar al-mujahid al-'arabi fi'l-jihad al-afghani', in *mawsu'at al-dhakha'ir*, vol. 3, pp. 358–364.
198. Abdallah Azzam, 'i'lan ila al-ikhwa al-mutabarri'in' [Announcement to Donor Brothers], *al-Jihad* no. 57 (July 1989): 21.
199. Mark Urban, *War in Afghanistan* (Basingstoke: Macmillan, 1988), p. 244.
200. Abdallah Anas said, "Only a very small fraction of that entered Afghanistan and participated in the fighting with the Mujahidin. The rest worked in Peshawar as doctors, drivers, cooks, accountants, and engineers": Anas, *wiladat*, p. 87.
201. Tam Hussein, 'Jihad, Then and Now', *Majalla*, 8 February 2014; author's telephone interview with Alastair Crooke, 23 March 2008.
202. Antonio Giustozzi, *War, Politics and Society in Afghanistan, 1978–1992* (Washington, DC: Georgetown University Press, 2000), p. 115.
203. In October 1987 *al-Bunyan al-Marsus* magazine published a list of all recorded Arab martyrs; it included forty-eight named individuals: *al-Bunyan al-Marsus* no. 16–17 (October 1987), pp. 30–36. An updated list published in March 1989 included seventy-nine individuals: *al-Bunyan al-Marsus* no. 26 (March 1986), pp. 48–51.
204. Noor Ahmad Khalidi, 'Afghanistan: Demographic Consequences of War, 1978–1987', *Central Asian Survey* 10, no. 3 (1 January 1991): 101–126, p. 106.
205. Anas, *wiladat*, p. 87.
206. al-Dhiyabi, 'Saudi Academic Recounts Experiences from Afghan War'.
207. Strick van Linschoten and Kuehn, *An Enemy We Created*, p. 54.
208. *al-Jihad* no. 54–55 (April 1989), p. 55.

209. Brown and Rassler, *Fountainhead*, pp. 73–74.
210. Strick van Linschoten and Kuehn, *An Enemy we Created*, p. 54.
211. See, for example, Mohammed M. Hafez, *Suicide Bombers in Iraq* (Washington, DC: USIP, 2007).
212. See, for example, Kristin M. Bakke, 'Help Wanted? The Mixed Record of Foreign Fighters in Domestic Insurgencies', *International Security* 38, no. 4 (1 April 2014): 150–187; Ben Rich and Dara Conduit, 'The Impact of Jihadist Foreign Fighters on Indigenous Secular–Nationalist Causes: Contrasting Chechnya and Syria', *Studies in Conflict and Terrorism* 38, no. 2 (2015): 113–131.
213. Edwards writes that "Arabs brought dissension with them, along with a ruthlessness that hadn't been there before," but he cites no sources or examples: Edwards, *Before Taliban*, pp. 270–271.
214. In the Bosnia war, for example, Arab fighters posed on camera next to beheaded enemy soldiers: see, for example, John Schindler, *Unholy Terror: Bosnia, al-Qa'ida, and the Rise of Global Jihad* (St. Paul, MN: Zenith Press, 2007), pp. 166–167. See also Ariel Koch, 'Jihadi Beheading Videos and their Non-Jihadi Echoes', *Perspectives on Terrorism* 12, no. 3 (2018): 24–34.
215. "We fed them the same food, gave them the same clothes and the same quality of life ... Through our conduct we showed them we were not bloodthirsty people": Hussein, 'Jihad, Then and Now'.
216. For example, in the spring of 1989 a group of Arab fighters reportedly "took prisoner dozens of Afghan Communist troops who had surrendered and, in direct contradiction to Afghan tradition, hacked them to bloody pieces and sent them back to the besieged Communist garrison at Jalalabad": Brian Glyn Williams, 'On the Trail of the "Lions of Islam": Foreign Fighters in Afghanistan and Pakistan, 1980–2010', *Orbis* 55, no. 2 (1 January 2011): 216–239, p. 220.
217. Rodric Braithwaite, *Afgantsy: The Russians in Afghanistan 1979–89* (New York: Oxford University Press, 2011), p. 232.
218. Jalali and Grau, *Afghan Guerrilla Warfare*, pp. 368–369.
219. al-Qandahari, *dhikrayat*, p. 130.
220. Grau and Jalali, 'The Campaign for the Caves', pp. 287 and 382. See also Braithwaite, *Afgantsy*, p. 233.
221. Torture was not the norm; al-Qandahari writes, "The Afghans treated their prisoners so well that the Arabs were always mad at them ... More strangely, they would not hesitate to kill them after all that. Not everything in Afghanistan can be understood": al-Qandahari, *dhikrayat*, p. 130.
222. Braithwaite, *Afgantsy*, p. 227.
223. Ibid., p. 212.

Resident

1. Lamb, *Waiting for Allah*, p. 181.
2. Author's interview with Jamal Isma'il, Islamabad, 18 March 2008.
3. Author's interview with Abdallah Anas, London, 1 December 2015.
4. "[When I was with the Fedayin in 1969] I had a large-print [Qur'an], and during the time in which I would stand guard at night, I would repeat what I had memorized during the day. So, if I mispronounced a word, I opened it, and I would read it using the light of the Moon. As for now, I cannot even see using the light of the Sun, so, we ask Allah to strengthen our eyesight": 'The Words of Abdallah Azzam', p. 2.
5. Author's interview with Sami' al-Haqq, Akora Khattak, 21 March 2008. Abdallah Anas also highlights Azzam's sporting ability: Anas and Hussain, *To the Mountains*, p. 24.
6. Author's interview with Ahmad Zaidan, Islamabad, 18 March 2008.
7. Azzam, *al-duktur al-shahid*, p. 78.
8. Ibid., p. 208.
9. Jarrar, *al-shahid*, p. 355.
10. Muhammad, *safahat*, p. 101.
11. Wright, *The Looming Tower*, p. 134.
12. Jarrar, *al-shahid*, pp. 353–354.
13. Azzam, *al-duktur al-shahid*, p. 200.
14. Ibid., p. 73.
15. *fi 'uyun mu'asira*, p. 98.
16. Ibid., p. 381.
17. Author's interview with Abu Harith, Amman, 8 May 2008.
18. Jarrar, *al-shahid*, p. 349.
19. Anas and Hussain, *To the Mountains*, p. 107.
20. Jarrar, *al-shahid*, p. 345.
21. Ibid., p. 88; Amir, *al-shaykh al-mujahid*.
22. His real name was Ahmad Muhammad al-Ahmadi. He was an uneducated Yemeni who had come to Pakistan in 1985 and was nicknamed "Nightly Predator" because of this courage. Azzam, who had known him personally, wrote his martyrdom biography in *al-Jihad* no. 32 (July 1987), pp. 26–29.
23. Author's interview with Jamal Isma'il, Islamabad, 20 March 2008.
24. Jarrar, *al-shahid*, p. 351.
25. Azzam, *wasiyat al-'abd al-faqir ila allah*.
26. Author's interview with Abdallah Anas, London, 1 December 2015. His will from 20 April 1986 refers to Fatima and Wafa as Umm al-Hasan and Umm Yahya: ibid.

27. Jarrar, *al-shahid*, p. 35.
28. *fi 'uyun mu'asira*, p. 169. At their engagement party, the groom gave out "300 Qur'ans at 81 Jordanian dinars each," which greatly pleased his father-in-law: Abdallah Azzam, 'wathiqa ila al-ikhwan al-muslimun fi'l urdun' [Document to the Muslim Brotherhood in Jordan], *mawsu'at al-dhakha'ir*, vol. 1, pp. 999–1006.
29. "When Abu Yahya asked for Wafa's hand, Azzam reportedly asked him, 'Do you realize how much the dowry is?' The suitor got a little nervous but said he was prepared to pay whatever the sheikh demanded. Azzam patted him on the shoulder and smiled and said, 'The dowry is that you carry the banner of la illaha illa allah and wage jihad in Afghanistan'. So he went and fought and married the sheikh's daughter": Jarrar, *al-shahid*, p. 52. See also Muhammad, *safahat*, p. 99. There are other stories of grooms waging jihad as dowry; al-Qandahari writes, "When I asked him one day why he had come to the Jihad, I understood that he wanted to marry the daughter of the sheikh in the village. Her dowry was the jihad in Afghanistan": al-Qandahari, *dhikrayat*, p. 119.
30. *fi 'uyun mu'asira*, p. 179.
31. Bergen, *The Osama Bin Laden I Know*, p. 28. Nir Rosen, *Aftermath: Following the Bloodshed of America's Wars in the Muslim World* (New York: Nation Books, 2010), p. 131.
32. Rosen, *Aftermath*, p. 131.
33. Mary Fitzgerald, 'The Son of the Father of Jihad', *The Irish Times*, 7 July 2006.
34. Hudhayfa Abdallah Azzam, 'min wahi surat al-anfal' [Inspiration from Surat al-Anfal], *al-Jihad* no. 43 (June 1988): 44.
35. Azzam, *al-duktur al-shahid*, p. 19.
36. See Twitter message from @LoveLiberty, 20 September 2015.
37. *fi 'uyun mu'asira*, p. 426.
38. Azzam, *al-duktur al-shahid*, pp. 19–20.
39. Abu Mujahid, *al-shahid*, p. 1 (Minbar edition).
40. Azzam, *al-duktur al-shahid*, p. 20.
41. Abdallah Azzam, 'shukr 'ala tu'az' [Thank you for the Condolences], *Luhayb al-Ma'raka* 34 (14 January 1989), in *mawsu'at al-dhakha'ir*, vol. 1, p. 798; Abdallah Azzam, *fi khidamm al-ma'raka* [In the Heat of Battle], 9 September 1989, in ibid., vol. 2, p. 2.
42. *fi 'uyun mu'asira*, p. 426.
43. Jarrar, *al-shahid*, p. 52; *fi 'uyun mu'asira*, p. 425.
44. Author's interview with Abu Harith, Amman, 8 May 2008.
45. Berger, *Beatings and Bureaucracy*, Kindle edition, location 671.
46. Amir, *al-shaykh al-mujahid*, p. 65.

47. 'The Words of Abdallah Azzam', pp. 62–63. Azzam later sold the cushions: ibid., p. 63. See also Jarrar, *al-shahid*, p. 30. And Azzam, *al-duktur al-shahid*, p. 92.
48. "I gave out the least expensive boxes of sweets in the store; I bought 150 boxes for the women and children at 18 dinars": Abdallah Azzam, 'wathiqa ila al-ikhwan al-muslimun fi'l urdun.
49. *fi 'uyun mu'asira*, p. 385.
50. Azzam, *al-duktur al-shahid*, p. 85.
51. Jarrar, *al-shahid*, p. 33.
52. Anas, *rihlati ma' al-jihad*, part 3.
53. Sami' al-Haqq (JUI) said he met Azzam several times at Sayyaf's home: author's interview with Sami' al-Haqq, Akora Khattak, 21 March 2008.
54. Bergen, *The Osama Bin Laden I Know*, p. 40.
55. Author's interview with Isam al-Attar, Aachen, 16 December 2009.
56. Badi, *afghanistan: ihtilal al-dhakira*, p. 113.
57. Jarrar, *al-shahid*, p. 343.
58. Azzam, *The Lofty Mountain*, p. 51.
59. Ibid., p. 9.
60. Author's interview with Ahmad Zaidan, Islamabad, 18 March 2008.
61. Author's interview with Rahimullah Yusufzai, Peshawar, 17 March 2008.
62. Author's interview with Ahmad Zaidan, Islamabad, 18 March 2008.
63. Author's interview with Abdallah Anas, London, 27 July 2009; author's interview with Ahmad Zaidan, Islamabad, 18 March 2008.
64. Author's interview with Hudhayfa Azzam, Amman, 12 November 2006.
65. al-Qandahari, *dhikrayat*, p. 229.
66. Ibid., p. 114.
67. Muhammad, *safahat*, p. 101.
68. Abdallah Azzam, 'masani' al-abtal' [Hero Factories], *al-Jihad* no. 36 (November 1987): 4–6.
69. Berger, *Beatings and Bureaucracy*, Kindle edition, location 622.
70. Umm Siddiq, 'suq khayri li-salih al-mujahidin al-afghan' [Charity Market for Afghan Mujahidin], *al-Bunyan al-Marsus* no. 5 (February 1986): 48–50.
71. There were couples where both husband and wife were in the writing business, for example, one issue of *al-Bunyan al-Marsus* had articles by both Umm Suhayb and Abu Suhayb: *al-Bunyan al-Marsus* no. 9 (September 1986), pp. 52 and 62.
72. Hamza, *qafilat da'wat jihad*, p. 149. Described as "very well educated," she also ran a girls' school in Jeddah when she was not on the road.

73. Pauline Lewis, 'Zainab al-Ghazali: Pioneer of Islamist Feminism', *Michigan Journal of History* 4, no. 2 (2007).
74. Tanwir, *Afghanistan*, vol. 2.
75. Anas and Hussain, *To the Mountains*, p. 120.
76. Muhammad, *safahat*, pp. 38 and 40–41; Aziz, "abdallah 'azzam wa juhuduhu', p. 49.
77. Zaidan, *The "Afghan Arabs" Media*, p. 66.
78. Abdallah Azzam, 'risala ila akhawatina al-mujahidat' [Letter to our Mujahid Sisters], *al-Jihad* no. 8 (June 1985): 41.
79. *al-Jihad* no. 9 (17 July 1985), p. 44.
80. She mentioned this in the two eulogies she wrote after Azzam's assassination: *fi 'uyun mu'asira*, pp. 384 and 386.
81. *Al-Bunyan al-Marsus* actually introduced a women's section a few months before *al-Jihad* did: see *al-Bunyan al-Marsus* no. 3 (September 1985), p. 54.
82. See, for example, A'ida Muhajir, 'da'wa ila jihad' [Call to Jihad], *al-Jihad* no. 20 (July 1986): 38 and A'ida Muhajir, 'hamsa fi udhn al-mutabarri 'in' [Whisper in the Ear of the Donors], *al-Jihad* no. 32 (July 1987): 40.
83. Ahlam, 'tahrir al-mar'a' [Women's Liberation], *al-Jihad* no. 18 (June 1986): 34.
84. Bergen, *The Osama Bin Laden I Know*, p. 43.
85. Bayan Kharabsha, 'risalat tifla li'l-jihad' [Letter from a Young Girl to the Jihad], *al-Jihad* no. 28 (March 1987): 38.
86. See Azzam's foreword to the first issue, reproduced in *mawsu'at al-dhakha'ir*, vol. 2, pp. 378–379.
87. The last issue I have seen referenced is number 11, published in 1991: *fi 'uyun mu'asira*, p. 409.
88. Abdallah Azzam, 'muqabala ma' al-da'iya: al-sayyida zaynab al-ghazzali' [Interview with a Preacher: Mrs Zaynab al-Ghazzali], *al-Jihad* no. 14 (December 1985): 38–40. Al-Ghazzali would visit again in the early autumn of 1986; on that occasion, *al-Bunyan al-Marsus* published an interview with her: *al-Bunyan al-Marsus* no. 7–8 (August 1986), pp. 58–60.
89. Hassan Abu Hanieh, *Women and Politics from the Perspective of Islamic Movements in Jordan* (Amman: Friedrich-Ebert-Stiftung, 2008), p. 58.
90. Azzam, *ilhaq bi'l-qafila*, p. 8 (Minbar edition).
91. Ibid., p. 29 (Minbar edition).
92. From Azzam's lecture titled 'ithaf al-'ibad bi-fada'il al-jihad' [Illustrating the Virtues of Jihad to God's Servants], translated by and cited in Nelly Lahoud, 'The Neglected Sex: The Jihadis' Exclusion of Women from Jihad', *Terrorism and Political Violence* 26, no. 5 (20 February 2014): 780–802, p. 785.

93. Ibid., p. 786.
94. Vikram Dodd, 'Roshonara Choudhry: Police Interview Extracts', *The Guardian* Online, 3 November 2010. See also Elizabeth Pearson, 'The Case of Roshonara Choudhry: Implications for Theory on Online Radicalization, ISIS Women, and the Gendered Jihad', *Policy and Internet*, 29 September 2015.
95. Åsne Seierstad, *To Søstre* [Two Sisters](Oslo: Kagge, 2016), p. 26.
96. For a rare exception, see Umm Yahya, 'fima tufakkir hadhihi al-tifla?' [What is this Girl Thinking About?]', *al-Jihad* no. 47 (October 1988): 30–31. Umm Yahya was the director of the women's department of the Canadian Islamic charity Human Concern International (Hay'at al-Ighatha al-Insaniyya al-'Alamiyya).
97. Hauslohner, 'Friend of Zawahiri'.
98. 'Bin-Ladin Associate Interrogated', *al-Sharq al-Awsat* (via FBIS), 24 June 1999; Hafsa al-Rashwan is also the sister of Abd al-Hamid Abd al-Salam, one of the men who participated in the assassination of Anwar Sadat in 1981.
99. Neighbour, *The Mother of Mohammed*, pp. 174–176.
100. Ibid., p. 179.
101. Ibid.
102. Ibid., pp. 184–185.
103. For more on the interaction between Arabs and Afghans, see Strick van Linschoten and Kuehn, *An Enemy we Created*, pp. 69–82, and Brown and Rassler, *Fountainhead*, pp. 78 ff.
104. Azzam, *al-duktur al-shahid*, p. 58.
105. al-Qandahari, *dhikrayat*, p. 235.
106. Azzam, *The Lofty Mountain*, pp. 71–72; Azzam, *'ibar wa basa'ir*, p. 108–109.
107. Ibid., p. 229.
108. Ibid., p. 188.
109. Ibid., p. 53.
110. Ibid., p. 252.
111. Ibid., p. 246.
112. Neighbour, *The Mother of Mohammed*, p. 188.
113. Azzam, *al-duktur al-shahid*, p. 57.
114. Jalali and Grau, *Afghan Guerrilla Warfare*, p. 129.
115. Ibid., pp. 314–315.
116. Ibid., p. 398.
117. Abu Rumman and Sa'id, *al-'alim*, p. 21.
118. For a description of the details, see Anas, *rihlati ma' al-jihad*, part 8, at 17'15".
119. al-Qandahari, *dhikrayat*, p. 85.

120. Azzam, *'ibar wa basa'ir*, p. 70.
121. Azzam, *al-duktur al-shahid*, p. 54.
122. Anas and Hussain, *To the Mountains*, p. 190.
123. al-Qandahari, *dhikrayat*, p. 171.
124. Ibid., p. 27.
125. Ibid., p. 215.
126. Azzam, *al-duktur al-shahid*, p. 52.
127. Anas, *rihlati ma' al-jihad*, part 8, at 17'15".
128. Azzam, *al-duktur al-shahid*, p. 55.
129. Abdallah Azzam, 'li'l-shabab al-dhahibin li-jabhat al-qital fi afghanistan' [To the Youth Going to the Battlefronts in Afghanistan], in *mawsu'at al-dhakha'ir*, vol. 1, p. 800.
130. *fi 'uyun mu'asira*, p. 105.
131. Ibid., p. 106.
132. al-Qandahari, *dhikrayat*, p. 85.
133. Ibid., p. 284.
134. Ibid., p. 285.
135. Interview with Vahid Mojdeh conducted by Anne Stenersen, Kabul, 18 October 2009. I am grateful to Anne Stenersen for sharing this information.
136. al-Qandahari, *dhikrayat*, p. 159.
137. Notin, *La Guerre de l'ombre*, p. 299.
138. Anas, *wiladat*, p. 63.
139. al-Qandahari, *dhikrayat*, p. 251.
140. Ibid., pp. 206–207.
141. Li, 'Taking the Place of Martyrs'.
142. Syed Shahzad says Jamaat-e Islami alone had thousands of Pakistani fighters in Afghanistan: Syed Saleem Shahzad, *Inside al-Qaeda and the Taliban: Beyond Bin Laden and 9/11* (New York: Pluto Press, 2011), p. 207. Arif Jamal says 4,000 Pakistanis joined the Harakat al-Jihad al-Islami alone: Jamal, 'The Growth of the Deobandi Jihad in Afghanistan'. However, we know from the Arab estimates that snapshot aggregate estimates tend to be inflated. Correcting for this tendency, it seems reasonable to suggest that the total number for all groups was very roughly in the order of 5,000.
143. Fair, Hoffman, and Reinares, 'Leader-Led Jihad in Pakistan', p. 577.
144. Hamid and Farrall, *The Arabs*, p. 174.
145. For example, *al-Jihad* occasionally featured fallen Pakistanis: see the martyrdom will of the Pakistani fighter Fakhr al-Islam in *al-Jihad* no. 29 (April 1987), p. 27.
146. Usmani, *Jihad in Afghanistan*, p. 193; see also p. 204.
147. Ibid., p. 251.

148. Shahzad, *Inside al-Qaeda and the Taliban*, p. 207. Mustafa Hamid also refers to two camps for Pakistanis in Khost at the end of the 1980s called Badr and Salman al-Farsi; Hamid and Farrall, *The Arabs*, p. 174.
149. Shahzad's number may well be too high. Abd Rabb al-Rasul Sayyaf later said that only "a small number of [Jamaat-e Islami members] participated. [In practice] they didn't participate." According to Abdallah Anas, Azzam used to complain in private that the Jamaat-e Islami did not do more on the military front. "Sheikh Abdallah had these questions," Abdallah Anas later said, "always he was saying I don't know why these people [aren't doing more], there's a blessed jihad on their doorstep and they are not part of it, either the level of muhajirin or in the level of frontlines": author's interview with Abd Rabb al-Rasul Sayyaf, Paghman, 8 December 2017; author's interview with Abdallah Anas, Paghman, 8 December 2017.
150. In addition to the figures highlighted in the main text, Hamza mentions Abu Ali al-Saudi, Abu Basir al-Filastini, Ibrahim al-Urduni, Abd al-Razzaq, Abu Jabir al-Saudi, Hudhayfa bin Yaman, Abu Rihan, and Abu Jihad: Hamza, *qafilat da'wat jihad*, pp. 64, 101, 123, 126–127, 171, and 205.
151. Ibid., pp. 121–122.
152. Ibid., p. 149. Abu Abd al-Aziz is described as later fighting in Bosnia, so he is probably the red-bearded fighter who became known in Bosnia as "Barbaros." That there were Arabs in Kunar who worked with MDI is corroborated by Tankel, who mentions a Saudi named Abd al-Rahman al-Surayhi, who "played a role in organizing MDI's early training camps in Afghanistan": Tankel, *Storming the World Stage*, p. 20.
153. Hamza, *qafilat da'wat jihad*, p. 138.
154. See, for example, Anas, *wiladat*; al-Qandahari, *dhikrayat*; Hamid and Farrall, *The Arabs*; Salah, *waqa'i' sanawat al-jihad*; Badi, *afghanistan: ihtilal al-dhakira*.
155. al-Qandahari, *dhikrayat*, pp. 23–24.
156. Anas and Hussain, *To the Mountains*, p. 160.
157. 'mukhayyamat tarbawiyya islamiyya' [Islamic Educational Camps], *al-Jihad* 21 (August 1986), pp. 33–35.
158. USA v. Usama bin Laden et al., Southern District of New York, 2001, day 2 (6 February 2001), p. 169 ff.
159. Anas, *rihlati ma' al-jihad*, part 7, at 14'.
160. Yousaf and Adkin, *Afghanistan: The Bear Trap*, p. 32.
161. Muhammad, *safahat*, p. 159.

162. Berger, *Jihad Joe*, pp. 14–15.
163. Badi, *afghanistan: ihtilal al-dhakira*, pp. 112–121.
164. al-Qandahari, *dhikrayat*, p. 192.
165. Anas, *wiladat*, p. 58.
166. al-Qandahari, *dhikrayat*, p. 111.
167. Azzam, *The Tawhid of Action*, p. 7.
168. 'The Words of Abdallah Azzam', pp. 2–3.
169. There is abundant evidence of aspirations to martyrdom among the Afghan Arabs; they are palpable in everything from the letters to the editor of magazines such as *al-Jihad*, in the wills that fighters wrote before being killed (many of which were published in jihadi magazines when they died), in interviews with fighters published in jihadi magazines, in the films recorded in the field by Isam Diraz, in memoirs and testimonies of former Afghan Arabs, and in other sources.
170. al-Qandahari, *dhikrayat*, p. 291.
171. Iain R. Edgar, *The Dream in Islam: From Qur'anic Tradition to Jihadist Inspiration* (New York: Berghahn Books, 2011).
172. al-Qandahari, *dhikrayat*, p. 188.
173. Ibid., p. 200.
174. Ibid., p. 282.
175. Ibid., p. 250.
176. Azzam, *The Lofty Mountain*, p. 45.
177. Miller, *The Audacious Ascetic*, pp. 95–97.
178. Anas and Hussain, *To the Mountains*, p. 163.
179. Muhammad, *safahat*, p. 122.
180. Ibid., p. 114.
181. *al-Jihad* no. 14 (December 1985), pp. 43–44.
182. *al-Jihad* no. 18 (May 1986), p. 28; *al-Jihad* no. 22 (September 1986), p. 42; *al-Jihad* no. 32 (July 1987), p. 44. *Al-Bunyan al-Marsus* published many similar letters; see, for example, no. 3 (September 1985), p. 56; no. 7–8 (August 1986), p. 57; and no. 10 (November 1986), pp. 48–49.
183. *al Jihad* no. 16 (February 1986), p. 36; *al-Jihad* no. 21 (August 1986), p. 38; *al-Jihad* no. 48 (November 1988), p. 39.
184. al-Qandahari, *dhikrayat*, p. 190.
185. Abdallah Anas, *rihlati ma' al-jihad*, part 7, at 35'40" ff.
186. *al-Bunyan al-Marsus* no. 30 (February 1990), p. 9.
187. *al-Jihad* no. 30 (May 1987), pp. 16–20.
188. Muhammad, *safahat*, p. 111.

189. Izzat Muhammad Ibrahim Hassan, 'al-jihad al-afghani fi manzur al-shu'ara' al-'arab 1979–1994' [The Afghan Jihad in the Eyes of Arab Poets, 1979–1994] (Baha al-Din Zakariya University, 1997).
190. Vahid Mojdeh, *afghanistan: panj sal sultat taliban* [*Afghanistan: Five Years under Taliban Power*] (Teheran: Nashreney, 2003), p. 27 (English translation by Sepideh Khalili and Saeed Ganji).
191. 'mukhayyamat tarbawiyya islamiyya' [Islamic Educational Camps], *al-Jihad* 21 (August 1986), pp. 33–35.
192. Nelly Lahoud, 'A Cappella Songs (anashid) in Jihadi Culture,' in *Jihadi Culture: The Art and Social Practices of Militant Islamists*, ed. Thomas Hegghammer (Cambridge: Cambridge University Press, 2017), pp. 42–62, p. 42.
193. Tareekh Osama 118.

Enemy

1. Al Shafey, '*Asharq al-Awsat* Interviews Umm Mohammed'.
2. Abdallah Anas later wrote, "The ISI knew full well what we were up to when Sheikh Azzam set up the office": Anas and Hussain, *To the Mountains*, p. 145.
3. Muhammad, *safahat*, p. 205. In an interview with Lawrence Wright, Muhammad Bayazid (Abu Rida al-Suri) also said that the Pakistanis began closing down the guest houses in Peshawar: Wright, *The Looming Tower*, pp. 116 and 400.
4. Muhammad, *safahat*, p. 112.
5. *fi 'uyun mu'asira*, p. 98.
6. Azzam, *al-duktur al-shahid*, p. 60. The account was corroborated by a former student of Azzam's at the IIUI, who added that Azzam was offered the position of dean at King Abd al-Aziz University: author's interview with Atiq-u-Zafar, Islamabad, March 2008.
7. The most accurate-looking version of this story appears in Azzam, *al-duktur al-shahid*, pp. 61–62, but variants feature in several other sources, notably Jarrar, *al-shahid*, pp. 346–347; Amir, *al-shaykh al-mujahid*, p. 12; and *fi 'uyun mu'asira*, p. 483.
8. Azzam, *al-duktur al-shahid*, p. 61.
9. Ibid., pp. 61–62.
10. *fi 'uyun mu'asira*, p. 107. It was notably during this exile that Azzam recorded the forty-five-lecture lecture series "In the Shade of Surat al-Tawba."
11. Ibid., pp. 482–483.
12. Azzam, *al-duktur al-shahid*, pp. 62–63; Anas and Hussain, *To the Mountains*, p. 188.

13. *al-Bunyan al-Marsus* no. 7–8 (August 1986), pp. 58–60.
14. Azzam, *al-duktur al-shahid*, p. 67.
15. *al-Jihad* no. 54–55 (April 1989), p. 37.
16. *al-Jihad* no. 42 (May 1988), p. 3.
17. *al-Jihad* no. 42 (May 1988), p. 41.
18. *al-Jihad* no. 60 (October 1989), p. 11.
19. *al-Jihad* no. 62 (December 1989), p. 12. This issue was prepared before Azzam's death, and possibly with his input, because his assassination is not mentioned.
20. See *al-Bunyan al-Marsus* no. 24 (September 1988).
21. Rabi' bin Hadi al-Madkhali, 'munadhara 'an afghanistan' [Discussion on Afghanistan], n.d., http://madkhalis.com/2010/02/rab-al-madkhalis-slander-of-abdullah-azzam/ (accessed 25 January 2018).
22. Wright, *The Looming Tower*, pp. 136, 402.
23. Notin, *La Guerre de l'ombre*, pp. 323–324.
24. Author's interview with Prince Turki al-Faisal, Princeton, 12 November 2009.
25. *al-Jihad* no. 19 (June 1986), p. 22.
26. Rougier, *Everyday Jihad*, p. 77.
27. Barnett R. Rubin, 'Arab Islamists in Afghanistan', in *Political Islam: Revolution, Radicalism, or Reform?* ed. John Esposito (Boulder: Lynne Rienner, 1997), 179–206, pp. 196–197; and Roy, *Islam and Resistance*, p. 118.
28. Kevin Bell, 'The First Islamic State: A Look Back at the Islamic Emirate of Kunar', *The Sentinel* 9, no. 2 (February 2016): 9–14.
29. Davis, 'Foreign Combatants in Afghanistan'; Bell, 'The First Islamic State', p. 11.
30. Author's interview with Mishari al-Dhaydi, Riyadh, 21 November 2005.
31. Davis, 'Foreign Combatants in Afghanistan'.
32. Ibid.; Barnett R. Rubin, *The Search for Peace in Afghanistan: From Buffer State to Failed State* (New Haven and London: Yale University Press, 1995), p. 261; Dorronsoro, *Revolution Unending*, p. 232. According to Bell, al-Rumi was a former Muslim Brotherhood member and had previously worked for *al-Jihad* magazine: Bell, 'The First Islamic State', p. 11.
33. Azzam, *al-duktur al-shahid*, pp. 65–66.
34. Ibid., pp. 65–66 and 152.
35. Ibid., p. 136. Prince Turki al-Faisal later insisted in an interview that Abdallah Azzam was banned from the kingdom "in the early 1980s." The date is clearly inaccurate given Azzam's many documented trips to Saudi Arabia throughout the 1980s, but there may have been a ban

toward the end of the decade: author's interview with Prince Turki al-Faisal, Princeton, 12 November 2009.
36. For Prince Salman's involvement with the Afghan and Bosnian jihads, see, for example, David Andrew Weinberg, 'King Salman's Shady History: Foreign Policy', *Foreign Policy* Online, 27 January 2015; Hegghammer, *Jihad in Saudi Arabia*, pp. 20, 25, 28 and 34.
37. Badi, *afghanistan: ihtilal al-dhakira*, pp. 197–198.
38. Twitter messages from Hudhayfa Azzam (@AzzamHuthaifa), 13 March 2018 (accessed 14 March 2018).
39. Badi, *afghanistan: ihtilal al-dhakira*, pp. 182–187.
40. Al-Qandahari later wrote, "What seized my attention was that the Arabs sharing the same nationality were closer to each other than to the Arabs from other nationalities and this was extremely surprising to me because I never had and still do not have any nationalistic feelings": al-Qandahari, *dhikrayat*, p. 234.
41. Anas and Hussain, *To the Mountains*, p. 151.
42. Ibid., pp. 117, 165–166.
43. Ibid., p. 117.
44. *fi 'uyun mu'asira*, p. 40; *al-Bunyan al-Marsus* no. 30 (February 1990), p. 29.
45. *fi 'uyun mu'asira*, p. 352; Anas and Hussain, *To the Mountains*, p. 117.
46. Al-Zawahiri's Salafi background is documented in Stéphane Lacroix's forthcoming history of Salafism in Egypt, which has the working title *A Social and Political History of Egyptian Salafism*.
47. Joas Wagemakers, *A Quietist Jihadi: The Ideology and Influence of Abu Muhammad al-Maqdisi* (Cambridge: Cambridge University Press, 2012).
48. Al-Qandahari later wrote, "I learned later on, that as [Abu Ayyub] was in Peshawar, he ran across a number of Algerians who carried the *takfiri* ideology, did not participate in the battles but settled in Peshawar preaching about the righteous path of Allah. Abu Ayyub thus started perceiving the Mujahidin as being sinners fighting the atheists": al-Qandahari, *dhikrayat*, p. 183.
49. Wagemakers, *A Quietist Jihadi*, p. 38.
50. Abd al-Qadir Bin Abd al-Aziz, *risalat al-'umda fi i'dad al-'udda li'l-jihad fi sabil allah* [Treatise on the Pillar of Military Preparation for Jihad in God's Path] (Minbar al-Tawhid wa'l-Jihad, 1988); Abu Muhammad al-Maqdisi, *millat ibrahim wa da'wat al-anbiya' wa'l-mursalin* [The Community of Abraham and the Call of the Prophets and the Messengers] (Minbar al-Tawhid wa'l-Jihad, 1984); Abu Muhammad al-Maqdisi, *al-kawashif al-jaliyya fi kufr al-dawla al-sa'udiyya* [The Blatant Proof of the Infidel Nature of the Saudi State]

(Minbar al-Tawhid wa'l-Jihad, 1989). See also Simon Wolfgang Fuchs, *Proper Signposts for the Camp: The Reception of Classical Authorities in the Ǧihādī Manual* al-'Umda fī I'dād al-'Udda (Würzburg: Ergon-Verlag, 2011); Nelly Lahoud, *The Jihadis' Path to Self-Destruction* (New York: Columbia University Press, 2010), pp. 132–137; Wagemakers, *A Quietist Jihadi*, p. 38; and Lacroix, *Awakening Islam*, pp. 101–102.

51. Lia, *Architect of Global Jihad*, p. 116.
52. Anas, *wiladat*, p. 73.
53. Bergen, *The Osama Bin Laden I Know*, p. 95.
54. Wright, *The Looming Tower*, p. 130.
55. Bergen, *The Osama Bin Laden I Know*, p. 69.
56. Abu Muhammad al-Maqdisi, *marhalat Afghanistan* [The Afghanistan Stage], Minbar al-Tawhid wa'l-Jihad, n.d.
57. Ibid.; see also Wagemakers, *A Quietist Jihadi*, pp. 38–39.
58. Author's interview with Abu Muhammad al-Maqdisi, Zarqa, 11 July 2018.
59. Anas and Hussain, *To the Mountains*, pp. 177 and 189.
60. Bergen, *The Osama Bin Laden I Know*, p. 67. According to Abdallah Anas, it was during al-Zawahiri's time in Jeddah around 1985 that he first met Usama Bin Ladin: Anas and Hussain, *To the Mountains*, p. 180. For more on al-Zawahiri's background see Wright, 'The Man Behind Bin Laden'; Muntassir al-Zayyat, *The Road to al-Qaeda: The Story of Bin Laden's Right-Hand Man* (London: Pluto Press, 2004); Youssef Aboul-Enein, *Ayman al-Zawahiri: The Ideologue of Modern Islamic Militancy* (Maxwell Air Force Base, AL: USAF Counterproliferation Center, Air University, 2004); Stéphane Lacroix, 'Ayman al-Zawahiri, le vétéran du jihad', in *al-Qaida dans le texte*, ed. Gilles Kepel et al. (Paris: Presses Universitaires de France, 2008), 221–242; Abd al-Rahim, *ayman al-zawahiri*; Abd al-Rahman Hallush, *al-shaykh wa'l-tabib: usama bin ladin wa ayman al-zawahiri* [The Shaykh and the Doctor: Usama Bin Ladin and Ayman al-Zawahiri] (Beirut: Riyadh al-Rayyis, 2011). For English translations of several of his writings, see Laura Mansfield, *His Own Words: A Translation of the Writings of Dr. Ayman al-Zawahiri* ([Old Tappan, NJ]: TLG Publications, 2006).
61. Wright, *The Looming Tower*, pp. 122 ff. For more on Dr. Fadl, see Lahoud, *The Jihadis' Path to Self-Destruction*, pp. 131–132.
62. Anas and Hussain, *To the Mountains*, p. 177. Ridwan Nammus went on to become one of the most long-serving al-Qaida members in the

group's history. After two decades with al-Qaida Central, he relocated to Syria around 2013, where he served in Jabhat al-Nusra until his death in 2016: Thomas Joscelyn, 'al Nusrah Front Confirms al Qaeda Veteran Killed in US Airstrike,' *The Long War Journal*, 6 April 2016.
63. Anas and Hussain, *To the Mountains*, p. 189.
64. Bergen, *The Osama Bin Laden I Know*, pp. 68 and 95.
65. Ahmad Sa'id Khadr was an Egyptian who had gone to Canada in the mid-1970s to study engineering. In Canada he married and obtained citizenship, but he also became more religious. In 1982 the family moved to Bahrain, and in the summer of 1983 he made his first trip to Pakistan. He went again in mid-1984, and in January 1985 he moved to Peshawar for good to work for a Kuwaiti organization called Lajnat al-Da'wa. Later, in 1988, he became involved with the Canadian NGO Human Concern International (Hay'at al-Ighatha al-Insaniyya al-'Alamiyya), which had been founded in 1980 by two Muslim doctors from Calgary. He presented himself not as a fighter but as a charity man, and unlike other Arabs in Peshawar, he wore Western trousers and dress shirts. In 1986 or 1987 he met Ayman al-Zawahiri and the two became close. Ahmad Khadr was killed in Afghanistan in 2003, and two of his sons ended up in Guantanamo: Michelle Shephard, *Guantanamo's Child: The Untold Story of Omar Khadr* (Mississauga, Ont: Wiley, 2008), *passim*. See also Tawil, *Brothers in Arms*, pp. 40–41.
66. The background story presented here is based on the written ruling produced by the adjudication committee in late December 1988: see Berger, *Beatings and Bureaucracy*, Kindle version, location 623 ff.
67. That the break-in occurred is undisputed; in the records from the adjudication, Wa'il Julaydan does not deny it, and most of the discussion is about issues arising from the documents taken from Khadr's office.
68. Berger, *Beatings and Bureaucracy*, Kindle version.
69. Wright, *The Looming Tower*, pp. 136–137. See also Anas's own, slightly less dramatic account in Anas and Hussain, *To the Mountains*, pp. 203–204.
70. Shephard, *Guantanamo's Child*, pp. 32–34. I thank Vahid Brown for alerting me to Shephard's account.
71. Berger, *Beatings and Bureaucracy*, Kindle version, location 623 ff.
72. It is not clear why Azzam was not present. Shephard says Bin Ladin advised Azzam to stay away for his own safety, but it could well be that the parties agreed that each should be represented by one person.
73. Berger, *Beatings and Bureaucracy*, Kindle version, location 623 ff.

74. Ayman al-Zawahiri, *The Exoneration*, 2008, https://fas.org/irp/dni/osc/exoneration.pdf, p. 246 (accessed 22 January 2018). I quote al-Zawahiri's quotation from Dr. Fadl's book.
75. Ibid., pp. 246–247. Incidentally, Usama Bin Ladin later reproached al-Zawahiri for airing the dirty laundry in this way; in a letter from the late 2000s found in the Abbottabad compound, he wrote, "Perhaps keeping quiet about Fadl's intent in his expression would have been better": "Letter to Abu Muhammad," www.dni.gov/files/documents/ubl2016/english/Letter%20to%20Shaykh%20Abu%20Muhammad.pdf (accessed 27 February 2018). Bin Ladin says in the same letter that he himself did not attend the al-Tahaddi trial.
76. Tawil, *Brothers in Arms*, p. 39.
77. 'liqa' zawjat al-shahid'.
78. Author's interview with Abdallah Anas, Kabul, 8 December 2017.
79. 'The Open Meeting with Sheikh Ayman al-Zawahiri – Part One', 2008, https://azelin.files.wordpress.com/2010/08/the-open-meeting-with-shaykh-ayman-al-zawahiri-1429h.pdf (accessed 22 January 2018), p. 16.
80. al-Zawahiri, *The Exoneration*, pp. 37, 106, and 247.
81. Hekmatyar was very hostile to Massoud, and openly accused him of being a Russian agent, among other things. For a taste of Hekmatyar's vitriol against Massoud, see Gulbuddin Hekmatyar, *Secret Plans Open Faces: From the Withdrawal of Russians to the Fall of the Coalition Government* (Peshawar: University of Peshawar, 2004).
82. Coll, *Ghost Wars*, pp. 107–119.
83. Massoud had attended the French high school Lycée Esteqlal in Kabul because his father had been a high-ranking officer in the Afghan army.
84. He gave the lecture in Lahore in November 1989: Azzam, *al-duktur al-shahid*, pp. 138 and 141.
85. Jamal Khashoggi said, "Azzam had a strategic mind. And he saw where the problem lay in Afghanistan. It was a problem between Massoud and Hekmatyar. If you bring those two together, then the problem of Afghanistan would be solved ... so he put so much effort on that front": Bergen, *The Osama Bin Laden I Know*, p. 97.
86. In mid-1985 Abdallah Azzam and Massoud exchanged letters via an envoy from the Services Bureau. Azzam's letter and Massoud's response, both of which contained mainly niceties, were published in *al-Jihad* no. 12 (October 1985), pp. 22–25.
87. Abdallah Azzam, *shahr bayna al-'amaliqa* [A Month among Giants] (Minbar al-Tawhid wa'l-Jihad, 1989). See also the report in *al-Jihad* no. 53 (March 1989), pp. 32–36.
88. al-Dhiyabi, 'Saudi Academic Recounts Experiences from Afghan War'.

89. Anas, *wiladat*, p. 77.
90. Bergen, *The Osama Bin Laden I Know*, p. 94.
91. Coll, *Ghost Wars*, pp. 202–203.
92. Abdallah Anas later said, "Osama told me in one meeting, 'I don't need you to exaggerate about Massoud. Nothing happened inside Afghanistan.' He was under the influence of Gulbuddin Hekmatyar, who hated Massoud": Bergen, *The Osama Bin Laden I Know*, pp. 70–71. Similarly, Coll noted that "increasingly, Osama bin Laden sided with Hekmatyar, alienating his mentor Abdullah Azzam": Coll, *Ghost Wars*, pp. 202–203.
93. Coll, *Ghost Wars*, p. 202; Anas, *wiladat*, pp. 74–75.
94. al-Dhiyabi, 'Saudi Academic Recounts Experiences from Afghan War'.
95. Anas and Hussain, *To the Mountains*, pp. 198–202; Anas, *wiladat*, p. 74; Tawil, *Brothers in Arms*, pp. 21–24; al-Dhiyabi, 'Saudi Academic Recounts Experiences from Afghan War'; author's telephone interview with Jamal Khashoggi, 14 September 2018.
96. al-Dhiyabi, 'Saudi Academic Recounts Experiences from Afghan War'.
97. Bergen, *The Osama Bin Laden I Know*, p. 69.
98. Anas, *wiladat*, pp. 77–80. See also Azzam, *al-duktur al-shahid*, p. 96; Barnett R. Rubin, *The Fragmentation of Afghanistan: State Formation and Collapse in the International System*, 2nd ed. (New Haven: Yale University Press, 2002), pp. 250–251; Coll, *Ghost Wars*, pp. 202–203; Yousaf and Adkin, *Afghanistan: The Bear Trap*, p. 129.
99. *al-Jihad* no. 59 (September 1989), p. 9; Coll, *Ghost Wars*, pp. 202–203; Bergen, *The Osama Bin Laden I Know*, p. 71.
100. The committee was led by Azzam and included Abd al-Majid al-Zindani, Qazi Hussain Ahmad, Zubayri Walfif, Fathi al-Rifa'i, Muhammad Umar Zubayr, Muhammad Sawwaf, and Yasin Qadhi: *fi 'uyun mu'asira*, pp. 115 and 280.
101. Ibid., p. 280.
102. Ibid., p. 115. The text of the agreement is reproduced in ibid., p. 136.
103. Ibid., p. 176.
104. *al-Jihad* no. 43 (June 1988), p. 8.
105. Jarrar, *al-shahid*, p. 74.
106. Ibid., p. 65.
107. Abu Harith says they overlapped at al-Azhar in the early 1970s and met briefly there, but this is uncertain: author's interview with Abu Harith, Amman, 8 May 2008.
108. Maliach, 'Abdullah Azzam, al-Qaeda, and Hamas', p. 87.
109. 'liqa' zawjat al-shahid'; Al Shafey, '*Asharq al-Awsat* Interviews Umm Mohammed'.

110. Author's interview with Jamal Isma'il, Islamabad, 20 March 2008; author's interview with Abu Harith, Amman, 8 May 2008.
111. Maliach, 'Abdullah Azzam, al-Qaeda, and Hamas', p. 84.
112. Azzam, *al-duktur al-shahid*, p. 150.
113. Abdallah Azzam, 'fi'l-ta'amur al-'alami – al-juz' al-thani' [On the Global Conspiracy – Part Two], in *mawsu'at al-dhakha'ir*, vol. 4, p. 637.
114. Author's interview with Jamal Isma'il, Islamabad, 20 March 2008.
115. Jarrar, *al-shahid*, p. 356.
116. Ibid., p. 65.
117. Author's interview with Jamal Isma'il, Islamabad, 20 March 2008. Isma'il's statement is corroborated by another source, which says that Azzam "made a special course for [the Palestinian trainees]": Jarrar, *al-shahid*, p. 356.
118. al-Dahshan, 'juhud al-duktur', p. 105.
119. Ehud Ya'ari, 'The Afghans Are Coming', *Jerusalem Report*, 2 July 1992: 30.
120. There are also cases of Palestinian attackers who reportedly confessed during interrogation to having links to Azzam, but such statements may have been made under duress. Asaf Maliach, for example, wrote that "a former member of the Engineers Union in Nablus and a well-known member of Hamas, 'Abd al-Hadi was arrested at the end of the 1980s by Israeli security forces, who suspected him of planning to detonate a car bomb inside Israel. During his interrogation, 'Abd al-Hadi confessed that he had been trained in Pakistan by 'Abdullah 'Azzam, and that 'Azzam had trained additional Palestinians, whom he sent back to the territories": Asaf Maliach, 'Bin Ladin, Palestine and al-Qa'ida's Operational Strategy', *Middle Eastern Studies* 44, no. 3 (May 2008): 353–375, p. 355.
121. Jarrar, *al-shahid*, p. 353.
122. 'From Kabul to al-Quds', video file in author's possession.
123. *al-Jihad* no. 60 (October 1989), p. 41.
124. 'liqa' zawjat al-shahid'.
125. 'Izz al-Din Subhi al-Shaykh Khalil', www.alqassam.net, n.d. (accessed 10 April 2018). I thank Alexander De la Paz for this reference.
126. 'Ibrahim Abd al-Karim Bani Awda', www.alqassam.net/arabic/martyrs/details/31, n.d. (accessed 10 April 2018). I thank Alexander De la Paz and Erik Skare for this reference.
127. Jarrar, *al-shahid*, p. 356.
128. Azzam, *hamas*, p. 81.
129. Ibid.
130. Author's interview with Jamal Isma'il, Islamabad, 20 March 2008.
131. Jarrar, *al-shahid*, p. 356.

132. Author's interview with Reuven Paz, London, 26 March 2012.
133. Author's interview with Shaul Shay, Hertzlia, 8 September 2013.
134. Shlomo Shpiro, 'Israeli Intelligence and al-Qaeda', *International Journal of Intelligence and CounterIntelligence* 25, no. 2 (2012): 240–259, p. 241.
135. Author's interview with Yonathan Fighel, Hertzlia, 8 September 2013.
136. Author's interview with Reuven Paz, London, 26 March 2012; author's interview with Ely Karmon, Hertzlia, 7 September 2013; author's interview with Yonathan Fighel, Hertzlia, 8 September 2013; author's interview with Shaul Shay, Hertzlia, 8 September 2013.
137. Author's interview with Yonathan Fighel, Hertzlia, 8 September 2013.

Martyr

1. *fi 'uyun mu'asira*, p. 132.
2. *al-Jihad* no. 28 (March 1987), pp. 28–32.
3. One Western official put the number at 400 per year: author's telephone interview with Alastair Crooke, 23 March 2008. My review of the reporting in *The Frontier Post*, a local English-language newspaper for the Peshawar area, identified over twenty major security incidents in 1988 alone.
4. Zaidan, *The "Afghan Arabs" Media*, p. 69. Adnan Ibrahim was a former Syrian military officer who made a name for himself as something of a military correspondent for *al-Jihad* magazine in the mid-1980s.
5. *fi 'uyun mu'asira*, p. 188.
6. For example, Mahmud Azzam later wrote that Azzam had been told by Pakistani authorities that the USA was out to kill him: Azzam, *al-duktur al-shahid*, p. 64. "The Palestinian ambassador in Pakistan, Mr. Ahmad Salmani, also warned Abdallah Azzam and advised him to look after himself because he had become a target of the Zionist enemy due to his training Palestinian youth and urging them to fight the Jews": Aziz, "abdallah 'azzam wa juhuduhu', p. 6.
7. FBIS, 'Compilation', p. 125.
8. *fi 'uyun mu'asira*, p. 66.
9. Author's interview with Abu Harith, Amman, 8 May 2008.
10. Author's telephone interview with Jamal Khashoggi, 14 September 2018.
11. *fi 'uyun mu'asira*, pp. 53 and 58.
12. 'Discovery of an Explosive Device in the Arabs' Mosque in Peshawar', *al-Jihad* no. 61 (November 1989), p. 13. See also Abu Rumman and Sa'id, *al-'alim*, p. 16; Amir, *al-shaykh al-mujahid*, p. 63; Azzam, *al-duktur al-shahid*, p. 206. Bin Ladin also mentioned this in a 1998 interview: see FBIS, 'Compilation', p. 125.

13. Most of what we know comes from eyewitness reports recorded in jihadi magazines and local newspapers right after the event. For a collection of descriptions of what happened, see *fi 'uyun mu'asira*, pp. 125–137. At least two different drawings of the blast area have been published: see Jarrar, *al-shahid*, p. 211; and *al-Bunyan al-Marsus* no. 30 (February 1990), pp. 6–7. A short, grainy video recording of the car wreckage features in Abu Hilala's documentary about Azzam. It shows a mangled red car with the number plate SLA 22, but little of the surroundings: Abu Hilala, *awwal al-afghan al-'arab*, part 1, at 2'40" and 6'46".
14. Jarrar, *al-shahid*, p. 211.
15. See, for example, Miniter, *Mastermind*, p. 110.
16. As Ahmad Zaidan noted, "It is inconceivable that Bin Ladin or Zawahiri killed Azzam. They needed him": author's interview with Ahmad Zaidan, Islamabad, 18 March 2008.
17. Bergen, *The Osama Bin Laden I Know*, p. 97. Jamal Isma'il said Usama was ordered back to Saudi Arabia by Saudi authorities after allegations that he helped fund a scheme to buy votes in the Pakistan National Assembly for a no-confidence vote in Benazir Bhutto: author's interview with Jamal Isma'il, Islamabad, 21 March 2008.
18. Bergen, *The Osama Bin Laden I Know*, p. 97.
19. From Bin Ladin's 1999 interview with al-Jazeera, transcribed in FBIS, 'Compilation', p. 125.
20. The information had come up in the context of their trying to turn Humam al-Balawi (aka Abu Dujana al-Khorasani) into an informant: Joby Warrick, *The Triple Agent: The al-Qaeda Mole who Infiltrated the CIA* (New York: Doubleday, 2011), p. 82; see also 'Interview with Abu Dujana al-Khorasani', al-Sahab media, posted on al-Tahaddi forum, 28 February 2010, www.atahadi.com/vb/showthread.php?t=13625 (accessed 28 February 2010).
21. Warrick, *The Triple Agent*, p. 82.
22. Author's interview with Hudhayfa Azzam, Amman, 11 September 2006; Azzam, *al-duktur al-shahid*, p. 98.
23. Coll, *Ghost Wars*, pp. 136 and 139.
24. Peter Bergen notes that "Mossad might also have wanted Azzam dead": Bergen, *The Osama Bin Laden I Know*, p. 92. Ahmad Zaidan also mentions Mossad as one of two main candidates, along with KHAD: ibid., p. 97.
25. FBIS, 'Compilation', p. 125; see also pp. 5, 8, and 14.
26. Between 1948 and 2000, Israel conducted around 500 targeted killing operations, killing at least 1,000 people: Ronen Bergman, *Rise and Kill First: The Secret History of Israel's Targeted Assassinations*

(New York: Random House, 2018), p. xxii. Most of these occurred in the Palestinian Territories; Bergman describes external Mossad operations as "sporadic" (p. 504). Most of the Mossad's victims in the 1970s and 1980s were leftist Palestinian militants, but it would later also go after Hamas leaders such as Khalid Mash'al in Amman in 1997.
27. Author's interview with Bruce Hoffman, Amman, 29 October 2015.
28. 'The Mossad and Imad Mughniyeh', *Jerusalem Post*, 19 February 2008.
29. Bergman, *Rise and Kill First*, p. 412.
30. Peter Bergen noted, "The more I looked into this, the more plausible it looked that it was ... a coalition of Egyptian hardliners and the Afghan leader Gulbuddin Hekmatyar, who had the strongest motives and inclination to murder Azzam": Bergen, *The Osama Bin Laden I Know*, p. 93.
31. Ibid., p. 94.
32. Ibid., p. 95.
33. See, for example, *mawsu'at al-jihad*, pp. 521–527. We do not know whether this section was written in the 1980s or later.
34. Peter Tomsen notably suggests that the assassination may have been orchestrated by Hekmatyar in collaboration with the ISI, because Azzam had moved closer to Massoud: Tomsen, *The Wars of Afghanistan*, pp. 387–388.
35. Author's interview with Prince Turki al-Faisal, Princeton, 12 November 2009.
36. Bergen, *The Osama Bin Laden I Know*, p. 97.
37. Dorronsoro, *Revolution Unending*, p. 158.
38. Lohbeck, *Holy War, Unholy Victory*, p. 128.
39. Lohbeck writes that "spokesmen for Hekmatyar warned Afghan refugees that those who supported Zahir Shah would share Professor Majrooh's fate": ibid., p. 236.
40. Coll, *Ghost Wars*, pp. 181–182.
41. For an account of Jamil al-Rahman's killing at hands of Abdallah al-Rumi, see al-Qandahari, *dhikrayat*, pp. 157–163 and Ali bin Ibrahim al-Nimla, *al-jihad wa'l-mujahidun fi afghanistan* [Jihad and Mujahidin in Afghanistan] (Riyadh: Maktabat al-Ubaykan, 1994), pp. 55–59.
42. Hamid and Farrall, *The Arabs*, p. 83.
43. Tomsen, *The Wars of Afghanistan*, pp. 384–385.
44. Author's telephone interview with Jamal Khashoggi, 14 September 2018.
45. Khashoggi is the only source to suggest that Hekmatyar saw it this way. Other sources (see the previous chapter) suggest the late 1989 process was straightforward peace negotiation and not an inquiry into the Farkhar massacre.

46. Bearden and Risen, *The Main Enemy*, p. 236.
47. Coll, *Ghost Wars*, p. 134.
48. Anas, *wiladat*, p. 61.
49. Author's interview with Abu Harith, Amman, 8 May 2008.
50. Author's interview with Ahmad Zaidan, Islamabad, 20 March 2008.
51. *fi 'uyun mu'asira*, p. 51. The "most recent long trip" refers to a trip earlier in 1989 that Abdallah Anas described in his book: "Hekmatyar asked Sheikh Azzam to accompany him on his tour into Afghanistan just as he had accompanied Rabbani . . . Indeed, Sheikh Azzam entered with Hekmatyar the territories of the Islamic Party on the outskirts of Kabul and the eastern areas, and I accompanied them on the tour based on a request from Sheikh Abdullah Azzam": Anas, *wiladat*, p. 78.
52. He was interviewed in issues 50 (December 1988), 51 (January 1988), and 60 (October 1989).
53. 'kalimat al-shaykh 'abdallah 'azzam' [The Word of Shaykh Abdallah Azzam], in *mawsu'at al-dhakha'ir*, vol. 4, pp. 1098–1102.
54. *fi 'uyun mu'asira*, pp. 51, 72, 336, and 378–379. Since then, however, he has not said much publicly about the Azzam assassination. His short book from 1999 about Afghan politics from 1988 to 1998 does not mention Azzam or other Arabs: Hekmatyar, *Secret Plans Open Faces*.
55. Among the people who have suggested KhAD or Russian intelligence are Rahimullah Yusufzai, Gilles Dorronsoro, Sami' al-Haqq, and Ahmad Zaidan. Author's interview with Rahimullah Yusufzai, Peshawar, 17 March 2008; author's interview with Gilles Dorronsoro, Amman, 28 October 2015; author's interview with Sami' al-Haqq, Akora Khattak, 21 March 2008; Bergen, *The Osama Bin Laden I Know*, p. 97.
56. Yousaf and Adkin, *Afghanistan: The Bear Trap*, p. 12.
57. Lohbeck, *Holy War, Unholy Victory*, p. 191; see also pp. 54 and 206. Lohbeck also writes that he interviewed a KhAD defector who "had been in charge of disbursing payments to KhAD agents and employees for various operations outside Afghanistan. The most significant was in early 1988 when he delivered money to a small group of Tui tribesmen in Pakistan. The men were paid to assassinate a prominent Shiite Mullah in Peshawar named Arif Husseini": ibid., p. 251.
58. Amir, *al-shaykh al-mujahid*, pp. 200 ff.
59. Interview with Vahid Mojdeh conducted by Anne Stenersen, Kabul, 18 October 2009.
60. *fi 'uyun mu'asira*, pp. 363–365.
61. Author's interview with Abdallah Anas, London, 28 March 2012.
62. *fi 'uyun mu'asira*, p. 363.
63. Ibid., p. 365.

64. Yousaf and Adkin, *Afghanistan: The Bear Trap*, pp. 146–147.
65. Coll, *Ghost Wars*, pp. 132–133.
66. Ibid., p. 135.
67. Interview with Vahid Mojdeh conducted by Anne Stenersen, Kabul, 18 October 2009.
68. Hamid and Farrall, *The Arabs*, p. 166.
69. Email correspondence with Hein G. Kiessling, 6 November 2017.
70. In March 2018 Abd Rabb al-Rasul Sayyaf indicated to *al-Sharq al-Awsat* that he knew who was behind Azzam's assassination. He said, cryptically, that he "had a lot of information regarding the Jihad in Afghanistan, including the killing of Azzam," and that "I will raise the curtain on time, in anticipation of the emergence of new sedition": Nasser al-Haqbani, 'Exclusive – Sayyaf to *Asharq al-Awsat*: I Know Who Killed Azzam', *al-Sharq al-Awsat* English Online, 20 February 2018.
71. Abu Rumman and Sa'id, *al-'alim*, pp. 125–134; Amir, *al-shaykh al-mujahid*, pp. 135–136.
72. Hatina, 'Warrior Saints', Kindle version, location 4768 ff.
73. Abu Rumman and Sa'id, *al-'alim*, p. 149.
74. *fi 'uyun mu'asira*, pp. 88 and 128.
75. Azzam, *al-duktur al-shahid*, p. 216.
76. Ibid., pp. 217–218.
77. Abu Rumman and Sa'id, *al-'alim*, p. 149.
78. Hatina, 'Warrior Saints', Kindle version, location 4787–4792.
79. *fi 'uyun mu'asira*, pp. 46–84 and 120.
80. Ibid., p. 350.
81. Bergen, *The Osama Bin Laden I know*, p. 96.
82. Ibid., pp. 132 and 284; Amir, *al-shaykh al-mujahid*, p. 305.
83. *al-Bunyan al-Marsus* no. 30 (February 1990), pp. 16–17.
84. *fi 'uyun mu'asira*, p. 351.
85. Ibid., pp. 335–336.
86. Azzam, *al-duktur al-shahid*, p. 147.
87. *fi 'uyun mu'asira*, p. 89 and 349.
88. Ibid., p. 272.
89. Maliach, 'Abdullah Azzam, al-Qaeda, and Hamas', p. 88. Amir, *al-shaykh al-mujahid*, pp. 159–160; Abu Rumman and Sa'id, *al-'alim*, pp. 135–136.
90. Rougier, *Everyday Jihad*, p. 70.
91. *fi 'uyun mu'asira*, p. 377.
92. Anas and Hussain, *To the Mountains*, p. 210.
93. Zaidan, *The "Afghan Arabs" Media*, p. 14.
94. That said, Anas hints at a degree of controversy also over his appointment: "In January 1990 *barring a few glitches* [my

emphasis], I was now running the Arab Services Bureau": Anas and Hussain, *To the Mountains*, p. 116.
95. Author's interview with Jamal Isma'il, Islamabad, 21 March 2008.
96. Author's interview with Jamal Isma'il, Islamabad, 21 March 2008. Noman Benothman says the Muslim Brotherhood "got involved to impose" Abbas; this is likely a reference to al-Zindani's role: author's interview with Noman Benothman, London, 29 September 2010.
97. Azzam, *al-duktur al-shahid*, p. 221; author's interview with Jamal Isma'il, Islamabad, 20 March 2008. Imad Ahmed moved to Jeddah. An Egyptian named Isam Abd al-Hakim took over, together with "one who had come recently from Jordan, a graduate [in] journalism from a Jordanian University."
98. Author's interview with Jamal Isma'il, Islamabad, 21 March 2008.
99. Author's interview with Jamal Isma'il, Islamabad, 21 March 2008.
100. Azzam, *al-duktur al-shahid*, p. 222.
101. *fi 'uyun mu'asira*, p. 190.
102. *al-Jihad* no. 82 (September 1991), p. 16.
103. Author's interview with Jamal Isma'il, Islamabad, 21 March 2008; Azzam, *al-duktur al-shahid*, p. 222.
104. Anas and Hussain, *To the Mountains*, p. 116. Gerald Posner, *Why America Slept: The Failure to Prevent 9/11* (New York: Ballantine Books, 2003), pp. 8–10.
105. Anas and Hussain, *To the Mountains*, p. 236.
106. Author's interview with Jamal Isma'il, Islamabad, 21 March 2008.
107. Author's interview with Jamal Isma'il, Islamabad, 21 March 2008.
108. Hamid and Farrall, *The Arabs*, p. 172.
109. Anas, *wiladat*, p. 90.
110. Bergen, *The Osama Bin Laden I Know*, p. 85.
111. Li, 'Taking the Place of Martyrs', p. 16.
112. Salah, *waqa'i' sanawat al-jihad*, p. 113.
113. Author's interview with Kamal al-Helbawy, London, 23 March 2008.
114. Author's interview with Jamal Isma'il, Islamabad, 21 March 2008.
115. For more on this typology, see Thomas Hegghammer, 'Jihadi Salafis or Revolutionaries? On Theology and Politics in the Study of Militant Islamism', in *Global Salafism: Islam's New Religious Movement*, ed. Roel Meijer (New York: Columbia University Press, 2009), 244–266.
116. See, for example, the "Letter from the wife of the martyr Abdallah Azzam to the leaders of the Afghan mujahidin" and her "Open letter from the wife of the martyr Abdallah Azzam to the Women's Islamic conference in America and Sweden": *mawsu'at al-dhakha'ir*, vol. 2, pp. 373–375.
117. Ibid., pp. 38 and 40–41; *fi 'uyun mu'asira*, pp. 165–170.

118. Yusuf al-Azm, 'al-shahid 'abdallah 'azzam: wuduh al-ru'ya wa sidq al-sira' [The Martyr Abdallah Azzam: Clarity of Vision and Sincerity of Conduct], *al-Sabil*, 8 August 1995 p. 2.
119. Neighbour, *The Mother of Mohammed*, p. 186.
120. Ibid., p. 193.
121. al-Dahshan, 'juhud al-duktur', p. 31.
122. Azzam, *al-duktur al-shahid*, p. 244.
123. Steven Emerson's 1994 PBS documentary 'Terrorists among us: Jihad in America' (https://cosmolearning.org/documentaries/terrorists-among-us-jihad-in-america-jihad-in-america-1049/) includes a segment showing Fayiz Azzam speaking at a fundraising rally in Atlanta in 1990.
124. Emerson, *American Jihad*, pp. 11–12. Emerson had gone to Jenin in 1993 and looked up one of Azzam's brothers-in-law. The brother-in-law told Emerson that Azzam had a nephew in Chicago named Abu Ayman who was in closer touch with the relatives in Peshawar. Emerson then went to visit the nephew in Bridgeview, Illinois. "He told me about Hudaifa, one of Abdullah's sons, and said he was trying to hold together his father's organization in Peshawar." Abu Ayman provided the introduction to Hudhyfa. Hudhayfa later regretted the decision to receive Emerson. The family felt misrepresented in Emerson's subsequent book and documentary, and they felt Emerson had not been honest about the true purpose of his visit: author's interview with Hudhayfa Azzam, Amman, 11 September 2006.
125. Ibid., pp. 62 and 64–72.
126. Ibid., pp. 71–72.
127. Ibid., p. 73.
128. Ibid., pp. 76–77.
129. Al Shafey, '*Asharq al-Awsat* Interviews Umm Mohammed'; 'liqa' zawjat al-shahid'.
130. Rosen, *Aftermath*, p. 132.
131. Ibid.
132. Fitzgerald, 'The Son of the Father of Jihad'.
133. Anas and Hussain, *To the Mountains*, pp. 141, 235, 237–238; author's interview with Abdallah Anas, London, 28 March 2012.
134. Hussein, 'Jihad, Then and Now'.
135. 'Jordanian Guantanamo Prisoner Released', UPI, 14 August 2004.
136. Azzam, *al-duktur al-shahid*, p. 21.

Icon

1. Author's interview with Abdallah Anas, Kabul, 8 December 2017.
2. al-Haddushi, 'nubdha mukhtasira'.

3. See, for example, the speech by the Afghan Mujahidin commander Muhammad Yasir in 1989: *fi ʻuyun muʻasira*, p. 76, or the female writer Umm al-Mathani: ibid., p. 390.
4. 'The Abdullah Azzam of Syria: A Profile of Abdallah Muhammad Bin Sulayman al-Muhaysini', Jamestown.org, 7 February 2017.
5. FBIS, 'Compilation', p. 125.
6. al-Zawahiri, *The Exoneration*, pp. 32–37. In fact, the extract was later published as a standalone document and circulated on jihadi websites under the title 'Abdullah Azzam: the Wounds of al-Quds on the Peaks of the Hindu Kush': document in author's possession.
7. al-Filastini, 'shaykh al-jihad'.
8. Miller, *The Audacious Ascetic*, p. 87.
9. Azzam features in seven of the approximately 260 Abbottabad documents released between May 2015 and January 2017: see 'Bin Laden's Bookshelf', www.dni.gov/index.php/features/bin-laden-s-bookshelf (accessed 27 February 2018). I have not systematically reviewed the much larger cache of Abbottabad documents released on 1 November 2017: see 'November 2017 Release of Abbottabad Compound Material', www.cia.gov/library/abbottabad-compound/index.html (accessed 27 February 2018).
10. 'Jihad in Pakistan', www.dni.gov/files/documents/ubl2016/english/Jihad%20in%20Pakistan.pdf (accessed 27 February 2018).
11. For example, in late August 2018 the channels Sham'ul Melahim, Livet i Sham, shabakat al-fida', Umm Ammara, and Mujahidah all posted Azzam materials, such as his book *Signs of the Merciful* (in both Arabic and English) and videotaped lectures (with English and French subtitles), in addition to memes featuring his picture and selected quotes.
12. See, for example, 'The Dr. Abdallah Azzam Academy', Meir Amit Intelligence and Terrorism Information Center, 6 April 2009, pp. 10–12, www.terrorism-info.org.il/Data/pdf/PDF_09_158_2.pdf (accessed 22 January 2018).
13. The quotation read: "If you want to liberate a land, place in your gun ten bullets: nine for the traitors and one for the enemy": Aymenn J. al-Tamimi, 'The Islamic State Billboards and Murals of Tel Afar and Mosul', Aymenn Jawad al-Tamimi's Blog, 7 January 2015 (accessed 10 April 2018). Incidentally, it is not clear whether this quotation is authentic; I have not seen it in Azzam's texts or heard it in his speeches.
14. *fi ʻuyun muʻasira*, pp. 501–598.
15. Abd al-Rahman al-Ashmawi, 'risala ila al-shahid ʻabdallah ʻazzam' [Letter to the Martyr Abdallah Azzam], 17 February 2017, www.facebook.com/permalink.php?story_fbid=1882314935338735&id=

1604990909737807 (accessed 27 May 2017). Al-Ashmawi had met Azzam in Riyadh in 1989: *fi 'uyun mu'asira*, p. 197.
16. Maliach, 'Abdullah Azzam, al-Qaeda, and Hamas', p. 89; Abu Hilala, *awwal al-afghan al-arab*.
17. Twitter message from @Weissenberg7 (Caleb Weiss), 5 February 2019.
18. Lucas Winter, 'The Abdullah Azzam Brigades', *Studies in Conflict and Terrorism* 34, no. 11 (2011): 883–895.
19. Anja Freudenthal, 'Abdallah Azzam Brigades', HS-community.org, 28 February 2016 [accessed 4 April 2018].
20. See, for example, their video statement posted on Youtube on 13 September 2014 at www.youtube.com/watch?v=RvCGyZ3HKak (accessed 28 May 2017).
21. *al-Safir* (Beirut), 11 August 1998.
22. Shafika Mattar, 'US Ship Attacked in Jordan Port', *Washington Post*, 20 August 2005.
23. 'New Group Takes Credit for Pakistan Blast', UPI.com, 11 June 2009; Iftikhar Firdous, 'Suicide Attack on Peshawar Police Station Leaves Four Dead', *Express Tribune*, 24 February 2012.
24. 'Japan Tanker was Damaged in a Terror Attack, UAE Says', BBC News Online, 6 August 2010.
25. 'The Dr. Abdallah Azzam Academy'.
26. Christopher Anzalone, 'al-Shabab's Tactical and Media Strategies in the Wake of its Battlefield Setbacks', *CTC Sentinel* 6, no. 3 (2013): 12–15; Christopher Anzalone, 'The Rise and Decline of al-Shabab in Somalia', *Turkish Review* 4, no. 4 (2014): 386–395.
27. Aymenn Jawad al-Tamimi, 'The Factions of Abu Kamal', Brown Moses Blog, 18 December 2013.
28. 'shahid takhrij dawra li-jabhat al-nusra min mu'askarat "abdallah 'azzam' fi dana bi-rif idlib' [Watch the Graduation of a Jabhat al-Nusra Unit from the Abdallah Azzam Training Camps in Dana in the Idlib Countryside], www.youtube.com/watch?v=nHfNV_VC-48, posted 8 May 2016 (accessed 12 September 2018).
29. A Twitter message by @Raqqa_SL on 2 November 2015 said IS forces were hit by coalition airstrikes on the way to the "Abdallah Azzam training camp." The camp was destroyed in airstrikes in 2016: see Twitter message from @obretix on 19 May 2018. The journalist Jenan Moussa later published a picture of the deserted camp's entrance gate with Azzam's name on it: Twitter message from @jenanmoussa, 13 May 2018.
30. Alexander Meleagrou-Hitchens, Seamus Hughes, and Bennett Clifford, *The Travelers: American Jihadists in Syria and Iraq* (Washington, DC: George Washington University Program on Extremism, February 2018), p. 60.

31. 'In Southeast Asian Recruitment Drive, IS Posts Video of Malay-Speaking Child Members', *Malay Mail* Online, 17 March 2015.
32. There are at least two Abdallah Azzam mosques in Amman, one in Suwailih where he used to live, and another (aka al-Shahid mosque) in the al-Hashmi al-Shamali district in eastern Amman. There are at least four Abdallah Azzam mosques in Gaza: one in Sabra (Gaza City), one in Nuseirat, one in Beit Hanoun, and another in Khan Yunis. There is at least one Abdallah Azzam mosque in Saudi Arabia, in Jeddah's Mutanazahat district, one in the Yemeni city of al-Ma'ala, and another one in Khartoum in Sudan.
33. The street is in the municipality of Ümraniye which is governed by the Turkish Islamist party AKP (Justice and Development Party): 'al-Qaeda Founder's Name Given to İstanbul's Street in Turkey', soL InternationaL Online, 17 July 2017.
34. Twitter message from @SeamusHughes, 22 June 2016.
35. Twitter message from @RomainCaillet, 30 June 2017.
36. For example, in September 2015 the user of the Twitter account @nightwalker_54 included in his biography a link to the IS media repository Isdarat while at the same time having a background picture with an Azzam quote ("Jihad and the Rifle Alone," in English) (accessed 20 September 2015).
37. Twitter message from @SeamusHughes, 13 January 2016.
38. Maliach, 'Abdullah Azzam, al-Qaeda, and Hamas', p. 90.
39. 'fi dhikraihi al-27 ... 'abdallah 'azzam shu'lat jihad la tuntafa' [On the 27th Anniversary ... Abdallah Azzam is a Flame of Jihad that Does Not Fade], www.alqassam.ps, n.d. (accessed 2 December 2016). Thanks to Chris Anzalone for alerting me to this source.
40. A facsimile of the statement is produced in 'The Dr. Abdallah Azzam Academy', p. 14.
41. Azzam, *al-duktur al-shahid*, pp. 5–9.
42. 'bayan na'iyan li'l-'allama al-da'iya 'abdallah 'azzam' [Death Notice for the Prominent Preacher Abdallah Azzam], 26 November 1989, http://hamas.ps/ar/post/81/ (accessed 26 January 2018).
43. 'risala min al-ikhwan al-muslimin: muqawama rashida wa basha'ir al-'awda' [Message from the Muslim Brothers: Rightly Guided Resistance and Tidings of Return], Ikhwan Online, 20 November 2018, www.ikhwanonline.com/Message/234913/Default.aspx (accessed 26 March 2019).
44. Author's interview with Yonathan Fighel, Hertzlia, 8 September 2013.
45. See, for example, Kim Cragin, 'Al Qaeda Confronts Hamas: Divisions in the Sunni Jihadist Movement and its Implications for US Policy', *Studies in Conflict and Terrorism* 32, no. 7 (29 July 2009): 576–590.

46. See, for example, Dore Gold, 'Hamas and al-Qaeda are the Same', Israel National News Online, 6 January 2010.
47. See, for example, Anas Altikriti, 'Hamas is not al-Qaida', *The Guardian* Online, 21 September 2009.
48. See, for example, 'Muslim Publics Share Concerns about Extremist Groups', Pew Research Center, 10 September 2013.
49. One example is Nabil Aqil, who joined al-Qaida in the 1990s while studying in Karachi and who was arrested in Gaza in 2000 on suspicion of recruiting for al-Qaida and plotting attacks in Israel: Daniel Benjamin and Steven Simon, *The Age of Sacred Terror* (New York: Random House, 2002), pp. 193–194.
50. al-Awadh, *afghanistan: tahaddiyat al-jihad al-akbar*, p. 68.
51. See, for example, Zaeef, *My Life with the Taliban*.
52. See, for example, Strick van Linschoten and Kuehn, *An Enemy we Created*.
53. See, for example, 'Tehrik-i Taliban Pakistan (Maulana Fazlullah Faction) Citing the Late 'Abdullah 'Azzam', http://ibnsiqilli.tumblr.com/post/120043010192/tehrik-i-taliban-pakistan-maulana-fazlullah (accessed 27 May 2015).
54. Author's interview with Iqbal Khattak, Peshawar, 17 March 2008.
55. Daud Khattak, 'The Complicated Relationship Between the Afghan and Pakistani Taliban', *CTC Sentinel* 5, no. 2 (2012): 14–15; Fernando Reinares, 'A Case Study of the January 2008 Suicide Bomb Plot in Barcelona', *CTC Sentinel* 2, no. 1 (2009): 5–7.
56. Sam Heller, 'Ahrar al-Sham's Revisionist Jihadism', War on the Rocks (blog), 30 September 2015.
57. Ben Hubbard, 'In Syria, Potential Ally's Islamist Ties Challenge US', *New York Times*, 25 August 2015.
58. Hudhayfa Azzam on Facebook, 13 August 2015; see also Heller, 'Ahrar al-Sham's Revisionist Jihadism'.
59. 'fi dhikra al-shahid 'abdallah 'azzam' [In Memory of the Martyr Abdallah Azzam], n.d., www.ikhwan-jor.com (accessed 25 November 2013). I thank Joas Wagemakers for bringing the *al-Sabil* articles to my attention.
60. Maréchal, *The Muslim Brothers in Europe*, pp. 87–88.
61. See, for example, the Azzam section in the online bookstore Beyaz Minare Kitap, at www.beyazminarekitap.com/yazar/abdullah-azzam (accessed 12 September 2018).
62. al-Madkhali, 'munadhara'.
63. Moazzam Begg, *Enemy Combatant: My Imprisonment at Guantanamo, Bagram, and Kandahar* (New York: New Press, 2006), p. 81.

64. Miller, *The Audacious Ascetic*, p. 87. Above Azzam on the list were Abd al-Rahim al-Tahhan, A'id al-Qarni, Ahmad al-Qattan, and Muhammad bin al-Uthaymin.
65. Wagemakers, *A Quietist Jihadi*, p. 137.
66. William McCants, ed., *Militant Ideology Atlas: Executive Report* (West Point, NY: United States Military Academy, 2006), p. 13.
67. William McCants, *Militant Ideology Atlas: Research Compendium* (West Point, NY: Combating Terrorism Center, 2006), pp. 8–20.
68. Donald Holbrook, *What Types of Media Do Terrorists Collect? An Analysis of Religious, Political, and Ideological Publications Found in Terrorism Investigations in the UK* (The Hague: International Centre for Counter-Terrorism, September 2017), p. 28.
69. Muhammad al-Salim, 39 *wasila li-khidmat al-jihad wa'l-musharaka fihi* [39 Ways to Serve Jihad and Take Part in it] (Sawt al-Jihad, 2003), p. 37. Muhammad al-Salim was a pseudonym used by Isa Al Awshan.
70. Vahid Brown, 'A Mujahid's Bookbag', Jihadica.com, 21 December 2009, www.jihadica.com/a-mujahids-bookbag/ (accessed 28 February 2018).
71. 'Course of Islamic Study for Soldiers and Members', www.dni.gov/files/documents/ubl2016/english/Course%20of%20Islamic%20Study%20for%20Soldiers%20and%20Members.pdf (accessed 27 February 2018).
72. Omar Nasiri, *Inside the Jihad: My Life with al-Qaeda* (Cambridge, MA: Perseus, 2006), p. 151.
73. Fadil Harun, *al-harb 'ala al-islam* [The War against Islam], part 2, 2009, p. 48, https://ctc.usma.edu/harmony-program/the-war-against-islam-the-story-of-fazul-harun-part-2-original-language-2/ (accessed 13 September 2018).
74. Ebrahim, *The Terrorist's Son*, p. 33.
75. Andrew Black, 'Featured Profile: Mokhtar Belmokhtar: The Algerian Jihad's Southern Amir', *Jamestown Terrorism Monitor*, 8 May 2009.
76. Harun, *al-harb*, p. 39.
77. Romain Caillet and Pierre Puchot, *"Le combat vous a été prescrit": une histoire de jihad en France* (Paris: Stock, 2017), p. 59.
78. Mark Kukis, *"My Heart Became Attached": The Strange Odyssey of John Walker Lindh* (Washington, DC: Brassey's, 2003), p. 24.
79. 'An al-Qaeda Love Story: From Morocco to Bosnia to Afghanistan and Saudi Arabia, Via New Jersey', *MEMRI Special Dispatch*, no. 984 (9 September 2005).
80. Fernando Reinares, *al-Qaeda's Revenge: The 2004 Madrid Train Bombings* (New York: Columbia University Press, 2017), pp. 60 and 82.

81. Peter R. Neumann and Ryan Evans, 'Operation Crevice in London', in *The Evolution of the Global Terrorist Threat: From 9/11 to Osama Bin Laden's Death*, ed. Bruce Hoffman and Fernando Reinares (New York: Columbia University Press, 2014), 61–80, p. 64.
82. Sally Neighbour, 'Operation Pendennis in Australia', in *The Evolution of the Global Terrorist Threat: From 9/11 to Osama Bin Laden's Death*, ed. Bruce Hoffman and Fernando Reinares (New York: Columbia University Press, 2014), 163–191, p. 176.
83. Haroon Siddique, 'Terror Suspect "Planned to Take Children on Suicide Attack"', *The Guardian* Online, 23 April 2008.
84. Abdul Ghaffar El Almani, 'Mein Weg nach Jannah', 2010, p. 60, www.scribd.com/doc/31071994/Schaheed-Abdul-Ghaffar-al-Almani-Mein-Weg-Nach-Jannah (accessed 20 November 2012).
85. Lori Lowenthal Marcus, 'Dzokhar Tsarnaev Inspired by Hamas Founder, Indictment Reveals', TheJewishPress.com, 28 June 2013.
86. David Thomson, *Les Français jihadistes* (Paris: Les Arènes, 2014), p. 146.
87. Vikram Dodd, 'Two British Men Admit to Linking Up with Extremist Group in Syria', *The Guardian* Online, 8 July 2014.
88. 'Exclusive Q & A with Junaid Hussain – British ISIS Fighter and Hacker', 5PillarsUK (blog), 24 September 2014, https://5pillarsuk.com/2014/09/24/exclusive-q-and-a-with-junaid-hussain-british-isis-fighter-and-hacker/.
89. 'Canadian ISIL Fighter Wanted by RCMP May Have Been Killed in Missile Strike in Syria: Document', NationalPost.com, 19 December 2016.
90. 'Brownsburg Man Charged with Attempting to Provide Resources to Terrorist Group Pleads Guilty', CBS4indy.com (CBS 4 Indianapolis News online), 23 May 2018.
91. See Twitter message from @SeamusHughes, 13 January 2016.
92. Caillet and Puchot, *"Le combat vous a été prescrit"*, p. 44.
93. Prachi Vyas, 'The Islamic State's Married Ideology: Something Borrowed, Something New', Lawfare Blog, 2 July 2017.
94. Mahmud Azzam describes the founding and running of the Center in Azzam, *al-duktur al-shahid*, pp. 243–255.
95. Nico Prucha, 'Celebrities of the Afterlife: Death Cult, Stars, and Fandom of Jihadist Propaganda', in *Jihadi Thought and Ideology*, ed. Rüdiger Lohlker and Tamara Abu-Hamdeh (Berlin: Logos, 2013), 83–137, pp. 114 ff.
96. Marisa Urgo, '"Martyrs in a Time of Alienation" – Complete Blogger's Cut', 28 December 2010, www.makingsenseofjihad.com/2010/12/martyrs-in-a-time-of-alienation-complete.html (accessed 20 July 2012).
97. Dominic Casciani, 'Babar Ahmad: The Godfather of Internet Jihad?', BBC News (online), 17 July 2014; Robert Verkaik, 'The Trials of

Babar Ahmad: From Jihad in Bosnia to a US Prison via Met Brutality', *The Guardian*, 19 March 2016. Ahmed was in Bosnia on and off between 1992 and 1995, and he was briefly in Chechnya in mid-1996, where he met Ibn Khattab.
98. Author's interview with Babar Ahmed, London, 31 May 2017.
99. Verkaik, 'The Trials of Babar Ahmad'; Andrew North, 'Pro-Jihad Website Draws Readers', BBC News Online, 15 February 2002; author's interview with Babar Ahmed, London, 31 May 2017.
100. 'Statement from Azzam.Com Regarding Closure of its Web-Site', TalibanNews.com, 24 September 2002, www.freerepublic.com/focus/news/756623/posts (accessed 27 May 2017). Partly as a result of an extradition battle between the USA and the UK, Babar Ahmed spent twelve years in detention, before finally being released in 2015 without a conviction.
101. Author's interview with Babar Ahmed, London, 31 May 2017.
102. Author's interview with Babar Ahmed, London, 31 May 2017.
103. Hatina, 'Warrior Saints', Kindle version, location 4758.
104. Author's interview with Babar Ahmed, London, 31 May 2017.
105. Richard A. Nielsen, *Deadly Clerics: Blocked Ambition and the Paths to Jihad* (Cambridge: Cambridge University Press, 2017), p. 122.
106. Fitzgerald, 'The Son of the Father of Jihad'.
107. Author's interview with Abdallah Anas, London, 28 March 2012.
108. Harun, *al-harb*, p. 53.
109. This perspective was illustrated in a photo montage posted on Twitter in 2017 which showed Azzam together with Ibn Khattab, Yahya Ayyash (the former Hamas operative), and Umar Mukhtar (the Libyan national resistance hero): see Twitter message from @sakti00sakti, 7 September 2017. Similarly, a montage posted in 2018 showed Ibn Khattab and Azzam Photoshopped into the same picture, accompanied with a quote from Abdallah al-Muhaysini saying, "Despite the fact that I did not see these two men in al-Sham, I did not benefit from someone as much as I have done from them": Twitter message from @ToreRHamming, 27 March 2018.
110. 'Jihad in Pakistan', pp. 5–6, www.dni.gov/files/documents/ubl2016/english/Jihad%20in%20Pakistan.pdf (accessed 27 February 2018).
111. Khattab bin Muhammad al-Hashimi, 'al-mujaddidan. ibn ladin wa 'azzam. naqidan am diddan' [The Renewers. Bin Ladin and Azzam: Contrasts or Opposites?], *Umma Wahida* no. 1 (April 2019): 25–33; Karam al-Hafyan, *al-jihad al-mu'asir bayna 'abdallah 'azzam wa usama bin ladin* [Contemporary Jihad between Abdallah Azzam and

Usama Bin Ladin] (Istanbul: Egyptian Institute for Studies, 5 March 2019).
112. 'liqa' zawjat al-shahid'.
113. Author's interview with Babar Ahmed, London, 31 May 2017.
114. Chris Heffelfinger, *Radical Islam in America: Salafism's Journey from Arabia to the West* (Washington, DC: Potomac Books, 2011), p. 39.
115. 'The Opinion of Shaykh Abdullah Azzam on the Issue of Taking Slaves', https://almuwahideenmedia.wordpress.com/2015/01/28/the-opinion-of-shaykh-abdullah-azzam-on-the-issue-of-taking-slaves/, 28 January 2015 (accessed 1 March 2018).
116. Mansur al-Shihri, 'ta'kidan lima asharat ilayhi 'ukaz: "al-qa'ida" ta'lan hallak arwa baghdadi' [Confirming *Ukaz*'s Indications: "al-Qaida" Announces (Responsibility for) the Destructive Arwa Baghdadi], '*Ukaz* Online, 8 February 2017.
117. See, for example, '"ukaz" tasif 'abdallah 'azzam bi'"l-irhabi al-halik" wa'l-nashitun: al-aqzam tatatawal 'ala 'azzam' [*Ukaz* Describes Abdallah Azzam as 'a Destructive Terrorist' and the Activists [Say]: The Midgets Dare to Attack Azzam], *The New Khalij* Online, 10 February 2017.
118. See the Twitter hashtag #*al-aqzam_tatatawal_'ala_'azzam* (in Arabic).
119. As'ad AbuKhalil, "Abdullah 'Azzam: Who Inspired Bin Laden and Scores of Other Terrorists', The Angry Arab News Service, 9 February 2017, https://angryarab.blogspot.no/2017/02/abdullah-azzam-who-inspired-bin-laden.html (accessed 12 September 2018); As'ad AbuKhalil, "Abdullah 'Azzam was a Reactionary Terrorist, and Idol of Bin Laden', The Angry Arab News Service, 10 February 2017, https://angryarab.blogspot.no/2017/02/abdullah-azzam-was-reactionary.html (accessed 12 September 2018).
120. '"ukaz" tasif 'abdallah 'azzam bi'"l-irhabi al-halik"'.
121. Twitter messages from @Azzam_Huthaifa, 24 April 2016. Hudhayfa said he was with Azzam at the time and that they had gone to Saudi Arabia to sort out their Saudi visas.
122. 'Jordanian Liberal Harshly Criticized for her Condemnation of University of Jordan for Naming Prayer Hall after al-Qaeda Ideologue 'Abdallah 'Azzam', *MEMRI Special Dispatch* no. 7483, 22 May 2018.
123. See, for example, Sean Yom and Wael Al-Khatib, 'Islamists are Losing Support in Jordan', *Washington Post* Online, 17 May 2018.
124. 'liqa' zawjat al-shahid'.
125. Fitzgerald, 'The Son of the Father of Jihad'.

126. Author's interview with Abdallah Anas, London, 28 March 2012.
127. Abdallah Azzam, 'mas'uliyyat al-'arab amam allah' [The Responsibility of Arabs before God], *al-Jihad* no. 7 (3 June 1985): 4–5, p. 5.
128. Azzam, 'maktab khidamat al-mujahidin'.
129. His wife said in 1990 that the family had kept the house and a car in Amman. Azzam himself was banned from entering Jordan in 1985, but his older sons and his grandfather appear to have gone back from time to time in the late 1980s: *fi 'uyun mu'asira*, p. 167.
130. Maliach, 'Abdullah Azzam, al-Qaeda, and Hamas', p. 86.
131. Bin Laden, Bin Laden, and Sasson, *Growing up Bin Laden*, p. 131.

Conclusion

1. Malet, *Foreign Fighters*.
2. Sidney Tarrow, *The New Transnational Activism* (Cambridge: Cambridge University Press, 2006), pp. 124–128.
3. Ibid., p. 127.
4. Hugh Thomas, *The Spanish Civil War*, rev. ed. (London: Penguin, 2001).
5. Thomas Hegghammer, 'Syria's Foreign Fighters', ForeignPolicy.com, 9 December 2013.
6. Margaret E. Keck and Kathryn Sikkink, *Activists beyond Borders: Advocacy Networks in International Politics* (Ithaca: Cornell University Press, 1998).
7. Idean Salehyan, *Rebels without Borders: Transnational Insurgencies in World Politics* (Ithaca: Cornell University Press, 2009).
8. Haroro J. Ingram, *The Charismatic Leadership Phenomenon in Radical and Militant Islamism* (London: Routledge, 2014), Kindle version, chapter 9.
9. On the fragmentation of authority in Islam, see, for example, Dale F. Eickelman and James P. Piscatori, *Muslim Politics* (Princeton: Princeton University Press, 2004), pp. 131 ff.
10. Great man theory is the nineteenth-century idea, associated with the writer Thomas Carlyle, that history can be largely explained by the actions of highly influential individuals.
11. Thomas Hegghammer and Joas Wagemakers, 'The Palestine Effect: The Role of Palestinians in the Transnational Jihad Movement', *Die Welt des Islams* 53, no. 3–4 (2013): 281–314; Hazim al-Amin, *al-salafi al-yatim: al-wajh al-filistini li'l-jihad al-'alami wa'l-qa'ida* [The Orphaned

Salafi: The Palestinian Dimension of Global Jihad and al-Qaida] (Beirut: Dar al-Saqi, 2011).
12. Thomas Hegghammer, 'Should I Stay or Should I Go? Explaining Variation in Western Jihadists' Choice between Domestic and Foreign Fighting', *American Political Science Review* 107, no. 1 (2013): 1–15.
13. Bearden and Risen, *The Main Enemy*, p. 366.

Bibliography

The 9/11 Commission Report. New York: W. W. Norton & Co., 2004.
Abd al-Rahim, Jamal. *ayman al-zawahiri: min qusur al-ma'adi ila kuhuf afghanistan* [Ayman al-Zawahiri: From the Palaces of Ma'adi to the Caves of Afghanistan]. Cairo: Madbuli al-Saghir, 2006.
Abdalla, Ahmed. *The Student Movement and National Politics in Egypt, 1928–1973.* 2nd ed. Cairo: American University in Cairo Press, 2009.
'Abdallah Azzam'. www.ikhwan.net/wiki, n.d.
'Abdallah Azzam's Son Says Bin Ladin Driven to Extremism by al-Zawahiri'. Al-Arabiyya Television (via FBIS), 2005.
Abdallah, Umar F. *The Islamic Struggle in Syria.* Berkeley: Mizan Press, 1983.
Abdelnasser, Walid M. 'Islamic Organizations in Egypt and the Iranian Revolution of 1979: The Experience of the First Few Years'. *Arab Studies Quarterly* 19, no. 2 (1997): 25–39.
'Abdullah Azzam Poem "Bakat 'Ayni – My Eyes Wept"'. Youtube. www.youtube.com/watch?v=u0yUiYZnHzI
Abou Zahab, Mariam. 'Salafism in Pakistan: The Ahl-e Hadith Movement'. In *Global Salafism: Islam's New Religious Movement,* edited by Roel Meijer, 126–142. London: Hurst, 2009.
Aboul-Enein, Youssef. *Ayman al-Zawahiri: The Ideologue of Modern Islamic Militancy.* Maxwell Air Force Base, AL: USAF Counterproliferation Center, Air University, 2004.
The Late Sheikh Abdullah Azzam's Books (3 parts). West Point, NY: Combating Terrorism Center, 2007.
Abu Amr, Ziyad. *Islamic Fundamentalism in the West Bank and Gaza: Muslim Brotherhood and Islamic Jihad.* Bloomington: Indiana University Press, 1994.
Abu Ghanima, Ziyad. *al-haraka al-islamiyya wa qadiyat filastin* [The Islamic Movement and the Palestine Issue]. Amman: Dar al-Furqan, 1989.
'Abu Hafs al Masri'. West Point, NY: Combating Terrorism Center, 2008. https://ctc.usma.edu/wp-content/uploads/2011/06/Abu_Hafs.pdf.
Abu Hanieh, Hassan. *Women and Politics from the Perspective of Islamic Movements in Jordan.* Amman: Friedrich-Ebert-Stiftung, 2008.

Abu Hilala, Yasir. *awwal al-afghan al-'arab* [The First Afghan Arab], 2009. https://archive.org/details/biographyofazzam.

Abu Iyad and Eric Rouleau. *My Home, My Land: A Narrative of the Palestinian Struggle*. New York: Times Books, 1981.

Abu Izza, Abdallah. *ma' al-haraka al-islamiyya fi'l-duwal al-'arabiyya* [With the Islamic Movement in the Arab States]. Kuwait: Dar al-Qalam, 1986.

Abu Mujahid. *al-shahid 'abdallah 'azzam bayna al-milad wa'l-istishhad* [The Martyr Abdallah Azzam from Birth to Martyrdom]. Peshawar: Markaz al-Shahid Azzam al-I'lami, 1991.

Abu Rumman, Bashir, and Abdallah Sa'id. *al-'alim wa'l-mujahid wa'l-shahid al-shaykh 'abdallah 'azzam* [The Scholar, Mujahid, Martyr and Sheikh Abdallah Azzam]. Amman: Dar al-Bashir, 1990.

Abu Rumman, Mohammad, and Hassan Abu Hanieh. *The "Islamic Solution" in Jordan: Islamists, the State, and the Ventures of Democracy and Security*. Amman: Friedrich-Ebert-Stiftung, 2013.

Jordanian Salafism: A Strategy for the "Islamization of Society" and an Ambiguous Relationship with the State. Amman: Friedrich-Ebert-Stiftung, December 2010.

'Abu 'Ubayda al-Banshiri'. West Point, NY: Combating Terrorism Center, 2008. https://ctc.usma.edu/wp-content/uploads/2011/06/Abu_Ubayda_al-Banshiri.pdf.

Ahlam. 'tahrir al-mar'a' [Women's Liberation]'. *al-Jihad* no. 18 (June 1986): 34.

Ajami, Fouad. *The Arab Predicament: Arab Political Thought and Practice since 1967*. Cambridge: Cambridge University Press, 1981.

'al-Albani about Qutb, Abdullah Azzam and al-Ikhwan al-Muslimun', n.d. www.youtube.com/watch?v=6LYAdAmUqlA&t=190s.

'al-'alim al-mujahid wa'l-shaykh al-shahid 'abdallah 'azzam' [The Scholar, Mujahid and Martyr Shaykh Abdallah Azzam]. *Iyha'at Jihadiyya* no. 1 (July 2015): 21–23.

Altikriti, Anas. 'Hamas is not al-Qaida'. *The Guardian* Online, 21 September 2009.

al-Amin, Hazim. *al-salafi al-yatim: al-wajh al-filistini li'l-jihad al-'alami wa'l-qa'ida* [The Orphaned Salafi: The Palestinian Dimension of Global Jihad and al-Qaida]. Beirut: Dar al-Saqi, 2011.

Amir, Muhammad Abdallah. *al-shaykh al-mujahid 'abdallah 'azzam: al-rajul alladhi tarjama al-aqwal ila af'al* [The Mujahid Sheikh Abdallah Azzam: The Man who Translated Words into Deeds]. 1st ed. Kuwait: Maktabat Dar al-Bayan, 1990.

Anas, Abdallah. *rihlati ma' al-jihad* [My Journey with the Jihad]. Al-Magharibia Channel, 2015, 9 parts, Youtube.com.

wiladat al-afghan al-ʿarab [The Birth of the Afghan Arabs]. London: Saqi, 2002.

Anas, Abdullah, and Tam Hussain. *To the Mountains: My Life in Jihad, from Algeria to Afghanistan*. London: Hurst, 2019.

Anonymous. *Through our Enemies' Eyes: Osama Bin Laden, Radical Islam and the Future of America*. Washington, DC: Brassey's, 2002.

al-Ansari, Abu Ibada. *mafhum al-hakimiyya fi fikr ʿabdallah ʿazzam* [The Concept of *Hakimiyya* in the Thought of Abdallah Azzam]. Peshawar: Markaz al-Shahid Azzam al-I'lami, n.d.

Antoun, Richard T. *Muslim Preacher in the Modern World: A Jordanian Case Study in Comparative Perspective*. Princeton: Princeton University Press, 1989.

Anzalone, Christopher. 'The Rise and Decline of al-Shabab in Somalia'. *Turkish Review* 4, no. 4 (2014): 386–395.

  'al-Shabab's Tactical and Media Strategies in the Wake of its Battlefield Setbacks'. *CTC Sentinel* 6, no. 3 (2013): 12–15.

Aql, Iyad Abd al-Hamid. 'maʿalim al-tarbiya al-jihadiyya fi dhaw' kitabat al-shaykh ʿabdallah ʿazzam' [Principles of Jihadi Education in Light of the Writings of Sheikh Abdallah Azzam]. Master's thesis, Islamic University in Gaza, 2008.

al-Arian, Abdullah. *Answering the Call: Popular Islamic Activism in Sadat's Egypt*. Oxford: Oxford University Press, 2014.

  'Commanding the Faithful: Frame Construction in Egyptian Islamist Periodicals, 1976–1981'. *Journal of Islamic Studies* 28, no. 3 (September 2017): 341–368.

Arnon, Itzhak, and Michael Raviv. *From Fellah to Farmer: A Study on Change in Arab Villages*. Rehovot: Settlement Study Centre, 1980.

Asʿad, Khalid Khalil. *muqatil min makka: al-qissa al-kamila li-usama bin ladin* [Warrior from Mecca: The Complete Story of Usama bin Ladin]. London: al-I'lam li'l-Nashr, 2000 (translation from 2002 by Foreign Broadcast Information Service).

'*Asharq al-Awsat* Interviews the Son of Bin Laden's Mentor'. *al-Sharq al-Awsat* English Online, 2 September 2005.

Ashour, Omar. *The De-Radicalization of Jihadists: Transforming Armed Islamist Movements*. London: Routledge, 2009.

Aust, Stefan. *Baader–Meinhof: The Inside Story of the RAF*, trans. Anthea Bell. Oxford: Oxford University Press, 2009.

al-Awadh, Yahya. *afghanistan: tahaddiyat al-jihad al-akbar* [Afghanistan: The Challenges of the Great Jihad]. Doha: Dar al-Sharq, 1992.

al-Azdi, Abu Jandal. *usama bin ladin: mujaddid al-zaman wa qahir al-amrikan* [Usama Bin Ladin: Renewer of the Century and Victor over the Americans], 2003. www.qa3edoon.com.

Aziz, Manal Abd al-Karim Hasan. "'abdallah 'azzam wa juhuduhu fi nashr al-'aqida al-islamiyya' [Abdallah Azzam and his Efforts to Spread the Islamic Doctrine]. Master's thesis, Islamic University in Gaza, 2012.

al-Azm, Yusuf. 'al-shahid 'abdallah 'azzam: wuduh al-ru'ya wa sidq al-sira' [The Martyr Abdallah Azzam: Clarity of Vision and Sincerity of Conduct]. *al-Sabil*, 8 August 1995.

Azzam, Abdallah. 'al-afghan bayna ta'yid al-rahman wa kunud al-insan' [Afghans between the Support of the Merciful and the Ingratitude of Man], *al-Mujtama'* no. 589 (5 October 1982).

al-'aqida wa atharuha fi bina' al-jil [The Creed and its Effect on Building the Generation]. Amman: Dar al-Aqsa, 1975.

"ashrun 'aman 'ala al-shahada' [Twenty Years of Martyrdom]. *al-Jihad* no. 23 (October 1986): 4–7.

al-as'ila wa'l-ajwiba al-jihadiyya [Jihadi Questions and Answers]. Minbar al-Tawhid wa'l-Jihad, n.d.

'ayat wa basha'ir wa karamat fi'l-jihad al-afghani' [Signs, Tidings, and Miracles in the Afghan Jihad]. *al-Mujtama'* no. 569 (4 May 1982): 28–30.

ayat al-rahman fi jihad al-afghan [Signs of the Merciful in the Afghan Jihad]. Peshawar: Ittihad Talabat al-Muslimin, 1983.

'ayna al-sahafi al-muslim?' [Where is the Muslim Journalist?]. *al-Jihad* no. 10 (August 1985): 4–8.

'azima wa tasmim' [Decision and Determination]. *al-Jihad* no. 34 (September 1987): 4–7.

basha'ir al-nasr [Tidings of Victory]. Minbar al-Tawhid wa'l Jihad, n.d.

dalalat al-kitab wa'l-sunna 'ala al-ahkam: min haythu al-bayan wa'l-ijmal aw al-zuhur wa'l-khafa' [The Implications of the Book and the Sunna for Legal Rulings: Regarding Demonstration and Generalization or the Apparent and the Concealed]. Jeddah: Dar al-Mujtama', 2001.

'dawr britania fi muharabat al-islam' [Britain's Role in Fighting Islam]. *Luhayb al-Ma'raka*, 29 April 1989.

'dhikrayat filastin' [Memories of Palestine]. Minbar al-Tawhid wa'l-Jihad, n.d.

'dhikrayat min sahat al-jihad' [Memories from the Field of Jihad]. *al-Bunyan al-Marsus* no. 4 (December 1985): 12–13.

al-difa' 'an aradi al-muslimin: ahamm furud al-a'yan [The Defense of Muslim Lands: The Most Important of Individual Duties]. Peshawar: Dawa and Jihad University, 1985.

'du'a wa thana'' [Supplication and Tribute]. *al-Jihad* no. 39 (February 1988): 40–41.

'al-duktur hasan al-turabi yadli li-jihad bi-tasrihat hamma hawla qadhiyat al-jihad' [Dr. Hasan al-Turabi Presents to *al-Jihad* Important Statements about the Issue of Jihad], *al-Jihad* no. 37 (December 1987): 10–13.

hamas: al-judhur al-tarikhiyya wa'l-mithaq [Hamas: Historical Roots and Charter]. Amman: unknown publisher, 1990.

'al-haqd al-yahudi al-salibi' [Jewish–Crusader Malevolence]. *Luhayb al-Ma'raka* no. 47 (23 April 1989).

'hatta la nu'idhdh asabi' al-nadam' [So That we Will Not Regret it]'. *al-Mujtama'* no. 168, 26 April 1983.

'*ibar wa basa'ir li'l-jihad fi'l-'asr al-hadir* [Lessons and Insights on Jihad in the Current Age]. 2nd ed. Amman: Maktabat al-Risala al-Haditha, 1987.

'*i'lan ila al-ikhwa al-mutabarri'in*' [Announcement to Donor Brothers]. *al-Jihad* no. 57 (July 1989): 21.

i'lan al-jihad [Declaring Jihad]. Minbar al-Tawhid wa'l-Jihad, n.d.

ilhaq bi'l-qafila [Join the Caravan]. Minbar al-Tawhid wa'l-Jihad, 1987.

'inhilal al-zawaj fi'l-fiqh wa'l-qanun' [Marriage Dissolution in Islamic Jurisprudence and Civil Law]. BA thesis, Damascus University, 1966 [from Minbar al-Tawhid wa'l-Jihad].

'isda' al-haraka al-kamaliyya wa in'ikasatuha 'ala al-'alam al-islami' [The Repercussions of the Kemalist Movement and its Consequences in the Muslim World], *al-Mujtama'* no. 574 (8 June 1982).

'al-islam huwa mustaqbal al-bashariyya' [Islam is the Future of Mankind]. *al-Mujtama'*, 11 November 1980.

al-islam wa mustaqbal al-bashariyya [Islam and the Future of Mankind]. Minbar al-Tawhid wa'l-Jihad, 1980.

ithaf al-'ibad bi-fada'il al-jihad [Illustrating the Virtues of Jihad to God's Servants]. Minbar al-Tawhid wa'l-Jihad, n.d.

jarimat qatl al-nafs al-muslima [The Crime of Killing a Muslim Soul]. Minbar al-Tawhid wa'l-Jihad, n.d.

fi'l-jihad adab wa ahkam [Proper Conduct and Rulings in Jihad]. Peshawar: unknown publisher, 1986.

'jihad wa hajat al-umma 'alayhi' [Jihad and the *Umma*'s Need for it]. Audio file in author's possession.

'jihad al-kafirin fard 'ayn' [Jihad against the Infidels is an Individual Obligation], *al-Mujtama'* no. 686 (9 October 1984).

The Lofty Mountain. London: Azzam Publications, n.d.

'maktab khidamat al-mujahidin' [The Services Bureau for the Mujahidin]. *al-Jihad* no. 50 (December 1988): 2.

al-manara al-mafquda [The Lost Beacon]. Peshawar: unknown publisher, 1987.

'masani' al-abtal' [Hero Factories]. *al-Jihad* no. 36 (November 1987): 4–6.

'ma'sat al-fikr al-gharbi' [The Crisis of Western Thought]. *al-Mujtama'*, 14 April 1981.

'mas'uliyyat al-'arab amam allah' [The Responsibility of Arabs before God]. *al-Jihad*, no. 7 (3 June 1985): 4–5.

'min kabul ila al-quds' [From Kabul to Jerusalem]. *al-Jihad* no. 52 (1989): 47.
'muqabala ma' al-da'iya: al-sayyida zaynab al-ghazzali' [Interview with a Preacher: Mrs Zaynab al-Ghazzali], *al-Jihad* no. 14 (December 1985): 38–40.
'*al-qa'ida al-sulba*' [The Solid Base]'. *al-Jihad*, no. 41 (April 1988): 4–6.
al-qawmiyya al-'arabiyya [Arab Nationalism]. Minbar al-Tawhid wa'l-Jihad, n.d.
'risala ila akhawatina al-mujahidat' [Letter to our Mujahid Sisters]. *al-Jihad* no. 8 (June 1985): 41.
'risala maftuha ila al-'ulama' [Open Letter to the Scholars]'. *al-Jihad* no. 5 (April 1985): 36–37.
The Ruling on Meat Slaughtered in the West. Translation of 2nd ed. Minbar al-Tawhid wa'l-Jihad, 1989.
al-saratan al-ahmar [The Red Cancer], 1st ed. Amman: Maktabat al-Aqsa, 1980.
'*sayyid qutb wa qawl bi-wihdat al-wujud*' [Sayyid Qutb and the Unity of Existence]. *al-Mujtama'* no. 525 (April 1981).
The Scales of Allah, n.d. www.khilafahbooks.com/the-scales-of-allah-swt-by-shaykh-abdullah-azzam/.
shahr bayna al-'amaliqa [A Month among Giants]. Minbar al-Tawhid wa'l-Jihad, 1989.
'al-tarbiya al-jihadiyya wa'l-bina" [Jihadi Education and Edification], 1992.
The Tawhid of Action. Tibyan Publications, n.d. www.khilafahbooks.com/the-tawhid-of-action-by-imam-abdallah-azzam/.
'*ushshaq al-hur* [Those who Love the Virgins of Paradise], n.d. www.almeshkat.net/book/1242.
'wasiyat al-'abd al-faqir ila allah ta'ala 'abdallah bin yusuf 'azzam' [The Will of God's Poor Servant Abdallah Yusuf Azzam]', 22 April 1986. Minbar al-Tawhid wa'l-Jihad.
'ya muslimiy al-'alam: intabahu' [Muslims of the World: Pay Attention]. *al-Mujtama'*, 30 August 1983.
fi zilal surat al-tawba [In the Shade of Surat al-Tawba]. Minbar al-Tawhid wa'l-Jihad, 1986.

Azzam, Ahmad Sa'id. *min manaqib al-imam al-shahid 'abdallah 'azzam* [Character Traits of the Martyred Imam Abdallah Azzam]. Peshawar: unknown publisher, 1990; repr. in *fi 'uyun mu'asira*, Peshawar: Markaz al-Shahid Azzam al-Islami, 1997, pp. 473–499.

Azzam, Hudhayfa Abdallah. 'min wahi surat al-anfal' [Inspiration from Surat al-Anfal]. *al-Jihad* no. 43 (June 1988): 44.

Azzam, Mahmud Sa'id. *al-duktur al-shahid 'abdallah yusuf 'azzam: shaykhi alladhi 'ariftu* [The Martyred Doctor Abdallah Yusuf Azzam: My

Shaykh as I Knew him]. Gaza: Mu'assasat Ibda' li'l-Abhath wa'l-Dirasat wa'l-Tadrib, 2012.

Badi, Mustafa. *afghanistan: ihtilal al-dhakira* [Afghanistan: The Occupation of Memory]. Sanaa: unknown publisher, 2004.

al-Bahri, Nasser, and Georges Malbrunot. *Dans l'ombre de Ben Laden: révélations de son garde du corps repenti*. Paris: Michel Lafon, 2010.

Bailey, Clinton. *Jordan's Palestinian Challenge 1948–1983: A Political History*. Boulder: Westview, 1984.

Baitenmann, Helga. 'NGOs and the Afghan War: The Politicisation of Humanitarian Aid'. *Third World Quarterly* 12, no. 1 (1 January 1990): 62–85.

Bakke, Kristin M. 'Help Wanted? The Mixed Record of Foreign Fighters in Domestic Insurgencies'. *International Security* 38, no. 4 (1 April 2014): 150–187.

Barfield, Thomas J. *The Central Asian Arabs of Afghanistan: Pastoral Nomadism in Transition*. Austin: University of Texas Press, 1981.

Bari, Zohurul. *Re-Emergence of the Muslim Brothers in Egypt*. New Delhi: Lancers Books, 1995.

Barraclough, Steven. 'al-Azhar: Between the Government and the Islamists'. *Middle East Journal* 52 (1998): 236–249.

Batatu, Hanna. 'Syria's Muslim Brethren'. *MERIP Reports* 12 (1982): 12–20.

Bearden, Milt, and James Risen. *The Main Enemy: The Inside Story of the CIA's Final Showdown with the KGB*. New York: Random House, 2003.

Begg, Moazzam. *Enemy Combatant: My Imprisonment at Guantanamo, Bagram, and Kandahar*. New York: New Press, 2006.

Bell, Kevin. 'The First Islamic State: A Look Back at the Islamic Emirate of Kunar'. *The Sentinel* 9, no. 2 (February 2016): 9–14.

Usama Bin Ladin's "Father Sheikh": Yunus Khalis and the Return of al-Qa'ida's Leadership to Afghanistan. West Point, NY: Combating Terrorism Center, 2013.

Benjamin, Daniel, and Steven Simon. *The Age of Sacred Terror*. New York: Random House, 2002.

Bergen, Peter. *The Osama Bin Laden I Know*. New York: Free Press, 2006.

Bergen, Peter, and Paul Cruickshank. 'Revisiting the Early Al Qaeda: An Updated Account of its Formative Years'. *Studies in Conflict and Terrorism* 35, no. 1 (1 January 2012): 1–36.

Berger, J. M. *Jihad Joe: Americans Who Go to War in the Name of Islam*. Washington, DC: Potomac, 2011.

Berger, J. M., ed. *Beatings and Bureaucracy: The Founding Memos of Al Qaeda*. Intelwire Press, 2012.

Bergman, Ronen. *Rise and Kill First: The Secret History of Israel's Targeted Assassinations*. New York: Random House, 2018.

al-Berry, Khaled. *Life is More Beautiful than Paradise: A Jihadist's Own Story*. Cairo: American University in Cairo Press, 2009.

Bianchi, Robert. *Guests of God: Pilgrimage and Politics in the Islamic World*. Oxford: Oxford University Press, 2004.

al-Bilali, Abu Umar. 'majallat al-jihad fi 'amiha al-khamis' [*al-Jihad* Magazine in its Fifth Year]. *al-Bunyan al-Marsus* no. 28 (July 1989): 41–43.

Bin Abd al-Aziz, Abd al-Qadir. *risalat al-'umda fi i'dad al-'udda li'l-jihad fi sabil allah* [Treatise on the Pillar of Military Preparation for Jihad in God's Path], Minbar al-Tawhid wa'l-Jihad, 1988.

Bin Baz, Abd al-Aziz. 'fadl al-jihad fi sabil allah wa'l-musabara fi dhalik' [The Merit of Jihad in God's Path and Perseverance in It] (parts 1 and 2)', *al-Jihad* no. 42–43 (June 1988): 38–40 and 24–27.

 'al-jihad fi'l-afghan jihad islami yajib '"ala jami'" al-muslimin da'muhu wa musanadatuhu' [The Jihad in Afghanistan is an Islamic Jihad and All Muslims Must Support and Assist it]. *al-Jihad* no. 22 (September 1986): 24–25.

 'risala ila aghniya' al-muslimin' [Letter to Wealthy Muslims]. *al-Jihad* no. 9 (July 1985): 36–37.

Bin Laden, Omar, Najwa Bin Laden, and Jean Sasson. *Growing up Bin Laden: Osama's Wife and Son Take us Inside their Secret World*. New York: St. Martin's Press, 2009.

Bin Ladin, Usama. 'Letter on Shura'. Bin Laden's Bookshelf, n.d. www.dni.gov/index.php/features/bin-laden-s-bookshelf?start=1.

'Bin-Ladin Associate Interrogated'. *al-Sharq al-Awsat* (via FBIS), 24 June 1999.

Bin Omar, Abdallah. 'The Striving Sheikh: Abdullah Azzam'. *Nida'ul Islam*, July 1996.

Bolton, Matthew. 'Goldmine: A Critical Look at the Commercialization of Afghan Demining'. Research paper. London School of Economics and Political Science: Centre for the Study of Global Governance, 2008.

Bonner, Michael. *Jihad in Islamic History: Doctrines and Practice*. Princeton: Princeton University Press, 2006.

Botiveau, Bernard. 'La Formation des oulémas en Syrie: la faculté de Sharî'a de l'université de Damas'. In *Les Intellectuels et le pouvoir : Syrie, Égypte, Tunisie, Algérie*, edited by Gilbert Delanoe, 67–87. Cairo: CEDEJ, 1986.

 Loi islamique et droit dans les sociétés arabes: mutations des systèmes juridiques du Moyen-Orient. Paris: Karthala, 1993.

Braithwaite, Rodric. *Afgantsy: The Russians in Afghanistan 1979–89*. New York: Oxford University Press, 2011.

Brown, Vahid. *Abu'l-Walid al-Masri: A Biographical Sketch*. West Point, NY: Combating Terrorism Center, 2007. www.ctc.usma.edu/v2/wp-content/uploads/2011/06/Abul-Walid.pdf.
  Cracks in the Foundation: Leadership Schisms in al-Qa'ida From 1989–2006. West Point, NY: Combating Terrorism Center, 2007.
  'A Mujahid's Bookbag'. Jihadica.com, 21 December 2009. www.jihadica.com/a-mujahids-bookbag/.
Brown, Vahid, and Don Rassler. *Fountainhead of Jihad: The Haqqani Nexus, 1973–2012*. Oxford: Oxford University Press, 2013.
'Brownsburg Man Charged with Attempting to Provide Resources to Terrorist Group Pleads Guilty', CBS4indy.com (CBS 4 Indianapolis News online), 23 May 2018.
Bruce, James. 'Arab Veterans of the Afghan War'. *Jane's Intelligence Review* 7 no. 1 (1995): 178–80.
Burr, J. Millard. 'Jordan's Muslim Brotherhood: A Short History'. American Center for Democracy, 2014.
Burr, J. Millard, and Robert O. Collins. *Alms for Jihad*. New York: Cambridge University Press, 2006.
Caillet, Romain, and Pierre Puchot. *"Le combat vous a été prescrit": une histoire du jihad en France*. Paris: Stock, 2017.
Cairncross, Frances. *The Death of Distance: How the Communications Revolution Will Change our Lives*. Cambridge, MA: Harvard Business School Press, 1997.
Calvert, John C. M. *Sayyid Qutb and the Origins of Radical Islamism*. New York: Columbia University Press, 2009.
  'The Striving Shaykh: Abdallah Azzam and the Revival of Jihad'. *Journal of Religion and Society* – Supplement Series (2007): 83–102.
'Canadian ISIL Fighter Wanted by RCMP May Have Been Killed in Missile Strike in Syria: Document'. NationalPost.com, 19 December 2016.
Carew, Tom. *Jihad! The Secret War in Afghanistan*. London: Mainstream, 2001.
Carré, Olivier. *Mystique et politique: lecture révolutionnaire du Coran par Sayyid Qutb, Frère Musulman radical*. Paris: Presses de la Fondation Nationale des Sciences Politiques, 1984.
Carré, Olivier, and Gerard Michaud. *Les Frères Musulmans: Égypte et Syrie*. Paris: Gallimard, 1983.
Casciani, Dominic. 'Babar Ahmad: The Godfather of Internet Jihad?' BBC News (online), 17 July 2014.
Centlivres, Pierre, and Micheline Centlivres-Demont. 'Les martyrs afghans par le texte et l'image (1978–1992)'. In *Saints et héros du Moyen-Orient contemporain. Actes du colloque des 11 et 12 décembre 2000*, edited by

Catherine Mayeur-Jaouen, 319–333. Paris: Maisonneuve et Larose, 2002.
Chaliand, Gérard. *The Palestinian Resistance*. London: Penguin, 1972.
Chamberlin, Paul Thomas. *The Global Offensive: The United States, the Palestine Liberation Organization, and the Making of the Post-Cold War Order*. New York: Oxford University Press, 2015.
Chevalérias, Alain. 'L'Afghanistan travaillé par les missionaires intégristes'. *Journal de Genève*, 26 November 1985.
Cohen, Amnon. *Political Parties in the West Bank under the Jordanian Regime, 1949–1967*. Ithaca: Cornell University Press, 1982.
Coll, Steve. *The Bin Ladens*. New York: Penguin, 2008.
 Ghost Wars: The Secret History of the CIA, Afghanistan and Bin Laden, from the Soviet Invasion to September 10, 2001. New York: Penguin, 2004.
 'Osama in America: The Final Answer'. *New Yorker*, 30 June 2009. www.newyorker.com/news/steve-coll/osama-in-america-the-final-answer
Conduit, Dara. 'The Syrian Muslim Brotherhood and the Spectacle of Hama'. *Middle East Journal* 70, no. 2 (15 April 2016): 211–226.
'Connecting the Dots – America's First al Qaeda Fighters'. New York: NEFA Foundation, April 2010. www.nefafoundation.org/miscellaneous/nefa_connectingthedots0410.pdf.
Cook, David B. 'Contemporary Martyrdom: Ideology and Material Culture'. In *Jihadi Culture: The Art and Social Practices of Militant Islamists*, edited by Thomas Hegghammer, 151–170. Cambridge: Cambridge University Press, 2017.
Cook, Michael. *Ancient Religions, Modern Politics: The Islamic Case in Comparative Perspective*. Princeton: Princeton University Press, 2014.
Cooley, John K. *Green March, Black September: The Story of the Palestinian Arabs*. London: Frank Cass, 1973.
 Unholy Wars: Afghanistan, America and International Terrorism. 1st ed. London: Pluto Press, 1999.
Cragin, R. Kim. 'Early History of al-Qa'ida'. *The Historical Journal* 51 (2008): 1047–1067.
 'Al Qaeda Confronts Hamas: Divisions in the Sunni Jihadist Movement and its Implications for US Policy'. *Studies in Conflict and Terrorism* 32, no. 7 (29 July 2009): 576–590.
Curtis, Adam. 'The Power of Nightmares: The Rise of the Politics of Fear'. London: BBC, 2004 [documentary].
Curtis, Mark. *Secret Affairs: Britain's Collusion with Radical Islam*. London: Serpent's Tail, 2010.

al-Dahshan, Sa'id Sha'ban Khalil. 'juhud al-duktur 'abdallah 'azzam fi nashr al-da'wa al-islamiyya' [Dr Abdallah Azzam's Efforts in Propagating the Islamic Call]. Master's thesis, Islamic University in Gaza, 2013.

Dalrymple, William. 'Nancy Hatch Dupree's Quest to Save Afghanistan's History'. *Newsweek*, 12 April 2013. http://newsweekpakistan.com/ill-just-finish-my-chips/.

Dasuqi, Abduh Mustafa. *nash'at al-tanzim al-duwali li'l-ikhwan al-muslimin: min al-nash'a hatta al-sab'inat* [The Emergence of the International Organization of the Muslim Brotherhood: From the Emergence to the 1970s]. Cairo: Mu'assasat Iqra' li'l-Nashr wa'l-Tawzi' wa'l-Tarjama, 2013.

Datta, S. K. *Inside ISI: The Story and Involvement of the ISI in Afghan Jihad, Taliban, al-Qaeda, 9/11, Osama Bin Laden, 26/11 and the Future of al-Qaeda*. New Delhi: Vij Books, 2014.

Davis, Anthony. 'Foreign Combatants in Afghanistan'. *Jane's Intelligence Review* 5 (1993): 327–331.

Da'war, Ghassan Muhammad. *qawa'id al-shuyukh: muqawamat al-ikhwan al-muslimin didd al-mashru' al-sahyuni* [The Bases of the Sheikhs: The Muslim Brotherhood's Resistance to the Zionist Project]. Beirut: Markaz al-Zaytuni li'l-Dirasat wa'l-Istisharat, 2018.

De la Paz, Alexander. 'Miracles, Jihad, and Propaganda'. Unpublished draft paper, 2017.

de Ponfilly, Christophe. *Vies clandestines: nos années afghanes*. Paris: Florent Massot, 2001.

'Death Tolls for the Major Wars and Atrocities of the Twentieth Century', n.d. http://necrometrics.com/20c1m.htm.

'Des Jordaniens rentrés d'Afghanistan inquiètent Amman'. Agence France Presse, 28 May 1993.

Devine, Jack, and Vernon Loeb. *Good Hunting: An American Spymaster's Story*. New York: Sarah Crichton Books, 2014.

al-Dhiyabi, Jamil. 'Saudi Academic Recounts Experiences from Afghan War'. *al-Hayat* (via Ariana News), 20 March 2006.

Dimitrakis, Panagiotis. *The Secret War in Afghanistan: The Soviet Union, China and Anglo-American Intelligence in the Afghan War*. London and New York: I. B. Tauris, 2013.

Diraz, Issam. *malhamat al-mujahidin al-'arab fi afghanistan* [The Epic of the Arab Mujahidin in Afghanistan]. Madinat al-Ashir min Ramadan: Dar al-Tiba'ah wa-l-Nashr al-Islamiyya, 1989.

'Director-General of Islamic Teaching Center Concludes Middle East Tour'. *Islamic Teaching Center News* 1, no. 1 (February 1978): 3.

Dodd, Peter, and Halim Barakat. 'Palestinian Refugees of 1967: A Sociological Study'. *Muslim World* 60, no. 2 (1970): 123–142.

Dodd, Vikram. 'Roshonara Choudhry: Police Interview Extracts'. *The Guardian* Online, 3 November 2010.
  'Two British Men Admit to Linking Up with Extremist Group in Syria'. *The Guardian* Online, 8 July 2014.
Dorronsoro, Gilles. *Revolution Unending: Afghanistan, 1979 to the Present*. New York: Columbia University Press, 2005.
Doumani, Beshara. *Rediscovering Palestine: Merchants and Peasants in Jabal Nablus, 1700–1900*. Berkeley: University of California Press, 1995.
'The Dr. Abdallah Azzam Academy'. Meir Amit Intelligence and Terrorism Information Center, 6 April 2009. www.terrorism-info.org.il/Data/pdf/PDF_09_158_2.pdf.
Dupree, Louis. 'Afghanistan in 1982: Still no Solution'. *Asian Survey* 23, no. 2 (February 1983): 133–142.
Ebrahim, Zak. *The Terrorist's Son: A Story of Choice*. New York: Simon & Schuster, 2014.
Eccel, Chris. *Egypt, Islam, and Social Change: al-Azhar in Conflict and Accommodation*. Berlin: Klaus Schwartz, 1984.
Edgar, Iain R. *The Dream in Islam: From Qur'anic Tradition to Jihadist Inspiration*. New York: Berghahn Books, 2011.
Edwards, David B. *Before Taliban: Genealogies of the Afghan Jihad*. Berkeley: University of California Press, 2002.
  Caravan of Martyrs: Sacrifice and Suicide Bombing in Afghanistan. Oakland: University of California Press, 2017.
  'Print Islam: Media and Religious Revolution in Afghanistan'. *Anthropological Quarterly* 68 (July 1995): 171–184.
Eickelman, Dale F., and James P. Piscatori. *Muslim Politics*. Princeton: Princeton University Press, 2004.
Eighmy, Thomas. 'Remembering USAID's Role in Afghanistan, 1985–1994'. *Foreign Service Journal*, December 2007.
Ekberg, Gunnar. *De ska ju ändå dö: Tio år i svensk underrättelsetjänst* [They're Going to Die Anyway: Ten Years in Swedish Foreign Intelligence]. Stockholm: Fischer & Company, 2009.
El Almani, Abdul Ghaffar. 'Mein Weg Nach Jannah', 2010. www.scribd.com/doc/31071994/Schaheed-Abdul-Ghaffar-al-Almani-Mein-Weg-Nach-Jannah.
El Awaisi, Abd al-Fattah M. *The Muslim Brothers and the Palestine Question, 1928–47*. London: I. B. Tauris, 1998.
Elpeleg, Zvi. *The Grand Mufti: Haj Amin al-Hussaini, Founder of the Palestinian National Movement*. London: Routledge, 1993.
El-Rayyes, Riad, and Dunia Nahas. Guerrillas for Palestine. London: Croom Helm, 1976.

Elshobaki, Amr. *Les Frères Musulmans des origines à nos jours*. Paris: Karthala, 2009.

Emerson, Steven. 'Abdullah Assam: The Man before Osama Bin Laden', *Journal of Counterterrorism and Security International* (1998), www.iacsp.com/itobli3.html.

American Jihad: The Terrorists Living among us. New York: Free Press, 2002.

'Inside the Osama Bin Laden Investigation'. *Journal of Counterterrorism and Security International 5*, no. 3 (1998): 16–26.

'The Suspect Ties of CAIR Officials, Fundraisers and Trainers'. The Investigative Project, 2008.

Ennab, Wael R. *Population and Demographic Developments in the West Bank and Gaza Strip until 1990*. New York: United Nations Conference on Trade and Development, United Nations, 1994.

Esposito, John L., ed. *The Oxford Dictionary of Islam*. Oxford: Oxford University Press, 2004.

'Exclusive Q & A with Junaid Hussain – British ISIS fighter and hacker'. 5PillarsUK (blog), 24 September 2014. https://5pillarsuk.com/2014/09/24/exclusive-q-and-a-with-junaid-hussain-british-isis-fighter-and-hacker/.

al-Fahd, Nasir. 'ayat al-rahman fi "ghazwat sibtimbar"' [Signs of the Merciful in the "September Raid"]. Minbar al-Tawhid wa'l-Jihad, 2002.

Fair, C. Christine, Bruce Hoffman, and Fernando Reinares. 'Leader-Led Jihad in Pakistan: The Case of Lashkar-e-Taiba'. In *The Evolution of the Global Terrorist Threat: From 9/11 to Osama Bin Laden's Death*, edited by Bruce Hoffman and Fernando Reinares. 571–599. New York: Columbia University Press, 2014.

Fandy, Mamoun. *Saudi Arabia and the Politics of Dissent*. New York: Palgrave Macmillan, 2001.

Farquhar, Michael. *Circuits of Faith: Migration, Education, and the Wahhabi Mission*. Stanford: Stanford University Press, 2016.

FBIS. 'Compilation of Usama bin Ladin Statements, 1994–January 2004'. Foreign Broadcast Information Service, 2004. www.fas.org/irp/world/para/ubl-fbis.pdf.

'fi dhikra al-shahid 'abdallah 'azzam' [In Memory of the Martyr Abdallah Azzam], n.d. www.ikhwan-jor.com.

fi 'uyun mu'asira: al-imam al-shahid 'abdallah 'azzam [Through Contemporary Eyes: The Martyred Imam Abdallah Azzam]. Peshawar: Markaz al-Shahid Azzam al-I'lami, 1997.

Fighel, Jonathan. 'Sheikh Abdullah Azzam: Bin Laden's Spiritual Mentor'. International Institute for Counter-Terrorism (blog, 27 September 2001). http://212.150.54.123/articles/articledet.cfm?articleid=388.

al-Filastini, Abu Qatada. 'shaykh al-jihad wa 'alam al-din wa'l-shahada 'abdallah 'azzam' [Shaykh of Jihad and Symbol of the Religion and Martyrdom Abdallah Azzam]. Justpaste.it, 23 September 2015. https://justpaste.it/nxcm.

Firdous, Iftikhar. 'Suicide Attack on Peshawar Police Station Leaves Four Dead'. *Express Tribune*, 24 February 2012.

Fitzgerald, Mary. 'The Son of the Father of Jihad'. *The Irish Times*, 7 July 2006.

Forest, James J. F., Jarret Brachman, and Joseph Felter. 'Harmony and Disharmony: Exploiting al-Qa'ida's Organizational Vulnerabilities'. West Point, NY: Combating Terrorism Center, 14 February 2006. https://ctc.usma.edu/harmony-program/.

Frampton, Martyn. *The Muslim Brotherhood and the West: A History of Enmity and Engagement*. Cambridge, MA: Harvard University Press, 2018.

Frantzman, Seth J. and Jovan Ćulibrk. 'Strange Bedfellows: The Bosnians and Yugoslav Volunteers in the 1948 War in Israel/Palestine', *Istorija 20. veka*, no. 1 (2009): 189–200.

Freer, Courtney. *Rentier Islamism: The Influence of the Muslim Brotherhood in Gulf Monarchies*. New York: Oxford University Press, 2018.

Fremont-Barnes, Gregory. *The Soviet–Afghan War 1979–89*. Oxford and Long Island City, NY: Osprey Publishing, 2012.

Freudenthal, Anja. 'Abdallah Azzam Brigades', HS-community.org, 28 February 2016.

Fuchs, Simon Wolfgang. 'Glossy Global Leadership: Unpacking the Multilingual Religious Thought of the Jihad'. In *Afghanistan's Islam: From Conversion to the Taliban*, edited by Nile Green, 189–206. Oakland: University of California Press, 2017.

Proper Signposts for the Camp: The Reception of Classical Authorities in the Ǧihādī Manual al-'Umda fī I'dād al-'Udda. Würzburg: Ergon-Verlag, 2011.

Gerges, Fawaz. *The Far Enemy: Why Jihad Went Global*. New York: Cambridge University Press, 2005.

Gershoni, Israel. 'The Muslim Brothers and the Arab Revolt in Palestine'. *Middle Eastern Studies* 22 (1986): 367–397.

Ghandour, Abdel-Rahman. *Jihad humanitaire: enquête sur les ONG islamiques*. Paris: Flammarion, 2002.

al-Ghannouchi, Rachid. "abdallah 'azzam namudhaj al-'ulama al-mujahidin' [Abdallah Azzam is a Model of Mujahidin Scholars]. *al-Sharq al-Awsat*, 3 December 1989.

al-hurriyat al-'amma fi'l-dawla al-islamiyya [Public Freedoms in the Islamic State]. Beirut: Markaz Dirasat al-Wihda al-Arabiyya, 1993.

nahnu wa'l-gharb [We and the West]. Unknown publisher, n.d.

tariqna ila al-nasr [Our Road to Victory]. Unknown publisher, n.d.

Ghusheh, Ibrahim. *The Red Minaret: Memoirs of Ibrahim Ghusheh (Ex-Spokesman of Hamas)*. Beirut: al-Zaytouna Centre for Studies and Consultations, 2013.

Gillan, Audrey. 'The Fantasy Life and Lonely Death of the SAS Veteran who Never Was'. *The Guardian*, 24 January 2009.

Girardet, Edward. *Killing the Cranes: A Reporter's Journey through Three Decades of War in Afghanistan*. White River Junction, VT: Chelsea Green Publishing, 2011.

Giustozzi, Antonio. *War, Politics and Society in Afghanistan, 1978–1992*. Washington, DC: Georgetown University Press, 2000.

Gold, Dore. 'Hamas and al-Qaeda are the Same'. Israel National News Online, 6 January 2010.

Grau, Lester W. *The Bear Went over the Mountain*. London: Routledge, 2005.

Grau, Lester W., and Ali Ahmad Jalali. 'The Campaign for the Caves: The Battles for Zhawar in the Soviet–Afghan War'. *Journal of Slavic Military Studies* 14, no. 3 (2001): 69–92.

Green, Abdurraheem. 'Abdurraheem Green: "Returning Jihadis Aren't so Bad, I Used to be one"'. 5Pillars (blog), 30 October 2014.

Grey, Stephen. 'Mint Tea with Terrorists'. *New Statesman*, 11 April 2005.

Hadawi, Sami. *Village Statistics 1945: A Classification of Land and Area Ownership in Palestine*. Beirut: Palestine Liberation Organization Research Center, 1970.

al-Haddushi, Umar. 'nubdha mukhtasira 'an hayat mujaddid al-jihad al-shaykh al-imam 'abdallah 'azzam' [Short Presentation of the Life of the Reviver of Jihad, the Sheikh and Imam Abdallah Azzam]. Shabakat al-Tahaddi al-Islami (posted on http://al-faloja1.com/vb/showthread.php?t=93030, 19 November 2009), n.d.

Hafez, Mohammed M. *Suicide Bombers in Iraq*. Washington, DC: USIP, 2007.

al-Hafyan, Karam. *al-jihad al-mu'asir bayna 'abdallah 'azzam wa usama bin ladin* [Contemporary Jihad between Abdallah Azzam and Usama Bin Ladin]. Istanbul: Egyptian Institute for Studies, 5 March 2019.

Hallush, Abd al-Rahman. *al-shaykh wa'l-tabib: usama bin ladin wa ayman al-zawahiri* [The Shaykh and the Doctor: Usama Bin Ladin and Ayman al-Zawahiri]. Beirut: Riyadh al-Rayyis, 2011.

'"al-hamdu li'llah rabb al-'alamayn", kanat awwal kalima nataqtu biha ba'd sama'i khabar istishhad zawji wa abna'i' ['Praise be to God' was the First Word I Uttered after Hearing the News of the Martyrdom of my Husband and Sons]. *al-Sabil*, 2 December 1997.

Hamid, Mustafa, and Leah Farrall. *The Arabs at War in Afghanistan*. London: Hurst, 2015.

Hamza, Mawlana Amir. *qafilat daʻwat jihad* [The Caravan of *Daʻwa* and Jihad]. n.p.: Dar al-Andalus, 2004.

al-Haqbani, Nasser. 'Exclusive – Sayyaf to *Asharq al-Awsat*: I Know Who Killed Azzam'. *al-Sharq al-Awsat* English Online, 20 February 2018.

Harakan, Muhammad Ali. 'Duty of Implementing the Resolutions'. *Journal of the Muslim World League* (1980): 48–49.

Harun, Fadil. *al-harb ʻala al-islam* [The War against Islam], part 2, 2009. https://ctc.usma.edu/harmony-program/the-war-against-islam-the-story-of-fazul-harun-part-2-original-language-2/.

al-Hashimi, Khattab bin Muhammad. 'al-mujaddidan. ibn ladin wa ʻazzam: naqidan am diddan' [The Renewers. Bin Ladin and Azzam: Contrasts or Opposites?]. *Umma Wahida* no. 1 (April 2019): 25–33.

Hassan, Hassan. 'Bin Laden Journal Reveals he was Shaped by the Muslim Brotherhood'. *The National* Online, 2 November 2017.

Hassan, Izzat Muhammad Ibrahim. 'al-jihad al-afghani fi manzur al-shuʻaraʼ al-ʻarab 1979–1994' [The Afghan Jihad in the Eyes of Arab Poets, 1979–1994]. Baha al-Din Zakariya University, 1997.

Hassan, Muhammad Haniff. *The Father of Jihad: ʻAbd Allah ʻAzzamʼs Jihad Ideas and Implications to National Security*. London: Imperial College Press, 2014.

 'Jihad ideas of "Abd Allah" Azzam and their implications for national security'. Ph.D. thesis, Nanyang Technological University, 2012.

Hatina, Meir. 'Warrior Saints: ʻAbdallah ʻAzzamʼs Reflections on Jihad and Karamat'. In *Martyrdom and Sacrifice in Islam: Theological, Political and Social Contexts*, edited by Meir Hatina and Meir Litvak. London: I. B. Tauris, 2017.

Hauslohner, Abigail. 'Friend of Zawahiri: The Tangled Tale of the Mild-Mannered Salafi'. *Time*, 11 July 2011.

Hawwa, Saʻid. *hadhihi tajribati ... wa hadhihi shahadati* [This is my Experience ... and This my Testimony]. Cairo: Dar al-Tawfiq al-Namudhajiyya, 1987.

al-Hawali, Safar. 'mafhum al-jihad' [The Concept of Jihad], 1989. www.alhawali.com.

Heffelfinger, Chris. *Radical Islam in America: Salafismʼs Journey from Arabia to the West*. Washington, DC: Potomac Books, 2011.

Hegghammer, Thomas. 'Abdallah Azzam: lʼimam du jihad'. In *al-Qaida dans le texte*, edited by Gilles Kepel, Thomas Hegghammer, Stéphane Lacroix, Jean-Pierre Milelli, and Omar Saghi, 115–138. Paris: Presses Universitaires de France, 2005.

'Abdallah Azzam and Palestine'. *Die Welt des Islams* 53, no. 3–4 (2013): 353–387.

Jihad in Saudi Arabia: Violence and Pan-Islamism since 1979. Cambridge: Cambridge University Press, 2010.

'Jihadi Salafis or Revolutionaries? On Theology and Politics in the Study of Militant Islamism.' In *Global Salafism: Islam's New Religious Movement*, edited by Roel Meijer, 244–266. New York: Columbia University Press, 2009.

'The Rise of Muslim Foreign Fighters: Islam and the Globalization of Jihad'. *International Security* 35, no. 3 (2010): 53–94.

'Should I Stay or Should I Go? Explaining Variation in Western Jihadists' Choice between Domestic and Foreign Fighting'. *American Political Science Review* 107, no. 1 (2013): 1–15.

'Syria's Foreign Fighters'. ForeignPolicy.com, 9 December 2013.

'Terrorist Recruitment and Radicalisation in Saudi Arabia'. *Middle East Policy* 13, no. 4 (2006): 39–60.

Hegghammer, Thomas, ed. *Jihadi Culture: The Art and Social Practices of Militant Islamists*. Cambridge: Cambridge University Press, 2017.

Hegghammer, Thomas, and Stéphane Lacroix. *The Meccan Rebellion: The Story of Juhayman al-'Utaybi Revisited*. London: Amal Press, 2011.

Hegghammer, Thomas, and Joas Wagemakers. 'The Palestine Effect: The Role of Palestinians in the Transnational Jihad Movement'. *Die Welt des Islams* 53, no. 3–4 (2013): 281–314.

Hekmatyar, Gulbuddin. *Secret Plans Open Faces: From the Withdrawal of Russians to the Fall of the Coalition Government*. Peshawar: University of Peshawar, 2004.

Heller, Sam. 'Ahrar al-Sham's Revisionist Jihadism'. War on the Rocks (blog), 30 September 2015.

al-Hindukushi, Abu al-Shaqra'. 'min kabul ila baghdad' [From Kabul to Baghdad], 2007. http://archive.org/details/fromcaboltobagdad.

Hinnebusch, Raymond. 'Empire and State Formation: Contrary Tangents in Jordan and Syria'. In *Sovereignty after Empire: Comparing the Middle East and Central Asia*, edited by Sally N. Cummings and Raymond Hinnebusch, 263–281. Edinburgh: Edinburgh University Press, 2011.

Hodson, Peregrine. *Under a Sickle Moon: A Journey through Afghanistan*. New York: Grove Press, 2002.

Hoffman, Bruce. *Inside Terrorism*. New York: Columbia University Press, 1998.

Holbrook, Donald. *What Types of Media Do Terrorists Collect? An Analysis of Religious, Political, and Ideological Publications Found in Terrorism*

Investigations in the UK. The Hague: International Centre for Counter-Terrorism, September 2017.

Hubbard, Ben. 'In Syria, Potential Ally's Islamist Ties Challenge US'. *New York Times*, 25 August 2015.

Hughes, Matthew. 'Collusion across the Litani? Lebanon and the 1948 War'. In *The War for Palestine*, edited by Eugene Rogan and Avi Shlaim, 204–227. Cambridge: Cambridge University Press, 2007.

Huntington, Samuel. *The Clash of Civilizations and the Remaking of the World Order*. New York: Touchstone, 1996.

Hussein, Tam. 'Jihad, Then and Now'. *Majalla* 8 February 2014.

Hyman, Anthony. 'Arab Involvement in the Afghan War'. *Beirut Review* no. 7 (1994): 73–90.

Ibrahim, Saad Eddin. 'Anatomy of Egypt's Militant Islamic Groups: Methodological Notes and Preliminary Findings'. *International Journal of Middle East Studies* 12 (1980): 423–453.

Ingram, Haroro J. *The Charismatic Leadership Phenomenon in Radical and Militant Islamism*. London: Routledge, 2014.

'An Insider's View of al-Qa'ida as Narrated by Abu-Jandal (Nasir al-Bahri), Bin-Ladin's Bodyguard (part 4)'. *al-Quds al-Arabi* (via FBIS), 22 March 2005.

'Interview with Sheikh Tameem al Adnani'. Lawrence Islamic Video, 1988. http://archive.org/details/interview-sheikh-tameem-adnani.

Jalali, Ali Ahmad, and Lester W. Grau. *Afghan Guerrilla Warfare: In the Words of the Mujahideen Fighters*. St. Paul, MN: MBI Publishing, 2001.

Jamal, Arif. *Call for Transnational Jihad: Lashkar-e-Taiba 1985–2014*, 1st South Asian ed. New Delhi: Kautilya, 2015.

'The Growth of the Deobandi Jihad in Afghanistan'. *Jamestown Terrorism Monitor* 8, no. 2 (14 January 2010).

Shadow War: The Untold Story of Jihad in Kashmir. New York: Melville House, 2009.

Jankowski, James. 'Egyptian Responses to the Palestine Problem in the Interwar Period'. *International Journal of Middle East Studies* 12 (1980): 1–38.

Jansen, Johannes. *The Neglected Duty: The Creed of Sadat's Assassins and Islamic Resurgence in the Middle East*. New York: Macmillan, 1986.

'Japan Tanker was Damaged in a Terror Attack, UAE Says'. BBC News Online, 6 August 2010, sec. Asia-Pacific.

Jarrar, Husni Adham. *al-shahid 'abdallah 'azzam: rajul da'wa wa-madrasat jihad* [The Martyr Abdallah Azzam: Man of Da'wa and School of Jihad]. Amman: Dar al-Diya, 1990.

al-Jasir, Jasir. 'qissat al-afghan al-sa'udiyyin' [The Story of the Saudi Afghans]. *al-Majalla*, 11 May 1996.

Jehl, Douglas. 'Mohammed al-Ghazali, 78, An Egyptian Cleric and Scholar'. *New York Times*, 14 March 1996.

Jenkins, Philip. 'Clerical Terror: The Roots of Jihad in India', *The New Republic*, 24 December 2008.

Johnson, Steve A. 'Political Activity of Muslims in America'. In *The Muslims in America*, edited by Yvonne Yazbeck Haddad, 111–124. New York: Oxford University Press, 1991.

Jomier, Jaques. 'Programme et orientation des études à la faculté de théologie d'al-Azhar: kulliyat usûl al-dîn'. *Revue des études islamiques* no. 44 (1976): 253–272.

'Jordanian Guantanamo prisoner released'. UPI, 14 August 2004.

'Jordanian Liberal Harshly Criticized for her Condemnation of University of Jordan for Naming Prayer Hall after al-Qaeda Ideologue 'Abdallah 'Azzam'. *MEMRI Special Dispatch* no. 7483, 22 May 2018.

'Jordan's Moslem Brotherhood Braces for In-House Elections'. *Mideast Mirror* 12, no. 72 (16 April 1998).

Joscelyn, Thomas. 'al Nusrah Front Confirms al Qaeda Veteran Killed in US Airstrike.' *The Long War Journal*, 6 April 2016.

Joshi, Shashank. 'Assessing Britain's Role in Afghanistan'. *Asian Survey* 55, no. 2 (2014): 420–445.

Kamal, Ahmad Adil. *al-nuqat fawqa al-huruf: al-ikhwan al-muslimun wa'l-tanzim al-khass* [The Points above the Letters: The Muslim Brotherhood and the Special Apparatus]. Cairo: al-Zahra li'l-I'lam al-Arabi, 1989.

Kaufman, Michael T. 'Mrs. Thatcher Visits Afghans on the Frontier'. *New York Times*, 9 October 1981.

Kaya, Ferzede. 'Turks who Fought in Afghanistan'. *Turkish Daily News*, 17 October 2001.

Keck, Margaret E., and Kathryn Sikkink. *Activists beyond Borders: Advocacy Networks in International Politics*. Ithaca: Cornell University Press, 1998.

Kepel, Gilles. *Jihad: The Trail of Political Islam*. Cambridge, MA: Belknap, 2002.

Muslim Extremism in Egypt. Berkeley: University of California Press, 1986.

Khalidi, Noor Ahmad. 'Afghanistan: Demographic consequences of war, 1978–1987'. *Central Asian Survey* 10, no. 3 (1 January 1991): 101–126.

Khalidi, Walid. *All that Remains: The Palestinian Villages Occupied and Depopulated by Israel in 1948*. Washington, DC: Institute for Palestine Studies, 1992.

Khalil, Imad al-Din. *fawda al-'alam fi'l-masrah al-gharbi al-mu'asir* [Chaos of the World in Contemporary Western Theater]. Beirut: al-Risala, 1977.

Khalili, Laleh. *Heroes and Martyrs of Palestine: The Politics of National Commemoration*. Cambridge: Cambridge University Press, 2007.

Khamahyar, Abbas. *iran wa'l-ikhwan al-muslimin: dirasa fi 'awamil al-iltiqa' wa'l-iftiraq* [Iran and the Muslim Brotherhood: A Study of the Causes of Confluence and Divergence]. Beirut: Markaz al-Dirasat al-Istratijiyya wa'l-Buhuth wa'l-Tawthiq, 1997.
'khamas sanawat fi sujun kabul' [Five Years in the Prisons of Kabul]. *al-Jihad* no. 46 (September 1988): 16–20.
Kharabsha, Bayan. 'risalat tifla li'l-jihad' [Letter from a Young Girl to the Jihad]. *al-Jihad* no. 28 (March 1987): 38.
Khashoggi, Jamal. 'Arab Youths Fight Shoulder to Shoulder with Mujahideen'. *Arab News*. 4 May 1988.
Khattak, Daud. 'The Complicated Relationship between the Afghan and Pakistani Taliban'. *CTC Sentinel* 5, no. 2 (2012): 14–15.
Kiessling, Hein. *Faith, Unity, Discipline: The Inter-Service-Intelligence (ISI) of Pakistan*. London: Hurst, 2016.
Kilpatrick, A. Jefferson. *Sayyid Qutb: A Selective Annotated Bibliography of Dissertations and Theses*. Annotated edition. CreateSpace Independent Publishing Platform, 2015.
Koch, Ariel. 'Jihadi Beheading Videos and their Non-Jihadi Echoes'. *Perspectives on Terrorism* 12, no. 3 (2018): 24–34.
Kuehn, Felix, Leah Farrall, and Alex Strick van Linschoten. 'Expert Report – US vs. Talha Ahsan; US vs. Babar Ahmad', April 2014. http://www.sacc.org.uk/sacc/docs/ba_expert_reports.pdf.
Kukis, Mark. *"My Heart Became Attached": The Strange Odyssey of John Walker Lindh*. Washington, DC: Brassey's, 2003.
Lacroix, Stéphane. 'al-Albani's Revolutionary Approach to Hadith'. *ISIM Review*, no. 21 (2008): 6–7.
  Awakening Islam: The Politics of Religious Dissent in Contemporary Saudi Arabia. Cambridge, MA: Harvard University Press, 2011.
  'Ayman al-Zawahiri, le vétéran du jihad'. In *al-Qaida dans le texte*, edited by Gilles Kepel, Thomas Hegghammer, Stéphane Lacroix, Jean-Pierre Milelli, and Omar Saghi, 221–242. Paris: Presses Universitaires de France, 2008.
  'Between Revolution and Apoliticism: Nasir al-Din al-Albani and his Impact on the Shaping of Contemporary Salafism'. In *Global Salafism: Islam's New Religious Movement*, edited by Roel Meijer, 58–80. London: Hurst, 2009.
  A Social and Political History of Egyptian Salafism (forthcoming).
Lahoud, Nelly. 'A Cappella Songs (*anashid*) in Jihadi Culture', in *Jihadi Culture: The Art and Social Practices of Militant Islamists*, edited by Thomas Hegghammer, 42–62. Cambridge: Cambridge University Press, 2017.
  The Jihadis' Path to Self-Destruction. New York: Columbia University Press, 2010.

'The Neglected Sex: The Jihadis' Exclusion of Women from Jihad'. *Terrorism and Political Violence* 26, no. 5 (20 February 2014): 780–802.

'The Pitfalls of Jihad as an Individual Duty (*fard 'ayn*)'. In *Jihad and its Challenges to International and Domestic Law*, edited by M. Cherif Bassiouni and A. Guellali, 87–106. The Hague: T.M.C. Asser Press, 2009.

Lamb, Christina. *Waiting for Allah: Pakistan's Struggle for Democracy*. New York: Viking, 1991.

'lamha 'an al-sila al-harithiyya' [Glance at al-Sila al-Harithiyya]. http://selahartiah.blogspot.no/p/blog-page_3241.html, n.d.

Landau, J. M. *The Politics of Pan-Islam: Ideology and Organization*. Oxford: University Press, 1990.

Landis, Joshua. 'Syria and the Palestine War: Fighting King 'Abdullah's "Greater Syria Plan"'. In *The War for Palestine*, edited by Eugene L. Rogan and Avi Shlaim, 176–203. Cambridge: Cambridge University Press, 2007.

Lappen, Alyssa A. 'The Muslim Brotherhood in North America'. In *The Muslim Brotherhood: The Organization and Policies of a Global Islamist Movement*, edited by Barry Rubin, 161–180. New York: Palgrave Macmillan, 2010.

Lauzière, Henri. *The Making of Salafism: Islamic Reform in the Twentieth Century*. New York: Columbia University Press, 2015.

Lea-Henry, Jed. 'The Life and Death of Abdullah Azzam'. *Middle East Policy* 25, no. 1 (2018): 64–79.

Lefèvre, Raphael. *Ashes of Hama: The Muslim Brotherhood in Syria*. New York: Oxford University Press, 2013.

Levenberg, Haim. *Military Preparations of the Arab Community in Palestine 1945–1948*. London: Frank Cass, 1993.

Lewis, Pauline. 'Zainab al-Ghazali: Pioneer of Islamist Feminism'. *Michigan Journal of History* 4, no. 2 (2007).

Li, Darryl. 'Lies, Damned Lies and Plagiarizing "Experts"'. *Middle East Report* 41, no.260 (11 September 2011): 5.

'Taking the Place of Martyrs: Afghans and Arabs under the Banner of Islam'. *Arab Studies Journal* 20, no. 1 (2012): 12–39.

Lia, Brynjar. *Architect of Global Jihad: The Life of al-Qaeda Strategist Abu Mus'ab al-Suri*. London: Hurst, 2007.

'The Islamist Uprising in Syria, 1976–82: The History and Legacy of a Failed Revolt'. *British Journal of Middle Eastern Studies* 43, no. 4 (8 February 2016): 541–559.

The Society of the Muslim Brothers in Egypt: The Rise of an Islamic Mass Movement, 1928–1942. Reading: Ithaca, 1998.

Lia, Brynjar, and Thomas Hegghammer. 'Jihadi Strategic Studies: The Alleged Al Qaida Policy Study Preceding the Madrid Bombings'. *Studies in Conflict and Terrorism* 27, no. 5 (2004): 355–375.

Lindecke, Fred W. '5,000 Muslim Students Spending Holidays at St. Louis Convention'. *St. Louis Post*, 25 December 1983.

'liqa' zawjat al-shahid 'abdallah 'azzam ma' sahifat al-waqt al-turkiya' [Interview with the Wife of Martyr Abdallah Azzam by the Turkish *Vakit* Newspaper], 2006.

Lobmeyer, Hans Günter. *Opposition und Widerstand in Syrien*. Hamburg: Deutsches Orient-Institut, 1995.

Lohbeck, Kurt. *Holy War, Unholy Victory: Eyewitness to the CIA's Secret War in Afghanistan*. Washington, DC: Regnery Gateway, 1993.

Lorentz, John H. 'Afghan Aid: The Role of Private Voluntary Organizations.' *Journal of South Asian and Middle Eastern Studies* 11 (1987): 102–111.

al-Madkhali, Rabi' bin Hadi. 'munadhara 'an afghanistan' [Discussion on Afghanistan], n.d. http://madkhalis.com/2010/02/rab-al-madkhalis-slander-of-abdullah-azzam/.

al-Mahdawi, Diyab Hasan. *ayat al-rahman fi filastin wa-lubnan* [Signs of the Merciful in Palestine and Lebanon]. Beirut: Dar al-Mahajja al-Bayda', 2007.

Maher, Shiraz. 'The Future of Unholy War'. *Standpoint Magazine*, November 2008. http://standpointmag.co.uk/node/584/full.

Salafi-Jihadism: The History of an Idea. Oxford: Oxford University Press, 2016.

al-Majdhub, Muhammad. *dhikrayat la tansa ma' al-mujahidin wa'l-muhajirin fi bakistan* [Unforgettable Memories with the Mujahidin and the Emigrants in Pakistan]. Medina: Nadi al-Madina al-Munawwara al-Adabi, 1984.

Malet, David. *Foreign Fighters: Transnational Identity in Civil Conflicts*. New York: Oxford University Press, 2013.

Maliach, Asaf. 'Abdallah Azzam and the Ideological Origins of Usama Bin Ladin's Worldwide Islamic Terrorism' [in Hebrew], Ph.D. dissertation. Bar-Ilan University, 2006.

'Abdullah Azzam, al-Qaeda, and Hamas: Concepts of Jihad and Istishhad'. *Military and Strategic Affairs* 2, no. 2 (2010): 79–93.

'Bin Ladin, Palestine and al-Qa'ida's Operational Strategy'. *Middle Eastern Studies* 44, no. 3 (May 2008): 353–375.

Malik, Jamal. 'Islamic Mission and Call: The Case of the International Islamic University, Islamabad'. *Islam and Christian–Muslim Relations* 9, no. 1 (1 March 1998): 31–45.

'man huwa fadilat al-shaykh 'abd al-ghani 'abd al-khaliq?' [Who is Shaykh Abd al-Ghani Abd al-Khaliq?], n.d. www.ahlalhdeeth.com/vb/showthread.php?t=106337.

Mandaville, Peter. *Global Political Islam*. London: Routledge, 2007.

Mansfield, Laura. *His Own Words: A Translation of the Writings of Dr. Ayman al-Zawahiri*. [Old Tappan, NJ]: TLG Publications, 2006.

Mansur, Ahmad. 'al-jihad al-afghani fi marhalat muwajahat al-nifaq' [The Afghan Jihad is in the Stage of Confronting Hypocrisy]. *al-Jihad* no. 59 (September 1989): 32–33.

al-Maqdisi, Abu Muhammad. *al-kawashif al-jaliyya fi kufr al-dawla al-sa'udiyya* [The Blatant Proof of the Infidel Nature of the Saudi State]. Minbar al-Tawhid wa'l-Jihad, 1989.

   marhalat afghanistan [The Afghanistan Stage]. Minbar al-Tawhid wa'l-Jihad, n.d.

   millat ibrahim wa da'wat al-anbiya' wa'l-mursalin [The Community of Abraham and the Call of the Prophets and the Messengers], Minbar al-Tawhid wa'l-Jihad, 1984

Marcus, Lori Lowenthal. 'Dzokhar Tsarnaev Inspired by Hamas Founder, Indictment Reveals'. TheJewishPress.com, 28 June 2013.

Maréchal, Brigitte. *The Muslim Brothers in Europe: Roots and Discourse*. Leiden: Brill, 2008.

Martin, Richard C., and Abbas Barzegar, eds. *Islamism: Contested Perspectives on Political Islam*. Stanford: Stanford University Press, 2009.

The Martyrs of Afghanistan. Azzam Publications, n.d. www.islamicline.com/islamicbooks/new/current/The_Shuhadaa_of_Afghanistan%28www.islamicline.com%29.pdf.

Masalha, Nur-eldeen. 'The 1967 Palestinian Exodus.' In *The Palestinian Exodus, 1948–1998*, edited by Ghada Karmi and Eugene Cotran, 63–110. Reading: Ithaca, 1999.

al-Masri, Abu Walid. 'laylat suqut qandahar: al-sumud al-'arabi al-akhir fi'l-waqt al-da'i'' [The Night Qandahar Fell: The Last Arab Resistance on Borrowed Time], 2009. http://mafa.maktoobblog.com/311555/%D8%AC%D9%85%D9%8A%25.

Mattar, Shafika. 'US Ship Attacked in Jordan Port'. *Washington Post*, 20 August 2005.

Matthiesen, Toby. 'The Iranian Revolution and Sunni Political Islam'. In *New Analysis of Shia Politics*, edited by Marc Lynch, 36–38. POMEPS Studies 28. Washington, DC: George Washington University Project on Middle East Political Science, 2017. https://pomeps.org/2017/12/21/the-iranian-revolution-and-sunni-political-islam/.

mawsu'at al-dhakha'ir al-'izam fima uthira 'an al-imam al-humam al-shahid 'abdallah 'azzam [Encyclopedia of the Relics of the Legacy of the Brave Martyred Imam Abdallah Azzam]. Peshawar: Markaz al-Shahid Azzam al-I'lami, 1997. https://archive.org/details/zakhaer3ozma.

mawsuʿat al-jihad [Encyclopedia of Jihad]. al-Imara al-Islamiyya fi Afghanistan; Maktab al-Khadamat (1st electronic ed.), 2002. http://unfulfilledduty.weebly.com/uploads/1/8/5/3/18537222/_1.pdf.

Mayer, Jane. 'Junior: The Clandestine Life of America's Top Al Qaeda Source'. New Yorker, 11 September 2006.

Mayer, Thomas. 'The Islamic Opposition in Syria, 1961–1982'. *Orient* 24 (1983): 589–610.

'The Military Force of Islam: The Society of the Muslim Brethren and the Palestine Question, 1945–1948'. In *Zionism and Arabism in Palestine and Israel*, edited by Elie Kedourie and Sylvia G. Haim, 100–117. London: Frank Cass, 1982.

McCants, William, ed. *Militant Ideology Atlas: Executive Report*. West Point, NY: United States Military Academy, 2006.

Militant Ideology Atlas: Research Compendium. West Point, NY: Combating Terrorism Center, 2006.

McGregor, Andrew. '"Jihad and the Rifle Alone": 'Abdullah 'Azzam and the Islamist Revolution'. *Journal of Conflict Studies* 23, no. 2 (2003): 92–113.

Meleagrou-Hitchens, Alexander, Seamus Hughes, and Bennett Clifford. *The Travelers: American Jihadists in Syria and Iraq*. Washington, DC: George Washington University Program on Extremism, February 2018.

Menshawy, Mustafa. *State, Memory, and Egypt's Victory in the 1973 War: Ruling by Discourse*. New York: Palgrave Macmillan, 2017.

'Midhat Mursi al-Sayyid 'Umar: Abu Khabab'. West Point, NY: Combating Terrorism Center, n.d. https://ctc.usma.edu/app/uploads/2011/06/Abu-Khabab.pdf.

Miller, Flagg. *The Audacious Ascetic: What the Bin Laden Tapes Reveal about al-Qaida*. London: Hurst, 2015.

Miniter, Richard. *Mastermind: The Many Faces of the 9/11 Architect, Khalid Shaikh Mohammed*. New York: Sentinel, 2011.

Mitchell, Alison. 'After Blast, New Interest in Holy-War Recruits in Brooklyn'. *New York Times*, 11 April 1993.

Mitchell, Richard P. *The Society of the Muslim Brothers*. London: Oxford University Press, 1969.

Mojdeh, Vahid. *afghanistan: panj sal sultat taliban* [Afghanistan: Five Years under Taliban Power]. Teheran: Nashreney, 2003.

Mokeddem, Mohamed. *Les Afghans algériens: de la Djamaâ à la Qa'îda*. Algiers: Éditions ANEP, 2002.

Morabia, Alfred. *Le Ǧihad dans l'Islam médiéval: le 'combat sacré' des origines au XIIième siècle*. Paris: Albin Michel, 1993.

Morris, Benny. *1948: A History of the First Arab–Israeli War*. New Haven: Yale University Press, 2008.

Righteous Victims: A History of the Zionist–Arab Conflict, 1881–2001. New York: Vintage, 2001.

'The Mossad and Imad Mughniyeh'. *Jerusalem Post*. 19 February 2008.

Mouline, Nabil. 'Enforcing and Reinforcing the State's Islam: The Functioning of the Committee of Senior Scholars', in *Saudi Arabia in Transition: Insights on Social, Political, Economic, and Religious Change*, edited by Bernard Haykel, Thomas Hegghammer, and Stephane Lacroix, 48–67. Cambridge: Cambridge University Press, 2015.

Mouline, Nabil. *The Clerics of Islam: Religious Authority and Political Power in Saudi Arabia*. New Haven: Yale University Press, 2014.

Muhajir, A'ida. 'da'wa ila jihad' [Call to Jihad]. *al-Jihad* no. 20 (July 1986): 38.

'hamsa fi udhn al-mutabarri'in' [Whisper in the Ear of the Donors]'. *al-Jihad* no. 32 (July 1987): 40.

Muhammad, Basil. *safahat min sijill al-ansar al-'arab fi afghanistan* [*Pages from the Record of the Arab Supporters in Afghanistan*]. 2nd ed. Riyadh: Lajnat al-Birr al-Islamiyya, 1991.

Müller, Mathias Ghyoot. 'Signs of the Merciful: 'Abdullah 'Azzam (d. 1989) and the Sacralization of History in Jihadist Literature, 1982–2002'. *Journal of Religion and Violence* (forthcoming, 2019).

Murphy, Caryle, and Steve Coll. 'The Making of an Islamic Symbol: US Spotlight has Elevated Radical Sheik's Status in Muslim World'. *Washington Post*, 9 July 1993.

Musallam, Adnan. *From Secularism to Jihad: Sayyid Qutb and the Foundations of Radical Islamism*. Westport, CT: Praeger, 2005.

'Muslim Publics Share Concerns about Extremist Groups'. Pew Research Center, 10 September 2013.

'Muslim Scholars Visit ITC'. *Islamic Teaching Center News*, February 1978.

Muslim World League. *qararat wa tawsiyat ahamm al-mu'tamarat allati 'aqadatha rabitat al-'alam al-islami mundhu 'am 1381–1412 hijriyya* [The Resolutions and Recommendations of the Most Important Conferences Organized by the Muslim World League, 1962–1992]. Mecca: Muslim World League, 1992.

al-Nahawi, Adnan. *'abdallah 'azzam: ahdath wa mawaqif* [Abdallah Azzam: Events and Positions]. Riyadh: Dar al-Nahawi, 1994.

Nasiri, Omar. *Inside the Jihad: My Life with al-Qaeda*. Cambridge, MA: Perseus, 2006.

Neighbour, Sally. *The Mother of Mohammed: An Australian Woman's Extraordinary Journey into Jihad*. Philadelphia: University of Pennsylvania Press, 2010.

'Operation Pendennis in Australia'. In *The Evolution of the Global Terrorist Threat: From 9/11 to Osama Bin Laden's Death*, edited by

Bruce Hoffman and Fernando Reinares, 163–191. New York: Columbia University Press, 2014.

Nesser, Petter. 'Abū Qatāda and Palestine'. *Die Welt des Islams* 53, no. 3–4 (1 January 2013): 416–448.

Islamist Terrorism in Europe: A History. London: Hurst, 2015.

Neumann, Peter R., and Ryan Evans. 'Operation Crevice in London'. In *The Evolution of the Global Terrorist Threat: From 9/11 to Osama bin Laden's Death*, edited by Bruce Hoffman and Fernando Reinares, 61–80. New York: Columbia University Press, 2014.

'New Group Takes Credit for Pakistan Blast'. UPI.com, 11 June 2009.

Nielsen, Richard A. *Deadly Clerics: Blocked Ambition and the Paths to Jihad*. Cambridge: Cambridge University Press, 2017.

al-Nimla, Ali bin Ibrahim. *al-jihad wa'l-mujahidun fi afghanistan* [Jihad and Mujahidin in Afghanistan]. Riyadh: Maktabat al-Ubaykan, 1994.

Nishino, Masami. 'Muhammad Qutb's Islamist Thought: A Missing Link between Sayyid Qutb and al-Qaeda?' *NIDS Journal of Defence and Security* 16 (2015): 113–145.

North, Andrew. 'Pro-Jihad Website Draws Readers'. BBC News Online, 15 February 2002.

Noth, Albrecht. 'Les 'ulama' en qualité de guerriers.' In *Saber religioso y poder político en el Islam*, ed. Manuela Marin, 175–195. Madrid: Agencía Espanola de Cooperación Internacional, 1994.

Notin, Jean-Christophe. *La Guerre de l'ombre des Français en Afghanistan: 1979–2011*. Paris: Fayard, 2011.

O'Ballance, Edgar. *Arab Guerilla Power, 1967–1972*. [Hamden, CT]: Archon Books, 1973.

Ochsenwald, William. 'Saudi Arabia and the Islamic Revival'. *International Journal of Middle East Studies* 13 (1981): 271–286.

Olidort, Jacob. 'In Defense of Tradition: Muhammad Nasir al-Din al-Albani and the Salafi Method'. Ph.D. dissertation, Princeton University, 2015.

O'Neill, Sean, and Daniel McGrory. *The Suicide Factory: Abu Hamza and the Finsbury Park Mosque*. London: HarperCollins, 2006.

'The Open Meeting with Sheikh Ayman al-Zawahiri – Part One', 2008. https://azelin.files.wordpress.com/2010/08/the-open-meeting-with-shaykh-ayman al-zawahiri-1429h.pdf.

Oren, Michael B. *Six Days of War: June 1967 and the Making of the Modern Middle East*. Oxford: Oxford University Press, 2002.

Overby, Paul. *Holy Blood: An Inside View of the Afghan War*. Westport, CT: Praeger, 1993.

Pappe, Ilan. *The Ethnic Cleansing of Palestine*. Oxford: Oneworld, 2007.

Pargeter, Alison. *The Muslim Brotherhood: The Burden of Tradition*. London: Saqi, 2010.

Pearson, Elizabeth. 'The Case of Roshonara Choudhry: Implications for Theory on Online Radicalization, ISIS Women, and the Gendered Jihad'. *Policy and Internet*, 2015.

Perrin, Jean-Pierre. 'Dans un camp souterrain des moudjahidin'. *Gazette de Lausanne*, 14 January 1986.

Pierret, Thomas. 'Les oulémas syriens aux XXe–XXIe siècles: la tradition comme ressource face aux défis du changement social et de l'autoritarisme', Ph.D. dissertation, Institut d'Études Politiques, Paris, 2009.

Religion and State in Syria: The Sunni Ulama from Coup to Revolution. Cambridge: Cambridge University Press, 2013.

Pilger, John. 'What Good Friends Left Behind'. *The Guardian*, 20 September 2003.

Piscatori, James. 'Imagining Pan-Islam'. In *Islam and Political Violence: Muslim Diaspora and Radicalism in the West*, edited by Shahram Akbarzadeh and Fethi Mansouri, 27–38. London: I. B. Tauris, 2007.

Posner, Gerald. *Why America Slept: The Failure to Prevent 9/11*. New York: Ballantine Books, 2003.

Prucha, Nico. 'Abdallah Azzam's Outlook for Jihad in 1988 – "al-Jihad between Kabul and Jerusalem"'. Research Institute for European and American Studies, 2010. www.rieas.gr/images/nicos2.pdf.

'Celebrities of the Afterlife: Death Cult, Stars, and Fandom of Jihadist Propaganda'. In *Jihadi Thought and Ideology*, edited by Rüdiger Lohlker and Tamara Abu-Hamdeh, 83–137. Berlin: Logos, 2013.

'al-Qaeda Founder's Name Given to İstanbul's Street in Turkey'. soL InternationaL Online, 17 July 2017.

'An al-Qaeda Love Story: From Morocco to Bosnia to Afghanistan and Saudi Arabia, Via New Jersey'. *MEMRI Special Dispatch* no. 984 (9 September 2005).

al-Qandahari, Abu Ja'far al-Misri. *dhikrayat 'arabi afghani* [Memoirs of an Afghan Arab]. Cairo: Dar al-Shuruq, 2002.

'qawa'id al-shuyukh' [The Bases of the Shaykhs]. Youtube, n.d. www.youtube.com/watch?v=EN4Ff8JrBkc.

'qissat hayat al-mujahid al-shaykh tamim muhammad al-'adnani' [The Story of the Life of the *Mujahid* Sheikh Tamim al-Adnani]. *al-Jihad* no. 62 (December 1989): 24–34.

Qutb, Amina. *rasa'il ila shahid* [Letter to a Martyr]. Amman: Dar al-Furqan, 1985.

'risala min amina qutb ila umm muhammad' [Letter from Amina Qutb to Umm Muhammad]. In *fi 'uyun mu'asira: al-imam al-mujahid al-shahid 'abdallah 'azzam,* 325–327. Peshawar: Markaz al-Shahid Azzam al-I'lami, 1997.

Qutb, Muhammad. *al-jihad al-afghani wa-dalalatuhu* [The Afghan Jihad and its Proofs]. Jeddah: Mu'assasat al-Madinah li'l-Sihafa wa'l-Tiba'a wa'l-Nashr, 1989.

Qutb, Sayyid. *Milestones*. Birmingham: Maktabah Booksellers and Publishers, 2006. www.kalamullah.com/Books/Milestones%20Special%20Edition.pdf.

Rabinovich, Itamar. *Syria under the Ba'th 1963–66: The Army–Party Symbiosis*. Jerusalem: Israel Universities Press, 1972.

rabitat al-'alam al-islami: 'ashrun 'aman 'ala tariq al-da'wa wa'l-jihad [The Muslim World League: Twenty Years on the Road of *Da'wa* and Jihad]. Mecca: Muslim World League, 1981.

Racius, Egdunas. 'The Multiple Nature of the Islamic Da'wa'. Ph.D. dissertation, University of Helsinki, 2004. https://helda.helsinki.fi/bitstream/handle/10138/19209/themulti.pdf?sequence=1.

Ramadan, Abd al-Azim. *al-ikhwan al-muslimun wa'l-tanzim al-sirri* [The Muslim Brotherhood and the Secret Apparatus]. Cairo: Ruz al-Yusif, 1982.

Rana, Muhammad Amir, and Mubasher Bukhari. *Arabs in Afghan Jihad*. Lahore: Pak Institute for Peace Studies, 2007.

'Reagan Praises Afghan Fighters'. Associated Press, 3 February 1983.

Reinares, Fernando. 'A Case Study of the January 2008 Suicide Bomb Plot in Barcelona'. *CTC Sentinel* 2, no. 1 (2009): 5–7.

al-Qaeda's Revenge: The 2004 Madrid Train Bombings. New York: Columbia University Press, 2017.

Reissner, Johannes. *Ideologie und Politik der Muslimbruder Syriens: Von den Wahlen 1947 bis zum Verbot unter Adib as-Sisakli 1952*. Freiburg: Klaus Schwartz, 1980.

Rich, Ben, and Dara Conduit. 'The Impact of Jihadist Foreign Fighters on Indigenous Secular–Nationalist Causes: Contrasting Chechnya and Syria'. *Studies in Conflict and Terrorism* 38, no. 2 (2015): 113–131.

Riedel, Bruce. 'The 9/11 Attacks' Spiritual Father'. *The Daily Beast* (11 September 2011). www.thedailybeast.com/articles/2011/09/11/abdullah-azzam-spiritual-father-of-9-11-attacks-ideas-live-on.html.

Robinson, Glenn E. 'Defensive Democratization in Jordan'. *International Journal of Middle East Studies* 30 (1998): 387–410.

Rogan, Eugene. *The Arabs: A History*. 2nd ed. London: Penguin, 2012.

Rosen, Nir. *Aftermath: Following the Bloodshed of America's Wars in the Muslim World*. New York: Nation Books, 2010.

Rougier, Bernard. *Everyday Jihad: The Rise of Militant Islam among Palestinians in Lebanon*. Cambridge, MA: Harvard University Press, 2007.

'Le jihad en Afghanistan et l'émergence du salafisme-jihadisme'. In *Qu'est-ce que le salafisme?*, edited by Bernard Rougier, 65–86. Paris: Presses Universitaires de France, 2008.

Roy, Olivier. *Islam and Resistance in Afghanistan*. 2nd ed. Cambridge: Cambridge University Press, 1990.

'The Origins of the Islamist Movement in Afghanistan'. *Central Asian Survey* 3 (1984): 117–127.

Rubin, Barnett R. 'Arab Islamists in Afghanistan'. In *Political Islam: Revolution, Radicalism, or Reform?* edited by John Esposito, 179–206. Boulder: Lynne Rienner, 1997.

The Fragmentation of Afghanistan: State Formation and Collapse in the International System. 2nd ed. New Haven: Yale University Press, 2002.

The Search for Peace in Afghanistan: From Buffer State to Failed State. New Haven and London: Yale University Press, 1995.

Rubin, Barry, and Judith Colp Rubin. *Yasir Arafat: A Political Biography*. New York: Oxford University Press, 2003.

al-Sabagh, Mahmud. *haqiqat al-tanzim al-khass* [The Truth about the Secret Apparatus]. Cairo: Dar al-I'tisam, 1989.

Salah, Muhammad. *waqa'i' sanawat al-jihad: rihlat al-afghan al-'arab* [Realities of the Years of Jihad: The Journey of the Arab Afghans]. Cairo: Khulud, 2001.

Salahi, Adil. 'Sayyid Sabiq: The Man who Wrote *Fiqh al-Sunna*'. *Arab News*, 22 July 2005.

Salehyan, Idean. *Rebels without Borders: Transnational Insurgencies in World Politics*. Ithaca: Cornell University Press, 2009.

Al-Salih, Huda. 'How al-Qaeda was Born in a Tiny Office in New York'. Al-Arabiya English, 14 October 2016. http://ara.tv/px8ak.

al-Salim, Muhammad. *39 wasila li-khidmat al-jihad wa'l-musharaka fihi* [39 Ways to Serve Jihad and Take Part in it]. Sawt al-Jihad, 2003.

Sandee, Ronald. *America's First al-Qa'ida Fighters*. New York: NEFA Foundation, April 2010. www.academia.edu/12893801/Americas_first_al-Qaida_Fighters.

Sayigh, Yezid. *Armed Struggle and the Search for State: The Palestinian National Movement 1949–1993*. Oxford: Oxford University Press, 1997.

Scheuer, Michael. *Osama Bin Laden*. New York: Oxford University Press, 2011.

Schindler, John. *Unholy Terror: Bosnia, al-Qa'ida, and the Rise of Global Jihad*. St. Paul, MN: Zenith Press, 2007.

Schnelle, Sebastian. 'Abdullah Azzam, Ideologue of Jihad: Freedom Fighter or Terrorist?' *Journal of Church and State* 54, no. 4 (1 December 2012): 625–647.

Schulze, Reinhard. *Islamischer Internationalismus im 20. Jahrhundert*. London: E. J. Brill, 1990.

Scott, Peter Dale. *The Road to 9/11: Wealth, Empire, and the Future of America*. Berkeley: University of California Press, 2007.

Scott, Rachel. 'An "Official" Islamic Response to the Egyptian al-Jihad Movement'. *Journal of Political Ideologies* 8, no. 1 (2003): 39–61.

Sedgwick, Mark. 'Jihadism, Narrow and Wide: The Dangers of Loose Use of an Important Term'. *Perspectives on Terrorism* 9, no. 2 (2015): 34–41.

Seidelin, Matias. *Allahs danske krigere* [Allah's Danish Warriors]. Copenhagen: Politiken forlag, 2012.

Seierstad, Åsne. *To Søstre* [Two Sisters]. Oslo: Kagge, 2016.

Sela, Avraham. 'State, Society and Transnational Networks: The Cases of Arab Volunteers in the Palestine War (1947–48) and the "Afghan Arabs"'. Department of International Relations, Hebrew University of Jerusalem, 2005.

al-Shafi'i, Muhammad. 'Gul, the Godfather of the Taliban, Tells *al-Sharq al-Awsat* that the Tribal Region in Pakistan is Accepting Money and Arms from the Americans'. *al-Sharq al-Awsat* Online (via FBIS), 25 April 2009.

'tharthara fawqa saqf al-'alam' [Chatter on the World's Rooftop], part III. *al-Sharq al-Awsat*, 28 October 2006.

Shafqat, Saeed. 'From Official Islam to Islamism: The Rise of Dawat-ul-Irshad and Lashkar-e-Taiba'. In *Pakistan: Nationalism without a Nation*, edited by Christophe Jaffrelot, 131–47. London: Zed Books, 2002.

Al Shafey, Mohammed. '*Asharq al-Awsat* Interviews Umm Mohammed: The Wife of Bin Laden's Spiritual Mentor'. *al-Sharq al-Awsat* English Online, 2005.

Shahzad, Syed Saleem. *Inside al-Qaeda and the Taliban: Beyond Bin Laden and 9/11*. New York: Pluto Press, 2011.

Shapira, Anita. *Yigal Allon, Native Son: A Biography*. Philadelphia: University of Pennsylvania Press, 2008.

'al-shaykh tamim al-'adnani yatahaddath li'l-jihad' [Sheikh Tamim al-Adnani Speaks to *al-Jihad*]. *al-Jihad* no. 32 (July 1987): 35–39.

'Sheikh Abdullah Azzam', n.d. www.azzam.com/html/storiesabdullahazzam.htm.

Sheikh, Naveed S. *The New Politics of Islam*. London: RoutledgeCurzon, 2003.

Shepard, William. *Sayyid Qutb: Oxford Bibliographies Online Research Guide*. [New York]: Oxford University Press, USA, 2010.

Shephard, Michelle. *Guantanamo's Child: The Untold Story of Omar Khadr*. 1st ed. Mississauga, Ont: Wiley, 2008.
al-Shihri, Mansur. 'ta'kidan li-ma asharat ilayhi 'ukaz. "al-qa'ida" ta'lan hallak arwa baghdadi' [Confirming *Ukaz*'s Indications: "al-Qaida" Announces (Responsibility for) the Destructive Arwa Baghdadi]. *Ukaz* Online, 8 February 2017.
Shlaim, Avi. 'Israel and the Arab coalition in 1948'. In *The War for Palestine*, edited by Eugene L. Rogan and Avi Shlaim, 79–103. Cambridge: Cambridge University Press, 2007.
Shpiro, Shlomo. 'Israeli Intelligence and al-Qaeda'. *International Journal of Intelligence and CounterIntelligence* 25, no. 2 (2012): 240–259.
Siddiqi, Abdurrahman. *The Military in Pakistan: Image in Reality*. Lahore: Vanguard Books, 1996. www.vanguardbooks.com/browsetitle.php?isbn=9694022827&subject=Bestsellers
Siddique, Haroon. 'Terror Suspect "Planned to Take Children on Suicide Attack"'. *The Guardian* Online, 23 April 2008.
Simon, Rachel. *'agudat ha-akhim ha-muslemim (jami'at al-ikhwan al-muslimin)* [The Society of Muslim Brothers]. In *miflagot politiot ba-gada ha-ma'aravit* [Political Parties in the West Bank], edited by Amnon Cohen, 274–407. Jerusalem: Hebrew University, 1980.
'In Southeast Asian Recruitment Drive, IS Posts Video of Malay-Speaking Child Members'. *Malay Mail* Online, 17 March 2015.
'Space Shuttle's Flight Dedicated to Afghans'. Reuters, 11 March 1982.
'Statement from Azzam.Com Regarding Closure of its Web-Site'. TalibanNews.com, 24 September 2002. www.freerepublic.com/focus/news/756623/posts.
Steinberg, Guido. 'Jihadi-Salafism and the Shi'is: Remarks about the Intellectual Roots of anti-Shi'ism'. In *Global Salafism: Islam's New Religious Movement*, edited by Roel Meijer, 107–125. London: Hurst, 2009.
Stemmann, Juan Jose Escobar. 'The Crossroads of Muslim Brothers in Jordan'. In *The Muslim Brotherhood: The Organization and Policies of a Global Islamist Movement*, edited by Barry Rubin, 57–71. London: Palgrave Macmillan, 2010.
Stenersen, Anne. *al-Qaida in Afghanistan*. Cambridge: Cambridge University Press, 2017.
Stephens, Joe, and David B. Ottaway. 'From US, the ABC's of Jihad'. *Washington Post*, 23 March 2002.
Storer, Cynthia. 'Working with al-Qaeda Documents: An Analyst's View before 9/11'. In *Ten Years Later: Insights on al-Qaeda's Past and Future through Captured Records*, edited by Lorry M. Fenner, Mark E. Stout, and Jessica L. Goldings, 41–52. Washington, DC: Johns Hopkins University Center for Advanced Governmental Studies, 2012.

Strick van Linschoten, Alex, and Felix Kuehn. *An Enemy we Created: The Myth of the Taliban–al Qaeda Merger in Afghanistan*. Oxford: Oxford University Press, 2012.
Suellentrop, Chris. 'Abdullah Azzam: The Godfather of Jihad'. Slate.com, 16 April 2002.
'ta'arruf 'ala al-sila al-harithiyya' [Getting to know al-Sila al-Harithiyya]. http://a6fal.7olm.org/t50-topic.
Tamam, Hossam. 'The International Organization of the Muslim Brotherhood'. In *Islamic Movements of Europe: Public Religion and Islamophobia in the Modern World*, edited by Frank Peter and Rafael Ortega, 89–94. London: I. B. Tauris, 2014.
al-Tamimi, Aymenn Jawad. 'The Factions of Abu Kamal'. Brown Moses Blog, 18 December 2013.
  'The Islamic State Billboards and Murals of Tel Afar and Mosul'. Aymenn Jawad al-Tamimi's Blog, 7 January 2015.
Tamimi, Azzam. *Hamas: Unwritten Chapters*. 2nd ed. London: Hurst, 2009.
Rachid Ghannouchi: A Democrat within Islamism. New York: Oxford University Press, 2001.
Tammam, Husam. 'al-tanzim al-duwali li'l-ikhwan ... al-wa'd wa'l-masira wa'l-mal' [The Brotherhood's International Organization ... its Promise, Path, and Fate?] *al-Hiwar* no. 962 (20 September 2004). www.ahewar.org/debat/show.art.asp?aid=23729.
Tankel, Stephen. *Storming the World Stage: The Story of Lashkar-e-Taiba*. Oxford: Oxford University Press, 2011.
Tanwir, M. Halim. *Afghanistan: History, Diplomacy and Journalism*. Kindle. Dartford: Xlibris, 2013.
Tarrow, Sidney. *The New Transnational Activism*. Cambridge: Cambridge University Press, 2006.
Tawfiq, Muhammad. *afghanistan al-jariha – afghanistan al-habiba* [Afghanistan the Wounded – Afghanistan the Beloved]. Riyadh: Mu'assasat al-Jazira, 1990.
Tawil, Camille. *Brothers in Arms: The Story of al-Qa'ida and the Arab Jihadists*. London: Saqi, 2011.
Tcitelbaum, Joshua. 'The Muslim Brotherhood and the "Struggle for Syria", 1947–1958: Between Accommodation and Ideology'. *Middle Eastern Studies* 40 (2004): 134–58.
Thomas, Hugh. *The Spanish Civil War*. Rev. ed. London: Penguin, 2001.
Thomson, David. *Les français jihadistes*. Paris: Les Arènes, 2014.
Tomsen, Peter. *The Wars of Afghanistan: Messianic Terrorism, Tribal Conflicts, and the Failures of Great Powers*. New York: PublicAffairs, 2011.

Toth, James. *Sayyid Qutb: The Life and Legacy of a Radical Islamic Intellectual*. Oxford: Oxford University Press, 2013.
Trofimov, Yaroslav. *The Siege of Mecca: The Forgotten Uprising in Islam's Holiest Shrine and the Birth of al Qaeda*. 1st ed. New York: Doubleday, 2007.
al-Ubaydi, Awni Judu'. *jama'at al-ikhwan al-muslimun fi'l-urdun wa filastin 1945–1970* [The Muslim Brotherhood in Jordan and Palestine, 1945–1970]. Amman: unknown publisher, 1991.
'"ukaz" tasif 'abdallah 'azzam' bi'"l-irhabi al-halik" wa'l-nashitun: al-aqzam tatatawal 'ala 'azzam' [*Ukaz* Describes Abdallah Azzam as 'a Destructive Terrorist' and the Activists [Say]: The Midgets Dare to Attack Azzam]. *The New Khalij* Online, 10 February 2017.
Umm Siddiq. 'suq khayri li-salih al-mujahidin al-afghan' [Charity Market for Afghan Mujahidin]. *al Bunyan al-Marsus* no. 5 (February 1986): 48–50.
Umm Yahya. 'fima tufakkir hadhihi al-tifla?' [What is this Girl Thinking About?]. *al-Jihad* no. 47 (October 1988): 30–31.
Urban, Mark. *War in Afghanistan*. Basingstoke: Macmillan, 1988.
Urgo, Marisa. '"Martyrs in a Time of Alienation" – Complete Blogger's Cut', 28 December 2010. www.makingsenseofjihad.com/2010/12/martyrs-in-a-time-of-alienation-complete.html.
USA v Usama bin Laden et al., Southern District of New York, 2001. https://cryptome.org/usa-v-ubl-dt.htm.
Usmani, Mufti Mohammad Rafi. *Jihad in Afghanistan against Communism*. Karachi: Darul-Ishaat, 2003.
Valencia, Milton J. 'Accused Al Qaeda Supporter's Defense Rests'. *Boston Globe*, 15 December 2011.
Van Dyk, Jere. *In Afghanistan: An American Odyssey*. New York: Coward-McCann, 1983.
Verkaik, Robert. 'The Trials of Babar Ahmad: From Jihad in Bosnia to a US Prison via Met Brutality'. *The Guardian*, 19 March 2016.
Vidino, Lorenzo. *The New Muslim Brotherhood in the West* (New York: Columbia University Press, 2010).
Vyas, Prachi. 'The Islamic State's Married Ideology: Something Borrowed, Something New'. Lawfare blog, 2 July 2017.
Wagemakers, Joas. *A Quietist Jihadi: The Ideology and Influence of Abu Muhammad al-Maqdisi*. Cambridge: Cambridge University Press, 2012.
  Salafism in Jordan: Political Islam in a Quietist Community. Cambridge: Cambridge University Press, 2016.
  'In Search of "Lions and Hawks": Abū Muḥammad al-Maqdisī's Palestinian Identity'. *Die Welt des Islams* 53, no. 3–4 (1 January 2013): 388–415.

al-Waʻi, Tawfiq Yusuf. *mawsuʻat shuhada' al-haraka al-islamiyya* [Encyclopedia of the Martyrs of the Islamic Movement]. Cairo: Dar al-Tawziʻ waʼl-Nashr al-Islamiyya, 2006.

Wardak, Commandant Amin. *Mémoires de guerre*. Paris: Arthaud, 2009.

Warrick, Joby. *The Triple Agent: The al-Qaeda Mole who Infiltrated the CIA*. New York: Doubleday, 2011.

Weaver, Mary Anne. 'The Children of the Jihad'. New Yorker, 12 June 1995.

Weinberg, David Andrew. 'King Salman's Shady History: Foreign Policy'. *Foreign Policy* Online, 27 January 2015.

Weiser, Benjamin, Susan Sachs, and David Kocieniewski. 'US Sees Brooklyn Link to World Terror Network'. *New York Times*, 22 October 1998.

Weissmann, Itzchak. 'Saʻid Hawwa: The Making of a Radical Muslim Thinker in Modern Syria'. *Middle Eastern Studies* 29 (1993): 601–623.

Wiig, Camilla Holte. 'Forpliktet til kamp: En studie av Abdullah Azzams fiendebilde og krigslegitimering [Bound to Fight: A Study of Abdallah Azzam's Enemy Picture and Legitimation for War]'.MA thesis, University of Oslo, 2007.

Wiktorowicz, Quintan. *The Management of Islamic Activism: Salafis, the Muslim Brotherhood, and State Power in Jordan*. New York: State University of New York Press, 2001.

Williams, Brian Glyn. 'On the Trail of the "Lions of Islam": Foreign Fighters in Afghanistan and Pakistan, 1980–2010'. *Orbis* 55, no. 2 (1 January 2011): 216–39.

Winter, Lucas. 'The Abdullah Azzam Brigades'. *Studies in Conflict and Terrorism* 34, no. 11 (2011): 883–895.

'The Words of Abdallah Azzam', n.d., www.scribd.com/doc/54242137/The-Words-of-Abdullah-Azzam.

Wright, Lawrence. 'The Man behind Bin Laden'. *New Yorker*, 16 September 2002.

  The Looming Tower: Al Qaeda and the Road to 9/11. New York: Knopf, 2006.

Ya'ari, Ehud. 'The Afghans Are Coming'. *Jerusalem Report*, 2 July 1992: 30.

Yasmeen, Samina. *Jihad and Dawah: Evolving Narratives of Lashkar-e-Taiba and Jamat ud Dawah*. London: Hurst, 2017.

Yom, Sean, and Wael Al-Khatib. 'Islamists are Losing Support in Jordan'. *Washington Post* Online, 17 May 2018.

Young, T. Cuyler. 'Pan-Islamism in the Modern World: Solidarity and Conflict among Muslim Countries'. In *Islam and International Relations*, edited by J. Harris Proctor, 194–221. London: Pall Mall, 1965.

Yousaf, Mohammad, and Mark Adkin. *Afghanistan: The Bear Trap*. 2nd ed. Barnsley: Leo Cooper, 2001.

'yusuf islam fi ard al-ribat' [Yusuf Islam in the Land of Ribat]. *al-Jihad* no. 17 (March 1986): 20–22.

Zaeef, Abdul Salam. *My Life with the Taliban*. London: Hurst, 2010

Zahid, Farhan. 'Influences of Abu Ala Maududi on Islamo-Jihadi Thoughts of Abdullah Azzam the Father of Modern Jihad Movement'. Centre Français de Recherche sur le Renseignement, Foreign Analysis 33, December 2015.

Zaidan, Ahmad Muaffaq. *The "Afghan Arabs" Media at Jihad*. Islamabad: ABC Printers, 1999.

al-Zawahiri, Ayman. *The Exoneration*, 2008. https://fas.org/irp/dni/osc/exoneration.pdf.

'fursan taht rayat al-nabi' [Knights under the Prophet's Banner'. *al-Sharq al-Awsat*, 2 December 2001.

'Knights under the Prophet's Banner', 2001. https://azelin.files.wordpress.com/2010/11/6759609-knights-under-the-prophet-banner.pdf.

al-Zaydi, Mshari. 'History of the Jordanian Muslim Brotherhood (Part 1)'. *al-Sharq al-Awsat* English Online, 27 December 2005.

'History of the Jordanian Muslim Brotherhood (Part 2)'. *al-Sharq al-Awsat* English Online, 30 December 2005.

al-Zayla'i, Abu Bakr. 'Verily, I am the Naked Warner'. al-Haqa'iq Media, 1 May 2013. http://jihadology.net/2013/05/01/release-from-shaykh-abu-bakr-al-zaylai-an-open-letter-verily-i-am-the-naked-warner/.

al-Zayyat, Muntassir. *The Road to al-Qaeda: The Story of Bin Laden's Right-Hand Man*. London: Pluto Press, 2004.

Zeghal, Malika. *Gardiens de l'Islam: les oulémas d'al-Azhar dans l'Égypte contemporaine*. Paris: Presses de Sciences-Po, 1996.

Zollner, Barbara. *The Muslim Brotherhood: Hasan al-Hudaybi and Ideology*. London: Routledge, 2008.

Index

Abbas, Fadl, 78
Abbas, Muhammad, 453–454, 458
Abbottabad, 117, 338, 461, 464, 475, 484
Abd al-Aziz, Abd al-Qadir (Dr. Fadl), 355, 357, 358, 383, 419, 421, 475
Abd al-Fattah, Ali, 264, 270
Abd al-Ghani, Hajj, 172
Abd al-Hadi, Shafiq As'ad, 32
Abd al-Hakim, Isam, 162, 231, 413
Abd al-Khaliq, 77
   Abd al-Ghani, 77
   Abd al-Rahman, 52, 70, 452
Abd al- Mannan, 77, 238
Abd al-Maqsud, Majdi, 265
Abd al-Mu'izz, 355
Abd al-Rahman, Umar (the "blind sheikh"), 78, 81, 168, 264, 418–419
Abd al-Raziq, 388
Abd al-Samad, 223
Abd al-Sami', 344
Abd al-Wahhab, 96
Abd al-Wahid, 225
Abdallah Azzam Academy, 467–468
Abdallah Azzam Brigades, 466–467, 472
Abdallah Azzam operations, 451, 468
Abdallah Azzam Street, 474
Abdallah Azzam training camps, 468, 470
Abduh, Muhammad, 137
Abu Abd al-Aziz, 396
Abu Abd al-Rahman, 396
Abu Abdallah. *See* Bin Ladin, Usama
Abu Adil. 6. *See* Azzam, Mahmud
Abu al-Adib, 223
Abu Akram, 201, 212–213, 215, 240, 379
Abu Amir al-Urduni, 379
Abu Ammar (Jordanian), 212–213, 333
Abu Ammar (Palestinian leader). 57. *See* Arafat, Yasir
Abu Amr (Salah Hasan), 42, 50, 55, 58–59, 231, 334
Abu Anas, 231
Abu Anis Group, 337
Abu Asim al-Iraqi, 404
Abu Ayyub, 217, 354–355
Abu Ayyub al-Iraqi, 357
Abu Ayyub al-Tayyib, 223
Abu Bakr al-Siddiq, 154, 249
Abu al-Bara', 215, 223–224, 396
Abu al-Burhan, 421
Abu Dawud, 213
Abu Dhabi, 149, 162–163, 166–167, 305
Abu Dharr, 78
Abu Dujana, 238, 401
Abu Durra, Yusuf, 13
Abu Faris, Muhammad, 82, 89–90, 93
Abu Faruq, 219
Abu al-Futuh, Abd al-Mun'im, 199–201
Abu Ghuda, Abd al-Fattah, 38
Abu Hafs, 358, 385
Abu Hamza (Mahir Shalbak), 207, 212, 214
Abu Hanifa, 391
Abu Hanieh, Hasan, 91–92, 93, 131–132
Abu al-Harith, 395
Abu Harith, 213, 373–374, 408, 431, 446, 457–458, 460
Abu Hasan, 238
Abu Hashim, 403
Abu Hilala, Yasir, 56

Index

Abu Hudhayfa, 212–213, 379
Abu Husayn, 223
Abu Ibada, 213
Abu Islam, 385
Abu Izza, Abdallah, 49, 60
Abu Jahl, 61
Abu Jandal, 432
Abu al-Jud, 406
Abu Majid, 102
Abu Mazin, 144, 181, 196
Abu Mu'adh, 401
Abu Mujahid, xviii. *See* al-Suri, Abu Mus'ab
Abu al-Nasr, Muhammad Hamid, 201, 451
Abu Qasim, 452
Abu Qura, Abd al-Latif, 17, 32
Abu Qutayba, 223
Abu Ratib, 406
Abu Rida, 197, 238, 355
Abu Rumman, Bashir, 5, 91–93, 131–132
Abu Sayyaf, 213
Abu Shahida, 265
Abu Shu'ayb, 223
Abu Suhayb, 240, 458
Abu Sulayman, 393, 402
Abu Tahla, 445
Abu Talhah, 385
Abu Tariq, 379
Abu Ubeidah, 385–386
Abu Umran, 213
Abu Uthman, 222
Abu Yahya, 373, 459
Abu Zant, Abd al-Mun'im, 51, 59
Abu Zayd, 213
Abu Zayd, Muhammad Fu'ad, 32
AbuKhalil, As'ad, 486
Adams, Joseph, 479
al-Adnani, Tamim, 215, 255–258, 348, 408, 437
    Azzam's personal relationship with, 376, 377
    Bin Ladin on, 404
    al-Qaida and, 362
    quoted, 304, 308, 346
    Services Bureau and, 353, 354, 362
Afghan war, 304, 346, 458
Afghanistan, 25–27, 120–122, 160–167, 179–192, 221–229, 254–256, 258–267, 313–315, 395–399, 410–414, 429–434, 454–456
    Arab fighters in, 2–3, 182–185, 266–288, 349–351, 365–370, 401–403, 404–408, 409–410, 435–436, 455–456
    Azzam's move to, 108, 119, 120–123
    Communist government, 147, 317, 319, 413, 446
    socio-political makeup, 174
    US policy toward, 186–187
African Islamic Coordination Council, 111
African-American Muslims, 192–194
Ahmed, Babar, 479–481, 485
Ahmed, Khurshid, 202
Ahmed, Qazi Hussain, 202, 233
Ahrar al-Sham, 467, 473, 483
Ajami, Fouad, 22
Akfan Brigade, 207
AKP (Justice and Development Party [Turkey]), 473
Alamdar, Tawfiq Khalid, 181, 197
al-Albani, Nasr al-Din, 44, 92–94, 130, 132, 409, 474
Aleppo, 37–38
Alexandria University, 71
Ali, Abd al-Aziz, 42, 51, 165, 198, 233, 336, 340, 482
Ali, Abdulla Ahmed, 477
Ali, Ahmad al-Hajj, 34
Alim, Muhammed, 149
Allon, Yigal, 18
Almqvist, Börje, 188
Amin, Sadiq, 130–131, 132, 231
al-Amriki, Abu Hafs, 397
al-Amriki, Abu Hamza, 346
al-Amush, Bassam, 63, 90, 487
Anas, Abdallah, 164–166, 176–177, 212–214, 365, 387–388, 399–400, 419–420, 423, 445–446, 452–454
anashid, 234, 344, 405–407, 433
Anis, Dhib, 51
Ansar Institute, 225, 234
al-Ansari, Abdallah, 159
Antonius, George, 137
Antoun, Richard, 30
al-Aqil, Abdallah, 121

Arab–Israeli conflict, 47, 298
Arab-Israeli war (1948), 14–18
al-Aradi, Abd al-Razzaq, 260
Arafat, Yasir, 57, 63
Arin, 339, 341, 347
Armed Islamic Group (GIA), 468–470, 482–483
As'ad, Khalid, 265
Asadallah, 403
al-Ashqar, Umar, 90
al-Assad, Hafiz, 26, 101, 319
al-Assal, Ahmad, 160
Atta, Abu Muhammad, 451
al-Attar, Isam, 36, 37, 49, 52, 96, 249, 269, 376
Awatila, Abdallah, 15
Awatila, Samira. 19. *See* Azzam, Samira
Awaynat, Muhammad, 260
Awda, Abd al-Qadir, 34
al-Awlaki, Anwar, 475, 478
Al Awshan, Isa, 475
Ayish, Kazim, 85
Ayn al-Hilweh camp, 452, 468
Ayyash, Yahya, 471, 484
Ayyub, Hasan, 201, 233
al-Azhar University, 35–36, 65–66, 70–71, 75–79, 88, 95, 123, 127
al-Azm, Yusuf, 90, 159
Azzad, Ibrahim, 9, 20, 436, 438, 440
Azzam, Abd al-Malik, 12
Azzam, Abdallah
  assassination, 436–439
    aftermath, 449–462
    potential perpetrators, 440–449
  early life, 11–13
  education
    Damascus University, 35–38
    Islamic Law studies, 30
    school, 18
    university study, 19
  family, 12, 107, 143, 361, 373, 425, 452, 458–461, 469
    children, 20, 372–373
    marriage, 19–20, 53, 54, 79, 82, 84, 105, 372, 425–426, 459
    parents, 12, 29, 53, 54, 263
    parents' religious beliefs, 29
  Fedayin membership
    combat, 57–58
    decision to join, 53–55
    training camps, 55–58
  ideology and writing, 125, 288–290, 511
    Afghan jihad, 294–299
    anti-Communism, 133–139
    anti-quietism, 130, 133
    anti-Westernism, 140, 320–327
    caliphate, 313–317
    ethics, 290–294
    foreign-fighter doctrine, 155, 288, 299–306, 488, 494–495, 499, 503–504
    Islamic education, 129–130
    Islamic Law, 126–129
    Islamic supremacism, 139–142
    martyrdom, 299
    militarism, 293–294
    on non-Islamist Muslim states, 317–320
    on Palestine, 23–27
    Qutb's influence, 40, 44–45
    readership, 474–478
    on women, 380–384
  image
    as fighting scholar, 328–330
  influence
    breadth of appeal, 468–474
    as heroic figure, 463–465
    jihadi organizations, 466–468
    legacy, 482–487
    as martyr, 481
    operational effects, 474–482
    tribute websites, 465–466
  intellectual influence, 4, 85, 367, 416, 433
  international travel and connections, 94–100
  in Jordan, 21
    expulsion from, 100–107
  lecture tours, 247–258
  lectures, 465
  lifestyle and friendships, 375–377
  marriage, 19, 372
  Massoud and, 426–429
  Muslim Brotherhood and
  joins Jenin Brotherhood, 31–35
  Muslim World League and, 374–375
  opposition to Arab militants, 418–426

Index 685

Israel, 429–435
Pakistan, 409–413
Saudi Arabia, 413–417
other figures and
Bin Ladin, 117–118
in Pakistan, 122–124
personality and friendships, 480
publications
as "Abu Muhammad", 231, 296
BA thesis, 35, 36, 126, 488
Defense of Muslim Lands, 199, 236, 288–289, 302, 384, 408, 426, 474–475, 477
Hamas: Historical Roots and Charter, 23, 430
online archives, 478–480
Red Cancer, 23, 45, 133–134, 137, 142
Signs of the Merciful, 60, 153, 169, 173, 203, 288, 295, 296, 301, 379
al-Qaida and, 327, 354–355, 361–362, 368, 434, 464, 484–487, 491, 504
recruitment efforts, 244–247
in Saudi Arabia, 116–117
teaching work, 18–19, 53, 146–147, 371
Azzam, Fayiz, 5–6, 54, 453, 458, 460
Azzam, Hamza, 20
Azzam, Hudhayfa, 9, 101, 209–210, 309, 373, 375, 417, 458–459, 486, 487
Azzam, Ibrahim, 9, 20, 408, 436, 438, 440
Azzam, Jamal, 213. *See* Abu Harith
Azzam, Mahmud, 213, 230, 232, 377, 410–412, 450, 453, 457–459, 460, 478–480
Azzam, Muhammad, 9, 20, 373, 436, 438, 440
Azzam, Mus'ab, 20, 373
Azzam, Salih Mahmud, 12
Azzam, Samira (Umm Muhammad, AA's wife), 19–20, 53, 54, 79, 82, 84, 105, 372, 425–426, 459
Azzam, Sumayya, 20, 373, 446, 460
Azzam, Wafa, 20, 68, 78, 373, 459
Azzam Publications, 465, 479–480, 485

Baader, Andreas, 62
Badr al-Sughra, 357
Badr training project, 168, 206–207, 212, 331, 343, 345, 370, 377, 392, 395
Baha, 69–70
Bakeer, Jihan, 83
Balata, Muhammad, 260
Baluchistan, 339
Bangladesh, 112, 235, 249, 266
Bani Awda, Ibrahim Abd al-Karim, 433
al-Banna, Abd ar-Rahman, 297
al-Banna, Hasan, 32, 34, 40, 50, 73, 121, 290, 293, 462, 466, 471, 531, 551, 562
Bannaism, 18, 38, 72–73, 80, 89–90
al-Banshiri, Abu Ubayda, 270, 338, 340, 343, 345, 350–351, 352–354, 355, 357, 358–360
Bashir, Zakariya, 456
Bayazid, Muhammad Lu'ay, 224. *See* al-Suri, Abu al-Rida
Bayt Abu Hamza, 214, 219
Bayt Abu Uthman, 214
Bayt al-Ansar, 219–220, 331, 357, 362, 370–371, 378, 397, 408, 419–420, 446
Bayt al-Maqdis, 50, 57, 207, 410
Bayt al-Muslimin, 213
Bayt al-Shuhada', 214
Bayt al-Tamwil al-Kuwayti, 300
Bayt Yafa, 50
Bearden, Milt, 183, 187
Bell, Kevin, 174
Ben-Gurion, David, 141
Benothman, Noman, 160, 202
Bergen, Peter, 350
al-Berry, Khalid, 264
Bhutto, Benazir, 325, 363, 413
Bin Abi Anas, Anas, 105
Bin Baz, Abd al-Aziz, 117, 165, 198 199, 233, 305, 416, 482
Bin Ladin, Usama, 333–334, 341, 345–346, 348–352, 356–364, 415–416, 464, 482–486, 488–490, 504–506
anti-Shiite position, 345
Azzam and, 209, 328
disagreement over training camps, 337–338
first meeting, 99, 117

Bin Ladin, Usama (cont.)
　al-Ma'sada camp, 341–344
　meeting in USA, 98
　Azzam's assassination and, 439–440
　CIA involvement, 184
　French intelligence awareness of, 185
　funding provided, 211, 214
　　Mujahidin, 153, 210, 212
　　Services Bureau, 209, 217, 234, 258
　al-Ma'sada camp and, 197–198, 328, 338–341, 344, 345
　Muslim Brotherhood and, 98
　MWL and, 195
　in Pakistan, 210–211, 213, 237, 334
　al-Qaida, 326, 350–364, 487, 504, 507, 509
　　anti-Americanism, 327
　al-Qaida and, 242
　Sada camp and, 335–336
　Saudi intelligence and, 181
　Saudi Relief Committee and, 197
　Services Bureau and, 205, 215–216, 239, 332
　in United States, 98
bin al-Uthaymin, Muhammad, 117
bint Abu Bakr, Asma, 333–334, 341, 345–346, 348–352, 356–364, 382, 415–416, 464, 482–485, 488–490, 504–506
bint al-Azwar, Khawla, 382
Black September, 24, 47–48, 60, 63, 64–65, 76, 89–90
"blind sheikh.", 78. *See* Abd al-Rahman, Umar
Boko Haram, 469
Bosnia-Herzegovina, 407–408, 454, 456, 459, 479, 483, 485, 487, 489–491, 492
Boston Marathon, 477
Brown, Vahid, 5, 167, 306
Brzezinski, Zbigniew, 178

Cairo, 41, 44, 49, 65, 70–71, 74, 76, 78, 80, 96
Camp David accords, 120, 135, 413
Canada, 257, 422
Carré, Olivier, 93
Carrel, Alexis, 140
Chaliand, Gérard, 56

charities, 194–197, 227, 228–229, 233, 237, 259, 260, 380, 506.
　See also non-governmental organizations
Choudhry, Roshonara, 383, 477
CIA (Central Intelligence Agency), 6–7, 179, 182–183, 184–187, 336, 363, 441, 448
Coll, Steve, 98, 181, 183, 186, 441, 445, 448
Colorado State College of Education, 41
Combating Terrorism Center, 355, 475
Comintern, 497
Communism, 133–135, 136, 178
Communist Party, 31, 367
Cooley, John, 179, 182
Crandall, Larry, 185, 187
Crevice Plot, 477
Crooke, Alastair, 182, 185, 191, 266
Crusader concept, 326
culture, 405–408, 433, 439, 444, 463, 466, 471, 502, 504
　Islamic, 117, 292, 315
　jihadi, 370, 405–408
　Western, 41, 320–321

Dabiq magazine, 470
Damascus, 19, 28, 30, 32–32, 35, 37–38, 59, 66, 70, 77
Damascus University, 19–20, 30, 32, 45, 66, 69, 77, 126, 453
　Muslim Brotherhood presence, 36–37
da'wa, 25, 33–34, 39, 59, 69, 79, 82, 85, 97, 104–105
Da'wa House, 32
al-Da'wa magazine, 42, 115
al-Dawsary, Abd al-Aziz, 255
Devine, Jack, 182
al-Dhahabi, Muhammad, 73
Dhat al-Nitaqayn, 382
diaspora, 22–23, 431
Dibbin woods camps, 49–51, 52, 55, 59, 63
al-Dik, Khalil bin Sa'id, 479
Diraz, Isam, 6, 360, 446
Doha, 249
Dönmeh, 134
Dorronsoro, Gilles, 160

Index

Dr. Fadl, 165, 246, 403–404, 450. *See* Abd al-Aziz, Abd al-Qadir
dreams, 165, 403–404
Dupree, Nancy, 194

Edwards, David, 188, 267, 297
Egypt, 38–39, 49–52, 71, 75, 88–90, 96, 115–116, 121–122, 263–265, 455–456
  Six Day War, 20, 23
Egyptian Doctors' Syndicate, 160, 263
Egyptian Islamic Group (EIG: al-Jama'a al-Islamiyya), 264, 359, 364, 418, 469
Egyptian Islamic Jihad (EIJ: Tanzim al-Jihad), 264, 298, 359–360, 418, 421, 469
Emerson, Steven, 458
Erbakan, Necmettin, 318

al-Fadl, Jamal, 354–355, 356–357, 359, 398
al-Falastini, Abu Shaleed, 398
al-Faransi, Maysara, 223
Farhan, Ishaq, 50, 64–65, 85, 89–90
Farkhar massacre, 429
al-Farooq mosque (Brooklyn), 259
Farrall, Leah, 5, 353, 362, 364
al-Faruq, Umar, 146
al-Faruq Camp/Military College, 357, 359
Faruqi, Amani, 270
Fatah movement, 47–49, 51, 57, 61, 162, 212
al-Fazari, Abu Ishaq, 329
FBI (Federal Bureau of Investigation), 7, 262
Fedayin, 47–52, 53, 58, 60–61, 63, 70, 130, 135, 298, 502
  areas of operation, 56
  Azzam's involvement, 53–54, 57, 71, 503
  bases, 56, 64
  Black September, 63, 64
  composition of group, 51
  leadership, 51–52
  leftist groups and, 60–62

Muslim Brotherhood and, 48–49, 52, 89
volunteers, 48
Fighel, Yonathan, 434, 471
al-Filastini, Abu A'id, 479
al-Filastini, Abu Qatada, 23, 290, 441, 464, 469, 475
al-Filastini, Abu Yusuf, 388
films, 6, 186, 208, 229–230, 246, 260, 263, 300, 371, 465
Finsbury Park mosque, 255
foreign-fighter doctrine, 155, 288, 299–306, 488, 494–495, 499, 503–504
Fort Worth, Texas, 250–251, 262
Foundation for Assisting Turkish Pilgrims and Muslims, 165
France, 112, 135, 162, 179, 189, 191–192, 235–236, 269, 324, 381
Franceschi, Patrice, 188
Front Islamique du Salut (FIS), 460
al-Fulayj, Yusuf, 159
al-Funaysan, Saud, 97

Gailani, Ahmad, 156, 166, 174–175, 233, 389
Gaza Strip, 22, 433, 467
Germany, 150, 251, 253–254, 269
al-Ghamidi, Abd al-Wahhab, 166
al-Ghamidi, Abdullah, 297
al-Ghamidi, Ahmad Sa'd, 396
Ghannouchi, Rachid, 7, 99, 140, 201, 233, 408, 452
Gharaybeh, Ibrahim, 89
al-Gharaybeh, Ruhayyil, 103
al-Gharbi, Nur al-Din, 165
al-Ghazzali, Muhammad, 116
al-Ghazzali, Zaynab, 79, 201, 233, 380, 382, 412
al-Ghazzi, Abu al-Hasan Ibrahim, 59
Ghusheh, Ibrahim, 48, 55, 99
Ghuti, Eveline, 191
Ghuzlan, Ali, 198
GIA., 468. *See* Armed Islamic Group
Gibb, Hamilton, 141
Girardet, Edward, 153, 192–193
global jihad, 483–484, 488

Golani Brigade, 14
Grau, Lester, 389
Green, Abdurraheem, 187
Green Line, 14
Guantanamo Bay, 460, 491
Guevara, Che, 61, 136, 466
Gul, Hamid, 179, 363

Habannaka, Abd al-Rahman, 116
Hadid, Marwan, 37–38, 52, 59, 421, 469
Hajj, 96, 208, 212
Hama, 59
Hamas, 27, 202, 430–432, 433, 442, 466–467, 468, 470–472, 482–484, 487
al-Hamid, Muhammad, 37
Hamid, Mustafa, 161–164, 166–167, 170–171, 208, 305–306, 330, 343, 364, 444–445, 454–455
al-Hamidi, Khalil, 157–158
Hampton-El, Clement, 401
al-Hamud, Muhammad, 144, 181, 196
Hamza, 20
Haniyeh, Isma'il, 471
Haq, Abdul, 366
ul Haq, Zia, 145, 322, 325, 368, 412–413, 441
Haqqani, Jalaluddin, 149–150, 163, 166–170, 173, 203, 208, 233, 306, 329, 332–334
Harakat al-Jihad al-Islami (HJI), 203, 395
Harun, Fadil, 476
Hasan, Salah. *See* Abu Amr
al-Hashimi, Khattab, 484
Hawa, Sa'id, 37–38, 158, 301
al-Hawali, Safar, 426
Hekmatyar, Gulbuddin, 156–157, 159, 174–177, 206, 408–409, 415, 426–429, 435–436, 443–446, 449–451
 Azzam's assassination and, 443–446
al-Helbawy, Kamal, 117–118, 199, 202, 420, 456
Hezb-i Islami, 444
Hijaz, 108, 109, 116, 247, 258, 493
 pan-Islamism, 108, 112, 114, 195, 495

Hizb al-Tahrir, 73, 90, 130–131, 132
Huntington, Samuel, 141
Hussain, Junaid, 477
Husayn bin Ali bin Abi Talib, 12
Hussein of Jordan, 48, 63, 90, 100
Hutchinson, Rabiah, 221, 385–387, 459

Ibn Baz, 198. *See* Bin Baz
Ibn Khattab, 466, 469, 483
Ibn Taymiyya, 40, 290, 329
Ibrahim, Adnan, 224
Ibrahim, Qari, 393
international Islamic organizations (IIOs), 107–108, 109–110, 114, 117, 123, 152, 496, 506. *See also* charities; non-governmental organizations
International Islamic Relief Organization (IIRO), 153, 157, 194–195, 197
International Islamic University in Islamabad (IUI), 108–109, 143, 144–147, 160, 202, 370, 374, 410, 451
al-Iraqi, Abu Hajir, 241, 242, 334–335, 340, 343, 345–346, 352–354, 355, 423, 461, 489
 on Azzam, 241
 on Bin Ladin, 332
 biographical details, 242
 leaves Services Bureau, 242
 proposes closing down Services Bureau, 241
 al-Qaida and, 242
 on Services Bureau, 223, 228, 238, 240
 as Services Bureau executive director, 215, 331
 Services Bureau roles, 215, 229, 241
 sets up Sada camp, 335–336
al-Iraqi, Abu Ibrahim, 242
Isa, Nasr, 59
ISI (Inter-Services Intelligence), 174, 179–180, 183–184, 186–187, 363, 366, 426, 428, 444, 446–449
Islam, Yusuf., 233. *See* Stevens, Cat

Islamabad, 123–124, 142–146, 180–181, 183, 210–211, 254, 370, 409–410, 451–452, 456–459
Islamic Group, 78, 136, 164, 264, 270, 291–292, 359, 418, 468; *See also* Egyptian Islamic Group
Islamic law, 19, 32, 35, 36, 69–71, 77, 80, 82, 99–100, 125–126
Islamic State (IS), 136–137, 314, 466, 468–470, 477–478, 483, 484–485, 486, 491
Islamism, vii. *See* pan-Islamism
Isma'il, Jamal, 6, 132–133, 211, 213, 227, 230, 431, 433, 453, 454
Israel, 11, 14, 15–16, 20, 25, 47–48, 323–324, 435, 442–443, 502
  Azzam's assassination and, 442–443
Izz al-Din, 357

al-Jafri, Abdallah, 210
Jaji, battle of, 169, 336, 337, 345, 347–349, 351, 363, 373, 389, 404
al-Jama'a al-Islamiyya. *See* Egyptian Islamic Group
Jama'at al-Da'wa, 265, 415
Jamaat-e Islami, 146, 151, 153, 157–158, 174, 176, 202, 210, 222, 305, 376, 395–396
Jarrar, Dawud, 59
Jarrar, Fayiz, 32–33
Jarrar, Husni, 5, 33, 438
Jarrar, Tawfiq, 32
al-Jawdar, Abd al-Rahman, 159
al-Jaza'iri, Abu Bakr, 164–165, 233
al-Jaza'iri, Ahmad, 421
al-Jaza'iri, Asad al-Rahman, 388
al-Jaza'iri, Nur al-Din, 164–166, 215, 333, 427
Jenin, battle of, 14
Jenin high school, 18
Jerusalem, 16, 22, 23–24, 32, 44, 50, 207, 249, 256, 324
al-Jihad magazine, 230–232, 236, 239, 413, 414–415, 430, 433, 437–438, 446–448, 453–454
  advertisements, 233–234
  Azzam's writing in, 24, 44, 191, 195, 199, 201, 307, 315, 325, 328
  content, 190, 220–221, 224, 232–234, 261, 326, 349, 363, 406, 408
    Afghan focus, 319, 323
    interviews, 79, 99, 202, 233, 305, 366, 382
    letters section, 297, 404
    martyr sections, 363
    photographs, 406
    poetry, 407
    women's section, 381
  contributors, 117, 216, 223, 226, 393
  distribution, 234–236, 259, 260–261, 262
  financing, 234
  foundation, 230–232
  production process, 232
jihadi culture, 370, 405–408
jihadism, 1, 2, 7, 326, 436, 470, 493, 506
Jordan, 16–22, 59–63, 81–82, 84–85, 88, 91–93, 94–97, 102–103, 105–106, 199–200
Jordan, intelligence agency, 441
Jordan University, 52, 71, 84–85, 90, 102–103, 106, 213, 220, 486, 493
Joshi, Shashank, 185
Julaydan, Wa'il, 195, 196–197, 215–216, 217, 256, 261, 376, 422–424, 425, 428
al-Jumayli, Tais, 97

Kadoorie, Ellis, 18
Kadoorie Agricultural School, 7, 18–19, 67, 126
al-Kanadi, Abd al-Rahman, 422, 424
Karachi, 112, 156–157, 163, 166, 203, 210, 249, 254, 305, 397
Karama, battle of, 47–48
Karmal, Babrak, 147, 317
al-Kawakibi, Abd al-Rahman, 137
KhAD (Khadamat-e Ittila'at-e Dawlati), 369, 416, 449
Khadr, Ahmad Sa'id, 422
Khalidi, Walid, 15
Khalifa, Jamal, 44, 195, 209, 224

Khalifa, Muhammad Abd al-Rahman, 34, 44, 52, 89, 102, 158, 200, 201, 322, 451
al-Khalili, Ahmad, 233
Khalis, Yunus, 156, 158, 159, 167, 174–175, 186, 450
Khan, Bakht Zameen, 395
Khan, Muhammad Dawud, 147, 317
Khanjani, Abd al-Rahim, 451
Khashoggi, Jamal, 131, 247, 437, 445, 455
Khawaja, Mahmud, 212
Khawaja, Mohammed Momin, 477
Khraysat, Ibrahim, 89, 90
al-Kifah Refugee Center, 259–261, 262
King Abd al-Aziz University, 97, 106, 108–109, 116–118, 122–123, 145, 410–411, 506
King Faisal mosque, 145
*kunya*s, 20, 397
Kuwaiti Red Crescent (KRC), 109, 153–154, 194–195, 197, 421, 425

Lafraie, Najibullah, 485
Lebanon, 14, 16, 47–48, 51, 120–121, 162, 235–236, 313–314, 466, 468
lectures, 5, 67–68, 82–83, 84–86, 92–93, 110–111, 248–250, 256–257, 296, 465
al-Libi, Abu Dharr, 394
al-Libi, Abu Yahya, 408, 475
al-Libi, Isam al-Din, 207, 212
logistics, 229
Lohbeck, Kurt, 187, 444, 446

al-Madani, Abu al-Hasan, 195, 196, 217, 238, 349
al-Madhun, Muhammad, 471
al-Mahlawi, Ahmad, 233
Majati, Abd al-Karim, 476
al-Majdhub, Muhammad, 156
al-Majid, Majid, 467
al-Malt, Ahmad, 115, 121, 158, 201
al-Maqdisi, Abu al-Hasan, 207, 212–213, 373, 459
al-Maqdisi, Abu Muhammad, 6, 23, 329, 418–420, 421, 440–441, 469, 475

Markaz al-Da'wa wa'l-Irshad (MDI), 203–204, 396
Martyr Azzam Media Center, 457
martyrdom, 5, 57–58, 59–60, 245, 294, 296–297, 298–299, 402–403, 481, 488
martyrdom biographies, 231, 268, 296, 312
martyrdom stories, 60
al-Ma'sada project, 197, 328, 339–342, 343–344, 345–347, 348–352, 355–356, 360, 412, 415–416
  foundation, 339–342
Mashhur, Mustafa, 115, 121, 158–159, 200–202, 233
Mashru', battle of, 58, 59, 62
al-Masri, Abd al-Rahman, 168
al-Masri, Abu Dujana, 219, 238
al-Masri, Abu Hafs, 166, 168, 340, 343, 345, 348–350, 354, 355, 357, 359–360
al-Masri, Abu Hamza, 255
al-Masri, Abu Khabib, 216–217, 394
al-Masri, Abu Khalid, 340, 343, 345, 354
al-Masri, Abu Walid, 162, 164
al-Masri, Assadallah, 403, 405
Massoud, Ahmed Shah, 185, 222, 371, 408, 419, 426, 444, 451, 452, 461
Mawdudi, Abu al-A'la, 293
MAYA (Muslim Arab Youth Association), 97–98, 248, 252, 259, 263
Mazar-e Sharif, 190, 221–222, 228, 387, 489
McCurry, Steve, 192
McWilliams, Ed, 444
Mecca incident (1979), 118
Medina, University of, 92, 109, 145, 156, 164, 247, 250
Melbourne Cell, 477
Miller, Flagg, 404
Minbar al-Tawhid wa'l-Jihad, 131, 475, 479, 509, 511
Mirror of the Afghan Jihad, 230, 234
al-Misri, Abu Usama., 51. *See* Ali, Abd al-Aziz

Mojdeh, Vahid, 213, 231, 393, 407, 447, 448
Morris, Benny, 14
Moscow, 312, 488, 507
Mossad, 442
al-Mu'ayyad, Abd al-Ilah, 159
Mubarak, Husni, 26, 72
Mughniyeh, Imad, 442
Muhajir, A'ida, 381
Muhammad, Basil, 6, 163, 168, 169, 196, 338, 343, 349, 358, 359
Muhammad, Mian Tufayl, 202
Muhammad Ali Pasha, 137
al-Muharib, Abdallah, 265
al-Muhaysini, Abdallah, 464
al-Mujahid newsletter, 230–231, 406, 415
Mujahidin, 150–154, 156–158, 170–176, 177–179, 183–184, 205–210, 225–229, 253–254, 294–295, 363–365
  Information Bureau, 150
  international outreach, 148–151
  leadership, 158, 163–164, 166, 253, 256, 426, 429, 444, 446, 449
  magazines, 151
  in Peshawar, 147
  publications, 150
  self-image, 148
  US support for, 178–179, 184, 186, 507
al-Mujtama' magazine, 42, 44, 92, 94, 115, 117, 119, 121, 160, 300
al-Munajjid, Muhammad, 304
music., 344. See *anashid*
Musleh, Akram, 477
Muslim Aid, 194–195, 233–234
Muslim Brotherhood, 30–36, 40–45, 48–53, 72–74, 90–96, 102–104, 105–108, 130–132, 157–161, 198–202
  Azzam's membership, 28, 45
  Consultative Council, 89, 215, 332
  Egypt, 72–73, 79, 95, 115–116, 157, 200, 336, 412, 418
  Fedayin and, 48–52
  Guidance Office, 115, 200
  Islamist Fedayin and, 52

Jenin, 18
Jordan, 31–32, 34, 44, 88–89, 91–92, 105–106, 200–201, 409, 451, 473
  membership numbers, 30
  magazines, 79, 115, 263
  other organizations and Fatah, 49–51
  Secret Apparatus (paramilitary wing), 31, 42, 121
  Syria, 28, 35–36, 37–38, 49, 92
Muslim Student Union, 213
Muslim World League (MWL), 95–96, 107–108, 110–112, 114, 154–156, 157, 195, 374, 411, 506
Mustafa, Mustafa Kamal, 255
al-Mutawwa', Abu Badr, 153, 159, 201
Muzamil, Muhammad Zaman, 151

al-Nafir al-Amm, 151
al-Nahrayn, battle of, 331
Nammus, Ridwan, 421
Nangarhar, 223, 356, 365, 446
Nasif, Umar Abdallah, 195, 411
Nasiri, Omar, 476
Nasser, Gamal Abdul, 31, 35, 39, 42–43, 71, 75, 80, 95, 319
Nawfal, Ahmad, 48, 50–51, 52, 56–57, 78, 82, 89, 90, 92, 201
New York Times, 178, 260
Nisar, Fu'ad, 134
non-governmental organizations (NGOs), 6, 107, 160, 187–188, 189–190, 194–195, 227, 326, 495, 507
  Islamic, 6, 172, 189, 195–196, 206, 246, 495. See also Services Bureau
Notin, Jean-Christophe, 192
Nur, Muhammad, 57, 59

Operation Pendennis, 477
Organization of the Islamic Conference (OIC), 108, 155

Pakistan, 122–123, 157–158, 178–183, 203–205, 246–249, 265–266, 410–413, 455–457, 459–461, 493–497

Pakistan (cont.)
  government, 180, 204, 363, 409–413, 448
    concerns about Azzam, 409–413
  ISI (Inter-Services Intelligence), 174, 179–180, 183–184, 186–187, 363, 366, 426, 428, 444, 446–449
  Islamist groups, 138, 194, 202, 204, 305, 376, 413
Paktia province, 161–163, 170, 204, 329, 330, 337, 343, 365, 393, 395–396
Palestine, 15–18, 19–20, 22–27, 50–51, 59, 133–134, 313–314, 429–430, 431–433, 484–485
  Azzam's views on, 23–27
  forced evictions, 21
  UN Partition Plan, 14
Palestine War, 2, 16
Palestinian Intifada, 85, 313, 368, 409, 434–435, 442
pan-Islamism, 107–108, 112, 114, 116, 123, 152, 493, 495–497, 500, 506
Peshawar, 143–144, 151–154, 156–160, 188–196, 213–217, 373–376, 377–380, 407–412, 417–420, 452–461
Peshawar Seven, 174
PLO (Palestine Liberation Organization), 24, 27, 35, 62–63, 152, 432, 471
poetry, 41, 139, 158, 233, 236, 381, 405–407, 466
prayer, 80, 86, 242, 370–372, 392, 397, 402, 403, 450, 486

al-Qaida, 326, 350–364, 487, 504, 507, 509
  Azzam and, 327, 354–355, 361–362, 368, 434, 464, 484–487, 491, 504
  Azzam's assassination and, 456
  bombings, 467
  early objectives, 356
  Egyptian involvement, 358–359, 361
  establishment, 352, 357
  founders, 345, 353–354, 359
  founding memos of, 351, 353–354
  Hamas and, 471–472
  Islamic State and, 469–470
  name, 352
  organizational structure, 355–356
  recruitment process, 357
  recruits and members, 476–477
  regional affiliates, 469
  Saudi involvement, 416
  secrecy of, 358
  Services Bureau and, 362–363, 439
  tactics, 357
  training camps, 357, 443, 475
Qana massacre, 489
Qandahar, 216, 223, 337, 338–339, 365, 368, 388, 390, 394, 405
al-Qandahari, Abu Ja'far, 217, 388, 397–400, 401, 402, 404
  on Arab fighters, 357, 364, 387, 392
  on al-Ma'sada, 356
  on Mujahidin personnel, 379, 387–388, 389, 393
  on al-Qaida recruitment, 357
  quoted, 226, 263, 364, 367, 378, 387
al-Qaradawi, Yusuf, 40, 127, 201, 233
al-Qarni, Musa, 366, 428, 437, 451
al-Qaryiouti, Abdullah, 92
al-Qatari, Abu Shahid, 357
al-Qattan, Ahmad, 233, 248, 252, 264
Qutb, Amina, 158
Qutb, Muhammad, 34, 40, 73, 79, 97, 116–117, 127, 141, 160
Qutb, Sayyid, 3, 4, 39–40, 42–44, 58, 72–73, 88–89, 93–94, 127, 468–469
  early life, 41–42
  execution, 39–40, 72, 80
  ideas, 43–44
  imprisonment, 43
  intellectual influence, 3
  publications
    Milestones, 43–44
  writing, 41
Qutbism, 38, 40, 44, 72–73, 89–91

Rabbani, Burhanuddin, 149, 151, 156, 174–175, 176, 390, 426–427, 429, 445, 449–451
Rabin, Yitzhak, 18
al-Rahman, Jamil, 204, 345, 393, 415

Ramadan, battle of, 345, 347
Ramadan, Sa'id, 32
Rashid, Abdullah, 401
al-Rashid, Nasir, 153
al-Rashidi, Amin Ali., 343. *See* Abu Ubayda al-Banshiri
Rassler, Don, 5, 167, 306
Reagan, Ronald, 178
Red Cross, 189–190, 322
refugees, 15, 21–22, 148, 153, 207, 218, 226, 326, 382
Rehman, Akhar Abdul, 179
religious inclinations, 31
al-Ridi, Isam, 229, 239
al-Rifa'i, Fathi, 226
rituals, 293, 370, 389, 392, 402
Rochman, Rachid (Rashid al-Rahman), 162, 193
Roy, Olivier, 147, 192
al-Rumi, Abdallah, 393, 415
Russia., 72. *See* Soviet Union
Russians, 154, 294

al-Sabuni, Abd al-Rahman, 126
Sa'd al-Din, Adnan, 38, 201, 233
Sada training camp, 292, 309, 329, 334–337, 353, 357, 371, 407
Sadat, Anwar, 71–72, 74–75, 120, 129, 295, 413
Saeed, Hafiz, 203
Sa'id, Abdallah, 5
Salafism, 70, 91, 92, 265, 290, 389, 393, 406, 415, 418, 474
Salamah, Shawqi, 385
Salih, Mohammed Ra'fat Sa'id, 90
Salim, Atiyya, 165
Salim, Mamduh Mahmud. 215. *See* Abu Hajir al-Iraqi
Salman al-Farsi camp, 331, 395
al-Sananiri, Muhammad Kamal al-Din, 42, 79, 115, 124, 158, 395, 500
Saqr, Abd al-Badi', 306
al-Sa'udi, Abu Mus'ab, 357
Saudi Arabia, 117–118, 150–152, 179–180, 235–236, 246–248, 250–251, 256–257, 264, 488–490, 495–497
    Azzam in, 107–110
    moves to (1967), 53
    government, 160, 180–181, 248, 318, 362, 415–416, 419, 440, 475, 489
    concerns about Azzam, 413–417
Saudi intelligence, 449
Saudi Red Crescent (SRC), 153, 160, 194, 197–198, 214, 216, 227, 234, 422
Saudi Relief Committee, 194–195, 196–197, 227
Saur Revolution, 147
Sawalha, Muhammad Kazim, 85
Sawt al-Jihad, 151
al-Sawwaf, Muhammad Mahmud, 17, 159, 201, 233
al-Sayis, Muhammad, 77
Sayyaf, Abd Rabb al-Rasul, 158–161, 167–170, 172–175, 176–177, 206–207, 221–223, 301, 347–349, 376–377, 449–451
    appointed head of Islamic Union, 159
    Azzam as houseguest, 144
    first hears of Azzam, 120
    first meets Azzam, 123
    meets MWL delegates, 156
    on al-Sananiri, 158
    travel and conferences, 149
al-Sayyid, Abdallah, 265
Scheuer, Michael, 361
Secret Apparatus, 31, 42, 121
Services Bureau, 205–208, 211–217, 221–223, 228–231, 237–240, 241–243, 257–262, 333–338, 362–363, 452–454
    activities, 217–219
        education, 224–226
        humanitarian aid, 226–228
        intelligence gathering, 221–224
        Mujahidin logistical assistance, 228–229, 331
        publishing, 229–237
        reception of incoming volunteers, 219–221
    competing organizations, 263–266
    foundation and financing, 208–214
    organizational structure, 214–217
        Consultative Council, 215, 332
        Medical Committee, 216, 226–227
        Orphans and Widows Committee, 216, 227

Services Bureau (cont.)
    Reception Committee, 216, 219
    Technical Committee, 216, 229
    Transportation Committee, 216, 228
  overseas branches, 258–263
  problems and disagreements, 237–243
"Seven Dwarfs", 174
al-Shabaab, 254, 467, 469
Sha'ban, battle of, 345, 346
Shafqat, 396
al-Shahada, 151
al-Shahawi, Ibrahim, 77
Shakir, Ahmed, 475
Shalabi, Mustafa, 454
Shalbak, Mahir, 207, 212–213
'Shaqra', Muhammad Ibrahim, 90, 92
al-Shar'a, Muhand, 236
Sharabini, Isam, 50
Shari'a, 36–37, 71, 102, 105, 108, 110, 116, 127, 128, 144–145
al-Sharif, Sayyid Imam, 355, 357, 358, 383, 419, 421, 475
al-Sharkasi, Abu Mu'adh, 212, 215, 224
al-Sharqawi, Muhammad Abd al-Rahim, 270, 384
al-Shatti, Isma'il, 7, 52, 77, 78, 117, 248
Shay, Shaul, 434
al-Shaybani, Abdallah, 260
al-Shishani, Darar, 432
al-Siba'i, Muhammad, 17
Siba'i, Mustafa, 36, 38, 95, 127
Siddique, Muhammad, 252, 254
al-Sila al-Harithiyya, 6, 11–13, 14–16, 19–21, 32–34, 39, 142, 373, 430, 460
al-Sila al-Harithiyya school, 18
al-Sindi, Badi al-Din, 420
Six Day War, 11, 20–22, 52, 502
Soviet Union, 323–325, 412
  withdrawal of troops from Afghanistan, 364–365, 442, 507
Stevens, Cat, 1, 233–234, 408
Storer, Cynthia, 187
Strick van Linschoten, Alex, 149, 362, 366

al-Sudani, Abu Muhammad, 240
al-Suri, Abu al-Rida, 195, 224, 261, 331, 345, 352
al-Suri, Abu al-Sa'id, 238
al-Suri, Abu Burhan, 204, 336, 342, 352–353, 357, 396, 448
al-Suri, Abu Faris, 396
al-Suri, Abu Firas, 421
al-Suri, Abu Mahmud, 345
al-Suri, Abu Mus'ab, 1, 51, 184, 248, 263, 320, 329, 336, 419, 458
al-Suri, Abu Usayd, 219
Syria, 16–17, 35–37, 38, 47–48, 51, 59–60, 92, 467–468, 477, 506–507

Tabligh movement, 130, 204, 265, 290–291
Tahir, Muhammad, 163
Taraki, Nur Muhammad, 147
Tawba, Muhammad, 260
Thatcher, Margaret, 178
Tsarnaev, Dzhokhar, 477
Tulkarm, 7, 15, 18, 31, 34, 126, 434
al-Turabi, Hasan, 304–305
al-Turkistani, Abd al-Aziz, 346

al-Ulwan, Abdallah, 301
United Kingdom, 112, 235
United Nations, Palestine Partition Plan, 14
United States, 249, 261, 442, 505
  Afghanistan and, 186–187
  Afghanistan policy, 412
    Mujahidin support, 178–179, 184, 186, 507
  Azzam travels to, 229, 248, 251–252, 324, 458
  Azzam's assassination and, 441–442
  Azzam's hostility to, 320, 322–325, 488
  fighter training in, 260
  foreign fighters from, 193, 261–262, 269, 401
  as Islam's opponent, 141
  Middle East involvement, 489
  Muslim immigration to, 96

al-Qaida attacks on, 242, 360, 456, 489
Qutb in, 41
Services Bureau in, 244, 246, 258–259, 261, 453
al-Urduni, Abu Dawud, 215
al-Urduni, Abu Hamza, 216
al-Urduni, Abu Hudhayfa, 215, 240, 242
al-Urduni, Abu Khalid, 334, 458
USAID (United States Agency for International Development), 185, 186–187, 189
Usmani, Mohammad Rafi, 203
al-Utaybi, Juhayman, 118, 420
Uthman, Usama, 257
Uthmani, Taqi, 305

Vallat, David, 476
Van Dyk, Jere, 153, 162

al-Wa'i, Tawfiq, 52
West Bank, 11, 14, 19–21, 26, 28, 31, 47, 53, 466, 468
Western volunteers in Afghanistan, 188–189
women, 380–384
World Association of Muslim Youth (WAMY), 108, 117

al-Yamani, Abu Faraj, 357
al-Yamani, Abu Ibrahim, 227
al-Yamani, Abu Salih, 390

Yasin, Ahmad, 79, 430, 466, 471, 484
al-Yasin, Ahmad Bazigh, 159
Yemen, 51, 59–60, 117, 119–120, 152, 452–453, 456, 458, 460, 461
Yousaf, Mohammad, 168, 334

Zaeef, Abdul Salam, 217
Zaidan, Ahmad, 6, 151, 196, 223, 231, 234, 239, 330, 439, 446
Za'im, Abd al-Sattar, 51, 59
al-Zarqawi, Abu Mus'ab, 408, 466, 470, 475
al-Zawahiri, Ayman, 154, 270, 355, 408, 421, 461
  on Azzam, 182, 464
  Azzam and, 418, 421–422, 425
  Azzam's assassination and, 443
  on Dr. Fadl's trial, 424
  prominence in Afghan Arab community, 359–360
  al-Qaida and, 357, 358
  quoted, 184
  Salafi background, 418
al-Zayid, Abdallah, 159
al-Zayla'i, Abu Bakr, 254
Zhawar, battle of, 168–169, 329, 332–333, 334, 337, 339, 372, 406
Zindani, Abd al-Majid, 119, 159, 233, 451, 452
Zionism, 14, 112, 136, 141, 323, 484
Ziyad, 213